# Globalization and Labour Markets
## Volume II

# The Globalization of the World Economy

*Series Editor:* Mark Casson
*Professor of Economics*
*University of Reading, UK*

Wherever possible, the articles in these volumes have been reproduced as originally published using facsimile reproduction, inclusive of footnotes and pagination to facilitate ease of reference.

For a list of all Edward Elgar published titles visit our site on the World Wide Web at
http://www.e-elgar.co.uk

# Globalization and Labour Markets
# Volume II

*Edited by*

# David Greenaway

*Professor of Economics and Pro-Vice Chancellor*
*University of Nottingham, UK*

*and*

# Douglas R. Nelson

*Professor of Economics and Political Economy*
*Tulane University, USA*

THE GLOBALIZATION OF THE WORLD ECONOMY

**An Elgar Reference Collection**
Cheltenham, UK • Northampton, MA, USA

Published by
Edward Elgar Publishing Limited
Glensanda House
Montpellier Parade
Cheltenham
Glos GL50 1UA
UK

Edward Elgar Publishing, Inc.
136 West Street, Suite 202
Northampton
Massachusetts 01060
USA


A catalogue record for this book
is available from the British Library

**Library of Congress Cataloguing in Publication Data**

Globalization and labour markets / edited by David Greenaway and Douglas R. Nelson.
        p. cm. — (Globalization of the world economy ; 10)
     Includes bibliographical references and index.
     1. Foreign trade and employment. 2. Investments, Foreign and employment. 3. Globalization—Economic aspects. 4. International business enterprises—Employees. 5. International trade—Social aspects. 6. International labor activities. 7. Labor market. 8. Free trade. I. Greenaway, David. II. Nelson, Douglas R. III. Series.

HD5710.7 .G5476 2001
331.1—dc21                                                                                   2001033431


ISBN   1 84064 132 0 (2 volume set)


Printed and bound in Great Britain by MPG Books Ltd, Bodmin, Cornwall

# Contents

# Acknowledgements

The editors and publishers wish to thank the authors and the following publishers who have kindly given permission for the use of copyright material.

American Economic Association for articles: Kristin F. Butcher and David Card (1991), 'Immigration and Wages: Evidence from the 1980's', *American Economic Review*, **81** (2), May, 292–6; Robert J. LaLonde and Robert H. Topel (1991), 'Immigrants in the American Labor Market: Quality, Assimilation, and Distributional Effects', *American Economic Review*, **81** (2), May, 297–302; Rachel M. Friedberg and Jennifer Hunt (1995), 'The Impact of Immigrants on Host Country Wages, Employment and Growth', *Journal of Economic Perspectives*, **9** (2), Spring, 23–44.

Blackwell Publishers Ltd for articles: James R. Markusen and Anthony J. Venables (1997), 'The Role of Multinational Firms in the Wage-Gap Debate', *Review of International Economics*, **5** (4), November, 435–51; Magnus Blomström, Gunnar Fors and Robert E. Lipsey (1997), 'Foreign Direct Investment and Employment: Home Country Experience in the United States and Sweden', *Economic Journal*, **107** (445), November, 1787–97; Noel Gaston (1998), 'The Impact of International Trade and Protection on Australian Manufacturing Employment', *Australian Economic Papers*, **37** (2), June, 119–36.

Lael Brainard and David A. Riker for their own article: (1997), 'Are U.S. Multinationals Exporting U.S. Jobs?', NBER Working Paper, No. 5958, March, 1–26.

Brookings Institution Press for article and excerpt: George I. Borjas, Richard B. Freeman and Lawrence F. Katz (1997), 'How Much Do Immigration and Trade Affect Labor Market Outcomes?', *Brookings Papers on Economic Activity*, **1**, 1–67, 86–90; Lori G. Kletzer (1998), 'International Trade and Job Displacement in U.S. Manufacturing, 1979–1991', in Susan M. Collins (ed.), *Imports, Exports, and the American Worker*, Chapter Ten, 423–72.

Elsevier Science for articles: Ciaran Driver, Andrew Kilpatrick and Barry Naisbitt (1986), 'The Employment Effects of UK Manufacturing Trade Expansion with the EEC and the Newly Industrialising Countries', *European Economic Review*, **30** (2), April, 427–38; Michael J. Greenwood, Gary L. Hunt and Ulrich Kohli (1997), 'The Factor-market Consequences of Unskilled Immigration to the United States', *Labour Economics*, **4** (1), 1–28; David Greenaway, Robert C. Hine and Peter Wright (1999), 'An Empirical Assessment of the Impact of Trade on Employment in the United Kingdom', *European Journal of Political Economy*, **15**, 485–500.

*Industrial and Labor Relations Review* for articles: Jean Baldwin Grossman (1984), 'Illegal Immigrants and Domestic Employment', *Industrial and Labor Relations Review*, **37** (2), January, 240–51; George J. Borjas (1987), 'Immigrants, Minorities, and Labor Market Competition', *Industrial and Labor Relations Review*, **40** (3), April, 382–92; David Card (1990), 'The Impact of the Mariel Boatlift on the Miami Labor Market', *Industrial and Labor Relations Review*, **43** (2), January, 245–57.

*International Labour Review* for article: Dieter Schumacher (1984), 'North–South Trade and Shifts in Employment: A Comparative Analysis of Six European Community Countries', *International Labour Review*, **123** (3), May–June, 333–48.

Robert Z. Lawrence for his own article: (1994), 'Trade, Multinationals, and Labor', *NBER Working Paper*, No. 4836, August, 1–52.

MIT Press Journals and the President and Fellows of Harvard College and the Massachusetts Institute of Technology for articles: Ana L. Revenga (1992), 'Exporting Jobs? The Impact of Import Competition on Employment and Wages in U.S. Manufacturing', *Quarterly Journal of Economics*, **107**, 255–84; Thomas L. Hungerford (1995), 'International Trade, Comparative Advantage and the Incidence of Layoff Unemployment Spells', *Review of Economics and Statistics*, **LXXVII**, 511–21; Robert C. Feenstra and Gordon H. Hanson (1999), 'The Impact of Outsourcing and High-Technology Capital on Wages: Estimates for the United States, 1979–1990', *Quarterly Journal of Economics*, **CXIV** (3), August, 907–40.

Organization for Economic Co-operation and Development for article: Patrick A. Messerlin (1995), 'The Impact of Trade and Capital Movements on Labour: Evidence on the French Case', *OECD Economic Studies*, **24**, 90–124.

University of Chicago Press for excerpt: Joseph G. Altonji and David Card (1991), 'The Effects of Immigration on the Labor Market Outcomes of Less-skilled Natives', in John M. Abowd and Richard B. Freeman (eds), *Immigration, Trade, and the Labor Market*, Chapter 7, 201–34.

Every effort has been made to trace all the copyright holders but if any have been inadvertently overlooked the publishers will be pleased to make the necessary arrangement at the first opportunity.

In addition the publishers wish to thank the Marshall Library of Economics, Cambridge University and the Library of the London School of Economics and Political Science for their assistance in obtaining these articles.

# Part I
# Trade and Employment

# [1]

International Labour Review, Vol. 123, No. 3, May-June 1984

# North-South trade and shifts in employment
## A comparative analysis of six European Community countries

Dieter SCHUMACHER *

## 1. Introduction

Exports are necessary for developing countries since they provide the bulk of foreign exchange earnings needed to finance the importation of goods and services. In view of the present scarcity of factors of production other than unskilled labour, the developing countries should for the time being expand exports of labour-intensive manufactures where they are competitive and can count on high market shares. This, in fact, was what many of them did in the 1970s, but they are now confronted by increasing numbers of trade barriers erected by the developed countries in an attempt to check declining employment in industries adversely affected by imports at a time of low overall growth rates and rising unemployment. Such protectionist measures have increasingly been conceived as a means of maintaining the structural status quo instead of being temporarily introduced merely to ease the transition to new patterns of production.

In this context it is relevant to assess the effects of imports from developing countries on employment in developed countries since this will indicate to what extent liberal foreign trade attitudes might conflict with internal employment objectives. The aim of this article is to provide empirical information on the relationship between employment on the one hand and imports and exports in trade with developing countries on the other.[1] There are, of course, many studies on the effects of trade with developing countries on employment in individual developed countries.[2] However, these differ widely with regard to methodology, sectoral break-down and the years they cover. Our subject is a comparative analysis applying a common methodology and covering six European Community countries (Federal Republic of Germany, France, Italy, United Kingdom, Netherlands, Belgium). An input-output model is used which takes into

---

* German Institute for Economic Research, Berlin (West).

account the direct effects in the industry whose products are exported or imported and, additionally, the indirect effects from inter-industrial linkages, i.e. the production of intermediate inputs generated by exports on the one hand and the decrease in demand for intermediate inputs if domestic production is replaced by imports on the other.

The analysis begins by presenting the theoretical basis of the calculations as well as the data used. It then highlights the main features of the division of labour between the EC countries and the Third World in the 1970s, and goes on to discuss the empirical results with regard to the impact on employment at the level of the total economy, by sex and qualification levels as well as by industries. Finally, some policy conclusions are drawn from the empirical analysis.

## 2. Theoretical considerations, the model and the data used

Changes in employment arise from a complex set of factors. As the effects due to the various determinants cannot be observed individually, they must be attributed by model calculations based upon more or less simplifying assumptions. A detailed discussion of the methodological problems involved lies beyond the scope of this article.[3] Here only the most important relationships are briefly stated to provide a background against which our approach can be seen.

Substituting imports for domestic production has an immediate effect on a number of economic variables and induces other repercussions at further points in time. The most important changes and their linkages are shown in the diagram, it being assumed for demonstration purpose that the world as a whole is subdivided into two entities – A (developed countries) and B (developing countries):

(1) If A replaces domestic output of a product by imports of the same product from B, the output of that product as well as employment and the value added in the industry concerned decrease in A while production, employment and value added in the same industry increase in B (direct or initial effects).

(2) Moreover, by virtue of inter-industrial linkages, production, employment and value added in other industries are affected negatively in A and positively in B (indirect or linkage effects). Here, an induced decrease in A's imports of intermediate goods from B and increased imports by B of intermediate goods from A must be taken into account as well.

(3) The net foreign exchange earnings accruing to B through the initial increase in exports after deduction of imports induced and exports of intermediate goods forgone permit an increase in aggregate final demand according to the marginal propensity to import. This can further increase employment in B (foreign-exchange multiplier effects).

## Employment effects arising from replacement of production in developed countries by imports from developing countries

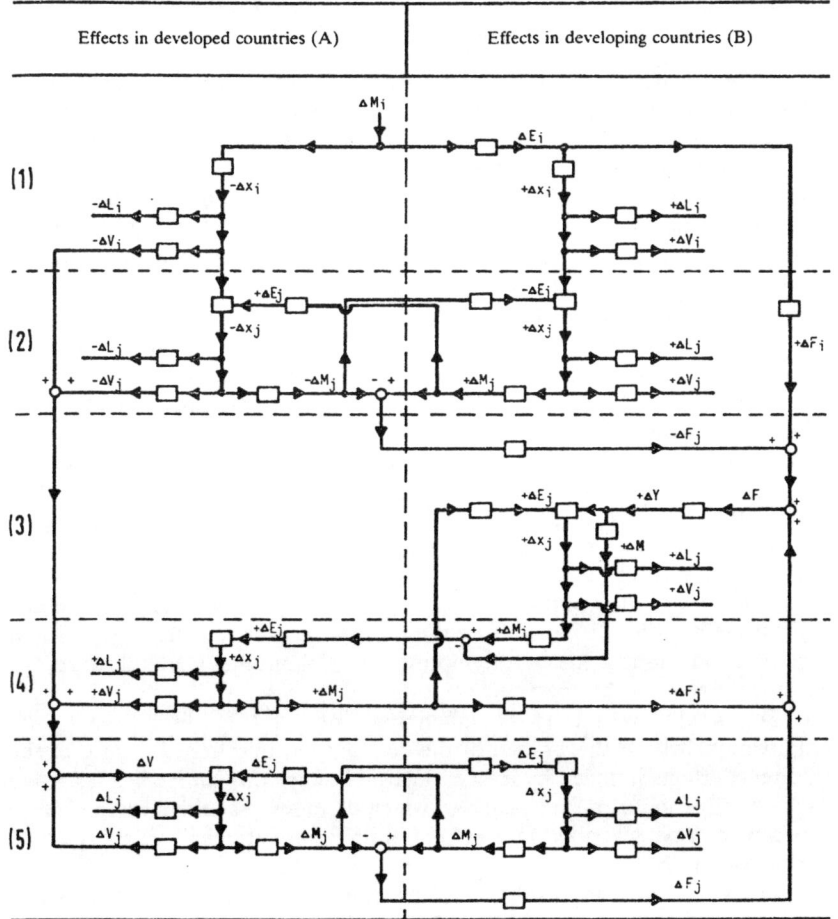

$\triangle M$, $\triangle E$, $\triangle x$, $\triangle L$, $\triangle V$, $\triangle F$ and $\triangle Y$ represent changes in imports, exports, gross value of production, employment, value added, foreign exchange and aggregate final demand, respectively. $i$ is the industry whose products are additionally imported, $j$ represents all industries $j = 1, \ldots, n$. The rectangles represent a functional relationship between the variables, the form of which is left open.

335

(4) Spending B's foreign exchange on imports increases A's production in export industries and in industries providing intermediate goods; it thus directly and indirectly exerts positive effects on employment and value added.

(5) The net changes in value added in A – which to judge by the results of empirical studies can be assumed to be positive – induce multiplier effects by changes in consumption which in turn affect production, employment and trade flows (income multiplier effects).

Further effects, though not considered here, arise from changes in prices, investment and growth in both developed and developing countries. Moreover, it must be remembered that the competitive position of individual countries within both A and B differs and influences the distribution among them of the effects described above. Ideally, all effects and repercussions due to internal and external linkages have to be taken into account simultaneously when the level and sectoral patterns of the employment impact in developed countries arising from increased imports from developing countries are calculated. Information must be available on the functional relationships between the variables; if the calculations are carried out for future trade flows, projections of these relationships are necessary.

For reasons of data availability and data-processing time, the empirical studies available provide only partial analyses concentrating on a few relationships between the variables mentioned above. Moreover, simplifying assumptions as to functional relationships are made. The present work is based on partial analyses for the individual EC countries concentrating on the direct and indirect (negative) employment effects of imports on the one hand – parts A (1) and A (2) in the diagram – and the corresponding (positive) effects of exports on the other – part A (4). The analysis proceeds from trade data for 1977, or from the difference between these figures and the 1970 position, without attempting to explain the trade flows or to establish a relationship between imports and exports.

To enable account to be taken not only of the (direct) effects on employment within the branch of the economy in question, but also of the (indirect) effects induced by inter-industrial linkages, recourse has been had to the tool of input-output analysis, which assumes that the structure of an economy can be described by a system of linear equations. This is explained in the Appendix.

In evaluating the results, account must be taken of the restrictive assumptions on which equations 10 and 11 are based. For example, the assumed constancy of the input coefficients means that we have ignored "economies of scale", the effect of prices, and changes in the degree to which industry is working to capacity. Distortions also arise from the fact that average sectoral values have been applied as the coefficients. On the export side, it has been assumed that all exports have been newly produced and are not merely existing assets that have been transferred (e.g. old aircraft or ships). On the import side, there is the problem of the division into competitive and non-competitive imports, as also the question of to what extent demand was first induced by the import, perhaps because of its lower price. In the method of estimating we have adopted, the effects of imports on employment have been overestimated to the extent that imports themselves bring demand into being; and underestimated to the extent that they squeeze out of the market home producers of below-average productivity.

The statistical data available allow the calculations to be disaggregated into 24 branches of the economy (16 of which are in the manufacturing sector), which have been differentiated in accordance with NACE-CLIO.[4] The coefficients for intermediate inputs have been derived from standardised input-output tables furnished by the Statistical Office of the European Communities for 1970.[5] Accordingly, the value data appearing in this paper – unless otherwise stated – are to be understood as being at 1970 prices. The unit of exchange is the United States dollar, which in 1970 corresponded to the common unit of account (EUR) applied in the standardised input-output tables. The sectoral labour-output ratios were estimated from figures provided by the Community's accounts, giving the figure for persons engaged per unit of gross output value in accordance with 1977 productivity. The division into male and female workers was also mainly based on data for 1977.[6] The breakdown according to qualification levels is based on data from a survey of industrial employees in 1972 and could only be done for the manufacturing sector;[7] however, it is here that more than 80 per cent of the direct and indirect effects of trade in industrial products are felt.

The foreign trade values were taken from the OECD statistics for 1970 and 1977[8] and aggregated in line with the selected sectoral scheme. The breakdown of imports into goods which could be produced at home and those not covered by any home-based industry is a difficult task and, additionally, could work out differently from country to country. A pragmatic solution was adopted: in view of the level of technology in the industrial countries basically all manufactured goods were regarded as being capable of being produced in the importing Community country. The only exceptions were foodstuffs and petroleum products. The categorising of foodstuffs as non-competitive products was founded on the consideration that imports from developing countries consist predominantly of tropical agricultural products which cannot be produced in Europe. The exclusion of petroleum products was made necessary because no separate information on the production function of these products was available.[9] Thus the definition of competitive imports chosen for use here coincides by and large with Standard International Trade Classification groups 5 to 8 (industrial products). To make comparison possible, on the export side too effects on employment were calculated only for industrial products, which in any case make up almost the entire range of exports from the EC countries. The 1977 trade figures have been deflated to the price basis of the 1970 input-output tables with the help of sectoral unit value indices.[10] On average the prices of

International Labour Review

industrial imports and exports in United States dollars just about doubled between 1970 and 1977.

Owing to the distortions brought about by the restrictive assumptions in the theoretical assessment and by inaccuracies in the data employed, the results of the mathematical models should not be interpreted with too high an expectation of accuracy. However, their order of magnitude and their direction allow a useful picture to be built up. Furthermore, the distortions should tend in the same direction for all the EC countries, so that a comparison of effects between them is not significantly prejudiced. One must, of course, interpret the figures as indicating only impact effects rather than actual changes in employment.

## 3. Foreign trade relations of the EC countries with the developing countries

In 1977 the six EC countries examined here imported more than $360,000 million worth of goods (at 1977 prices). Of those imported from fellow EC and other Western industrialised countries, from the newly industrialised countries of south-east Asia and from the developing countries of southern Europe 70 to 80 per cent were industrial products; imports of industrial goods from the rest of the developing world, however, accounted on average for only 20 to 30 per cent of total imports from those countries.

The structure of imports of industrial goods themselves also differs from one group of countries to another. The imports of the EC from all the groups of developing countries dealt with here are dominated by consumer goods, with textiles, clothing and consumer durables as the most important items. On the other hand, imports from the Western industrialised countries are dominated by the products of the capital goods industries.

Exports of the six EC countries taken together reached a value of $360,000 million in 1977 (at 1977 prices). They were for the most part products of the capital goods industries and were mostly traded with other industrialised countries; foodstuffs and other agricultural products also play an important role in trade between the EC countries themselves.

In the 1970s the developing countries considerably increased their share of the foreign trade of the six EC countries under review. This was due essentially to the higher cost of the oil supplies from OPEC countries but also to increased imports of finished goods – especially from the more advanced newly industrialised countries – and in the other direction to larger exports, in particular to the OPEC countries. A comparison of the actual make-up of exports and imports in trade with the developing countries shows the following: The EC countries export a large assortment of products of the capital goods and chemical industries. In return they purchase almost nothing but crude oil from the OPEC countries and primarily other raw materials, especially agricultural products, from the bulk of the other non-European developing countries. Here, the traditional complementary specialisation pattern of North and South has therefore been retained up to now, although a trend towards diversifying the division of labour is evident in that the exchange of semi-manufactures and finished goods has become the dominant form of trade between the North and some of the more highly developed countries of the South, where there is by now to a great extent an exchange of investment goods for consumer goods, although the mutual trade in products of the investment goods sectors increased markedly in the 1970s. As a whole, however, the developing countries are still of greater importance to the European Community as a market for industrial products and as suppliers of raw materials than as a source of semi-manufactures and finished goods.

## 4. Overall employment effects

Aided by the model computations, we can estimate that in 1977 over 1 million gainfully employed persons in the United Kingdom and nearly 1 million in the Federal Republic of Germany depended on exports of industrial goods to developing countries (including the OPEC group), directly or through production of intermediate goods. In Italy and France their number was close to 700,000 and in the Netherlands and Belgium over 120,000 each (see table 1). In all countries these exports accounted for approximately 3-4 per cent of total employment. Of those employed by manufacturing industry about 10 per cent were generally working on exports for the Third World – in the United Kingdom as many as 13 per cent. The "employment equivalent" of the imports of industrial goods from the Third World in the same year, on the other hand, is to be put for the four large EC countries at around one-third and for the two smaller ones (Belgium and the Netherlands) at just over one-half of the employment effect of the exports. The employment forgone owing to the increase in imports between 1970 and 1977 may be estimated to amount to 0.6 per cent of the total employment in the six countries together.

In order to provide a better comparison the employment effects of exports and imports were related to units of $1,000 million (at 1970 prices).[11] For this amount of exports the United Kingdom needed the largest number of workers in 1977, nearly 150,000; Italy followed next with over 110,000; in the Federal Republic of Germany and France almost 90,000 were needed, and in Belgium and the Netherlands only 60,000. The figures differ because of divergent sectoral export patterns, import intensities and labour productivities. In the two smaller EC countries, for instance, imported intermediate inputs accounted directly and indirectly for 40 per cent of the value of the exports, leaving only 60 per cent as the contribution to the gross domestic product; the effect on employment is correspondingly small. In the large EC countries, on the other hand, 75-85 per cent of the export value is home-produced; the proportion is highest in France. The high manpower requirements in Italy and the United Kingdom arise chiefly as a result of low productivity. The domestic product per worker in manufacturing industry

Table 1.  Overall employment effects of trade with developing countries in industrial
          goods, 1977

| Breakdown | Germany (Fed.Rep. of) | France | Italy | United Kingdom | Nether-lands | Belgium |
|---|---|---|---|---|---|---|
| *Workers dependent on exports to developing countries* | | | | | | |
| Number of persons ('000) | 956.8 | 679.9 | 685.4 | 1,124.9 | 124.8 | 121.3 |
| % of total employ-ment | 3.8 | 3.2 | 3.4 | 4.5 | 2.7 | 3.2 |
| Number of persons ('000) per US$1,000 million of exports [1] | 85.8 | 89.2 | 111.5 | 145.7 | 62.0 | 60.4 |
| of whom (%): | | | | | | |
| Men | 72.2 | 71.6 | 75.5 | 73.9 | 84.9 | 76.0 |
| Women | 27.8 | 28.4 | 24.5 | 26.1 | 15.1 | 24.0 |
| Skilled [2, 3] | 58.2 | 58.6 | 46.6 | . | 60.7 | 44.4 |
| Semi-skilled and unskilled [2] | 41.8 | 41.4 | 53.4 | . | 39.3 | 55.6 |
| *Employment equivalent of imports from developing countries* | | | | | | |
| Number of persons ('000) | 358.0 | 233.6 | 181.1 | 362.7 | 69.1 | 62.6 |
| % of total employ-ment | 1.4 | 1.1 | 0.9 | 1.5 | 1.5 | 1.7 |
| Number of persons ('000) per US$1,000 million of imports [1] | 93.6 | 102.0 | 121.9 | 146.1 | 73.7 | 64.1 |
| of whom (%): | | | | | | |
| Men | 54.0 | 61.0 | 57.9 | 61.7 | 74.3 | 69.5 |
| Women | 46.0 | 39.0 | 42.1 | 38.3 | 25.7 | 30.5 |
| Skilled [2, 3] | 43.7 | 48.8 | 43.6 | . | 49.9 | 38.8 |
| Semi-skilled and unskilled [2] | 56.3 | 51.2 | 56.4 | . | 50.1 | 61.2 |

[1] At 1970 prices; commodity structure in 1977.  [2] In manufacturing industry only: approximately 80 per cent of the total employment effect arose here.  [3] Salaried employees and skilled workers.

Sources: Model computations based on OECD and EC data. OECD: *Trade by commodities*, Series C (Paris, 1977); EC Commission: Print-outs with revised national accounts figures; Eurostat: *Input-output tables*, The Nine and the Community, 1970, Special Series, Vol. 8 (Luxembourg, 1978); idem: *Employment and unemployment, 1972-1978* (Luxembourg, 1979); idem: *Censuses of population in the Community countries, 1968-1971* (Luxembourg, 1977); idem: *Social statistics. Structure of earnings in industry, 1972*. Special Series (Luxembourg, 1975).

amounted in 1977 to no more than $5,600 in the United Kingdom and to $6,600 in Italy as compared with $9,500-10,000 in the other countries (at 1970 prices).

A breakdown of the employment effect from the production of goods for export by sex and levels of skill also reflects the general differences between the economies of the EC countries. The workers in the Netherlands, the Federal Republic of Germany and France are trained to a very high level; in these countries skilled workers account for approximately 60 per cent of the employment generated by the exports, against only about 45 per cent in Italy and Belgium.[12] The Netherlands has the lowest female participation in such employment: at 15 per cent it is not much more than half of that in the other EC countries.

The (negative) employment effects of imports deviate considerably from the manpower requirements for exports owing to the differences in the composition of the supplies and purchases of industrial goods to and from developing countries. The number of workers needed for the production of export goods for the Third World in the six EC countries is on average about 10 per cent lower than the employment content of the domestic production displaced by an equal amount of imports. In the Netherlands the difference is greatest (16 per cent); in the United Kingdom an equal amount of manpower is needed for both. The proportion of women in the labour force required for the production of exports is on average only about two-thirds of that in import-replaced production. The production of export goods for developing countries also generally involves a markedly smaller proportion of unskilled and semi-skilled labour; it thus absorbs more human capital.

Intensifying the division of labour with developing countries accordingly entails substantial shifts in manpower requirements. An especially important aspect is that most of the redundancies due to the imports occur among groups of workers who are in any case disadvantaged: if imports from the Third World substitute for domestic production and an equal amount of goods is produced instead for export, the result is that on balance – corresponding to their present shares of employment in the various industries – women are made redundant while the demand for male labour rises. Similarly, the redundancies hurt those at the lower end of the wage scale while more openings arise at the upper end. The structural change induced thus implies a need for training more women in jobs hitherto regarded as men's and training to a higher level of skill for the workforce in general.

## 5. Sectoral employment effects

The sectoral shifts in employment behind the above-mentioned changes at the level of the economy as a whole are shown in table 2. Despite all the differences of detail, the structural changes induced by exchange of goods with developing countries point in the same direction in the EC countries under review. These changes are in the main characterised by a shift of manpower requirements from the consumer goods sector to the investment goods industries. Redundancies occur chiefly in the textile, clothing, timber, wooden products, furniture and leather industries, while the mechanical engineering industry is the principal beneficiary from the shift in employment.

Table 2.  Net effect on employment by industry, sex and level of skill per US$1,000 million[1] of imports and exports of industrial goods from and to developing countries, 1977 ('000 workers)

| Industry/employment category | Germany (Fed. Rep. of) | France | Italy | United Kingdom | Nether-lands | Belgium |
|---|---|---|---|---|---|---|
| *Agriculture, forestry, fisheries* | -0.8 | -3.5 | -1.1 | -0.1 | -0.2 | -0.2 |
| *Mining and energy* | 0.2 | – | 0.1 | 0.3 | 0.1 | -0.2 |
| *Manufacturing industries* | -7.3 | -9.0 | -9.5 | -1.2 | -10.1 | -3.2 |
| Basic materials and producer goods | 2.1 | -0.2 | 1.6 | 2.1 | 1.6 | -3.3 |
| Ferrous and non-ferrous ores and metals | 0.8 | -1.2 | -1.5 | 1.6 | 0.7 | -4.1 |
| Minerals and non-metallic mineral products | -0.4 | -0.5 | 2.9 | -1.5 | -2.4 | -1.2 |
| Chemical products | 1.7 | 1.5 | 0.3 | 2.0 | 3.2 | 1.9 |
| Investment goods | 28.7 | 21.8 | 33.0 | 45.0 | 21.2 | 13.4 |
| Metal goods (excluding machinery and transport equipment) | 2.7 | 5.2 | 10.0 | 5.6 | 1.3 | 3.1 |
| Agricultural and industrial machinery | 17.2 | 8.9 | 16.0 | 18.7 | 7.0 | 6.2 |
| Office and data-processing machines, precision and optical instruments | 0.6 | 0.4 | 0.7 | -0.7 | 2.2 | 1.0 |
| Electrical products | 2.4 | 3.3 | 2.7 | 4.2 | 3.7 | 2.4 |
| Motor vehicles and parts | 4.8 | 1.2 | 2.7 | 13.3 | 0.8 | 0.8 |
| Other transport equipment | 1.1 | 2.7 | 1.0 | 3.9 | 6.1 | – |
| Food, beverages, tobacco products | – | – | – | -0.1 | – | – |

*Employment effects of North-South trade*

| Industry/employment category | Germany (Fed. Rep. of) | France | Italy | United Kingdom | Netherlands | Belgium |
|---|---|---|---|---|---|---|
| Consumer goods | -38.1 | -30.5 | -44.2 | -48.3 | -32.7 | -13.3 |
| Textiles, clothing | -32.1 | -20.3 | -32.0 | -35.8 | -21.9 | -10.5 |
| Leather and leather goods, footwear | -3.7 | -3.5 | -7.4 | -4.9 | -2.8 | -1.0 |
| Timber, wooden products and furniture | -2.9 | -6.9 | -9.5 | -6.8 | -9.2 | -2.4 |
| Paper and printing products | – | -0.6 | -0.4 | 0.4 | 0.3 | 0.1 |
| Rubber and plastic products | 1.7 | 1.7 | 2.6 | 1.3 | 2.4 | 0.9 |
| Other manufactures | -1.0 | -1.0 | 2.5 | -2.5 | -1.6 | -0.5 |
| *Building and construction* | 0.1 | 0.1 | 0.1 | 0.5 | 0.3 | -0.1 |
| *Services* | | | | | | |
| Trade, recovery and repair services | 0.1 | -0.4 | -0.1 | 0.2 | -1.9 | -0.1 |
| Transport and communication services | 0.1 | -0.9 | -0.9 | – | -1.4 | -0.2 |
| Banking and insurance services | – | – | 0.7 | -0.1 | -0.2 | -0.4 |
| Other market services | – | 0.5 | 0.2 | } 0.2 | -0.3 | 0.5 |
| Non-market services | – | – | – | } | – | – |
| **Total** | **-7.8** | **-12.8** | **-10.4** | **-0.4** | **-11.7** | **-3.7** |
| Men | 11.5 | 1.6 | 13.6 | 17.5 | -2.1 | 1.4 |
| Women | -19.2 | -14.4 | -24.0 | -17.9 | -9.6 | -5.1 |
| Skilled[2,3] | 6.8 | 2.6 | -1.4 | . | 0.7 | 1.6 |
| Semi-skilled and unskilled[2] | -14.1 | -11.6 | -8.1 | . | -10.8 | -4.8 |

[1] At 1970 prices; commodity structure in 1977. [2] In manufacturing industry only; almost all intersectoral shifts occur in this area. [3] Salaried employees and skilled workers.
Sources: As for table 1.

These structural effects are manifest in the trade with virtually all groups of Third World countries. They are in general most prominent in the exchange of goods with south-east Asia but relatively small in the exchanges with the three countries which were candidates for accession to the EC in 1977 (Spain, Greece,[13] Portugal).

The extent of the structural change induced can be characterised by the sum of the sectoral "net gains" in employment on the one hand and the sectoral "net losses" on the other. The smaller of these two amounts, i.e. here the sum of net gains as calculated from table 2, indicates the number of workers no longer required owing to imports who – purely mathematically and on the basis of isolated consideration of the trade with the relevant group of countries – must "change" sector in order to find a job in export production. On the basis of the composition of the trade with developing countries in 1977 an expansion of imports and exports by $1,000 million involves the greatest number of job changes in the United Kingdom (52,000) and Italy (42,000); next come the Federal Republic (33,000), the Netherlands (28,000) and France (26,000) while Belgium comes last (17,000). With increased division of labour with the Third World, 30-40 per cent of the additional jobs in export production arise in other economic sectors – at the level of disaggregation chosen here – than those in which labour is made redundant by the imports. Owing to the high level of intrasectoral division of labour in the EC countries' trade with industrialised Western countries outside the EC, the corresponding figure in this case is below 20 per cent; for the trade within the EC it is as low as 10 per cent.[14]

Model computations based on the *actual* increase in imports and exports show that in the 1970-77 period the expansion of the trade in industrial goods with developing countries resulted in quite as large – or even larger – shifts in the sectoral structure as the increase in the exchange of goods with the industrialised Western countries inside and outside the EC, even though the volume of trade with the Third World was far smaller than that with the industrialised countries. In relation to overall employment the expansion of trade with the developing countries caused the biggest shifts in the Netherlands (0.5 per cent) and the Federal Republic of Germany (0.3 per cent) and the smallest in Italy (below 0.1 per cent). The changes have thus had very little effect indeed on total employment; they are also small in relation to the overall changes in the sectoral employment pattern arising during the period under review from changes in technology, domestic demand and foreign trade combined.[15] In the future the changes induced in the employment pattern by additional trade with developing countries will probably also be relatively minor: even if imports doubled compared with 1977 and exports grew by a similar amount, the change would not affect more than 0.5 per cent of all workers in any of the six EC countries considered, assuming that the commodity pattern of trade remained the same as in 1977.

## 6. Conclusions

The effects induced are in fact so limited that the course now being taken by trade with developing countries cannot be regarded as a significant cause of unemployment in the EC countries; measures to oppose imports of industrial goods from the Third World are thus not a suitable means for reducing unemployment. The positive effect of trade barriers on employment is small and only short-term; over the longer term they will have a negative effect because they tend to conserve structures which are no longer competitive and, besides, curtail the potential for growth on the export side. Since developing countries have as a rule, except for the OPEC countries, always imported more from the developed countries than they have exported, it is reasonable to assume that, overall, for each dollar of foreign exchange earned by additional exports of manufactures to developed countries at least one dollar is spent on products from the developed countries, offsetting to a considerable extent the displacement effects due to imports. Thus, considering the positive net income multiplier effects as well, the overall net employment effect might tend to be zero, leaving developed countries none the less with the task of restructuring. In order to meet the problems which arise when shifting employment from import-competing to export industries and which are likely to occur even after provision is made for normal departures, an appropriate adjustment policy must be conceived, in particular including retraining measures.

However, the induced structural effect differs in degree between the individual EC countries, increasing with differences in the respective composition of imports and exports, low productivity of labour and low import intensity of the economy. Overall, the largest structural changes – assuming an equal volume of trade and measured by the number of workers affected – would be felt in the United Kingdom and Italy. Again, the individual EC countries' chances of securing additional orders from the Third World differ. The Federal Republic of Germany and the Netherlands would probably be in the most favourable position owing to their high level of productivity and the competitive range of goods they offer, the emphasis being on capital goods and chemical products. Next, no doubt, would be France, where labour productivity is similarly high and whose international position in the field of capital goods improved considerably in the 1970s. The situation of Belgium is less favourable because the supply structure is unsatisfactory (the emphasis being on metals and textiles). The prospects of the United Kingdom appear even worse because productivity in all sectors is low. Italy's position would probably also be unfavourable, as the country has not only a low level of productivity but also an adverse supply structure (with the emphasis on textiles, clothing and leather goods).

A liberal trade policy towards the Third World is necessary from the point of view of development, and, having regard to the orders of magnitude revealed, there are no important employment objections to this. However, owing to the different attitudes of the individual EC member States, it is doubtful whether free access for the developing countries to the entire European market can be achieved quickly. On the contrary, although formally trade policy has now been substantially unified on a Community basis, as stipulated in the Treaty of Rome, individual member States have erected further import barriers. Indeed, the Community itself is becoming increasingly protectionist. In such an unfavourable trade policy climate, and given the national differences described above, it is difficult to submit unified proposals for a liberalisation of imports capable of being seriously discussed by political decision-makers and having any prospects of implementation, particularly since opinions will differ from country to country about the extent to which the contraction of threatened industries is deemed socially acceptable.

For these reasons, any offer by the European Community to the developing countries to dismantle the barriers to imports in accordance with a binding schedule identical for all member States would have to be accompanied by a structural policy taking account of the important differences between EC countries. One possibility would be preferential active support by the Community for structural change in countries with comparatively serious problems. Sector-related restructuring aids are in fact already provided or are being prepared for by legislation. However, until the growing budgetary constraints of the Community are eliminated by a comprehensive reform of the agricultural policy, the scope for a common structural policy will remain very small indeed. Additional funds might, however, be raised from tariff revenues, particularly if tariffs are substituted for quantitative restrictions.

## Appendix

The open static Leontief model used in this article can be represented in matrix form as follows:

(1) $\quad Ax + y = x$

where $x$ is the column vector of the gross production values for the sectors, $y$ the column vector of the deliveries to final demand from the individual branches of the economy, and $A$ the matrix of the intermediate input coefficients $a_{ij}$ (taken as constant). The entire "technologically" dependent gross output for an exogenously given final demand can thus be calculated as

(2) $\quad x = (I - A)^{-1}y = Cy$

where $I$ is the unit matrix of the $n$th order and $C$ is the inverse of the Leontief matrix $(I - A)$.

Just as the direct and indirect effects of final demand on output can be calculated, it is also possible to work out the primary inputs necessary for this output. If we again base ourselves on constant input coefficients and adopt the following notations for the people employed for each unit of gross output in the separate branches $j = 1,..., n$ of the economy:

$l_j$ all persons employed (labour-output ratio)
$l_j^m$ males employed
$l_j^w$ females employed
$l_j^q$ persons employed of qualification level $q$   $(q=1,...,Q)$,

then the figure for employees needed in the various branches of the economy for given sectoral output values can be given as

(3)   $L_j = l_j x_j$   $(j = 1,..., n)$

and in all sectors as

(4)   $L = \sum_{j=1}^{n} l_j x_j$

This requirement can be broken down into the figures for men and women employed:

(5)   $L^m = \sum_{j=1}^{n} l_j^m x_j$

and

(6)   $L^w = \sum_{j=1}^{n} l_j^w x_j$

and according to qualification levels:

(7)   $L^q = \sum_{j=1}^{n} l_j^q x_j$   $(q = 1,..., Q)$.

If the results on the left-hand side of equations (3) to (7) are condensed to a column vector $p$ and the coefficients on the right-hand side of these expressions to a matrix $A_p$, labour requirements can be written as

(8)   $p = A_p x$.

In the light of (2), the direct and indirect labour input for a given final demand vector $y$ is given as

(9)   $p = A_p C y$.

If into this equation we now insert exports $E$ as the final demand, then using (9) the labour force needed for producing the exports can be calculated. It appears as

(10) $p^E = A_p C E$.

A reduction in the labour requirement resulting from imports can likewise be calculated, if the imported goods could have been produced by home industries (competitive imports). If it is assumed that one value unit of imports will always replace one value unit of demand for domestically produced goods, the effects of imports on employment can be given as

(11) $p^M = -A_p C M$.

where $M$ is the column vector of the competitive imports.

## Notes

[1] This article is based on a more comprehensive study. See D. Schumacher: *Trade with developing countries and employment in the European Community*, A comparative analysis for six EEC countries on the basis of current import and export flows in trade with industrial products, Programme of Research and Actions on the Development of the Labour Market, Study No. 82/22 (Brussels, Commission of the European Communities, 1982). Selected findings of the research project were first published in *Wochenbericht des DIW* (Berlin), No. 17/81, and in English in *Intereconomics* (Hamburg), July-Aug. 1981.

[2] For analyses of empirical studies cf. UNIDO: *The impact of trade with developing countries on employment in developed countries*, Empirical evidence from recent research, UNIDO Working Papers on Structural Changes, No. 3 (Vienna, doc. UNIDO/ICIS.85, Oct. 1978; mimeographed); OECD: *The impact of the newly industrialising countries on production and trade in manufactures*, Report by the Secretary-General (Paris, 1979), Annex II; Centre Interuniversitaire de Recherches en Sciences Humaines: *Effet sur l'emploi dans la Communauté Economique Européenne de l'évolution de la division internationale du travail entre la C.E.E. et les pays en voie de développement*, Etude n° 77/37 (Lille, 1978). A bibliography is given in Schumacher, op. cit., pp. 82-84.

[3] A very detailed treatment of the methodological questions is given by W. S. Salant and B. N. Vaccara: *Import liberalization and employment*, The effects of unilateral reductions in United States import barriers (Washington, Brookings Institution, 1961). See also H. F. Lydall: *Trade and employment*, A study of the effects of trade expansion on employment in developing and developed countries (Geneva, ILO, 1975), pp. 17-35. Some notions from the latter have been used in the representation of the effects described here.

[4] Eurostat: *Classification of products used in the European System of Integrated Economic Accounts (ESA)* (Luxembourg, 1972; doc. 931/ST/72 E).

[5] idem: *Input-output tables*, The Nine and the Community, 1970, Special Series, Vol. 8 (Luxembourg, 1978).

[6] In the case of manufacturing industry use has been made of data on the breakdown of employees in 1977 according to sex (idem: *Employment and unemployment, 1972-1978* (Luxembourg, 1979)); for the other sectors information was obtained from population censuses taken around 1970 (idem: *Censuses of population in the Community countries, 1968-1971* (Luxembourg, 1977)).

[7] idem: *Social statistics. Structure of earnings in industry, 1972*, Special Series (Luxembourg, 1975). For a detailed description of the various qualification levels cf. Vol. 1 (Methods and definitions), pp. 30-38.

[8] OECD: *Trade by commodities*, Series C (Paris).

[9] They are included in the mining and energy sector.

[10] Indices calculated from the comparison of value and quantity data in the OECD statistics were kindly made available by the EC Commission.

[11] About $2,000 million at 1977 prices.

[12] Comparable figures for the United Kingdom are not available.

[13] Greece has been an EC member since 1 January 1981.

[14] Only in Italy are major intersectoral changes caused by the trade with industrialised countries.

[15] For further details see Schumacher, op. cit., pp. 28 ff.

# [2]

## EXPORTING JOBS?
### THE IMPACT OF IMPORT COMPETITION ON EMPLOYMENT AND WAGES IN U. S. MANUFACTURING*

ANA L. REVENGA

This paper investigates the effect of increased import competition on U. S. manufacturing employment and wages, using data for a panel of manufacturing industries over the 1977–1987 period. The empirical analysis uses previously unavailable industry import price data and an instrumental variables estimation strategy. The estimates suggest that changes in import prices have a significant effect on both employment and wages. The dramatic appreciation of the dollar between 1980 and 1985 is estimated to have reduced wages by 2 percent, and employment by 4.5–7.5 percent on average in this sample of trade-impacted industries.

## I. INTRODUCTION

During the last two decades the United States has become an increasingly open economy. This has been reflected in a strong and steady increase in import penetration ratios throughout manufacturing. Between 1975 and 1985 the ratio of manufacturing imports to total domestic supply doubled, rising from 6.6 percent to 13.1 percent. During the same period U. S. manufacturing employment fell steadily, as did the standards of living of a large segment of American labor. These parallel developments have led some observers to link increased import competition with the "deindustrialization" of America and have fostered a renewed interest in the merits of protectionism. Calls for more protectionist trade policy were heard widely in the political arena throughout the 1980s. Despite recent improvements in the trade balance, such calls will continue to be heard throughout the 1990s.

This paper examines whether increased import competition has been a major factor behind declining employment and sluggish real wage growth in U. S. manufacturing. Despite the political rhetoric surrounding the issue, the links between trade and structural change in the labor market have not been convincingly

*I am grateful to Lawrence Katz for invaluable advice and to Lawrence Summers, Richard Freeman, Joshua Angrist, and an anonymous referee for many helpful comments. Seminar participants at the National Bureau of Economic Research; Harvard, Cornell, and Stanford Universities; the University of California, Berkeley and Los Angeles; the University of Chicago; the Fundacion Empresa Publica; and the Bank of Spain provided comments and suggestions on an earlier draft. The opinions expressed in this paper are solely those of the author and should not be attributed to the World Bank.

demonstrated. Previous empirical work has produced ambiguous results; earlier studies tend to find only weak correlations between increased import competition and employment decline, and similarly weak relationships between changes in import competition and manufacturing wages.[1]

These results might seem to undercut politicians' arguments that import competition has been damaging to U. S. labor. Alternatively, the failure to find a strong relationship between increased import competition and employment decline may be associated with problems in research design. This paper introduces some improvements in the methodology used to study the labor market impact of import competition and finds that changes in techniques seem to matter greatly. In contrast to most previous studies, this paper finds sizable and statistically significant effects of import competition on both employment and wages in U. S. manufacturing.

The empirical analysis is based on industry-level data for a panel of manufacturing industries over the 1977–1987 period. This period is of particular interest because of the strong appreciation of the dollar during the early 1980s, and its subsequent sharp depreciation. These wide exchange rate swings provide a natural experiment for examining the relationship between international competition and the labor market.[2] Two features distinguish this analysis from previous empirical work. First, it uses a data set that combines employment and earnings data with previously unavailable data on import prices and with industry-specific exchange rates. The import price data are based on a survey of actual transactions prices of importers, and to the extent possible reflect c.i.f. (cost, insurance, freight) prices at the U. S. border. Unlike the

---

1. Grossman [1987] examines nine manufacturing industries for the 1969–1979 period and finds a significant effect of import competition on employment in only one of the nine industries, and a significant impact of imports on wages in only two. In a similar analysis of the steel industry (see Grossman [1986]), he concludes that most of the loss in steel industry employment during the 1976–1983 period cannot be attributed to international competition. Mann [1984] also finds a small impact of import prices on employment, but finds that import share has a larger effect. Other studies have been more successful in finding a significant relationship: Freeman and Katz [1991] find a significant correlation between volume of imports and employment, and a small but statistically significant relation between imports and wages. Branson and Love [1986] find substantial effects of the real exchange rate on employment.

2. Among previous empirical studies of the labor market effects of international competition, only the papers by Branson and Love [1986, 1987] have explicitly examined the role of the appreciating dollar. This paper differs from theirs in using industry prices and source-weighted industry exchange rates rather than the aggregate exchange rates as the measure of changing international competitiveness.

unit value indexes used in previous studies, these data avoid many problems of shifting composition of goods within the aggregate category.

Second, the analysis relies on an instrumental variables (IV) estimation strategy to control for the potential correlation between import prices and the disturbances in the estimating equations. The paper proposes and tests two alternative IV strategies. One approach uses source-weighted industry exchange rates and source-weighted industry indices of foreign production costs as the instruments for the import price.[3] The alternative IV strategy is to use the unweighted exchange rates, interacted with industry group dummies, directly as the excluded instruments.

The empirical analysis shows that changes in import prices have had a significant effect on both employment and wages. The two-stage least squares (2SLS) estimates of import price elasticities range from 0.24 to 0.39 for employment, and from 0.06 to 0.09 for wages. Thus, changes in import prices appear to have a sizable effect on employment and a smaller, but significant, effect on wages. The relative size of the wage and employment elasticities suggests that labor is quite mobile *across* industries—the impact on the return to labor of an adverse trade shock in a particular industry seems to be quite small, with most of the adjustment occurring through employment.[4] Another interesting implication of the results is that exchange rate misalignments can have real effects. According to the point estimates, the 1980–1985 appreciation of the dollar reduced employment on average by 4.5–7.5 percent and wages by 1–2 percent in this sample of trade-impacted industries.

The remainder of the paper is organized as follows. Section II lays out the framework for the analysis and discusses the main econometric problems that arise in the empirical implementation. Section III presents the data and some basic, stylized facts. Section IV presents and contrasts the OLS and 2SLS results. Section V

---

3. The industry exchange rate is defined as a geometric average of the nominal exchange rates of countries accounting for more than 2 percent of industry imports. As weights, I use the share of each foreign country's goods in total U. S. imports for that particular industry category in 1984. The industry index of foreign production costs is constructed analogously and equals the import share weight times each country's aggregate producer price index. Both variables are deflated by the aggregate U. S. producer price index.

4. This analysis does not capture the effects of industry demand shifts on relative wages *within* industries. These are likely to be important if workers of different skills are imperfect substitutes.

examines the robustness of the results to changes in the specification of the estimating equations. Finally, Section VI concludes.

## II. Import Competition, Employment, and Wages: An Empirical Framework

The link between import competition and industry employment and wages is, in principle, straightforward. A change in import competition that shifts industry product demand will tend to shift employment in the same direction, with wage adjustments dampening the employment response. The magnitude of the employment and wage effects will depend on the nature of the labor market in question and on the wage-setting mechanism. In a standard competitive labor market, in which wages move to equate labor demand and labor supply, the extent of wage and employment adjustment to a shift in the demand for labor will be given by supply and demand elasticities. In a unionized labor market, where wages diverge from market-clearing rates, the patterns may be more complex. Union wages in excess of outside opportunities may allow for greater wage responsiveness to shifts in demand than do competitively determined wages—a union may choose to offer wage concessions in order to preserve jobs. Alternatively, a union may opt to maintain wages at the expense of employment. In this case, wages may prove to be less responsive to demand shocks than competitively determined wages.[5] Union wages may also respond "perversely" to shifts in demand—for example, if the industry is characterized by "endgame bargaining," in which unions, seeing little future to an industry, seek to extract as much as they can in a short period.

Other considerations may be important in determining how wages and employment adjust. If workers of different skill levels are imperfect substitutes, adjustment to shifting industry demand could occur through changes in skill-group wage differentials and through changes in the skill composition of the industry workforce. The recent literature on wage structure suggests that the within-industry component of adjustment is, in fact, important. Katz and Revenga [1989] and Bound and Johnson [1989] find that most changes in relative wages by skill group in the 1970s and 1980s occurred *within* industries. Murphy and Welch [1988] and Katz

---

5. For example, if senior workers exert a disproportionate influence on wage-setting.

and Murphy [1992] find that much of the largely within-industry expansion in education and experience wage differentials in the United States during the 1980s can be linked to changing patterns of international trade. This paper focuses exclusively on movements in relative industry employment and wages, and does not address the within-industry changes. However, the results obtained here seem to be consistent with the facts outlined above, and lend support to the claim that changes in the pattern of relative wages have *not* occurred primarily across industries.

Consider first a simple competitive labor market, in which wages adjust to equate labor demand and labor supply. Let the demand for labor in industry $i$ and year $t$ $(L_{it})$ be given, in first difference form, by

(1)        $d\ln L_{it} = dZ_{it} \sqcap + \theta_1 d\ln P_{it}^m - \theta_2 d\ln W_{it} + w_{1it},$

where $Z_{it}$ is a vector of observable factors that shift the demand for labor in industry $i$ and year $t$, $\sqcap$ is a vector of parameters, $P_{it}^m$ is the domestic currency price of the import good, $W_{it}$ is the industry wage, and $w_{1it}$ is an error term reflecting unmeasured labor demand shocks.

Let labor supply to the industry be represented, in first difference form, by a smooth upward sloping supply curve:

(2)        $d\ln L_{it} = c \cdot d\ln W_{it} + dH_{it}\lceil + w_{2it},$

where $H_{it}$ is a vector of observed factors that shift labor supply and $w_{2it}$ reflects other unmeasured labor supply shocks. Labor market clearing then yields the following quasi-reduced-form equations for changes in employment and wages:

(3)        $d\ln L_{it} = \gamma_1 dZ_{it} \sqcap + \gamma_2 d\ln P_{it}^m + \gamma_3 dH_{it}\lceil + u_{it}$

(4)        $d\ln W_{it} = \beta_1 dZ_{it} \sqcap + \beta_2 d\ln P_{it}^m + \beta_3 dH_{it}\lceil + v_{it}.$

The terms $u_{it}$ and $v_{it}$ represent unmeasured components of employment and wage variation, and are combinations of the unmeasured labor demand and labor supply shocks.

Although I have used a competitive supply and demand model to derive equations (3) and (4), their interpretation need not be limited to this approach. Similar equations could be derived from different models of union wage setting and from other noncompetitive models.

Equations (3) and (4) can, in principle, be estimated by OLS, and be used to infer employment and wage elasticities with respect to the import price. However, if the import price variable $(d\ln P_{it}^m)$ is correlated with any of the components of the disturbance term, OLS estimation will yield biased and inconsistent parameter estimates. While it seems reasonable to assume that the labor supply shocks $(w_{2it})$ will be orthogonal to the import price, it seems less likely that the orthogonality assumption will hold for the unobservable demand shocks. Correlation between the import price $d\ln P_{it}^m$ and the errors $u_{it}$ and $v_{it}$ will arise, for example, if there is an unobservable worldwide cost shock that affects the price of the import good (e.g., an unmeasured shock to the cost of materials). Alternatively, a correlation between the import price and the error could arise if, because of the size of the domestic market, taste or demand shifts in the United States had an effect on the world import price. A similar problem would exist if import prices were not set on the world market, but rather set specifically for the U. S. market.

Consistent estimates of the import price elasticity may be obtained by using instrumental variables, if an instrument that is correlated with the price of imports but not with the unobserved determinants of industry employment and wages is available. One variable that seems to satisfy these requirements is the source-weighted industry exchange rate, which is defined as a geometric average of the nominal exchange rates of countries accounting for more than 2 percent of industry imports. As weights, I use the share of each foreign country's goods in total U. S. imports for that particular industry category in 1984. This variable is correlated with the import price but, to the extent that it is primarily determined by macroeconomic factors, is likely to be orthogonal to the unobservable components of industry wage variation. This is especially true when the econometric specification includes time-period dummies, so that the estimates are driven primarily by relative wage and employment changes. An additional potential instrument is the source-weighted industry index of foreign costs. This variable is constructed analogously to the industry exchange rate and equals the import share weights times each country's aggregate producer price index.[6] As a proxy of the level of foreign costs, it should be correlated with the price of imports. Yet, because it is constructed using aggregate producer price indexes for the exporting countries, it should be orthogonal to industry-specific

---

6. Both the industry exchange rate and the industry index of foreign costs are deflated by the U. S. aggregate PPI.

shocks. Assuming that the exchange rate is always an appropriate instrument, it is possible to test the exclusion restrictions implicit in the use of this additional instrumental variable by conventional overidentification tests.

An alternative to using these source-weighted variables as the excluded instruments is to enter all the country exchange rates directly into the first-stage equation and to let the data themselves pick the weights.[7] To maintain some flexibility in the specification and to allow the weights on the country exchange rates to vary across industries, one may introduce some interaction terms between the exchange rate variables and some broad industry groupings.

Consequently, the first-stage equation becomes

(5)    $d\ln P_{it}^m = dZ_{it}\mu_1 + dH_{it}\mu_2 + \Sigma_j\Sigma_k\,\mu_{jk}\cdot(ID_k\cdot dXR_{jt}) + \xi_{it}\,,$

where $ID_k$ is an industry dummy for industry group $k$ and $XR_{jt}$ is the exchange rate for country $j$ at time $t$. Using (5), one may estimate equations (3) and (4) by two-stage least squares. While this approach greatly reduces the degrees of freedom of the first-stage estimates, it offers the advantage of not relying on an arbitrary year for constructing the weighted exchange rates. On the other hand, the first IV strategy allows each industry to have its own weighted exchange rate instrument, while this procedure allows the weighted exchange rate to vary only across broad industry categories. An additional limitation of this alternative IV strategy is that one can no longer include period effects in the second-stage equation, since doing so would introduce perfect collinearity with the exchange rate instruments.

## III. DATA DESCRIPTION

This study examines wage, employment, exchange rate, and import price data for a panel of 38 three- and four-digit SIC manufacturing industries during the 1977–1987 period. The panel is restricted to the subset of U. S. manufacturing industries for which import price series starting in or before 1980 are available. As a group, these industries accounted for 72 percent of total imports in 1985 and 35 percent of employment. A summary of sources and definitions for the different variables is presented in the Appendix.

---

7. A broadly similar estimation strategy can be found in Angrist and Krueger [1989].

The industry import price variable is a quarterly fixed-weight Laspeyres index of transactions prices based on a 1980 import market basket. Following Mann [1986], the industry exchange rate variable is defined as a geometric average of the nominal exchange rates of countries accounting for more than 2 percent of industry imports. As weights, I use the share of each foreign country's goods in total U. S. imports for that particular industry category in 1984. The indexes of foreign production costs are constructed analogously and equal the import share weights times each country's producer price index. Both variables are deflated by the U. S. aggregate Producer Price Index (PPI).

As measures of industry employment I use (1) the number of production workers in each industry and (2) average person-hours per week. The latter is constructed as the product of the number of production workers and the average number of hours worked by production workers per week. For the wage variable I use average hourly earnings for production workers in each industry, and I use (1) average hourly earnings in services and (2) average hourly earnings in trade as two different measures of the alternative wage. All wage variables are deflated by the U. S. aggregate CPI. Although these data are all available on a monthly basis, they were converted to quarterly averages for consistency with the available import price indexes.

To capture cyclical fluctuations in demand, I use two alternative aggregate measures: (1) the aggregate quarterly unemployment rate and (2) quarterly real GDP. As measures of other factor prices I consider (1) an index of the cost of materials in manufacturing and (2) an index of energy prices. I have made no attempt to measure directly the user cost of capital. Variation in the user cost of capital is assumed to be absorbed by the industry and time effects in the empirical specification.

Table I presents a complete listing of the industries included in the analysis, along with information on selected industry characteristics. The table shows employment declining between 1980 and 1985 in all but three industries. During the same period import prices fell, and import shares increased in most industries, suggesting a potential association between increased import competition and employment decline.

Table I also reveals substantial variation in the share of imports in total output across industries. To the extent that the share of imports in total output is a good measure of the intensity of import competition, its magnitude is likely to have implications

## TABLE I
### SAMPLE OF U. S. MANUFACTURING INDUSTRIES, DESCRIPTIVE STATISTICS 1980–1985

| Industry (SIC) | (1) Employment ('000s) | (2) Δ Employment[a] 1980–1985 | (3) Δ Imports[b] 1980–1985 | (4) Import share, 1985 | (5) Δ I. Share[c] 1980–1985 | (6) Δ I. Prices 1980–1985 | (7) Δ Exchange rate 1980–1985 | (8) Δ Wage 1980–1985 | (9) Δ Sales 1980–1985 | (10) Δ Consumption 1980–1985 |
|---|---|---|---|---|---|---|---|---|---|---|
| Meat products (2010) | 311.7 | 0.03 | -0.08 | 0.04 | -0.01 | -0.33 | .57 | -0.23 | 0.06 | 0.05 |
| Fruits, vege. (2030) | 192.9 | -0.08 | 2.68 | 0.31 | 0.28 | -0.06 | 0.91 | 0.02 | 0.05 | 0.41 |
| Sugar (2060) | 84.9 | -0.02 | -0.12 | 0.12 | -0.02 | -0.65 | 1.07 | 0.01 | 0.04 | 0.03 |
| Beverages (2080) | 90.1 | -0.15 | 0.11 | 0.08 | 0.004 | 0.01 | 0.56 | 0.07 | 0.06 | 0.06 |
| Textiles I (2220) | 76.7 | -0.29 | 0.42 | 0.09 | 0.03 | -0.06 | 0.40 | 0.02 | -0.08 | 0.01 |
| Textiles II (2290) | 42.5 | -0.20 | -0.07 | 0.09 | -0.01 | -0.24 | 0.34 | 0.02 | 0.00 | 0.03 |
| Apparel I (2310) | 54.0 | -0.23 | 0.60 | 0.23 | 0.10 | -0.04 | 0.33 | -0.05 | -0.08 | 0.04 |
| Apparel II (2320) | 270.8 | -0.11 | 0.63 | 0.23 | 0.09 | 0.04 | 0.33 | -0.04 | 0.01 | 0.14 |
| Apparel III (2380) | 34.9 | -0.33 | 2.24 | 0.70 | 0.52 | -0.10 | 0.33 | -0.06 | -0.12 | 0.90 |
| Lumber (2421) | 139.9 | -0.10 | 0.35 | 0.19 | 0.05 | -0.13 | 0.27 | -0.03 | -0.02 | 0.08 |
| Millwork (2430) | 192.5 | -0.16 | 0.38 | 0.08 | 0.01 | -0.20 | 0.44 | -0.04 | 0.17 | 0.19 |
| Furniture (2500) | 398.2 | 0.07 | 0.92 | 0.10 | 0.05 | -0.13 | 0.49 | 0.02 | 0.10 | 0.20 |
| Pulp mill (2610) | 148.6 | -0.03 | 0.15 | 0.30 | 0.001 | -0.32[d] | 0.44 | 0.09 | 0.15 | 0.23 |
| Paper mill (2620) | 129.6 | -0.01 | 0.32 | 0.17 | 0.02 | 0.06 | 0.49 | 0.11 | 0.16 | 0.20 |
| Tires & inner tubes (3010) | 62.9 | -0.21 | 0.34 | 0.16 | 0.02 | -0.16 | 0.19 | 0.02 | 0.15 | 0.21 |
| Footwear (m) (3143) | 34.4 | -0.35 | 0.62 | 0.31 | 0.14 | -0.09 | 0.42 | -0.04 | -0.07 | 0.03 |
| Footwear (w) (3144) | 31.2 | -0.38 | 1.04 | 0.53 | 0.27 | -0.04 | 0.42 | -0.05 | -0.15 | 0.31 |
| Ceramics (3260) | 29.5 | -0.22 | 0.25 | 0.38 | 0.09 | -0.06 | 0.18 | 0.06 | -0.17 | -0.03 |

a. Changes are log-changes for 1980:4 to 1985:4.
b. Sales and imports are deflated by the Annual Survey of Manufacturers's shipments deflator. Import prices and Exchange rates are deflated by the U. S. aggregate Producer Price Index. Wages are deflated by the U. S. aggregate Consumer Price Index.
c. Changes in import shares are *not* in logs.
d. 1981–1985.

*Source:* Data on imports, sales, and import shares are from the NBER Trade and Immigration Data Base, 1980–1985. Data on Employment and Wages are from the BLS; Establishment Survey. Data on Import Prices are from the BLS; *U. S. Import and Export Price Indexes.* Industry Exchange Rates are constructed by the author and described in Appendix A.

TABLE I
U.S. MANUFACTURING INDUSTRIES, DESCRIPTIVE STATISTICS 1980–1985 (CONTINUED)

| Industry (SIC) | (1) Employment ('000s) | (2) Δ Employment[a] 1980–1985 | (3) Δ Imports[b] 1980–1985 | (4) Import share, 1985 | (5) Δ I. Share[c] 1980–1985 | (6) Δ I. Prices 1980–1985 | (7) Δ Exchange rate 1980–1985 | (8) Δ Wage 1980–1985 | (9) Δ Sales 1980–1985 | (10) Δ Consumption 1980–1985 |
|---|---|---|---|---|---|---|---|---|---|---|
| Iron & steel I (3310) | 222.5 | −0.55 | 0.08 | 0.18 | 0.06 | −0.16 | −0.04 | −0.12 | −0.42 | −0.33 |
| Iron & steel II (3330) | 30.2 | −0.56 | −0.03 | 0.30 | 0.08 | −0.28[d] | −0.02 | −0.03 | −0.44 | −0.28 |
| Nonferrous metals (3350) | 130.9 | −0.13 | 0.71 | 0.07 | 0.04 | −0.17 | −0.02 | −0.07 | −0.05 | 0.02 |
| Nuts & screws (3450) | 71.2 | −0.12 | 0.32 | 0.10 | 0.03 | −0.23 | 0.15 | −0.00 | −0.01 | 0.05 |
| Wire products (3496) | 39.8 | −0.04 | 0.54 | 0.15 | 0.03 | −0.14 | 0.24 | −0.01 | 0.28 | 0.34 |
| Machinery I (3531) | 51.4 | −0.58 | 0.62 | 0.12 | 0.08 | −0.18 | .27 | −0.05 | −0.43 | −0.08 |
| Machinery II (3540) | 219.3 | −0.20 | 0.32 | 0.15 | 0.06 | −0.11 | 0.15 | −0.00 | −0.26 | −0.15 |
| Machinery III (3552) | 12.4 | −0.42 | −0.11 | 0.42 | 0.07 | −0.15 | 0.37 | 0.01 | −0.42 | −0.23 |
| Machinery IV (3560) | 164.4 | −0.23 | 0.13 | 0.13 | 0.05 | −0.15 | 0.30 | −0.04 | −0.12 | −0.02 |
| Computers (3570) | 178.3 | −0.05 | 2.31 | 0.16 | 0.08 | −0.16 | −0.04 | 0.06 | 1.53 | 1.68 |
| Wiring & light (3640) | 144.6 | −0.04 | 0.34 | 0.06 | 0.02 | −0.15 | −0.11 | 0.02 | 0.04 | 0.08 |

TABLE I
(CONTINUED)

| Industry (SIC) | (1) Employ-ment ('000s) | (2) Δ Employ-ment[a] 1980–1985 | (3) Δ Imports[b] 1980–1985 | (4) Import share, 1985 | (5) Δ I. Share[c] 1980–1985 | (6) Δ I. Prices 1980–1985 | (7) Δ Exchange rate 1980–1985 | (8) Δ Wage 1980–1985 | (9) Δ Sales 1980–1985 | (10) Δ Consump-tion 1980–1985 |
|---|---|---|---|---|---|---|---|---|---|---|
| Radios & TVs (3650) | 57.6 | -0.31 | 1.12 | 0.58 | 0.19 | -0.27 | -0.05 | 0.12 | 0.33 | 0.78 |
| Telephone equip. (3661) | 81.7 | -0.27 | 1.49 | 0.12 | 0.05 | -0.33 | 0.03 | -0.03 | 0.22 | 0.32 |
| Electrical mch. (3690) | 109.4 | -0.01 | 0.77 | 0.15 | 0.05 | -0.14 | 0.06 | -0.03 | 0.29 | 0.38 |
| Autos & parts (3710) | 694.3 | 0.15 | 0.59 | 0.25 | 0.04 | 0.07[d] | -0.11 | 0.00 | 0.35 | 0.43 |
| Instruments I (3820) | 137.8 | -0.12 | 0.48 | 0.09 | 0.03 | -0.10 | 0.09 | 0.02 | 0.03 | 0.11 |
| Instruments II (3830) | 16.7 | -0.09 | 0.73 | 0.16 | 0.01 | -0.16 | 0.09 | 0.04 | 0.63 | 0.72 |
| Photo equipment (3860) | 56.2 | -0.18 | 0.57 | 0.17 | 0.06 | -0.17 | 0.09 | 0.05 | 0.05 | 0.18 |
| Watches (3870) | 8.6 | -0.60 | -0.01 | 0.60 | 0.16 | -0.22 | -0.01 | -0.01 | -0.65 | -0.29 |
| Toys & sport (3940) | 68.3 | -0.21 | 0.69 | 0.38 | 0.16 | -0.05 | 0.24 | 0.02 | -0.07 | 0.20 |
| Total mfg. | 13,092.0 | -0.08 | 0.56 | 0.13 | 0.04 | --- | 0.33[e] | 0.02 | 0.11 | --- |

e. Aggregate real exchange rate.

for the relationship between import competition, employment, and wages. To investigate this, I classify the thirty-eight industries into three broad groups corresponding to high import-share, moderate import-share, and low import-share industries.[8] Table II gives the 1980–1985 and 1985–1987 mean percentage changes for the full panel and by import-share group.

The descriptive statistics presented in Table II reinforce the patterns revealed in Table I. Employment appears to decrease substantially between 1980 and 1985 for all industry groups, with the decline being significantly more marked (in percentage terms) in the high import-share industries.[9] Import prices fall uniformly across industries during that period, as expected, given the appreciation of the exchange rate. However, the declines in import prices do not appear to reflect the full magnitude of the exchange rate changes: the standard deviation of the industry exchange rate exceeds the standard deviation of the import price for all industry groups. This is consistent with previous research by Mann [1986] and Hooper and Mann [1987], which finds evidence of incomplete pass-through from exchange rates to prices. On the whole, the data confirm our vision of the 1980–1985 period as one of intensified import competition resulting from an appreciated exchange rate, and of falling employment.

The statistics reported in Table II reveal substantial variation in the patterns of exchange rate movements across industries. The standard deviation of the industry exchange rate is quite large for both the 1980–1985 and 1985–1987 periods. This indicates that there is substantial variance across industries in the pattern of exchange rate movements, the fact that the U. S. dollar moves quite differently vis-à-vis the currencies of different countries. Figure I brings out this point. This set of graphs plots the U. S. real exchange rate against the currencies of some major trading

8. Import share is defined as imports/(domestic output + imports). High import share industries are defined to be those in which imports comprised at least 20 percent of total new supply in 1984. Medium import share industries have import shares of 10 to 20 percent. Low import share industries have import shares of less than 10 percent.

9. To some extent, this may reflect the secular decline of these high-import share industries: between 1970 and 1980 employment in this group of industries declined by 24 percent on average, while employment in the medium import-share and low import-share groups increased by 2 percent and 5 percent, respectively. However, it is worth noting that, during the same period, the mean import share in the high import industries increased by ten percentage points, whereas it increased by only three percentage points and one percentage point, respectively, in the other two groups of industries.

TABLE II
LONG-PERIOD CHANGES, 1980–1987

| Variable | All industries | High import share | Medium import share | Low import share |
|---|---|---|---|---|
| | (a) Mean log changes, 1980–1985 (S.D. log changes) | | | |
| Employment | −0.171 | −0.278 | −0.138 | −0.078 |
| | (0.177) | (0.154) | (0.173) | (0.153) |
| Real wage | −0.005 | −0.003 | −0.001 | −0.017 |
| | (0.063) | (0.054) | (0.052) | (0.099) |
| Import price | −0.185 | −0.139 | −0.203 | −0.203 |
| index | (0.119) | (0.109) | (0.135) | (0.107) |
| Industry exchange | 0.332 | 0.335 | 0.262 | 0.421 |
| rate | (0.244) | (0.191) | (0.254) | (0.266) |
| Aggregate exchange | | | | |
| rate | 0.327 | 0.327 | 0.327 | 0.327 |
| Materials prices | −0.022 | −0.022 | −0.022 | −0.022 |
| Import share | 0.080 | 0.150 | 0.051 | 0.045 |
| | (0.098) | (0.129) | (0.042) | (0.078) |
| | (b) Mean log changes, 1985–1987 (S.D. log changes) | | | |
| Employment | 0.007 | 0.012 | −0.010 | 0.034 |
| | (0.078) | (0.078) | (0.084) | (0.061) |
| Real wage | −0.011 | −0.016 | −0.010 | −0.006 |
| | (0.028) | (0.037) | (0.023) | (0.023) |
| Import price | 0.174 | 0.191 | 0.156 | 0.180 |
| index | (0.085) | (0.092) | (0.089) | (0.065) |
| Industry exchange | −0.133 | −0.174 | −0.087 | −0.146 |
| rate | (0.435) | (0.372) | (0.527) | (0.407) |
| Aggregate exchange rate | −0.370 | −0.370 | −0.370 | −0.370 |
| Materials prices | 0.038 | 0.038 | 0.038 | 0.038 |

*Notes.* Employment is measured in average person-hours per week. Sales and Imports are deflated by the ASM's shipments deflator. Industry import prices and exchange rates are deflated by the U. S. aggregate PPI. Wages are deflated by the aggregate CPI. The aggregate exchange rate is the IMF's Relative Unit Labor Costs Index. Import shares are defined as imports/(domestic output + imports). High import share industries are defined as those with import shares greater than or equal to 0.20 in 1984. Medium import share industries are those with import shares greater than or equal to 0.10 but less than 0.20. Low import share industries are those with import shares less than 0.10.

partners. Figure II shows similar plots of movements in industry exchange rates. Clearly the different movements of the dollar vis-à-vis the currencies of different trading partners imply significantly different patterns of exchange rate changes across industries.

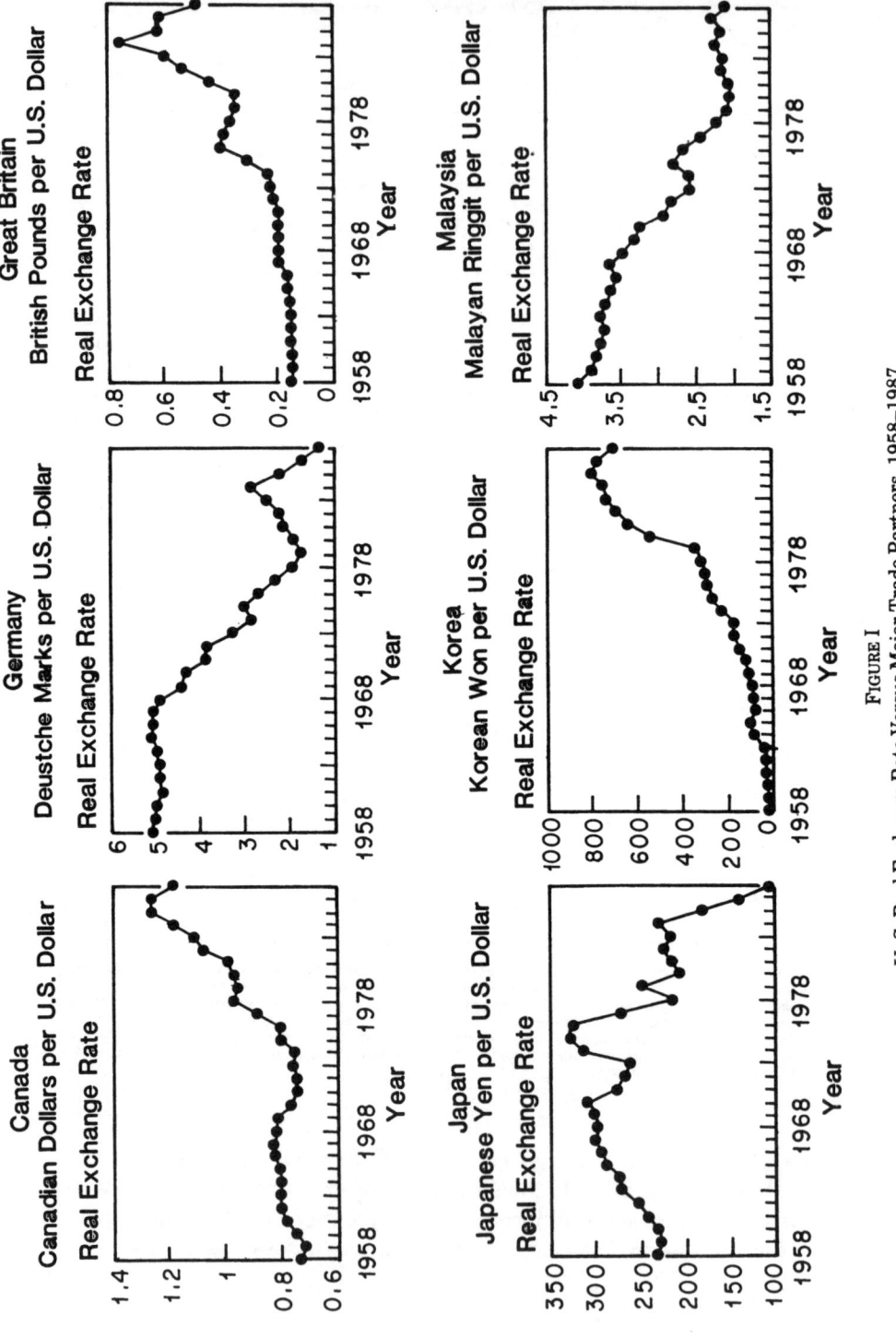

FIGURE I

U. S. Real Exchange Rate Versus Major Trade Partners, 1958–1987

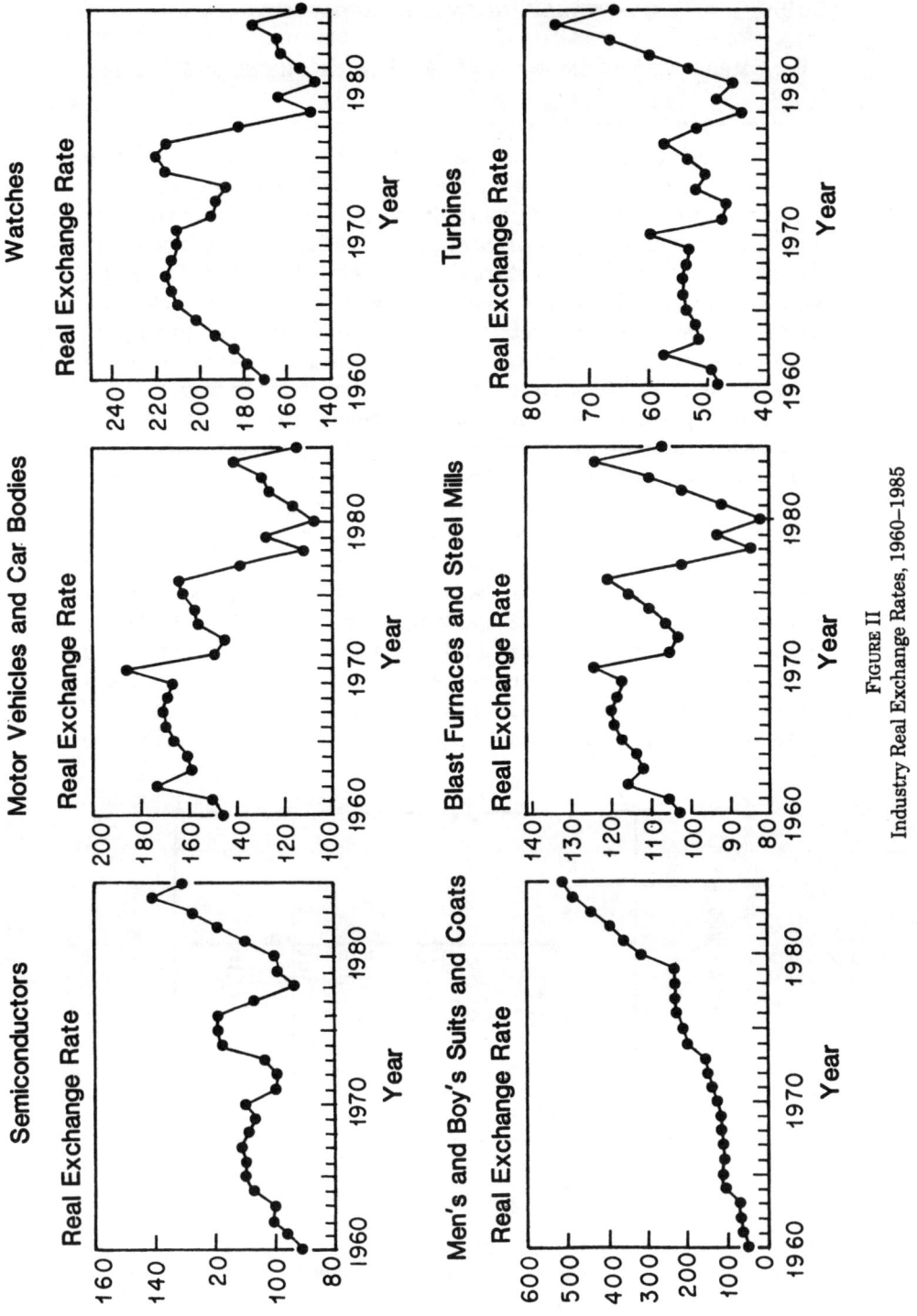

FIGURE II
Industry Real Exchange Rates, 1960–1985

## IV. EMPIRICAL EVIDENCE FOR U. S. MANUFACTURING INDUSTRIES

### A. *Long-Period Changes*

Figures III and IV plot the 1981–1985 changes in industry employment and wages against the 1981–1985 changes in industry import prices. I chose 1981 as the base year because it is the first full year for which import price data are available for all industries (some import price series start during 1980). I chose 1985 as the comparison point because it marks the peak of the dollar cycle. The plots suggest a positive relationship between changes in import prices and changes in employment, and a similar positive relationship between changes in import prices and changes in wages.

These patterns are confirmed by regressing the 1981–1985 changes in log industry employment and log industry wages on a constant and on the 1981–1985 changes in log industry import prices. OLS estimation yields an import price elasticity of 0.79 ($SE = 0.31$) for employment, and an import price elasticity of 0.03 ($SE = 0.11$) for wages. When industry exchange rates and industry foreign production costs are used as instruments for import prices, the estimated import price elasticities are 1.74 ($SE = 1.31$) for employment and 0.40 ($SE = 0.38$) for wages. As a first cut, these results indicate a likely relationship between increased import competition—as reflected in lower relative import prices—and employment and wage decline in U. S. manufacturing during the

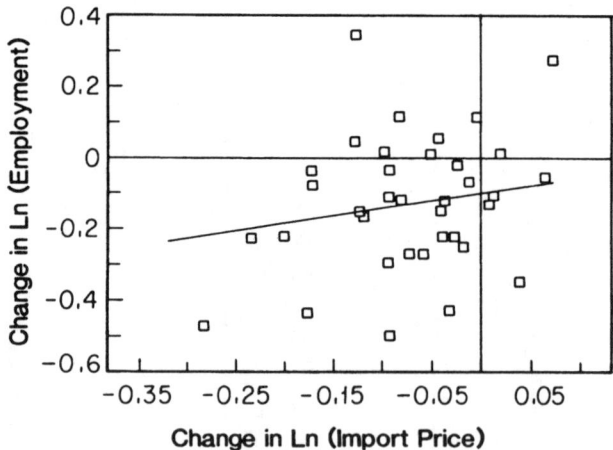

FIGURE III
Long-Period Changes, 1981–1985

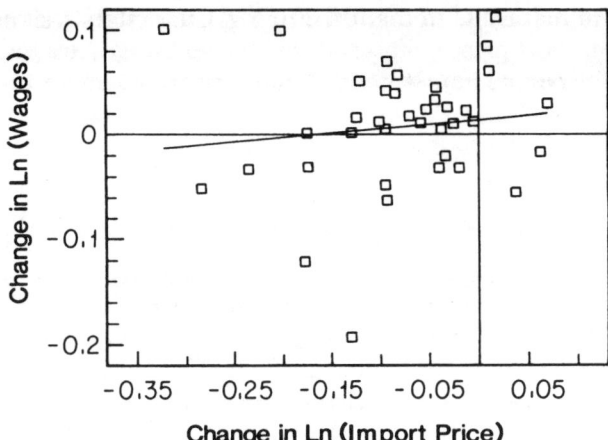

FIGURE IV
Long-Period Changes, 1981–1985

early 1980s. With these basic facts in mind, I turn now to the more detailed quarterly analysis.

*B. Quarterly Changes*

The quarterly analysis is based on equations (3) and (4), as developed in Section II. The equations include industry fixed effects to capture industry-specific differences in the rates of growth of employment and wages.[10] Regressions are estimated using pooled cross-section time-series quarterly data on 38 three- and four-digit SIC industries for the 1977–1987 period. Standard errors are corrected for arbitrary conditional heteroskedasticity.

Table III presents the estimation results for the (first-differenced) quasi-reduced-form wage and employment equations. The dependent variable in column (1) is average weekly person-hours. The dependent variable in column (2) is the number of production workers. The dependent variable in column (3) is the industry wage. The determinants of industry wages and employment include a cyclical variable (the aggregate unemployment rate), the real domestic currency price of the import good, the alternative real wage (the average real wage in services), and the

10. The sensitivity of the results to the inclusion of industry or time fixed effects is discussed in Section V.

real cost of materials in manufacturing. Current as well as lagged values of import prices, materials prices, and wages are included to account for partial adjustment of industry employment to demand shocks.

TABLE III
WAGE AND EMPLOYMENT EQUATIONS, FIRST DIFFERENCES[a]
ALL INDUSTRIES, 1977–1987

| | (a) Ordinary least squares estimates | | |
|---|---|---|---|
| | Employment | | |
| Variable | Hours (1) | Workers (2) | Wages (3) |
| Unemployment | −0.311 | −0.192 | −0.006 |
| | (0.030) | (0.027) | (0.006) |
| Import price | 0.059 | 0.070 | −0.007 |
| | (0.085) | (0.074) | (0.016) |
| Alternative wage | −0.026 | −0.011 | 0.485 |
| | (0.021) | (0.018) | (0.057) |
| Materials prices | −0.377 | −0.510 | −0.117 |
| | (0.231) | (0.203) | (0.102) |
| Industry dummies | yes | yes | yes |
| $R^2$ | 0.157 | 0.117 | 0.125 |
| $N$ | 1,243 | 1,243 | 1,287 |

| | (b) Instrumental variables estimates 1[b] (IV1) | | |
|---|---|---|---|
| | Employment | | |
| Variable | Hours (1) | Workers (2) | Wages (3) |
| Unemployment | −0.293 | −0.177 | −0.005 |
| | (0.033) | (0.029) | (0.006) |
| Import price | 0.387 | 0.351 | 0.085 |
| | (0.257) | (0.225) | (0.044) |
| Alternative wage | −0.036 | −0.019 | 0.463 |
| | (0.022) | (0.019) | (0.058) |
| Materials prices | −0.462 | −0.584 | −0.324 |
| | (0.241) | (0.212) | (0.143) |
| Industry dummies | yes | yes | yes |
| $N$ | 1,243 | 1,243 | 1,243 |
| $\chi^2$ statistic for | | | |
| GMM specification test | 8.64 | 6.17 | 5.99 |
| [prob. value] | [0.17] | [0.29] | [0.30] |

TABLE III
(CONTINUED)

| | (c) Instrumental variables estimates $2^c$ (IV2) Employment | | |
| Variable | Hours (1) | Workers (2) | Wages (3) |
|---|---|---|---|
| Unemployment | −0.296 | −0.170 | −0.009 |
| | (0.030) | (0.026) | (0.006) |
| Import price | 0.285 | 0.236 | 0.062 |
| | (0.132) | (0.116) | (0.026) |
| Alternative wage | −0.016 | −0.008 | 0.460 |
| | (0.030) | (0.027) | (0.054) |
| Materials prices | −0.310 | −0.520 | −0.299 |
| | (0.205) | (0.181) | (0.090) |
| Industry dummies | yes | yes | yes |
| N | 1,343 | 1,343 | 1,345 |
| $\chi^2$ statistic for | | | |
| GMM specification test | 112.3 | 96.1 | 39.3 |
| [prob. value] | [0.05] | [0.28] | [0.10] |

a. All equations estimated in log differences. The sample covers 38 three- and four-digit SIC industries over the 1977:1–1987:4 period. Equation (1): the dependent variable is average weekly person-hours. Equation (2): the dependent variable is number of production workers. Equation (3): the dependent variable is the real wage for production workers. The employment equations allow for three lags on the import price, one lag on the alternative wage, and one lag on the cost of materials. The wage equation is identical but includes only one lag on the import price. The reported coefficients are the sums of the lag coefficients. The equations in panel (c) do not include any lags on the import price. Standard errors (in parentheses) are corrected for arbitrary conditional heteroskedasticity and MA(1) error.

b. Instrumental variables for the import price include industry-specific source-weighted foreign PPIs and industry-specific source-weighted exchange rates.

c. These equations do not allow for any lags on the import price. The instruments for the contemporaneous import price are the unweighted exchange rates for six countries (Canada, West Germany, the United Kingdom, Japan, Korea, and Singapore), interacted with five broad industry group dummies. In the employment equations the instruments also include first and second lags on the full set of interacted exchange rates.

The top panel of Table III presents the OLS estimates. In both the employment and wage equations, the correlation between import prices and the dependent variable is close to zero. Employment is negatively related to the aggregate unemployment rate, weakly negatively related to the alternative wage, and negatively related to materials prices. Wages are negatively correlated with the price of materials and weakly negatively correlated with the aggregate unemployment rate, but positively correlated with alternative wage.

Panel (b) in Table III presents similar specifications which control for the endogeneity of import prices through an instrumental variables approach. Instruments for the price of imports include current and lagged values of the industry-specific exchange rate, and current and lagged values of industry-specific foreign production costs. The 2SLS estimates are quite different from those obtained using OLS. The estimated effect of import prices on employment is positive, much larger in magnitude and nearly significant at conventional levels. The effect of import prices on wages is positive and significant, although smaller in magnitude than the employment effect.

The point estimate of the elasticity of employment with respect to import prices is 0.39 when one uses person-hours as a measure of employment, and 0.35 when one uses production worker employment instead. These estimates imply that a 10 percent reduction in the price of the import substitute reduces employment by 3.5 to 3.9 percent, depending on the employment measure used. Since import prices during the 1980–1985 period fell by 19 percent on average, the appreciation of the dollar appears to have reduced employment by approximately 6.5 to 7.5 percent. The estimated wage elasticity is substantially smaller: the point estimate is 0.09. This associates the real appreciation of the dollar with a 2 percent drop in industry wages. This result is consistent with findings by Freeman and Katz [1991], who estimate a small but significant response of industry wages to weighted changes in import penetration. Similarly, Revenga [1990] finds a significant relationship between changes in industry wages and changes in domestic industry sales.[11]

The specification tests reported at the bottom of panel (b) examine the assumption of the orthogonality of the instruments and the error terms in the wage and employment equations. The Generalized Method of Moments (GMM) error-orthogonality test involves regressing the two-stage least squares residuals on the set of instrumental variables; $N$ times the $R^2$ from this regression, where $N$ equals the degrees of freedom from the original equation, asymptotically follows a chi-squared distribution. A weak relationship between the residuals and the instruments would indicate that the equation is properly specified.[12] The reported chi-squared

---

11. Revenga [1990] closely follows the analytical approach developed in Freeman and Katz [1991], but uses an instrumental variables estimation strategy similar to that developed here, to control for the potential simultaneity bias arising from the impact of wages on industry prices and output, and therefore on sales. The IV estimates tend to reinforce the findings of Freeman and Katz and suggest that OLS estimation significantly underestimates the true response of wages to trade-induced demand shocks.

12. Or, alternatively, that the test has little power.

test of the null hypothesis of no misspecification fails to reject at the 0.10 level in all three cases.

Panel (c) in Table III shows the elasticities obtained using the alternative instrumental variables estimation strategy. This strategy consists of entering all the unweighted country exchange rates directly into the first-stage equation, thus letting the data themselves pick the weights attached to each exchange rate. To maintain some flexibility in the specification, and to allow the weights to vary across industries, I introduce interaction terms between the exchange rate variables and dummies for broad industry groupings. To conserve degrees of freedom, I limit the exchange rate variables to six countries, and divide the sample of industries into five broad groups.[13] This yields thirty excluded instruments for the contemporaneous import price: six exchange rates interacted with five industry group dummies.[14]

The 2SLS estimates shown in panel (c) are similar to those shown in panel (b). The estimated import price elasticities are all positive and significant at conventional levels. The estimates for employment are 0.28 for the hours equation, and 0.24 for the workers equation. The estimated import price elasticity for wages is 0.062. All of these estimates appear to be slightly smaller in magnitude than those obtained with the alternative IV procedure. However, the equations in panel (c) do not allow for any lags on the import price, so the estimates are not directly comparable to those in top and middle panels. When the regressions in panel (b) are estimated without lags in the import price, the estimated elasticities are 0.30 (0.19) for employment and 0.07 (0.04) for wages. Thus, both sets of 2SLS estimates are actually very similar. The GMM specification tests of instrument-error orthogonality, re-

13. The six countries are Canada, West Germany, the United Kingdom, Japan, Korea, and Singapore. The five industry groups are the following. Group 1 includes food and raw materials related manufacturing industries: SICs 2010, 2030, 2060, 2080, 2421, 2430, 2500, 2610, 2620, and 3010. Group 2 includes the textile, apparel, footwear, and ceramic industries: SICs 2220, 2290, 2310, 2320, 2380, 3143, 3144, and 3260. Group 3 covers the primary metals and fabricated metal products industries: SICs 3310, 3330, 3350, 3450, and 3496. Group 4 includes all the machinery industries: SICs 3531, 3540, 3552, 3560, 3570, 3640, 3650, 3661, 3690, and 3710. Finally, group 5 includes instruments and other miscellaneous SICs: 3820, 3830, 3860, 3870, and 3940. The results are not very sensitive to altering the countries included in the analysis and to changing the industry groupings.

14. In the employment equations the instruments for the import price also include first and second lags of the full set of exchange rates and interactions. This yields 90 excluded instruments for the contemporaneous import price. Note that the equations in panel (c) do not allow for any lags in the import price. Including lagged import prices would require using additional excluded instruments, and this would seriously reduce the degrees of freedom of the analysis.

ported at the bottom of panel (c), are below conventional significance levels, suggesting that the exchange rates interacted with the industry group dummies are a valid set of instruments for these equations.

One potential criticism of the GMM test is that it is unlikely to detect a single deviation from the null when there are numerous overidentifying restrictions. An alternative is to test whether the overall exchange rate (weighted for all industries together) is orthogonal to the residuals in panels (b) and (c) of Table III (as opposed to testing whether all the instruments are jointly orthogonal to the residuals).[15] Regressing the 2SLS residuals from panel (b) (IV1 approach) on the overall exchange rate yields a coefficient of $-0.001$ ($SE = 0.002$) for wages, and of $-0.001$ ($SE = 0.01$) for employment. A similar regression for the residuals in panel (c) (IV2 approach) yields coefficients of $-0.003$ ($SE = 0.002$) for wages and $-0.002$ (0.002) for employment. In all cases, the coefficient on the overall exchange rate is not significantly different from zero, suggesting that the exchange rate can be considered exogenous. However, the evidence supporting the exogeneity of the instruments for the models in panel (c) is a bit weak, particularly for the wage equation. The coefficient on the aggregate exchange rate, although very small, is nearly significant.

The results from Table III seem to suggest that the OLS coefficients are significantly downward biased. There appears to be a simultaneous relationship between import prices and industry wages, and possibly a similar simultaneous relationship between import prices and industry employment. The failure to consider this potential endogeneity of import prices in the wage and employment equations may explain in part the weakness of the results reported in previous studies.[16]

Table IV presents the coefficients obtained from regressing the wage and employment equations with import prices interacted with industry import shares. This set of estimates suggests that the responsiveness of employment and wages to changes in import prices varies positively with the degree of import penetration in the industry. The elasticity with respect to the import price for an industry with an 18 percent import penetration ratio (sample

---

15. This specification test was suggested by an anonymous referee.
16. To test more formally for the endogeneity of import prices, I performed Hausman [1978] specification tests on all the reduced-form equations. The results suggest a strong simultaneous relationship between import prices and industry wages. However, the results for employment are much weaker.

TABLE IV
WAGE AND EMPLOYMENT EQUATIONS, FIRST DIFFERENCES[a]
IMPORT PRICE INTERACTED WITH IMPORT SHARE

|  | Employment | | Wages | |
|---|---|---|---|---|
|  | IV1 | IV2 | IV1 | IV2 |
| Import price * import share | 0.89 | 0.56 | 0.32 | 0.24 |
|  | (0.48) | (0.33) | (0.19) | (0.11) |
| Import price elasticity evaluated at: | | | | |
| Import share[b] = 0.18 (sample mean) | 0.16 | 0.10 | 0.06 | 0.04 |
| Import share = 0.32 (1 SD above mean) | 0.29 | 0.18 | 0.10 | 0.08 |
| Import share = 0.03 (1 SD below mean) | 0.03 | 0.02 | 0.01 | 0.01 |

a. The equations are identical to those presented in Table IV, but include the import price interacted with the industry import share.

b. Import share = Imports/(imports + domestic output). Mean import share for the sample (whole period) is 0.18. Mean import share in 1977 was 0.09. In 1985 it was 0.22.

average) is of 0.16 for employment and 0.06 for wages. The corresponding elasticities for an industry with a 32 percent import penetration ratio (one standard deviation above the mean) are 0.29 for employment and 0.10 for wages.

Tables III and IV suggest several conclusions. The main finding is that import competition has had a significant effect on both employment and wages. Although OLS estimation fails to detect any significant import price effect on either employment or wages, both alternative 2SLS procedures yield positive and significant or nearly significant import price elasticities. These estimated 2SLS import price elasticities range from 0.24 to 0.39 for employment, and from 0.06 to 0.09 for wages. Thus, all else equal, a 10 percent reduction in the price of the competing import good is associated, on average, with a drop of about 2.5 to 4 percent in employment, and of about 0.5 to 1 percent in wages. Taken together with the findings of Murphy and Welch [1988] among others, these results suggest that workers are highly mobile across industries but not across skill groups.

## V. SENSITIVITY ANALYSIS

Tables V and VI present the results of estimating the wage and employment equations with and without time-varying covariates, and with or without industry and time-period dummies. Table V

TABLE V

WAGE AND EMPLOYMENT EQUATIONS, FIRST-DIFFERENCES[a]

SENSITIVITY OF THE RESULTS TO PERIOD AND INDUSTRY FIXED EFFECTS

Instrumental variables estimates 1[b]

| Variable | Employment | | | | | | Wages | | | | | |
|---|---|---|---|---|---|---|---|---|---|---|---|---|
| | (1) | (2) | (3) | (4) | (5) | (6) | (1) | (2) | (3) | (4) | (5) | (6) |
| Import price | 0.713 | 0.239 | −0.462 | 0.747 | 0.387 | 0.766 | 0.082 | 0.053 | 0.053 | 0.097 | 0.085 | 0.082 |
| | (0.285) | (0.273) | (0.624) | (0.251) | (0.257) | (0.706) | (0.042) | (0.046) | (0.024) | (0.038) | (0.044) | (0.054) |
| Unemployment rate | ... | −0.297 | ... | ... | −0.293 | ... | ... | −0.007 | ... | ... | −0.005 | ... |
| | | (0.034) | | | (0.033) | | | (0.006) | | | (0.006) | |
| Alternative wage | ... | −0.016 | ... | ... | −0.036 | ... | ... | 0.521 | ... | ... | 0.463 | ... |
| | | (0.016) | | | (0.022) | | | (0.059) | | | (0.058) | |
| Materials prices | ... | −0.474 | ... | ... | −0.462 | ... | ... | −0.249 | ... | ... | −0.324 | ... |
| | | (0.237) | | | (0.241) | | | (0.109) | | | (0.143) | |
| Industry dummies | no | no | yes | yes | yes | yes | no | no | yes | yes | yes | yes |
| Time dummies | no | no | yes | no | no | yes | no | no | yes | no | no | yes |
| N | 1,242 | 1,242 | 1,242 | 1,242 | 1,242 | 1,242 | 1,242 | 1,242 | 1,242 | 1,242 | 1,242 | 1,242 |

a. All equations estimated in log differences. The dependent variable in the employment equations is average weekly person-hours. The dependent variable in the wage equations is the real wage for production workers. The econometric specification includes three lagged values of the import price for employment and one lagged value of the import price for wages. The equations also include one lagged value of the alternative wage and one lagged value of materials prices. The reported coefficients are the sums of the lags.
b. Instrumental variables for the import price include industry-specific PPIs and industry-specific source-weighted foreign PPIs and industry-specific source-weighted exchange rates.

TABLE VI
WAGE AND EMPLOYMENT EQUATIONS, FIRST-DIFFERENCES[a]
SENSITIVITY OF THE RESULTS TO INDUSTRY FIXED EFFECTS

| | Instrumental variables estimates 2[b] | | | | | | | |
| | Employment | | | | Wages | | | |
| Variable | (1) | (2) | (3) | (4) | (1) | (2) | (3) | (4) |
|---|---|---|---|---|---|---|---|---|
| Import price | 0.222 | 0.171 | 0.246 | 0.285 | 0.095 | 0.064 | 0.091 | 0.062 |
| | (0.097) | (0.098) | (0.098) | (0.132) | (0.023) | (0.027) | (0.023) | (0.026) |
| Unemployment | ... | −0.314 | ... | −0.170 | ... | −0.010 | ... | −0.009 |
| rate | | (0.027) | | (0.026) | | (0.006) | | (0.006) |
| Alternative | ... | −0.010 | ... | −0.008 | ... | 0.468 | ... | 0.460 |
| wage | | (0.028) | | (0.027) | | (0.053) | | (0.054) |
| Materials prices | ... | −0.439 | ... | −0.310 | ... | −0.277 | ... | −0.299 |
| | | (0.203) | | (0.181) | | (0.090) | | (0.090) |
| Industry dummies | no | no | yes | yes | no | no | yes | yes |

a. All equations estimated in log differences. The dependent variable in the employment equations is average weekly person-hours. The dependent variable in the wage equations is the real wage for production workers. The econometric specifications do not allow for any lags on the import price.

b. The instruments for the contemporaneous import price are the unweighted exchange rates for six countries (Canada, West Germany, the United Kingdom, Japan, Korea, and Singapore), interacted with five broad industry group dummies. The instruments also include first and second lags on the full set of interacted exchange rates.

shows the 2SLS estimates obtained using source-weighted industry exchange rates and source-weighted industry indices of foreign costs as the instruments for the price of imports. Table VI presents the results of estimating similar equations using unweighted exchange rates interacted with industry group dummies as the excluded instruments for the import price. Both sets of 2SLS estimates are, once again, quite similar. However, entering the exchange rate variables directly into the first-stage equation, rather than using the source-weighted series, tends to yield smaller standard errors and therefore more precise estimates.

Columns (1) and (2) in both tables present the estimates from the pooled cross-section time-series models, with both slope and intercept coefficients restricted to be constant over time and across industries. These specifications do not allow for parameter heterogeneity among industries or over time, but offer the advantage of drawing on all sources of variation—cross-section and time-series—in the data. The estimates obtained with the simplest specification (column (1)) are positive and strongly significant for both employment and wages. With no other controls included in the equation, decreases in import prices—implying increases in import competition—are strongly associated with declines in employment and wages. A comparison of columns (1) and (2) shows that adding other time-varying covariates significantly decreases the estimated import price elasticity for both employment and wages. This is to be expected given that adding the other covariates serves to control for much of the time-series variation in the data.

Because these restricted specifications do not allow for any heterogeneity in trend growth rates across industries, the estimates are likely to be biased. Columns (4) and (5) present less-restrictive specifications that allow for industry fixed effects. By including industry dummies in the difference equations, I allow the rate of growth of employment and wages to differ across industries. The other explanatory variables then serve to explain the deviations from that rate. This approach uses the within-industry, purely time-series variation in the data to estimate the parameters. Column (4) presents the results of estimating a first-difference equation, which includes import prices and industry fixed effects, but no other time-varying covariates. All the time-series variation in employment and wages is then linked to the variation in the price of imports. Not surprisingly, this approach yields larger and significant import price effects. Adding other time-varying explanatory variables again decreases the magnitude of the estimated import price elasticities, which, however, remain positive and significant. These sets of estimates, which correspond to the regressions estimated in Section IV, are presented in column (5) of both tables.

An alternative to including other time-varying covariates in the regression is to include time dummies instead. These time fixed-effects capture period-specific shocks that are common to all industries. The resulting estimates are then primarily driven by the cross-industry variation in the data. The advantage of this approach is that you control for any excluded time-varying variables, and thus reduce the problems with omitted variable bias. These estimates are shown in columns (3) and (6) of Table V. No period effects are included in the regressions presented in Table VI because doing so would introduce perfect collinearity between the fixed-effects and the exchange rate instruments.

Including period effects in the employment equation tends to increase the estimated import price elasticity. However, the addition of period effects also seems to increase the standard error more than proportionately. This suggests that despite substantial cross-industry variation in the data, the employment results are driven primarily by time-series changes. That is, most of the identification in the employment equation seems to be coming from the large time-series movements in import prices. This is not surprising given the large real exchange rate swings that characterize this period. Introducing the period effects in the wage equation does not have much of an impact. The estimates reported in column (3) and (6) are practically identical to those shown in columns (2) and (5), which rely instead on the time-varying covariates.

## V. CONCLUSIONS

This paper has investigated the impact of increased import competition on employment and wages, using data for a panel of U. S. manufacturing industries over the 1977–1987 period. This period is of particular interest because it captures the dollar's appreciation during the early 1980s, and its subsequent deprecia- tion. It thus provides a natural experiment for examining the relationship between import prices, employment, and wages.

The main empirical finding is that changes in import prices have had large and significant effects on both employment and wages. The estimated import price elasticities range from 0.24 to 0.39 for employment, and from 0.06 to 0.09 for wages. The relative size of the wage and employment effects suggests that the impact of an adverse trade shock on average wages in a particular industry is quite small, with most of the adjustment occurring through employment. This seems to imply that labor is quite mobile across industries. However, since these estimates represent averages for the panel of industries, they may hide substantial variation across sectors.[17] Note also that the estimates do not reflect within- industry changes in employment and wages, which we know have represented a large fraction of the movements in the wage struc- ture during the 1980s.

An interesting implication of the results is that exchange rate misalignments can have real effects. These estimates suggest that the misalignment of the dollar between 1980 and 1985 reduced employment on average by 4.5–7.5 percent and wages by 1–2 percent in this sample of trade-impacted industries.

Finally, the results also offer a useful insight on methodology.

---

17. Evidence provided by Freeman and Katz [1991] and Revenga [1990] suggests that the extent of wage adjustment does vary significantly across sectors.

282          *QUARTERLY JOURNAL OF ECONOMICS*

The comparison of the OLS and 2SLS estimates suggests the existence of a simultaneous relationship between industry employment and the price of the import substitute, or of an omitted variable that is jointly correlated with employment and the import price. The evidence suggests that a similar simultaneous relationship exists between import prices and industry wages. The OLS estimates of the import price elasticities seem to be significantly downward biased, which may help explain why previous studies of the labor market effects of import competition have usually found weak results.

APPENDIX: DATA SOURCES AND VARIABLE DEFINITIONS

*A. Import Prices*

Import price data on a disaggregated SIC basis are taken from the Bureau of Labor Statistics, *U. S. Import and Export Price Indexes*. The industry import price variable is a quarterly fixed-weight Laspeyres price index based on a 1980 import market basket. These indexes are based on a survey of actual transactions prices of importers, and to the extent possible reflect c.i.f. (cost, insurance, freight) prices at the U. S. border.

*B. Industry Exchange Rates and Industry Foreign Costs*

Following Mann [1986], the exchange rate index for each industry is defined as a geometric average of the nominal exchange rates of countries accounting for more than 2 percent of industry imports. The weights are the share of each foreign country's goods in total U. S. imports for that particular industry category in 1984. The indexes of foreign production costs are constructed analogously, and equal the import share weights times each country's aggregate producer price index. Both variables are deflated by the aggregate U. S. PPI.

The construction of both of these variables was complicated by the lack of data on import volumes on a SIC basis. Import volumes by country are available only according to the Standard International Trade Classifications (SITC) system, and a usable concordance between the two classifications schemes does not exist. As a consequence, constructing the desired exchange rate and foreign costs variables involved a three-step procedure. First, I calculated country weights on an SITC basis, using import volumes derived from the United Nations COMTRADE data base. Then, I developed a concordance between the two classification systems using the Commerce Department's *U. S. Foreign Trade Statistics: Classifications and Cross-Classifications,* which provides separate concordances between Schedule A classifications (which generally parallel those of the SITC) and those of the Tariff Schedules of the United States Annotated (TSUSA), and between the latter and the SIC scheme. I then used this concordance to determine what SITC categories to aggregate to derive the SIC categories. Once the import share weights were determined, calculating the exchange rate and foreign costs indexes was straightforward.

## C. Employment and Earnings

Data for the following industry-level variables are taken from the Bureau of Labor Statistics (BLS), Establishment Survey: (1) production worker employment; (2) average weekly hours for production workers; (3) average hourly earnings for production workers; (4) average hourly earnings in services; (5) average hourly earnings in trade. All wage variables are deflated by the U. S. consumer price index (CPI).

## D. Energy Prices, Materials Costs, and Aggregate Demand Variables

Data for the following aggregate variables were taken from the Data Resources, Inc. *U. S. Central* data base: (1) aggregate quarterly unemployment rate; (2) quarterly real GDP; (3) quarterly index of energy prices; (4) quarterly index of the cost of materials in manufacturing.

THE WORLD BANK

## REFERENCES

Angrist, Joshua, and Alan B. Krueger, "Why Do World War II Veterans Earn More Than Non-Veterans?" NBER Working Paper No. 2991, 1989.

Bound, John, and George Johnson, "Changes in the Structure of Wages During the 1980's: An Evaluation of Alternative Explanations," unpublished paper, University of Michigan, 1989.

Branson, William H., and James P. Love, "Dollar Appreciation and Manufacturing Employment and Output," NBER Working Paper No. 1972, 1986.

____, and ____, "U. S. Manufacturing and the Real Exchange Rate," in R. Marston, ed., *Misalignment of Exchange Rates: Effects on Trade and Industry* (Chicago: The University of Chicago Press, 1988).

Freeman, Richard B., and Lawrence F. Katz, "Industrial Wage and Employment Determination in an Open Economy," in John M. Abowd and Richard Freeman, eds., *Immigration, Trade and the Labor Market* (Chicago: University of Chicago Press, 1991), pp. 235–59.

Grossman, Gene M., "Imports as a Cause of Injury: The Case of the U. S. Steel Industry," *Journal of International Economics,* XX (1986), 201–23.

284 *QUARTERLY JOURNAL OF ECONOMICS*

——, "The Employment and Wage Effects of Import Competition," *Journal of International Economic Integration,* II (1987), 1–23.

Hausman, J. A., "Specification Tests in Econometrics," *Econometrica,* XLVI (1978), 1251–71.

Hooper, Peter, and Catherine L. Mann, "The U. S. External Deficit: Its Causes and Persistence," International Finance Discussion Paper No. 316, 1987.

Katz, Lawrence F., and Kevin M. Murphy, "Changes in Relative Wages, 1963–1987: Supply and Demand Factors," *Quarterly Journal of Economics,* CVII (1992), 35–78.

Katz, Lawrence F., and Ana L. Revenga, "Changes in the Structure of Wages: The U. S. vs. Japan," *Journal of the Japanese and International Economies,* III (1989), 522–53.

Mann, Catherine L., "Employment and Capacity Utilization in Import Sensitive U. S. Industries," Ph.D. thesis, M.I.T., 1984, Chapter 3.

——, "Prices, Profit Margins, and Exchange Rates," *Federal Reserve Bulletin,* VII (1986), 306–79.

Murphy, Kevin, and Finis Welch, "Wage Differentials in the 1980s: The Role of International Trade," unpublished paper, University of Chicago, 1988.

Revenga, Ana L., "Wage Determination in an Open Economy: International Trade and U. S. Manufacturing Wages," unpublished paper, Harvard University, 1990.

# [3]

European Economic Review 30 (1986) 427–438. North-Holland

## THE EMPLOYMENT EFFECTS OF UK MANUFACTURING TRADE EXPANSION WITH THE EEC AND THE NEWLY INDUSTRIALISING COUNTRIES

Ciaran DRIVER, Andrew KILPATRICK and Barry NAISBITT*

*National Economic Development Office, London SW1P 4QX, UK*

Received August 1984, final version received July 1985

This paper uses an input–output framework to consider the employment effects in the U.K. of a balanced trade expansion with the Newly Industrialising Countries and the EEC. Both the overall net effects and the results by industry are presented. They are subdivided into the direct effects on an industry due to the trade change in that industry and the indirect effects arising from that part of the industry's production which is sold as an intermediate input to other industries. The exercise, carried out for 1979, finds small negative net overall employment effects in each case examined, but important differences in the inter-industry pattern of employment changes are reported.

## 1. Introduction

Recent developments in the pattern and nature of international trade of the U.K. have given rise to concern about the consequences for domestic employment. In particular since joining the EEC U.K. exports of manufactured goods to EEC countries have increased at an annual growth rate of 15.5% from 1973 to 1983, but imports from the EEC have increased by 18.9% p.a.; and the Western industrialised economies in general have been concerned about structural changes necessitated by the recent industrialisation of the less developed countries (LDCs). The purpose of this paper is to examine these issues in a particular context, by investigating the employment effects of a balanced expansion of manufacturing trade by the U.K. with three country groups, the EEC and two definitions of the group of Newly Industrialising Countries (NICs).

Despite the fact that U.K. manufacturing trade with each of the three groups is not balanced, the assumption of a balanced trade expansion provides a reference point with which to measure a loss or gain to the U.K.

*Thames Polytechnic and National Economic Development Office (NEDO), NEDO, and Liverpool University and NEDO respectively. The views expressed in this paper are those of the authors and should not be taken to represent those of any institutions with which they are associated.

economy. This implies that an increase in imports acting as a substitute for domestic production is compensated for by the revenue being spent by the appropriate group of nations on purchasing U.K. exports. The proposed method is also of interest in that, although any unbalanced increase in trade carries obvious immediate implications for both national income and the exchange rate, a marginal increase in balanced trade has implications which are only rarely evaluated. Such an evaluation can be seen as corresponding to the concept of balanced budget tax incidence in the public finance literature and it provides important information for discussions of conditions for the orderly expansion of world trade.

## 2. Analytical framework

The evaluation of the effects of a balanced trade expansion in the Heckscher–Ohlin full-employment trade model in terms of changes in relative factor prices and the usage of factors in different sectors has been thoroughly examined in the literature [see Caves and Jones (1981)]. The methodological approach followed in this paper differs from this standard treatment in that a short-run analysis with fixed production coefficients and factor prices and demand-determined employment is utilised. This particular approach has been used previously by Baldwin (1976), De Grauwe et al. (1979), and Driver, Kilpatrick and Naisbitt (1984a) in the context of examining industrial patterns of employment changes due to trade changes.

The present analysis makes use of the 1979 U.K. input–output tables, the latest available. The large amount of detail contained in the $100 \times 100$ matrices in these tables has been aggregated in order to match the individual categories for which import and export data were readily available. This resulted in a summary input–output table covering 26 sectors. Using this table the employment effects of trade changes were calculated from

$$e = \hat{E}[I - A]^{-1}t, \tag{1}$$

where

$\hat{E}$ = diagonal matrix of industry employment/output ratios,
$A$ = matrix of technical coefficients,
$t$ = column vector of trade changes,
$e$ = resulting column vector of employment changes.

The vector of trade changes was calculated by first obtaining the shares of U.K. exports (imports) in total manufacturing exports (imports) for each of the 21 manufacturing industry categories identified in the input–output matrix to (from) each of the three country groupings in 1979. A marginal expansion of equal total value in both exports and imports was then applied pro rata across these sectors to obtain the trade vectors. This is, of course, only an approximation to what might occur if a trade expansion took place, in that it ignores the effects of relative price or real income movements on the pattern of trade. Because of the linearity of eq. (1) the precise numerical values of the overall trade changes are of limited importance in the analysis, and it was decided to use aggregate expansions which in each case were equal to approximately 10% of the 1979 level of trade. Hence the tables presented can be compared since they use trade changes of similar proportions. The derivation of the manufacturing trade changes are discussed in appendix 1.

In order to complete the consideration of the effects of trade expansion the induced change in total value added was also calculated by using

$$g = v[I - A]^{-1}t, \tag{2}$$

where

$v$ = row vector of ratios of value added to gross output,
$g$ = resulting scalar value of value added change.

The changes to value added will themselves have further employment implications. However, we have not sought to analyse this, nor have we attempted to investigate any departures from balanced trade that might result either from the change in value added and final demand or from any change in induced intermediate demands that might be implied by the new trade vector with unchanged production coefficients. A fuller analysis could consider these effects, along with the other second-round effects, through the use of a disaggregated macroeconomic model.

In Driver, Kilpatrick and Naisbitt (1984a) it was argued that the contrast between direct and indirect employment effects was of importance for considering the impact of trade changes. In particular, the study indicated that there was no significant correlation between the direct employment effects of the trade changes, that is to say the employment change in an industry due to the trade change in that industry, and the indirect effects, which measure the employment generated in an industry through its production being used as an intermediate input in other industries. These two effects can be calculated from

$$e_1 = \hat{E}[\widehat{I-A}]^{-1}t \tag{3}$$

and where $e_1$ = vector of direct employment effects and where $[\widehat{I-A}]^{-1}$ consists of the diagonal elements of $[I-A]^{-1}$ and has zeros elsewhere.

$$e_2 = e - e_1, \tag{4}$$

where $e_2$ = vector of indirect employment effects.

Finally, three country groupings were chosen for the calculations. These were the EEC and two widely used definitions of the Newly Industrialising Countries (NICs). The first of these, denoted NIC, is the narrow definition of a group of eleven countries and is commonly found in OECD publications. The second, denoted NICH, is a wider definition of twenty-three countries which encompasses the first group and includes additional countries largely from Asia and Eastern Europe and is often associated with the Hayes Report [Foreign and Commonwealth Office (1979)]. This report also presented some estimates of the employment effects of trade with the NICs but a rather different methodology from that presented here was used. The definitions are given in appendix 2.

## 3. Empirical results

Table 1 presents the aggregate results of the analysis described in the previous section. It is noticeable immediately that because of the linearity of the model and the greater scale of trade with the EEC than the NICs, the absolute employment figures are greater in the EEC case than the other cases. However, the net employment effects which are based on the overall changes in the trade balances are perhaps surprisingly all of the same magnitude and are all negative. The similarity of effects contrasts with the results presented by De Grauwe et al. (1979) for Belgium, but their findings for 1970 and 1975 also indicated negative effects on employment for the two types of country groups.

Table 1

Employment and value added effects of an approximate 10% balanced change in U.K. exports and imports of manufactured goods, 1979.

| | Total employment | of which | | Value added £m |
|---|---|---|---|---|
| | | direct | indirect | |
| *NIC* | | | | |
| Exports | 32482 | 19805 | 12677 | 212.6 |
| Imports | 36424 | 23786 | 12638 | 204.3 |
| Net effects (exports minus imports) | −3942 | −3981 | 39 | +8.3 |
| *NICH* | | | | |
| Exports | 43809 | 26896 | 16913 | 282.8 |
| Imports | 47858 | 30732 | 17126 | 271.5 |
| Net | −4090 | −3836 | −213 | +11.3 |
| *EEC* | | | | |
| Exports | 201532 | 120631 | 80901 | 1347.5 |
| Imports | 205999 | 110512 | 95487 | 1382.0 |
| Net | −4467 | 10119 | −14586 | −34.5 |

In all of the cases the direct employment effects were larger than the indirect but the importance of estimating the latter is shown by the the fact that in the most extreme case it still accounts for 35% of the total employment change. In the case with the largest relative indirect effect, it accounts for 46% of the total employment change. Therefore the omission of the indirect effects of the trade changes would seriously underestimate in each case the magnitude of the resultant employment changes.

The pattern of the net direct and indirect changes is also of interest in that the net direct effects are, in fact, positive for the case of trade with the EEC as can be seen from table 1. However in this case the negative net indirect effects outweigh the direct employment gains to produce an overall employment loss. Thus it appears that the pattern of inter-industry linkages in the U.K. is such that the result of increased trade is to reduce domestic intermediate demand and hence employment sufficiently to overcome the positive direct employment effects of the trade change. In the cases of the NIC groupings, the net indirect changes are very small, with that for the smaller NIC group being marginally positive, and the overall consequences are dominated by the negative net direct employment effects.

An alternative presentation of these results is given in table 2 which examines the employment effects of a balanced trade expansion of equal value (£100m) with each of the groups. Given the different values of U.K. trade with these groups, such an expansion would, in terms of exports, amount to an increase with the NIC group of 3.7%, 2.3% with NICH, and

Table 2

Employment and value added effects of a £100m increase in U.K. exports and imports of manufactured goods, 1979.

| | Total employment | of which | | Value added £m |
| --- | --- | --- | --- | --- |
| | | direct | indirect | |
| *NIC* | | | | |
| Exports | 10827 | 6602 | 4226 | 70.9 |
| Imports | 12141 | 7929 | 4213 | 68.1 |
| Net effects (exports minus imports) | −1314 | −1327 | 13 | +2.8 |
| *NICH* | | | | |
| Exports | 10952 | 6724 | 4228 | 70.7 |
| Imports | 11965 | 7683 | 4282 | 67.9 |
| Net | −1012 | −959 | −53 | +2.8 |
| *EEC* | | | | |
| Exports | 10077 | 6032 | 4045 | 67.4 |
| Imports | 10300 | 5526 | 4774 | 69.1 |
| Net | −223 | 506 | −729 | −1.7 |

0.7% with the EEC on the 1979 level. The results indicate that the total employment gain from exports is greatest for the NICH group and the employment loss from imports is largest for trade with the NIC group. The two NICs groups produce similar employment figures but these contrast strongly with those for the EEC where a direct employment gain is outweighed by an indirect employment loss to produce only a marginal overall employment loss of approximately one fifth of the size of that associated with the trade expansion with the NICs.

The results on the value-added effects shown in both tables 1 and 2 are perhaps to be expected, indicating that the U.K. exports relatively higher value-added goods to the NICs than it imports, but the position is reversed with respect to the EEC. It appears that the U.K. both in terms of employment and value added loses from a balanced trade expansion with the EEC, whereas the same degree of expansion of trade with the NICs produces real income gains to set against the employment losses.

The sectoral results are presented in tables 3 to 5. The basic patterns of total effects for the two NICs categories are very similar, with the only major difference being in the other manufacturing category which has a higher export share to the NICH group than the NIC group, and this yields an overall positive employment effect for this sector. In general in the two NICs categories the import competing items are the textiles, food, and timber industries, which is exactly the pattern suggested by the Hayes Report (1979). The pattern of trade with the EEC is rather different, however, with large direct net employment losses occurring in particular in motor vehicles, and iron and steel; although large gains are recorded in other manufacturing and aerospace. It is also of interest to note in this case that there is a loss of service sector employment which occurs through the indirect effects. Thus it appears that the domestically produced manufactured goods which are replaced by EEC import competition are more service-intensive in their production profiles than the exported goods.

The tables reveal that on average the direct employment effects by industry are larger than the indirect, but in several individual cases the indirect outweigh the direct. In particular, the paper and printing industry and the iron and steel industry generally have larger indirect than direct employment effects. The largest direct employment changes for exports in each case are due to mechanical engineering, with the largest indirect effects being found in the services sector which has no direct effects because the analysis is based on an expansion of manufacturing trade only. The largest direct employment losses due to increased import substitution arise in the clothing and textile industries in the case of trade with the NICs, and for textiles these losses are reinforced by the indirect effects. Nonetheless it must be recognised that the operation of trading agreements such as the Multi-Fibre Arrangement will influence the outcome of any trade expansion in practice. For imports from

Table 3

Employment generated by an approximate 10% balanced change in U.K. manufacturing trade with the NIC group.

| Industry | Exports | | Imports | | Net |
|---|---|---|---|---|---|
| | Total employ-ment | of which indirect | Total employ-ment | of which indirect | Total employ-ment |
| *Primary industries* | | | | | |
| Agriculture, Forestry and Fishing | 338 | 338 | −751 | −751 | −413 |
| Mining & Quarrying | 265 | 265 | −218 | −218 | 47 |
| *Manufacturing industries* | | | | | |
| Food | 339 | 83 | −789 | −72 | −450 |
| Drink & Tobacco | 348 | 11 | −319 | −12 | 29 |
| Textiles | 1180 | 226 | −5188 | −1495 | −4008 |
| Clothing, Furs & Footwear | 360 | 68 | −7379 | −43 | −7037 |
| Leather, etc. | 257 | 18 | −682 | −144 | −425 |
| Timber & Furniture | 196 | 131 | −1806 | −104 | −1610 |
| Paper & Printing | 820 | 542 | −1134 | −599 | −314 |
| Chemicals | 1778 | 329 | −705 | −486 | 1073 |
| Petroleum & Coal Products | 60 | 44 | −58 | −32 | 2 |
| Bricks, Pottery, Glass, etc, | 511 | 215 | −338 | −157 | 173 |
| Iron and Steel | 1510 | 849 | −913 | −466 | 597 |
| Non Ferrous Metals | 442 | 316 | −259 | −161 | 183 |
| Metal products | 1469 | 614 | −1243 | −506 | 226 |
| Mechanical Engineering | 5366 | 468 | −1248 | −305 | 4118 |
| Electrical Engineering | 2571 | 534 | −1984 | −247 | 587 |
| Shipbuilding, etc. | 2011 | 53 | −521 | −31 | 1490 |
| Motor Vehicles, etc. | 2192 | 84 | −931 | −63 | 1261 |
| Aerospace Equipment | 488 | 22 | −97 | −12 | 391 |
| Other Vehicles | 433 | 17 | −47 | −12 | 386 |
| Instrument Engineering | 1150 | 30 | −978 | −23 | 172 |
| Other Manufacturing | 1250 | 274 | −2303 | −183 | −1053 |
| *Other non-manufacturing industries* | | | | | |
| Construction | 195 | 195 | −182 | −182 | 13 |
| Gas, Electricity & Water | 320 | 320 | −257 | −257 | 63 |
| Services | 6632 | 6632 | −6077 | −6077 | 555 |

the EEC, the large direct losses in textiles and mechanical engineering are balanced by large direct gains via exports, but for motor vehicles this proves not to be the case, resulting in a net loss of employment. As in the case of clothing and textiles trade with the NICs some EEC trade is characterised by controls of various kinds and, in particular, the large negative employment effect due to indirect agricultural trade consequent upon trade expansion with the EEC might, given the existence of the Common Agricultural Policy, turn out differently in practice. The existence of various forms of trade agreements or restrictions could be expected to affect the response to an external trade change. No attempt is made in this paper to model the implications of this feature of international trade.

434        C. Driver et al., *Employment effects of UK manufacturing trade expansion*

Table 4

Employment generated by an approximate 10% balanced change in manufacturing trade with the NICH group.

| Industry | Exports | | Imports | | Net |
| | Total employ-ment | of which indirect | Total employ-ment | of which indirect | Total employ-ment |
| --- | --- | --- | --- | --- | --- |
| *Primary industries* | | | | | |
| Agriculture, Forestry and Fishing | 380 | 380 | −1487 | −1487 | −1107 |
| Mining & Quarrying | 361 | 361 | −285 | −285 | 76 |
| | | | | | |
| *Manufacturing industries* | | | | | |
| Food | 381 | 108 | −1648 | −90 | −1267 |
| Drink & Tobacco | 371 | 14 | −307 | −16 | 64 |
| Textiles | 1397 | 289 | −7166 | −1790 | −5769 |
| Clothing, Furs & Footwear | 392 | 90 | −8698 | −57 | −8306 |
| Leather, etc. | 235 | 23 | −1081 | −178 | −846 |
| Timber & Furniture | 236 | 179 | −2746 | −132 | −2510 |
| Papers & Printing | 1165 | 742 | −1416 | −808 | −251 |
| Chemicals | 2313 | 457 | −981 | −663 | 1332 |
| Petroleum & Coal Products | 76 | 60 | −75 | −44 | 1 |
| Bricks, Pottery, Glass, etc. | 686 | 291 | −425 | −206 | 261 |
| Iron & Steel | 2460 | 1112 | −1138 | −593 | 1322 |
| Non Ferrous Metals | 579 | 418 | −383 | −199 | 196 |
| Metal Products | 1958 | 817 | −1571 | −684 | 387 |
| Mechanical Engineering | 7360 | 584 | −1571 | −406 | 5789 |
| Electrical Engineering | 3221 | 705 | −2271 | −327 | 950 |
| Shipbuilding, etc. | 2218 | 73 | −790 | −44 | 1428 |
| Motor Vehicles, etc. | 2784 | 115 | −1030 | −85 | 1754 |
| Aerospace Equipment | 764 | 29 | −213 | −15 | 551 |
| Other Vehicles | 370 | 23 | −62 | −16 | 308 |
| Instrument Engineering | 1537 | 44 | −1126 | −28 | 411 |
| Other Manufacturing | 2924 | 358 | −2655 | −238 | 269 |
| | | | | | |
| *Other non-manufacturing industries* | | | | | |
| Construction | 261 | 261 | −245 | −245 | 16 |
| Gas, Electricity & Water | 439 | 439 | −346 | −346 | 93 |
| Services | 8941 | 8941 | −8142 | −8142 | 799 |

Given the importance of the indirect effects in generating the total employment effects, the results for the manufacturing sector were examined further to discover whether a knowledge of the more readily calculable direct effects would permit useful inferences to be made about the indirect effects. Correlation coefficients between the direct and indirect employment effects for each of the six cases were calculated and were all positive but in no case was a correlation coefficient significantly different from zero at the 5% level. Therefore a knowledge of the direct effects alone would not permit an accurate assessment of the indirect and hence total effects of the trade changes.

*C. Driver et al., Employment effects of UK manufacturing trade expansion*          435

Table 5

Employment generated by an approximate 10% balanced change in manufacturing trade with the EEC.

| Industry | Exports Total employ- ment | of which indirect | Imports Total employ- ment | of which indirect | Net Total employ- ment |
|---|---|---|---|---|---|
| *Primary industries* | | | | | |
| Agriculture, Forestry and Fishing | 3890 | 3890 | −7280 | −7280 | −3390 |
| Mining Quarrying | 2824 | 2824 | −2438 | −2438 | 386 |
| | | | | | |
| *Manufacturing industries* | | | | | |
| Food | 4335 | 509 | −8406 | −481 | −4071 |
| Drink & Tobacco | 1327 | 71 | −1535 | −80 | −208 |
| Textiles | 11634 | 2196 | −12187 | −2133 | −553 |
| Clothing, Furs & Footwear | 6421 | 374 | −5779 | −380 | 642 |
| Leather, etc. | 1246 | 184 | −845 | −181 | 401 |
| Timber & Furniture | 2387 | 807 | −3005 | −851 | −618 |
| Paper & Printing | 6610 | 3702 | −6795 | −3755 | −185 |
| Chemicals | 11519 | 2367 | −10728 | −2466 | 791 |
| Petroleum & Coal Products | 1075 | 271 | −814 | −284 | 261 |
| Bricks, Pottery, Glass, etc. | 3013 | 1258 | −3094 | −1339 | −81 |
| Iron & Steel | 8429 | 4540 | −9930 | −4744 | −1501 |
| Non Ferrous Metals | 3231 | 1586 | −2735 | −1778 | 496 |
| Metal Products | 8685 | 3774 | −7745 | −3943 | 940 |
| Mechanical Engineering | 26207 | 2293 | −25831 | −2530 | 376 |
| Electrical Engineering | 10703 | 2696 | −9779 | −2773 | 924 |
| Shipbuilding, etc. | 4277 | 314 | −4083 | −353 | 194 |
| Motor Vehicles, etc. | 10177 | 493 | −18553 | −485 | −8376 |
| Aerospace Equipment | 3930 | 114 | −2662 | −118 | 1268 |
| Other Vehicles | 444 | 97 | −450 | −103 | −6 |
| Instrument Engineering | 5909 | 200 | −5443 | −173 | 466 |
| Other Manufacturing | 18405 | 1486 | −8911 | −1846 | 9494 |
| | | | | | |
| *Other non-manufacturing industries* | | | | | |
| Construction | 1332 | 1332 | −1368 | −1368 | −36 |
| Gas, Electricity & Water | 2051 | 2051 | −2092 | −2092 | −41 |
| Services | 41470 | 41470 | −43512 | −43512 | −2042 |

## 4. Conclusions

The principal conclusion of the study is that a balanced expansion of manufacturing trade with both the NICs and the EEC results in the first round in small reductions in U.K. employment. These results, which are derived using a model based on fixed production coefficients and factor prices, are interesting for several reasons. First, the overall net effects mask relatively large employment changes in individual industries. Thus the effect of the manufacturing trade expansion with the NICs is to promote employment on a broad base (for the NIC case in 18 of the 26 sectors) with the mechanical engineering industry having a large positive total employment effect; while the employment loss is narrowly concentrated, mainly in the textiles and clothing industries. The pattern is dramatically changed when considering trade with the EEC which sees a more varied picture of net gains and losses with the two largest effects being on the negative side for motor vehicles and, on the positive side, for the catch-all category, other manufacturing industries.

The distinction between the direct and indirect employment effects of the trade changes is of considerable importance for calculating the overall employment changes. For trade with the EEC overall, the direct employment effects were positive but outweighted by the negative indirect effects, which contrasts with the results for the NIC groups where the net direct effects were negative. The individual pattern of indirect effects differs markedly from that of the direct effects and a calculation of only the direct effects appears to carry no information that can be readily used to make inferences about the indirect effects. Thus the use of an input–output framework is crucial to the estimation of the total employment changes.

Although the results presented are clearly model-specific, the general findings are perhaps surprisingly similar to those of De Grauwe et al. (1979) for Belgium in terms of the overall employment effects, but not the value-added effects which are here negative for trade with the EEC. It should be recognised, of course, that in general balanced trade expansion is not an observed phenomenon but rather a conceptual benchmark. Should U.K. trade develop in such a way that manufactured imports from these country groupings grow at a faster rate than exports to them, then, without a degree of domestic factor price adjustment, these employment losses would be magnified.

The employment changes derived in the analysis are based upon average productivity figures for each industry. This is however a rather limiting (if standard) assumption since it might be expected that output expansion would in general be achieved by firms with higher than average productivity. By a similar argument, it might also be expected that contractions in trade would occur via a contraction of the least productive plants. The omission of these effects would be expected to cause an upwards bias in the employment calculations, particularly for the case of the NICs. It is, however, unclear how the appropriate marginal productivity coefficients should be calculated. A further discussion of this issue is contained in Driver, Kilpatrick and Naisbitt (1984b).

Finally, it is necessary to review some caveats to the analysis carried out in the paper. The trade data, input–output matrix and the employment–output coefficients used are all for 1979, the choice being constrained by the need to provide consistent figures. There have however been major changes in the structure of U.K. manufacturing industry since 1979 in terms of both productivity and trade behaviour which the analysis of necessity does not reflect. In addition, it can be argued that if overall manufacturing trade increased by 10%, as in the reference case considered in this paper, it would not be plausible as a practical outcome for each component of the trade vector to change by the same proportion. The aim of the paper has been to provide illustrative conceptual examples of the effects of two marginal manufacturing trade changes in order to assess their implications for employment within a static framework at a given point in time; to address completely the full range of issues concerning impacts of changes in trade patterns would require a much more complicated and ambitious model, a project which lies outside the scope of this paper.

## Appendix 1

Details of U.K. trade vectors

In each case the proportion of total manufactured exports (imports) to (from) the country groupings in 1979 for each of the 21 manufacturing industries used in the study was calculated.

As both a reference point for comparisons and a representation of a balanced expansion in trade, values were chosen which represented approximately a 10% increase of exports or imports with the country group. Therefore since the value of trade with the EEC is much greater than with the NICs, the absolute size of the trade expansion considered was larger.

Since the method assumes a balanced trade expansion, total exports and imports were increased by the same amount for each country group with the proportions of 1979 exports and imports being used to allocate the totals to the individual industries.

The totals used in the exercise and their relative magnitudes were:

| Country group | Trade change (£m) | % of 1979 export value | % of 1979 import value |
|---|---|---|---|
| NIC | 300 | 11.0 | 11.7 |
| NICH | 400 | 9.1 | 10.9 |
| EEC | 2,000 | 13.5 | 10.9 |

## Appendix 2

Definitions of the Newly Industrialising Country Groups
NIC: Greece, Portugal, Spain, Turkey, Yugoslavia, Mexico, Brazil, Singapore, South Korea, Taiwan, Hong Kong.

NICH: As NIC but also includes Poland, Hungary, Romania, Malta, Argentina, Israel, Iran, Pakistan, India, Thailand, Malaysia, Philippines.

438     *C. Driver et al., Employment effects of UK manufacturing trade expansion*

## References

Aho, C.M. and J.A. Orr, 1981, Trade-sensitive employment: Who are the affected workers?, Monthly Labour Review 104, no. 2, Feb., 29–35.

Baldwin, R.E., 1976, Trade and employment effects in the United States of multilateral tariff reductions, American Economic Review 66, May, Papers and proceedings, 142–148.

Baldwin, R.E. and W.E. Lewis, 1978, US tariff effects on trade and employment in detailed SIC industries, in: W.G. Dewald, The impact of international trade and investment on employment (Bureau of International Labour Affairs, Washington, DC).

Brech, M., 1984, Some evidence on the role of innovation in UK trade and competitiveness, NEDO economic working paper, forthcoming.

Cable, V., 1977, British protectionism and LDC imports, Overseas Development Institute Review, no. 2, 29–48.

Cable, V., 1978, Sources of employment displacement in UK industries competing with LDC imports, Overseas Development Institute Mimeo.

Caves, R.E. and R.W. Jones, 1981, World trade and payments, 3rd revised ed. (Little, Brown, Boston, MA).

De Grauwe, P., W. Kennes, T. Peeters, T. and R. Van Straelen, 1979, Trade expansion with the less developed countries and employment: A case study of Belgium, Weltwirtschaftliches Archiv, Band 115, Heft 1, 99–115.

Driver, C., A. Kilpatrick and B. Naisbitt, 1984a, An investigation of the employment effects of changes in UK trade structure using an input–output framework, NEDO economic working paper no. 11.

Driver, C., A. Kilpatrick and B. Naisbitt, 1984b, An example of the use of marginal versus average coefficients in input–output studies, Mimeo.

Foreign and Commonwealth Office Working Group, 1979, The newly industrialising countries and the adjustment problem, Government Economic Service working paper no. 18, (HMSO, London).

Hayes, J.P. et al., 1979, *see* Foreign and Commonwealth Office Working Group.

Leontief, W., 1966, Input–output economics (Oxford University Press, New York).

Martin, J.P., and J.M. Evans, 1981, Notes on measuring the employment displacement effects of trade by the accounting procedure, Oxford Economic Papers 33, March, 154–164.

NEDO, 1983, British industrial performance (National Economic Development Office, London).

OECD, 1979, The impact of the newly industrialising countries (OECD, Paris).

# [4]

European Journal of Political Economy
Vol. 15 (1999) 485–500

European Journal of
POLITICAL
ECONOMY

ELSEVIER

# An empirical assessment of the impact of trade on employment in the United Kingdom

David Greenaway *, Robert C. Hine, Peter Wright

*Centre for Research on Globalisation and Labour Markets, School of Economics, University of Nottingham, Nottingham NG7 2RD, UK*

Received 1 February 1998; received in revised form 1 September 1998; accepted 1 January 1999

## Abstract

A large number of studies have recently attempted to evaluate the impact of trade on employment, many relying on either the factor content or growth accounting approaches. With some notable exceptions, this work finds limited evidence of strong direct effects but stronger effects through induced productivity changes. This study models the effects of trade on employment in the UK in a dynamic labour demand framework, on a panel of 167 manufacturing industries. We find that when we introduce trade, increases in trade volumes, both in terms of imports and exports, cause reductions in the level of derived labour demand. When we disaggregate by origin of imports we find stronger effects in trade with the EU and US compared to trade with East Asia. This provides supportive evidence for the idea that trade affects $x$-inefficiency, with the strongest competition for UK manufacturers coming from producers in the EU and US. © 1999 Elsevier Science B.V. All rights reserved.

*JEL classification:* F16

*Keywords:* Trade and employment

## 1. Introduction

Between 1979 and 1991, more than two million jobs were lost in UK manufacturing. Table 1 shows, however, that the extent of the job losses differed

---

* Corresponding author. E-mail: david.greenaway@nottingham.ac.uk

*Globalization and Labour Markets II*

486     D. Greenaway et al. / European Journal of Political Economy 15 (1999) 485–500

Table 1
Trade, production, wages and employment in UK manufacturing industries, 1979 and 1991
Source: ONS Business Monitor PA1002, various years.

| SIC Division | Employment ('000s) | | | Production[a] (£million) | | | Wage rates[b] | | | Import penetration[c] | | | Export share[d] | | |
|---|---|---|---|---|---|---|---|---|---|---|---|---|---|---|---|
| | 1979 | 1991 | % change 1979–1991 | 1979 | 1991 | % change 1979–1991 | 1979 | 1991 | % change 1979–1991 | 1979 | 1991 | % change 1979–1991 | 1979 | 1991 | % change 1979–1991 |
| 43 | 368.0 | 181.7 | −50.6 | 79.4 | 52.3 | −34.1 | 4788 | 7000 | 46.22 | 0.29 | 0.47 | 62.1 | 0.23 | 0.32 | 39.1 |
| 35 | 491.2 | 245.8 | −50.0 | 155.3 | 149.2 | −3.9 | 6875 | 10,976 | 59.63 | 0.35 | 0.46 | 31.4 | 0.32 | 0.42 | 31.3 |
| 32 | 967.5 | 547.0 | −43.5 | 255.2 | 221.6 | −13.2 | 6684 | 10,367 | 55.11 | 0.21 | 0.30 | 42.9 | 0.30 | 0.33 | 10.0 |
| 2 | 1045.5 | 613.9 | −41.3 | 482.2 | 419.3 | −13.1 | 6986 | 11,039 | 58.0 | 0.21 | 0.31 | 47.6 | 0.24 | 0.31 | 29.2 |
| 44 and 45 | 448.3 | 269.6 | −39.9 | 76.1 | 56.5 | −25.9 | 3894 | 5416 | 39.09 | 0.25 | 0.44 | 75.0 | 0.17 | 0.26 | 52.6 |
| 31 | 498.1 | 307.9 | −38.2 | 116.9 | 102.1 | −12.7 | 5863 | 8517 | 45.25 | 0.08 | 0.15 | 87.5 | 0.10 | 0.13 | 30.0 |
| 36 | 383.6 | 251.3 | −34.5 | 81.2 | 110.2 | 35.7 | 6903 | 11,315 | 63.92 | 0.14 | 0.14 | 0.0 | 0.19 | 0.17 | −10.5 |
| 34 and 37 | 797.2 | 547.4 | −31.3 | 184.4 | 210.0 | 13.9 | 6027 | 9594 | 59.19 | 0.31 | 0.56 | 77.9 | 0.32 | 0.52 | 60.1 |
| 46 | 245.6 | 188.9 | −23.1 | 69.2 | 67.0 | −3.0 | 5777 | 7914 | 37.00 | 0.25 | 0.23 | −8.0 | 0.06 | 0.06 | 0.0 |
| 42 | 265.9 | 216.8 | −18.5 | 222.9 | 246.2 | 10.5 | 6508 | 10,241 | 57.36 | 0.08 | 0.12 | 50.0 | 0.08 | 0.13 | 62.5 |
| 47 | 533.0 | 441.9 | −17.1 | 151.9 | 201.0 | 32.3 | 6924 | 10,776 | 55.64 | 0.15 | 0.17 | 13.3 | 0.08 | 0.10 | 25.0 |
| 48 | 267.5 | 223.5 | −16.5 | 75.7 | 91.3 | 20.7 | 6117 | 9108 | 48.90 | 0.15 | 0.24 | 60.0 | 0.17 | 0.20 | 17.7 |
| 49 | 90.9 | 76.9 | −15.4 | 22.2 | 23.2 | 4.5 | 4878 | 7098 | 45.51 | 0.23 | 0.35 | 52.2 | 0.22 | 0.22 | 0.0 |
| 41 | 394.4 | 359.8 | −8.8 | 168.9 | 187.8 | 11.2 | 5013 | 7173 | 43.11 | 0.17 | 0.18 | 5.9 | 0.05 | 0.07 | 40.0 |
| 33 | 46.9 | 64.4 | 37.3 | 21.0 | 58.8 | 179.7 | 7531 | 13,209 | 75.41 | 0.50 | 0.51 | 2.0 | 0.44 | 0.49 | 11.4 |

*SIC description*

2 Extraction of minerals, manufacture of metals and mineral products
31 Manufacture of metal goods
32 Mechanical engineering
33 Manufacture of office machinery
34 and 37 Electrical and instrument engineering
35 Manufacture of motor vehicles
36 Manufacture of other transport equipment
41/42 Food drink and tobacco
43 Textiles
44 and 45 Manufacture of leather, footwear and clothing
46 Processing of rubber and plastics
47 Timber and wooden furniture
48 Manufacture of paper and paper products
49 Other manufacturing industries

*D. Greenaway et al. / European Journal of Political Economy 15 (1999) 485–500*      487

substantially across two-digit SIC industry divisions. The manufacture of office machinery and the processing of rubber and plastics, for example, recorded increases in their workforces while three divisions — including textiles and motor vehicle manufacturing — experienced job losses of more than 50%. Such large-scale losses reflect a period of major adaptation and organisational change, particularly as the value of UK manufacturing output remained stable in real terms. At a disaggregated level, though, it is clear that the production experience of industries was very mixed, with about equal numbers of those shown in Table 1 recording an expansion or contraction over the period as a whole. The sharpest declines occurred in textiles, leather, footwear and clothing where competition from low wage economies has been particularly intense for the established industrialised countries.

The combination of falling employment and stable production in manufacturing necessarily implies rising output per person. Even at the two-digit SIC level, however, productivity improvements varied widely — for example, the value of output per person in the manufacture of office machinery rose eight times faster than in the leather industry. Relative movements in productivity appear to be reflected in changes in wages in Table 1, but the range of wage changes across industries is much more restricted than is the range of employment or production change. Thus, half of the industries had a growth in average wages per worker of between 55% and 60% over the 12-year period.

UK industry has become increasingly integrated into the international economy through trade and foreign direct investment. Between 1979 and 1991, this was particularly marked for imports, as shown in Table 1. Their (unweighted) average share in apparent consumption rose from 26% to 37%, while for exports as a share of production the proportion rose from 23% to 31%. Once again, there was a wide diversity of experiences across industries, although only one division recorded a decline in import penetration (SIC 46, timber and wooden furniture) and only one a decline in export shares (SIC 36, other transport equipment). Reflecting the dominance of intra-industry trade (IIT), movements in import penetration and export shares were positively correlated at the two-digit level. Thus, divisions 36 and 46 were ranked lowest in both import and export growth, and at the upper end, instrument and electrical engineering exemplified the growing trade orientation of most sectors of UK manufacturing.

Summing up, the UK has been through a particularly turbulent period in the development of its manufacturing industry with a combination of sharply reduced employment, stable production and marked improvements in output per person

---

Notes to Table 1:

[a] 1985 prices.

[b] Per person per year, 1985 £ prices.

[c] Imports as a share of apparent consumption (production + imports − exports).

[d] Exports as a share of production.

employed. This was a period also of increasing openness in the UK economy. An important issue, therefore, is the possible link between greater exposure to trade and labour market adjustments. This is explored econometrically later in this paper, taking advantage of the wide diversity of experience of individual industries which is apparent even at the two-digit level in Table 1. By combining trade, labour market and industrial organisation data, we assemble a panel of data for 167 (four-digit) industries in the UK to evaluate the impact of imports and exports on productivity and employment. This is a unique dataset and provides the opportunity to advance on the more limited factor content and accounting approaches to the problem and we would argue yields more robust and more credible results. In addition, however, our dataset also permits us to investigate the impact of trade with different groups of countries.

The remainder of the paper is organised as follows. Section 2 reviews previous evidence on trade and employment and points up the particular contribution which this paper makes. Section 3 explains our modelling strategy and sets out details of our dataset. Section 4 reports on and discusses our results, while Section 5 concludes.

## 2. Trade and employment: A review of previous work

The Heckscher–Ohlin–Samuelson (H-O-S) framework yields some fairly clear predictions regarding the effect of trade on employment across sectors. When trade barriers are reduced, the import substitute sector contracts while the export sector expands; ceteris paribus employment in the former declines, while in the latter it increases. The simple H-O-S message therefore is that trade results in a redistribution of employment away from the import substitute sector and towards the export sector.

This is a useful starting point. However, given that much international trade appears to be driven by non-H-O-S factors, how do these results need to be adjusted for a world of IIT, where a large proportion of trade is between countries with similar factor endowments and where the products concerned might be vertically or horizontally differentiated? [1] In principle, one might assume that increased imports (exports) are associated with employment reductions (increases), ceteris paribus. There are some differences, however. First, because expansions/contractions occur largely within industries the analysis becomes more complicated. Nevertheless, one would still be trying to establish how trade impacts differentially across industries depending upon differences between them in exposure to trade and changes therein. Second, it is conceivable that technical change, on average, affects IIT industries more than non-IIT industries because more

---

[1] Greenaway et al. (1994, 1995) evaluate empirically the relative importance of horizontal and vertical IIT in the UK.

*D. Greenaway et al. / European Journal of Political Economy 15 (1999) 485–500* 489

(product and process) innovation occurs. Third, the sensitivity of IIT industries may be greater in the sense that adjustment to trade expansion occurs more rapidly.

There have been a number of attempts to evaluate empirically the impact of trade on employment. Two principal methodologies have been used: *factor content* and *growth accounting* approaches. In factor content studies, estimates are made of the labour required to produce a given amount of exports or being displaced by a given amount of imports. For instance, following this approach, Sapir and Schumacher (1985) show that a balanced expansion of EC trade with other OECD countries would have only minor effects on employment [2] — imports and exports have similar labour contents. However, in trade with developing countries the job intensity of European exports was only around 0.8 of the import level in the period studied (1970–1981). A balanced expansion of trade with developing countries in value terms would therefore lead to an erosion of jobs. More recently, Wood (1991, 1994) has contended that the employment impact of such trade would be greater on the grounds that imports from developing countries are 'non-competing'. As a result, conventional factor content methodologies underestimate the amount of labour in the North which imports from the South displace. He estimates that North–South trade has resulted in a net loss of nine million jobs in the North compared with one million using the standard methodology, and compared with a jobless total in the OECD countries of 35 million in 1994. However, Wood's findings have been criticised by Baldwin (1995) for overstating the extent to which imports are non-competing, and for the assumption that similar production technologies are employed in the North and South. Although they concede that the potential biases identified by Wood could result in factor content analysis underestimating the employment impact of trade with developing countries, Cortes et al. (1996) still conclude that the labour market impact of trade with low wage economies in France has been modest.

Krugman (1995) sets up a mini-CGE model to explore the employment impact of increased trade with developing countries. He argues that with rigid relative wages of unskilled and skilled labour, increased imports of unskilled labour intensive products will have two components. The first is the standard factor content effect from an increase in net imports of unskilled-labour intensive products. This is supplemented by a general equilibrium multiplier effect whose magnitude depends on the level of net exports of skilled labour intensive products and the unskilled to skilled ratio in aggregate employment. The combined effect is double that of the usual factor content estimate alone. However, the impact on employment of increased trade with developing countries remains small — an estimated 1.43% fall in employment from an import penetration rate for manufac-

---

[2] A small increase in Italy and decline in Germany, the Netherlands and Belgium; no change in the UK and France.

490 *D. Greenaway et al. / European Journal of Political Economy 15 (1999) 485–500*

tures from Newly Industrialising Countries of 1.75% of GDP (current level in OECD countries).

In the growth accounting approach, the sources of employment change are decomposed into domestic demand, trade and productivity elements. It is generally found that trade factors have played only a minor role in recent job losses — productivity growth has been the main factor displacing labour (in the short run). Indeed, an OECD (1992) study concluded that between 1970 and 1985 trade — including trade in services — was a net source of employment gains in Denmark, France, Germany and the Netherlands, but a source of loss in the UK. For the more recent period, 1979 to 1990, Gregory and Greenhalgh (1997) found that the UK also had a gain in employment from trade changes — though this was achieved by an increase in financial services, and primary and extractive employment, and losses in manufacturing. For France, Messerlin (1995) observed again a modest and mostly positive employment effect from foreign trade between 1980 and 1992 ( +0.8% per year on average), though the effect was negative during the economic expansion of 1988 to 1991.

A well-known problem with the growth accounting approach is that it is assumed that the components of change are independent. Clearly, for example, if rising imports stimulated faster productivity growth, there would be additional effects of trade not picked up by this method (see Martin and Evans, 1981; Wood, 1994). [3] There is evidence linking the growth of trade to the growth of labour productivity. For example, Cortes and Jean (1996) find a clear link for the US, France and Germany as does Lawrence (1996) for the US. Moreover, there are good reasons for believing that such an effect will be important. Trade-induced productivity growth might be stimulated via various channels. Caves and Krepps (1993) emphasise the pro-competitive impact of trade on $x$-efficiency while Borgas and Ramey (1994) point to reduced rents and employment of unionised labour. As Feenstra and Hanson (1996) argue, trade may also result in the relocation abroad of the most labour intensive stages of the production process. Neven and Wyplosz (1996) find substantial evidence of defensive changes in technique and output prices to meet competition from imports.

Clearly, therefore, theory and empirical evidence lays considerable stress on induced productivity effects. It is the principal aim of this study to quantify the importance of the trade stimulus to productivity growth and employment in the UK. [4]

---

[3] Some critics (e.g., Leamer, 1994; Courakis et al., 1997) argue that the growth accounting approach is flawed in an even more fundamental way. In their view, trade is not capable of 'explaining' changes in aggregate employment since employment in the tradeables sector is a residual after changes in factor supplies, factor demands by non-tradeables and technology. Since both trade and technology play a role, and the critical issue is the growing globalisation of the world economy, the attempt to apportion relative importance to the two factors is seen as irrelevant.

[4] Surveys of what is now a very substantial literature can be found in Lawrence (1996), Cline (1997) and Slaughter (1999).

*D. Greenaway et al. / European Journal of Political Economy 15 (1999) 485–500*        491

## 3. Modelling employment effects

As documented in Section 2, there are important limitations associated with the two most widely used approaches to investigating the employment effects of increased trade: the factor content and accounting decomposition methods. Instead of relying on either, we adopt a regression based approach grounded in a dynamic model of labour demand [5] to quantify possible employment losses resulting from a more efficient use of labour.

We begin by assuming a Cobb–Douglas production function where for the representative firm in industry $i$ in period $t$:

$$Q_{it} = A^{\gamma} K_{it}^{\alpha} N_{it}^{\beta} \tag{1}$$

where $Q$ = real output; $K$ = capital stock; $N$ = units of labour utilised; and where $\alpha$ and $\beta$ represent the factor share coefficients and $\gamma$ allows for factors changing the efficiency of the production process. A profit-maximising firm will employ labour and capital at such levels that the marginal revenue product of labour equals the wage $(w)$ and the marginal revenue product of capital equals its user cost $(c)$. Solving this system simultaneously to eliminate capital from the expression for firm output allows us to obtain the following expression:

$$Q_{it} = A^{\gamma} \left( \frac{\alpha N_{it}}{\beta} \frac{w_i}{c} \right)^{\alpha} N_{it}^{\beta}. \tag{2}$$

Taking logarithms and rearranging Eq. (2) allows us to derive the firm's, and therefore the industry's, derived demand for labour as

$$\ln N_{it} = \phi_0 + \phi_1 \ln(w_i/c) + \phi_2 \ln Q_{it} \tag{3}$$

where $\phi_0 = -(\gamma \ln A + \alpha \ln \alpha - \alpha \ln \beta)/(\alpha + \beta)$; $\phi_1 = -\alpha/(\alpha + \beta)$; $\phi_2 = 1/(\alpha + \beta)$.

One might expect that the technical efficiency of the production process increases over time and that the rate of technology adoption and increases in $x$-efficiency would be correlated with trade changes, therefore it is hypothesised that parameter $A$ in the production function varies with time in the following manner:

$$A_{it} = e^{\delta_0 T_i} M_{it}^{\delta_1} X_{it}^{\delta_2}, \quad \delta_0, \delta_1, \delta_2 > 0, \tag{4}$$

---

[5] There are a limited number of previous studies which use regression based techniques, the majority of which are based on US data. Abowd (1987) examines the impact of import competition on collectively bargained wage and employment outcomes in the US, with Abowd and Lemieux (1990) and Caves (1990) providing a comparison with Canada. Denny and Machin (1991) and Konings and Vandenbussche (1995), using firm-level data for the UK, also examine the impact of increased foreign competition on wages and employment.

where $T$ = time trend; $M$ = import penetration; $X$ = export penetration which implies:

$$\ln N_{it} = \phi_0^* - \mu_0 T - \mu_1 \ln M_{it} - \mu_2 \ln X_{it} + \phi_1 \ln(w_i/c) + \phi_2 \ln Q_{it} \quad (5)$$

with $\phi_0^* = -(\alpha \ln \alpha - \alpha \ln \beta)/(\alpha + \beta)$; $\mu_0 = \mu \delta_0$; $\mu_1 = \mu \delta_1$; $\mu_2 = \mu \delta_2$; $\mu = \gamma/(\alpha + \beta)$.

### 3.1. Dynamics in the employment equation

If there are costs associated with employment adjustment then the level of employment may deviate from its steady state as adjustment to equilibrium takes place. This leads to the introduction of a lag on employment into the employment function. If the employment measure is an aggregation across workers with differing adjustment costs then additional lags may be necessary to allow for heterogeneity effects (Nickell, 1986). A longer lag structure may also be necessary if serially correlated technology shocks are present. Lags may also be introduced into the labour demand function once bargaining considerations are taken into account — such as sequences of bargains or expectations formation about future wage and output levels.

Purely specifying dynamics in terms of lags of the dependent variable implicitly imposes a common evolution for employment following a change in an explanatory variable. This restriction may be relaxed by additionally introducing a distributed lag structure for the independent variables. This is the approach which we adopt since we are agnostic about the source of the dynamics in the employment equation.

### 3.2. Data and implementation

The dataset we use has been specially assembled using a diversity of sources in order to allow the construction of an integrated database of industrial, labour market and trade statistics. Thus, we have a panel of 167 manufacturing industries, corresponding approximately to a four-digit ISIC level of aggregation, from 1979 to 1991. [6] Since the dataset has both cross-sectional and time series elements the general dynamic estimating equation for the panel of industries in our study is of the form [7]

$$\ln N_{i,t} = \lambda_i - \mu_0 T - \sum_j \mu_{1j} \ln M_{i,t-j} - \sum_j \mu_{2j} \ln X_{i,t-j} + \sum_j \phi_{0j} \ln N_{i,t-j}$$
$$+ \sum_j \phi_{1j} \ln w_{i,t-j} + \sum_j \phi_{2j} \ln Q_{i,t-j} + \varepsilon_{it} \quad (6)$$

---

[6] Details of the data are available from the authors on request.

[7] Assuming perfect capital markets, the user cost of capital will only vary over time, so that in estimation its variation will be captured by time dummies.

where $N_{it}$ = total employment in industry $i$ in time $t$; $w_{it}$ = average real wage in industry $i$ in time $t$; $Q_{it}$ = real output in industry $i$ in time $t$; $\lambda_i$ = industry specific effect.

Note that in this equation explanatory variables are assumed to have common impacts across industries. The industry specific effects allow for unaccounted differences between sectors which are constant over time.

For the purposes of estimation, the employment equation is differenced so as to transform out the industry specific fixed effects, and a dynamic equation implemented of the form

$$\Delta \ln N_{i,t} = -\mu_0 - \sum_j \mu_{1j}\Delta \ln M_{i,t-j} - \sum_j \mu_{2j}\Delta \ln X_{i,t-j} + \sum_j \phi_{0j}\Delta \ln N_{i,t-j}$$

$$+ \sum_j \phi_{1j}\Delta \ln w_{i,t-j} + \sum_j \phi_{2j}\Delta \ln Q_{i,t-j} + \Delta \varepsilon_{it}. \tag{7}$$

However, since the differencing will induce a bias in the coefficient on the lagged dependent variable because of the correlation between it and the unobserved fixed effects in the residual, an instrumental variable approach must be adopted. The one used is the generalised method of moments technique of Arellano and Bond (1991). This uses lags of the endogenous variables dated $t - 2$ and earlier as instruments, but is efficient in the sense that it expands the instrument set as the panel progresses and the number of potential lags increases. This equation will give unbiased and consistent estimates of the regression coefficients as long as the differenced equation is free of second and higher order serial correlation. Thus, test statistics, which are distributed normally under the null of no serial correlation, are calculated and presented in the tables. The validity of the instrument set is checked using a Sargan test based on the correlation between the instruments and the residuals from the model. This is asymptotically distributed as chi-squared under the null.

## 4. Results

The results of our model estimations are presented in Tables 2 and 3. The first reports three sets of estimates: for the base specification alone, for the base specification augmented by total trade and for the latter also including some analysis of interactions between trade and wage effects. There are some a priori reasons for thinking that origin might matter and, as we saw, some earlier empirical work has pointed to stronger employment effects being associated with North–South trade than North–North trade. Table 3 therefore reports on our analysis when UK trade is decomposed by origin.

In the first panel of Table 2, we report on our base specification where both output and wages have the expected impacts. Output causes increases in the level of derived labour demand both in the short run and the long run whereas increases

Table 2
Employment Equations for UK manufacturing: total trade

|  | 1 | | 2 | | 3 | |
|---|---|---|---|---|---|---|
|  | Coefficient | $t$-ratio | Coefficient | $t$-ratio | Coefficient | $t$-ratio |
| Constant | 0.0001 | 0.0054 | −0.0033 | −0.4540 | −0.0088 | −1.2891 |
| $\Delta \ln N_{t-1}$ | 0.4309 | 2.7136 | 0.3980 | 2.6628 | 0.3243 | 2.4432 |
| $\Delta \ln N_{t-2}$ | 0.0469 | 0.7318 | 0.0419 | 0.7178 | 0.0120 | 0.2060 |
| $\Delta \ln Q_t$ | 0.6082 | 8.7225 | 0.5255 | 7.5387 | 0.5067 | 7.2180 |
| $\Delta \ln Q_{t-1}$ | −0.2039 | −1.7798 | −0.1819 | −1.6488 | −0.1377 | −1.3855 |
| $\Delta \ln Q_{t-2}$ | −0.0053 | −0.0798 | 0.0368 | 0.5843 | 0.0676 | 1.0790 |
| $\Delta \ln (W/c)_t$ | −0.3350 | −3.4110 | −0.3141 | −3.1464 | −0.2843 | −2.3993 |
| $\Delta \ln (W/c)_{t-1}$ | 0.2451 | 1.5078 | 0.2831 | 1.8030 | 0.2533 | 1.6026 |
| $\Delta \ln (W/c)_{t-2}$ | 0.0102 | 0.0879 | 0.0121 | 0.1057 | 0.0093 | 0.0751 |
| $\Delta \ln$ concentration | −0.0324 | −1.3046 | −0.0234 | −0.9419 | −0.0213 | −0.8531 |
| $\Delta \ln$ import$_t$ |  |  | −0.0449 | −3.1716 | −0.0667 | −2.5131 |
| $\Delta \ln$ import$_{t-1}$ |  |  | 0.0002 | 0.0200 | 0.0030 | 0.3454 |
| $\Delta \ln$ import$_{t-2}$ |  |  | 0.0101 | 0.7810 | 0.0110 | 0.9025 |
| $\Delta \ln$ export$_t$ |  |  | −0.0317 | −2.4592 | −0.0086 | −0.6292 |
| $\Delta \ln$ export$_{t-1}$ |  |  | 0.0108 | 1.4381 | 0.0082 | 0.9962 |
| $\Delta \ln$ export$_{t-2}$ |  |  | −0.0055 | −0.3536 | −0.0015 | −0.0978 |
| $\Delta \ln (W/c)_t \cdot \Delta \ln$ import$_t$ |  |  |  |  | −0.3724 | −0.9219 |
| $\Delta \ln (W/c)_{t-1} \cdot \Delta \ln$ import$_{t-1}$ |  |  |  |  | 0.2398 | 0.6729 |
| $\Delta \ln (W/c)_{t-2} \cdot \Delta \ln$ import$_{t-2}$ |  |  |  |  | 0.0401 | 0.1048 |
| $\Delta \ln (W/c)_t \cdot \Delta \ln$ export$_t$ |  |  |  |  | 0.2567 | 1.1450 |
| $\Delta \ln (W/c)_{t-1} \cdot \Delta \ln$ export$_{t-1}$ |  |  |  |  | −0.4128 | −1.4395 |
| $\Delta \ln (W/c)_{t-2} \cdot \Delta \ln$ export$_{t-2}$ |  |  |  |  | −0.3824 | −0.9412 |
| Instrumental validity |  | 0.76673 |  | 0.85355 |  | 0.90328 |
| 2nd order serial correlation |  | 0.203 |  | −0.022 |  | 0.734 |

Notes:
1. The dependent variable is $\Delta \ln N_t$.
2. Heteroskedastic consistent $t$-ratios in parentheses.
3. All models are estimated in differences by instrumental variables.
4. Coefficients on time dummies are not reported.

in wages have a negative effect. The positive coefficient on the lagged dependent variable indicates persistence in both the wage and output effects on the level of employment. Finally, we note that the equation performs well in conventional statistical terms with no second order serial correlation and with the Sargan test for instrumental validity indicating that the instrument set and the residuals are not correlated.

Panel 2 of Table 2 reports the results of introducing import and export penetration into the base employment equation. The specification is robust to such change with the signs of the coefficients remaining unchanged and of broadly similar magnitudes. Turning to trade shares we see that the impact effect of import penetration is negative, as expected, and significant at the 1% level. What are the employment implications of these results? Over the period 1981–1991 employ-

D. Greenaway et al. / European Journal of Political Economy 15 (1999) 485–500     495

Table 3
Employment equations for UK manufacturing: trade by origin

| | 1 | | 2 | |
|---|---|---|---|---|
| | Coefficient | t-ratio | Coefficient | t-ratio |
| Constant | −0.0015 | −0.1863 | −0.0002 | −0.0234 |
| $\Delta \ln N_{t-1}$ | 0.4002 | 2.3935 | 0.3988 | 2.3888 |
| $\Delta \ln N_{t-2}$ | 0.0635 | 1.0188 | 0.0555 | 0.8865 |
| $\Delta \ln Q_t$ | 0.5257 | 7.5628 | 0.5318 | 7.6063 |
| $\Delta \ln Q_{t-1}$ | −0.1784 | −1.5180 | −0.1784 | −1.5262 |
| $\Delta \ln Q_{t-2}$ | 0.0148 | 0.2149 | 0.0181 | 0.2624 |
| $\Delta \ln (W/c)_t$ | −0.2826 | −2.8327 | −0.2820 | −2.8536 |
| $\Delta \ln (W/c)_{t-1}$ | 0.2822 | 1.7271 | 0.2768 | 1.7561 |
| $\Delta \ln (W/c)_{t-2}$ | 0.0146 | 0.1269 | 0.0176 | 0.1508 |
| $\Delta \ln$ concentration | −0.0218 | −0.8742 | −0.0241 | −0.9766 |
| $\Delta \ln$ Japan$_t$ | 0.0059 | 1.3495 | 0.0049 | 1.0538 |
| $\Delta \ln$ Japan$_{t-1}$ | 0.0004 | 0.1059 | −0.0004 | −0.0893 |
| $\Delta \ln$ Japan$_{t-2}$ | −0.0072 | −1.2507 | −0.0074 | −1.2737 |
| $\Delta \ln$ USA$_t$ | −0.0036 | −0.5458 | −0.0052 | −0.7877 |
| $\Delta \ln$ USA$_{t-1}$ | −0.0155 | −2.8229 | −0.0157 | −2.8529 |
| $\Delta \ln$ USA$_{t-2}$ | 0.0045 | 0.6479 | 0.0061 | 0.8773 |
| $\Delta \ln$ E. Asia$_t$ | −0.0057 | −0.8758 | | |
| $\Delta \ln$ E. Asia$_{t-1}$ | 0.0025 | 0.6785 | | |
| $\Delta \ln$ E. Asia$_{t-2}$ | 0.0019 | 0.3728 | | |
| $\Delta \ln$ Dragons$_t$ | | | −0.0051 | −0.7811 |
| $\Delta \ln$ Dragons$_{t-1}$ | | | 0.0005 | 0.1226 |
| $\Delta \ln$ Dragons$_{t-2}$ | | | 0.0032 | 0.7435 |
| $\Delta \ln$ Tigers$_t$ | | | 0.0003 | 0.1128 |
| $\Delta \ln$ Tigers$_{t-1}$ | | | −0.0068 | −1.8473 |
| $\Delta \ln$ Tigers$_{t-2}$ | | | 0.0038 | 0.9531 |
| $\Delta \ln$ EU$_t$ | −0.0348 | −2.8779 | −0.0314 | −2.5963 |
| $\Delta \ln$ EU$_{t-1}$ | 0.0129 | 1.2515 | 0.0119 | 1.5086 |
| $\Delta \ln$ EU$_{t-2}$ | 0.0156 | 0.9583 | 0.0151 | 0.9140 |
| $\Delta \ln$ export$_t$ | −0.0250 | −1.6909 | −0.0244 | −1.6475 |
| $\Delta \ln$ export$_{t-1}$ | 0.0111 | 1.7048 | 0.0116 | 1.7146 |
| $\Delta \ln$ export$_{t-2}$ | −0.0085 | −0.5233 | −0.0108 | −0.6757 |
| 2nd order serial correlation | | 0.88772 | | 0.89507 |
| Instrumental validity | | 0.160 | | 0.297 |

Notes:
1. The dependent variable is $\Delta \ln N_t$.
2. Heteroskedastic consistent t-ratios in parentheses.
3. All models are estimated in differences by instrumental variables.
4. Coefficients on time dummies are not reported.

ment in manufacturing decreased from 6.107 million to 4.623 million, a reduction of 24.3%. Of this fall, our results indicate that changes in the efficiency of the use of labour as a result of increases in import penetration caused a short-run decline of 86,074 and a long run decline of 94,887. This accounts for 5.8% and 6.4%, respectively, of the 1.484 million fall in employment over the period. This

496        *D. Greenaway et al. / European Journal of Political Economy 15 (1999) 485–500*

excludes the direct employment displacement effects of trade which have been calculated in studies such as Wood (1991, 1994) (see Section 2). Table 4 shows the two-digit industries particularly affected by the impact of increased import penetration. The extraction of other minerals and ores (SIC 22, 23, 24) has suffered an increase in penetration of over a third, as have the leather and metal goods industries.

Perhaps more surprising, however, is the result that the sign on current export share is also negative and significant and would have accounted for declines in employment of 56,543 (3.8%) in the short run and 69,900 (4.71%) in the long run. Although the magnitude of this effect is smaller than for imports it is nonetheless notable. It suggests that there are also trade induced efficiencies in the use of labour in export oriented industries. Note that there is no strong evidence that the extent of domestic competition affects efficiency since, although the coefficient on seller market concentration is negative, it falls short of significance. [8]

The final panel of Table 2 focuses on the impact of trade changes on the slope of the derived labour demand function since, as we noted earlier, some analysts have suggested increased openness may make it easier to substitute foreign workers for domestic workers. Thus, in panel 3, import and export volumes are interacted with the wage rate. For both, the effect is to increase the wage elasticity though none of the impact effects are statistically significant at conventional levels.

In Table 3, we investigate whether UK trade with different regions impacts differentially on the derived demand for labour. Column one disaggregates imports into those originating from the European Union, United States, Japan and East Asia, which on average accounted for 80% of UK imports over the sample period. The European Union and the United States are the UK's most important trading partners and much of the trade in question is of an intra-industry type. Japan and East Asia have become increasingly important and trade here is more typically inter-industry. The second thing we do is to disaggregate the East Asian countries into the established newly industrialising countries (NICs) (Korea, Taiwan, Hong Kong and Singapore) and the new exporting countries (NECs) (Thailand, Malaysia and Indonesia). These are referred to in the table as the 'Tigers and Dragons', respectively.

Refer first to the broad country results. For all the groupings, the long run impact of import penetration is negative. These effects are rather badly determined however as import change among the regions is somewhat collinear. What is apparent, however, is that the timing and magnitude of impacts differs between regions. As can be seen from Table 5, imports from Japan and East Asia have increased proportionately faster than that from other regions over the sample period. Indeed, import penetration from the United States declined between 1981

---

[8] This possibility is suggested by Konings and Vandenbussche (1995).

*D. Greenaway et al. / European Journal of Political Economy 15 (1999) 485–500*   497

Table 4
Changes in import penetration by industry

| $\Delta \ln M < 0$ | $0 \leq \Delta \ln M \leq 1/3$ | $\Delta \ln M > 1/3$ |
|---|---|---|
| 26 Production of man-made fibres | 25 Chemical industries | 22 Metal manufacturing |
| 33 Manufacture of office machinery | 32 Mechanical engineering | 23 Extraction of minerals |
| 36 Manufacture of other transport equipment | 34 Electrical engineering | 24 Manufacture of non-metallic mineral products |
| 46 Timber and wooden furniture | 35 Manufacture of motor vehicles | 31 Manufacture of metal goods |
| 47 Manufacture of paper and paper products | 37 Instrument engineering | 44 Manufacture of leather |
| 49 Other manufacturing industries | 41 Food, drink, tobacco | |
| | 43 Textile industry | |
| | 45 Footwear and clothing | |
| | 48 Processing of rubber and plastics | |

Table 5
Changes in import penetration by region

| Country | Average annual increase 1981–1991 |
| --- | --- |
| United States | −1.04 |
| Japan | 3.04 |
| European Union | 0.97 |
| East Asia | 4.98 |

and 1991. However, the strongest induced efficiency effects are associated with imports from the USA and the European Union, though those from the EU have a more immediate impact. When one disaggregates between 'dragons' and 'tigers' the negative effect of import penetration persists with the coefficient for 'dragons' higher than that for 'tigers'. The stronger impacts from the European Union and the United States are perhaps contrary to the work of Wood (1994) and others. This may reflect the fact that imports from Asia are in those industries which have already declined in importance in the United Kingdom. Labour from the United States and the European Union however more directly competes with that currently extant in the UK. [9] As a result, $x$-efficiency effects are stronger in these sectors. Our results may also be influenced by the fact that we model aggregate employment, rather than focusing on skilled and unskilled workers separately.

## 5. Conclusions

Throughout the post-war period, the growth in trade has consistently outstripped the growth in real output resulting in a growing integration of the world's economies. The UK has featured prominently in this process. Recently, the impact of expanding trade on labour markets and labour market adjustment has generated growing interest. In particular, there has been concern about the effect on jobs of the growth of trade in general and the rapid expansion with low wage economies of East Asia. This interest has been acute in the UK given the sharp decline in manufacturing employment in the 1980s. Up until now, however, it has not been empirically investigated.

In this paper, we have investigated the impact of trade on industry level outcomes for a sample of 167 manufacturing industries. We build on a dynamic labour demand equation by incorporating imports and exports in a panel framework using a specially constructed database. Our base equation is well defined and robust to changes in specification. When we introduce trade we find that increases

---

[9] At the suggestion of an anonymous referee, we investigated whether a differential response existed between high and low IIT industries. Evidence was found that the efficiency impact of imports is stronger in high IIT industries and it is also more rapid. UK trade with the US and EU is predominantly IIT. This will be investigated further in future work.

in trade volumes, both in terms of imports and exports, cause reductions in the level of derived labour demand. This is consistent with the view that increased openness serves to increase the efficiency with which labour is utilised in the firm. Among other things, it could imply that previous work has underestimated the impact of trade by ignoring the extent to which increased import penetration induces the elimination of $x$-inefficiency and the take up of new technology. Our results, however, find limited evidence to support the proposition advanced in Rodrik (1997) that the potential for substituting foreign for domestic workers increases the wage elasticity of the derived labour demand function.

Our database allowed us to disaggregate the import data in order to see whether the region of origin affected labour demand differentially. Some evidence was reported to suggest that this may very well be the case. However, our results suggest very clearly that the disciplining effects of trade with East Asia and Japan appears to be less marked than that associated with imports from the EU. This reinforces the idea that trade affects $x$-inefficiency, with the strongest competition for UK producers coming from the EU and US rather than East Asia.

Finally, the paper points up some potentially interesting avenues for future research. Given more finely graded data, it would be useful to explore the relationship for different categories of labour. Given the extensive literature on the skill gap, disaggregation into different categories of labour is worth pursuing. Aggregating industries into a range of alternative groupings by relative factor intensities would also be worth exploring. In addition, the links between the speed of adjustment and the importance of IIT merit further investigation. This is an issue which has attracted much comment but little serious research.

## Acknowledgements

The authors wish to acknowledge financial support from The Leverhulme Trust under Progamme Grant F114/BF and helpful comments from two anonymous referees on an earlier draft of the paper.

## References

Abowd, J.M., 1987. The Effects of International Competition on Collective Bargaining Agreements in the United States. Princeton University, Princeton, NJ, unpublished.

Abowd, J.M., Lemieux T., 1990. The effects of international competition on collective bargaining outcomes: A comparison of the United States and Canada. Working Paper 3352, NBER, Cambridge, MA.

Arellano, M., Bond, S., 1991. Some tests of specification for panel data: Monte Carlo evidence and an application to employment equations. Review of Economic Studies 58 (2), 277–297.

Baldwin, R.E., 1995. The effects of trade and foreign direct investment on employment and relative wages. OECD Economic Studies 23, 7–53.

Borgas, G.J., Ramey, V.A., 1994. The relationship between wage inequality and international trade. In: Bergstrand, J. et al. (Eds.), The Changing Distribution of Income in an Open US Economy. North-Holland, Amsterdam.

Caves, R.E., 1990. Adjustment to International Competition: Short run relations of prices, trade flows and inputs in Canadian manufacturing industry. Economic Council of Canada, Ottawa.

Caves, R., Krepps, M., 1993. Fat: The displacement of nonproduction workers from US manufacturing industries. Brookings Papers, Macroeconomics, 2 pp.

Cline, W., 1997. Trade and Income Distribution. Institute for International Economics, Washington, DC.

Cortes, O., Jean, S., 1996. International trade spurs productivity. Mimeo, OECD Development Centre, Paris.

Cortes, O., Jean, S., Pisani-Ferry, J., 1996. Trade with emerging countries and the labour market: The French case. Document de travail, no. 96-04, CEPII, Paris.

Courakis, A., Maskus, K.E., Webster, A., 1997. Occupational employment and wage changes in the UK: Trade and technology effects. In: Borkakoti, J., Milner, C.R. (Eds.), 1997. International Trade and Labour Markets. Macmillan, London.

Denny, K., Machin, S., 1991. The effects of import competition on wages and employment. Mimeo, Institute for Fiscal Studies, London.

Feenstra, R., Hanson, G.H., 1996. Foreign investment outsourcing and relative wages. American Economic Review 86, 252–257.

Greenaway, D., Hine, R.C., Milner, C.R., 1994. Country specific factors and the pattern of horizontal and vertical intra-industry trade in the UK. Weltwirtschaftliches Archive 131, 77–100.

Greenaway, D., Hine, R.C., Milner, C.R., 1995. Horizontal and vertical intra-industry trade: a cross industry analysis for the UK. Economic Journal 105, 1505–1518.

Gregory, M., Greenhalgh, C., 1997. International trade, de-industrialisation and labour demand — an input–output study for the UK 1979–1990. In: Borkakoti, J., Milner, C.R. (Eds.), 1997. International Trade and Labour Markets. Macmillan, London.

Konings, J., Vandenbussche, H., 1995. The effect of foreign competition on UK employment and wages: evidence from firm-level panel data. Weltwirtschaftliches Archiv 131, 655–671.

Krugman, P., 1995. Growing world trade: Causes and consequences. Brookings Papers on Economic Activity (1), 327–377.

Lawrence, R., 1996. Single World, Divided Nations. OECD, Paris.

Leamer, E.E., 1994. Trade, wages and revolving door ideas. Working Paper 4716. National Bureau of Economic Research, Cambridge, MA.

Martin, J.P., Evans, J.M., 1981. Notes on measuring the employment displacement effects of trade by the accounting procedure. Oxford Economic Papers 33, 154–164.

Messerlin, P.A., 1995. The impact of trade and capital movements on labour: Evidence of the French case. OECD Economic Studies 24, 89–124.

Neven, D., Wyplosz, 1996. Relative prices, trade and restructuring in European Industry. Discussion Paper No. 1451, CEPR, London, August.

Nickell, S., 1986. Dynamic models of labour demand. In: Ashenfelter, O., Layard, R. (Eds.), Handbook of Labour Economics, Vol. 1. North-Holland, Amsterdam.

OECD, 1992. Structural Change and Industrial Performance: A Seven Country Growth Decomposition Study. OECD, Paris.

Rodrik, D., 1997. Has Globalization Gone too Far? Institute for International Economics, Washington, DC.

Sapir, A., Schumacher, D., 1985. The employment impact of shifts in the composition of commodity and services trade. In: Employment Growth and Structural Change. OECD, Paris.

Slaughter, M., 1999. Globalisation and Employment: Will There be a Protectionist Backlash? The World Economy, Vol. 22, forthcoming.

Wood, A., 1991. The factor content of North–South trade in manufactures reconsidered. Weltwirtschaftliches Archiv 127, 719–743.

Wood, A., 1994. North–South Trade, Employment and Inequality: Changing Fortunes in a Skill-Driven World. Clarendon Press, Oxford.

# [5]

# INTERNATIONAL TRADE, COMPARATIVE ADVANTAGE AND THE INCIDENCE OF LAYOFF UNEMPLOYMENT SPELLS

## Thomas L. Hungerford*

*Abstract*—The gains and losses to factors of production from trade are discussed primarily within the context of the Stolper-Samuelson theorem which focuses on factor rewards. But policy makers are more concerned about employment effects of trade. This paper focuses on the short-run effects of trade on the incidence of layoffs in U.S. manufacturing industries. A probit model with endogenous switching is employed to estimate the effects of trade shocks and explore the role of comparative advantage on layoffs. The evidence suggests that trade shocks play a minor role in the incidence of layoff spells. However, net importing industries tend to adjust their labor force through layoffs to a greater extent than net exporting industries.

## I. Introduction

THE gains and losses to the factors of production due to trade are discussed primarily within the context of the Stolper-Samuelson theorem which is based on a timeless and, hence, long-run model. A version of this theorem (in a two-good, two-factor model) states that anything that raises the relative price of a good also raises the real wage of the factor used intensively in its production and lowers the real wage of the other factor. The reverse will be true for a fall in the relative price. Generally, increased import competition leads to a fall in the relative price of the competing domestic good.

Underlying this theorem is the assumption of full employment of factors. But policy makers are more concerned about employment effects of trade. Before assuming away employment effects, Stolper and Samuelson (1941) note that "second only in political appeal to the argument that tariffs increase employment is the popular notion

that the standard of living of the American worker must be protected against the ruinous competition of cheap foreign labour." The President of the UAW claimed that "more than 300,000 U.S. jobs would be lost if Japan shipped all the cars it is capable of sending to our market."[1] And the implicit assumption of the Trade Adjustment Assistance (TAA) program is that workers in import impacted industries have greater probabilities of being laid off (Corson, et al. 1979).

Furthermore, in the U.S., trade protection is generally offered only as temporary relief from short-run trade difficulties. Before trade protection can be granted, many of the U.S. trade laws (e.g., escape clause, antidumping, and countervailing duties) not only require that imports be increasing but also that the increasing imports be an important cause of injury to the industry. In the determination of serious injury under the escape clause, one of the factors that the ITC considers is "significant unemployment or underemployment within the industry."

However, Grossman (1986) and Pindyck and Rotemberg (1987) examined two escape clause cases and found that increasing imports were not the most important cause of serious injury. In another case, the International Trade Commission (ITC, 1980) ruled that the recession with falling demand was a greater cause of injury to the auto industry than increasing imports. Kruse (1988) found that the unemployment duration of workers displaced from manufacturing industries varied directly with the long-term rise in the industry's import share. However, he points out that this relationship is apparently due to the fact that the work force in these industries (import competing) tends to have "demographic characteristics associated with labor market adjustment difficulties."[2]

Received for publication June 28, 1993. Revision accepted for publication July 26, 1994.

* U.S. General Accounting Office and American University.

I would like to thank Frank Stafford, Alan Deardorff, Jim Levinsohn, Charlie Brown, Michael Baker, seminar participants at the University of Michigan, Wayne State University, American University, and the Midwest International Economics Conference, and two anonymous referees for comments on an earlier draft. Any remaining errors are my own. The views presented here do not necessarily represent the views of the U.S. General Accounting Office.

[1] Ownen Bieber, Letters, *The New York Times*, March 13, 1986.

[2] Other studies examining the long-run effect of trade on employment are described and summarized in OECD (1979) and Dickens (1988). Most of these studies find that the overall net effect of import competition on employment was relatively small in the 1970s.

Layoffs are a significant component of unemployment and over the past several years various researchers have investigated factors leading to layoffs. However, one potential contribution to the incidence[3] of layoff unemployment has been largely ignored: international trade. Knowing the extent to which trade adversely affects the labor market in the short-run has implications for the granting of temporary trade protection to injured industries and the making of weekly cash payments to laid off workers under the TAA program.

Most discussions of the link between trade and layoffs have implicitly assumed that the employment decisions of firms in exporting industries are insulated from trade and are different from firms in import competing industries. This paper focuses on the short-run effects of trade (both import and export) shocks on the incidence of layoffs in U.S. manufacturing industries from 1980 to 1985. U.S. comparative advantage is incorporated to yield an endogenous switching model. In general, the evidence presented in this paper suggests that trade shocks play a minor role in the incidence of layoff spells. The rest of the paper is organized into four sections. The following section lays the theoretical foundation for the empirical work and the data are described in section III. The results are presented in section IV and concluding remarks are offered in the final section.

## II.  Theoretical Background and Empirical Strategy

It is quite possible that trade has had important short-run labor market effects. Contract theories of unemployment start from the premise that workers are indefinitely attached to the firm and firms accommodate demand fluctuations by laying off workers (Azariadis, 1975 and Baily, 1974). It is generally well accepted that workers remain attached to their employers and most workers who are laid off eventually return to their original employers (Feldstein, 1976). Matusz (1985) shows in a simple general equilibrium trade

---

[3] By incidence, I am referring to the number of people on layoff at a point-in-time rather than to the initiation of new layoff unemployments spells. Thus, the results reported do not distinguish between the effects on the initiation of layoffs and the duration of layoff spells.

model with uncertainty and implicit contracts that the Stolper-Samuelson theorem may not hold and that in low productivity states of nature there will be layoffs.

The model examined here is a short-run model of the firm. The firm, when faced with changing product market conditions, will adjust its labor force. When conditions change for the better the firm will recall workers, and lay off workers when conditions take a turn for the worse. Market conditions are reflected in the product price. The product price is straightforwardly determined in the market. Let

$$D^d = D^d(P, \delta)$$
$$D^f = D^f(P, \nu)$$
$$S^d = S^d(P, \sigma)$$
$$S^f = S^f(P, \mu)$$

where $D^d$, $D^f$, $S^d$, and $S^f$ are domestic demand, foreign demand, domestic supply, and foreign supply, respectively, and $P$ is price. The shock terms $(\delta, \nu, \sigma, \mu)$ are defined such that positive shocks will shift out their respective curves and can be thought of as deviations from trend. In addition to reflecting changes in consumers' tastes and changes in input prices, the foreign demand and supply shocks also include fluctuations in exchanges rates and changes in tariffs and non-tariff barriers.

The price is implicitly defined by the market equilibrium condition:

$$D^d(P, \delta) + D^f(P, \nu) = S^d(P, \sigma) + S^f(P, \mu)$$

to yield:

$$P = P(\delta, \nu, \sigma, \mu)$$

with

$$\frac{\partial P}{\partial \delta} > 0, \qquad \frac{\partial P}{\partial \nu} > 0,$$
$$\frac{\partial P}{\partial \sigma} < 0, \quad \text{and} \quad \frac{\partial P}{\partial \mu} < 0.$$

Before the realization of the shocks, firms choose their labor forces to maximize expected profits. After the realization of the shocks the firms adjust their labor forces. Increases in product price (e.g., a positive foreign demand shock and increased exports) should lead to increases in labor demand and decreases in the price (e.g., a positive foreign supply shock and increased imports) should lead to declining labor demand (i.e., layoffs).

Oi (1962) argues that labor is a quasi-fixed factor in the short run and differences in the degree of fixity among labor implies differences in unemployment and layoff rates. The degree of fixity depends on the amount of fixed employment costs such as hiring costs, training costs, separation costs, and unemployment compensation taxes paid by the firm. The higher the fixed employment costs the higher the degree of fixity. He notes (p. 547) that "the high-wage, highly skilled jobs appear to be associated with higher degrees of fixity," and thus experience relatively smaller demand shifts as a result of short-run changes in market conditions.

Oi's finding was reaffirmed by Mincer and Higuchi (1988), who examined the proposition that human capital formation (e.g., continuous training) is the basic reason for lower labor turnover in Japan. They found that rapid technological change induces grater training and is partly responsible for less labor turnover in both the United States and Japan. In general, workers with more human capital should face a relatively lower probability of layoff than other workers.

This model also indicates that the higher the unemployment compensation tax is the lower the proportion of the firm's labor force that is on layoff. In the United States, unemployment payments are made by the government through the Unemployment Insurance (UI) program. The UI program is financed by payments from firms based on the amount of UI payments their workers have received. The methods of experience rating[4] in the United States are very imperfect with the effect that the UI tax does not reflect the true costs of laying off workers. This imperfection leads to increased layoffs (Brechling, 1981).

There are other factors which affect a firm's propensity to lay off workers but are not directly captured in the foregoing model. Research by Medoff (1979) shows that in manufacturing industries labor "adjustment through layoffs is substantially greater in unionized firms than in comparable nonunionized firms." This could be be-

cause unionized firms tend to incur higher fixed employment costs.

Katz and Summers (1989) examined interindustry wage differential and trade. They found that the top net exporting industries paid wages that were above the average even after controlling for worker characteristics while the top net importing industries paid wages that were below the average. They note that these differentials could arise because of differences in motivating and training workers, among other unobservable differences. Most likely the factors that affect wages in the long run will affect employment levels in the short run. Clearly net importing and net exporting industries differ in ways that are not observed by the analyst.

The Heckscher-Ohlin (H-O) theorem of international trade essentially states that countries tend to export those goods which use relatively intensively their relatively abundant factors of production. Many researchers have tried to determine the validity of this theorem. In a review of the literature, Deardorff (1984) states "it is now quite clear that U.S. comparative advantage derives from the knowledge possessed by its workers or its firms." Leamer (1984), on the other hand, finds that the "abundance of human capital was important in 1958 but not very important in 1975" in explaining the pattern of U.S. trade. Bowen (1983), however, concluded "that relative availability of skilled versus unskilled labor is an important determinant of U.S. comparative advantage." While the strong H-O theory may not provide a particularly reliable description of trade, Staiger (1988) provides evidence that trade patterns are consistent with a more general endowment based model.

Net exporting industries will tend to use human capital more intensively than net importing industries. Unfortunately, human capital is not easy to measure, and, as discussed above, is an important determinant of layoffs. The type of industry (net importing or net exporting) the individual works in should have important affects on the probability of being laid off—net exporting industries should have fewer layoffs holding all other observables constant because of unobservable differences. It is, therefore, reasonable to include industry trade type as an explanatory variable in an equation examining layoffs to pick up unobserved differences in human capital, motivational

---

[4] Brechling (1981) states "experience rating means that a firm's tax rate rises (falls) in response to increases (decreases) in benefit payments to the firm's own ex-employees."

techniques, and training. However, the type of industry that an individual works in is a choice variable, not an exogenous variable and the coefficient estimate would be biased. Instrumental variables techniques could be employed, but the model would be very restrictive.

A more general model is a switching model which consists of three equations:

$$l_{1i}^* = X_{1i}\beta_1 - \epsilon_{1i} \tag{1}$$

$$l_{2i}^* = X_{2i}\beta_2 - \epsilon_{2i} \tag{2}$$

$$t_i^* = Z_i\gamma - \mu_i. \tag{3}$$

Equations (1) and (2) are the basic layoff models for workers in net importing and net exporting industries, respectively. Let $l_{ji}^*$, $j = 1, 2$ be an individual's unobserved propensity to be laid off from a job. However, we observe only whether or not the worker is laid off. An individual is on layoff if $l_{ji}^*$ is greater than some threshold and working otherwise. Since $X_i$ includes a constant the threshold can be arbitrarily set to zero.[5] This relationship can be summarized as

$$l_{ji} = \begin{cases} 1 & \text{if } l_{ji}^* \geq 0 \\ 0 & \text{otherwise}. \end{cases}$$

The $X_{ji}$ vectors contain variables denoting the worker's characteristics, industry variables, and state level variables that affect layoffs. These variables are described in the next section.

Equation (3), the selection equation, models the type of industry the worker is employed in. An individual will work in a net exporting industry if the net returns are higher than working in a net importing industry. Specifically, a worker will be employed in a net importing industry if $t_i^* < 0$ and in a net exporting industry if $t_i^* \geq 0$. The variables in the $Z_i$ vector, including both the worker's and industry's characteristics, are described in the next section. The type of industry an individual works in depends on choices made by both the individual and the firm. In the United States, workers with more human capital will tend to work in net exporting industries, suggesting that $\epsilon_1$ and $\mu$ as well as $\epsilon_2$ and $\mu$ will be correlated.

It is assumed that

$$(\epsilon_1, \epsilon_2, \mu)' \sim N(0, \Sigma)$$

where

$$\Sigma = \begin{pmatrix} 1 & \sigma_{12} & \rho_1 \\ \sigma_{12} & 1 & \rho_2 \\ \rho_1 & \rho_2 & 1 \end{pmatrix}.$$

Given this model, a worker can be (1) laid off from a net exporting industry (a member of set $N_{11}$), (2) working in a net exporting industry (a member of set $N_{01}$), (3) laid off from a net importing industry (a member of set $N_{10}$), or (4) working in a net importing industry (a member of set $N_{00}$). The contributions to the likelihood function for each type of worker are

$$P(X_{1i}\beta_1 \geq \epsilon_{1i} \ \& \ Z_i\gamma \geq \mu_i)$$
$$= \int_{-\infty}^{Z_i\gamma} \int_{-\infty}^{X_{1i}\beta_1} f(\epsilon, \mu, \rho_1) \, d\epsilon \, d\mu$$

$$P(X_{1i}\beta_1 < \epsilon_{1i} \ \& \ Z_i\gamma \geq \mu_i)$$
$$= \int_{-\infty}^{Z_i\gamma} \int_{X_{1i}\beta_1}^{+\infty} f(\epsilon, \mu, \rho_1) \, d\epsilon \, d\mu$$

$$P(X_{2i}\beta_2 \geq \epsilon_{2i} \ \& \ Z_i\gamma < \mu_i)$$
$$= \int_{Z_i\gamma}^{+\infty} \int_{-\infty}^{X_{2i}\beta_2} f(\epsilon, \mu, \rho_2) \, d\epsilon \, d\mu$$

$$P(X_{2i}\beta_2 < \epsilon_{2i} \ \& \ Z_i\gamma < \mu_i)$$
$$= \int_{Z_i\gamma}^{+\infty} \int_{X_{2i}\beta_2}^{+\infty} f(\epsilon, \mu, \rho_2) \, d\epsilon \, d\mu$$

where $f(\epsilon, \mu, \rho)$ is the bivariate standard normal distribution. The likelihood function can now be written as

$$L = \prod_{i \in N_{11}} P_i \prod_{i \in N_{01}} P_i \prod_{i \in N_{10}} P_i \prod_{i \in N_{00}} P_i.$$

The model will be identified as long as there are variables in $Z$ that are not in $X$.[6] The covariance, $\sigma_{12}$, does not appear in the likelihood function and is therefore not identified.

### III.  Data Description

The data set used in this study is a time-series of cross-sections of individual workers. The advantage of this data is that not only are the cross-sectional differences among industries controlled for but also changes in these variables over time. The source of the individual worker data comes from the March Current Population

---

[5] The model allows this threshold to vary over time.

[6] Formally, functional form is sufficient to identify the correlation between the $\epsilon$'s and $\mu$. Full Information Maximum Likelihood estimation was employed to maximize the log likelihood function. The standard errors were calculated using the Berndt, Hall, Hall, and Hausman (1974) method.

LAYOFF UNEMPLOYMENT SPELLS                              515

Survey (CPS) for 1980 through 1985.[7] Only individuals working in or laid off[8] from manufacturing industries are included in the sample. Individuals in the CPS are interviewed for four consecutive months, sit out for the next eight months and then are interviewed again for the next four months. In order to avoid the problem of workers appearing in the sample twice, only individuals who are in their fifth through eighth interview months are included so the error terms will not be correlated. The CPS sample was then merged with detailed 3-digit Census Industrial Classification (CIC) manufacturing data and state-specific unemployment and unemployment insurance (UI) data (appendix table A.1 lists the sources of all the data). Unfortunately in 1982, the Census Bureau changed their CIC system. The final data set includes 32,146 individuals in the 66 industries (of 77 total) there are the same in the two CIC systems. The variables used in the analysis are listed and defined in table 1.

## A.  Layoff Model

The variables used in the layoff model control for worker and industry characteristics. Some of the worker's characteristics control for human capital which include education (*EDUC*), potential work experience (*EXPER*), and whether or not the worker has a blue collar occupation (*BLUCOL*). Other worker characteristics included are whether or not the worker is female (*FEMALE*), black (*BLACK*), or married (*MARRIED*). Industry variables include the percentage of unionized workers (*UNION*), the average industry wage (ln *W*), and the capital-labor ratio (*K/L*). Lastly, the one year labor productivity shock (*PRDSHK*) is designed to capture, to some extent, domestic supply shocks.

Another variable is designed to capture the variation in state UI systems. UI payments are financed by a payroll tax which is typically partially experience rated. With imperfect experience rating firms are subsidized for laying off workers. The variable used here is the ratio of benefits paid to unemployed workers to employer contributions (*BENCON*) in each state. The idea

---

[7] Limitations on the availability of industry level data prevented using a longer time-series.
[8] The CPS defines a person on layoff as "a person who is unemployed but expects to be called back to a specific job."

TABLE 1.—VARIABLE DEFINITIONS AND MEANS

| Variable | Description | Mean (Std. Dev.) |
|---|---|---|
| MARRIED | = 1 if married | 0.759 (0.4287) |
| BLACK | = 1 if black | 0.0806 (0.272) |
| FEMALE | = 1 if female | 0.332 (0.471) |
| EDUC | years of education | 12.971 (2.910) |
| EXPER | potential work experience (age − EDUC − 6) | 21.751 (11.727) |
| EXPERSQRD | EXPER squared | 610.634 (576.276) |
| BLUCOL | = 1 if blue collar worker | 0.650 (0.477) |
| K/L | capital-labor ratio | 24.0470 (30.560) |
| UNION | percent workers unionized in industry | 28.221 (14.341) |
| IPR | import penetration ratio shock: time-series regression residual | 0.0512 (0.0850) |
| XS | export share shock: time-series regression residual | 0.0389 (0.0574) |
| PRICE | = 1 if percent change in output deflator less than mean | 0.411 (0.492) |
| IPRP | = IPR if PRICE = 1 and IPR greater than zero or if PRICE = 0 and IPR less than zero = 0 otherwise | 0.0226 (0.0635) |
| XSP | = XS if PRICE = 1 and XS greater than zero or if PRICE = 0 and XS less than zero = 0 otherwise | 0.0176 (0.0472) |
| MPRISHK | import price index shock: time-series regression residual | 0.0510 (4.397) |
| XPRISHK | export price index shock: time-series regression residual | 0.159 (2.792) |
| PRDSHK | labor productivity (value added per hour) shock: time-series regression residual | −0.783 (4.172) |
| ln W | log average real wage in industry | 2.163 (0.285) |
| PRDGWTH | 5 year average of industry labor productivity (value added per hour) growth | 3.180 (5.415) |
| BENCON | state UI benefits to contribution ratio | 115.234 (53.200) |

is that the higher the benefit to contribution ratio the higher will be the UI subsidy (a greater proportion of firms will be at the maximum tax rate) and the higher the layoff probability.

Price is a function of the various supply and demand shocks, but these shocks are not measured. One possible way of capturing the effects of imports and exports would be to include the one year changes in the import penetration ratio and the export share. However, this strategy has two drawbacks. First, the change in these variables includes anticipated and unanticipated components. It is the unanticipated component that should affect layoffs. Second, both the import penetration ratio and export share can change for a number of reasons including some that have purely domestic origins. The idea behind the injury test in U.S. and international trade law is that trade policy should be used only in the event of harm due to foreign developments.

Grossman (1987) used an import price index to measure changes in imports. Under the assumption of perfectly elastic foreign supply, a change in the import price is due solely to a change in foreign supply. However, the assumption of perfectly elastic foreign supply may not be correct given the size of U.S. markets, distributional inertia, and the short-run focus of the model. In the case of less than perfectly elastic foreign supply, import prices can change due to changes in domestic supply and demand as well as changes in foreign supply.

In this paper two methods are used to measure import and export shocks. The first is to create import and export price index shocks (*MPRISHK* and *XPRISHK*, respectively). These price index shocks are the residuals from time-series regressions of either the industry import price index or the industry export price index on time and time squared for the period 1977 to 1986.[9]

The second method drops the assumption of perfectly elastic foreign supply and uses observable variables to create the trade shocks.[10] Focusing first on imports in the domestic market, total supply (both foreign and domestic) will equal domestic demand in equilibrium. If the domestic demand curve were to shift out (a positive demand shock), the quantity supplied by both domestic firms and foreign firms would increase. If foreign supply is more elastic than domestic supply then imports would increase relative to the

market. In this case, the product price would increase as well as domestic production and the increase in imports (both relative and absolute) would have no harmful effects on firms. On the other hand, if the foreign supply curve were to shift out (a positive foreign supply shock), ceteris paribus, imports would also increase relative to the market, but product price would fall. Lastly, in some industries characterized by learning by doing both the domestic and foreign supply curves will be shifting out resulting in an increasing import penetration ratio and falling price.

In order to distinguish the first situation from the last two, 3 variables were created from the observable variables output, price deflator, and imports. The import penetration ratio shock (*IPR*) is the residual from a time-series regression of the import penetration ratio (ratio of imports to new supply) for each industry on time and time squared for the period 1977 to 1986. A binary variable was created that is equal to one if the percentage change in the industry price deflator was less than the manufacturing mean (*PRICE*), since it is whether or not the product price decreased that is important. The third variable (*IPRP*) is equal to *IPR* if *IPR* is greater than zero and *PRICE* is equal to one or if *IPR* is less than zero and *PRICE* is equal to zero, and equal to zero otherwise. In this way, the coefficient estimate of *IPR* will capture the effects of domestic demand changes on the import penetration ratio while the sum of the coefficient estimates of *IPR* and *IPRP* will capture the effects of changes in foreign supply.

The analysis of exports is not as straightforward as it may initially seem. Again focusing on a simple partial equilibrium model: in equilibrium, total domestic output will be equal to domestic plus foreign demand. Policymakers generally talk about exports in a favorable light, and view unanticipated increases in exports as indicators of an industry's health. However, an unanticipated increase in exports could be an indication of weakening domestic demand and falling output.[11] For example, if the domestic demand curve were to shift in the new equilibrium would have a lower price, increased exports and decreased output. On the other hand, if the foreign demand curve

---

[9] These prices indices are the implicit import and export price indices constructed from data furnished by the Bureau of Labor Statistics.

[10] Conversations with Frank Stafford helped to clarify my thinking for this section.

[11] I thank Alan Deardorff for suggesting this possibility to me.

were to shift out the equilibrium would include a higher price, increased exports, and increased output.

In order to distinguish between these two situations three variables were created. The export share shock ($XS$) is the residual from a time-series regression of export share on time and time squared. The last variable ($XSP$) is equal to $XS$ if $XS$ is greater than zero and $PRICE$ is equal to one or if $XS$ is less than zero and $PRICE$ is equal to zero, and equal to zero otherwise. The sum of the coefficient estimates of $XS$ and $XSP$ will capture the effects of domestic demand shocks on exports, while the coefficient estimate of $XS$ will capture foreign demand shocks.

### B. Selection Model

The selection model reflects the workers' choice of industry type[12] which depends on the worker's characteristics and the characteristics of the industry chosen by the worker. The later set of variables include the capital–labor ratio ($K/L$) and the 5-year average (prior to each observation) of labor productivity growth ($PRDGWTH$).[13] Mincer and Higuchi (1988) show that the demand for human capital increases as productivity grows. The basic distinction between the $X$ and $Z$ vector is that variables reflecting the worker's choice of industry type and the long-run trade position of an industry appear in $Z$ and variables affecting short-run employment decisions appear in $X$.

### IV. Results

The variable means by industry type are shown in table 2 and the estimation results of the switching model are contained in table 3. As can be seen from table 2, the layoff rate is higher in net importing industries. Furthermore, net importers

---

[12] The industry type was determined by calculating the 9-year average of net exports. If this average is less than zero the industry is a net importer.

[13] Productivity growth ($PRDGWTH$) is the only variable to appear in the $Z$ vector and not the $X$ vector. This helps to identify the model and can be justified since long-run productivity growth reflects the type of workers employed in an industry, while short-run productivity shocks affect layoffs. Total factor productivity growth is not available for manufacturing industries at the required level of disaggregation, thus forcing the use of labor productivity growth. Labor productivity growth incorporates not only total factor productivity growth but also changes in factor intensity.

face greater positive import shocks, on average, while net exporters face larger positive export shocks. The degree of unionization, the proportion of female workers, and the proportion of blue collar workers are higher in net importing industries which fits with the Corson et al. (1979) general description of TAA recipients. As expected, the average years of education and the average (ln) hourly wage are greater in net exporting industries. Interestingly, the capital–labor ratio is higher in net importing industries, which may suggest that capital tends to complement unskilled labor.[14]

The coefficient estimates for the switching or selection equation are reported in the last column of table 3.[15] The signs of the coefficient estimates, for the most part, fit with expectations. Workers with more education tend to work for net exporters and industries with higher productivity growth tend to be net exporters. Female workers and blue collar workers are more likely to work in net importing industries. Consistent with the means, industries with higher capital–labor ratios tend to be net importers.

The results for the layoff models are also reported in table 3 and the implied effects of selected variables on the conditional probability of layoff are reported in table 4. The probability of layoff conditional on industry type was determined with these coefficient estimates using the same variable values (see the note in table 4 for specific values). In this way the probabilities can be compared holding all (observable) variables constant. The conditional layoff probability for workers in net importing industries is 35% greater than it is for workers in net exporting industries

---

[14] Branson (1980) has observed that physical capital plays a relatively neutral role in U.S. comparative advantage, "combining relatively more with human capital in exports and unskilled labor in imports." More recently, Berman, Bound and Griliches (1993) have found "strong correlations between within-industry skill upgrading and ... increased investment in computers," suggesting that recent capital investment and skilled labor tend to be complementary.

[15] In an initial estimation, year dummies were included in the switching equation, but all five coefficient estimates were small, not statistically significant (individually or jointly) and were dropped from subsequent specifications. This suggests that the threshold for the choice of industry type (net exporter or net importer) remained constant over this period. Various specifications of the switching model were estimated and the results are very robust.

TABLE 2.—MEANS: NET EXPORTERS AND NET IMPORTERS

| Variable | Net Exporters | Net Importers |
|---|---|---|
| %Layoffs | 2.44 | 3.31 |
| IPR | 0.02545 | 0.06738 |
|  | (0.03825) | (0.1008) |
| IPRP | 0.01018 | 0.03042 |
|  | (0.02856) | (0.07671) |
| XS | 0.05362 | 0.02969 |
|  | (0.07553) | (0.03963) |
| XSP | 0.02572 | 0.01253 |
|  | (0.06567) | (0.02921) |
| PRICE | 0.3709 | 0.4353 |
|  | (0.4831) | (0.4958) |
| MPRISHK | −0.0269 | 0.0996 |
|  | (3.9124) | (4.6739) |
| XPRISHK | 0.2244 | 0.1186 |
|  | (2.4926) | (2.9631) |
| PRDSHK | −0.8669 | −0.7310 |
|  | (3.9224) | (4.3200) |
| K/L | 20.4130 | 26.3182 |
|  | (17.1045) | (36.3510) |
| UNION | 25.0516 | 30.2020 |
|  | (12.2451) | (15.1752) |
| ln W | 2.2328 | 2.1196 |
|  | (0.2817) | (0.2790) |
| EDUC | 13.3945 | 12.7060 |
|  | (2.7244) | (2.9896) |
| EXPER | 21.0114 | 22.2138 |
|  | (11.5210) | (11.8304) |
| BLUCOL | 0.5889 | 0.6889 |
|  | (0.4921) | (0.4630) |
| FEMALE | 0.2808 | 0.3634 |
|  | (0.4494) | (0.4810) |
| BLACK | 0.07392 | 0.08477 |
|  | (0.2617) | (0.2786) |
| MARRIED | 0.7539 | 0.7622 |
|  | (0.4308) | (0.4257) |
| BENCON | 114.5927 | 115.6344 |
|  | (53.1275) | (53.2432) |
| N | 12,364 | 19,782 |

(2.9% compared to 2.2%), holding everything constant.

It is noteworthy that the correlation coefficients ($\rho_1$ and $\rho_2$) are large and statistically significant at the 1% level in the case of net importing industries. The error terms are correlated between the layoff equations and the selection equation, implying that selection into a particular industry is important in determining the probability of being laid off. For example, estimating a simple probit model shows that years of education has a negative and statistically significant effect on the probability of being on layoff. However, the coefficient estimates on the education variable in the selection and layoff models suggest that it is the fact more educated individu-

TABLE 3.—RESULTS: SWITCHING MODEL
(standard errors in parentheses)

| Variable | Net Exporters | Net Importers | Switching |
|---|---|---|---|
| **A. MODEL I** | | | |
| CONSTANT | −3.0401$^c$ | −1.2381$^c$ | −0.4229$^c$ |
|  | (0.4247) | (0.3118) | (0.06154) |
| IPR | 1.2057 | −0.1141 | |
|  | (1.3884) | (0.2479) | |
| IPRP | −13.2149$^c$ | 0.1937 | |
|  | (2.5984) | (0.3089) | |
| XS | −0.1509 | −0.1772 | |
|  | (0.8236) | (0.6137) | |
| XSP | 5.1764$^c$ | −1.2375 | |
|  | (1.2138) | (0.8751) | |
| PRICE | 0.1226$^a$ | −0.008429 | |
|  | (0.06515) | (0.03342) | |
| PRDSHK | 0.006015 | −0.001534 | |
|  | (0.01035) | (0.006779) | |
| PRDGWTH | | | 0.02904$^c$ |
|  | | | (0.001778) |
| K/L | −0.001436 | −0.005490$^c$ | −0.005844$^c$ |
|  | (0.001615) | (0.0007615) | (0.0003626) |
| UNION | 0.005128$^b$ | 0.003298$^b$ | |
|  | (0.002176) | (0.001332) | |
| ln W | 0.07154 | 0.1253$^a$ | |
|  | (0.1519) | (0.07252) | |
| EDUC | −0.01374 | 0.004399 | 0.02916$^c$ |
|  | (0.01224) | (0.007098) | (0.003212) |
| EXPER | −0.02092$^b$ | −0.01037$^b$ | 0.004971$^a$ |
|  | (0.008807) | (0.005109) | (0.002705) |
| EXPERSQRD | 0.0002549 | 0.0001075 | −0.0001171$^b$ |
|  | (0.0001786) | (0.00009564) | (0.00005505) |
| FEMALE | 0.06763 | −0.07595 | −0.2963$^c$ |
|  | (0.05811) | (0.04689) | (0.01613) |
| BLACK | 0.08840 | 0.07450$^a$ | −0.004314 |
|  | (0.07353) | (0.04103) | (0.02703) |
| MARRIED | 0.02495 | −0.05757$^b$ | −0.06370$^c$ |
|  | (0.05364) | (0.02838) | (0.01748) |
| BLUCOL | 0.4650$^c$ | 0.3125$^c$ | −0.1581$^c$ |
|  | (0.06837) | (0.09859) | (0.01742) |
| BENCON | 0.001059$^a$ | 0.0003263 | |
|  | (0.0005950) | (0.0003176) | |
| D81 | 0.1555$^a$ | 0.09172$^b$ | |
|  | (0.09277) | (0.04359) | |
| D82 | 0.3160$^c$ | 0.1862$^c$ | |
|  | (0.09509) | (0.05170) | |
| D83 | 0.4861$^c$ | 0.2369$^c$ | |
|  | (0.1032) | (0.06691) | |
| D84 | 0.3760$^c$ | 0.1400$^b$ | |
|  | (0.1099) | (0.06027) | |
| D85 | 0.1736 | 0.1289$^b$ | |
|  | (0.1148) | (0.06042) | |
| $\rho$ | 0.8718 | 0.8760$^c$ | |
|  | (0.6424) | (0.06281) | |
| ln L | −24538.2 | | |
| **B. MODEL II** | | | |
| MPRISHK | −0.004277 | −0.0006124 | |
|  | (0.01830) | (0.005672) | |
| XPRISHK | −0.008443 | 0.002414 | |
|  | (0.01620) | (0.006283) | |
| ln L | −24564.4 | | |

Note: $N = 32,146$.
$^a$ Significant at the 10% level.
$^b$ Significant at the 5% level.
$^c$ Significant at the 1% level.

TABLE 4.—EFFECTS OF INCREASE IN SELECTED VARIABLES
ON CONDITIONAL PROBABILITY OF LAYOFF

| Variable | Net Exporters | Net Importers |
|---|---|---|
| Base Case-Layoff Probability | 2.16 | 2.91 |
| IPR at PRICE = 0 by 1 Std. Dev. | +0.68 | −0.11 |
| IPR at PRICE = 1 by 1 Std. Dev. | −2.16 | +0.10 |
| XS at PRICE = 0 by 1 Std. Dev. | −0.05 | −0.11 |
| XS at PRICE = 1 by 1 Std. Dev. | +7.48 | −1.27 |
| PRDSHK by 1 Std. Dev. | +0.15 | −0.07 |
| K/L by 1 Std. Dev. | −0.24 | −1.47 |
| UNION by 1 Std. Dev. | +0.47 | +0.58 |
| ln W by 1 Std. Dev. | +0.12 | +0.43 |
| EDUC by 1 Year | −0.14 | −0.18 |
| EXPER by 1 Year | −0.44 | −1.50 |
| BENCON by 1 Std. Dev. | +0.35 | +0.20 |

Note: Base case was evaluated at means of all continuous variables and year dummies, *PRICE*, *FEMALE* and *BLACK* were set equal to zero, and *MARRIED* and *BLUCOL* were set equal to one. Other table entries show increase or decrease in the layoff probability from the base case.

als tend to work in net exporting industries that leads to a lower incidence of layoffs among educated workers, and not the effects of education per se. The same general pattern holds for female workers: female workers have a higher probability of layoff than male workers because they tend to work in net importing industries.

The coefficient estimates for the capital–labor ratio ($K/L$) are different between the two industry types. Apparently, changes in the capital–labor ratio do not affect the incidence of layoffs in net exporting industries. However, a higher capital–labor ratio in a net importing industry leads to a reduced incidence of layoffs. This result raises the possibility that capital and unskilled labor in net importing industries may be complementary. But regression evidence suggests that blue collar workers in net importing industries tend to work in industries with lower capital–labor ratios,[16] thus providing weak confirmation of Berman,

[16] The coefficient estimate from regressing $K/L$ on *BLUCOL* is −3.8328(0.5576). However, blue collar workers are not necessarily unskilled workers.

Bound and Griliches' (1993) finding of complementarity between skilled labor and capital.

The results also indicate that the UI system has little effect on layoffs since the coefficient estimates for the benefit–contribution ratio (*BENCON*) are fairly small and only significant at the 10% level in the case of net exporting industries. This could be due, in part, to the crudeness of the UI measure. A standard deviation increase in the benefit–contribution ratio will increase the conditional layoff probabilities by 0.35 percentage points for workers in net exporting industries and 0.20 points for workers in net importing industries. Unsurprisingly, blue collar workers are more likely to be laid off than workers in other occupations. The proportion of unionized workers has a relatively small positive effect on the incidence of layoffs.

The results from using the two methods to measure trade shocks are reported. Model I, the more general model in that no assumptions are made concerning the elasticities of the foreign supply and demand curves, includes *IPR*, *IPRP*, *XS*, and *XSP* to measure trade shocks. The second model, model II, is based on the assumption that both foreign supply and demand are completely elastic and includes the import shock (*MPRISHK*) and the export price shock (*XPRISHK*). Only the coefficient estimates for the two trade variables are shown in table 3 since the coefficient estimates for the other variables are virtually identical to those reported for model I.

It appears, in model I, that once selection into industries and observed worker and industry characteristics are taken into account, trade shocks do not significantly affect the incidence of layoff spells in net importing industries (all trade coefficient estimates are fairly small and not statistically significant). For example, import penetration ratio shocks that appear to be caused by shifts in foreign supply have little affect on layoffs: the implied coefficient estimate is 0.0796 (−0.1141 + 0.1937) with a standard error of 0.3961. In this case, an increase in the import penetration ratio shock by one standard deviation leads to a 0.10 point increase in the conditional layoff probability.

The situation is very different for net exporting industries. A positive export share shock combined with a real price decline increases the

probability of layoffs (the implied coefficient estimate is positive (5.0255) and statistically significant (S.E. 1.4668)) and an increase in this variable by one standard deviation increases the conditional layoff probability by almost 8 percentage points. This suggests that exporting firms may compensate for failing domestic demand by trying to "dump" their output overseas.

It may seem strange at first that a positive import penetration ratio shock combined with a real price decline leads to a large decrease in the layoff probability (the implied coefficient estimate is negative ($-12.0092$) and statistically significant (S.E. 2.9461)) and an increase in the import penetration ratio shock by one standard deviation reduces the conditional layoff probability to virtually zero. The likely explanation for this may be that both the domestic and foreign supply curves are shifting out. This would lead to falling price, an unexpectedly high import penetration ratio, and expanding domestic output. In fact, this appears to be the case in over three-quarters of the cases with *IPRP* > 0.

In model II, the coefficient estimates of both *MPRISHK* and *XPRISHK* are very small and not statistically significant for either type of industry. This result, combined with those from model I, suggest that trade shocks do not significantly affect layoffs.

### V.  Concluding Remarks

This paper has focused on the short-run layoff behavior of manufacturing industries in the United States. In particular the role of trade shocks and comparative advantage were examined using a probit model with endogenous switching. Surprisingly, the short-run layoff behavior of net importing industries does not appear to be affected by international trade shocks. However, the layoff behavior of net exporting industries appear to be somewhat affected by trade shocks. But it appears that the trade shocks are due more to domestic phenomena than to overseas developments. These results, however, should not be interpreted as showing that trade has no labor market effects in these industries: there may be long-run employment and wage effects.

Many of the other results in this paper are, for the most part, not surprising: blue collar workers

and workers with less work experience tend to be at greater risk of being laid off than other workers regardless of industry type. As expected, workers with more human capital tend to work in net exporting industries which is consistent with a factor proportions theory of comparative advantage. It appears that net importing industries tend to make short-run work force adjustments through layoffs to a greater extent than net exporting industries. The results also suggest that workers with less education and female workers face a greater probability of layoff because they tend to work in net importing industries. These findings also suggest that both Kruse's (1988) and Mincer and Higuchi's (1988) results are not inconsistent with a factor proportions theory of comparative advantage.

The results reported in this paper call into question the desirability of using temporary trade protection to maintain employment levels in injured industries since trade shocks don't appear to be the cause of layoffs. Also, to the extent that international trade leads to permanent displacement of workers, then the current focus of the TAA program on worker retraining and relocation is the correct one. Income maintenance for laid off workers should come through the Unemployment Insurance system rather than through the TAA program.

### REFERENCES

Azariadis, Costas, "Implicit Contracts and Underemployment Equilibria," *Journal of Political Economy* 83 (6) (1975), 1183–1202.

Baily, Martin Neil, "Wages and Employment under Uncertain Demand," *Review of Economic Studies* 41 (1) (1974), 37–50.

Berman, Eli, John Bound, and Zvi Griliches, "Changes in the Demand for Skilled Labor within U.S. Manufacturing Industries: Evidence from the Annual Survey of Manufacturing," NBER working paper no. 4255 (1993).

Berndt, Ernest, Bronwyn Hall, Robert Hall, and Jerry Hausman, "Estimation and Inference in Nonlinear Structural Models," *Annals of Economic and Social Measurement* 3 (1974), 653–665.

Bowen, Harry P., "Changes in the International Distribution of Resources and Their Impact on U.S. Comparative Advantage," this REVIEW 65 (3) (1983), 402–414.

Branson, William H., "Trends in U.S. International Trade and Investment since World War II," in Martin Feldstein (ed.), *The American Economy in Transition*, Chicago: University of Chicago Press, 1980.

Brechling, Frank, "Layoffs and Unemployment Insurance," in Sherwin Rosen (ed.), *Studies in Labor Markets* (Chicago: University of Chicago Press, 1981).

## LAYOFF UNEMPLOYMENT SPELLS 521

Corson, Walter, Walter Nicholson, David Richardson, and Andrea Vayda, *Final Report: Survey of Trade Adjustment Assistance Recipients*, report to the Office of Foreign Economic Affairs, Bureau of International Labor Affairs, U.S. Department of Labor. Mathematica Policy Research, Inc. (1979).

Deardorff, Alan V., "Testing Trade Theories and Predicting Trade Flows," in Ronald Jones and Peter Kenan (eds.), *Handbook of International Economics* (Amsterdam: North-Holland, 1984).

Dickens, William T., "The Effects of Trade on Employment: Techniques and Evidence," in Laura D'Andrea Tyson, William T. Dickens and John Zysman (eds.), *The Dynamics of Trade and Employment* (Cambridge, MA: Ballinger Publishing Co., 1988).

Feldstein, Martin, "Temporary Layoffs in the Theory of Unemployment," *Journal of Political Economy* 84 (5) (1976), 937–957.

Grossman, Gene M., "Imports as a Cause of Injury: The Case of the U.S. Steel Industry," *Journal of International Economics* 20 (1986), 201–223.

Grossman, Gene M., "The Employment and Wage Effects of Import Competition," *Journal of International Economic Integration* 2 (1987).

Katz, Lawrence F., and Lawrence H. Summers, "Can Interindustry Wage Differential Justify Strategic Trade Policy," in Robert C. Feenstra (ed.), *Trade Policies for International Competitiveness*, (Chicago: University of Chicago Press, 1989).

Kruse, Douglas L., "International Trade and the Labor Market Experience of Displaced Workers," *Industrial and Labor Relations Review* 41 (3) (1988), 402–217.

Leamer, Edward E., *Sources of International Comparative Advantage* (Cambridge, MA: MIT Press, 1984).

Matusz, Steven J., "The Heckscher-Ohlin-Samuelson Model with Implicit Contracts," *Quarterly Journal of Economics* 100 (4) (1985), 1312–1329.

Medoff, James L., "Layoffs and Alternatives under Tade Unions in U.S. Manufacturing," *American Economic Review* 69 (3) (1979), 380–395.

Mincer, Jacob, and Yoshio Higuchi, "Wage Structure and Labor Turnover in the United States and Japan," *Journal of the Japanese and International Economies* 2 (1988), 97–133.

OECD Secretariat, "Measuring the Employment Effects of Changes in Trade Flows: A Survey of Recent Literature," in *The Impact of Newly Industrializing Countries on Production and Trade in Manufactures* (Paris: OECD, 1979).

Oi, Walter Y., "Labor as a Quasi-fixed Factor," *Journal of Political Economy* 70 (1962), 538–555.

Pindyck, Robert S., and Julio J. Rotemberg, "Are Imports to Blame?: Attribution of Injury under the 1974 Trade Act," *Journal of Law and Economics* 30 (1) (1987), 101–122.

Staiger, Robert W., "A Specification Test of the Heckscher-Ohlin Theory," *Journal of International Economics* 25 (1988), 129–141.

Stolper, Wolfgang, and Paul A. Samuelson, "Protection and Real Wages," *Review of Economic Studies* 9 (1941), 58–73.

U.S. International Trade Commission, *Certain Motor Vehicles*, TA-201-44, publication #1110 (1980).

## APPENDIX

### TABLE A.1.—DATA SOURCES

1. Product shipments, production worker hours, and value added: Annual Survey of Manufacturers: Statistics for Industry Groups and Industries, Bureau of the Census, various issues.
2. Output deflators: 1982 = 100, unpublished Bureau of Labor Statistics (BLS) data obtained from the Division of Economic Growth, BLS, U.S. Department of Labor.
3. Imports (c.i.f.), Exports (f.o.b.), Import Price Index and Export Price Index: unpublished BLS data obtained from the Division of Economic Growth, BLS, U.S. Department of Labor.
4. State unemployment data, and Unemployment Insurance data: Statistical Abstract of the United States, various years, Bureau of the Census.
5. Wages: *Supplement to Employment and Earnings*, BLS, U.S. Department of Labor.
6. Union estimates and capital stock: NBER Trade and Immigration Database. The 1985 union estimate was obtained by linear extrapolation.

# [6]

TEN

# International Trade and Job Displacement in U.S. Manufacturing, 1979–1991

*Lori G. Kletzer*

THE DOMESTIC labor market consequences of expansions of international trade is an area of long-standing national concern. The United States has become an increasingly open economy over the past three decades. Between 1965 and 1993, imports as a share of real gross domestic product (GDP) rose from 5 to 13.2 percent, while the share of exports rose from 4.8 to 11.6 percent.[1] Over the latter half of this period (1979–93), employment in the manufacturing sector (the one most affected by trade) fell by 15 percent. Millions of workers have lost their jobs following plant closures, plant relocations, or large-scale reductions in operations. Many labor market participants and observers have linked the growth of international trade to the decline of manufacturing employment and the stagnation of real wages. As evidenced by

This research was supported by the Brookings Institution and the Social Sciences Division and the Academic Senate Committee on Research of the University of California, Santa Cruz. I am grateful to Jeannine Bailliu for her excellent research assistance, and to Henry S. Farber, Larry Mishel, Robert Bednarzik, Gregory Schoepfle, Susan Collins, Rob Fairlie, and Ken Kletzer for their comments and suggestions.

1. *Economic Report of the President* (February 1994, table B-22, p. 293).

424                                                        LORI G. KLETZER

the recent debate about the North American Free Trade Agreement (NAFTA), there is a clear public perception that "trade costs jobs."[2] As nations move on their current course of economic integration, there will be heated discussion about the domestic employment costs. Amidst calls for protection, it is increasingly important to understand the facts about trade and job loss.

In this chapter I examine the relationship between international merchandise trade and job displacement. As commonly defined, job displacement is an involuntary (from the worker's perspective) termination of employment based on the employer's operating decisions, and not on a worker's individual performance. Many job displacements occur through plant closings or the employer going out of business. Although there are now a number of studies on trade and employment (and wages), many motivated by an interest in the effects of trade on currently employed workers, there are virtually no studies of trade and displacement.[3] Most of the literature on trade and employment focuses on industry net employment changes. These net employment changes are a result of changes in the gross flows of new hires, recalls, quits, displacements, temporary layoffs, and retirements (accessions minus separations). My focus here on one of the gross flows, displacement, is motivated by the perspective that the amount of social and private adjustment to freer trade greatly depends on gross employment changes. It is precisely the job loss component of employment change that concerns workers, the general public, and policymakers. Job displacements are arguably the most policy-relevant component of gross separations. For example, the private welfare implications of an employment reduction undertaken through (voluntary) quits together with no replacement hiring are vastly different from the welfare implications of the same percentage employment reduction undertaken through displacements. These costs and concerns play an important role in the domestic political economy of free trade, as evidenced by the strong historical support for transfer programs such as Trade Adjustment Assistance (TAA).

This examination of trade and job displacement joins and complements recent work on trade, wages, and employment. The role of international trade in accounting for declining manufacturing employment (particularly

2. The notion that trade costs jobs has a long history in the labor movement. Organized labor's official position has alternated between strong calls for protection and quiet support for trade liberalization (support eased by the passage of workers adjustment-assistance legislation, including the recent NAFTA Transitional Adjustment Assistance Program). See Mitchell (1976) for a review and analysis of labor issues in international trade.

3. Exceptions are recent. See Haveman (1994); Addison and others (1995).

low-skill employment) and increasing income inequality between high-skill and low-skill workers is still debated. There are two excellent reviews of this extensive and diverse literature: one by Dickens, with a focus on trade and employment, and another by Belman and Lee, with a more general review of trade, wages, employment, and wage inequality.[4] Dickens assessed the literature up to the mid-1980s as reaching a common conclusion that import competition caused only a small fraction of employment losses. Most employment change was judged to result from changes in domestic demand, real wages, and productivity.[5] In their review of more recent studies, Belman and Lee reach a different assessment—that increased import competition negatively affects both employment and wages, with the employment effects several times larger than the wage effects.[6] It may be fair to conclude that the jury is still out with respect to whether trade has a large or small impact on the domestic labor market. However, virtually all studies conclude that increasing internationalization alone cannot explain the large changes in employment and relative wages that have occurred in the U.S. labor market since the late 1970s.

The relationship between international trade and job displacement is examined in two related parts. These two approaches together provide a framework for examining both the incidence and consequences of trade-related job displacement. In the first part of the chapter, I treat measures of trade influence and job displacement as industry characteristics and examine the cross-section and time series evidence for manufacturing industries. This approach basically asks, "Is the incidence of job displacement across industries related to trade?" There is considerable variation across industries in job displacement, and I attempt to control for industry characteristics not related to trade. As a caveat, I note that the analysis is empirical; no formal model of job loss (how firms implement a reduction in desired employment) is presented.

In the second part of my analysis, I turn to individual-level data to consider how the "trade" characteristics of the lost job are related to the consequences of job displacement. To isolate the impact of trade, it is

---

4. Dickens (1988); Belman and Lee (1996).

5. Grossman (1986, 1987) is widely cited on this point. A number of studies written after Dickens (1988) reach a similar conclusion. See Mann (1988); Krugman and Lawrence (1993); Lawrence and Slaughter (1993); Lawrence (1994). Berman, Bound, and Griliches (1994) conclude that trade plays a small role in increasing the relative employment of skilled workers.

6. See Borjas, Freeman, and Katz (1992); Freeman and Katz (1991); Leamer (1993, 1994); Murphy and Welch (1991); Revenga (1992); Sachs and Shatz (1994); Wood (1994).

important to control for individual characteristics. Import-competing industries such as apparel, textiles, and footwear employ many lesser-skilled, low-wage, disadvantaged workers, making it important to try to separate general labor market difficulties from difficulties related to trade. This part of the analysis considers the question, "Are trade-displaced workers different from other displaced workers?"[7] Answers to this question will be informative about the social desirability of trade-displacement-assistance policies.

The empirical analysis is based on industry-level trade data for manufacturing industries over the 1979–91 period. This was a period of increased trade flows and large swings in the value of the dollar, thus making it an interesting time to study both trade flows and trade prices. This period was also characterized by widespread permanent job loss, particularly in manufacturing. Over the 1980s, knowledge about the consequences of job displacement was greatly expanded by the availability of the Displaced Worker Surveys (DWS), biennial supplements to the Current Population Survey (CPS) first released in 1984. Almost every study of job displacement completed in the last ten years has noted, at least in passing, the likely role of increased international competition in manufacturing job loss.[8]

## Measuring Industry Trade Sensitivity

What is the best indicator of how changes in international trade affect domestic labor? The trade and employment literature is divided on the answer to this question, with some studies measuring trade changes and increasing foreign competition as changes in import prices, and other studies using changes in import share quantities. There is no unique "best" measure in the sense that the choice of a proxy for an exogenous shock in the foreign sector is model specific (more on this point below). Causality aside, there is also a question in the literature about how to classify industries as "trade sensitive" or "trade impacted." In this section I take a somewhat agnostic approach and discuss the various measures available and how the measures may (or may not) be related to changes in employment and job loss.

7. This part of the study is linked to an established tradition of examining the worker characteristics of import-competing and exporting industries. Kruse (1988) asked similar questions using the 1984 Displaced Worker Survey. Other papers include Aho and Orr (1981); Schoepfle (1982); Bednarzik (1993). See Neumann (1978); Corson and Nicholson (1981); and Decker and Corson (1995) for studies of recipients of TAA.

8. There is now a sizable literature on the consequences of job displacement. This literature is reviewed in Kletzer (1995).

TRADE AND JOB DISPLACEMENT IN U.S. MANUFACTURING        427

Import penetration ratios (or import shares) provide an intuitively appealing way to categorize industries facing significant foreign competition. More generally, industries with a large (or rising) share of output (or supply) internationally traded are often labelled "trade sensitive" (or import/export sensitive) on the basis of calculated import (and export) penetration ratios. If the flow of imports reduces domestic employment, high-import-penetration-ratio industries are where that result is most likely to be found.[9] Using these measures of trade sensitivity, Freeman and Katz find that a 10 percent increase in imports reduces industry employment by 5 percent and industry wages by up to 0.64 percent.[10]

Causality does not necessarily follow from the intuitive appeal of a quantity-based categorization of industries. From a theoretical perspective, there is no simple causal link between the volume of trade and employment changes, because the rise in import share could indicate a number of foreign or domestic developments. A few examples may be illustrative. Take the case of perfect competition, increasing but different marginal costs of production for both domestic and foreign firms, with substitutability between domestic and foreign goods. Let foreign supply expand, perhaps from technological diffusion (or an export promotion scheme) that lowers foreign costs while domestic costs remain unchanged. This reduces the foreign-good price and imports rise. With constant demand, the rise in imports reduces price, domestic output, and domestic employment. With declining domestic output, import share also rises. How much import share rises depends on the elasticity of domestic supply. As domestic supply becomes more elastic, a given increase in imports produces a bigger reduction in domestic quantity (and presumably employment), and rising import share.

9. An import penetration ratio is calculated by dividing industry imports by the sum of industry output plus imports (the denominator is industry supply). An export penetration ratio is calculated by dividing industry exports by industry output. See Schoepfle (1982) for classifications in 1972–79 and Bednarzik (1993) for the period 1982–87. Davis, Haltiwanger, and Schuh (1994) find high rates of job destruction for plants in industries with very high import penetration ratios in 1972–88. Plants in the top quintile of industries ranked by import penetration ratios had average annual employment reductions of 2.8 percent.

10. Freeman and Katz (1991, table 8-2, p. 245). Borjas, Freeman, and Katz (1992) estimate the factor content (effective labor supply) of imports and exports as a way of estimating how trade affects the wages of U.S. workers. There are a number of studies of the effects of trade on the labor market through estimates of the factor (labor) content of imports. The direct and indirect labor content of trade is calculated by allocating imports and exports to input-output sectors and then using average output/employment ratios to derive employment requirements. See Aho and Orr (1980); U.S. International Trade Commission (1986).

When trade is measured as quantity flows, it is important also to consider (or control for) demand. In the perfectly competitive case, imports may also rise if domestic demand increases. Price moves accordingly, and if foreign supply is more elastic than domestic supply, import share will also rise because the increase in imports will exceed the increase in domestic output. Alternatively, if domestic supply is more elastic than foreign supply, the rise in imports will be accompanied by a decline in import share. Here, the use of quantities reveals an ambiguity. Rising imports and import share are associated with increased domestic employment and presumably less displacement, and rising imports may not be associated with rising import share. These two cases imply that over time, industry import shares will differ as a result of differences in supply elasticities as well as the varying competitiveness of domestic firms relative to foreign firms.

In a standard Heckscher-Ohlin (HO) model, industries face increasing import price competition when import prices fall—hence the appeal of using a price measure to examine whether job loss occurs when imports become more competitive. The link between import price competition and industry employment is fairly straightforward. If the price of an imported (substitutable) good falls, labor's marginal-revenue product falls. This drop in the derived demand for labor reduces employment (on an upward-sloping labor supply curve). Flexible wages dampen the fall in employment. If wages adjust fully to equate labor demand and labor supply (a competitive labor market), employment falls to desired levels through (employee-initiated) quits. How much wages and employment change will depend on supply and demand elasticities, but there will be no displacement. Only if prices fall enough that firms find it more profitable to shut down than to continue to operate will displacements occur (through plant closings).

In a market where wages differ from market clearing, the likely consequences of increasing import competition are a bit more complicated. In unionized labor markets, if current wages exceed opportunity wages, the presence of rents may leave room for wage concessions. These concessions may dampen employment loss.[11] Alternatively, senior union members may prefer to maintain wages (and their jobs), with layoffs reducing the employment of junior workers.[12] In a limited number of cases, unions may even push for higher wages as labor demand falls, with an "endgame" bargaining strategy that tries to get as much for the union as possible before the industry disappears. If wages diverge from market clearing for efficiency

11. Although direct evidence is difficult to find, there is a common belief that workers are limited in their ability to offer wage decreases.
12. Unionized firms most often operate with inverse-seniority layoff rules. These rules are also common in the nonunion sector; see Abraham and Medoff (1984).

TRADE AND JOB DISPLACEMENT IN U.S. MANUFACTURING          429

wage reasons, firms may be reluctant to impose wage reductions if they anticipate negative productivity consequences.

Studies using import price measures reach conflicting conclusions. Grossman examined nine manufacturing industries over the 1969–79 period and found a significant effect of declining import prices on employment in only one.[13] In a separate study of the steel industry, Grossman concluded that most of the employment reduction in 1976–83 was due to the appreciation of the dollar and not increasing international competition.[14] Revenga shows that for a sample of manufacturing industries in 1977–87, changes in import prices have a sizable effect on employment and a smaller yet significant effect on wages.[15] She concludes that most of the adjustment in an industry to an adverse trade shock occurs through employment. With somewhat inflexible wages (consistent with her finding that the elasticity of industry wages with respect to import prices is smaller than the employment elasticity), these employment reductions must be occurring through involuntary separations (unless industry quits are high).

There are at least two reasons to think that price, conceivably the preferred measure, is not completely informative about the effect of changes in trade policy or foreign supply. The first is that during the study period some industries had quota protection (apparel, footwear, radio, and television). Import price changes will not necessarily reflect these quantity restraints. More important, these quota restraints imply that market share (import share) is likely to be a determinant of foreign and domestic supply.

The second difficulty with price alone is more fundamental. Using a monopolistically competitive dominant/fringe model, Mann shows how market share is likely to be a determinant of both foreign and domestic supply.[16] First, quantity is a key variable in monopolistic competition with heterogeneous outputs.[17] Second, she notes that in a three-factor, Cobb-Douglas production function with no restrictions on returns to scale and with capital fixed in the short run, increasing returns to scale are an important determinant of price. In her empirical analysis, Mann finds that foreign competition (measured as both import prices and import share) plays a small role in determining employment relative to the role played by domestic demand and prices.[18]

13. Grossman (1987).
14. Grossman (1986).
15. Revenga (1992).
16. Mann (1988).
17. See Spence (1976).
18. For footwear (leather and rubber) and radio and TV, Mann does find that competition in both import price and import share is important for employment determination.

430                                                    LORI G. KLETZER

Trade, Employment, and Displacement:
An Empirical Relationship

In this section I develop a simple empirical framework for examining the
relationship between international trade, changes in employment, and job
displacement. The discussion of trade and employment change is similar to
Revenga's study.[19] A model of labor turnover is used to relate employment
change to displacement.

To simplify the analysis, assume wages adjust to equate labor supply and
labor demand. Using first differences, the demand for labor in industry $i$ in
year $t$ ($N_{it}$) can be written

$$\text{dln } N_{it} = \beta_1 \text{dln } W_{it} + \beta_2 \text{dln } X^1_{it} + \beta_3 \text{dln } X^2_{it} + v_{1it}, \tag{10-1}$$

where $W_{it}$ is the industry wage, $X^1_{it}$ is a vector of trade-related factors
(discussed in more detail below) that shift labor demand for industry $i$ in
year $t$, $X^2_{it}$ is a vector of non-trade-related factors, and $v_{1it}$ is the error term.
Also in first differences, labor supply can be written as

$$\text{dln } N_{it} = \alpha_1 \text{dln } W_{it} + \alpha_2 \text{dln } H_{it} + v_{2it}, \tag{10-2}$$

where $H_{it}$ is a vector of factors that shift labor supply and $v_{2it}$ is an error term.
Labor market clearing implies

$$\text{dln } N_{it} = \gamma_1 \beta_2 \text{dln } X^1_{it} + \gamma_2 \alpha_2 \text{dln } H_{it} + \gamma_3 \beta 3 \text{dln } X^2_{it} + \varepsilon_{it}, \text{ and} \tag{10-3}$$

$$\text{dln } W_{it} = \lambda_1 \beta_2 \text{dln } X^1_{it} + \lambda_2 \alpha_{2d} \text{ln } H_{it} + \lambda_3 \beta_3 \text{dln } X^2_{it} + u_{it}. \tag{10-4}$$

Equation 10-3 is a basic reduced-form equation for net changes in employment. This relationship must be modified and narrowed to focus on displacement, which is just one of the gross flow components of net employment
change. A simple model of turnover is helpful. Firms implement net employment reductions through the use of displacements and unreplaced attritions.
Attritions are separations due to quits, discharges (for cause), retirements, and
deaths. Attritions that are not replaced by employers are called unreplaced
attritions.[20] For an industry, net employment change in year $t$ can be written as

$$DIS + ATT = -\delta N, \tag{10-5}$$

where $DIS$ is displacements and $ATT$ is unreplaced attritions (Quits +
Discharges) minus Accessions.[21] This change in employment can be expressed as a proportion of total employment:

19. Revenga (1992).
20. The term, "unreplaced attritions," appears in Brechling (1978).
21. Accessions are new hires and rehires.

$$DIS/N_{t-1} = \text{Displacement Rate} = -(N_t - N_{t-1})/N_{t-1} - ATT/N_{t-1} \qquad (10\text{-}6)$$

Relying on the approximation of the rate of change of employment, $(N_t - N_{t-1})/N_{t-1}$, to the change in log employment, $(\ln N_t - \ln N_{t-1})$, for small changes, equation 10-6 is approximately equal to

$$\text{Displacement Rate}_t = - \, d\ln N_t - ATT \, \text{Rate}, \qquad (10\text{-}7)$$

where $ATT \, \text{Rate} = ATT/N_{t-1}$.

Equations 10-3 and 10-7 can be combined to yield a reduced-form equation for industry displacement:

$$\text{Displacement Rate}_{it} = \gamma_1\beta_2 d\ln X^1_{it} + \gamma_2\alpha_{2d}\ln H_{it} + \gamma_3\beta_3 d\ln X^2_{it} \qquad (10\text{-}8)$$
$$+ \, \gamma_4 ATT \, \text{Rate}_t + (\varepsilon_{t} + \eta_t),$$

where $\eta_t$ captures unobservable factors related to displacement.

A key difficulty with this specification is that it attempts to isolate just one of the endogenous turnover flows that together constitute net employment change. In the context of a turnover model, it is inappropriate to include quits, discharges, and accessions (summed here as $ATT$ Rate) as independent variables in a displacement relationship. Quits are likely to be influenced by conditions within the industry.[22] Reducing (or eliminating) replacement hiring, influencing quits, and implementing displacements are all measures under the firm's control as ways of changing employment levels in response to changes in the international trade environment. Firms and industries are likely to differ in their use of the various components of turnover to implement desired changes in employment.[23]

For the purposes of this chapter, a practical way of recognizing differential turnover by industry is to include industry fixed effects in the displacement rate specification. Separate industry constants will capture industry-specific differences in the rate of displacement that result from industry differences in turnover, and more generally, other interindustry differences in displacement.

The elements of the vector $X^1$ need be specified. As I discussed in the previous section, there are two alternatives. The first, using relative import prices, yields

---

22. Brechling (1978) presents a model of turnover with endogenous quits. In that model, quits rise and fall with industry employment growth and the state of the overall economy. In depressed industries, workers are much less likely to quit; therefore, "normal" attrition cannot be counted on to reduce employment.

23. The likely interdependence of the various components of turnover indicate the desirability of a more complete model of turnover in response to changing labor demand. Such a model is beyond the scope of this chapter.

432                                                           LORI G. KLETZER

Displacement Rate$_{it}$ = $\delta_1$dln $P^m_{it}$ + $\gamma_i$ + $e^1_{it}$,                    (10-9)

where $P^m_{it}$ is the domestic price (\$) of the import good (relative to the aggregate price level).[24] The elements of $X^2$ and *ATT* Rate are subsumed in the industry fixed effect $\gamma_i$, $\delta_1$ is a coefficient to be estimated, and $e^1_{it}$ is the error term.

An alternative specification uses import (and export) share. The discussion in the previous section suggests that import share be used along with controls for domestic demand. Studies have shown that changes in domestic sales and the overall level of domestic economic activity have significant effects on industry employment.[25] One option, following Freeman and Katz, is to decompose total sales into its component parts: the domestic market (Domestic = Sales − Exports + Imports); exports; and import share.[26] A first-order approximation gives

dSales = $w_1$dln (domestic) + $w_2$dln exports − $w_3$d(import share),   (10-10)

where $w_1$ = (sales − exports)/sales, $w_2$ = exports/sales, and $w_3$ = domestic/sales. The weights adjust changes in the three components for the difference in the absolute magnitude of sales generated by the domestic side as compared to the trade side.[27] The following equation relates changes in sales to displacement:

Displacement Rate = $\delta_{2w1}$dln (domestic) + $\delta_{3w2}$dln (exports)       (10-11)
$$+ \delta_{4w3}\text{d(importshare)} + \Pi_{i+e}2_{ib}$$

where the $\delta$'s are coefficients to be estimated, $\Pi_i$ is the industry fixed effect, and $e^2_{it}$ is the error term.[28]

24. The aggregate price level is measured as the aggregate Producer Price Index (PPI).
25. See Mann (1988); Freeman and Katz (1991).
26. Freeman and Katz (1991).
27. This decomposition of sales is explained in detail by Freeman and Katz (1991).
28. Equations 10-9 and 10-11 will be estimated by ordinary least squares (OLS). In Revenga's (1992) estimation of the elasticity of net industry employment change to changes in import prices, she discusses the potential correlation of the import price variable with the components of the disturbance term. Several factors may induce this correlation, such as unmeasured, worldwide shocks to material costs or unobserved and unmeasured taste or demand shifts in the United States that influence import prices due to the size of the U.S. market. With this correlation, OLS parameter estimates will be biased and inconsistent. Revenga uses an instrumental-variables procedure to obtain consistent estimates of the import price elasticity, and she shows that the OLS estimates appear downwardly biased. A similar case could be made here when industry displacement is the dependent variable. Correlations between import price and the error term for displacement may be weaker than in the net employment change model however, because displacement is just one of the components of net employment change.

## Data: Measuring International Trade and Job Displacement

The task of constructing a data set with industry trade measures and individual displacement information presents a number of challenges. Data are available on imports, exports, and total shipments starting in 1958 for four-digit Standard Industrial Classification (SIC) manufacturing industries. Coverage into the late 1980s is problematic because of changes in the SIC system in 1987 that changed the scope of many four-digit industries. The new industry definitions changed the allocation of imported and exported goods across industries. Post-1987 trade flow data, using 1987 SIC codes, cannot be compared with early 1980s trade data that used 1972 SIC codes.[29]

Import and export price indices are available for many four-digit SIC manufacturing industries starting in 1983–84, with coverage of some industries available from 1978. The price measure is a fixed-weight Laspeyres index with a 1985 base period. Relative import and export prices are obtained by deflating by the PPI as a proxy for the aggregate price level.

Combining trade measures with displacement information at the industry level requires considerable aggregation. Individual information on job loss is available from the biennial DWSs. In these household surveys, industries are classified according to the Census of Population Industrial Classification (CIC) system, and the most detailed level is three digit. Therefore the SIC-based trade data must be aggregated up to a three-digit CIC level to conform to the industries for which displacement information is available. As a consequence, the industry trade effects studied here may be different from other recent work on trade, wages, and employment where no individual information is used and industries are defined on a more disaggregated basis.

Aggregating the import, export, and shipments data up from the four-digit SIC level yields fifty-eight, three-digit CIC industries, covering the period 1975–85. Aggregation is more "costly" for the price data. Price

---

29. The appendix to this chapter contains more information on the trade flow data. The National Bureau of Economic Research (NBER) Trade and Immigration data set is the source of the import, export, and total shipments data used to calculate import and export shares and domestic demand. That file contains trade data for the period 1958–85. Import and export data for 1986–87 are available from the Department of Commerce (1987 shipments data are not available). In that data release, the Department of Commerce warns that data are not consistent with earlier department trade releases (which are the source of the NBER files). This means that an NBER-based trade data set cannot be extended with the Department of Commerce data, as the two are inconsistent.

index coverage is not complete for all manufacturing industries, so that not all four-digit SIC industries within a three-digit CIC industry have information available for constructing an aggregate CIC industry price index. I calculated a three-digit CIC index if approximately 40 percent or more of the underlying four-digit industry price indices were available. I adopted this decision rule recognizing that inaccuracies may be introduced by calculating an aggregate index from only a subset of constituent four-digit industries. This rule produced a sample of 24 three-digit CIC industries with an import price index for some part of the period 1978–91, and a total of 213 industry and year observations. More details are available in the appendix to this chapter.

### Identifying Displaced Workers

I draw my sample of displaced workers from the DWSs of 1984, 1986, 1988, 1990, and 1992. The DWSs were administered as supplements to the January CPS. In each survey, adults (aged twenty years and older) in the regular, monthly CPS were asked if they had lost a job in the preceding five-year period due to "a plant closing, an employer going out of business, a layoff from which he/she was not recalled, or other similar reasons." If the answer was yes, a series of questions followed concerning the old job and period of joblessness.[30]

A common understanding of displacement is that it occurs without personal prejudice; terminations are related to the operating decisions of the employer and are independent of individual job performance. In the DWSs, this definition can be implemented by drawing the sample of displaced from individuals who respond that their job loss was due to the reasons noted above. Other causes of job loss, such as quits or firings, are not considered displacements.[31] This operational definition is not without ambiguity. The displacements are "job" displacements, in the sense that an individual displaced from a job and rehired into a different job with the same employer is considered displaced.[32]

The job loss measured in the DWSs is permanent. These job losses, though a small fraction of total job loss and of total turnover and employ-

---

30. My sample construction and measures of incidence follow the discussion in Farber (1993). There is a sizable literature of DWS-based studies of the consequences of job displacement. Examples include Podgursky and Swaim (1987); Kletzer (1989); Topel (1990); Gibbons and Katz (1991); Farber (1993).

31. Individuals may also respond that their job loss was due to the end of a seasonal job or the failure of a self-employed business. These individuals are not considered displaced.

32. The survey instrument provides no information that would allow these workers to be removed from the displaced sample.

ment change, may well account for much unemployment and individual suffering.[33] At the same time, some of the distinctions may be too narrow or arbitrary. The distinction between quits and displacements is muddied by the ability of employers to reduce employment by reducing or failing to raise wages. Wage changes may induce some workers to quit (and not be in the sample), whereas others opt to stay with the firm (and are displaced and enter the sample).[34] This distinction means that the displaced worker sample will underestimate the amount of job change "caused" by trade. If the workers who stay on with the firm until displacement are those who face the worst labor market outcomes of all those at risk of displacement, then the displaced sample will be potentially nonrandom and will overstate the costs of job loss. Without data on quits, these questions cannot be answered.[35]

The analysis sample is limited to workers displaced from manufacturing industries who were ages twenty to sixty-four at the time of displacement. Because the information is retrospectively gathered, it has potential recall error. Problems of recall are compounded by the overlapping coverage of years of displacement by surveys, with some years covered in two or three surveys.[36] This bias is believed to be significant.[37] As Topel and Farber show, it is likely that the surveys seriously underestimate job loss that occurred long before the survey date because of inaccuracies in recall as well as question design.[38] This makes it desirable to have nonoverlapping recall periods (that is, each year of displacement drawn from only one survey).

A solution to recall bias that is easy to implement in this context was advanced by Farber.[39] He restricted his sample to displacements occurring

33. Permanent job losers account for a rising share of unemployment; see Medoff (1992).

34. Recent work by Jacobson, LaLonde, and Sullivan (1993) shows that wages fall for displaced workers before they are displaced.

35. I do not distinguish between layoffs without recall and plant closings. See Gibbons and Katz (1991) for a discussion of whether workers displaced by layoff are less able than workers displaced by plant closings (because employers have some discretion over whom to lay off while the plant remains open, and presumably plant closings involve all workers).

36. The 1984 DWS covered the period 1979–83; the 1986 survey, 1981–85; the 1988 survey, 1983–87; the 1990 survey, 1985–89; and the 1992 survey, 1987–91. Displacements that occurred during the survey month (January) were also counted, but it is common to omit these workers.

37. Events far back in the past may be less likely to be remembered. On the other hand, with time, events that result in serious economic and psychological costs may be more likely to be remembered. See Akerlof and Yellen (1985) for a discussion of research on recall bias.

38. If more than one job was lost, information is gathered only for the job held longest. See Topel (1990); Farber (1993).

39. Farber (1993).

in the two-year period preceding each survey. This makes recall periods shorter and eliminates overlapping-year coverage. I follow the spirit of his construction by restricting the analysis sample to displacements occurring in the two-year period in the middle of each survey's time coverage. From the 1984 survey, I drew individuals displaced during 1981–82; from the 1986 survery, 1983–84; from the 1988 survey, 1985–86; from the 1990 survey, 1987–88; and from the 1992 survey, 1989–90. This sampling framework differs somewhat from Farber, whose two years preceding the survey date design drew 1982–83 from the 1984 survey. Interest in the consequences of displacement guided my choice of years drawn. By starting three years before the survey date, I have a sample with "enough" time to become reemployed, at the cost of including workers who reported displacements three years in the past. Because the trade flows data currently end in 1985, I drew a larger sample from the 1984 survey by also including workers displaced during 1979–80. Although recall for these workers may be questionable, I included them to get the displacement data and the trade flows data to overlap as much as possible in years covered. Unless the early displacements are included, the two time series analyses overlap only for 1981–85.

### Job Loss and Trade by Industry: A First Look at the Data

To study the link between an industry's trade indicators (import and export share and prices) and industry job loss, I calculated industry displacement rates by dividing the number of workers displaced from a three-digit CIC industry in a year by the number of workers employed in that industry in that year. The annual industry employment numbers were calculated from merged CPS Outgoing Rotation Group data files, and are a proxy for industry workers at risk of displacement.[40] Figure 10-1 plots an annual manufacturing displacement rate for 1979–91. This aggregate displacement rate is the ratio of the number of workers who report a manufacturing displacement in a year divided by the number of individuals employed in manufacturing in the same year. In 1979, 2.7 percent of manufacturing workers were displaced; the rate rose to slightly less than 7 percent in 1982. It then fell steadily down to 2.4 percent in 1988, rising again in the late

40. All cell counts were weighted using the CPS final weights. A proper measure of workers at risk of displacement (the denominator of the displacement rate) requires interviewing workers at two points in time to ascertain jobs held and jobs lost. The DWS only asks displaced workers about the job lost; for non-displaced workers, there is no retrospective information about jobs not lost.

TRADE AND JOB DISPLACEMENT IN U.S. MANUFACTURING        437

Figure 10-1. *Annual Displacement Rate for Manufacturing, 1979–91*

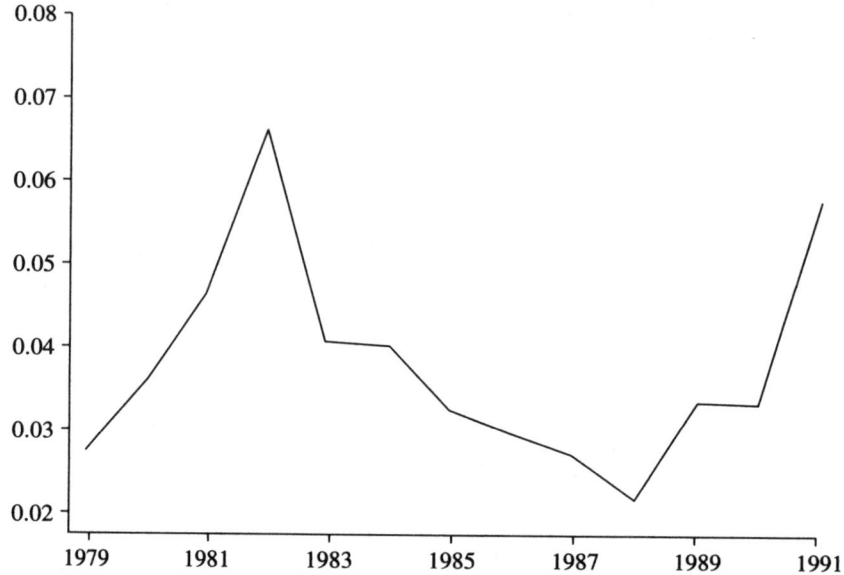

Sources: Current Population Survey; and merged OGRG files.

1980s, to 5.7 percent in 1991. Displacements follow a business cycle pattern, reaching a peak during the 1981–82 recession and then falling continuously throughout the recovery. Displacement rates rose again during the early 1990s recession.

Univariate classifications are a useful way to examine the link between displacement and international trade at the industry level. As a first step, I stay within the tradition of using import and export shares to classify industries as "trade sensitive." Mean import share for the industries in the sample was 8.2 percent in 1975–85, ranging from 0.07 percent to 67.2 percent.[41] If industries with average import penetration ratios of 15 percent or higher in 1975–85 are considered "import sensitive," the table below shows that displacement rates were high for some of these industries in 1979–86 (the mean industry displacement rate was 5.1 percent), although there was considerable variation and some industries had quite low displacement rates.[42]

41. Author's calculations based on data from NBER Trade and Immigration data set (see appendix).
42. Schoepfle (1982) adopted a similar definition of "import sensitive." Bednarzik (1993) uses a 30 percent import penetration ratio cutoff.

| Import-sensitive industry (CIC) | Displacement rate |
|---|---|
| Knitting mills (132) | 0.029 |
| Apparel and accessories (151) | 0.051 |
| Tires and inner tubes (210) | 0.046 |
| Footwear, except rubber/plastic (221) | 0.094 |
| Pottery and related products (261) | 0.100 |
| Blast furnaces, steelworks (270) | 0.078 |
| Other primary metal products (280) | 0.039 |
| Metalworking machinery (320) | 0.045 |
| Computers (322) | 0.027 |
| Radio, TV, and communication equipment (341) | 0.031 |
| Electrical machinery (342) | 0.045 |
| Motor vehicles (351) | 0.044 |
| Cycles and miscellaneous transport (370) | 0.047 |
| Scientific instruments (371) | 0.026 |
| Toys and sporting goods (390) | 0.072 |
| Miscellaneous manufacturing (391) | 0.042 |

As I discussed, one difficulty with this simple import share classification is that it ignores the role of domestic demand. If domestic demand increases and foreign supply increases faster than domestic supply, then import share will rise without a reduction in employment or a rise in displacement. In fact, the industries on this list with low displacements rates and high import share were those with strong domestic demand in 1975–85.

This method of classifying industries as import sensitive cannot address the question of whether *changes* in imports are associated with job loss— that is, does an increase in import share lead to job displacement? Changes in import and export penetration ratios and changes in domestic demand are examined in tables 10-1 to 10-3. These three tables report classifications of industries by changes in import share, export share, and domestic demand, respectively, over the period 1975–85, and for each industry, report an average displacement rate for 1979–86.[43] For each of the three quantity measures, industries were classified by their quantity change quartile, from highest to

43. The analysis sample does not include all three-digit CIC industries. Some industries were excluded due to incomplete time series information on displacement, employment, or trade flows. The displacement numbers may be "noisy." There are a few industry/year observations where the reported number of displaced in a year equals zero. It seems unlikely that the actual number displaced would truly be zero. Recall error and sampling may account for some of this, as well as errors in the recording of industry. Some "smoothing" of the industry displacement series is an attractive alternative, although one would be more confident if there was another source of displacement information to serve as a check.

TRADE AND JOB DISPLACEMENT IN U.S. MANUFACTURING          439

lowest. For example, table 10-1 reports a categorization of industries by their median import share change quartile (from highest to lowest) and, for each industry, its mean displacement rate. There is substantial variation in changes in import and export share and domestic demand across industries. This classification offers a simple perspective on the question of whether industries facing import share increases had high average displacement rates.

The average displacement rates reported in the last row of table 10-1 do not appear to rise systematically with increasing industry import share. High-displacement-rate industries are somewhat evenly spread across the table by import share. Industries with the highest displacement rates, such as footwear (CIC 221), wood buildings and mobile homes (CIC 232), and railroad locomotives (CIC 361) faced medium to low changes in imports. A number of industries with large positive changes in import share had low displacement rates over the period, including paperboard containers and boxes (CIC 162), aircraft and parts (CIC 352), and photographic equipment (CIC 380).

The strength of the dollar over the latter half of the 1975–85 period is a concern when considering the link between increases in export share and job displacement. The average annual change in export share was 8.6 percent, with a range of 0.04 percent to 60.5 percent. Table 10-2 classifies industries by average changes in export penetration ratios. Given the level of industry aggregation, it is not surprising that some industries have both large positive increases in import share and large positive increases in export share. As in table 10-1, high-displacement-rate industries are somewhat evenly spread across the table by changes in export share. Based on quartile average displacement rates, there is little suggestion that displacement falls as export share increases.

Table 10-3 reports an industry classification based on average annual changes in domestic demand. In this table we see that strong growth in domestic demand was associated with lower rates of displacement over the study period. High-average-displacement-rate industries are clustered in the lowest domestic demand change quartile. These industries include wood buildings and mobile homes (CIC 232), with an average displacement rate of 0.118; iron and steel foundries (CIC 271), 0.069; fabricated structural metal products (CIC 282), 0.061; construction and material handling machines (CIC 312), 0.080; and railroad locomotives and equipment (CIC 361), 0.140.

Figures 10-2 and 10-3 are scatterplots of annual industry displacement rates and percent changes from the previous year, in import penetration ratios (figure 10-2) and in relative import prices (figure 10-3). Each plot contains a regression line for the simple regression of the displacement rate on the chosen trade indicator. Turning first to figure 10-2 for 1979–85, there are

Table 10-1. *CIC Industries Classified by Median Annual Change in Import Penetration Ratio, 1975–85, with Mean Annual Displacement Rate for 1979–86*

| Highest import change (≥ 0.115) | High import change (0.078–0.115) | Medium import change (0.040–0.078) | Low import change (< 0.040) |
| --- | --- | --- | --- |
| Miscellaneous fabricated textiles (152) 0.044 | Canned, frozen fruits and vegetables (102) 0.034 | Dairy products (101) 0.046 | Meat products (100) 0.041 |
| Miscellaneous paper and pulp products (161) 0.035 | Bakery products (111) 0.022 | Grain mill products (110) 0.033 | Sugar and confectionery (112) 0.063 |
| Paperboard containers and boxes (162) 0.021 | Knitting mills (132) 0.029 | Yarn, thread, fabric mills (142) 0.046 | Beverages (120) 0.014 |
| Newspaper publishing and printing (171) 0.033 | Apparel and accessories (151) 0.051 | Drugs (181) 0.018 | Miscellaneous food preparations (121) 0.036 |
| Plastics and synthetics (180) 0.032 | Industrial and miscellaneous chemicals (192) 0.028 | Tires and inner tubes (210) 0.046 | Carpets and rugs (141) 0.061 |
| Soaps and cosmetics (182) 0.036 | Miscellaneous plastics (212) 0.040 | Other rubber products (211) 0.037 | Pulp, paper, paperboard (160) 0.017 |
| Paints, varnishes, related products (190) 0.042 | Leather products, except footwear (222) 0.074 | Footwear, except rubber and plastic (221) 0.094 | Printing, publishing (172) 0.028 |
| Furniture and fixtures (242) 0.043 | Glass and glass products (250) 0.045 | Sawmills and millwork (231) 0.051 | Petroleum refining (200) 0.030 |
| Cement, concrete, gypsum (251) 0.053 | Miscellaneous nonmetallic mineral and stone (262) 0.043 | Wood buildings and mobile homes (232) 0.118 | Logging (230) 0.044 |

(continued overleaf)

| | | | |
|---|---|---|---|
| Iron and steel foundries (271) 0.069 | Other primary metal (280) 0.039 | Miscellaneous wood products (241) 0.041 | Screw machine products (290) 0.038 |
| Miscellaneous fabricated metals (300) 0.043 | Cutlery, hand tools (281) 0.032 | Pottery and related products (261) 0.100 | Ordnance (292) 0.043 |
| Construction and material handling machines (312) 0.080 | Fabricated structural metal products (282) 0.061 | Blast furnaces and steelworks (270) 0.078 | Engines and turbines (310) 0.047 |
| Household appliances (340) 0.049 | Metal forgings and stampings (291) 0.048 | Primary aluminum (272) 0.034 | Farm machinery and equipment (311) 0.079 |
| Aircraft and parts (352) 0.019 | Metalworking machinery (320) 0.045 | Office and accounting machines (321) 0.031 | Radio, TV, and communication equipment (341) 0.031 |
| Ship- and boatbuilding (360) 0.053 | Computers and related equipment (322) 0.027 | Machinery, except electrical (331) 0.050 | Railroad locomotives and equipment (361) 0.140 |
| Photographic equipment (380) 0.029 | Electrical machinery, equipment (342) 0.045 | Motor vehicles and equipment (351) 0.044 | Guided missiles and parts (362) 0.033 |
| Miscellaneous manufacturing (391) 0.042 | Scientific and controlling instruments (371) 0.026 | Cycles and miscellaneous transportation equipment (370) 0.047 | Medical, dental, optical instruments (372) 0.033 |
| | Toys and sporting goods (390) 0.072 | | |

Mean displacement rate for import change quartile

| | | | |
|---|---|---|---|
| 0.042 | 0.042 | 0.053 | 0.046 |

Sources: Author's calculations from sample of industries drawn from the NBER Trade and Immigration data set; and the Displaced Worker Survey.

Table 10-2. *CIC Industries Classified by Median Annual Change in Export Penetration Ratio, 1975–85, with Mean Annual Displacement Rate for 1979–86*

| Highest export change (≥ 0.017) | High export change (+0.017–−0.021) | Medium export change (−0.021–−0.044) | Low export change (< −0.044) |
|---|---|---|---|
| Meat products (100) 0.041 | Dairy products (101) 0.046 | Canned, frozen fruits and vegetables (102) 0.036 | Knitting mills (132) 0.029 |
| Bakery products (111) 0.022 | Grain mill products (110) 0.033 | Miscellaneous paper and pulp products (161) 0.035 | Carpets and rugs (141) 0.061 |
| Sugar and confectionery (112) 0.063 | Beverages (120) 0.014 | Printing, publishing (172) 0.028 | Yarn, thread, fabric mills (142) 0.046 |
| Paperboard containers and boxes (162) 0.021 | Miscellaneous food preparations (121) 0.036 | Other rubber products (211) 0.037 | Miscellaneous fabricated textiles (152) 0.044 |
| Newspaper publishing (171) 0.033 | Apparel and accessories (151) 0.051 | Miscellaneous plastics (212) 0.040 | Pulp, paper products (160) 0.017 |
| Plastics and synthetics (180) 0.032 | Drugs (181) 0.018 | Miscellaneous wood products (241) 0.041 | Tires and inner tubes (210) 0.046 |
| Soaps and cosmetics (182) 0.036 | Paints, varnishes, related products (190) 0.042 | Primary aluminum (272) 0.034 | Sawmills and millwork (231) 0.051 |
| Industrial and miscellaneous chemicals (192) 0.028 | Petroleum refining (200) 0.030 | Other primary metal (280) 0.039 | Wood buildings and mobile homes (232) 0.118 |
| Footwear, except rubber and plastic (221) 0.094 | Logging (230) 0.044 | Cutlery, hand tools (281) 0.032 | Cement, concrete, gypsum (251) 0.055 |

(continued overleaf)

| | | | |
|---|---|---|---|
| Leather products, except footwear (222) 0.074 | Glass and glass products (250) 0.045 | Fabricated structural metal products (282) 0.061 | Blast furnaces and steelworks (270) 0.078 |
| Furniture and fixtures (242) 0.043 | Misc. nonmetallic mineral and stone (262) 0.043 | Engines and turbines (310) 0.047 | Iron and steel foundries (271) 0.069 |
| Pottery and related products (261) 0.100 | Metal forgings and stampings (291) 0.048 | Metalworking machinery (320) 0.045 | Screw machine products (290) 0.038 |
| Ship- and boatbuilding (360) 0.053 | Farm machinery and equipment (311) 0.079 | Machinery, except electrical (331) 0.050 | Ordnance (292) 0.043 |
| Railroad locomotives and equipment (361) 0.140 | Construction and material handling machines (312) 0.080 | Radio, TV, and communication equipment (341) 0.031 | Misc. fabricated metals (300) 0.043 |
| Cycles and miscellaneous transportation equipment (370) 0.047 | Computers and related equipment (322) 0.027 | Motor vehicles and equipment (351) 0.044 | Office and accounting machines (321) 0.031 |
| Toys and sporting goods (390) 0.072 | Household appliances (340) 0.049 | Scientific and controlling instruments (371) 0.026 | Aircraft and parts (352) 0.019 |
| | Electrical machinery, equipment (342) 0.045 | Medical, dental, optical instruments (372) 0.033 | Guided missiles and parts (362) 0.033 |
| Mean displacement rate for export change quartile | | | |
| 0.056 | 0.043 | 0.038 | 0.048 |

Sources: Author's calculations from sample of industries drawn from the NBER Trade and Immigration data set; and the Displaced Worker Survey.

Table 10-3. *CIC Industries Classified by Median Annual Change in Domestic Demand, 1975–85, with Mean Annual Displacement Rate for 1979–86*

| Highest domestic demand change (≥ 0.098) | High domestic demand change (0.086–0.098) | Medium domestic demand change (0.064–0.086) | Low domestic demand change (< 0.064) |
|---|---|---|---|
| Miscellaneous paper and pulp (161) 0.035 | Carpets and rugs (141) 0.061 | Canned, frozen fruits and vegetables (102) 0.036 | Meat products (100) 0.041 |
| Newspaper publishing and printing (171) 0.033 | Apparel and accessories (151) 0.051 | Bakery products (111) 0.022 | Dairy products (101) 0.046 |
| Printing, publishing (172) 0.028 | Miscellaneous fabricated textiles (152) 0.044 | Beverages (120) 0.014 | Grain mill products (110) 0.033 |
| Plastics and synthetics (180) 0.032 | Pulp, paper, paperboard (160) 0.017 | Yarn, thread, fabric mills (142) 0.046 | Sugar and confectionary (112) 0.063 |
| Drugs (181) 0.018 | Paperboard containers and boxes (162) 0.021 | Soaps and cosmetics (182) 0.036 | Miscellaneous food preparations (121) 0.036 |
| Miscellaneous plastics (212) 0.040 | Industrial and miscellaneous chemicals (192) 0.028 | Paints, varnishes, related products (190) 0.042 | Knitting mills (132) 0.029 |
| Pottery and related products (261) 0.100 | Footwear, except rubber and plastic (221) 0.094 | Tires and inner tubes (210) 0.046 | Petroleum refining (200) 0.030 |
| Ordnance (292) 0.043 | Logging (230) 0.044 | Other rubber products (211) 0.037 | Sawmills and millwork (231) 0.051 |
| Computers and related equipment (322) 0.027 | Miscellaneous nonmetallic mineral and stone (262) 0.043 | Leather products, except footwear (222) 0.074 | Wood buildings and mobile homes (232) 0.118 |
| Radio, TV, and communication equipment (341) 0.031 | Blast furnaces and steelworks (270) 0.078 | Miscellaneous wood products (241) 0.041 | Glass and glass products (250) 0.045 |

(continued overleaf)

| Industry | Rate | Industry | Rate | Industry | Rate | Industry | Rate |
|---|---|---|---|---|---|---|---|
| Motor vehicles and equipment (351) | 0.044 | Primary aluminum (272) | 0.034 | Furniture and fixtures (242) | 0.043 | Cement, concrete, gypsum (251) | 0.053 |
| Aircraft and parts (352) | 0.019 | Other primary metal (280) | 0.039 | Screw machinery products (290) | 0.038 | Iron and steel foundries (271) | 0.069 |
| Guided missiles and parts (362) | 0.033 | Cutlery, hand tools (281) | 0.032 | Metal forgings and stampings (291) | 0.048 | Fabricated structural metal (282) | 0.061 |
| Scientific and controlling instruments (371) | 0.026 | Engines and turbines (310) | 0.047 | Miscellaneous fabricated metals (300) | 0.043 | Farm machinery and equipment (311) | 0.079 |
| Medical, dental, and optical instruments (372) | 0.033 | Metalworking machinery (320) | 0.045 | Household appliances (340) | 0.049 | Construction and material handling machines (312) | 0.080 |
| Photographic equipment (380) | 0.029 | Office and accounting machines (321) | 0.031 | | | Railroad locomotives and equipment (361) | 0.140 |
| Miscellaneous manufacturing (391) | 0.042 | Machinery, except electrical (331) | 0.050 | | | Cycles and miscellaneous transportation equipment (370) | 0.047 |
| | | Electrical machinery, equipment (342) | 0.045 | | | | |
| | | Ship- and boatbuilding (360) | 0.053 | | | | |
| | | Toys and sporting goods (390) | 0.072 | | | | |
| Mean displacement rate for domestic demand change quartile | 0.036 | | 0.043 | | 0.041 | | 0.060 |

Sources: Author's calculations from sample of industries drawn from the NBER Trade and Immigration data set; and the Displaced Worker Survey.

Figure 10-2. *Industry Displacement Rate and Change in Import Share, 1979–85*

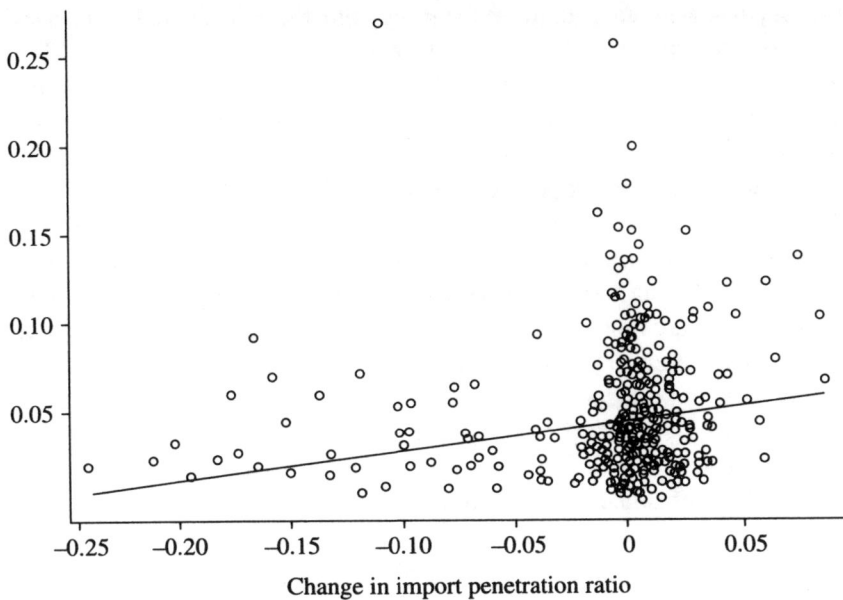

Change in import penetration ratio

Source: Author's calculations from sample drawn from NBER Trade and Immigration dataset and the Displaced Worker Surveys.

Figure 10-3. *Industry Displacement Rate and Change in Relative Import Price, 1981–91*

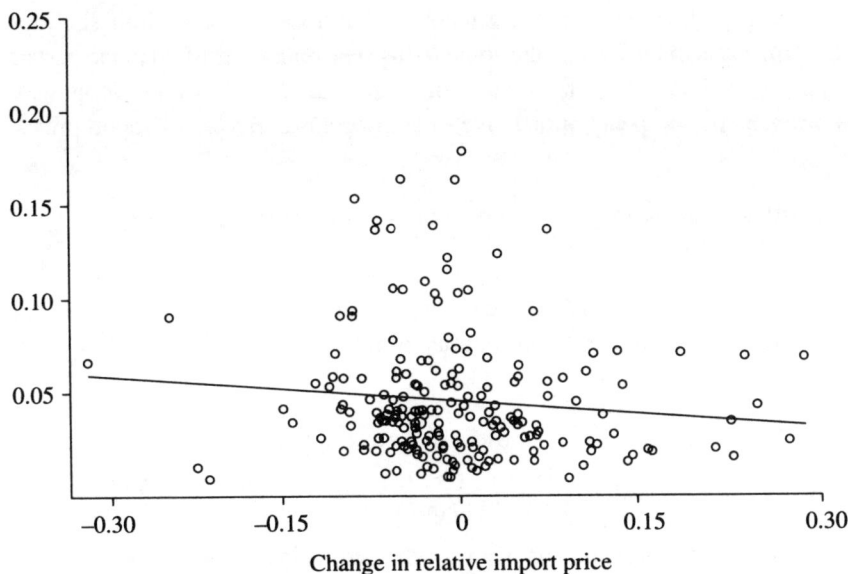

Change in relative import price

Source: Author's calculations from sample drawn from NBER Trade and Immigration dataset and the Displaced Worker Surveys.

a number of industry and year observations where import share changes little and displacement is high. At the same time, there are enough industries where positive (negative) changes in import share are associated with a high (low) displacement rate so that the regression line has a positive slope (with *t*-statistic of 1.761 for the estimated slope coefficient).[44] A few traditionally trade-sensitive industries, such as footwear and apparel, are important in determining the slope of the regression line.

Figure 10-3 presents the plot of industry displacement rate against the percent change in relative import price. The price coverage is far less comprehensive than the trade flow coverage (only twenty-four three-digit CIC industries are included), and the period of coverage is 1981–91. There are a cluster of industry observations where an increase in import prices (a reduction in import competition) is associated with lower displacement rates. The regression line has a negative slope, with a *t*-statistic of –1.520.[45] There are also a number of industry observations with high displacement rates and little change in relative import prices.

### *Remarks on the Simple Evidence on Trade and Displacement*

A few observations stand out from these descriptive figures and tables. Considerable variation in job displacement exists both within and across industries. There are a sizable number of industry observations where displacement is high in the absence of exposure to increasing foreign competition. To this end, controls for industry-specific effects will be used in the next section. Second, the perception that trade displaces domestic jobs has some basis in fact. There are some industries, many identified in the past as import sensitive, where high rates of displacement are found along with increases in import penetration ratios and/or decreases in relative import prices.

### Multivariate Analysis of the Cross-Industry Evidence on Trade and Jobs

Table 10-4 reports OLS and weighted least squares (WLS) estimates of a simple specification relating annual industry displacement rates to two

---

44. The estimated regression, with standard errors in parentheses, is:

$$\text{Displacement rate} = 0.0460 + 0.1722 \,(\% \, \Delta \text{ import penetration ratio}).$$
$$(0.0017) \quad (0.0978)$$

45. The estimated regression, with standard errors in parentheses, is:

$$\text{Displacement rate} = 0.0458 - 0.0418 \,(\% \, \Delta \text{ relative import price}).$$
$$(0.0023) \quad (0.0275)$$

Table 10-4. *Industry Displacement Rates, Import Penetration Rates, and Import Price*[a]

| | (1) | (2) | (3) | (4) |
|---|---|---|---|---|
| Estimation technique | OLS | WLS | OLS | WLS |
| Dependent variable | Displacement rate | Displacement rate | Displacement rate | Displacement rate |
| **Panel A** | | | | |
| Log change relative to import price index | −0.0489 (0.0246) | −0.0489 (0.0206) | −0.0328 (0.0286) | −0.0328 (0.0242) |
| Log change GDP | −1.8917 (0.6436) | −1.8917 (0.7866) | −1.8226 (0.7492) | −1.8226 (1.2094) |
| Industry effects | Yes | Yes | No | No |
| $R^2$ | 0.799 | 0.799 | 0.027 | 0.027 |
| N | 213 | 213 | 213 | 213 |
| **Panel B** | | | | |
| Weighted log change in import share | 0.0081 (0.0080) | 0.0081 (0.0078) | 0.0162 (0.0091) | 0.0162 (0.0117) |
| Weighted log change in exports | −0.1833 (0.0566) | −0.1833 (0.0469) | −0.1965 (0.0608) | −0.1964 (0.0511) |
| Weighted log change in domestic demand | −0.0708 (0.0174) | −0.0708 (0.0193) | −0.1038 (0.0188) | −0.1038 (0.0241) |
| Industry effects | Yes | Yes | No | No |
| $R^2$ | 0.789 | 0.789 | 0.099 | 0.099 |
| N | 401 | 401 | 401 | 401 |

Sources: Author's calculations from the NBER Trade and Immigration data set; U.S. Bureau of Labor Statistics U.S. Import and Export Price Indices; and the DWS.

a. Standard errors are shown in parentheses.

industry trade indicators.[46] Panel A reports estimates from a specification using changes in relative import price indices. Industry-specific characteristics, such as differential quits and accessions, and changes in technology that may be related to industry displacement are captured by the industry fixed effects in columns 1 and 2. There is some evidence that as relative import prices fall and imports become more competitive, displacement rises. The coefficient on the log change in relative import price is negative and statistically significant. The sensitivity of displacement rates to the business cycle is captured by the log change in GDP,

46. With a displacement rate as the dependent variable, error terms are potentially heteroscedastic.

with the estimated coefficient showing the countercyclical nature of displacement.[47]

Panel B of table 10-4 reports estimates from a specification of trade flows and domestic demand. Despite the increasing openness of the U.S. economy, the domestic market still represents the vast majority of demand for almost all industries.[48] Import and export share and domestic demand changes are weighted, using 1985 values, to adjust for the difference in the magnitude of sales generated domestically. Displacement rates are lower with increases in export share and domestic demand. Increases in import share are positively correlated with industry displacement rate although the coefficient is imprecisely estimated ($P$ value = 0.305 in the column 2 estimate).

Columns 3 and 4 report estimates from specifications without industry fixed effects. Overall, the coefficient estimates are modestly sensitive to the inclusion of the industry-specific constants. However, industry-specific effects do account for a substantial amount of the variation in displacement rates. Further work will attempt to measure this interindustry variation more directly, using proxies for technological change, changes in capital stock, changes in investment, and perhaps unionization. Industry-level protectionist policies, such as tariff and nontariff barriers (NTBs), may be important industry characteristics for this time period.[49]

## Who Are the Workers Displaced from "Import-Sensitive" Industries?

Although this analysis does not settle the debate about trade and displacement, a natural next question is whether workers displaced from import-sensitive industries face different (or worse) postdisplacement outcomes than workers displaced from manufacturing industries less influenced by trade.[50] To distinguish a set of import-sensitive industries, I use

47. The log change in GDP also captures some of the time variation in displacement rates.

48. The highest average export share in the analysis sample is 0.38.

49. See Gaston and Trefler (1994) for an analysis of the effects of trade protection policies on industry wages.

50. This is not a new question. The Bureau of International Labor Affairs (ILAB) of the U.S. Department of Labor (DOL) sponsored a number of empirical studies of trade-affected workers in the 1970s and early 1980s. An alternative comparison, not implemented here, is to compare workers displaced from trade-sensitive industries to workers displaced from all other, including nonmanufacturing, industries.

the common measure of a high import penetration ratio. My choice of this measure is for descriptive purposes only, and it is not meant to convey causality.

Table 10-5 presents summary statistics of worker characteristics by displacement industry. Industries are classified according to their average import penetration ratio for 1975–85, with workers displaced during 1979–86. High-import industries are those with import penetration ratios above 20 percent, medium-import industries those with import penetration ratios between 10 and 20 percent, and low-import industries those with penetration ratios less than 10 percent. Workers in high-import-share industries are younger, less educated, less tenured, and more likely to be female than workers in medium- and low-import-share industries. These characteristics are commonly found for import-sensitive industries.[51] Average predisplacement, real weekly earnings are significantly lower in high-import industries, and a smaller proportion of high-import displaced workers had health insurance on their old jobs than was the case for workers displaced from less-import-sensitive industries. There is no difference in fraction displaced from full-time employment.

Turning to the consequences of displacement, the lower part of table 10-5 lists survey date labor-force status and mean change in real weekly earnings. Reemployment proportions are significantly lower for workers displaced from high-import industries, and a larger share of these workers were not in the labor force at the time of the survey.[52] The log changes in earnings are sizable, and there is no significant difference in mean earnings changes by industry import sensitivity.

Table 10-6 reports coefficient estimates from a logit estimation of the probability of survey date employment.[53] The trade sensitivity of an industry is measured by its mean import or export penetration rate in 1975–85. With just mean import share as a regressor, column 1 shows that reemployment probability falls as import share rises. Column 2 uses mean export share along with mean import share and controlling for level of imports, larger export share is associated with a higher probability of reemployment. Columns 3, 4, and 5 add the individual characteristics of educational attainment, age, job tenure, and race, and account for time since displacement. The addition of these characteristics slightly changes the

51. See Aho and Orr (1980, and 1981).
52. Differences in survey date labor market status by industry import sensitivity are significant at $\alpha = 0.05$.
53. Employment is defined as either full-time or part-time employment.

TRADE AND JOB DISPLACEMENT IN U.S. MANUFACTURING         451

Table 10-5. *Worker Characteristics by Displacement Industry, 1979–86*[a]

|  | High import share (>20 percent) | Medium import share (10–20 percent) | Low import share (<10 percent) |
|---|---|---|---|
| Proportion female | 0.615 | 0.435 | 0.319 |
| Proportion nonwhite | 0.127 | 0.151 | 0.148 |
| Age at displacement |  |  |  |
| 20–30 years | 0.449 | 0.407 | 0.444 |
| 31–40 years | 0.288 | 0.291 | 0.274 |
| 41–50 years | 0.166 | 0.155 | 0.142 |
| 51+ years | 0.096 | 0.146 | 0.139 |
| Education |  |  |  |
| Less than high school | 0.121 | 0.076 | 0.083 |
| High school | 0.671 | 0.625 | 0.633 |
| Some college | 0.156 | 0.174 | 0.165 |
| College degree | 0.044 | 0.086 | 0.075 |
| Post-B.A. | 0.008 | 0.039 | 0.044 |
| Previous job tenure |  |  |  |
| <3 years | 0.551 | 0.520 | 0.557 |
| 4–6 years | 0.226 | 0.159 | 0.168 |
| 7–10 years | 0.123 | 0.131 | 0.110 |
| 11–15 years | 0.055 | 0.086 | 0.071 |
| 16–20 years | 0.013 | 0.038 | 0.039 |
| 21+ years | 0.031 | 0.065 | 0.054 |
| Employed full-time on previous job | 0.948 | 0.965 | 0.954 |
| Mean real weekly earnings on previous job | $291.52 (179.88) | $405.58 (246.24) | $390.33 (203.37) |
| Health insurance on previous job | 0.682 | 0.791 | 0.758 |
| N | 328,029 | 1,893,348 | 3,458,894 |
| Labor-force status |  |  |  |
| Employed | 0.596 | 0.665 | 0.685 |
| Unemployed | 0.069 | 0.070 | 0.079 |
| Not in labor force | 0.335 | 0.265 | 0.236 |
| Mean log change in real weekly earnings | −0.403 (1.286) | −0.386 (1.126) | −0.378 (1.148) |

Source: Author's calculations from the DWS.

a. Observations are weighted by final sampling weights. Reported nominal earnings are deflated using the Personal Consumption Expenditures deflator (1987 U.S. dollars).

452    LORI G. KLETZER

Table 10-6. *Logit Estimates of the Probability of Survey Date Employment: Effect of Import Penetration, Export Share, and Worker Characteristics*[a]

| Variable | (1) | (2) | (3) | (4) | (5) | (6) |
|---|---|---|---|---|---|---|
| Import penetration | −0.8540 | −0.9404 | −0.7994 | −0.8194 | −0.9292 | −0.2439 |
| ratio | (0.5000) | (0.4992) | (0.5120) | (0.5123) | (0.5161) | (0.5275) |
| Export share | | 1.2006 | 0.7128 | 0.7613 | 0.6991 | 0.3068 |
| | | (0.4818) | (0.4946) | (0.4956) | (0.4978) | (0.5034) |
| Education | | | | | | |
| High school | | | 0.2215 | 0.2239 | 0.2178 | 0.2427 |
| | | | (0.1331) | (0.1332) | (0.1341) | (0.1355) |
| Some college | | | 0.5203 | 0.5264 | 0.5223 | 0.5029 |
| | | | (0.1574) | (0.1575) | (0.1586) | (0.1602) |
| B.A. degree | | | 1.1861 | 1.1925 | 1.1857 | 1.1295 |
| | | | (0.2041) | (0.2042) | (0.2053) | (0.2067) |
| Post-B.A. | | | 1.1519 | 1.1561 | 1.1451 | 1.0893 |
| | | | (0.2645) | (0.2646) | (0.2658) | (0.2674) |
| Age at displacement | | | | | | |
| 20–30 years | | | 0.6578 | 0.6535 | 0.7041 | 0.6330 |
| | | | (0.1236) | (0.1237) | (0.1247) | (0.1262) |
| 31–40 years | | | 0.9110 | 0.9149 | 0.9646 | 0.9335 |
| | | | (0.1239) | (0.1240) | (0.1252) | (0.1264) |
| 41–50 years | | | 0.8141 | 0.8093 | 0.8547 | 0.8597 |
| | | | (0.1345) | (0.1346) | (0.1356) | (0.1371) |
| Job tenure at displacement | | | | | | |
| 0–3 years | | | 0.1902 | 0.1016 | 0.1190 | 0.2767 |
| | | | (0.1151) | (0.1152) | (0.1161) | (0.1191) |
| 4–6 years | | | 0.3619 | 0.3587 | 0.3872 | 0.5240 |
| | | | (0.1354) | (0.1355) | (0.1364) | (0.1389) |
| 7–10 years | | | 0.1363 | 0.1322 | 0.1481 | 0.2734 |
| | | | (0.1432) | (0.1433) | (0.1443) | (0.1470) |
| Years since displacement | | | | 0.678 | 0.0710 | 0.0772 |
| | | | | (0.403) | (0.0406) | (0.0410) |
| Nonwhite | | | | | −0.7084 | −0.6616 |
| | | | | | (0.1064) | (0.1075) |
| Female | | | | | | −0.6016 |
| | | | | | | (0.0792) |
| Constant | 0.7309 | 0.6370 | −0.4562 | −0.6143 | −0.5609 | −0.4569 |
| | (0.0568) | (0.0676) | (0.1585) | (0.1844) | (0.1858) | (0.1881) |
| Log likelihood | −2190.50 | −2187.34 | −2109.93 | −2107.91 | −2086.12 | −2057.22 |

Source: Author's calculations from the 1984–86 DWS.

a. Asymptotic standard errors in parentheses. Base group in last column is white men older than fifty (at the time of displacement), with less than twelve years of education and previous job tenure exceeding ten years. Sample size is 3,414.

TRADE AND JOB DISPLACEMENT IN U.S. MANUFACTURING          453

negative coefficient on imports, with a somewhat larger change for the estimated coefficient on export share. As expected, the correlation between education and reemployment is strongly positive. Older workers (ages fifty-one and over) are less likely to be reemployed than younger workers, and reemployment probability falls with job tenure. Nonwhites are considerably less likely to be reemployed following displacement (15 percentage points).[54] The probability of survey date employment increases with time since displacement (1.5 percentage points for each year since displacement).

Column 6 shows that the negative correlation between this measure of trade sensitivity and reemployment is largely the result of import-competing industries employing large numbers of women. With the addition of the dummy variable for female workers, the estimated coefficient on import share falls considerably. Women and nonwhites are approximately equally unlikely to be reemployed (about 14 percent). Comparing estimates in column 6 with the other estimates shows that it is the correlation between female employment share and trade sensitivity that is important for understanding the simple finding that "trade-displaced" workers are less likely to be reemployed.

Briefly, the determinants of the log change in real weekly earnings for the reemployed are examined in table 10-7.[55] As is typical for earnings change regressions, only a small fraction of the variance is explained by the regressors. Earnings changes are not significantly related to the trade sensitivity of the predisplacement industry. Earnings losses rise with previous job tenure and are smaller for more educated workers. Full-time or part-time status before and after displacement plays an important role in postdisplacement earnings changes. Workers reemployed in part-time jobs have significantly larger earnings losses than workers reemployed full-time. Because these differences in hours worked are due to both labor supply and labor demand influences, they are difficult to interpret.[56]

54. The derivative of the probability in the logit model is $\beta P(1 - P)$. The sample average value of $P$ for the period 1979–86 is 0.654.

55. An important weakness of the DWS is the lack of a control group. The proper measure of earnings loss is not the comparison between pre- and postdisplacement earnings; rather, it is the difference in earnings between observationally similar displaced and not-displaced workers. Future research will include the construction of a control group of not displaced from the CPS. See Ruhm (1991) and Jacobson, LaLonde, and Sullivan (1993) for two different displaced worker studies using control groups.

56. The inclusion of these variables also complicates interpretation of the estimated coefficient on female workers. A comparison of columns 3 and 4 indicates that there is also an important correlation between educational attainment and hours worked.

454                                                    LORI G. KLETZER

Table 10-7. *OLS Estimates of Log Change in Real Weekly Earnings for Reemployed Displaced Workers, 1979–86*[a]

| Variable | (1) | (2) | (3) | (4) |
|---|---|---|---|---|
| Import penetration ratio | −0.0562 (0.1639) | 0.0540 (0.1615) | 0.0663 (0.1638) | 0.0996 (0.1550) |
| Export share | −0.0727 (0.1480) | −0.1608 (0.1463) | −0.1720 (0.1477) | −0.1712 (0.1398) |
| Education | | | | |
| High school | | 0.0581 (0.0459) | 0.0585 (0.0459) | 0.0012 (0.0437) |
| Some college | | 0.1214 (0.0513) | 0.1207 (0.0514) | 0.0392 (0.0490) |
| B.A. degree | | 0.1922 (0.0575) | 0.1916 (0.0575) | 0.0867 (0.0549) |
| Post-B.A. | | 0.2053 (0.0690) | 0.2041 (0.0691) | 0.1105 (0.0657) |
| Job tenure at displacement | | | | |
| 0–3 years | | 0.2412 (0.0331) | 0.2434 (0.0334) | 0.2248 (0.0316) |
| 4–6 years | | 0.1748 (0.0396) | 0.1772 (0.0397) | 0.1695 (0.0376) |
| 7–10 years | | 0.0748 (0.0439) | 0.0768 (0.0441) | 0.0692 (0.0417) |
| Nonwhite | | | −0.0128 (0.0367) | 0.0107 (0.0349) |
| Female | | | −0.0130 (0.0246) | 0.0044 (0.0238) |
| Previous job part-time | | | | 0.6015 (0.0742) |
| Current job part-time | | | | −0.3911 (0.0304) |
| Both jobs part-time | | | | 0.2147 (0.1154) |
| Years since displacement | | | | −0.0118 (0.0117) |
| Constant | −0.1478 (0.0217) | −0.4075 (0.0519) | −0.4037 (0.0523) | −0.2638 (0.0575) |
| Adjusted $R^2$ | −0.0008 | 0.039 | 0.039 | 0.139 |

Source: Author's calculations from the 1984–88 DWS.
a. The base group in the last column is white men with less than twelve years of education, previous job tenure exceeding ten years, whose previous jobs were full-time. Nominal earnings are deflated by the Personal Consumption Expenditures deflator (1987 U.S. dollars). Standard errors in parentheses. Sample size is 2,107.

## Conclusion

In this chapter I have investigated the relationship between international trade and job displacement for a sample of manufacturing industries over the period 1979–91. Although the results are perhaps best viewed as preliminary, they are broadly consistent with the perception that imports displace some domestic jobs. This broad consistency appears to be a result

TRADE AND JOB DISPLACEMENT IN U.S. MANUFACTURING          455

of a reasonably strong positive relationship between increases in import share and job displacement for industries long identified as import sensitive— industries such as apparel, footwear, and textiles. Aside from these industries, the relationship between increasing foreign competition and permanent job loss appears much less systematic. What is unknown is whether the trade versus job loss relationship might be stronger within more narrowly defined industries. The displacement data do not allow further industry detail.[57]

Across industries, increasing foreign competition accounts for a small share of job displacement. There are high rates of job loss for industries with little trade. This conclusion would be highlighted if the analysis sample included trade and service industries, where rates of job loss are high while the services produced are mostly nontradables. These industries cannot be included in the analysis sample to date, as there is little time series information on trade outside of manufacturing.

There is an important limitation to this analysis. Displacement is just one of the flows that contribute to net changes in employment. It is likely that firms use all the components of turnover (quits and new and replacement hiring, as well as displacement) to move actual employment toward its desired level as foreign competition changes. It may be difficult for the data to isolate one flow in the absence of the others.

Results from the individual-level analysis may contribute to the "displaced versus disadvantaged" debate about the appropriate "targets" of adjustment assistance programs. Although workers displaced from high-import-share industries are less likely to be reemployed, their lower reemployment probabilities are accounted for by individual characteristics such as education, age, race, and (in particular) gender. Trade-displaced workers may have more difficult labor market adjustments, but the source of the difficulty is their otherwise disadvantaged characteristics, not the characteristics of their displacement industry.[58]

I conclude with a comment about the likely direction of future research. An important element in the relationship between increasing globalization and job displacement may be the geographic concentration of trade-sensitive industry employment. By major industrial sector, mining is the most concentrated geographically, followed by agriculture. Perhaps surprisingly, manufacturing is justly slightly less concentrated than agriculture. High-export-penetration-ratio industries tend to be in the West (Pacific region),

---

57. For related studies using establishment- and plant-level data, see Davis, Haltiwanger, and Schuh (1994); Bernard and Jensen (1995).

58. See Kruse (1988, 1991) for more on this point.

456                    LORI G. KLETZER

whereas high-import-penetration-ratio industries are concentrated in the Mid-Atlantic and New England regions.[59] These concentrations imply that a downturn in a highly concentrated, import-sensitive industry can adversely affect the local economy and make individual adjustments to permanent job loss more difficult. Although import- and export-sensitive industries have both job losses and job gains, these general characteristics imply that trade-related job losses occur in separate labor markets from trade-related job gains. Previous research on job displacement reveals the importance of local labor markets.[60] Measures of industry geographic concentration offer a way to further understand how local labor markets are influenced by trade flows and changes in trade policy.

## Appendix

### *Import and Export Penetration Rates*

The NBER Trade and Immigration data set contains information on imports, exports, and the value of shipments by four-digit 1972 SIC industry from 1958 to 1985. The basic classification system for imports and exports is by commodity type (using the Tariff Schedule of the U.S. Annotated (TSUSA). A concordance between TSUSA and SIC categories allows the development of an industry-based trade data set. The NBER data file is described in detail in Abowd (1991).

### *Import Prices*

Import price data are available by four-digit SIC industry in *U.S. Import and Export Price Indices,* published by the U.S. Bureau of Labor Statistics. This variable is a quarterly, fixed-weight, Laspeyres price index based on a 1985 import market basket. These indices are described in more detail in U.S. Bureau of Labor Statistics (1992). They are based on a survey of actual transactions prices, and to the degree possible, they reflect c.i.f (cost, insurance, and freight) prices. Robert Z. Lawrence provided me with annual average tabulations for a collection of two-, three-, and four-digit SIC industries for the period 1980–91, and the NBER trade data were used to aggregate up to three-digit CIC. When aggregation was needed, the SIC indices were weighted by their relative shares in total imports. Quarterly

---

59. See Shelburne and Bednarzik (1993). See Krugman (1991) for a more general discussion of industry geographical concentration.
    60. See Carrington (1993).

TRADE AND JOB DISPLACEMENT IN U.S. MANUFACTURING      457

U.S. Bureau of Labor Statistics data (available on-line from the BLS via ftp) were used to extend the Lawrence data back to 1978 for as many three-digit CIC industries as possible.

### Industry Employment

Data on industry employment used to construct the industry displacement rates were obtained from the merged 1979–91 CPS Outgoing Rotation Group files.

---

## Comment by Henry Farber

Lori Kletzer has carried out an interesting analysis of the relationship between international trade and the extent and consequences of job loss. This is an important and difficult problem. I will comment briefly on the theoretical framework and then more extensively on the empirical analysis.

The theoretical framework is based on a standard supply-demand equilibrium model. Equilibrium employment and wages are derived as a function of demand and supply factors, including trade-related factors. Simple first-differencing yields employment change as a function of changes in the demand and supply factors, including changes in the trade-related factors. A difficulty with this approach is job displacement (job loss due to layoff), rather than employment change, is the focus of the analysis. Kletzer notes that displacement is only one component of the gross flows that make up net employment change, the others being quits, accessions (new hires and rehires), and firing for cause. There are at least two reasons why displacement is likely to understate any effect of international trade on employment. Workers might quit in anticipation of being laid off, and these workers will not be counted as displaced. There is also a background level of worker attrition due to factors such as geographic relocation for family reasons or retirement. Firms may adjust employment in response to demand shifts at least in part by adjusting the rate at which they replace workers who leave voluntarily. For example, it is common for firms that want to reduce the size of their work force by a moderate amount to do so through attrition.

Nevertheless, Kletzer is correct in stating the job loss component of employment change is of considerable concern to policymakers and the public. Though the analysis of displacement cannot answer the question of

how trade affects employment, Kletzer therefore performs a valuable service with her analysis of job loss.

The empirical analysis has two parts. The first part uses data aggregated
to the industry level to examine the relationship between the incidence of
displacement and measures of international trade. The second part of the
analysis uses individual-level data from the DWSs to investigate the extent
to which postdisplacement employment and earnings are related to international trade.

Table 10-1 presents industry-level displacement rates for four categories
of industry defined by the extent of change in import penetration ratio. It is
clear that there is no systematic relationship here. The industries with larger
increases in their import penetration ratio do not have displacement rates
systematically different from those of other industries. Table 10-2 carries
out the analogous exercise for change in the export penetration ratio; again,
there is no systematic relationship with displacement rates. Table 10-3
examines the relationship between change in domestic demand and displacement rates. Not surprisingly, there is a strong relationship; industries
with large increases in domestic demand have lower displacement rates, on
average. Despite Kletzer's assessment that "the perception that trade displaces domestic jobs has some basis in fact," this preliminary analysis
shows little evidence of a systematic relationship between international
trade and job loss.

Next, Kletzer carries out a multivariate analysis of the relationship
between job loss and international trade using industry-level data. This
analysis uses changes in four criteria: an import price index, the import
penetration ratio, the export penetration ratio, and domestic demand as
measures of international trade. Only the latter two show a significant
relationship with job loss at the industry level as measured by the DWSs.
Basically, increases in either exports or domestic demand yield less job loss.
This is not surprising; both are direct products of domestic production and
employment.

In my view, the most interesting part of the analysis relates to the
characteristics of displaced workers and the consequences of displacement.
The tabulations in table 10-5 make it clear that workers in high-import-
share industries are less skilled (younger, less educated, with lower earnings) and more likely to be female than workers in low- and
medium-import-share industries. Essentially, our less-skilled workers are
competing for jobs with similar workers in other countries.

The simple tabulations in table 10-5 also show that the postdisplacement
employment probabilities of displaced workers is related to import share,

with workers displaced from jobs in high-import-share industries having significantly lower reemployment probabilities. This may be because these workers are relatively less skilled. Kletzer presents a multivariate logit analysis of postdisplacement reemployment probabilities in table 10-6 designed to get at this issue. The results are quite striking. The negative relationship between postdisplacement employment probabilities and the import penetration ratio is not due to the relatively low skill level of displaced workers. In fact, the relationship seems entirely because a much higher fraction of workers displaced from high-import-share industries are female and that females have a significantly lower probability for postdisplacement reemployment. This is not explored further by Kletzer. However, part of the explanation is that females are more likely than males to withdraw from the labor force after displacement from the work force. This is only partially offset by the fact that males are more likely than females to be unemployed after displacement.

The chapter concludes with a brief analysis of the relationship between the change in real weekly earnings of displaced workers. Kletzer finds no relationship between the import penetration ratio and the change in earnings. She concludes that this is partly because the data do not permit precise control of hours.

There is a potential problem of interpretation with the analysis of both reemployment probabilities and earnings change. Kletzer interprets the difference in outcomes between industries with high and low import-penetration ratios as the effect of being "trade displaced." But, as Kletzer makes clear in her earlier analysis, it is *changes* in international trade that could lead to job loss. The level of imports ought not lead to job loss, and workers who lose jobs in industries with high import penetration are not necessarily trade displaced. It is more likely that workers who lose jobs in industries with rising import penetration are trade displaced. It would therefore have been more relevant to consider the effect of changes in the import penetration ratio on outcomes.

Overall, we learn that job loss at the industry level is related to changes in domestic production and in exports in the expected directions. There is a weaker relationship between job loss and changes in imports. These are interesting patterns, but, as Kletzer notes, they do not make a strong case for large effects of international trade on job loss. What does seem clear is that job loss is inversely related to changes in domestic production and, presumably, changes in domestic employment. Thus the link between domestic employment and international trade would seem to be the key to understanding how international trade affects the labor market.

460                                                    LORI G. KLETZER

## Comment by Lawrence Mishel

This chapter deserves high marks for attempting to plough new ground. Lori Kletzer clearly labels the analysis "preliminary," so it is possible that more will be learned and these remarks can be taken as suggestions for further work.

Kletzer examines the relationship between trade sensitivity and rising import penetration on industry displacement rates and on displaced workers' reemployment experiences. The topic is thus a subset of how trade affects employment levels and the employment structure (the distribution of jobs across industries). This is because the employment impact of trade is also the result of net changes in employment accommodated by changes in new hires and voluntary attrition. Consequently, this research, though interesting, is only tangentially related to the larger questions of trade's impact on living standards and inequality. The strength of the research is the light it can shed on the extent of the short-term and medium-term adjustment costs that accompany increased trade.

Before reviewing the findings, it is worthwhile to reflect on several data questions. The first is conceptual and relates to whether the sample should be limited to manufacturing workers. When asking the question, "Are trade-displaced workers different from other displaced workers?" it is understandable to want to select industries for which trade measures are available. Nevertheless, even if trade-displaced manufacturing workers have similar displacement experiences to other manufacturing workers, it is still possible that trade-displaced workers have more adverse experiences relative to workers displaced from service industries or the average displaced worker. Much of the effect of trade on wages is based on differences between manufacturing and other sectors and not on any within-manufacturing impact (import and export jobs have similar characteristics). The analysis therefore needs to examine the degree to which manufacturing workers have more adverse displacement experiences.

Two technical data issues concern me. First is the use of the retrospective data for 1979 and 1980 (years four and five from the 1984 DWSs). Because it is acknowledged that these data have serious recall-bias problems, it is worth excluding these years to see whether the results are sensitive to their inclusion. Second, the use of the middle two years of the five-year retrospective seems reasonable for examining reemployment experiences. However, it would be better to use a sample of the first two years when constructing displacement rates.

TRADE AND JOB DISPLACEMENT IN U.S. MANUFACTURING          461

The first set of results comes from the multivariate analysis of changes in imports and exports on industry displacement rates (table 10-4). We learn that trends in domestic sales, exports, and imports explain little of the variation in displacement rates, but that industry fixed effects explain a great deal. Imports are associated with greater displacement, but the relationship does not achieve statistical significance when industry-specific effects are included.

These results raise an issue of interpretation. Is there really a question whether industry displacements are greater when import penetration grows, if growth in demand and other factors are held constant? That is, is there any dispute about whether imports displace domestic jobs in import-competing industries? If the empirical work finds that imports displace workers, then it seems it proves the obvious. If the results are otherwise, then it might call into question whether there is a proper set of controls or other measurement problems. In fact, if rising import penetration is not accompanied by displacement, then all of the adjustment is absorbed by attrition, or increased trade does not generate any reallocation of employment (and therefore no gains in allocative efficiency).

I suspect that in this instance the import variable does not adequately capture the structural shifts toward greater import competition. One reason is that it is specified as a percent change in import share. A 50 percent increase from 2 percent import penetration (a rise of 1 percentage point) is treated as equivalent to a 50 percent increase from 20 percent import penetration (a rise of 10 percentage points). Also, the change in import penetration is measured over one year, too short a time to reflect structural shifts. In addition, the use of a linear specification of import share imposes an overly strict test, asking whether a marginal growth in imports raises displacement rates. A less imposing specification would be to use a step function reflecting a small, moderate, or large growth in import penetration. Note that age, tenure, and education are all specified in a similar manner in the other estimations, and that import penetration is treated qualitatively in the descriptive tables.

The final results focus on the relationship between import sensitivity and worker displacement outcomes. The analysis switches from an examination of the effect of *growing* import penetration on displacement to one examining whether higher *levels* of import penetration (the average over the period) are associated with different displacement outcomes. As such, it is not clear to me that the analysis examines whether workers displaced from the growth of import penetration fare differently from other workers displaced from manufacturing. As a result, I would like to see imports specified in the reemployment and earnings loss equations in the same manner as I proposed for the industry displacement estimations—a step function reflecting long- or medium-term growth in import share.

The chapter finds that workers displaced from import-sensitive industries (that is, those with greater import penetration rates) have a lower chance of reemployment. When a gender control is added, however, the coefficient on imports becomes statistically insignificant. Kletzer interprets this trade sensitivity as unrelated to reemployment problems—rather, that trade-sensitive industries employ workers (that is, women) who have reemployment difficulties. I suspect the relationship between trade sensitivity and reemployment is driven by the high propensity women displaced from the apparel and textile industries have toward withdrawing from the labor force. An appropriate interpretation of these findings might be that workers displaced from trade-sensitive industries do have more negative reemployment prospects, primarily because of the types of workers that tend to be employed in trade-sensitive industries. Does this not follow from the usual analysis of what types of industries are likely to be affected by imports (requiring low-skilled workers, and so on)?

My last suggestion is that it would be worth examining the displacement experience of women separately from men and examining non-college-educated workers separately from those with college degrees.

## The Wage Inequality Literature

Let me turn to some general comments about the wage inequality literature and the evaluation of trade's impact on living standards.

There is an unspoken assumption that the forces causing wage inequality (either trade, technology, and perhaps even weakened labor market institutions) are somehow associated with "progress" or are at least leading to an overall growth in living standards. In fact, after examining trends in productivity or investment, one is hard put to find a superior performance in the 1980s or 1990s than in the 1970s (nonfarm, business-sector productivity was roughly 1.0 percent in each period). It may be that the post-1979 period is "all pain, no gain." If so, then the efficiency benefits of a range of laissez faire policies—deregulation, expanded openness to trade, erosion of the social safety net, weakened unions and minimum-wage protections, and privatization—must be small. One could argue that productivity would have collapsed further in the absence of these policies. But I am not sure why recent circumstances were more adverse than the 1970s, an era beset by a deep recession and several energy and food supply shocks. It may be that the productivity boost is not captured in our statistics, but I have not seen any credible analysis showing that *aggregate* productivity is measured more poorly for recent years than for earlier ones.

In addition, there is the presumption that we have been shifting employment toward more-skilled work, as seen in the relative growth of college graduate and white-collar (or nonproduction) employment. This framework suggests that what we need to explain is why skilled employment is rising even though the relative price of skill is also rising. One gets quite a different feel, however, after examining the share of workers earning low, middle, and high wages, especially men. As table 10-8 shows, the work force did shift toward higher-education groups over the 1973–93 period. However, since 1979 there has been a sizable shift from middle-wage to low-wage employment among men. At the same time, there was no significant growth in the number of high earners. There has also been an erosion of middle-wage earners among women since 1979, but the shift has been to both high- and low-wage employment. Perhaps the question (especially for men) is why there is an erosion of middle-wage earners and an increase in low-wage earners despite the increases in education and white-collar work.

This is another way of saying that we need to be careful to distinguish between shifts in education premiums and shifts in wage inequality. Rising education premiums explain only half the growth of wage inequality in the 1979–89 period and, according to Burtless, only about one-third of the growth of wage inequality in the 1969–93 period.[61] This means that one must explain the growth of within-group wage inequality (among workers with similar education and experience) to explain the overall growth in wage inequality.

It is also important to be careful in the rhetoric used to describe the dynamics of wage inequality. The usual description—"the wages of the more educated/skilled workers being bid up relative to the wages of less educated/skilled workers due to [pick your choice of factor]"—is both misleading and uninformative. It is misleading on two counts. This description leaves the impression that skilled, educated workers are faring well, when they are not—the real wages of "college-only" or white-collar workers, especially men, have been stagnant or falling since about 1987. The ninetieth-percentile male wage has been essentially flat since 1979. This group is only doing well in *relative* terms.

61. Burtless (1995).

LORI G. KLETZER

Table 10-8. *Educational Upgrading and Changes in Wage Structure, 1973–93*
Percent

| | Share of employment | | | | Percentage point change | | |
|---|---|---|---|---|---|---|---|
| | *1973* | *1979* | *1989* | *1993* | *1973–79* | *1979–89* | *1989–93* |
| Education[a] | | | | | | | |
| Men | | | | | | | |
| Less than high school | 30.6 | 22.4 | 15.9 | n.a. | –8.2 | –6.5 | n.a. |
| High school | 38.1 | 38.6 | 38.7 | n.a. | 0.5 | 0.1 | n.a. |
| Some college | 15.6 | 18.7 | 21.0 | n.a. | 3.1 | 2.3 | n.a. |
| College | 8.9 | 11.5 | 14.2 | n.a. | 2.6 | 2.7 | n.a. |
| More than college | 4.5 | 6.1 | 7.8 | n.a. | 1.6 | 1.7 | n.a. |
| Women | | | | | | | |
| Less than high school | 25.4 | 17.2 | 11.2 | n.a. | –8.2 | –5.0 | n.a. |
| High school | 47.2 | 46.8 | 42.7 | n.a. | –0.6 | –4.1 | n.a. |
| Some college | 14.5 | 19.6 | 23.9 | n.a. | 5.1 | 4.3 | n.a. |
| College | 8.8 | 10.4 | 13.9 | n.a. | 1.6 | 3.5 | n.a. |
| More than college | 2.3 | 3.5 | 5.8 | n.a. | 1.2 | 2.3 | n.a. |
| Percentile wage range[b] | | | | | *Annualized* | | |
| Men | | | | | | | |
| 1–20 | 18.9 | 20.0 | 26.1 | 33.6 | 0.18 | 0.60 | 1.51 |
| 21–50 | 34.6 | 30.0 | 30.0 | 28.3 | –0.78 | 0.00 | –0.34 |
| 51–75 | 26.1 | 25.8 | 20.9 | 17.9 | –0.06 | –0.48 | –0.61 |
| 76–90 | 11.7 | 15.0 | 13.2 | 10.4 | 0.54 | –0.17 | –0.56 |
| 91–100 | 8.6 | 9.3 | 9.8 | 9.7 | 0.11 | 0.05 | –0.00 |
| Women | | | | | | | |
| 1–20 | 23.3 | 20.6 | 25.6 | 27.9 | –0.46 | 0.50 | 0.46 |
| 21–50 | 28.1 | 29.4 | 17.3 | 20.3 | 0.22 | –1.21 | 0.60 |
| 51–75 | 26.7 | 25.1 | 22.6 | 20.3 | –0.27 | –0.25 | –0.47 |
| 76–90 | 14.4 | 14.9 | 16.1 | 13.7 | 0.09 | 0.12 | –0.48 |
| 91–100 | 7.5 | 10.0 | 18.3 | 17.7 | 0.42 | 0.83 | –0.11 |

Source: Mishel and Bernstein (1994, tables 3.10, 3.19).

n.a. Not available.

a. Excludes those with seventeen years of schooling.

b. Wage ranges are defined relative to 1979 wage distribution. For men, the wage ranges (in 1989 U.S. dollars) correspond to: $1.00–$6.98, $6.98–$11.06, $11.06–$15.08, $15.08–$20.11, and $20.11–$100.00. For women, the wage ranges (in 1989 dollars) correspond to: $1.00–$5.03, $5.03–$6.74, $6.74–$9.22, $9.22–$12.32, and $12.32–$100.00.

It is also misleading to put the "unskilled" label on groups comprising 80 percent (for example, production or nonsupervisory workers) or 75 percent (non-college-educated workers) of the work force, especially those with two-year college degrees or skills based on long apprenticeships. Unfortunately, "unskilled" frequently gets translated in the media as the losers being uneducated, miseducated, or poorly educated. This terminology is especially misleading, because the public believes that less than one-fourth of the work force is "unskilled" (based on my nonrandom sampling of audiences and classes over the last few years). Finally, the empirical work that uses a broad category for "unskilled" workers is also uninformative; the usual suspects (trade, technology, unions, and so on) affect the various subgroups differently.

## Trade and Wage Inequality

The consensus estimate of the impact of trade and globalization on wage inequality has been rising in recent years and now falls in the 10 to 25 percent range (that is, the share of the rise in overall wage inequality explained by "trade"). However, there is little analytical discipline in the choice of adjectives used to describe this impact. Is it small, modest, or large? One could argue that if trade explains 20 percent of the growth of wage inequality, then it explains as much as any other identifiable factor. Or one could say that trade explains only a "small part of the problem/ phenomenon." Let me strongly suggest that analysts be clear about what yardstick they are applying when they attribute an adjective to the role of any factor. Let me also suggest some yardsticks. If trade explains 10 to 25 percent of the 15 percentage point change in the male 90/50 wage differential over the 1979–93 period, then trade can be said to have cost the median male a 1.5 to 3.75 percent wage loss (note that the 90-percentile wage was flat over this time period). Is this small or large?

There are several possible comparisons. One would be to compare the loss to the benefits of expanded trade, which would have to be estimated for various income classes or "skill" groups. Unfortunately, there are no studies available that quantify benefits from expanded trade by income group.

Another yardstick could be to judge losses from trade relative to the benefits of various policies that economists highly recommend, such as the General Agreement on Tariffs and Trade (GATT) and deficit reduction. With this yardstick, the losses from trade would seem large.

466                                                    LORI G. KLETZER

Unanswered Questions

The topic of whether trade (or other factors) has altered the income split between labor and capital has been prematurely tabled. The basis for believing that there is no profit versus wages story is that national income shares reveal no shift in the 1980s. This analysis is too simple and shallow for several reasons. First, in contrast with most topics in economics, there is no comparison of actual outcomes relative to what one might expect given a *model* of what drives factor income shares. This means we need to look at the current period relative to earlier periods, and we should examine variables that affect income shares.

Several factors suggest that, other things being equal, capital's share should have declined. One is that the capital-to-output ratio has fallen rapidly since the early 1980s. Computations of capital income relative to assets, rather than total income, show that the return to capital has achieved near-record highs in the 1990s.[62] The Organization for Economic Cooperation and Development (OECD) finds the same trends for the United States and for most other advanced countries.[63] There has also been a strong advance in the quality of labor (that is, human capital) that should have led to upward pressure on labor's share. That is, as the ratio of human capital to output rises, there is a tendency for labor's share to expand.

Another factor is the growth of the government and nonprofit share of national income, which grew by 2.3 percentage points of national income from 1979 to 1993 but fell 1.0 percentage points from 1973 to 1979.[64] Because the government and nonprofit sector has labor income but no capital income, this trend makes shares of national income a misleading indicator of private sector trends. The bias is to understate the growth of labor's share in the 1970s and overstate it in the 1980s.

Finally, it is curious that much of the analysis of trade and technology trends has focused on manufacturing, but the discussion of factor shares focuses on national income. It is noteworthy that labor's share of income in manufacturing fell rapidly in the 1980s and early 1990s, and that the return to capital in manufacturing has risen strongly. My conclusion is that there is evidence that capital is benefiting from the structural changes since 1979, and it is worthy to inquire why.

A second area of needed research is on the role of capital mobility and trade flows in weakening the general bargaining power of workers. The

62. See Baker (1996); Poterba and Samwick (1995).
63. OECD (1995a).
64. Mishel and Bernstein (1994, p. 50).

issue is how prevalent are threats, implicit or explicit, to move production offshore in collective bargaining and in the wage expectations of nonunion workers. Likewise, how much does the message, "we have to keep labor costs down to maintain or improve our competitiveness with our import or export competition," play a role in wage determination?

A third area that might be explored is to contrast European and North American outcomes because of their varied experiences with trade with low-wage countries. Specifically, low-wage-country import penetration in manufacturing nearly doubled in North America in the 1980s, whereas in Europe and Japan the level of penetration was less and did not increase.[65]

The assumption that trade pressures on wages only arise from imports from low-wage countries should also be reexamined. The tough labor negotiations at Boeing and Caterpillar suggest that an export orientation can increase the need to curtail labor costs and constrain prices (certainly a benefit of trade). Moreover, increased global competition can put pressure on wages whenever an import can potentially displace production and jobs, which is true of imports from both low-wage and high-wage countries.

## General Discussion

Steven Davis related the results in this chapter to his recent work (with John Haltiwanger) on employment using plant-level data at the four-digit industry level. These data provide a longer time period (1972–88) and avoid the problem of recall bias. It is worth noting that they suggest a job destruction rate two to three times as large as the displacement rates that come from CPS data. Their analysis finds high rates of job creation and job destruction everywhere and little evidence of any difference among trade-exposed industries. The exception is the highest quintile of import penetration ratios, including textiles and apparel. However, job turnover is strongly inversely related to the wage level. Once wages are controlled for, even this result disappears, leaving no relationship between trade exposure and job displacement.

Davis expressed the view that it is interesting to examine the relationship of job displacement to the level of international openness as well as to changes in openness over time. He noted that, theoretically, a greater level of openness could lead to more or to less employment volatility, because

65. OECD (1995b).

openness helps to insulate producers from disturbances in domestic demand. This ambiguity makes it a good empirical question. Finally, he argued that neither the import penetration (quantity) nor the import price indicators are satisfactory measures of trade exposure. In particular, relative import price changes need not reflect a purely foreign disturbance—they may reflect changes in technology in both the United States and abroad. He advocated construction of more direct measures of openness, such as indicators based on measures of transport costs.

Marina Whitman raised the point that difficult welfare issues are implicit in the discussion of this chapter as well as others in this book. She, like many participants, believed that there are typically real costs to adjustment, such as the kind of job displacement studied in Lori Kletzer's chapter. Such an adjustment process can also bring about longer-run gains—for instance, through more rational allocation of resources. However, we do not have an adequate framework for assessing the net effects of these adjustments. Other participants also recognized this as an important area meriting more study.

Adrian Wood was struck by the differences in findings for males versus females. Kletzer's chapter found that female concentration explained most of the finding that workers displaced from high-import-penetration sectors fared poorly. Wood found this puzzling, given Richard Freeman's chapter 3, which found that women had been doing better than men (in terms of wages). He suggested that part of the explanation for the puzzle might be that women who are displaced appear to be relatively easily reabsorbed—in other parts of manufacturing and also in the service sector. In this context, he also cautioned against interpreting an industry as a labor market.

Some comments focused on the role of business cycles. James Tybout noted that the measure of import penetration used will tend to rise during recessions, because domestic output (which is in the denominator) will fall. Marina Whitman wondered whether including year dummies would capture the systematic variations in displacements and quits over the business cycle. Catherine Mann suggested that this issue is important; the appropriate policy response to a finding that associates foreign competition with particularly severe job displacement may be quite different, depending on whether the linkage reflects cyclical or secular trends.

Mann also noted that those sectors that have high import penetration and have experienced high displacement (apparel/textiles and footwear) are also sectors that are heavily protected. Thus, if one were to conclude that trade were a problem in terms of causing employment volatility, trade protection cannot be the answer.

TRADE AND JOB DISPLACEMENT IN U.S. MANUFACTURING     469

Edward Leamer stressed the importance of distinguishing between short- and long-run developments. Although apparel and textiles is in long-term decline, other industries such as transportation equipment, are experiencing increased volatility and uncertainty as a result of increased exposure to foreign shocks. He interpreted the regressions that omitted industry fixed effects as primarily capturing longer-run industry trends, and regressions that include industry fixed effects as being dominated by the shorter-term effects.

Finally, Woodhead questioned Kletzer's characterization of the AFL-CIO as being strongly protectionist. He also reiterated the dissatisfaction, previously expressed by Robert Blecker and others, about how well our measures capture actual differences in worker skills.

## References

Abowd, John M. 1991. "The NBER Immigration, Trade, and Labor Markets Data Files." In *Immigration, Trade, and the Labor Market,* edited by John M. Abowd and Richard B. Freeman, 407–22. University of Chicago Press.

Abraham, Katharine G., and James L. Medoff. 1984. "Length of Service and Layoffs in Union and Nonunion Work Groups." *Industrial and Labor Relations Review* 38 (October): 87–97.

Addison, John T., Douglas A. Fox, and Christopher J. Ruhm. 1995. "Trade and Displacement in Manufacturing." *Monthly Labor Review* 118 (April): 58–67.

Aho, C. Michael, and James A. Orr. 1980. "Demographic and Occupational Characteristics of Workers in Trade-Sensitive Industries." Economic Discussion Paper 2. U.S. Department of Labor, Bureau of International Labor Affairs (April).

———. 1981. "Trade-Sensitive Employment: Who Are the Affected Workers?" *Monthly Labor Review* 104 (February): 29–35.

Akerlof, George A., and Janet L. Yellen. 1985. "Unemployment through the Filter of Memory." *Quarterly Journal of Economics* 100 (August): 747–73.

Baker, Dean. 1996. "Trends in Corporate Profitability: Getting More for Less." Economic Policy Institute (February).

Bednarzik, Robert W. 1993. "An Analysis of U.S. Industries Sensitive to Foreign Trade, 1982–87." *Monthly Labor Review* 116 (February): 15–31.

Belman, Dale, and Thea M. Lee. 1996. "International Trade and the Performance of U.S. Labor Markets." In *U.S. Trade Policy and Global Growth: New Directions in the International Economy,* edited by Robert A. Blecker. M. E. Sharpe.

Berman, Eli, John Bound, and Zvi Griliches. 1994. "Changes in the Demand for Skilled Labor within U.S. Manufacturing: Evidence from the Annual Survey of Manufactures." *Quarterly Journal of Economics* 109 (May): 367–97.

Bernard, Andrew B., and J. Bradford Jensen. 1995. "Exporters, Jobs, and Wages in U.S. Manufacturing: 1976–1987." *Brookings Papers on Economic Activity: Microeconomics* 67–112.

Borjas, George J., Richard B. Freeman, and Lawrence F. Katz. 1992. "On the Labor Market Effects of Immigration and Trade." In *Immigration and the Work Force:*

*Economic Consequences for the United States and Source Areas,* edited by George J. Borjas and Richard B. Freeman, 213–44. University of Chicago Press.

Brechling, Frank. 1978. "A Time Series Analysis of Labor Turnover." In *The Impact of International Trade and Investment on Employment: A Conference on the Department of Labor Research Results,* edited by William G. Dewald and others, 67–86. U.S. Department of Labor, U.S. Bureau of International Labor Affairs.

Burtless, Gary. 1995. "Widening U.S. Income Inequality and the Growth in World Trade." Paper presented at Tokyo Club meeting in Dresden, Germany. Brookings.

Carrington, William J. 1993. "Wage Losses for Displaced Workers: Is It Really the Firm that Matters?" *Journal of Human Resources* 28 (Summer): 435–62.

Corson, Walter, and Walter Nicholson. 1981. "Trade Adjustment Assistance for Workers: Results of a Survey of Recipients under the Trade Act of 1974." In *Research in Labor Economics,* vol. 4, edited by Ronald Ehrenberg, 417–69. Greenwich, Conn.: JAI Press.

Davis, Steven J., John C. Haltiwanger, and Scott Schuh. 1994. *Gross Job Flows.* U.S. Department of Commerce. U.S. Bureau of the Census, Center for Economic Studies.

Decker, Paul T., and Walter Corson. 1995. "International Trade and Worker Displacement: Evaluation of the Trade Adjustment Assistance Program." *Industrial and Labor Relations Review* 4B (July): 758–74.

Dickens, William T. 1988. "The Effects of Trade on Employment: Techniques and Evidence." In *The Dynamics of Trade and Employment,* edited by Laura D'Andrea Tyson, William T. Dickens, and John Zysman, 41–85. Cambridge, Mass.: Ballinger.

Farber, Henry S. 1993. "The Incidence and Costs of Job Loss: 1982–91." *Brookings Papers on Economic Activity: Microeconomics: 1,* 73–119.

Freeman, Richard B., and Lawrence F. Katz. 1991. "Industrial Wage and Employment Determination in an Open Economy." In *Immigration, Trade, and the Labor Market,* edited by John M. Abowd and Richard B. Freeman, 235–60. University of Chicago Press.

Gaston, Noel, and Daniel Trefler. 1994. "Protection, Trade, and Wages: Evidence from U.S. Manufacturing." *Industrial and Labor Relations Review* 47 (July): 574–93.

Gibbons, Robert, and Lawrence F. Katz. 1991. "Layoffs and Lemons." *Journal of Labor Economics* 9 (October): 351–80.

Grossman, Gene M. 1986. "Imports as a Cause of Injury: The Case of the U.S. Steel Industry." *Journal of International Economics* 20 (May): 201–23.

———. 1987. "The Employment and Wage Effects of Import Competition in the United States." *Journal of International Economic Integration* 2 (Spring): 1–23.

Haveman, Jon D. 1994. "The Influence of Changing Trade Patterns on Displacements of Labor." Purdue University, Krannert School of Management.

Jacobson, Louis, Robert LaLonde, and Daniel Sullivan. 1993. *The Costs of Worker Dislocation.* Kalamazoo, Mich.: W. E. Upjohn Institute for Employment Research.

Kletzer, Lori G. 1989. "Returns to Seniority after Permanent Job Loss." *American Economic Review* 79 (June): 536–43.

———. 1995. "What Have We Learned about Job Displacement?" Working Paper 333. University of California, Santa Cruz, Department of Economics (October).

Krugman, Paul R. 1991. *Geography and Trade.* MIT Press.

Krugman, Paul R., and Robert Z. Lawrence. 1993. "Trade, Jobs, and Wages." Working Paper 4478. Cambridge, Mass.: National Bureau of Economic Research (September).

Kruse, Douglas L. 1988. "International Trade and the Labor Market Experience of Displaced Workers." *Industrial and Labor Relations Review* 41 (April): 402–17.

————. 1991. "Displaced versus Disadvantaged Workers." In *Job Displacement: Consequences and Implications for Policy,* edited by John T. Addison, 279–96. Wayne State University Press.

Lawrence, Robert Z. 1994. "Trade, Multinationals, and Labor." Working Paper 4836. Cambridge, Mass.: National Bureau of Economic Research (August).

Lawrence, Robert Z., and Matthew J. Slaughter. 1993. "International Trade and American Wages in the 1980s: Giant Sucking Sound or Small Hiccup?" *Brookings Papers on Economic Activity: Microeconomics* 2:161–210.

Leamer, Edward E. 1993. "Wage Effects of a U.S.-Mexican Free Trade Agreement." In *The Mexico-U.S. Free Trade Agreement,* edited by Peter M. Garber, 57–125. MIT Press.

————. 1994. "Trade, Wages and Revolving-Door Ideas." Working Paper 4716. Cambridge, Mass.: National Bureau of Economic Research (April).

Mann, Catherine L. 1988. "The Effect of Foreign Competition in Prices and Quantities on the Employment in Import-Sensitive U.S. Industries." *International Trade Journal* 2 (Summer): 409–44.

Medoff, James. 1992. "The New Employment." Harvard University Department of Economics paper for the Joint Economic Committee.

Mitchell, Daniel J. B. 1976. *Labor Issues of American International Trade and Investment.* Johns Hopkins University Press.

Mishel, Lawrence R., and Jared Bernstein. 1994. *The State of Working America 1994–95.* Economic Policy Institute Series. Armonk, N.Y.: M.E. Sharpe.

Murphy, Kevin M., and Finis Welch. 1991. "The Role of International Trade in Wage Differentials." In *Workers and Their Wages: Changing Patterns in the United States,* edited by Marvin H. Kosters, 39–69. Washington: American Enterprise Institute.

Neumann, George R. 1978. "The Labor Market Adjustments of Trade-Displaced Workers: The Evidence from the Trade Adjustment Assistance Program." In *Research in Labor Economics,* vol. 2, edited by Ronald G. Ehrenberg, 353–81. Greenwich, Conn.: JAI Press.

Organization for Economic Cooperation and Development. 1995a. *OECD Economic Outlook.* No. 57. Paris: Organization for Economic Cooperation and Development (June).

Organization for Economic Cooperation and Development. 1995b. *Linkages: OECD and Major Developing Economies.* Paris: Organization for Economic Cooperation and Development.

Podgursky, Michael, and Paul Swaim. 1987. "Job Displacement and Earnings Loss: Evidence from the Displaced Worker Survey." *Industrial and Labor Relations Review* 41 (October): 17–29.

Poterba, James M., and Andrew A. Samwick. 1995. "Stock Ownership Patterns, Stock Market Fluctuations, and Consumption." *Brookings Papers on Economic Activity* 2: 295–357.

Revenga, Ana L. 1992. "Exporting Jobs? The Impact of Import Competition on Employment and Wages in U.S. Manufacturing." *Quarterly Journal of Economics* 107 (February): 255–84.

Ruhm, Christopher J. 1991. "Are Workers Permanently Scarred by Job Displacements?" *American Economic Review* 81 (March): 319–24.

Sachs, Jeffrey D., and Howard J. Shatz. 1994. "Trade and Jobs in U.S. Manufacturing." *Brookings Papers on Economic Activity* 1: 1–69.

Schoepfle, Gregory K. 1982. "Imports and Domestic Employment: Identifying Affected Industries." *Monthly Labor Review* 105 (August): 13–26.

Shelburne, Robert C., and Robert W. Bednarzik. 1993. "Geographic Concentration of Trade-Sensitive Employment." *Monthly Labor Review* 116 (June): 3–13.

Spence, Michael. 1976. "Product Selection, Fixed Costs, and Monopolistic Competition." *Review of Economic Studies* 43 (June): 217–35.

Topel, Robert. 1990. "Specific Capital and Unemployment: Measuring the Costs and Consequences of Job Loss." *Carnegie-Rochester Conference Series on Public Policy* 33 (Autumn): 181–214.

U.S. Bureau of Labor Statistics. 1992. *BLS Handbook of Methods for Surveys and Studies.* Bulletin 2414.

U.S. International Trade Commission. 1986. *U.S. Trade-Related Employment: 1978–84.* Report on investigation 332–217 under section 332 of the Tariff Act of 1980.

Wood, Adrian. 1994. *North-South Trade, Employment and Inequality: Changing Fortunes in a Skill-Driven World.* Oxford, England: Clarendon Press.

# [7]

# THE IMPACT OF TRADE AND CAPITAL MOVEMENTS ON LABOUR: EVIDENCE ON THE FRENCH CASE

**Patrick A. Messerlin**

## INTRODUCTION

The emergence of high and persistent unemployment in many OECD countries and widening wage inequality in some has generated a lively debate as to the culprits. In particular, much research interest and political debate has focused on the question of the role of trade and foreign direct investment (FDI) flows in accounting for these phenomena. Views are divided on this question. The OECD *Jobs Study* reviewed the available evidence on the impact of trade and FDI on employment and relative wages and concluded that it was very small relative to other influences such as technological progress. But this conclusion has been disputed by other authors.

The debate has been hampered by the fact that most of the empirical work on the topic relates to the case of the United States whereas the labour market phenomena in question are common to many other OECD countries. Consequently, this paper seeks to add another country case study by examining the evidence for France. This example is particularly pertinent given the intense interest that the topic has evoked in France recently.

The past two years have witnessed an increasingly heated debate among French policy-makers about the impact of foreign trade and FDI on French jobs. The debate has been fuelled by reports suggesting that foreign trade and capital out-flows have dramatically reduced the number of jobs available to French workers.[1] It has revealed a widespread and strong belief among French policy-makers (and many industrialists as well) that imports from "dissimilar" countries (*i.e.* countries with wages significantly lower than French wages) are much more costly in terms of numbers of French jobs "lost" than imports from "similar" countries and are leading to a substantial decline in French wages, especially for low-skilled labour.

This paper aims at providing more information about the impact of trade and capital flows on French employment and wages. As underlined by Baldwin (1994), most of the recent empirical literature on these issues tests the hypothesis that growing integration of the world economy is driving a process of worldwide factor price equalisation – hence driving down the relative wage of unskilled labour to skilled labour in OECD countries. This paper does not follow this approach because it seems rather extreme on both theoretical and empirical grounds. First, factor price equalisation requires stringent assumptions if the theorem is to hold. For example, the existence of large labour migration or capital flows reflects the lack of effective factor price equalisation (Woodland, 1982). Second, French labour markets do not exhibit the flexible functioning which is necessary for a rapid process of factor price equalisation. Indeed, evidence which would reveal ongoing factor price equalisation at work in France is just not there, as shown below.[2]

Rather, the paper relies on an approach based on three other lessons suggested by pure trade theory. First, trade has a small impact (if any) on the **total** number of jobs available in an economy: total unemployment is mainly driven by macroeconomic forces and the functioning of labour and product markets itself. Second, changes in the relative prices of traded goods and services have a noticeable impact on the relative wages paid to skilled labour by import-competing and export industries – rather than on the relative wage paid to unskilled labour by both industries. Lastly, capital outflows and inflows are based on very complex motives: as a result, simple relations – such as a decline of domestic jobs as a result of capital outflows – are unlikely. These lessons lead to the following conclusion: most of the employment and wage developments that the French debate on trade policy focuses on are more related to domestic causes than to international trade and FDI.

The paper is organised as follows. The first section examines the relationships between trade and employment in the French case. It starts by looking at the link between exports and employment: it shows the extent to which during the last 15 years, world demand for French exports (the derived demand for French labour by foreign consumers) has driven French growth. Then it takes into account imports by estimating the number of French jobs lost because French consumers prefer foreign goods (the derived "non-demand" for French labour by French consumers). Combining these two derived demands for French labour allows us to make an estimate of the **net** impact of foreign trade on French employment. As expected by the theory, the estimated net impact of trade on total employment is very small and (for most of the period examined) positive. But the net impact on employment **by industry** can be substantial in both directions – negative as well as positive.

The section on trade, terms of trade, wages and skills (see below) explores the relationships between trade and the composition of employment defined in terms of skill requirements – shifting the focus to the links between trade and relative wages. It provides two main results. First, trade is unlikely to have a straightforward impact on the relative wages of French skilled and unskilled labour because France is not characterised by a high relative endowment of skilled labour (with respect to unskilled labour) when compared with the rest of the world: if she exports relatively skill-intensive goods and services to certain countries, she exports relatively unskilled labour-intensive goods and services to other countries. The second result is that, by contrast, there are substantial differences in the evolution (from 1984 to 1991) of the relative wages paid to **skilled** labour: the wages paid to skilled labour by export industries have increased substantially with respect to the wages paid to skilled labour by import-competing industries.

Lastly, the section on FDI, domestic investment, and jobs examines French FDI flows and provides three results. First, the shares of French outward and inward FDI flows in domestic gross investments are small for most industrial sectors – and in particular, for those exhibiting net job losses. Second, FDI flows tend to have the same geographical pattern as trade flows (with a dominant proportion of flows

*OECD Economic Studies No. 24, 1995/1*

towards and from the EC and other OECD countries) and job-contracting industries are no exception to this fact. Third, job-contracting industries do not invest in the rest of the world more than other industries, and they tend to receive as much foreign investment as other sectors.

## THE LINKS BETWEEN TRADE AND TOTAL EMPLOYMENT

Trade theory does not predict a strong link between trade openness and the aggregate level of employment even when employment is not fully flexible – for instance, when factors of production are specific to industries (Jones, 1971) or when domestic factors are not flexible because of the existence of minimum wages (Brecher, 1974).[3]

Indeed, Figure 1 clearly suggests that there is no strong link between trade and **total** unemployment. Between 1976 and 1992, the French unemployment rate increased by almost 300 per cent, whereas the openness ratio (defined as the sum of exports and imports of goods and services to GDP) of the French economy increased by only 10 to 20 per cent. These diverging evolutions suggest that French unemployment is more related to domestic macroeconomic variables and/or to poorly functioning labour and product markets than to foreign trade.[4]

Figure I. **French unemployment and openness**
*Index 1976 = 100*

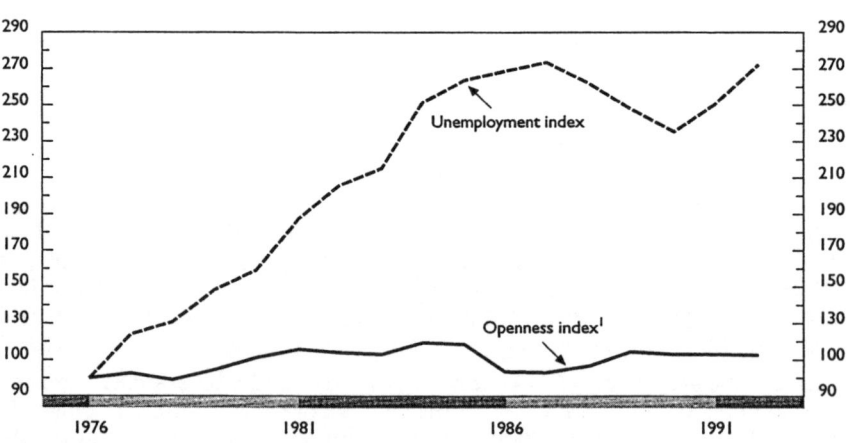

1. The openness index is defined as the ratio of the sum of exports and imports to GDP.

In this context, this section examines more closely two issues: the link between exports and jobs, and the net impact of trade on employment. It analyses not only the links with aggregate employment but it also focuses on individual industries: although foreign trade is not expected to have an impact on total employment, it is expected to have an impact on its composition (the specialisation process requires some reallocation of labour between industries).

The analysis is based on input-output accounting methods. The Annex describes these methods and their limits. However, these methods have a crucial advantage for our purposes: their capacity to link political and economic aspects. Indeed, they provide results easy to interpret in terms of votes (jobs mean votes) and are thus useful for understanding the public debate. And, they offer a close approximation to the results of standard trade theory, as underlined by Krugman and Lawrence (1993).

## French jobs supported by exports

In the context of GATT negotiations such as the Uruguay Round, each negotiating country tries hard to improve market access for its exporters. This focus on exports is explained by the fact that policy-makers aim at expanding the derived demand for domestic labour. This first look at the possible links between trade and jobs relies on the method developed by Davis (1992) which is based on the concept of value-added multipliers within an input-output accounting framework (see the Annex for a detailed description of this method). All the figures presented in the section are in constant prices (1980 French franc prices) and are based on data including service industries as well as manufacturing and agricultural sectors.

### Exports: the engine of French growth

Table 1 shows the important role of exports in French GDP and the degree to which exports of goods and services have been increasingly the engine of growth. It suggests that the prerequisite for an impact of trade on jobs – the existence of large trade flows – is met by the French case.

The share of exports of goods and services in total GDP has increased from 20 to 27 per cent between 1977 and 1992. However, export growth did not evolve smoothly over the period: between 1982 and 1986 it was erratic, whereas it was consistently positive before this period and has been since.

Increases of exports represented about 37 per cent (on average) of GDP increases in the late 1970s, and almost 75 per cent for the period 1987-92 (exceeding 100 per cent in 1991 and 1992). That export growth has represented a very large proportion of (or even surpassed) GDP growth underscores the extent to which exports have been a crucial growth engine in France (a feature shared with the vast majority of other OECD countries).

*OECD Economic Studies No. 24, 1995/I*

Table 1.  **Annual shares and changes in shares in real French GDP
and total employment supported by French exports**

|  | Export: share of total GDP % | Export-supported jobs [a] | | Number of jobs supported by 1 Bio FF of exports |
|---|---|---|---|---|
|  |  | Total number '000 | Share of employment |  |
| 1977 | 20.0 | 3 211.5 | 14.8 | 6 210 |
| 1978 | 20.5 | 3 253.0 | 14.9 | 5 940 |
| 1979 | 21.3 | n..a. | n..a. | n..a. |
| 1980 | 21.5 | 3 392.4 | 15.5 | 5 613 |
| 1981 | 22.1 | 3 494.4 | 16.0 | 5 576 |
| 1982 | 21.1 | 3 299.9 | 15.1 | 5 356 |
| 1983 | 21.8 | 3 395.9 | 15.5 | 5 316 |
| 1984 | 23.0 | 3 503.8 | 16.2 | 5 126 |
| 1985 | 23.0 | 3 457.5 | 16.0 | 4 964 |
| 1986 | 22.1 | 3 307.4 | 15.2 | 4 818 |
| 1987 | 22.3 | 3 259.8 | 15.0 | 4 608 |
| 1988 | 23.0 | 3 298.1 | 15.0 | 4 314 |
| 1989 | 24.4 | 3 425.0 | 15.4 | 4 065 |
| 1990 | 25.0 | 3 539.7 | 15.7 | 3 989 |
| 1991 | 25.8 | 3 633.9 | 16.2 | 3 944 |
| 1992 | 27.1 | 3 730.5 | 16.7 | 3 801 |
|  | cgr [b] | cgr [b] | cgr [b] | avg [c] |
| 1977-92 | 2.1 | 1.0 | 0.8 | 4 909 |
| 1977-81 | 2.5 | 2.1 | 2.0 | 5 723 |
| 1982-86 | 1.1 | 0.1 | 0.3 | 5 116 |
| 1987-92 | 4.0 | 2.7 | 2.2 | 4 120 |

a) See annex for the definition of "export-supported jobs".
b) cgr: annual compound growth rate.
c) avg: average.
*Source:* INSEE, *Comptes de la nation.* Author's computations.

## The impact of exports on jobs: an economy-wide view

Exports support "direct" jobs: a French car exported to the rest of the world embodies a direct content of French labour. In addition to this direct derived demand for labour, exports also support "indirect" jobs: the French exported car has required the production of intermediate inputs (steel plates, tires, etc.), capital goods (plant and equipment) and service inputs in France – all derived demands for French labour which should also be taken into account.[5]

Table 1 provides a crude estimate of the sum of direct and indirect jobs supported by total French exports: this amounted to over 3.7 million jobs in 1992 – about 16 per cent more than in 1977. Another way to express these results is provided by an estimate of the average number of jobs supported by exports of FF 1 billion: roughly 4 000 jobs in 1990 (*i.e.* roughly 25 000 jobs for US$1 billion which is close to the US figure of 19 000 jobs for US$1 billion estimated by Davis).[6] Table 1 shows that export-supported jobs represent an increasing share of total civilian employment – up from almost 15 per cent in 1977 to almost 17 per cent in 1992.

### Export impact on jobs: a sectoral view

Since much of the concern in the debate on the impact of trade on employment is fuelled by sectoral arguments, Table 2 decomposes the export-supported jobs into four broad sectors: manufacturing, agriculture, energy and services. It provides three main results:

First, the shares of export-supported jobs in the labour force vary widely among these sectors. In 1992 (the latest year for which data are available), half of the jobs in French manufacturing industry depended upon exports – compared with 35 per cent in agriculture, 25 per cent in energy and only 7 per cent in services.

Second, the growth rates of the export-supported jobs vary widely among the four sectors and over time. The only sector in which they are continuously (and highly) positive is the services sector.

Third, these share increases occurred in very different employment contexts. In industry, agriculture and energy, there has been a strong decline in total jobs (annual compound growth rates of –1.9, –2.8 and –1.2, respectively) accompanied by small increases or decreases of export-supported jobs (at annual rates of 0.1, –0.1 and –0.9 per cent, respectively). All these trends are in sharp contrast with what has occurred in services. In this sector, employment has increased by an annual

Table 2.  **Export-supported jobs by sector**

|  | Total economy | Manufacturing | Agriculture [a] | Energy | Services |
|---|---|---|---|---|---|
|  | Shares in total civilian employment | | | | |
| 1977-92 | 15.5 | 43.2 | 30.4 | 24.2 | 5.5 |
| 1977-81 | 15.3 | 39.3 | 26.2 | 23.7 | 4.9 |
| 1982-86 | 15.6 | 42.9 | 29.3 | 24.1 | 5.5 |
| 1987-92 | 15.7 | 46.0 | 34.0 | 24.7 | 6.0 |
|  | Annual compound growth rates [b] | | | | |
| 1977-92 | 1.0 | 0.1 | –0.1 | –0.9 | 4.0 |
| 1977-81 | 2.1 | 0.8 | 3.4 | 0.2 | 4.9 |
| 1982-86 | 0.1 | –1.3 | 1.7 | –1.7 | 2.1 |
| 1987-92 | 2.7 | 2.3 | –1.3 | –1.8 | 6.5 |

a) Agriculture includes forestry, fishing, food industries.
b) The year 1979 is not available.
*Source:* INSEE: *Comptes de la nation.* Author's computations.

OECD Economic Studies No. 24, 1995/1

growth rate of 1.2 per cent whereas export-supported jobs have increased at a 4 per cent rate.

### Export impact on jobs: a country view

As mentioned in the introduction, there is a widespread belief among French policy-makers that trade with countries with very different labour intensities (countries with "low" wages) is more costly in terms of jobs than trade with countries with similar labour intensities (*i.e.* the other OECD countries). It is thus interesting to redo the exercise of computing export-supported jobs for French trade flows disaggregated by trading partners.

Table 3.  **Exports and export-supported jobs by major trading zones**

| | French exports to | | | | Export-supported jobs | | |
|---|---|---|---|---|---|---|---|
| | EC | Other OECD | Rest of World | | EC | Other OECD | Rest of World |
| | | | DAEs[a] | Other | | | |
| | Millions US dollars | | | | Thousands | | |
| 1985 | 52.5 | 18.5 | 2.4 | 21.3 | 1 858.5 | 737.1 | 618.9 |
| 1986 | 69.1 | 21.8 | 2.6 | 25.2 | 1 872.2 | 702.9 | 544.0 |
| 1987 | 86.6 | 25.7 | 3.3 | 27.0 | 1 920.1 | 684.8 | 505.3 |
| 1988 | 99.7 | 29.3 | 4.1 | 29.2 | 1 964.8 | 696.1 | 502.8 |
| 1989 | 105.7 | 30.0 | 4.9 | 32.6 | 2 004.0 | 712.0 | 564.0 |
| 1990 | 131.5 | 34.9 | 6.1 | 36.2 | 2 107.8 | 732.6 | 543.7 |
| 1991 | 134.4 | 35.0 | 6.5 | 33.4 | 2 234.2 | 699.4 | 545.7 |
| 1992 | 145.5 | 37.0 | 7.8 | 36.3 | 2 279.9 | 726.8 | 573.8 |
| | Annual compound growth rates | | | | | | |
| 85-92 | 15.7 | 10.4 | 18.1 | 7.9 | 3.0 | −0.2 | −1.1 |
| 87-92 | 10.9 | 7.5 | 18.6 | 6.1 | 3.5 | 1.2 | 2.6 |
| | Percentage of total exports[b] | | | | Percentage of total export-supported jobs | | |
| 1985 | 51.6 | 18.2 | 2.4 | 21.0 | 53.8 | 21.3 | 17.9 |
| 1986 | 55.3 | 17.5 | 2.1 | 20.1 | 56.6 | 21.3 | 16.4 |
| 1987 | 58.4 | 17.3 | 2.2 | 18.2 | 58.9 | 21.0 | 15.5 |
| 1988 | 59.4 | 17.5 | 2.4 | 17.4 | 59.6 | 21.1 | 15.2 |
| 1989 | 58.9 | 16.7 | 2.7 | 18.2 | 58.5 | 20.8 | 16.5 |
| 1990 | 60.7 | 16.1 | 2.8 | 16.7 | 59.5 | 20.7 | 15.4 |
| 1991 | 61.9 | 16.1 | 3.0 | 15.4 | 61.5 | 19.2 | 15.0 |
| 1992 | 61.7 | 15.7 | 3.3 | 15.4 | 61.1 | 19.5 | 15.4 |

a)  DAEs (Dynamic Asian Economies): Hong Kong, Indonesia, Korea, Malaysia, Singapore, Taiwan-RoC, Thailand.
b)  Totals do not add to 100 (see footnote 7 in the text).
Source: INSEE, *Comptes de la nation.* IMF, Trade data. Author's computations.

Table 3 presents a breakdown of French trade by trading partners in four major zones in order to address these issues.[7] Two zones involve countries relatively similar to France: the EC countries (with which French trade flows are not hindered by trade barriers) and the other OECD zone. In addition, there is the Rest of World (RoW) zone which can be further divided between the Dynamic Asian Economies (DAEs) and the other RoW countries. During the period 1987-91, export flows shown in Table 3 (they concern all goods and services recorded by the IMF) exhibit very different annual compound growth rates: more than 18 per cent to the DAEs, almost 12 per cent to the EC, 8 per cent to the other OECD countries and less than 6 per cent to the rest of the RoW zone.

Table 3 also presents the computed export-supported jobs. These results do not support the above-mentioned widespread belief, but they match well the results expected from standard economic analysis. In particular, French export-supported jobs for all goods and services have increased at a higher rate with the RoW zone than with the other OECD zone. This evolution may reflect ongoing trade liberalisation as well as domestic growth differentials: during the late 1980s, the RoW zone experienced substantial unilateral trade liberalisations at the level of individual countries, such as Mexico, or at the level of regions, such as in Pacific Asia.

## Jobs and trade: a wider perspective

In sharp contrast to the above approach which makes sense only in the context of trade negotiations, economic theory shows that gains from trade flow from imports: French consumers prefer foreign goods and services because they are less expensive than French corresponding items or because they are better designed to suit their tastes than French goods and services. As a result of the choices of French consumers, there is less demand for French labour. Combining these two forces – the foreign derived demand for French labour and the French derived "non-demand" for French labour – allows us to estimate the **net** impact of trade on French jobs.

### French trade and net job creation

According to standard trade theory, the economic impact of foreign trade is on real incomes, not on total employment. However, since trade is closely related to growth opportunities existing in the entire world as well as in the country under consideration, one should not be surprised if trade has an impact on total employment.

Table 4 allows us to quantify this impact in the case of France. It gives the number of jobs (as a percentage of total employment) "created" by exports and the number of jobs "lost" by imports as well as the net number of jobs. These estimates are derived by using an accounting method (see Annex). It leads to three observations.

*OECD Economic Studies No. 24, 1995/I*

Table 4.    **Net job creation by trade in goods and services**[a]

Per cent of total French civilian employment

| | World | | | Intra-EC | | | Extra-EC | | |
|------|------|------|------|------|------|------|------|------|------|
| | M | X | Net | M | X | Net | M | X | Net |
| 1980 | −14.2 | 15.5 | 1.2 | | | | | | |
| 1981 | −14.0 | 16.0 | 2.0 | | | | | | |
| 1982 | −14.2 | 15.1 | 0.9 | | | | | | |
| 1983 | −13.8 | 15.5 | 1.8 | | | | | | |
| 1984 | −13.7 | 16.2 | 2.4 | | | | | | |
| 1985 | −13.9 | 16.0 | 2.1 | | | | | | |
| 1986 | −14.4 | 15.2 | 0.8 | | | | | | |
| 1987 | −14.9 | 15.0 | 0.0 | | | | | | |
| 1988 | −15.3 | 15.0 | −0.2 | | | | | | |
| 1989 | −15.7 | 15.4 | −0.3 | −9.2 | 9.1 | −0.06 | −6.5 | 6.3 | −0.2 |
| 1990 | −16.2 | 15.7 | −0.5 | −9.6 | 9.5 | −0.03 | −6.7 | 6.2 | −0.4 |
| 1991 | −16.6 | 16.2 | −0.4 | −9.6 | 10.1 | 0.50 | −7.0 | 6.1 | −0.9 |
| 1992 | −16.5 | 16.7 | 0.1 | −9.6 | 10.3 | 0.70 | −6.9 | 6.3 | −0.6 |
| Averages | | | | | | | | | |
| 80-92 | −14.9 | 15.7 | 0.8 | | | | | | |
| 87-92 | −15.9 | 15.7 | −0.2 | −9.49 | 9.77 | 0.28 | −6.75 | 6.22 | −0.5 |

a)   Estimates based on 81 sectors.
*Source:* INSEE, *Comptes de la nation.* Author's computations.

First, as expected, the **net** impact of trade on jobs is modest. It is on average about 0.8 per cent of French total employment, that is, almost 170 000 jobs – though it peaked at 2.4 per cent in 1984 (about 450 000 jobs).

Second, trade tends to be a net creator of jobs. In only four out of the fifteen years for which estimates are available was there a negative net impact of trade on jobs. These negative figures are very small: they never exceeded half a percentage point of total employment (less than 100 000 jobs in 1990).

Lastly, all four years in which trade led to net job losses are clustered in the period 1988-91. This may help to explain the increase in protectionist sentiment observed in France during recent years – though it is somewhat hard to believe that French politicians could be sensitive to such small figures.[8]

### A breakdown of net job creation by sector

Table 5 presents a breakdown of net job creation by sector. Rather than present all sectors, we have chosen to focus on the extremes, *i.e.* the ten sectors with the highest net job gains and the ten sectors with the highest net job losses. The former set is characterised by higher wages (on average) than the latter. If one excludes

Table 5. **Net job gains and losses by selected sectors ('000), 1992**

| Industries [a] | Zones | | | | | Average wages '000 FR [b] |
|---|---|---|---|---|---|---|
| | World | European Community | Other OECD | RoW | OPEC zone | |
| | The ten sectors with the highest net job gains | | | | | |
| Agriculture | 147.3 | 154.3 | 6.9 | −24.6 | 10.6 | |
| Car | 45.0 | 28.1 | 1.2 | 10.0 | 5.6 | 175.3 |
| Aircraft | 42.2 | 0.2 | 11.7 | 22.7 | 7.6 | 256.0 |
| Services to firms | 39.2 | 18.1 | 7.1 | 8.8 | 5.2 | |
| Electric machines | 23.4 | 4.9 | −1.5 | 13.3 | 6.7 | 179.6 |
| Tyres | 19.8 | 12.9 | 3.4 | 1.2 | 2.3 | 169.0 |
| Maritime transports | 14.4 | 0.7 | 9.6 | 2.7 | 1.4 | |
| Specialty chemicals | 14.2 | 3.7 | 1.1 | 7.4 | 2.0 | 214.5 |
| Foundry | 13.2 | 5.7 | −0.2 | 4.9 | 2.9 | 156.9 |
| Railway equipement | 12.9 | 9.7 | 0.7 | 1.7 | 0.8 | 183.1 |
| | The ten sectors with the highest net job losses | | | | | |
| Plastics | −18.3 | −13.8 | −5.2 | −0.8 | 1.4 | 149.3 |
| Construction | −19.2 | −1.4 | −3.1 | −5.2 | −9.4 | |
| Crude oil | −22.3 | −1.6 | −3.4 | −6.1 | −11.1 | |
| Scientific equipment | −23.6 | −7.1 | −18.9 | −0.5 | 2.9 | 159.4 |
| Natural gas | −24.7 | −3.9 | −3.7 | −6.1 | −11.1 | |
| Shoes | −25.1 | −14.8 | 2.8 | −12.1 | −1.0 | 124.3 |
| Fishing | −25.9 | −8.5 | −12.7 | −4.6 | −0.1 | |
| Coal | −26.7 | −1.2 | −16.8 | −8.0 | −0.7 | 212.5 |
| Hosiery | −29.4 | −7.7 | −4.8 | −15.6 | −1.2 | 120.5 |
| Office machines | −34.4 | 6.4 | −31.8 | −9.7 | 0.7 | 220.7 |
| All sectors | 30.9 | 124.3 | −119.7 | −32.3 | 58.6 | 180.0 |

a) Sectors are defined in terms of French Industrial Classification NAP 90. Agriculture excludes forestry, fishing and food industries.
b) Average wages (sectoral labour costs as defined by SESSI divided by sectoral employment) are available only for industrial sectors.
*Source:* INSEE, *Comptes de la nation.* Ministère de l'Industrie (SESSI). Author's computations.

agriculture, there is a relative balance in terms of size between the two sets of sectors.

Looking at the set of sectors creating net jobs, one can distinguish between sectors which create net jobs essentially through intra-EC trade (for instance, agriculture or railway equipment) and sectors which create net jobs through extra-EC trade. Agriculture shows the most marked contrast: net gains from intra-OECD trade, but net losses from trade with the rest of the world – a feature which may help to explain why it was one of the leading members of the protectionist coalition in France during the debate on the Uruguay Round.

*Globalization and Labour Markets II*

OECD Economic Studies No. 24, 1995/I

Sectors with net job losses can be distinguished by two criteria. A few of them are natural-resources based, such as coal, fishing and natural gas, with heavy losses arising from extra-EC trade. By contrast, traditional industries in difficulties (hosiery, shoes) are characterised by high losses arising from both intra-EC trade and non-OECD trade.

### A breakdown of net job creation by trading zone

In addition to examining net job gains and losses by sector, it is also instructive to examine the breakdown of net gains and losses by trading partners. Table 4 shows a different impact of intra-EC trade and extra-EC trade on French jobs. Net job losses seem to be more associated with extra-EC trade and net job gains with intra-EC trade for the period 1989-92 (the only years for which French National Accounts provide consistent trade data for the world and for the EC). This observation requires a more thorough examination.

Table 6 relies on a different set of trade data than those used so far. This data set (provided by the French Customs) permits a distinction to be drawn between the EC zone and the other OECD zone for the period 1980-92, and between these zones and the OPEC and RoW zones for the period 1985-92. Trade with the OPEC zone is associated with high net job creation, illustrating the fact that France imports non - competing goods from this zone. The EC zone also shows net job creation – except for 1989 and 1990 – at the level of disaggregation considered.[9] Lastly, trade with both the other OECD and the RoW zones exhibits a negative impact on jobs. It is

Table 6. **Estimates of net job gains and losses by trading zones**

Thousand of jobs

|  | World | European Community | Other OECD | RoW | OPEC |
|---|---|---|---|---|---|
| 1980 | 269.4 | 99.1 | −99.9 | n.a. | n.a. |
| 1981 | 442.9 | 57.6 | −69.5 | n.a. | n.a. |
| 1985 | 452.0 | 117.6 | 70.0 | 126.9 | 137.5 |
| 1986 | 183.9 | 36.4 | 12.7 | 45.6 | 89.2 |
| 1987 | 6.7 | 4.7 | −21.9 | −28.2 | 52.1 |
| 1988 | −51.0 | 10.2 | −44.2 | −56.8 | 39.8 |
| 1989 | −61.3 | −49.7 | −62.7 | 7.5 | 43.6 |
| 1990 | −104.4 | −49.2 | −80.2 | −29.6 | 54.6 |
| 1991 | −88.2 | 80.5 | −159.6 | −56.1 | 47.0 |
| 1992 | 30.9 | 124.3 | −119.7 | −32.3 | 58.6 |
| Averages |  |  |  |  |  |
| 80-92 | 108.1 | 43.2 | −57.5 | −2.3 | 52.2 |
| 87-92 | −44.6 | 20.1 | −81.4 | −32.6 | 49.3 |

Source: NSEE, *Comptes de la nation*. French customs. Author's computations.

noteworthy that trade with the RoW zone has a less strong impact in terms of net job losses for a given amount of trade than does trade with the other OECD zone – a fact that does not match with current French preconceptions.

### Comparison with other studies

Before turning to the section on trade, terms of trade, wages and skills, it is useful to compare the results of this section with the main results provided by the few available papers which have examined the impact of trade on French labour. Vimont (1993), who used a methodology similar to our approach (at a less disaggregated industrial classification), ended up with an estimate of net job creation of 106 000 jobs in 1991, compared with our estimate of a net job destruction of 88 000 jobs. However, this discrepancy can be easily explained by the treatment of the tourism sector: Vimont estimated net job gains from tourism at about 274 000 jobs whereas we were obliged to ignore the trade aspects of this industry because they were not included in the data set provided by the French National Accounts.

Two papers by Mathieu and Sterdyniak (1994) and by the Direction de la Prévision (1994) lead to results more radically different from our estimates: they suggest net job losses, ranging from 190 000 to 330 000, related to trade with developing countries alone (our corresponding result is 56 000 net job losses for 1991). This difference stems from the fact that both papers assume that one franc of imports from developing countries is equivalent to **more** than one franc of domestic production in the sense that one franc of imports represents, say, two T-shirts, whereas one franc of domestic production represents only one T-shirt. As a result, both papers assume that one franc of imports should eliminate more than one franc of domestic production: using data on imports and domestic production of shoes, both papers state that one thousand francs of imports (say, two pairs of shoes) should eliminate two thousand francs of domestic production (which correspond to the same quantity of two pairs of shoes).

Even if one accepts this assumption about the substitution of imported to domestic shoes and the ratio of two to one (see the Annex for a discussion about this ratio), the results offered by these two studies are subject to the following remarks. These authors have estimated domestic prices from export unit values and import prices from import unit values. These estimates are likely to be biased towards overestimates in the case of domestic prices and underestimates in the case of import prices. The second bias is the most severe: products like clothing, shoes and electronics are subject to quotas, and quota premiums have been ignored in these computations (in other words, import unit values are likely to be depressed by the expected quota premium). Small changes in these biases could change the final results radically. For instance, if export unit values are 10 per cent higher than domestic prices, and if import unit values are 30 per cent lower than import-competing prices (a plausible premium for quotas), the price differential would be only 1.5 instead of 2.1 which is the differential adopted by these two

OECD Economic Studies No. 24, 1995/I

studies. With such a lower price differential, their upper-bound estimate of net job losses would decrease from 330 000 to 107 000 jobs (close to our estimate).

## TRADE, TERMS OF TRADE, WAGES AND SKILLS

The previous section focuses on quantity relationships – namely the impact of trade flows on (aggregate and sectoral) levels of employment. Such an approach treats jobs with different levels of skills as similar and ignores the role of relative prices of goods and services (the terms of trade) on factor rewards. As a result, it cannot address the other crucial issue raised in the debate about the Uruguay Round: does French trade (in particular, trade with countries with low wages) tend to depress French wages? This general question leads to two very different approaches.

The first approach assumes that labour is very mobile between industries. In such a context, the impact of trade on French wages is mostly determined by the level of skills and is independent of the sectors involved. If France is relatively abundant in skilled labour (and if the terms of trade of skill-intensive goods increase), the wages paid to French unskilled labour should decline. The evidence provided below does not support the existence of this relation.

This negative result suggests the adoption of an alternative approach which recognises that labour is relatively immobile between sectors, especially in the short run. More precisely, skilled labour is assumed to be "specific" to an industry: it is less mobile between industries than unskilled labour. In this context, the specific-factor model of trade predicts that changes in the terms of trade will have a more noticeable impact on the relative wages paid to skilled labour by export sectors and by import-competing industries respectively than on the relative wages of unskilled labour (see Annex). Evidence provided below tends to support this result, although it also shows that French relative wages are heavily influenced by specific features of the domestic labour market – in particular, minimum wages and early retirement schemes.

### Trade and wages

The assertion that trade depresses the average wage of unskilled French labour is based on two different interpretations about the nature of French trade.

#### Trade patterns and average wages

The first (and most frequent) interpretation is that trade with low-wage countries has a depressing effect on the French **average** wage (first because workers in these countries allegedly compete directly with French unskilled workers, then because competition in terms of wages allegedly spreads to skilled labour). This interpretation does not generally rely upon the traditional "factor price equalisation" argument – and indeed it does not need to do so (Krueger, 1977).

However, such a direct relation between trade patterns and the average French wage has to take into account the fact that France trades not only with countries with lower wages, but also with countries with higher wages. If trade flows have any impact on the average wage, there is no reason to exclude France's trading partners with higher wages from the analysis.

As suggested by Krugman and Lawrence (1993), one simple figure can capture the whole argument: it is the average wage of France's trading partners weighted by French imports from all her partners. Using the estimates of labour costs provided by the US Bureau of Labor Statistics suggests that the weighted wage faced by France is close to **one**. This result flows from the fact that almost half of French trade is with countries with higher wages – the other half being with countries with lower wages (and the lower the trading partners' wages are, the less important are trade flows between France and the trading partners in question).

### Terms of trade and relative wages

The second interpretation states that French trade reduces the **relative** wages paid to French unskilled and skilled labour, drawing on the traditional "factor price equalisation" approach. This interpretation rests on two crucial hypotheses: *i)* France should be relatively well endowed with skilled labour (relatively to unskilled labour) vis-à-vis RoW (as a whole); and *ii)* the relative price of skill-intensive goods should have increased.

The first hypothesis cannot be taken for granted. France is both relatively well endowed with skilled labour vis-à-vis certain countries **and** relatively rich in unskilled labour vis-à-vis other trading partners.[10]

A simple extension of the work done in the section on the links between trade and total employment provides evidence supporting the ambiguity of French relative endowments. Following the approach suggested by Borjas, Freeman and Katz (1992) (see Annex for details), it is possible to calculate the skilled and unskilled labour "embodied" in French trade, *i.e.* to estimate a trade content in terms of "labour efficiency units" defined as jobs weighted by a variable mirroring the level of skills (namely, average wages). If French exports were systematically intensive in skilled labour, their content in terms of labour efficiency units should be higher than their content in jobs. And if French imports were systematically intensive in unskilled labour, their content in terms of labour efficiency units should be lower than their content in jobs.[11]

Table 7 presents the skill embodiment of French trade based on this method. It shows that there is no clearcut evolution in the French case: **both** exports and imports have contents in labour efficiency units higher than their contents in jobs. That leads to the conclusion that differences in relative endowments between France and RoW are not large to the point that they can generate noticeable changes in French relative (skilled/unskilled) wages.

It is also noticeable from Table 7 that French exports and imports have contents in labour efficiency units higher than their contents in jobs roughly in the

OECD Economic Studies No. 24, 1995/I

Table 7.  **Implicit labour input in goods and services trade flows**[a]

|  | As a % of total French labour input in number of jobs | | | As a % of total French labour input in efficiency units | | |
|---|---|---|---|---|---|---|
|  | Import | Export | Net | Import | Export | Net |
| 1985 | −14.3 | 16.4 | 2.1 | −20.6 | 23.7 | 3.1 |
| 1986 | −14.8 | 15.7 | 0.9 | −21.6 | 22.8 | 1.2 |
| 1987 | −15.3 | 15.4 | 0.1 | −22.6 | 22.5 | −0.1 |
| 1988 | −15.7 | 15.5 | −0.2 | −22.9 | 22.2 | −0.6 |
| 1989 | −16.1 | 15.9 | −0.1 | −23.4 | 22.9 | −0.5 |
| 1990 | −16.6 | 16.2 | −0.3 | −24.1 | 23.3 | −0.8 |
| 1991 | −16.9 | 16.6 | −0.2 | −24.7 | 24.1 | −0.5 |
| 1992 | −16.8 | 17.1 | 0.4 | n.a. | n.a. | n.a. |
| Averages |  |  |  |  |  |  |
| 85-86 | 14.5 | 16.0 | 1.5 | 21.1 | 23.2 | 2.1 |
| 87-92 | 16.2 | 16.1 | −0.1 | 23.5 | 23.0 | −0.5 |

a)  These estimates are based on 38 sectors. The results are slightly different from those of Table 4 because of this change in the level of disaggregation.
*Source:* INSEE, *Comptes de la nation* and DADS. Author's computations.

same proportion. As a result, the **net** trade impact in terms of "labour efficiency units" is still small when compared with total employment (expressed itself in terms of labour efficiency units) though it is higher than the net trade impact in terms of jobs. In sum, the conclusion suggested by the section on the links between trade and total employment (above) (that the trade impact on total employment is small) still appears to be valid when allowance is made for the skill composition of the work force.

### Skill-intensities of French industries

The previous discussion can be usefully completed by ranking French industries by wage levels. Such a ranking mirrors the income gains from trade. And if one assumes that the average wage in relatively skilled-labour-intensive industries is higher than the average wage in relatively unskilled-labour-intensive sectors, it is also a ranking in terms of skill contents which can be seen as a test confirming what has just been said about French relative endowments. Wage data consistent with the trade data used in the section on the links between trade and total employment (above) have been collected for 81 industries (see Annex for details). For the sake of simplicity, Table 8 aggregates the 81 industries into three groups: export industries, import-competing sectors and non-trading industries (defined as those which have no or very small trade flows – *de facto*, only services industries).[12]

Table 8.   **Relative wages among French industries, 1985-1991**

| Industries | 1985 | 1986 | 1987 | 1988 | 1989 | 1991 [a] |
|---|---|---|---|---|---|---|
| A. All sectors (except agriculture) [b] | | | | | | |
| World | | | | | | |
| Import-competing | 103.3 | 101.2 | 102.8 | 101.5 | 102.0 | 102.1 |
| Exporting | 100.3 | 102.4 | 100.3 | 105.1 | 102.1 | 105.6 |
| Non trading | 77.9 | 82.1 | 76.6 | 72.4 | 73.1 | 66.0 |
| European Community | | | | | | |
| Import-competing | 101.6 | 104.1 | 104.5 | 104.2 | 102.6 | 101.6 |
| Exporting | 97.7 | 93.1 | 93.6 | 99.6 | 100.4 | 103.3 |
| Other OECD | | | | | | |
| Import-competing | 102.2 | 104.3 | 101.2 | 101.2 | 101.1 | 104.5 |
| Exporting | 98.0 | 98.3 | 98.8 | 101.4 | 99.3 | 98.5 |
| RoW | | | | | | |
| Import-competing | 97.6 | 97.4 | 98.1 | 98.4 | 99.6 | 101.0 |
| Exporting | 101.8 | 101.8 | 101.9 | 106.2 | 103.5 | 106.2 |
| B. Manufacturing sector (including food processing) [c] | | | | | | |
| World | | | | | | |
| Import-competing | 99.2 | 97.0 | 98.2 | 98.1 | 98.5 | 98.5 |
| Exporting | 101.3 | 104.4 | 104.3 | 105.1 | 104.1 | 104.5 |
| Non trading | 95.2 | 101.1 | 90.9 | 92.0 | 89.2 | 85.0 |
| European Community | | | | | | |
| Import-competing | 96.3 | 97.9 | 99.4 | 100.8 | 98.1 | 98.1 |
| Exporting | 105.0 | 99.6 | 98.6 | 99.1 | 106.9 | 108.8 |
| Other OECD | | | | | | |
| Import-competing | 102.5 | 104.0 | 102.0 | 103.0 | 103.4 | 103.4 |
| Exporting | 96.1 | 96.1 | 95.4 | 95.7 | 93.2 | 93.0 |
| RoW | | | | | | |
| Import-competing | 98.6 | 98.6 | 100.3 | 99.8 | 101.4 | 97.4 |
| Exporting | 100.0 | 100.4 | 100.0 | 102.2 | 101.3 | 103.5 |

a) Data for 1990 are not available. See text for details.
b) Index 100 for the whole economy (agriculture excluded).
c) Index 100 for the whole manufacturing (including food processing).
*Source:* INSEE, *Comptes de la nation* and DADS. Authors' computations.

Table 8 illustrates French income gains from trade. Workers in export manufacturing sectors gain on average 6 per cent more than workers in import-competing manufacturing sectors (taking into account services).[13] Combined with the result from the section on the links between trade and total employment (above), this result mirrors the saying about the impact of freer trade: "Better jobs rather than more jobs."

*OECD Economic Studies No. 24, 1995/1*

This result requires a *caveat*: the observed link between French exports and wages may also reflect protection. For instance, trade barriers in textiles and apparel are imposed by all OECD countries on exports from the newly industrial and developing countries. Such trade barriers exclude non-OECD competitors from OECD markets and substitute for them competitors from other OECD countries with the closest factor endowments to those of the industrializing countries. France, which is a large exporter of textiles and clothing, is one of these OECD countries which benefits indirectly the most from such protection. Large French exports of apparel to the other OECD zone may thus mirror the OECD pattern of protection as well as her relative endowments. A similar argument could be made about protection in agriculture and French agricultural exports to the EC.

Table 8 also confirms that France tends to export low-skill-intensive products to the EC and the other OECD zones. This result holds for the other OECD zone for every year irrespective of whether services are included or excluded (though services tend to reduce the strength of the result). The conclusion is less stable for the EC than for the other OECD trading partners, in particular when services are excluded. In sharp contrast with this feature of French trade with industrial countries, France tends to export goods and services which are relatively skill intensive to the RoW zone. This conclusion is relatively stable and it is more marked when services are included.

In sum, these results confirm that France is not the country with the highest relative endowment in skilled labour. Compared with its OECD trading partners (among which there are all the skill-rich countries), France tends to rely on relatively low-skill-intensive exports. When facing industrializing or developing countries which are relatively rich in unskilled labour, France tends to export high-skill-intensive exports.

## Terms of trade and relative wages

Examining the impact of the terms of trade on relative wages requires some estimate of the changes in the relative prices of traded goods and services which have triggered changes in relative factor rewards (as is well known, fixed relative prices of traded goods and services and fixed technology lead to constant relative factor rewards, as in the Rybczynski case).[14] Figure 2 suggests that the French terms of trade improved between 1984 and 1991 – with most of the increase occurring between 1984 and 1986 (and essentially because the relative prices of imported goods decreased).

### The analytical framework

Examining the impact of the terms of trade on French relative wages also requires an analytical framework which is better adapted than the traditional factor price equalisation theorem. In what follows, we assume some "specificity" (different rates of adjustment) for different types of labour (supposed to be the only factor). More precisely, we rely upon the following hypothesis: skilled labour is specific to

Figure 2. **French terms of trade**

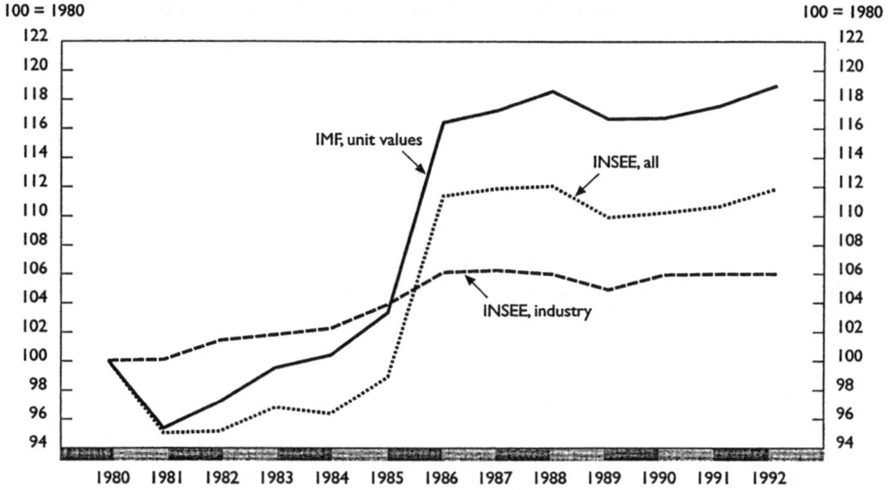

100 = 1980                                                                                              100 = 1980

*Source:* OECD.

the sector where it works, whereas unskilled labour is assumed to be mobile between all sectors.

It must be recognised that this working hypothesis can be criticised on several grounds: labour regulations (such as the minimum wage or employment protection legislation) also create rents which tend to limit the potential mobility of unskilled labour; some skills (for instance, managerial skills) can be more flexible than technical skills (skilled managers could be more mobile between sectors than skilled engineers); higher skills may be associated with better capacities to learn, thus with more flexibility, etc. Because of lack of information (for instance, on the proportion of managers compared with engineers in the skilled labour force, on the proportion of older workers with different skills, etc.) the working hypothesis cannot be tested directly on the data used in this paper.[15] However, the results presented below are consistent with the hypothesis that skilled labour is more sector-specific than unskilled labour in the French case.

If factors are sector-specific to a different extent (adjust at different speeds), economic analysis shows that changes in the terms of trade will trigger magnified reactions of the factor rewards of the specific factors (see Annex for details). For instance, improved terms of trade will have the following consequences: wages paid to skilled labour by export industries will improve by more than export prices; wages paid to skilled labour used in import-competing industries will decline by

*OECD Economic Studies No. 24, 1995/I*

more than import prices; and wages paid to unskilled (and mobile between industries) labour will stay within the range set by the changes of the export and import prices.

In sum, the analytical framework and the hypothesis adopted about the relative specificity of skilled *versus* unskilled labour predict that the difference between the growth rate of the wages paid to skilled labour by French export industries and the growth rate of the wages paid to skilled labour by French import-competing sectors would be positive, and that the differential would be highest for the highest skill category and decrease as the level of skill diminishes – for a given level of experience (age). It is also expected that the bulk of this change would have occurred between 1984 and 1986 (when the terms of trade improved strongly). Lastly, it is expected that the wages paid by French export and import-competing industries to unskilled labour would be broadly similar.

### Evidence

Table 9 aims at testing these predictions. It gives the changes (between 1984 and 1991) of French relative wages by skill and experience (based on detailed data by industry, sex, skills and experience kindly made available by INSEE and described in more detail in the annex). For each year, industries have been aggregated into export, import-competing and non-trading industries according to the sectoral trade balances observed for the year involved. However, the results of Table 9 are only based on export and import-competing sectors. As a result, they *de facto* cover only manufacturing sectors because evidence about services is rather unclear.[16]

Concerning male wages, Table 9 provides two interesting results. First, it shows that growth differentials between skilled labour wages in the export and import-competing industries fit the predictions of the standard trade theory only for two groups of workers, *i.e.* the segments III and IV of the male workers who are aged 36-45 and 46-55 years old. The wage growth differentials are highest for managers (roughly 15 per cent over eight years) and they decline as skills decrease. The bulk of the relative changes in wages occurs between 1984 and 1986 (that is, the period during which French terms of trade changed the most). Lastly, the differentials between the growth rates of the wages paid to unskilled labour by the export and the import-competing industries are very small (this last result is consistent with the choice of skilled labour as the specific factor of production).

Second, Table 9 suggests that domestic features of the French labour market are much stronger than the trade impact in the three remaining segments of the labour market: segments I and II of male workers (aged 18-25 and 26-35 years old, respectively) and segment V of male workers (older than 55 years).[17]

The case of segment V is consistent with the expected impact of existing early retirement schemes. These schemes offer the possibility of paying a reduced portion of wages to workers who accept a reduction of their working time. As the

Table 9.  **The evolution of relative wages:**
**Differentials between the growth rates of wages in the export**
**and import-competing industries (1984-1991)**

| Levels of skills | Levels of experience [a] | | | | |
|---|---|---|---|---|---|
| | I<br>18-25 years | II<br>26-35 years | III<br>36-45 years | IV<br>46-55 years | V<br>> 56 years |
| **Males** | | | | | |
| Managers | 51.8 | −47.9 | 15.8 | 15.0 | −8.6 |
| High level staff | −4.7 | −2.2 | 3.6 | 4.5 | −2.3 |
| Medium level staff | 1.1 | 1.7 | −1.0 | 0.1 | −5.2 |
| Low level staff | −4.0 | 2.1 | 1.4 | −5.2 | −22.0 |
| Workers | −4.1 | 0.2 | 1.5 | −0.0 | −11.2 |
| **Females** | | | | | |
| Managers | 66.7 | −64.3 | −8.5 | 102.4 | −4.4 |
| High level staff | −47.3 | −8.2 | −12.0 | 8.1 | −17.3 |
| Medium level staff | 3.5 | −1.1 | −3.6 | −0.6 | 5.1 |
| Low level staff | −6.3 | −8.0 | −8.3 | −8.2 | −8.6 |
| Workers | −5.4 | −3.8 | 0.9 | −1.7 | −4.4 |

a)  Levels of experience are measured by age.
*Source:* INSEE, DADS. Author's computations.

portion of the retained wage is higher than the reduction of the working time, these retirement schemes are equivalent to increases of real hourly wages. Such schemes are likely to be more intensively used in import-competing industries which have to restructure than in export sectors which have benefitted from growth. It is also likely that these schemes are more intensively used by unskilled workers and that they are less generously granted to the higher levels of skills. Lastly, the fact that the wage growth differential for low-level staff is negative already in the segment IV (−5.2 per cent) is not inconsistent with the previous relations.[18]

The case of segments I and II may be related to another feature of the French labour market, namely minimum wage regulations.[19] By contrast to the retirement schemes which target import-competing (contracting) industries, the SMIC covers both export and import-competing sectors. The question is thus to know whether the SMIC has a greater influence on import-competing industries than on export sectors – hence weakening the expected wage differentials. Data from French Ministry of Labour show in 1993 that SMIC earners represented 5.6 per cent of the labour force in industries we classify as import-competing sectors compared with 4.4 per cent in industries we classify as export sectors. INSEE data show that "unskilled workers" (ouvriers non qualifiés) represent 17 per cent of jobs in our import-competing sectors compared with 14.7 per cent in our export sectors.[20] That may explain why segments I and II do not show the pattern of skilled/unskilled wage differentials suggested by the specific-factors model.

Concerning female wages, Table 9 provides broadly similar, though less clear, results. The major difference with male wages is that domestic features dominate all the segments of the labour markets but one (segment IV).

In sum, Table 9 leads to the conclusion that, when disaggregated by skill level and gender, the evolution of French relative wages (in terms of skills) appears to be more influenced by domestic features of the labour market than by trade flows. The sole exceptions to this are the central segments of the work force (persons aged between 36 and 56 years old). In these two segments, skilled labour employed by export industries gains whereas skilled labour employed by import-competing industries loses (in relative wage terms). It should be kept in mind that these evolutions are the necessary signals for a reallocation of the French labour force which takes into account changing relative world prices.

## FOREIGN DIRECT INVESTMENT, DOMESTIC INVESTMENT, AND JOBS

The heated debate about France's signature of the Uruguay Round reached a peak with the arguments about "délocalisation". This issue centred on the fear that French outward FDI was worsening the allegedly negative trade impact on the number of jobs (and on relative wages).

Figure 3 helps to understand the emergence of this fear. It shows that it is only recently that outward FDI flows have become a noticeable feature of the French

Figure 3. **FDI shares in gross domestic investment**

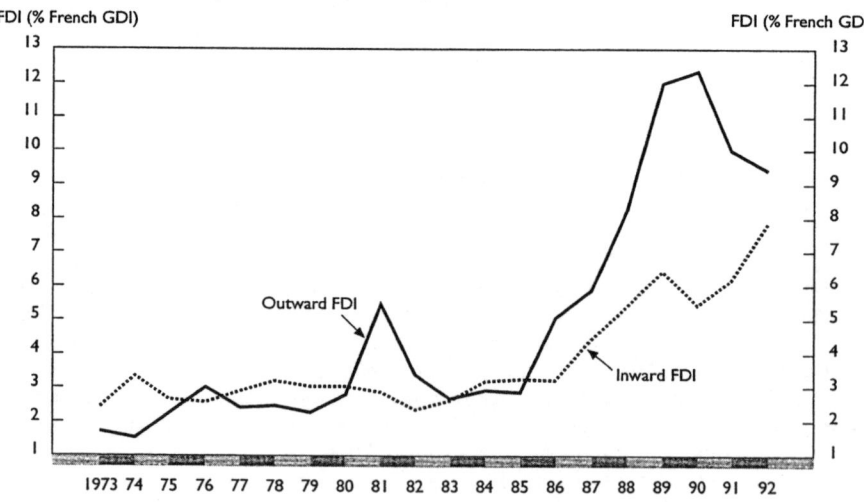

Source: OECD.

economy. Until 1986, outward FDI was insignificant (it represented less than 3 per cent of domestic gross investment defined by the "formation brute de capital fixe") whereas since 1986, French outward FDI has accounted for 8 to 12 per cent, with a peak in 1990.

However, Figure 3 also shows that inward FDI has followed the same evolution as outward FDI flows. After some lags between 1986 and 1990, the inward FDI share of domestic gross investment has converged towards the outward FDI share since 1991. The imbalance between inward and outward flows was never larger than 7 per cent of French gross domestic investment, and it declined to less than 2 per cent of domestic investment in 1992. These features were generally ignored in the French debate about outward FDI flows. As well as neglecting inward FDI flows by its misplaced focus on outward FDI, the "délocalisation" debate has also ignored the relative importance by industry of the outward FDI flows.

This section examines three issues. First, it provides some basic evidence about relationships between (inward and outward) FDI and gross domestic investment **by industry**. Second, it looks at the FDI geographical patterns by industry – in particular, checking whether import-competing industries have FDI patterns different from other French industries. Lastly, it provides some evidence about the relationships between FDI and structural changes in jobs by industry.

The section is based on detailed data about FDI by industry from the Balance of Payments statistics which are available only for the period 1989-92. As annual data on such a short period are not very meaningful, the section relies on averages over the four years. As usually in Balance of Payments statistics, data are in terms of flows and they concern residents and non-residents. This last point is crucial for a correct interpretation of the results provided below: they capture the relations between French savings and their use for investment purposes either in France or in the rest of the world. They do not capture the investment strategies of French (or foreign) multinationals which could (and indeed, do) rely on funds which are available elsewhere.

## Capital flows and gross investment by industry

Table 10 presents French gross domestic investment and FDI for 38 industries (goods and private as well as public services).[21] It provides three results.

First, even during these peak years (1989-92) the share of outward FDI relative to domestic gross investment by industry is on average small: 11 per cent for the whole French economy, 16 per cent for manufacturing as a whole and 12 per cent for services (excluding retail and wholesale, and public services).

Second, these shares vary widely among industries: ranging from almost zero for agriculture, coal, and several services (such as hotels or consumers services) to very high percentages (50 per cent and more) for some industries (oil and gas or ferrous metals) and services (business services or insurance and banking services).[22] It is interesting to note that those industries which have been the most vocal in the French debate about "délocalisation" and protection are **not** among the

*111*

Table 10.    **Outward and inward foreign direct investment (1988-92)**

Per cent of Gross Domestic Investment[a]

| Industries | | Outward FDI[b] | | | | | Inward FDI[b] | | | | |
|---|---|---|---|---|---|---|---|---|---|---|---|
| | | World | EC[c] | Other[c] | DAEs[c] | RRoW[c] | World | EC[c] | Other[c] | DAEs[c] | RRoW[c] |
| T01 | Agriculture | 0.3 | 0.2 | 0.1 | 0.0 | 0.0 | 0.4 | 0.3 | 0.1 | 0.0 | 0.0 |
| T02 | Meat and milk | 2.4 | 1.7 | 0.6 | 0.0 | 0.2 | 0.3 | 0.2 | 0.1 | 0.0 | 0.0 |
| T03 | Other food manuf. | 18.3 | 13.9 | 3.5 | 0.1 | 0.9 | 14.3 | 13.4 | 0.7 | 0.0 | 0.1 |
| T04 | Coal and coke | 0.1 | 0.1 | 0.0 | 0.0 | 0.0 | 0.8 | 0.0 | 0.8 | 0.0 | 0.0 |
| T05 | Oil | 59.0 | 4.7 | 13.9 | 0.5 | 39.8 | 1.8 | 0.5 | 1.3 | 0.0 | 0.0 |
| T06 | Utilities | 4.3 | 2.9 | 0.9 | 0.0 | 0.4 | 0.2 | 0.1 | 0.1 | 0.0 | 0.0 |
| T07 | Ferrous metals | 47.0 | 37.9 | 8.1 | 0.0 | 1.0 | 5.3 | 3.1 | 0.4 | 0.8 | 0.9 |
| T08 | Non ferrous metals | 6.5 | 2.8 | 2.0 | 0.0 | 1.7 | 2.0 | 1.6 | 0.3 | 0.0 | 0.1 |
| T09 | Mat. construction | 25.4 | 7.5 | 12.6 | 0.2 | 5.1 | 10.7 | 6.5 | 4.1 | 0.0 | 0.2 |
| T10 | Glass | 7.1 | 1.4 | 5.5 | 0.3 | 0.0 | 1.9 | 1.1 | 0.8 | 0.0 | 0.0 |
| T11 | Basic chemicals | 11.4 | 9.3 | 0.6 | 0.1 | 1.3 | 22.2 | 17.7 | 3.6 | 0.0 | 1.0 |
| T12 | Other chemicals | 21.8 | 7.3 | 3.7 | 0.3 | 10.5 | 26.5 | 16.3 | 5.2 | 0.0 | 5.0 |
| T13 | Foundries | 5.2 | 3.4 | 1.5 | 0.1 | 0.2 | 4.3 | 2.9 | 0.7 | 0.0 | 0.7 |
| T14 | Machinery | 19.3 | 10.9 | 1.7 | 0.4 | 6.3 | 20.3 | 9.0 | 7.4 | 2.1 | 1.8 |
| T15a | Professional electronics | 35.5 | 23.3 | 6.9 | 0.4 | 4.8 | 15.5 | 11.2 | 2.7 | 0.0 | 1.6 |
| T15b | Consumers electronics | 8.6 | 7.1 | 0.2 | 0.1 | 1.1 | 3.3 | 2.4 | 0.9 | 0.0 | 0.0 |
| T16 | Cars, transport mach. | 22.4 | 6.0 | 15.9 | 0.0 | 0.5 | 21.8 | 4.2 | 17.6 | 0.0 | 0.0 |
| T17 | Aircraft, ships | 14.9 | 9.7 | 1.6 | 0.1 | 3.5 | 8.1 | 7.9 | 0.1 | 0.0 | 0.0 |
| T18 | Textile, clothing | 14.8 | 8.4 | 3.6 | 0.7 | 2.1 | 8.2 | 3.7 | 3.0 | 0.1 | 1.4 |
| T19 | Leather, shows | 3.2 | 1.3 | 1.3 | 0.3 | 0.3 | 4.4 | 0.1 | 4.3 | 0.0 | 0.0 |
| T20 | Wood, furniture | 3.2 | 1.9 | 0.7 | 0.0 | 0.6 | 4.0 | 2.9 | 1.0 | 0.0 | 0.1 |
| T21 | Paper, board | 5.6 | 3.2 | 1.8 | 0.0 | 0.6 | 19.2 | 11.4 | 7.8 | 0.0 | 0.0 |
| T22 | Publishing | 10.6 | 4.2 | 6.1 | 0.0 | 0.3 | 5.3 | 3.2 | 1.9 | 0.0 | 0.2 |
| T23 | Rubber products | 12.2 | 10.4 | 0.9 | 0.5 | 0.3 | 5.7 | 3.8 | 1.3 | 0.0 | 0.6 |
| T24 | Construction | 7.9 | 4.1 | 2.1 | 0.0 | 1.8 | 1.3 | 0.7 | 0.3 | 0.0 | 0.3 |
| T25-8 | Wholesale, retail | 8.1 | 5.7 | 1.5 | 0.1 | 0.8 | 11.1 | 6.0 | 3.4 | 0.3 | 1.5 |
| T29 | Car retail, garage | 0.6 | 0.4 | 0.1 | 0.1 | 0.0 | 10.7 | 4.4 | 6.0 | 0.0 | 0.2 |
| T30 | Hotels, restaurants | 1.7 | 1.1 | 0.5 | 0.0 | 0.1 | 2.0 | 0.8 | 0.3 | 0.3 | 0.7 |
| T31 | Transportation serv. | 1.2 | 0.8 | 0.2 | 0.0 | 0.1 | 1.2 | 1.0 | 0.2 | 0.0 | 0.1 |
| T32 | Telecoms, mail | 0.2 | 0.0 | 0.1 | 0.0 | 0.0 | 0.0 | 0.0 | 0.0 | 0.0 | 0.0 |
| T33 | Business services | 76.9 | 48.8 | 24.4 | 0.4 | 3.3 | 31.2 | 20.8 | 7.6 | 0.4 | 2.3 |
| T34 | Consumers services | 1.4 | 0.7 | 0.6 | 0.0 | 0.2 | 1.3 | 0.8 | 0.4 | 0.0 | 0.1 |
| T35 | Housing | 0.4 | 0.3 | 0.1 | 0.0 | 0.0 | 0.4 | 0.2 | 0.1 | 0.0 | 0.1 |
| T36 | Insurance | 62.5 | 45.9 | 11.8 | 0.4 | 4.5 | 50.9 | 48.8 | 2.0 | 0.0 | 0.1 |
| T37 | Financial services | 76.9 | 50.1 | 19.7 | 1.2 | 5.9 | 30.2 | 14.2 | 3.9 | 0.5 | 11.7 |
| T38 | Public services | 2.8 | 1.8 | 0.7 | 0.0 | 0.3 | 6.9 | 4.1 | 2.0 | 0.4 | 0.4 |
| Total | | 11.0 | 6.6 | 3.1 | 0.1 | 1.1 | 6.8 | 4.2 | 1.8 | 0.1 | 0.7 |
| Industry (NAP 2,3,7-23) | | 16.1 | 9.0 | 4.8 | 0.2 | 2.1 | 12.3 | 7.3 | 4.1 | 0.1 | 0.7 |
| Services (NAP 25-37) | | 12.1 | 7.8 | 3.5 | 0.1 | 0.7 | 6.2 | 3.9 | 1.4 | 0.1 | 0.8 |

a)  Gross domestic investment is defined as "formation brute de capital fixe" (in FF millions).
b)  Shares of FDI (foreign direct investment) are in percentage of gross domestic investments.
c)  EC: European Community 12. Other: Other OECD. DAEs: Dynamic Asian Economies. RRoW: RoW excluding DAEs.
Source: Banque de France. *Comptabilité nationale*. Author's computations.

most active investors in foreign countries: consumer electronics, textiles and clothing, wood and furniture, leather and shoes exhibit shares of outward FDI with respect to gross domestic investment which are lower than the average share for the manufacturing sector as a whole.

Lastly, against a background of inward FDI flows that are globally smaller than outward FDI, there is a noticeable difference between the manufacturing sector (inward FDI is 75 per cent of outward FDI) and the services sector (the corresponding ratio is 50 per cent). Inward FDI flows are also less concentrated by individual sector than the corresponding outward FDI flows. It is interesting to note that job-losing industries receive substantial inward FDI flows: these flows are even larger than outward FDI flows for some import-competing industries (leather and shoes, wood and furniture).

## Geographical patterns of FDI flows by industry

The French debate about "délocalisation" has focused almost completely on investment (funded by French savings) in countries with low wages. It is thus worth checking whether a significant share of the French outward FDI is going to such countries, and, if so, whether this phenomenon is more marked for import-competing industries which exhibit high net losses in terms of jobs. Table 10 provides two answers to these questions.

First, the geographical pattern of French outward FDI is very similar to that of French merchandise trade. Most of the outward FDI is exported to the EC and to other OECD countries. Less than 20 per cent of outward FDI – *i.e.* the equivalent of barely 3 per cent of French gross domestic investment – goes to non-OECD countries. Thus, the idea that "délocalisation" represents a great threat to the French industrial base is not substantiated by the facts.

Second, it is essential to note that the geographical pattern of outward FDI is broadly the same for all French industries. In particular, labour-intensive industries do not exhibit an outward FDI pattern more oriented towards low-wage countries than other French industries. For instance, the shares of outward FDI (in French gross domestic investment) invested in non-OECD countries range from 2.8 through 1.2 to 0.6 per cent for textile and clothing, consumer electronics, and leather and shoes or wood and furniture, respectively.[23]

Table 10 also provides some information about the geographical sources of inward FDI (though this information is much less easy to interpret than the geographical pattern of outward FDI flows because sources of inward FDI may refer to the places where financing packages have been arranged rather than the places where funds have been effectively raised). With this caveat in mind, inward FDI flows come mostly from the EC and other OECD countries. Inward FDI flows from developing or newly industrialised countries represent a very small proportion of French gross domestic investment in manufacturing, except in ferrous metals, machinery, professional electronics, and textile and clothing.

*OECD Economic Studies No. 24, 1995/I*

That outward FDI flows have the same geographical pattern for all industries may seem, at a first glance, counter-intuitive. There are several possible explanations for this fact. Two seem particularly relevant. First, technological and factor price changes induce unskilled-labour-intensive industries to evolve towards capital or skill-intensive techniques. For instance, clothing can be designed and made electronically, and shoes can be manufactured by capital-intensive techniques (gluing instead of stitching). In such cases, outward FDI flows reveal the appropriate technological changes which take place in these industries and which will allow their future growth in developed countries. The second explanation is that inputs other than the two classical factors of production (capital and labour) may be crucial: for instance, gaining good information about markets and their evolution (fashion) may require a lot of investment. If that is the case, then the large and sophisticated markets – the OECD markets – will attract most of the investment, even for import-competing and job-losing industries (Oman, 1993).

## Capital flows and jobs

The debate over "délocalisation" aimed at addressing the issue of the impact of outward FDI flows on total employment: do these flows reinforce the allegedly negative impact of trade flows on employment? It does not seem very logical to limit this kind of question to outward FDI alone, thereby eliminating the possible impact of inward FDI on employment. Hence, this section examines this issue by combining estimates from the section on the links between trade and total employment with available data on French FDI – both inward and outward.

Table 11 presents the shares of French FDI held by industries grouped by their net situation in terms of job losses or gains (as computed in the section on the links between trade and total employment, above). It is based on a breakdown of all the sectors into four different types: those characterised by large job gains, those marked by large job losses and those with relatively small job gains or losses. It suggests two results.

First, outward FDI flows are concentrated in industries exhibiting net job **gains**. This feature is very clear if two industries (financial services for investment in the EC, and oil and gas extraction for investment in the non-OECD countries) are excluded for obvious reasons (the first is related to the Single Market programme and the second is related to the location of oil and gas deposits). Table 11 provides no evidence to support the assertion that "délocalisation" is concentrated in industries experiencing net job losses.

Second, inward FDI flows offer a more complex pattern. Inward FDI flows from the EC are disproportionately invested in French industries suffering substantial net job losses. By contrast, inward FDI flows from non-OECD countries are essentially directed to French industries exhibiting net job gains, while inward FDI flows from the other OECD countries are in-between. These investment patterns suggest two remarks. Inward FDI flows from developed countries seem to be largely consistent with the argument that French comparative advantages are complex vis-à-vis other OECD countries which are mostly capital and skilled labour-rich countries. By

Table 11.   **Shares of French foreign direct investment by industry ranked by net job gains and losses**

| Trading partners | Industries with net job losses | | Industries with net job gains | |
|---|---|---|---|---|
| | Industries having lost more than 5 000 jobs | all industries with net job losses | all industries with net job gains | Industries having gained more than 5 000 jobs |
| **Outward foreign direct investment** | | | | |
| World | 13.9 | 34.2 | 65.8 | 53.4 |
| EC | 21.3 | 32.0[a] | 68.0 | 48.4 |
| Other OECD | 5.4 | 16.6 | 83.4 | 57.2 |
| RoW | 31.6 | 38.7[b] | 61.3 | 28.4 |
| **Inward foreign direct investment** | | | | |
| World | 10.9 | 30.6 | 69.4 | 37.7 |
| EC | 16.3 | 29.1 | 70.9 | 31.9 |
| Other OECD | 8.6 | 19.1 | 80.9 | 43.5 |
| RoW | 2.1 | 2.9 | 97.1 | 26.5 |

*a)*  15% for the "Financial services" sector alone.
*b)*  24.5% for the "Oil & Gas" sector alone.
*Source:* Banque de France. Author's computations.

contrast, inward FDI flows from newly developed or developing countries mirror the more clear-cut comparative advantages.

## CONCLUSION

This paper examines the impact of trade and capital movements on French employment and relative wages. It provides three results which tend to support standard economic analysis.

First, trade has had, at most, a modest impact on **total** employment which depends more upon macroeconomic factors and policies as well as upon the structure of labour and product markets (and the ways in which labour and product market policies influence these structures). When the calculations are disaggregated between skilled and unskilled labour embodied in French trade, this result does not change. Contrary to what some observers believe, French exports are not particularly skilled-labour intensive compared with the rest of the world. Indeed, France is both relatively well endowed with skilled labour vis-à-vis certain trading partners (for instance, developing countries) and relatively intensive in unskilled labour vis-à-vis other countries (for instance, the major OECD countries).

Second, trade has had an impact on relative wages: the paper provides evidence supporting the saying that liberal trade is associated with better jobs rather than more jobs. But the paper also shows that the influence of trade on relative

OECD Economic Studies No. 24, 1995/I

wages was dampened by domestic labour market policies and regulations, especially for young workers and for those close to retirement.

Lastly, the paper shows that focusing on outward foreign direct investment (FDI) by import-competing industries is misleading: outward FDI is essentially done by exporting sectors, and inward FDI (which is broadly of the same magnitude) occurs in downsizing industries as well as in the exporting sectors – suggesting that French firms ignore opportunities to invest in France that foreign investors find profitable.

The first and third results of this paper are thus close to those provided by the existing literature on the US case (Baldwin, 1994). Taking into account the fact that French labour markets are characterised by more wage and quantity rigidities than US labour markets, this similarity is interesting. It confirms that trade policy is the wrong instrument for addressing labour issues, a message particularly useful if one takes into account the fact that the United States and France have been among the staunchest supporters of the introduction of a "social clause" in the GATT arena.

To our knowledge, the existing literature on the US case has not examined the relationship between trade and labour in a factor-specific environment which supports our second result. It would be interesting to see to which extent a crude method, like the one used in this paper, would provide similar or dissimilar results in an economy where labour market flexibility is more marked.

## NOTES

1.  See the Arthuis Report (1993) which was prepared by a member of the French Senate. For an opposite stance, see the Devedjian Report (1993).

2.  For a more detailed analysis of the relations between trade and factor movements, see Faini and Venturini (1993).

3.  Beyond these results of pure trade theory, economists tend to see trade as an engine of growth – a dynamic element of competition powerful enough to generate new jobs in the national economy (Edwards, 1993). However, the limited period for which data are available suggests that this argument should be put to one side in the context of this paper.

4.  The year 1976 has been chosen as the starting point because it is the first year with the French unemployment rate higher than 3 per cent (its average during the 20 previous years).

5.  At the level of disaggregation chosen (81 sectors), French national accounts allow to take into account requirements in terms of intermediate goods and services – but not in terms of capital goods.

6.  Since 1977, the decline in this ratio mirrors the increasing role of exports in French GDP.

7.  For the sake of simplicity, Table 3 does not show the number of export-supported jobs related to trade with the OPEC countries. Jobs supported by French exports to OPEC countries can be computed by subtracting the amount of export-supported jobs related to the zones shown in Table 3 from the total amount of export-supported jobs provided by Table 1.

8.  The same observation can be drawn from the results obtained in the United States by Borjas *et al.* (1991).

9.  Intra-industry trade opens the possibility of a more complex picture at a more disaggregated level of sectors than the 81 industries considered here.

10. Indeed, Krugman and Lawrence (1993) have shown that in the US case, factor price equalisation is dominated by more powerful domestic causes.

11. Indeed, such changes are observed by Borjas *et al.* in the US case: the implicit labour input in US exports is higher in efficiency units than in jobs, and the implicit labour input in US imports is lower.

*OECD Economic Studies No. 24, 1995/I*

12. Table 8 excludes agriculture (but not food industries) because wage data are not very reliable for this sector.

13. The wage differentials are smaller when services are included. That may be due to the fact that services are protected and workers in these sectors can share in the associated rents.

14. That remains true when the recent empirical literature has also added immigration in a relatively straightforward manner: the entry of more low-skilled immigrants is assumed to depress unskilled wages relatively to skilled wages. Again, however, a simple Heckscher-Ohlin model based on skilled and unskilled labour shows that this is not the case unless the terms of trade vary.

15. Again, what counts is not the absolute specificity of each factor, but the fact that some factors are assumed to be **less** mobile than others. Kraft (1994) found that German data (1965-90) show a negative correlation between skilled workers and mobility (as suggested by the human capital theory).

16. Only four service sectors may be considered as tradables (two as exportables and two as importables).

17. It should be emphasized that segment I accounts for a small share of the French work force.

18. It may suggest that these schemes are already shaping labour markets for employees aged between 45 and 55 years old (probably between 50 and 55 years old).

19. The impact of the minimum wage regulation on French employment has been thoroughly analyzed. See Rosa (1985) and Bazen and Martin (1991).

20. These figures are unweighted averages of the shares by sector provided by INSEE (1993).

21. FDI flows differ from gross domestic investment flows because they are also used to finance other purposes, in particular mergers and acquisitions.

22. These high figures (50 per cent and more) require some explanations. In manufacturing, there are only two cases (oil and non-ferrous mining) which are easy to explain: they clearly correspond to the absence of the raw materials in question in France. In the case of services, there are two plausible explanations. The ways data are recorded by the Banque de France may aggregate capital flows from some industries with capital flows of the services industry involved – in particular, for banking and insurance services. The other explanation is the huge foreign investments made by French banks and insurance companies in order to adjust to the Single Market exercise.

23. It may be argued that this result mirrors a statistical problem due to the fact that Table 10 aggregates capital and labour-intensive industries together (for instance, textiles and clothing). However, additional computations concerning the geographical FDI pattern at a higher level of disaggregation (81 industries) confirm the results of Table 10.

*Annex*

# METHODOLOGY AND SOURCES

## Standard trade propositions

The Heckscher-Ohlin-Samuelson model is based the assumption of perfect factor mobility among sectors. It predicts the following "magnification" effect of the link between factor and product prices:

$$w_s > p_s > p_u > w_u \qquad [1]$$

where $p_s$ is the price of the good intensive in skilled labour, $w_s$ the wage paid to skilled labour, $w_u$ the wage paid to unskilled labour, and $p_u$ the price of the good intensive in unskilled labour.

The specific-factor model (Jones, 1971) is based on imperfect factor mobility among sectors. It predicts the following magnification effect:

$$w_x > p_x > w_u > p_m > w_m \qquad [2]$$

where x and m refer to the exported and imported goods, and $w_x$ and $w_m$ to the skilled labour forces used in the exporting and import-competing sectors, respectively.

## Methodology: a short description

Tables 1 to 5 are based on the method suggested by Davis (1992) by computing the employment content of trade according to the following formula:

$$E = [I - (1 - m/s)A]^{-1}{}^*e \qquad [3]$$

where E is the vector of total (direct and indirect) domestic output of goods and services required to produce exports, e the direct output required, I the diagonal unit matrix, $(1 - m/s)$ the diagonal matrix comprising the domestic shares of outputs delivered to intersectoral and to final demands (m is imports and s the total supply of outputs), A the direct labour requirements coefficients matrix.

Sakurai (1993) who has done similar computations on a much more aggregate industrial classification gets results for the French economy which are very close to our results.

The methodology used in the Table 7 of the paper combines the approaches suggested by Borjas, Freeman and Katz (1991) (hereafter BFK) and by Davis. Following BFK, the implicit labour supply related to trade flows can be expressed as:

$$L_t = \text{SUM}_i \ (L_{it}/Q_{it})^*T_{it} = \text{SUM}_i \ L_{it}{}^*(T_{it}/Q_{it}) \qquad [4] \qquad \underline{\mathit{119}}$$

OECD Economic Studies No. 24, 1995/I

where $L_i$ is the number of employees (adjusted for hours worked) in the industry i, $Q_i$ the domestic output of the industry i and $T_i$ the net trade flow (imports minus exports) for this industry. All these variables are for the year t (from 1977 until 1992). When $T_{it}$ corresponds to net imports of the industry i, $L_t$ has a negative sign. When it corresponds to net exports of the industry i, $L_t$ has a positive sign.

BFK then refine their approach by introducing a broad distinction between two types of employees: "production workers" and "non-production workers." In the French case, this distinction has been interpreted as that between workers ("ouvriers") and other wage earners. As a result, the implicit supply of each type of labour related to trade flows can be expressed as:

$$L_{jt} = SUM_i \, [a_{ij} * L_{it} * (T_{it}/Q_{it})] \tag{5}$$

where $a_{ij}$ is the **average** proportion of employees of type j (j = 1, 2) by the industry during the period examined.

The second refinement introduced by BFK is the concept of "efficiency units." The number of employees $L_i$ is split into 64 efficiency units, according to three criteria: sex, skills and experience. In the French case, male and female workers in each industry i are divided in six levels of "socio-professional categories" which are the closest proxies for levels of education (managers, high-level staff, medium-level staff, low-level staff, workers, apprentices and trainees) and experience (given by five age-groups: under 26, from 26 to 35, from 36 to 45, from 46 to 55, above 56). Employees from the unit u in the industry i were weighted by the average hourly wage during the period 1984-91. As a result, the implicit supply of each type of labour efficiency unit related to trade flows can be expressed as:

$$L_{ut} = (1/U) * \, SUM_i \, [e_{iu} * U_{it} * (T_{it}/Q_{it})] \tag{6}$$

where $e_{iu}$ is the **average** proportion of employees of type u employed by the industry during the period 1984-91 and where $U_{it}$ is the total number of labour efficiency units used by the industry i.

The BFK computations are based on total output $O_i$. Following Davis (1992), this paper is based on domestic output $Q_i$ only. Before assessing the pros and cons of this methodology, it is useful to describe the statistical sources.

### Statistical sources

Data on output, trade flows and total employment by industry were taken from the French National Accounts. The NAP 90 level of the French Industrial Classification (NAP 90) was used. It is a relatively disaggregated level since it distinguishes 54 agricultural and manufacturing branches and 27 services branches (the 9 branches of "public services" have been aggregated into one branch). The breakdown of trade flows between trade with the European Community and trade with the Rest of the World is also based on the National Accounts for the period 1988-92.

For the years 1977-87, this breakdown is based on (unpublished) data processed by the Direction de la Prévision of the Ministry of the Economy.

All the detailed data on employment and wages were kindly provided by the Division Emploi of INSEE. Wages include all components (including taxable compensation) effectively paid after deduction of social charges (for social security, unemployment and retirement). As a result, they are taxable wages (except for compensations paid in kind). These wages are transformed into average wages by taking into account the corresponding number of hours worked. These data were available at the level of NAP 40 (based on 38 sectors).

Data on outward and inward capital flows between 1989 and 1993 were kindly provided by the Banque de France. These data, which follow the IMF guidelines on Balance of Payments statistics, were made available in terms of the French industrial classification (NAP).

## Some limitations of the methodology

The methodology used in this paper has attracted several criticisms (Cortes et Jean, 1994). The two most frequent criticisms are as follows: the methodology assumes homogeneous domestic and foreign goods; it is based on average and static input-output coefficients. It seems to us that none of these criticisms are decisive and, as a result, that this methodology can provide acceptable results for the French case.

The homogeneity of the goods included in each industry has two interpretations. First, sectors (even in a classification relying on 81 sectors) can be very broad, such as, for instance, the sector "machines-outils" or "matériel électrique". Second, domestically produced and imported goods pertaining to the same sector are considered as homogeneous.

The first dimension is a purely statistical problem which leads to the following question: would a more disaggregated classification provide very different results? This paper provides an indirect (though incomplete) answer to this question. In order to use the BFK methodology, it was necessary to shift from the NAP 90 classification to the NAP 40 classification. However, comparing Table 4 (based on the 81 NAP 90 sectors) to Table 7 (based on the 38 NAP 40 sectors) shows that the orders of magnitude are very close. As a result, it seems unlikely that further disaggregation would necessarily lead to very different results.

The second interpretation of homogeneity implicitly assumes that developing countries export low-quality goods and developed countries high-quality goods (as indeed implicitly assumed by Mathieu and Sterdyniak, 1994; and Direction de la Prévision, 1994). This assumed correlation between labour-intensity and low-quality versions of the good concerned on the one hand, and on the other hand between

*OECD Economic Studies No. 24, 1995/I*

capital-intensity and high-quality of the good in question is far from certain. For instance, clothing would provide many counter-examples.

The second major criticism concerns the fact that the methodology is based on **average** input-output coefficients. It is argued that imports eliminate the least efficient plants and exports rely on the most efficient plants (Driver *et al.*, 1988). As a result, marginal input-output coefficients should be used rather than average coefficients. Moreover, it is argued that the least efficient plants are labour-intensive and that the most efficient plants are capital-intensive.

This criticism could be valid in the standard Heckscher-Ohlin-Samuelson framework, with two countries, two goods and two factors of production. It is less convincing in a world where it is difficult to locate the relative endowments of a country with respect to the others. As suggested in the text, France is likely to be more labour-abundant than some OECD countries, but less labour-abundant than the other OECD countries and developing countries. In this case, it seems difficult to assume that firms will always eliminate labour-intensive plants and that exports will always be based on capital-intensive plants.

## BIBLIOGRAPHY

ARTHUIS, Jean (1993), *Rapport d'information sur les délocalisations des activités industrielles et de services hors de France*, Sénat.

BALDWIN, Robert E. (1994), The effects of trade and foreign direct investment on employment and relative wages, *OECD Economic Studies* No. 23, Winter.

BAZEN, Stephen and John P. MARTIN (1991), The impact of the minimum wage on earnings and employment in France, *OECD Economic Studies* No. 16, Spring.

BORJAS, George J., Richard B. FREEMAN and Lawrence F. KATZ (1991), On the labour market effects of immigration and trade, *NBER*, Working Paper No. 3761.

BRECHER, R. (1974), Minimum wage rates and the pure theory of international trade, *Quarterly Journal of Economics*, 88: 98-116.

CORTES, O. et S. JEAN (1994), Commerce international, emploi et salaires, *CEPII*, Document de travail 94-08, mimeo, Paris.

DAVIS, Lester A. (1992), US jobs supported by merchandise exports, *US Department of Commerce*, Economics and Statistics Administration, April.

DEVEDJIAN, Patrick (1993), *Le libre-échange, une chance pour la France* No. 774, Assemblée Nationale.

DIRECTION DE LA PRÉVISION (1994), Le contenu des emplois des échanges industriels de la France avec les pays en développement, Ministère de l'Économie, mimeo, Paris.

DRIVER, Ciaran, Andrew KILPATRICK and Barry NAISBITT (1988), The sensitivity of estimated employment effects in input-output studies, *Economic Modelling*, Vol. 5, No. 2, April, pp. 145-150.

EDWARDS, Sebastian (1993), Openness, trade liberalization and growth in developing countries, *Journal of Economic Literature*, September, XXXI: 1358-1393.

FAINI, Ricardo and A. VENTURINI (1993) Trade, aid and migrations: some basic policy issues, *European Economic Review*, 37, pp. 435-442.

INSEE (1993), Structure des emplois au 31 décembre 1991, Résultats détaillés, INSEE Résultats, *INSEE*, Paris.

JONES, Ronald W. (1971), A three-factor model in theory, trade and history, in J.N. Bhagwati *et al.*, (eds.), *Trade, Balance of Payments, and Growth*, Essays in honor of C.P. Kindleberger, North Holland, Amsterdam.

KRAFT, K. (1994), Wage differentials between skilled and unskilled workers, *Weltwirtschaftliches Archiv*, Vol. 130/2, pp. 329-349.

*OECD Economic Studies No. 24, 1995/I*

KRUGMAN, Paul and Robert Z. LAWRENCE (1993), Trade, jobs, and wages, *NBER*, Working Paper n° 4478.

KRUEGER, Anne O. (1977), *Growth, Distortions and Patterns of Trade Among Many Countries*, Princeton Studies in International Finance, Princeton University.

MATHIEU, C. and H. STERDYNIAK (1994), L'émergence de l'Asie en développement menace-t-elle l'emploi en France?, *Observations et diagnostics économiques*, No. 48, January.

ROSA, Jean-Jacques (1985), Les effets du SMIC sur l'emploi des jeunes: une analyse bien confirmée, mimeo, *FNSP*, Paris.

SAKURAI, Norihisa (1993), Structural change and employment: empirical evidence for eight OECD countries, *OECD*, October.

VIMONT, C. (1993), *Le commerce extérieur français créateur ou destructeur d'emplois?*, Institut de l'entreprise, *Economica*, Paris.

WOODLAND, A.D. (1982), *International Trade and Resource Allocation*, North Holland, Amsterdam.

# [8]

# THE IMPACT OF INTERNATIONAL TRADE AND PROTECTION ON AUSTRALIAN MANUFACTURING EMPLOYMENT*

NOEL GASTON
*Bond University*

The labour market consequences of trade and protection have only recently come under the scrutiny of labour economists. This paper seeks to accomplish two things - to survey the recent research and to provide estimates of the effect that reductions in effective rates of assistance afforded to Australia's manufacturing industries have had on employment. Recent labour market developments reveal a downward trend in manufacturing employment levels. The declines appear to have been associated with lower levels of assistance. However, the estimates of the effect of lower levels of protection are generally small - about a one per cent reduction in employment for each ten per cent reduction in the effective rate of industry assistance. In addition, the manufacturing employment developments appear to be only weakly linked to real wage resistance. Overall, an overriding impression from the findings presented in this paper is the strength of the structural adjustments ongoing in Australia.

Increased globalisation and the recent liberalisation of trading relationships are among the more significant events ever to affect national labour markets. The expected impact on labour markets has been, and continues to be, one of the more controversial features of freer trade. This paper investigates how imports, exports, and trade barriers have affected employment outcomes for Australian manufacturing industry.

Compared to countries such as the United States, Australia has long been a relatively open economy. However, since the early 1970s there has been a significant change in the trade orientation of its manufacturing industry. There was a 25 per cent across-the-board cut in tariff protection in July 1973; and in the last 25 years, the share of production exported has more than doubled, while the import share of domestic production has increased from approximately 18 per cent to over 30 per cent (Industry Commission, 1995a). The last thirty years has also witnessed the rapid growth and industrialisation of Japan and the East Asian 'Tigers'.

While it is tempting to search for clear-cut answers as to the potential benefits of liberalised trade, a theme to emerge from this study is that the impact is unlikely to be uniform across industries. Some industries will win, while others will lose. For Australia,

* The author is grateful to Sue Richardson, Peter Summers and two anonymous referees for their helpful comments. Unfortunately, responsibility for errors still rests with the author.

it seems that industries with strong links to natural resources, industries in which Australia has a comparative advantage, have increased their share of manufacturing output at the expense of industries such as passenger motor vehicles, textiles, clothing and footwear (Industry Commission, 1995a). If losers and beneficiaries can be identified this would seem to have at least two implications. First, the concentration of job losses may explain the resistance by some groups of workers (e.g. unions in certain industries) to trade liberalisation and continued microeconomic reform. In turn, this may assist in the formulation of appropriate policy responses. For example, there may be deficiencies in job retraining programs that can be addressed. Secondly, identifying categories of jobs and industries that are most affected by trade liberalising policies influences the very nature and direction of ongoing microeconomic reforms. For example, is it the high-paying, high value-added 'good jobs' or the low-paying, low value-added jobs that are most affected by trade and trade liberalisation?

## I.  EXISTING EVIDENCE ON TRADE, PROTECTION AND EMPLOYMENT

This section briefly reviews the existing literature that has taken a predominantly labour economics perspective on the effect of international trade and protection on labour markets. The primary emphasis is on recently published work on the impact of trade and protection on manufacturing workers. The labour market consequences of trade and protection have only recently come under scrutiny by labour economists. This was fuelled by the events of the 1980s which saw dramatic upheavals in North American labour markets together with an increased sensitivity of the US economy to foreign pressures. A key event of the 1980s was the 1980-85 Volker fight against inflation that led to a dollar appreciation of 35 per cent and to a trade deficit of unprecedented magnitude. The promise of the Plaza accord in 1985 to bring down the dollar took over three years to fulfil, a period of time during which the deficit actually increased.

Another important development during the 1980s was the significantly slower growth in average real wages in a number of industrialised countries. In addition, the wedge between skilled and unskilled wages widened. This increased wage dispersion, which has been associated with increased income inequality, was particularly evident in the United States and the United Kingdom, but was quite evident in other OECD countries as well, including Australia.[1] Given the coincidence of developments such as these, it is not surprising that labour economists identified international factors as crucial for explaining these trends. For example, some commentators have linked recent labour market developments to increasing import penetration and trade with labour-abundant developing countries (e.g. Murphy and Welch, 1992 and Wood, 1994). The labour economics literature spawned by these events is selectively and briefly reviewed in the remainder of this section, for it sets the stage for the evidence presented from Australia in the following sections.

---

[1] For example, average real wages fell slightly in the United States during the 1980s, but this disguised marked trends in real wages among disaggregated groups of workers: younger workers lost ground to older workers; less-skilled/less-educated workers lost ground to skilled/educated workers; and the male-female wage gap narrowed (Bound and Johnson, 1992; Borjas *et al.*, 1992), See Davis (1992) and OECD (1993) for international comparisons. Borland (1992) provides findings for Australia.

a) *Trade flows and employment*

There is a long history of research into the effects of trade flows on employment.[2] Recent regression-based studies that have come out of the labour literature clearly indicate that trade flows have a large impact on employment.[3] Setting aside differences in research design, the main conclusions are: (i) exports have a large and positive impact on employment, (ii) imports have a large and negative impact on employment, (iii) higher values of unit-value import price indexes lead to higher employment, and (iv) trade flows and import prices have a more pronounced impact on employment than on wages.

Employment responses to trade are consistently found to be larger than wage responses to trade. This feature is clearest in studies that estimate both wage and employment equations, e.g. Grossman (1987), Abowd and Lemieux (1991), Freeman and Katz (1991), and Revenga (1992). Thus, changes in employment tend to be the dominant adjustment factor in the labour market. This picture is altered when attention is confined to union workers. Gaston and Trefler (1995) show that in response to changing tariffs and imports, union workers make much greater wage adjustments than their non-union counterparts. In a competitive labour market, the dominant adjustment factor must be employment: workers respond to lower wages by switching industries. However, unions are in a position to accept lower wages in return for employment guarantees. Increased product market competition translates into increased labour market competition and eroding union-non-union wage differentials.

It is well-known that export-oriented industries pay higher average wages than do import-competing industries in the United States (e.g. Dickens and Lang, 1988 and Katz and Summers, 1989). This means that increased trade flows have been associated with increased employment in high-wage manufacturing industries and decreased employment in low-wage manufacturing industries. Thus, Dickens and Lang (1988, p.78) noted that 'it appears that trade is eliminating low-wage jobs and creating relatively high-wage jobs'. In contrast, by comparing within-industry and inter-industry employment effects, Berman *et al.* (1994) concluded that trade has not had a significant impact on labour-intensive manufacturing industries.

Since the early to mid-1980s, there has been concern over 'deindustrialisation' in many industrialised countries. The concern is that the continuing shift out of manufacturing and into the service sector is linked to increased import competition and that cheap foreign labour is stealing domestic manufacturing jobs (e.g. Revenga, 1992 and Wood, 1994). Abowd and Freeman (1991) argued that the decline in manufacturing employment means that fewer workers are now exposed to international competition than was previously the case. Nevertheless, deindustrialisation remains controversial. Manufacturing industry, in particular, has clearly had to adjust to the rapid onset of changes in technology. Technological progress has been identified as the leading candidate for explaining the structural

---

[2] More extensive literature surveys are provided by Gunderson (1992) and Gaston and Trefler (1994a).
[3] Another relevant genre of research should be mentioned here, namely computable general equilibrium and macro models. Until recently, one problem with these models has been the use of highly-aggregated labour market data and their treatment of the labour market. However, labour market features such as the mobility of labour across occupations or industries and the significant differences in union and non-union wage and employment determination are likely to be crucial for estimating the labour market response to trade liberalisation.

122                          AUSTRALIAN ECONOMIC PAPERS                          JUNE

shift from manufacturing to services and the increasing income inequality (for males, in particular) described above. Unfortunately, the difficulties with the policy implications of deindustrialisation are analogous to the difficulties of the policy implications of inter-industry wage differentials (see Krueger and Summers, 1988; Gaston and Trefler, 1994b). In the latter case, it is contentious whether high wages are a feature of the industry, as predicted by efficiency wage models, for instance, or whether high wages are due to unobserved worker sorting that attracts high-productivity workers to high-wage industries. If high wages are an industry characteristic then deindustrialisation may be a real concern: losing jobs in high-wage industries amounts to lowering average wages. On the other hand, if high wages reflect the high unobserved quality of workers employed in these industries, then deindustrialisation is less worrisome. As high-quality workers are forced to switch to new industries, they will raise both productivity and wages in their destination industries.

### b) *Trade protection and employment*

The employment effects of tariff cuts have generally escaped the attention of labour economists. A recent exception is Gaston and Trefler (1997) who estimated the Canadian employment response to the tariff cuts mandated by the Canada-US Free Trade Agreement (FTA). Canada suffered a staggering 19 per cent employment loss in its non-agricultural tradeables sector following the implementation of the FTA in 1988. Gaston and Trefler (1997) attempted to identify those jobs lost to the tariff cuts and those lost to other non-FTA factors: the recession, the Bank of Canada fight against inflation that led to high interest rates and a strong Canadian dollar, deindustrialisation, and deteriorating labour costs and productivity in Canada relative to the United States. Free trade was expected to create trade by promoting specialisation: tradeables-sector industries with a comparative advantage would expand employment, tradeables-sector industries with a comparative disadvantage would contract employment. This did not occur. Employment contracted in every tradeables-sector industry after 1988. Both exports and imports contracted for most of this period. The primary explanation for these events is the recession on both sides of the border.

In addition, Gaston and Trefler (1997) found that the tariff cuts were not the primary factor responsible for the Canadian recession. If the tariff cuts were recessionary, then one would expect the mechanism to be via increased import competition, yet real imports declined. Second, the recession was preceded by an unusually long period of expansion, suggesting that a recession was due. Third, Canadian and US recessions typically move together, suggesting that a Canadian recession was due at about the same time as the US recession. Of course, neither of the latter two points explain why the recession came right on the heels of the FTA implementation. What does explain the timing and depth of the recession is the fight against inflation that raised interest rates and strengthened the Canadian dollar. These non-FTA factors were most important.

However, Gaston and Trefler (1997) did find that mandated tariff cuts accounted for nine to fourteen per cent of the lost jobs. The FTA left real earnings unchanged, but had reduced employment by about 55,000 jobs. Particularly striking was the fact that unlike US earnings, Canadian earnings did not decline in the wake of massive job losses. Finally, they pointed to the fact that the impact of tariff cuts had not been uniform across industries: some industries were hurt by the tariff cuts while others were hurt by non-FTA factors such as high interest rates and the strong dollar.

## II. TRADE, PROTECTION AND EMPLOYMENT IN AUSTRALIAN MANUFACTURING INDUSTRY

The first goal of this section is to document the major trends in employment and average industry wages in the Australian manufacturing industry. The second goal is to relate these trends to the broad features of the economic environment that include: falling tariffs, changing levels of imports and exports, the business cycle, the changing value of the $A, and interest rate movements. The aim is to isolate the impact of trade and protection on employment. As we shall see below, there have been significant manufacturing industry employment losses since the early 1970s. The more recent employment losses have provided ammunition for the opponents of the movement towards more liberalised trade and ongoing microeconomic and labour market reform.

The employment elasticity estimates presented below are the first using actual trade and protection data for Australia. Together with some of the features of the complex relationship between labour market outcomes and trade barriers that were identified above, the goal is an increased understanding of potential employment consequences of globalisation for Australia.

### a) *Data preview*

The data for twelve two-digit ASIC manufacturing industries are yearly for the period 1973-74 to 1991-92. In July 1973 there was an across-the-board 25 per cent cut in tariff protection. The choice of 1973-74 as the base year for the following analysis is significant because manufacturing employment has never since achieved similar levels. Table I records the relevant features and performance of the twelve manufacturing industries over the sample period. The reported numbers are yearly percentage changes. For example, the clothing and footwear industry experienced an average yearly employment loss of 4.42 per cent over the entire sample period. A program of general tariff reductions was announced in the May 1988 Economic Statement. Table I also records (in italics) the averages over the four years from 1988-89 to 1991-92, for example, the clothing and footwear industry experienced a steeper 9.58 per cent per year decline.

One of the more striking features of Table I is the uniform employment losses in all twelve manufacturing industries. Underlying structural change is leading to the steady decline of employment in manufacturing industry. There is a well-known shift of employment from manufacturing to services, as indicated by the rise in services industry employment.[4] It should also be noted that, in percentage terms, employment losses accelerated in the last four years of the sample period.

While Table I does provide evidence of contraction of manufacturing industries, the

---

[4] From August 1983 to August 1992, total employment in all Australia industries rose from 6.24 million to 7.62 million workers or 22.1 per cent. Over this same time period manufacturing employment fell by 3.4 per cent and employment in services (fire, property and business services plus community services plus recreation, personal and other services) rose by an astonishing 47 per cent. Over the more recent and shorter time span from August 1988 to August 1992, total employment rose 3.6 per cent, manufacturing employment fell 9.1 per cent, and services employment rose 13.6 per cent. Calculations are based on data taken from The Labour Force, Australia (6203.0), ABS.

Globalization and Labour Markets II

Table I   Manufacturing industry employment and earnings growth, 1973–74 to 1991–92

| ASIC | Industry | $\Delta L_j$ | $\%\Delta L_j$ | | $\%\Delta w_j$ | | $\%\Delta X_j$ | | $\%\Delta M_j$ | | $\Delta t_j$ | | $\Delta ERA_j$ | |
|---|---|---|---|---|---|---|---|---|---|---|---|---|---|---|
| | | | 73–92 | 88–92 | 73–92 | 88–92 | 73–92 | 88–92 | 73–92 | 88–92 | 73–92 | 88–92 | 73–92 | 88–92 |
| 24 | C&F | -60,339 | -4.42 | -9.58 | 2.20 | 3.08 | 4.76 | 19.42 | 6.36 | 3.71 | 0.23 | 0.93 | 4.59 | -20.50 |
| 23 | Textiles | -28,345 | -4.08 | -7.24 | 2.30 | 1.72 | 7.00 | 4.89 | 2.07 | -4.00 | -0.18 | 0.45 | 0.47 | -4.75 |
| 32 | Transport | -77,127 | -3.07 | -7.20 | 1.51 | 2.40 | 3.79 | 8.10 | 7.61 | -9.06 | 0.16 | -1.00 | 0.06 | -3.75 |
| 33 | Machinery | -84,224 | -2.69 | -4.05 | 1.55 | 1.85 | 4.84 | 9.94 | 6.37 | -0.07 | -0.42 | -0.93 | -1.35 | -1.75 |
| 29 | Metal | -33,146 | -1.95 | -4.47 | 2.15 | 3.07 | 6.91 | 3.64 | 8.61 | 11.79 | -0.39 | -1.08 | -1.12 | 0.00 |
| 28 | Nonmetal | -17,546 | -1.90 | -1.72 | 1.44 | 1.29 | 8.42 | 17.26 | 3.63 | -1.31 | -0.64 | -1.05 | -0.65 | -0.25 |
| 34 | Miscellaneous | -19,532 | -1.89 | -2.88 | 2.05 | 1.05 | 4.75 | 9.41 | 6.03 | 0.45 | -0.65 | -1.10 | -0.88 | -2.00 |
| 31 | Fab Metal | -32,189 | -1.85 | -4.12 | 1.12 | 1.06 | 7.24 | 32.06 | 5.97 | 3.07 | -0.74 | -1.18 | -2.35 | -1.50 |
| 27 | Chemical | -17,411 | -1.36 | -1.79 | 2.03 | 1.78 | 16.10 | 7.20 | 5.81 | 1.24 | -0.35 | -0.58 | -1.47 | -1.25 |
| 21 | F, B&T | -39,514 | -1.25 | -1.38 | 1.44 | 0.38 | -1.73 | -0.03 | 6.52 | 2.16 | -1.05 | -0.80 | -0.88 | -0.75 |
| 25 | Wood | -13,752 | -0.86 | -3.04 | 1.35 | 0.86 | 5.22 | -0.34 | 6.64 | 0.11 | -0.46 | -1.00 | -0.71 | -1.50 |
| 26 | Paper | -9,599 | -0.57 | -2.14 | 1.87 | 1.38 | 5.93 | 9.80 | 4.04 | -1.91 | -0.12 | -0.58 | -2.59 | -2.00 |
| | Manufacturing | -432,724 | -2.08 | -3.87 | 1.70 | 1.64 | 3.11 | 3.98 | 5.58 | 1.91 | -0.31 | -0.72 | -1.12 | -1.50 |

Notes: $j$ indexes industries, $L_j$ is employment, $w_j$ is real earnings, $X_j$ is exports, $M_j$ is imports, $t_j$ is the average tariff rate and $ERA_j$ is the effective rate of assistance. $\Delta L_j$ is the 1991–92 employment level less the 1973–74 employment level. Figures for $\%\Delta L_j$, $\%\Delta w_j$, $\%\Delta X_j$ and $\%\Delta M_j$ are the average of year-to-year percentage changes. For $\Delta t$ and $\Delta ERA$ the figures are the average of year-to-year changes. Figures in columns labelled '73–92' are averages for 1973–74 to 1991–92 and figures in columns labelled '88–92' are averages for 1988–89 to 1991–92. Abbreviations: C&F is clothing and footwear; F, B&T is food, beverages and tobacco.

impression that these losses are attributable to cuts in trade protection is ostensibly mistaken. Over the entire period, the columns containing the protection data reveal no obvious relationship between the cuts in either tariffs or effective rates of assistance and changes in industry employment levels. If anything, there appears to be some evidence that industries that have experienced the largest long term declines in their employment levels have had their levels of protection maintained or even increased. This provides a preliminary indication of 'endogenous protection'. In Australia, it has been the case that 'distressed' industries can apply for temporary assistance. Much of this temporary assistance has taken the form of quantitative import restrictions. For example, the effect of the 1977 Multilateral Trade Negotiations tariff cuts on the textiles, clothing and footwear industry and the passenger motor vehicle industry were largely offset by increases in quotas between the mid-70s and mid-80s (see Industry Commission, 1995b, pp. 32-34). On the other hand, focusing on the later 1988-92 period, reveals that the industries with the largest job losses tend to have experienced the steepest cuts in their effective rates of assistance.

For real earnings, no clear picture of the effects of either trade or trade protection emerges from Table I. It is apparent that real earnings growth has been remarkably resilient over the entire sample period, particularly given the unabated employment decline in each manufacturing industry. This occurred even though Australian manufacturing industry was trimming its labour costs. (This is seen by adding the two columns labelled %$\Delta L$ and %$\Delta w$ of Table I, to get the percentage fall in the average wage bill or average labour costs.) While it is tempting to conclude that the continued decline of manufacturing industry employment and real wage resistance are importantly interrelated (see Phipps and Sheen, 1995), it should be borne in mind that the change in real earnings figures reported here also reflect increases in real labour productivity.

The data in Table I do not reveal any obvious relationship between either changes in real earnings or employment levels and changes in import or export levels. From Australia's vantage point, with few exceptions neither imports nor exports have surged across the board since 1988. In fact, in all but two industries, average annual import growth was actually lower in the later period, compared to the full sample period. Export growth fell in four industries. These features are probably best explained by the 1989-91 recession.

b) *Methodology*

As is evident from Section I, the increasing importance of international competition has lead to a wealth of new research on the effects of imports and exports on labour market outcomes. Recent and widely-cited regression-based studies dealing with the dynamic effects of trade flows on industry employment include Grossman (1987), Abowd and Lemieux (1991), Freeman and Katz (1991), and Revenga (1992). Apart from Gaston and Trefler (1994a, 1997), however, there have been no regression-based studies of the employment response to changes in industry assistance or trade policy. Similarly, to my knowledge, there have been no regression-based studies of the employment response to changes in trade policy and trade flows performed for Australia.

Whether motivated by market-clearing models of the labour market or models of union-firm bargaining, each of the aforementioned studies consider reduced-form employment equations taking the following general form

$$\Delta \ln L_{jt} = a_0 + a_1 \Delta X_t + a_2 \Delta Z_{jt} + a_3 \Delta T_{jt} + v_{jt} \qquad (1)$$

where $L_{jt}$ is industry employment; $\Delta$ is the first-difference operator (e.g. $\Delta Y_{jt} = Y_{jt} - Y_{jt-1}$); $X_t$ is a vector of time-varying regressors common to all industries; $Z_{jt}$ is a vector of time-varying industry regressors. First-differencing eliminates time-invariant industry effects. The random disturbance $v_{jt}$ is assumed iid normal. $T_{jt}$ is the vector containing the variables of interest such as trade flows.

For this study, data limitations necessitate the exclusion of the usual supply and demand regressors such as the price of non-labour inputs. Gunderson (1992) argues that this is reasonable because the mobility of non-labour factors of production will equalise factor prices across industries. Largely motivated by the desire for comparability across studies, I follow Gaston and Trefler (1997), by specifying $X_t =$ (interest rate, exchange rate). The exchange rate is included to capture external economic conditions. In addition, a weaker \$A may have buffered growing employment problems. Adverse interest rate movements may affect firms embarking on major capital expenditures and thus affect employment prospects. In the next section, I also consider other 'macro' variables. Second, I include average real earnings to capture the effects of changing real labour costs on employment developments, i.e. $Z_{jt} =$ (lagged average real wage). Finally, $T_{jt} =$ (tariffs, imports, exports, and domestic consumption). The reasons for including both tariffs *and* trade flows in $T_{jt}$ are provided by Gaston and Trefler (1994b, 1995).[5] While unambiguous and comprehensive policy measures of the government's stance towards freer trade probably don't exist, I use the average tariff rate and the effective rate of assistance as alternative measures of industry protection. Most of the data were taken from a recently published Industry Commission (1995a) information paper. The data for the macro variables are from EconData's *DX* database. The CPI was used to deflate all nominal values; industry price deflators may have been preferable, but were not available for all the years of my sample. The descriptive statistics for the pooled sample of twelve industries are described in Appendix Table A.I and the data correlations are reported in Appendix Table AII.

I follow Freeman and Katz (1991) and Abowd and Lemieux (1991) in their treatment of the adjustment of earnings and employment to domestic and international demand shocks. They decompose industry output into weighted components of imports, exports, and domestic consumption. The definition of domestic consumption is $DOM \equiv S + M - X$ where $S$ is the industry value of shipments, $X$ is exports and $M$ is imports. This can be written in first differences as $\Delta S \equiv \Delta DOM + \Delta X - \Delta M$. Dividing by $S$ and converting variables to natural logs yields: $\Delta s = (DOM/S)\Delta dom + (X/S)\Delta x - (M/S)\Delta m$ (where lower-case variables are logs). Hence, changes in domestic consumption, imports and exports are scaled by their contributions to total industry shipments.

Estimation of equation (1) raises a variety of specification issues. First, the coefficients are assumed to be stable over time. To examine this assumption the sample is split at 1988-89. As mentioned, a program of general tariff reductions was announced in the May 1988

---

[5] With perfectly competitive product markets, the best-known channel through which trade barriers affect the labour market is that lower protection stimulates imports, which in turn decreases the demand for domestic labour. With imperfectly competitive product markets, trade and protection can affect the strategic interaction between firms, thus affecting firm performance and hence employment levels. This channel is especially interesting for it provides reasons why protection may affect earnings and employment independently of any effect that protection may have on trade flows. Overall, lower protection is likely to have an effect that is far more complicated than that captured by an export- or import-induced shift in product demand.

Economic Statement. Second, the data are pooled across 12 two-digit ASIC industries. That is, we assume that $\alpha_j = \alpha$ for $j = 1, 2, 3$. To investigate the legitimacy of pooling, the sample is stratified by certain industry characteristics. In particular, we investigate high tariff industries and high import industries. Third, the assumed lag structure is one year. While longer lags may be desirable, parsimony precludes them. Fourth, many of the above regressors are potentially endogenous. The endogeneity of average earnings is particularly obvious and hence is introduced in its lagged form. Less obvious is the political economy bias associated with endogenous protection. From Section I, we suspect that policy-makers react to employment conditions when setting levels of protection, so that contemporaneous measures of trade protection are endogenous in the employment equation.

c) *Regression analysis*

Estimates of the employment equation are reported in Table II. Recall that the regressions relate changes in log employment to changes in a variety of macroeconomic and industry-specific variables. Across all specifications, the adjusted-$R^2$ is excellent. A basic specification is reported in column (1). With the exception of the coefficient on the effective rate of assistance (ERA), all significant coefficient signs are as expected, consistent with the

**Table II**  Regression results for manufacturing employment changes, 1973–74 to 1991–92

|  | (1) $ERA_t$ | (2) $ERA_{t-1}$ | (3) $Tariff_{t-1}$ | (4) High Tariff | (5) High import | (6) High export | (7) 1988–92 |
|---|---|---|---|---|---|---|---|
| ERA/Tariff | −0.021 | 0.095 | 0.201 | 0.093 | 0.100 | −0.028 | 0.250 |
|  | (0.831) | (3.892) | (2.012) | (3.009) | (1.424) | (0.296) | (4.409) |
| Imports | −0.445 | −0.420 | −0.434 | −0.424 | −0.376 | −0.388 | −0.388 |
|  | (6.606) | (6.482) | (6.518) | (3.360) | (3.984) | (2.928) | (2.457) |
| Exports | 0.170 | 0.183 | 0.161 | 0.235 | 0.231 | 0.178 | 0.089 |
|  | (1.792) | (1.996) | (1.707) | (1.424) | (1.864) | (1.832) | (0.489) |
| Domestic consumption | 0.527 | 0.508 | 0.516 | 0.526 | 0.481 | 0.480 | 0.433 |
|  | (13.656) | (13.622) | (13.487) | (7.221) | (8.094) | (7.491) | (4.550) |
| Real wage | −0.097 | −0.101 | −0.101 | −0.151 | −0.200 | −0.093 | −0.169 |
|  | (1.405) | (1.538) | (1.482) | (1.335) | (1.658) | (0.806) | (0.966) |
| Interest rate | −0.054 | −0.077 | −0.077 | −0.100 | −0.353 | −0.153 | −0.160 |
|  | (0.555) | (0.841) | (0.820) | (0.555) | (2.236) | (0.980) | (0.415) |
| Exchange rate | 0.023 | 0.048 | 0.026 | 0.013 | 0.084 | −0.037 | −0.060 |
|  | (0.760) | (1.627) | (0.876) | (0.225) | (1.696) | (0.745) | (0.455) |
| Intercept | −0.021 | −0.020 | −0.020 | −0.029 | −0.018 | −0.025 | −0.020 |
|  | (6.911) | (6.797) | (6.682) | (4.978) | (3.140) | (4.622) | (2.758) |
| Observations | 192 | 192 | 192 | 64 | 64 | 64 | 48 |
| Adjusted $R^2$ | 0.634 | 0.664 | 0.644 | 0.701 | 0.711 | 0.611 | 0.615 |
| F | 49.048 | 54.944 | 50.417 | 22.135 | 23.084 | 15.147 | 11.713 |

*Notes*: Absolute value of *t*-statistics in parentheses; The dependent variable is the first difference of log employment; The interest rate and the first differences of tariffs and ERA are in percentage points. The exchange rate and real wage are first differences of logs. The real wage is lagged. Domestic consumption, imports and exports are first differences of logs and are weighted as described in the text; High tariff, high import and high export industries are described in text.

literature surveyed in the previous section. Domestic consumption and exports are positively related to employment growth and import penetration has a large and significant negative impact on employment.

The measure of protection in column (1) is contemporaneous. However, due to suspected political economy bias, replacing this with its lagged value (i.e. $ERA_{t-1}$) yields a statistically significant positive coefficient. That is, lower levels of industry protection have had a negative effect on employment levels. However, the effect is not large economically. For example, the point estimate for ERA in column (2) implies that a ten percentage point reduction in the effective rate of industry assistance is associated with a less than one per cent reduction in employment. The standardised beta coefficient on ERA is 0.17 - indicating that a one standard deviation reduction in protection lowers log employment by approximately 0.17 standard deviations. In column (3), the tariff rate is used in place of the ERA. The impact of this measure of protection on employment growth is still positive and significant.

Manufacturing employment is strongly procyclical. The standardised beta coefficient on domestic consumption is 1.07. However, import competition has had a surprisingly large adverse influence (standardised beta $= -0.47$) and exports have had a surprisingly small positive effect on employment (standardised beta $= 0.09$). These features may indicate that the effects of import competition within Australia's manufacturing industry have increased in low labour productivity (probably labour intensive) goods while export effects have been concentrated in relatively high productivity (low labour intensity) goods.[6] Fluctuations in the exchange rate and the real interest rate do not appear to have had significant effects on employment. Finally, there is evidence of the expected negative relationship between wages and employment levels. While this suggests that real wage resistance may have contributed somewhat to declining manufacturing industry employment - the evidence for this possibility is far from overwhelming (*cf.* Phipps and Sheen, 1995).

To investigate the legitimacy of pooling across industries, three additional specifications are reported - those for high ERA industries, high import industries and high export industries. The high ERA industries are the four industries that had the highest ERAs in 1987-88. In all cases, these industries had ERAs greater than 25 per cent.[7] From an endogenous political economy perspective, high protection industries have characteristics that may make employment respond more adversely to imports and trade liberalisation. However, confining our attention to high ERA industries, note that industry assistance has had similar effects in promoting and discouraging employment.

The sample is also stratified according to high imports and high exports. The same argument is true for high import and high export industries as for high ERA industries - they may be more susceptible to trade pressures than less trade-exposed industries. The four industries with the highest import-sales and four highest export-sales ratios were chosen.[8]

---

[6] I am grateful to one of the journal's referees for this observation.

[7] The high protection ASIC industries are: 23 (textiles), 24 (clothing and footwear), 32 (transport), and 34 (miscellaneous).

[8] The high import ASIC industries are: 23 (textiles), 27 (chemicals), 32 (transport), and 33 (machinery), They all had import-sales ratios of at least 40 per cent in 1987-88. The high export ASIC industries are: 21 (food, beverages, and tobacco), 23 (textiles), 27 (chemicals), and 29 (metal), They all had export-sales ratios of at least 14 per cent in 1987-88. (Industries appearing in both lists have high levels of intra-industry trade.)

As for the high import industries - there are no sign changes (*cf.* column (2)). The only difference seems to be the increased sensitivity to the real interest rate and exchange rate. Gaston and Trefler (1997) report similar findings for high import Canadian industries. The notable features for the high export industries are the loss of significance for the ERA and the sign swap on real wages (albeit insignificant). The latter feature may possibly indicate some degree of rent-sharing occurring in high-wage export industries.

Overall, what does seem clear from Table II is that the estimated effects of trade barriers and trade flows across different subsamples are extremely similar to the estimates obtained by pooling the data across all industries.[9] The same is not true for the assumption about pooling the sample across time. Specification instability over time can be investigated by separately estimating models for the period 1973-74 to 1987-88 and the period 1988-89 to 1991-92. This allows slopes, intercepts, and regression standard errors to differ. The results appear in the last column (7) of Table II. The null of equal slopes in the two periods is easily rejected (*F*-statistic = 16.92). Column (7) reveals an increased sensitivity of employment to changes in the ERA since the announcement of the program of general tariff reductions announced in the May 1988 Economic Statement. In addition, the effect is economically larger - in the more recent period, each one percentage point reduction in the ERA has been associated with a 0.25 per cent reduction in manufacturing employment.

## III.  SENSITIVITY ANALYSIS

So far the regression specification has been treated with far greater confidence than is warranted given that the model, like any other, is unlikely to satisfy the many assumptions upon which the desirable properties of OLS rest. In this section I address these specification issues. In so doing I distinguish between robust and fragile results and highlight the features of the data that drive the conclusions.

### a) *Choice of regressors*

Since there is no well-defined supply-demand model underlying the reduced form employment equation, a strong case can be made for omitting some regressors and adding others. Given the relatively short duration of the data set and the desire for comparability with other studies, I opted for a parsimonious set of macro variables (ones that vary over time, but not across industries). I chose the interest rate and the exchange rate because adverse movements in these variables are common explanations for the employment losses (e.g. Phipps and Sheen, 1995). However, the omission of other determinants of employment could bias our estimates. Hence, I also considered the following regressors: the ratio of the federal government budget deficit to GDP, the ratio of immigrants to employees, and a dummy for Liberal vs Labor in political office. (Data for the first two variables are from EconData's *DX* database.) The results appear in Table III. Line 1

---

[9] More formally, the assumption of common slope and intercept coefficients across industries was tested by estimating industry fixed effects and random coefficient models (see Hsiao, 1986), *F*-tests indicated that the null of equal industry slopes ($F(11, 173) = 0.84$) and common intercept ($F(11, 173) = 1.50$) was unable to be rejected at the five per cent significance level.

**Table III** Sensitivity analysis

| | $ERA_{t-1}$ | Imports | Exports | Domestic Consumption | Real Wage | Interest Rate | Exchange Rate | Adj. $R^2$ |
|---|---|---|---|---|---|---|---|---|
| 1. Full model | 0.095** | −0.420** | 0.183* | 0.508** | −0.102 | −0.001 | 0.048 | 0.664 |
| **Choice of Regressors** | | | | | | | | |
| 2. 5 macro variables[a] | 0.073** | −0.358** | 0.183* | 0.443** | −0.021 | −0.001 | 0.032 | 0.693 |
| 3. No protection variable | | −0.440** | 0.168 | 0.524** | −0.101 | −0.001 | 0.028 | 0.638 |
| 4. No macro variables | 0.087** | −0.429** | 0.188* | 0.518** | −0.082 | | | 0.661 |
| 5. No trade variables | 0.106** | | | 0.313** | −0.126 | 0.0003 | 0.084** | 0.587 |
| 6. Unweighted demand | 0.104** | −0.049 | 0.025 | 0.465** | −0.097* | 0.0001 | 0.063 | 0.584 |
| 7. Sales[b] | 0.102** | | | 0.509** | −0.081 | 0.0001 | 0.065* | 0.631 |
| **Influential observations** | | | | | | | | |
| 8. Omit Clothing & Foot. | 0.111* | −0.381** | 0.157 | 0.479** | −0.099 | −0.001 | 0.056* | 0.675 |
| 9. Omit Transport | 0.087** | −0.466** | 0.205 | 0.520** | −0.105 | −0.001 | 0.032 | 0.657 |
| **Measurement error** | | | | | | | | |
| 10. Omit 1982–83 | 0.147** | −0.392** | 0.120 | 0.484** | −0.127* | −0.001 | 0.049 | 0.633 |
| 11. Omit 1990–91 | 0.041 | −0.417** | 0.156 | 0.496** | −0.150** | −0.001 | 0.051 | 0.669 |

*Notes: a.* Regression also included Government Deficit-GDP ratio, Immigrant-Employees Ratio and a dummy for whether Labor or Liberal was in government. *b.* Coefficient estimate reported in the Domestic Consumption column is for Sales. ** (*) Statistically significant at the 1 (5) per cent level. All regressions contained an intercept.

reports the model presented in Section II (transcribed from column (2) of Table II). To save space, as the regressor set is varied, I only report the coefficients on the regressors from the basic specification (i.e. line 1). Line 2 reports the result of including all five macro regressors in the regression. This leads to a slight decrease in the effects of cuts in protection on employment. Once again, a ten per cent cut in the ERA is associated with less than a one per cent reduction in employment. Of most importance, the coefficients on the non-macro variables (ones that vary across industries and time) do not switch signs when the macro regressor set is expanded.

I now turn to the non-macro regressors. The estimation in the previous section also raises the issue of collinearity between many of the regressors. Appendix Table A.II reports the data correlations. Out of concern about the degree of collinearity between the ERA and demand conditions, line 3 reports the effects of omitting any measure of industry assistance. Line 4 explores the effects of omitting the interest rate and exchange rate regressors. Line 5 omits imports and exports on the grounds that the primary impact of tariffs is via trade. Line 6 examines whether the weighting scheme used for imports, exports and domestic consumption matters by using unweighted imports, exports and domestic consumption. Line 7 investigates the effects of restricting imports, exports and domestic consumption to have identical slopes. This might be expected if all that mattered were the level of demand and not the source of demand. The $F$-statistic for the restriction of equality of these three coefficients is 10.26, which does not support the null of equal magnitudes. Overall, there are no statistically significant sign swaps for any of the included regressors. In addition, varying the choice of regressors does not appear to affect the conclusion that each one percentage point reduction in the industry assistance has been associated with an approximately 0.1 per cent reduction in manufacturing employment.

b) *Influential observations*

Pooling data across industries is not ideal because it imposes homogeneity of technology and demand structures across industries. Indeed, in connection with Table II we discussed the heterogeneity in the performance of, for example, export-oriented versus high import industries. Another approach to parameter stability investigates whether industries are influential in the sense of Belsley *et al.* (1980). Consider what happens to coefficient estimates when all the observations corresponding to, say, the clothing and footwear industry are omitted. As reported in line 8 of Table III the ERA coefficient rises from 0.095 to 0.111. That is, reductions in industry assistance have greater prominence. More generally, 12 regression models were estimated, each corresponding to the omission of one of the twelve industries in the sample. It was found that the coefficients on the ERA, imports and domestic consumption were insensitive to the omission of observations, and the coefficients on exports, the interest rate and exchange rate were somewhat sensitive. The ERA coefficient attains its largest magnitude when the clothing and footwear industry is omitted. At the other extreme, the ERA coefficient attains its smallest magnitude when the transport industry is omitted (see line 9 of Table III). This suggests that the transport industry has been relatively harder hit by reductions in industry assistance. While there is some variation across industries in the impact of reductions in protection, the variation is much less than that reported by Gaston and Trefler (1997) for Canada's manufacturing industries.

c) *Measurement error*

As in any study, there is good reason to be concerned about data quality. By their very nature, trade protection data are always suspect. For example, aggregating the tariffs of industries with different demand elasticities is dubious: a five per cent tariff on price-sensitive cheap radios is much more restrictive than a 20 per cent tariff on inelastically-demanded high-end consumer electronics. More specifically, there are a number of concerns specific to the data used for this paper. For example, in 1974-75, 1978-79 and 1982-83 new series of effective rates of assistance were introduced. Additionally, there are a number of other potential sources of series breaks in the key data (see Appendix B, Industry Commission, 1995a). In order to investigate the effects of changing definitions, the use of different trade and industry concordances, and so on, 18 regression models were estimated, each corresponding to the omission of one of the years of data in the sample. In line 10 of Table III, the results for the regression that yielded the largest coefficient on the ERA are reported and in line 11 the results for the regression that yielded the smallest coefficient on the ERA are reported. The results indicate that the largest impact of declining industry assistance was felt in 1990-91, during the most recent recession. This is in line with the findings discussed in connection with splitting the sample into pre- and post-1988 periods, at the end of the last section.

IV. CONCLUSION

The labour market consequences of trade and protection have only recently come under the scrutiny of labour economists. This paper has sought to accomplish two things - to survey this recent research and to provide estimates of the effect that reductions in the effective rates of assistance afforded to manufacturing industries have had on employment. This paper adopted what may be termed a labour market approach to this question. In particular, attention has been confined to how trade flows and trade protection have affected labour market outcomes.

Recent labour market developments in Australia revealed a continuing downward trend in manufacturing employment levels. These developments were relatively uniform across all manufacturing industries. This undoubtedly is a matter for concern, for manufacturing industry has long provided high-wage employment opportunities and 'good jobs' for less-skilled workers. The government seems to have recognised this fact by pursuing a relatively reactive policy of industry assistance. Unfortunately, this latter feature also made the isolation of the effect of tariff phasing and decreased industry assistance particularly difficult.

The more recent manufacturing employment declines do seem to have been associated with lower levels of assistance. While the estimates are generally small (i.e. a less than one per cent reduction in employment for each ten per cent reduction in the effective rate of industry assistance), the effect has approximately doubled in the time period since the program of general tariff reductions was announced in the May 1988 Economic Statement. In addition, Australian real earnings have been extremely resilient in view of the most recent recession and trade liberalisation. However, the adverse employment developments appear to be only weakly linked to this real wage resistance. This is an significant observation for any proposed explanation of the continuing manufacturing job losses in Australia, for not only does it suggest the importance of other, perhaps more fundamental, factors at work in the economy, but it also underscores the necessity of further research into Australia's rapidly changing labour market. Overall, the overriding impression from the findings presented in this paper has been the underlying strength of the structural adjustments ongoing in Australia.

## APPENDIX

**Table AI** Descriptive statistics: annual percentage changes, 1973–74 to 1991–92

| Variable | Mean | Standard deviation | Minimum | Maximum |
|---|---|---|---|---|
| Employment | −2.159 | 4.906 | −20.904 | 7.954 |
| Real earnings | 1.751 | 3.497 | −5.203 | 15.464 |
| Exports | 6.105 | 19.351 | −32.984 | 117.158 |
| Imports | 5.804 | 15.364 | −42.895 | 65.225 |
| Tariffs | −0.384 | 2.176 | −12.500 | 10.900 |
| ERA | −0.574 | 8.852 | −58.000 | 64.000 |
| Sales | 1.017 | 7.304 | −23.833 | 18.863 |
| Domestic consumption | 1.422 | 8.264 | −29.443 | 24.083 |
| Exchange rate | −1.848 | 8.082 | −15.130 | 13.603 |
| Interest rate | 0.046 | 2.661 | −4.550 | 4.220 |
| Real interest rate | 0.569 | 2.671 | −4.316 | 4.358 |

*Sources:* Industry-level data are from *Australian Manufacturing Industry and International Trade Data 1968–69 to 1992–93*, Industry Commission Information Paper, February 1995. The data for the exchange rate, interest rates, and the CPI (1989–90 = 100), used to deflate all nominal values, are from EconData's *DX* database.

*Notes: i.* For tariffs, effective rate of assistance (ERA), and interest rates, the means are average annual percentage point changes; *ii.* the exchange rate is $US per $A, the interest rate is the yield on 13-week Treasury Notes; *iii.* data are for 12 industries and the years 1973–74 to 1991–92 (the data for 1985–86 were not available). Hence, $n = 204$ (17 years by 12 industries).

**Table AII**   Correlation matrix

| | Employment | a. | b. | c. | d. | e. | f. | g. | h. | i. |
|---|---|---|---|---|---|---|---|---|---|---|
| a. Real wage | -0.183 / 0.009 | 1 | | | | | | | | |
| b. Exports | 0.167 / 0.017 | -0.092 / 0.191 | 1 / 0.0 | | | | | | | |
| c. Imports | 0.439 / 0.0001 | 0.167 / 0.017 | 1.114 / 0.105 | 1 / 0.0 | | | | | | |
| d. Tariffs | -0.125 / 0.075 | -0.088 / 0.213 | -0.0001 / 0.999 | -0.492 / 0.0001 | 1 / 0.0 | | | | | |
| e. ERA | -0.011 / 0.875 | -0.031 / 0.655 | -0.133 / 0.058 | -0.089 / 0.206 | 1.179 / 0.010 | 1 / 0.0 | | | | |
| f. Sales | 0.780 / 0.0001 | -0.057 / 0.418 | 0.255 / 0.0002 | 0.457 / 0.0001 | -0.099 / 0.160 | 1.043 / 0.544 | 1 / 0.0 | | | |
| g. Domestic consumption | 0.739 / 0.0001 | -0.010 / 0.886 | 0.105 / 0.136 | 0.717 / 0.0001 | -0.223 / 0.001 | 0.006 / 0.930 | 0.875 / 0.0001 | 1 / 0.0 | | |
| h. Exchange rate‡ | 0.534 / 0.027 | -0.012 / 0.963 | 0.367 / 0.148 | 0.336 / 0.188 | -0.499 / 0.041 | -0.420 / 0.093 | 0.533 / 0.028 | 0.507 / 0.038 | 1 / 0.0 | |
| i. Interest rate‡ | 0.381 / 0.132 | 0.179 / 0.491 | -0.128 / 0.624 | 0.586 / 0.014 | -0.297 / 0.246 | -0.034 / 0.895 | 0.236 / 0.361 | 0.457 / 0.065 | 0.113 / 0.666 | 1 / 0.0 |
| j. Real interest rate‡ | 0.202 / 0.436 | -0.437 / 0.079 | -0.101 / 0.681 | 0.016 / 0.953 | 0.252 / 0.330 | 0.431 / 0.084 | 0.214 / 0.409 | 0.267 / 0.300 | -0.103 / 0.693 | 0.354 / 0.163 |

*Notes*: Pearson correlation coefficients/Prob $> |R|$ under Ho: Rho $= 0/n = 204$.
‡Correlations are for industry averages ($n = 17$).
Sources and data definitions are given in Table AI.

REFERENCES

Abowd, John M. and Freeman, Richard B. (1991), 'Introduction and Summary', in John M. Abowd and Richard B. Freeman (eds), *Immigration, Trade and Labor Markets* (Chicago: NBER), pp. 1-25.

Abowd, John M. and Lemieux, Thomas (1991), 'The Effects of International Trade on Collective Bargaining Outcomes: A Comparison of the United States and Canada', in John M. Abowd and Freeman, Richard B. (eds), *Immigration, Trade, and Labor Markets* (Chicago: NBER), pp. 343-367.

Belsley, David A., Kuh, Edwin and Welsch, Roy E. (1980), *Regression Diagnostics* (New York: Wiley).

Berman, Eli, Bound, John and Griliches, Zvi (1994), 'Changes in the Demand for Skilled Labor Within US Manufacturing: Evidence From the Annual Survey of Manufacturers', *Quarterly Journal of Economics*, vol. 91, pp. 367-397.

Borjas, George J., Freeman, Richard B. and Katz, Lawrence F. (1992), 'On the Labor Market Effects of Immigration and Trade', NBER Working Paper no. 3761.

Borland, Jeff (1992), 'Wage Inequality in Australia', presented at the NBER Universities Conference on the Labor Market in International Perspective, Cambridge.

Bound, John and Johnson, George (1992), 'Changes in the Structure of Wages in the 1980s: An Evaluation of Alternative Explanations', *American Economic Review*, vol. 82, pp. 371-392.

Davis, Steven J. (1992), 'Cross-Country Patterns of Change in Relative Wages', in Olivier J. Blanchard and Stanley Fischer (eds), *1992 NBER Macroeconomic Annual* (Cambridge: MIT Press), pp. 239-292.

Dickens, William T. and Lang, Kevin (1988), 'Why it Matters What We Trade: A Case for Active Policy', in Laura Tyson, William T. Dickens and John Zysman (eds), *The Dynamics of Trade and Employment* (Cambridge: Ballinger Publishing), pp. 87-112.

Freeman, Richard B. and Katz, Lawrence F. (1991), 'Industrial Wage and Employment Determination in an Open Economy', in John M. Abowd and Richard B. Freeman (eds), *Immigration, Trade, and Labor Markets* (Chicago: NBER), pp. 235-259.

Gaston, Noel and Trefler, Daniel (1994a), 'The Role of International Trade and Trade Policy in the Labour Markets of Canada and the United States', *The World Economy*, vol. 17, pp. 45-62.

Gaston, Noel and Trefler, Daniel (1994b), 'Protection, Trade, and Wages: Evidence from US Manufacturing Industry', *Industrial and Labor Relations Review*, vol. 47, pp. 574-593.

Gaston, Noel and Trefler, Daniel (1995), 'Union Wage Sensitivity to Trade and Protection: Theory and Evidence', *Journal of International Economics*, vol. 39, pp. 1-25.

Gaston, Noel and Trefler, Daniel (1997), 'The Labour Market Consequences of the Canada-US Free Trade Agreement', *Canadian Journal of Economics*, vol. 30, pp. 18-41.

Grossman, Gene M. (1987), 'The Employment and Wage Effects of Import Competition in the United States', *Journal of International Economic Integration*, vol. 2, pp. 1-23.

Gunderson, Morley (1992), 'Wage and Employment Impacts Related to the North American Free Trade Agreement', Working Paper, Fraser Institute, Vancouver, Canada.

Hsiao, Cheng (1986), *Analysis of Panel Data* (New York: Cambridge University Press).

Industry Commission (1995a), *Australian Manufacturing Industry and International Trade Data 1968-69 to 1992-93*, Information Paper, February (Canberra: AGPS).

Industry Commission (1995b), *Assistance to Agricultural and Manufacturing Industries*, Information Paper, March (Canberra: AGPS).

Katz, Lawrence F. and Summers, Lawrence H. (1989), 'Can Inter-Industry Wage Differentials Justify Strategic Trade Policy?' in Robert C. Feenstra (ed.), *Trade Policies for International Competitiveness* (Chicago: University of Chicago Press), pp. 85-116.

Krueger, Alan B. and Summers, Lawrence H. (1988), 'Efficiency Wages and the Inter-Industry Wage Structure', *Econometrica*, vol. 56, pp. 259-293.

Murphy, Kevin M. and Welch, Finis (1992), 'The Structure of Wages', *Quarterly Journal of Economics*, vol. 107, pp. 285-326.

OECD (1993), *Employment Outlook* (Paris: OECD).

136                        AUSTRALIAN ECONOMIC PAPERS                        JUNE

Phipps, A.J. and Sheen, J.R. (1995), 'Macroeconomic Policy and Employment Growth in Australia', *Australian Economic Review*, vol. 109, pp. 86-104.

Revenga, Ana L. (1992), 'Exporting Jobs? The Impact of Import Competition on Employment and Wages in US Manufacturing', *Quarterly Journal of Economics*, vol. 107, pp. 255-284.

Wood, Adrian (1994), *North-South Trade, Employment and Inequality: Changing Fortunes in a Skill-Driven World* (Oxford: Clarendon Press).

# Part II
# Migration and Labour Market Adjustment

# [9]

# ILLEGAL IMMIGRANTS AND DOMESTIC EMPLOYMENT

## JEAN BALDWIN GROSSMAN*

This paper develops and tests a simple general equilibrium model to explore the common allegation that illegal immigrants take jobs away from native-born workers. A simulation of the effect of an increase in illegal immigration shows that the distribution of the immigrants among industries is critical in determining their effect on employment. If two-thirds of the illegal immigrants are employed in the agricultural service sector, for example, an increase in illegal immigration would increase domestic unskilled employment, but if only half are employed in that sector, an increase would lead to a decline in domestic unskilled unemployment.

POLICYMAKERS in the United States have recently been examining the costs and benefits of immigration. Extremely important to this analysis is an evaluation of the impact on the labor sector of unskilled immigrants, yet this form of immigration is the most difficult to analyze. At present, most unskilled workers entering the United States arrive as unsanctioned (illegal) immigrants, and most experts estimate that between two and five million unsanctioned immigrants work in this country.[1]

In some regions of the country, domestic workers, fearing that immigrants are replacing them in their jobs, are energetically lobbying to stop the flow of these foreign workers or, at least, to reduce it. Yet these feelings are far less prevalent in other regions. Surprisingly, isolationist sentiments are centered in the Northeast rather than the Southwest, where illegal immigrants are most common. In January 1979, the New York Times, in conjunction with CBS News, conducted a survey of U.S. citizens' attitudes toward illegal immigrants and job displacement. The survey uncovered striking regional differences in responses.[2] In the Northeast, 45 percent of those interviewed believed that illegal immigrants took jobs away from Americans, whereas only 28 percent of Westerners thought job displacement occurred. And many small employers throughout the United States fear that their livelihood would be threatened if immigrants were prevented from participating in the labor market, since immigrants' wages are lower than those of domestic workers.[3]

*The author is Research Economist at Mathematica Policy Research, Princeton, New Jersey. She would like to thank Gene Grossman for many useful discussions and comments. The paper has also benefited from comments offered at seminars at Princeton University and Mathematica Policy Research. The author also thanks Marjorie Mitchell for typing the many drafts of this paper.

[1]See, for example, Walter Fogel, "Illegal Alien Workers in the United States," *Industrial Relations*, Vol. 16, No. 3 (October 1977), pp. 243-63.

[2]See William K. Stevens, "Millions of Mexicans View Illegal Entry to U.S. as Door to Opportunity," *New York Times*, February 12, 1979, p.A-1.

[3]See Robert E. Taylor, "The Immigrants: U.S. Policy on Whom to Admit Draws Fire as Outdated and Feudal," *Wall Street Journal*, September 13, 1980, p. 1; and "The Economic Consequences of a New Wave," *Business Week*, June 23, 1980, pp. 80-86.

*Industrial and Labor Relations Review*, Vol. 37, No. 2 (January 1984). © 1984 by Cornell University.
0019-7939/84/3702 $01.00

Cornelius attributes the regional differences in attitudes described above to "a kind of 'personal unfamiliarity' gradient, or a 'relative-dependence-on-Mexican-labor' gradient."[4] This paper suggests that regional differences in the interindustry distribution of illegal immigrants would cause the inflow of immigrants to have different effects in different regions. A simulation of the effect of an increase in illegal immigration is conducted, using parameters appropriate to the United States and different distributional assumptions to illustrate these effects.

## Theoretical Considerations

The theoretical literature on immigration abstracts from several important features of the market for unsanctioned immigrants, because that literature deals with permanent legal immigrants. Most of the research fails to distinguish between skilled and unskilled labor, or does so only in a partial-equilibrium setting.[5] Although the population of permanent legal immigrants has approximately the same skill mix and level of human capital as the general public, unsanctioned workers usually have little education and low skill levels.[6] These illegal immigrants tend to accept jobs at the bottom of the economic ladder, and they are often paid less than the minimum wage. Thus, fluctuations in unsanctioned immigration would be expected to have profoundly different effects on the markets for domestic skilled and unskilled labor.

In the model that is briefly presented in the next two sections and that underlies the simulation, three distinctly different labor groups are identified, namely, domestic skilled labor, domestic unskilled labor, and foreign labor. No constraints are imposed on their substitutability. The minimum wage plays an important role in the market for domestic unskilled labor, inducing unemployment in the model. The model also characterizes a two-sector economy, in order to represent the belief that unsanctioned migrants work primarily in the labor-intensive agricultural and service sectors, while domestic unskilled workers are relatively more heavily employed in the more capital-intensive mining and manufacturing sectors.[7]

The simulation, presented in the penultimate section, reveals that domestic unskilled employment increases in response to an increase in illegal immigration, if approximately two-thirds of the immigrants are employed in the agricultural and service sector, as a survey done by the Immigration and Naturalization Service (INS) indicates.[8] But if immigrant employment is evenly split between the two sectors, as a study by North and Houstoun shows, domestic employment decreases in response to increased immigration.[9]

---

[4]Wayne Cornelius, "Building the Cactus Curtain: Mexican Migration and U.S. Responses," in U.S. Congress, Senate, *Hearings Before the Committee on the Judiciary*, 69th Cong., 1st sess., October 17 and 26, 1979 (Washington, D.C.: GPO, 1979), p. 287.

[5]One exception is George E. Johnson, "Labor Market Effects of Immigration," *Industrial and Labor Relations Review*, Vol. 33, No. 3 (April 1980), pp. 331–41. Johnson disaggregates labor into skilled, unskilled, and foreign labor groups and develops some interesting distributional implications. The major problem with his paper is that he constrains foreign and domestic unskilled labor to receive the same wage. Although this may be an appropriate model for permanent immigrants, it is not appropriate for unsanctioned immigrants, since unsanctioned workers embody far less human capital than native workers.

[6]The National Commission for Manpower Policy, *Manpower and Immigration Policies in the United States*, Special Report No. 20 (Washington, D.C.:

GPO, February 1978), p. 90, concludes, "In summary, the personal characteristics of legal immigrants that have a strong bearing on their role in the labor market, such as sex, marital status, and education, formerly were quite different from those of the U.S. population as a whole, but are now very close to that norm." Later in the same publication (p. 126), the average educational attainments of three groups of illegal immigrants are given as 4.9 years of schooling for Mexican illegal aliens, 8.7 years for other illegal aliens from the Western Hemisphere, and 11.9 years for those from the Eastern Hemisphere. It is believed that approximately 80 percent of illegal immigrants in the United States are Mexicans. The model developed here applies to the less-educated illegal workers.

[7]See Michael Piore, *Birds of Passage* (New York: Cambridge University Press, 1979), chap. 2, in particular pp. 40–41.

[8]Immigration and Naturalization Service, Office of Planning and Evaluation, "*Illegal Alien Study, Part I Fraudulent Entrance Study; A Study of Malafide Applicants at Selected Southwest Border Ports, 1976* (Washington, D.C.: U.S. Department of Justice, September 1976).

[9]See David North and Marion Houstoun, "Characteristics and Roles of Illegal Aliens in the U.S. Labor

242             INDUSTRIAL AND LABOR RELATIONS REVIEW

## The Model

The model underlying the results derived in this paper is similar to that developed by Jones.[10] Two sectors, A and B, produce goods $X_A$ and $X_B$, respectively, using three labor factors, domestic skilled labor $(L_s)$, domestic unskilled labor $(L_u)$, and unsanctioned immigrant labor $(L_m)$, with a constant-returns-to-scale production function. Capital has been suppressed in this model; however, $L_s$ can be thought of as a composite of human and nonhuman capital, assuming that relative prices within the capital composite remain constant. Labor factors receive their marginal products: skilled labor receives $w_s$; unskilled labor receives $w_u$; and immigrant labor receives $w_m$. The relative price of good $X_A$ in terms of $X_B$ is $P_A$.

It is assumed that because of enforced minimum-wage legislation, the wages paid to domestic unskilled workers are fixed at a level greater than the market clearing price, thereby creating unemployment. The wages of both domestic skilled and immigrant labor are flexible and adjust to clear their labor markets. Thus, the wages of immigrants can fall below the legal floor. More simply stated, we assume that minimum-wage laws are not enforced in the case of illegal immigrants.

This model may easily be extended to allow for minimum-wage noncompliance penalties and the costs of Immigration and Naturalization Service raids, but although both would enrich the model, they add unnecessary complication.[11] Because we are modeling the effects of changes in the number of immigrants, we can assume the supply of immigrants to be fixed at any given time and to be exogenously deter-

mined. This assumption is consistent with Craig's finding that conditions in immigrants' country of origin are the most significant factors accounting for the supply of those immigrants.[12]

Equilibrium in the economy is described by five constraints: the amount of skilled labor demanded in sectors A and B, at its equilibrium wage $(w_s)$, is equal to the fixed supply of skilled labor; the amount of immigrant labor demanded in sectors A and B, at its equilibrium wage $(w_m)$, is equal to its fixed supply; the price of $X_A$ $(P_A)$ is a weighted average of the wages of skilled labor $(w_s)$, of unskilled labor $(w_u)$, and of immigrant labor $(w_m)$, where the weights associated with each wage are the amounts of that labor used to produce one unit of $X_A$; the price of $X_B$ is likewise determined and will be normalized to one; and, finally, the relative supply of $X_A$ and $X_B$ equals the relative demand. The employment of unskilled labor $(N_u)$, which does not have to equal its supply, is determined by the amount of unskilled labor needed to produce the equilibrium of $X_A$ and $X_B$. The equilibrium and later comparative static are stated mathematically in the appendix.

The next three sections examine the comparative static effects of an increase in the stock of unsanctioned labor, under various assumptions about wage and price flexibility. First, the relative price of $X_A$ is assumed to be given exogenously. Price exogeneity obtains if $X_A$ and $X_B$ are traded in other markets and if the market under consideration (a city, state, or country) is relatively small compared to the total product market. In the next section, the fixed-price assumption is relaxed.

### Immigration into a Small Market

Suppose there is a small inflow of immigrants, induced perhaps by adverse conditions existing in their country of origin or by a relaxation of the receiving country's border-patrol policy. In a small market, the relative output price is as-

---

Markets: An Exploratory Study," monograph (Washington, D.C.: Linton and Company, March 1976), for more details.

[10]See Ronald Jones, "The Structure of Simple General Equilibrium Models," *Journal of Political Economy*, Vol. 73, No. 6, (December 1965), pp. 557-72.

[11]The omission of the costs of INS raids is not a serious one, since, as stated in Piore, *Birds of Passage*, pp. 167-80, the de facto strategy of the border patrol is actually to concentrate its resources on apprehending *incoming* unsanctioned immigrants and, for the most part, to leave already-employed immigrants alone.

---

[12]See John Craig, "Push-Pull in Recent Mexican Migration to the United States," *Journal of International Migration*, Vol. 10, No. 1 (February 1977), pp. 17-26.

sumed to be fixed and determined exogenously. The receiving economy must therefore adjust to an influx of immigrants without changing product prices. Because prices do not change, wages do not change, and, therefore, the combination of factors that minimize costs does not change.

As more immigrant labor becomes available to both sector A and sector B, more of it is employed in the relatively skilled, labor-intensive sector A. Skilled labor must be released from sector B to join the new immigrants in sector A. The production of $X_B$ must therefore fall to accommodate this shift of resources. The size of the fall will depend on the relative use of immigrant labor to skilled labor in both sectors. The more skilled workers per immigrant worker that are employed to produce one unit of $X_A$, the more $X_B$ shrinks relative to $X_A$. This relationship can be stated, more precisely, as:

$$(1) \qquad \hat{X}_A - \hat{X}_B = \frac{1}{|\lambda|} \hat{L}_m.$$

$\hat{X}_j$ is the proportional change in output $X_j$. $|\lambda|$ is a measure of factor intensities in the two sectors equal to $\lambda_{mA} \lambda_{sB} - \lambda_{mB} \lambda_{sA}$, where $\lambda_{ij}$ is the fraction of the supply of $i$ employed in sector $j$. And $\hat{L}_m$ is the proportional change in the stock of migrants.

The change in output induced by an increase in a relative factor endowment, at fixed prices, is known as the Rybczynski effect. The employment of unskilled labor increases if and only if sector A (the expanding sector) uses unskilled labor more intensively relative to skilled workers than sector B does. Mathematically, this relationship takes the form:

$$(2)(1 + k)\hat{N}_u = \frac{1}{|\lambda|} (\lambda_{uA}\lambda_{sB} - \lambda_{uB}\lambda_{sA}) \hat{L}_m,$$

where $(1 + k)$ is an income multiplier. If unskilled employment changes, income changes and, therefore, the level of demand changes. The factor $(1 + k)$ represents the multiplicative impact of a change in unskilled employment. The employment impact can thus also be summarized as follows: unskilled labor

employment will increase if sector B uses more skilled labor relative to unskilled labor than does sector A and if sector B uses more skilled labor relative to immigrant labor than does sector A.

### Equilibrium with Flexible Prices

Now assume that immigrants' wages and output prices are flexible. The effect of an influx of foreign labor when prices are flexible can be decomposed into two parts: the effect of an increase in the labor factor, holding prices constant; and the effect of the induced price change. The first is the Rybczynski effect examined above; that is, holding output prices constant, an increase in the relative supply of a labor factor increases the relative output of the industry that uses that factor intensively. Although the concept of factor intensity is less natural when there are three labor factors, we have assumed that compared to sector A, sector B uses both a greater ratio of skilled to unskilled labor and a greater ratio of skilled to immigrant labor. Thus, sector B is said to use skilled labor more intensively than sector A. An inflow of immigrants decreases the relative supply of skilled labor, which leads to a decrease in $X_B$ relative to $X_A$. To eliminate excess demand for $X_B$ at constant prices, the relative price of $X_B$ must rise.

This relationship leads to the second effect: the price effect. The price effect is a generalization of the Stolper-Samuelson theorem, which states that an increase in the output price of an industry causes an increase in the real return to the factor used intensively in that industry. Thus, when the relative price of $X_B$ increases to clear the goods market, it induces an increase in the real wage for skilled labor. Both parts of the adjustment increase the return to skilled labor relative to the return to the immigrants; the increased supply of immigrants lowers the immigrant wage; and the increase in the price of $X_B$ increases the wages of skilled workers. The proportional changes (again denoted by a hat) in the wages, the relative outputs, and the relative prices of $X_A$ are given in Equations 3 through 6 below. Their derivation is shown in the appendix.

244                INDUSTRIAL AND LABOR RELATIONS REVIEW

(3)     $\hat{P}_A = \dfrac{-1}{|\lambda|(\sigma_p + \sigma_D)} \hat{L}_m;$

(4)     $\hat{X}_A - \hat{X}_B = \dfrac{\sigma_D}{|\lambda|(\sigma_p + \sigma_D)} \hat{L}_m;$

(5)     $\hat{w}_m = \dfrac{-\Theta_{sB}}{|\lambda| \, |\Theta|(\sigma_p + \sigma_D)} \hat{L}_m;$

(6)     $\hat{w}_s = \dfrac{\Theta_{mB}}{|\lambda| \, |\Theta|(\sigma_p + \sigma_D)} \hat{L}_m.$

$\sigma_D$ is the elasticity of substitution in consumption between sector A and sector B; and $\sigma_p$ is the elasticity of the relative production of goods, $X_A/X_B$, with respect to a change in their relative price, $P_A$, induced by an influx of immigrants.[13]

If skilled workers substitute for unskilled and immigrant labor in a similar manner (that is, if the partial elasticities of substitution between skilled and unskilled labor and between immigrant and skilled labor have the same sign, as one would expect), $\sigma_p$ can be shown to be positive. $|\lambda|$ is defined as before, and $|\Theta|$ is a similar measure of the factor shares in unit cost equal to $\Theta_{mA}\Theta_{sB} - \Theta_{sA}\Theta_{mB}$, where $\Theta_{ij}$ is the share of labor factor $i$ in the unit cost of $X_j$.

The change in unskilled employment is best understood if it is decomposed into three parts:

(7)     $(1 + k)\hat{N}_u = \dfrac{\lambda_{uA}\lambda_{sB} - \lambda_{uB}\lambda_{sA}}{|\lambda|} \hat{L}_m$

$+ \dfrac{\delta_u^s \hat{w}_s + \delta_u^m \hat{w}_m}{|\lambda| \, |\Theta|(\sigma_D + \sigma_p)}$

$+ [(\lambda_{uA}\lambda_{sB} - \lambda_{uB}\lambda_{sA})\sigma_1$

$+ (\lambda_{uA}\lambda_{mB} - \lambda_{uB}\lambda_{mA})\sigma_2]\hat{L}_m.$

$\sigma_1$ and $\sigma_2$ are measures of the substitution induced by the changes in skilled and

immigrant wages.[14] The first part of Equation 7 is the change in employment caused by a wave of immigration holding prices fixed, and it is identical to the expression in Equation 2. Since prices are not fixed, however, an influx causes the immigrants' wage to fall and the skilled wage to increase. Both sectors will use a greater ratio of unskilled to skilled labor and a smaller ratio of unskilled to immigrant labor.

The second part of Equation 7 represents the net impact on unskilled employment of these changes in labor ratios, holding the output levels of $X_A$ and $X_B$ constant. The last part of the equation represents an additional employment impact, because output levels do not need to change as much as when prices are fixed. Relative wages change, dampening the expansion of sector A and the contraction of sector B. This effect in turn implies that unskilled employment will not increase as much as it would have if prices had been fixed.

### Numerical Simulation

The magnitudes of the effects of illegal immigration can be estimated using Equations 3 through 7. In this section, those effects will be calculated using ranges of variables that are appropriate for the United States. Let sector B primarily consist of goods-producing sectors — manufacturing, mining, and construction; and let sector A consist of agriculture and the service-producing sector — trades, transportation and utilities, finance, public administration, and other services.

Labor's factor shares in unit cost ($\Theta_{ij}$s) and the fraction of their supply employed in each sector ($\lambda$s) are derived using the *Handbook of Labor Statistics: 1973; Current Population Reports (CPR)*; and the *Input-Output Structure of the U.S. Economy: 1967.*[15] The input-output table

---

[13]     $\sigma_p = \dfrac{1}{|\lambda| \, |\Theta|} \, [\Theta_{sB}(\delta_s^m + \delta_m^s + \delta_m^u)$

$+ \Theta_{mB}(\delta_m^s + \delta_s^m + \delta_s^u)],$

between factors $i$ and $k$ in sector $j$, where $\delta_i^k = \lambda_{iA}\Theta_{kA}\sigma_{ki}^A + \lambda_{iB}\Theta_{kB}\sigma_{ki}^B$. $\sigma_{ki}^i$ is the Allen-Uezawa partial elasticity of substitution between factors $i$ and $k$ in sector $j$. $\delta_i^k$ can be interpreted as the change in average unit cost in the economy caused by the change in the use of factor $k$ relative to the use of factor $i$.

[14]Let $\sigma_1 = (\delta_m^s + \delta_m^u)\Theta_{sB} + \delta_m^s \Theta_{mB}$, and $\sigma_2 = (\delta_s^m + \delta_m^u)\Theta_{sB} + \delta_m^s \Theta_{mB}$, where $\delta_k^i$ is as defined in the previous footnote.

[15]The total amount of value added in each industry is given in the U.S. Department of Commerce, Social and Economic Statistics Administration, Bureau of Economic Analysis, *Input-Output Structure of the U.S. Economy: 1967, Volume II-Direct Requirements of*

was used to obtain the total value added, the *CPR* gave employee compensation, and the *Handbook* was used to determine the ratio of skilled employment (professional and technical workers, managers, crafts workers, and nontransport operatives) to unskilled employment (laborers, service and clerical workers, and transport operatives) within each industry.

The report *Manpower and Immigration Policies in the United States* provided information used to determine the distribution of illegal immigrants across industries ($\lambda_{m.}$ and $\Theta_{m.}$).[16] Between January 1 and March 30, 1975, the Immigration and Naturalization Service (INS) surveyed 47,947 apprehended unsanctioned migrants and gathered industry and wage data. The sample comprises mostly southwestern labor markets and mostly Mexican nationals. The INS found that 33 percent of the immigrants apprehended worked in the goods-producing sector and 67 percent worked in the agricultural and service sector.[17]

North and Houstoun (N-H) conducted a similar study a few months later. To account for the fact that apprehended immigrants are not a representative sample of all

immigrants, they weighted the information from border apprehendees less heavily than information from within-border apprehendees. The N-H estimates indicated that in March 1976, illegal immigrants were employed evenly between the two sectors.[18] Both the INS and N-H estimates are very tentative, since neither is derived from a random sample.

The values for all the relevant variables are shown in Table 1. Compensation shares are constructed under two alternative scenarios: one set of values is based on the assumption that there are four million illegal immigrants employed in the United States—the single number that most experts use; and the other set assumes that there are twelve million illegal immigrants—the highest estimate that has been made.[19]

To determine reasonable values for the elasticities of labor factor substitution and consumption, let us now turn to the previous literature. Empirical estimates of the elasticities of substitution between domestic skilled labor, domestic unskilled labor, and illegal immigrants has not been possible, since accurate economic information about the illegal immigrants is not available.[20] The disaggregation of labor by education analyzed by Grant comes closest in spirit to the disaggregation needed here.[21] Illegal immigrants differ from do-

---

*Detailed Industries* (Washington, D.C.: GPO, 1974), various pages. U.S. Bureau of Labor Statistics, *Handbook of Labor Statistics: 1973*, Bulletin 1966 (Washington, D.C.: GPO, 1973), p. 69, Table 20, gives the number of unskilled workers employed in each major industry by occupational class. U.S. Department of Commerce, *Current Population Reports: Consumer Income Series, Money Income in 1972 of Families and Persons in the United States*, Series P-60, No. 90 (Washington, D.C.: GPO, December 1973), pp. 140–45, Table 59, gives the mean earnings of employees in each major industry by occupational class. The product of earnings and number of employees, summed over a sector, gives an approximation of unskilled labor compensation by sector. Unskilled labor compensation can then be divided by the value added in the sector to give $\Theta_{u+m,j}$. One minus $\Theta_{u+m,j}$ gives $\Theta_{s,j}$. $\Theta_{m,j}$ is derived using wage estimates reported in the National Commission on Manpower Policies, *Manpower and Immigration Policies*, p. 140. The composite human and physical capital shares ($\Theta_{s,j}$) are approximated by the formula $\Theta_{sj}/(\Theta_{sA} + \Theta_{sB})$. The unskilled labor fraction ($\lambda_{u,j} + \lambda_{m,j}$) is easily obtained from Table 20 of the *Handbook of Labor Statistics*.

[16] See National Commission on Manpower Policy, *Manpower and Immigration Policies*, pp. 138–41.

[17] Immigration and Naturalization Service, *Illegal Alien Study*, p. 46.

[18] North and Houstoun, "Characteristics and Roles," pp. 105–112.

[19] Charles E. Keely, "The Shadows of Invisible People," *American Demographics*, Vol. 2, No. 3 (March 1980), p. 29.

[20] Elasticities of complementarity among native-born labor, second-generation immigrants, and foreign-born immigrants are presented in Jean Baldwin Grossman, "The Substitutability of Natives and Immigrants in Production," *Review of Economics and Statistics*, Vol. 54, No. 4 (November 1982), pp. 596–603. These estimates pertain to *legal* immigrants, however.

[21] See the estimates in James Grant, "Substitution Among Labor, Labor, and Capital in United States Manufacturing," Ph.D. dissertation (Lansing: Michigan State University, 1979). Those estimates may also be found in Daniel S. Hamermesh and James Grant, "Econometric Studies of Labor-Labor Substitution and Their Implications for Policy," *Journal of Human Resources*, Vol. 14, No. 4 (Fall 1980), pp. 518–42, along with an excellent review of other estimated elasticities of substitution among factors disaggregated in many alternative manners.

Table 1. Employment and Compensation Share Values,
Using the INS and N-H Estimates.[†]

|  | INS Estimates | | N-H Estimates | |
|---|---|---|---|---|
|  | 4 Million Illegals | 12 Million Illegals | 4 Million Illegals | 12 Million Illegals |
| $\lambda_{sB}$ | .43 | .43 | .43 | .43 |
| $\lambda_{sA}$ | .57 | .57 | .57 | .57 |
| $\lambda_{mB}$ | .33 | .33 | .50 | .50 |
| $\lambda_{mA}$ | .67 | .67 | .50 | .50 |
| $\lambda_{uB}$ | .15 | .15 | .15 | .15 |
| $\lambda_{uA}$ | .85 | .85 | .85 | .85 |
| $\Theta_{mB}$ | .02 | .06 | .03 | .10 |
| $\Theta_{uB}$ | .09 | .05 | .08 | .01 |
| $\Theta_{mA}$ | .03 | .10 | .02 | .06 |
| $\Theta_{uA}$ | .16 | .09 | .17 | .13 |
| $\Theta_{sB}$ | .89 | .89 | .89 | .89 |
| $\Theta_{sA}$ | .81 | .81 | .81 | .81 |

Legend:

$\lambda_{ij} = \dfrac{L_{ij}}{L_i}$, the employment share of factor $i$ in sector $j$.

$\Theta_{ij} = \dfrac{w_i a_{ij}}{p_j}$, the compensation share of factor $i$ in the unit cost of $j$.

[†]Assuming that the elasticity of substitution in production between skilled and unskilled labor in both sectors is 1.16; between immigrants and skilled workers in both sectors is .21; and between immigrants and unskilled workers in both sectors is .77. The elasticity of substitution in consumption between the outputs of the goods-producing sectors (B) and the agricultural and service sector (A) is assumed to be .5.

Source: Daniel S. Hamermesh and James Grant, "Econometric Studies of Labor-Labor Substitution and Their Implications for Policy," Journal of Human Resources, Vol. 14, No. 4 (Fall 1979), pp. 518–42.

mestic unskilled labor primarily in the amount of human capital they embody. Several studies, such as those by Cornelius and by North and Houstoun, have shown that most illegal immigrants are very unskilled and have little formal education.[22] As a rough approximation of the elasticities of substitution between labor factors, the following correspondence is used: immigrants are associated with workers with eight years of education or fewer; domestic unskilled labor with workers with nine to twelve years; and the skilled labor and capital aggregate is associated with the workers with thirteen or

more years of education.[23] The resulting elasticities are shown in Table 1.

An approximation of the elasticity of substitution between goods and consumption can be determined if the conpensated cross-price elasticity between $X_A$ and $X_B$ were available and if we knew the expendi-

[22]See Wayne Cornelius and Juan Diaz-Canedo, "The Mexican Migration to the United States: The View from Rural Sending Communities," mimeo, Center for International Studies (Cambridge, Mass.: Massachusetts Institute of Technology, 1976). Also see North and Houstoun, "Characteristics and Roles."

[23]Grant's estimates of the partial Allen elasticities of substitution are:

|  | Education (in years) | | | |
|---|---|---|---|---|
| Education | 0–8 | 9–12 | 13+ | Capital |
| 0–8 Years | −8.58 | .77 | .21 | .94 |
| 9–12 Years |  | −1.62 | 1.16 | .38 |
| 13+ Years |  |  | −2.12 | .04 |
| Capital |  |  |  | −.39 |

Although separability tests cannot reject the aggregation of capital and more highly educated labor, the reader may wish to interpret the effects of immigration presented here as short-run impact effects, holding capital fixed.

ture share of $X_A$ and $X_B$. Abbott and Ashenfelter estimate demand functions for several aggregates,[24] but unfortunately, the values they obtain seem to be sensitive to the functional form. Nonetheless, a range of elasticities of consumption substitution of between 0.5 and 1.5 seems reasonably consistent with their work.

In estimating this elasticity of substituting, two base cases are first calculated and then key parameters are varied to discover the sensitivity of the results. In the first base case it is assumed that four million illegal immigrants are employed in the United States and that, as indicated by the INS survey, one-third of them are in the goods-producing sector and two-thirds of them are in the agricultural and service sector. The second base case has the same total number of illegal immigrants, but it assumes that the allocation between the two sectors is, as in the N-H survey, 50 percent in each. The elasticity assumptions for both cases are those at the bottom of Table 1.

The information in Table 1 and in Equations 3 through 7 yields an estimate that a one percent increase in the number of immigrants (40,000) would cause skilled wages to increase 0.08 percent if the INS distribution were correct, or 0.11 percent if the N-H distribution were correct. The immigrants' wage falls by 3.40 percent under the INS assumptions, or 3.43 percent under the N-H assumptions. In both cases, the wage changes induced by an influx of immigrants are similar. The effect of immigration on unskilled labor employment differs radically, however, depending on the distribution of immigrants. Under the INS estimates, a one percent increase in the stock of immigrants would induce a 2.89 percent increase in unskilled employment if there is no income effect (that is, if $k = 0$), whereas under the N-H distribution estimates, unskilled employment falls 3.69 percent if there is no income effect. A large income effect would reduce the response under both scenarios by $1/(1 + k)$, but the directions of the change are not

affected. The major determinants of the impact on domestic employment are the intensities of the sectors' labor factors.

The two cases differ because the relative intensities of immigrant and skilled labor differ drastically under the two distributional assumptions. Under the INS assumption, sector A, the agricultural and service sector, employs more immigrants per skilled worker—approximately 1.2 to 1—than does sector B—approximately a .77 to 1 ratio. The inflow of immigrants causes the immigrant-intensive sector, A, to expand. As sector A expands, skilled labor must be released from sector B to go to sector A. Concomitantly, unskilled labor will also be released from B as the sector contracts. Sector A uses approximately 1.5 unskilled workers per skilled worker, whereas sector B uses only .35 unskilled worker per skilled worker. The expanding sector A therefore absorbs the unskilled labor released from B and demands more in addition. Although the total number of immigrants is equally split between the sectors under the N-H distributional assumptions, sector B now employs relatively more immigrants per skilled worker than does sector A—approximately 1.2 to 1—as opposed to .88 to 1. An influx of immigrants thus causes sector B to expand and *total* unskilled employment to fall.

Under both distributional assumptions, the secondary price effects enhance domestic unskilled employment. Had output prices been fixed, an N-H distribution of immigrants would predict a fall in employment of 4.0 percent. This drop is mitigated to 3.69 percent when prices are flexible. Likewise, an INS distribution of immigrants predicts an employment increase of 2.8 percent if prices are fixed and a 2.89 percent increase if prices are flexible. Again, note that an income effect reduces the magnitudes but does not alter the relative sizes of the employment changes.

Now consider the sensitivity of these base results to changes in the parameters. The primary effects of illegal immigration on employment can be seen as holding prices constant. The results for ranges of relative factor intensities with fixed prices are shown in Table 2. The most important

---

[24]Michael Abbott and Orley Ashenfelter, "Labor Supply, Commodity Demand, and the Allocation of Time," *Review of Economic Studies*, Vol. 43, No. 3 (October 1976), pp. 389–411.

*Table 2.* The Percent Change in Unskilled Employment Induced by a One Percent Increase in the Stock of Immigrants under Alternative Factor-Intensity Assumptions, with Fixed Prices.

(asterisks denote base results)

| Relative Immigrant Employment Shares | Relative Unskilled Employment Shares in B vs. A | | |
| --- | --- | --- | --- |
| | .4/.6 | .43/.57 | .45/.55 |
| Relative Unskilled Compensation Shares in B vs. A = .15/.85 | | | |
| .5/.5 (N-H) | −2.50 | −4.00* | −6.00 |
| .4/.6 | − | 9.33 | 6.00 |
| .33/.67 (INS) | 3.57 | 2.80* | 2.50 |
| Relative Unskilled Compensation Shares in B vs. A = .2/.8 | | | |
| .5/.5 (N-H) | −2.00 | −3.29 | −5.00 |
| .4/.6 | − | 7.67 | 5.00 |
| .33/.67 (INS) | 2.86 | 2.30 | 2.08 |

result is that the more similar the relative factor intensities of skilled and immigrant labor in each sector, the larger the negative impact of immigration. This is because the more the immigrant-intensive sector expands, the more the other sector must contract before it can release the requisite number of skilled workers. Thus, the relative production and factor utilization change to a greater extent.

As can be seen in Equation 4, the adjustment in production is directly related to the similarity or dissimilarity of the sectors. Similar factor intensities implies that $|\lambda|$ is small and, therefore, the relative production adjustment is large. Employment increases if the expanding sector employs more unskilled labor per skilled worker than does the contracting sector, as it does under the INS assumptions, but not under the N-H assumptions. The larger the change in relative production, the larger the change in employment. As shown in the bottom half of Table 2, however, the more similar the employment of unskilled labor, the smaller the change in total employment.

Table 3 displays variations in the elasticity-of-substitution assumptions. Changes in the elasticities affect only the secondary price effect; thus, it is not surprising that the results do not change qualitatively under these variations. The first row of the table presents the base cases. The second row is the same as the base cases, except that the consumption elasticity is 1.5 rather than 0.5. This change has a negligible effect (a third-place decimal effect), since factor shifts dominate the employment shifts. The third row constitutes a doubling of the base elasticities. This has no effect on the fixed-price portion of the change in employment. When the economy is twice as responsive, however, factor and commodity prices respond half as much as before to a given immigration inflow. The change in aggregate unskilled employment, holding output constant, is half as large as it was in the less elastic case, but when the relative outputs are allowed to adjust, total employment increases. Under the INS assumptions, total employment increases relative to the base, whereas under the N-H assumptions, the output effect just offsets the substitution effect.

In the last row of Table 3, the elasticity of substitution between immigrants and domestic unskilled labor is made to be greater than the substitutability between domestic

## ILLEGAL IMMIGRANTS AND DOMESTIC EMPLOYMENT          249

*Table 3.* The Percent Change in Unskilled Employment Induced
by a One Percent Change in the Stock of Immigrants.[a]

(asterisks denote base results)

| Elasticities of Substitution[b] | Relative Immigrant Employment Shares in Sector B Versus Sector A | |
|---|---|---|
| | .5/.5(N-H) | .33/.67 (INS) |
| $\sigma_D = .50$ $\sigma_{su} = 1.16$ $\sigma_{sm} = .21$ $\sigma_{mu} = .77$ | −3.69* | 2.89* |
| $\sigma_D = 1.50$ $\sigma_{su} = 1.16$ $\sigma_{sm} = .21$ $\sigma_{mu} = .77$ | −3.69 | 2.89 |
| $\sigma_D = 1.00$ $\sigma_{su} = 2.32$ $\sigma_{sm} = .42$ $\sigma_{mu} = 1.54$ | −3.69 | 2.98 |
| $\sigma_D = .50$ $\sigma_{su} = 1.16$ $\sigma_{sm} = .21$ $\sigma_{mu} = 2.00$ | −3.94 | 2.77 |

[a]All calculations in this table assumed base variables unless stated otherwise. Thus, $\lambda_{uB}/\lambda_{uA} = .15/.85$, and $\Theta_{sB}/\Theta_{sA} = .89/.81$.

[b]$\sigma_{ij}$ is the elasticity of substitution between factors $i$ and $j$. $\sigma_D$ is the elasticity of substitution between goods in consumption.

unskilled and skilled labor. As one would expect, unskilled employment is smaller under this configuration of production techniques than under the base-case configuration.

Table 4 presents results testing the sensitivity of the base results to variations in the compensation shares. The compensation shares could differ from the base shares for two reasons: either the wage that was imputed to a labor factor was not correct; or in the case of immigrants, more of them were employed than had been assumed in the base case. Changing the compensation shares affects unskilled employment primarily by its influence on the skilled wage. If there are twelve million illegal immigrants employed in the United States, rather than the assumed four million, a one percent increase in the immigrant stock (a larger inflow) will cause the skilled wage to increase more than in the base case. Both

sectors therefore employ a smaller ratio of skilled to unskilled labor, implying that, if output is held constant, skilled labor is released. The contracting sector will have to shrink less to provide the immigrant-intensive sector the skilled labor it needs, and in addition, the expanding sector expands less.

Under the INS assumptions, the expanding sector employs relatively more unskilled labor than the contracting sector, therefore; and although domestic employment increases, it does not increase as much as in the base case. Under the N-H assumptions, the sector employing relatively more unskilled labor is the contracting sector; employment will therefore shrink, and shrink less than it does in the base case.

Similarly, the increase in the skilled wage is greater in the cases presented in the second column of Table 4, where the skilled-labor and capital-compensation

250                 INDUSTRIAL AND LABOR RELATIONS REVIEW

*Table 4.* The Percent Change in Employment Induced by a One Percent
Increase in the Stock of Immigrants under Alternative
Factor-Compensation-Share Assumptions.[†]

(asterisks denote base results)

| *Relative Migrant Compensation Shares in Sector B vs. Sector A* | *Relative Share of Compensation Going to Capital and Skilled Labor in Sector B versus Sector A* | |
|---|---|---|
| | *.8/.7* | *.89/.81* |
| With Four Million Immigrants | | |
| .03/.02 (N-H) | −3.73 | −3.69* |
| .02/.03 (INS) | 2.92 | 2.89* |
| With Twelve Million Immigrants | | |
| .10/.06 (N-H) | −3.35 | −3.11 |
| .06/.10 (INS) | 2.63 | 2.59 |

[†]The other variables besides compensation shares take on the values in the base cases.

shares are larger than they are in the first column. The expanding sector expands less, and the contracting sector contracts less, in the second-column cases than in the first-column cases.

In summary, varying most parameters makes little difference in the results, but seemingly small changes in the relative factor intensities have a large effect on the results. In particular, changes in the relative employment of immigrants can qualitatively change the effect of illegal immigration on the employment of domestic unskilled labor. If the INS estimates are a representative picture of the distribution of illegal immigrants in the Southwest and if the N-H estimates are more representative of the distribution in the Northeast, the regional difference in attitudes toward immigrants could be economically explained. This paper suggests that a regional difference in the interindustry distribution of illegal immigrants would provide an economic basis for different regional perceptions of the immigrants' influence on the labor market.

## Summary and Conclusion

A model that allows for the commonly asserted changes in domestic unemployment that result from illegal immigration has been developed and examined in this paper. The results show that the distribu-

tion of immigrants among industries is critical in determining their impact on U.S. employment. Regional differences in relative factor intensities could account for differences in the region-specific effects of immigration. The simulation shows that if two-thirds of the illegal immigrants are employed in the agricultural and service sector, a one percent increase in illegal immigration (40,000) would increase unskilled domestic employment between 2.08 and 3.57 percent. If only half of the illegal immigrants were employed in the agricultural and service sector, on the other hand, unskilled domestic employment would fall between 2 and 6 percent. Under both distributional assumptions, the immigrants' wages are fairly sensitive to their own supply (an elasticity of greater than 3 percent), whereas the skilled wage is fairly insensitive to the supply of immigrants (a cross-elasticity of approximately 0.1).

The model presented here is a very simplified view of the economy. If there were domestic workers whose wages could fall below the minimum wage (such as employees of very small firms) and who were perfect substitutes for the immigrants, their wage would fall as did the immigrants'. We would expect these workers to oppose the liberalization of immigration laws. Chicano and black citizens are more likely to find themselves in this economic situation than whites. The New York

## ILLEGAL IMMIGRANTS AND DOMESTIC EMPLOYMENT 251

Times/CBS News survey cited earlier supports this conjecture, since 55 percent of the blacks interviewed believed that most illegal immigrants took jobs away from Americans, whereas only 34 percent of the whites interviewed expressed this sentiment.[25]

As many others have said, more information is needed on the number, location, earnings, industry, and occupation of the immigrants before conclusive results can be determined. Nonetheless, this paper has illustrated the importance of their inter-industry distribution in determining the impact of immigration on domestic employment. It suggests that in a world with limited resources, the government should first determine where unsanctioned immigrants are employed. Other employment-related information will aid policymakers in refining their estimates of unemployment, but the broader picture can be discerned simply by knowing the immigrants' distribution among industries.

### Mathematical Appendix

This appendix outlines the derivations of fixed- and flexible-price equilibriums. Following the notation developed by Jones,[26] the proportional change in $X$, $dx/x$, is denoted by $\hat{X}$; the share of labor factor $i$ in unit cost is $\Theta_{ij}$ (which equals $a_{ij}w_i/p_j$, where $a_{ij}$ is the amount of labor factor $i$ employed to produce one unit of $j$); and the fraction of the supply of factor $i$ employed to produce good $j$ is $\lambda_{ij}$, or $a_{ij}X_j/L_i$, where $X_j$ is the amount of $j$ produced and $L_i$ is the supply of factor $i$). Total differentiation of the two full-employment constraints (for skilled labor and for immigrants) and the two price equations with respect to an increase in the supply of immigrants yields:

$$(1') \qquad \lambda_{mA}\hat{X}_A + \lambda_{mB}\hat{X}_B = \hat{L}_m - (\lambda_{mA}\hat{a}_{mA} + \lambda_{mB}\hat{a}_{mB});$$

$$(2') \qquad \lambda_{sA}\hat{X}_A + \lambda_{sB}\hat{X}_B = 0 - (\lambda_{sA}\hat{a}_{sA} + \lambda_{sB}\hat{a}_{sB});$$

$$(3') \qquad \Theta_{mA}\hat{w}_m + \Theta_{sA}\hat{w}_s = \hat{P}_A - (\Theta_{mA}\hat{a}_{mA} + \Theta_{sA}\hat{a}_{sA} + \Theta_{uA}\hat{a}_{uA});$$

$$(4') \qquad \Theta_{mB}\hat{w}_m + \Theta_{sB}\hat{w}_s = -(\Theta_{mB}\hat{a}_{mB} + \Theta_{sB}\hat{a}_{sB} + \Theta_{uB}\hat{a}_{uB}).$$

When prices are fixed, $\hat{P}_A$ is zero. By cost minimization, the expressions within the parentheses of Equations 3' and 4' are also zero. The only solution that simultaneously satisfies both equations is $\hat{w}_m = \hat{w}_s = 0$. Because the input prices do not change, the optimal factor mix also does not change. The expressions within the parentheses of Equations 1' and 2' are therefore equal to zero. The changes in the output and employment levels are now given by Equations 1 and 2 in the text.

If prices are flexible, factor ratios will change. The changes can be expressed as a function of the Allen-Uezawa partial elasticities of substitution ($\sigma_{ij}$).[27]

$$(5') \qquad \hat{a}_{mj} = -\Theta_{sj}\sigma_{ms}^j(\hat{w}_m - \hat{w}_s) - \Theta_{uj}\sigma_{mu}^j\hat{w}_m;$$

$$(6') \qquad \hat{a}_{sj} = \Theta_{mj}\sigma_{ms}^j(\hat{w}_m - \hat{w}_s) - \Theta_{uj}\sigma_{su}^j\hat{w}_s;$$

$$(7') \qquad \hat{a}_{uj} = \Theta_{mj}\sigma_{mu}^j\hat{w}_m + \Theta_{sj}\sigma_{su}^j\hat{w}_s.$$

Substituting Equations 5' through 7' into Equations 1' through 4' and simplifying, we obtain:

$$(8') \qquad \lambda_{mA}\hat{X}_A + \lambda_{mB}\hat{X}_B - (\delta_m^s + \delta_m^u)\hat{w}_m + \delta_m^s\hat{w}_s = \hat{L}_m;$$

$$(9') \qquad \lambda_{sA}\hat{X}_A + \lambda_{sB}\hat{X}_B + \delta_s^m\hat{w}_m - (\delta_s^m + \delta_s^u)\hat{w}_s = 0;$$

$$(10') \qquad \Theta_{mA}\hat{w}_m + \Theta_{sA}\hat{w}_s - \hat{P}_A = 0;$$

$$(11') \qquad \Theta_{mB}\hat{w}_m + \Theta_{sB}\hat{w}_s = 0,$$

where $\delta_i^k = \lambda_{iA}\Theta_{kA}\sigma_{ki}^A + \lambda_{iB}\Theta_{kB}\sigma_{ki}^B$. Consumers' behavior is summarized by:

$$(12') \qquad \hat{X}_A - \hat{X}_B - \sigma_D\hat{P}_A = 0.$$

Solving this system of equations yields Equations 3 through 7 in the text.

---

[25] This relationship is derived in Raveendra Batra and Francisco Casas, "A Synthesis of the Hecksher-Ohlin and the Neoclassical Models of International Trade," *Journal of International Economics*, Vol. 6, (February 1976), pp. 21 - 38, by (a) totally differentiating the unit-cost function,

$$a_{ij} = \Theta_{mj}\sigma_{mi}^j w_m + \Theta_{sj}\sigma_{si}^j w_s + \Theta_{uj}\sigma_{ui}^j w_u,$$
$$i = m, s, u, \quad j = A, B;$$

(b) by realizing that the cost functions are homogeneous of degree zero in $w_m$, $w_s$, and $w_u$, such that,

$$\Theta_{mj}\sigma_{mi}^j + \Theta_{sj}\sigma_{si}^j + \Theta_{uj}\sigma_{ui}^j = 0,$$
$$i = m, s, u, \quad j = A, B;$$

and (c) by substituting in for $\sigma_{ii}^j$.

[26] See Stevens, "Millions of Mexicans."

[27] See Jones, "The Structure of Simple General Equilibrium Models."

# [10]

# IMMIGRANTS, MINORITIES, AND LABOR MARKET COMPETITION

GEORGE J. BORJAS*

This paper investigates the extent of labor market competition among immigrants, minorities, and the native population. An analysis of 1980 U.S. Census data reveals that immigrants tend to be substitutes for some labor market groups and complements for others. The effects of shifts in immigrant supply on the earnings of native-born men are, however, very small. On the other hand, increases in the supply of immigrants do have a sizable impact on the earnings of immigrants themselves: an increase of 10 percent in the supply of immigrants, for example, reduces the immigrant wage by about 10 percent.

THE literature on the economics of immigration has, in the past decade, been dominated by analyses of two questions: How do immigrants do *in* the U.S. labor market and what do immigrants do *to* the U.S. labor market? Beginning with the work of Chiswick (1978), most of the empirical studies have focused on the first of these issues (see also Borjas 1985). The literature on the second question is much less developed. Little is known about the labor market adjustments caused by the large influx of immigrants in the last twenty years. Some studies (e.g., Johnson 1980) have constructed theoretical models of the labor market interaction between the native- and the foreign-born populations. In effect, these models build on the basic assumption that the two groups are substitutes in production, even though the type of technological relationship between the two groups is *entirely* an empirical question.

The empirical determination of the extent of substitutability or complementarity between any two labor inputs is, of course, based on neoclassical input demand theory. The main methodological tool of such studies is the estimation of the production technology in which various race, gender, and other (demographically defined) labor inputs, as well as capital, enter as inputs in the production process (see Borjas 1983; Grant and Hamermesh 1981; and the survey by Hamermesh, 1986). The parameters of the production technology provide important information about the technological relationships among the various inputs, and are used to infer the extent of substitutability or complementarity between any two inputs.

This framework has been used to study the relationship between native- and foreign-born workers by Borjas (1986a, 1986b) and Grossman (1982). Despite major differences in methodological approach and in the data sets analyzed, these studies conclude that immigrants have a very small numerical impact on the earnings of the native-born population.[1] These studies,

*The author is Professor of Economics at the University of California–Santa Barbara and Research Associate at the National Bureau of Economic Research. He thanks Daniel Hamermesh for helpful comments on an early draft of this paper and the Rockefeller Foundation for financial assistance.

[1] One crucial difference between the Borjas and Grossman studies is the use of different functional

however, aggregate rather different immigrant groups (Mexicans, Vietnamese, Chinese, Cubans, Italians, etc.) into a single population. Since it is well known that the national origin of the immigrant population (as well as the racial/ethnic background of native-born men) is an important characteristic in the determination of earnings, the conclusion that immigrants have had little impact on native earnings may well be masking important country- or race-specific distinctions in the extent of substitutability. This paper presents estimates of the extent of labor market competition between immigrants and natives in which both populations have been disaggregated by race and ethnic origins.

### Framework

Assume that the production technology is characterized by the Generalized Leontief production function (Diewert 1971):

$$(1) \qquad Q = \sum_j \sum_i \gamma_{ij}(X_i X_j)^{1/2},$$

where $Q$ is output, $X_i$ is the quantity of input $i$, and $\gamma_{ij}$ is the technology coefficient. The production function in (1) is linearly homogeneous and restricts the values of the technology parameters so that $\gamma_{ij} = \gamma_{ji}$.[2] The sign of $\gamma_{ij}$ determines whether inputs $i$ and $j$ are substitutes ($\gamma_{ij} < 0$) or complements ($\gamma_{ij} > 0$).

The assumption that firms in the labor market maximize profits and face constant input prices leads to the following system of labor demand functions:

$$(2) \qquad r_i = \gamma_{ii} + \sum_{j \neq i} \gamma_{ij}(X_j/X_i)^{1/2}.$$

---

forms (the Generalized Leontief versus the translog) to describe the production process. There is no *a priori* reason to prefer one function over the other, since both are second-order approximations to any arbitrary production function. Moreover, experiments by Griffin (1982) and Wales (1977) show that the translog function provides a better fit over certain ranges of data and the Generalized Leontief equation over others.

[2] In addition, diminishing marginal productivity for input $l$ requires that not all $\gamma_{lj}(j = 1, \ldots, l-1, l+1, \ldots, n)$ be negative. For a discussion of this and other related restrictions see Diewert (1971) and Sato and Koizumi (1973).

The system of equations in (2) illustrates the usefulness of the Generalized Leontief functional form: wage equations are linear-in-parameters and hence can be easily estimated by standard least squares techniques. Further, the functional form in (2) provides an intuitive understanding of the underlying process. In particular, the wage of group $i$, $r_i$, is affected by the number of type $j$ individuals in the labor market *per* member of group $i$ ($X_j/X_i$). Thus, the relative quantities of other factors of production affect group $i$'s wage through the technology parameter $\gamma_{ij}$, and when group $i$ is complementary (substitutable) with group $j$, an increase in the supply of group $j$ increases (decreases) group $i$'s wage. Finally, the simplicity of the wage equation arising from the production function (1) indicates that the Generalized Leontief technology may provide a much-needed link between demand theory and the many studies of wage determination in the literature.

Although the signs of the parameters $\gamma_{ij}$ contain useful information about the possibilities for technical substitution among the $n$ inputs, it is instructive to transform these parameters into quantities that are more tractable. Let us define the Hicks partial elasticity of complementarity (Hicks 1970):

$$(3) \qquad c_{ij} = \frac{QQ_{ij}}{Q_i Q_j}$$

where $Q_i = \partial Q/\partial X_i$, $Q_{ij} = \partial^2 Q/\partial X_i \partial X_j$. The Hicks elasticity of complementarity measures the effect on the relative price of factor $i$ of a change in the relative quantity of factor $j$, holding constant the marginal cost and the quantities of other factors. Since the analysis in this paper is mainly concerned with estimating the impact of changes in the supply of immigrants on the earnings of the native-born population, the elasticity of complementarity (rather than its dual, the elasticity of substitution) is the natural measure to quantify this impact.

A useful property of the elasticity of complementarity is given by:

(4)
$$\frac{d \ln r_i}{d \ln X_j} = s_j c_{ij},$$

where $s_j = r_j X_j / Q$, the relative share of income accruing to factor $j$. Hence the elasticity of factor price $(d\ln r_i / d\ln X_j)$, which measures the percentage change on the earnings of group $i$ due to a one-percent increase in the supply of group $j$, is proportional to the elasticity of complementarity. Knowledge of the elasticities of complementarity, therefore, provides a complete picture of price shifts occurring among the native-born as a result of a supply shift in the immigrant population.

It can be shown that under the Generalized Leontief technology, the elasticities of complementarity are given by:

(5)
$$c_{ij} = \frac{\gamma_{ij}}{2(s_i s_j r_i r_j)^{1/2}} \quad \text{for } i \neq j,$$

and

(6)
$$c_{ii} = \frac{\gamma_{ii} - r_i}{2 s_i r_i} \quad \text{for } i = j.$$

As implied by the earlier discussion, the sign of $\gamma_{ij}$ determines the sign of the (cross) elasticity of complementarity, which, in turn, determines the sign of the elasticity of factor price.

The estimation of the demand system in (2) is affected by two major econometric problems. First, equations (2) are not wage-determination functions unless (relative) supply conditions are also specified. It is common in the input demand literature (see, for example, Grant and Hamermesh 1981:355) to estimate the production technology under the assumption that input supply is exogenous. The usual justification for this assumption is that the supplies of age-specific sex/race groups are essentially fixed at any given time. But this assumption ignores the fact that although the total stock of specific labor inputs may be treated as fixed, its distribution across labor markets is likely to be guided by input price differentials. In the empirical analysis below, the assumption of inelastic relative supplies will be used, and the sensitivity

of the results to more complex supply models will be addressed.

The second econometric problem that has been ignored in the labor demand literature concerns the aggregation of workers into the labor inputs $X_i$. An implicit assumption in specifying production functions such as (1) is that all group $i$ workers are homogeneous within *and* across labor markets. Of course, individuals within each of these groups vary markedly in skills, and these differences may lead to group $i$ individuals having different average skills across different labor markets. Hence wage differentials across labor markets may simply reflect an unequal distribution of skill levels, seriously biasing the estimates of the production function.

This problem can be approached (in the Generalized Leontief framework) by characterizing an individual's effective labor supply in terms of a fixed effect indicating the skill level of the individual. In particular, the wage paid to individual $l$ in group $i$, $r_{il}$, depends on: (a) the market-determined wage level for the average group $i$ person, $r_i$; and (b) how the skills of individual $l$ differ from the skills of the average group $i$ person, $f_l$. Hence, in general, $r_{il} = r_{il}(w_i, f_l)$, and the individual's wage rate depends both on market forces and on his (relative) skill level.

To make this approach useful it is necessary to add structure to the model. Two possible simplifications are $r_{il} = r_i f_l$ and $r_{il} = r_i + f_l$. The additive fixed effect assumes that the wage premium due to differential skills is independent of the demographic characteristics of the labor market, whereas the multiplicative specification allows for the possibility of an interaction.[3] For simplicity, the analysis in this paper uses the additive specification. If it is assumed that $f_l$ can be written in terms both of observable socioeconomic characteristics, $Z_l$, and a random uncorrelated error, $\epsilon_l$, the stochastic equivalent of (5) is given by:

---

[3]Note that the definition of the fixed effect requires that $E(f_l)$ equal one in the multiplicative specification and zero in the additive model.

## IMMIGRANTS, MINORITIES, AND LABOR MARKET COMPETITION    385

(7)   $r_{it} = Z_{i}\beta_{i} + \sum_{j \neq i} \gamma_{ij} (X_{j}/X_{i})^{1/2} + \epsilon_{t},$

$$i = 1, \ldots, n.$$

Equation (7) specifies the wage-determination process at the individual level and will be used throughout the empirical analysis. It is important to note that estimates of the demand system in (7) control for observable differences in socioeconomic variables *within* each of the labor inputs, but do not control for differences in these variables across the groups. It is these differences in socioeconomic variables, as well as differences in unobserved characteristics captured by the error term, that prevent the production technology from degenerating into a system in which all inputs are perfect substitutes.

### Data and Basic Results

The data set used in the analysis is the 1980 5/100 A Sample from the U.S. Census.[4] The analysis was restricted to working-age individuals (18–64 years) who (a) were not in the military, (b) were not self-employed or working without pay, and (c) had records containing complete information on the variables used in the analysis. The "local labor market" is defined to be the SMSA in which the individual resides.

To account for the differences in ethnicity and race among persons, as well as for the difference between native- and foreign-born status, the analysis is initially conducted using a nine-way breakdown of the labor force: white native males (WN), black native males (BN), Hispanic native males (HN), Asian native males (AN), white immigrant males (WI), black immigrant males (BI), Hispanic immigrant males (HI), Asian immigrant males (AI), and females (F).

Three points should be made regarding this particular decomposition of the labor force. First, the analysis allows for the disaggregation of the four largest racial/eth-

nic groups that can be identified in the 1980 Census. Second, all women are aggregated into one group because previous research (e.g., Smith 1977) shows that earnings differentials among different types of women are much narrower than earnings differentials among different types of men. This fact suggests that employer differentiation of women is likely to be less important than employer differentiation of men. Finally, the samples defined as "white" contain all non-black, non-Asian, non-Hispanic observations.

The employment data necessary for the estimation of equations (2) were obtained from the Census files. The labor input $X_{i}$ (in the SMSA) is defined as the number of individuals in group $i$ who were of working age and were employed in 1979. Finally, the capital ($K$) data are drawn from Grant (1979), who calculated the capital stock in each of 84 SMSAs for the ten years up to 1969 using the *Census of Manufactures* and the *Annual Survey of Manufactures*.[5] The capital data used below, for 1979, are extrapolated from the time-series.[6]

It is well known that capital stock calculations are subject to large measurement errors. To complicate matters, the capital data are available only for manufacturing industries. Since the analysis in this paper is conducted over all industries, the capital data lead to biased parameter estimates unless it is assumed that the aggregate capital stock in the SMSA is (roughly) proportional to the manufacturing capital stock. Because the capital data are available for only 84 SMSAs, the analysis is restricted to persons residing in these labor markets.

Before proceeding to the estimation of the demand system, it is useful to present summary statistics on the earnings and relative sizes of the nine labor groups under

---

[4]Since the Census data set is quite large, random samples were drawn for some of the larger population groups. The sampling proportions used are available from the author on request.

[5]The 84 SMSAs used by Grant (1979) to construct the capital time series are not a random sample of the 310 SMSAs identified in the A sample of the 1980 Census; they tend, rather, to be the largest SMSAs in the country.

[6]The analysis also experimented with using the 1969 level of the capital stock, rather than the 1979 extrapolation made from the 1959–1969 trend. The impact of this change in the definition of the capital variable on the estimated coefficients was trivial.

*Table 1.* Summary Statistics: Labor Force Characteristics of Native and Immigrant Groups.

| Group | Mean 1979 Annual Earnings | Percent of Labor Force | Number of Observations |
|---|---|---|---|
| White Native Men | $18,892 | 42.6 | 5,831 |
| Black Native Men | 13,660 | 5.2 | 4,136 |
| Hisp. Native Men | 13,702 | 2.5 | 25,726 |
| Asian Native Men | 18,393 | .3 | 4,247 |
| White Immigrant Men | 20,293 | 2.3 | 1,902 |
| Black Immigrant Men | 12,261 | .3 | 1,747 |
| Hisp. Immigrant Men | 11,600 | 2.3 | 23,253 |
| Asian Immigrant Men | 16,487 | .8 | 13,557 |
| Women | 9,305 | 43.7 | 62,710 |

*Source*: 1980 U.S. Census of Population, A Sample.

study. Table 1 presents these basic statistics, which illustrate the well-known differences in earnings across the groups and also show how the large Hispanic immigration is creating a labor force with almost as many Hispanics as blacks.

Equation (2) was estimated on the micro Census data using 1979 annual earnings as the dependent variable. The estimation was conducted by stacking the data for all nine labor force groups (so that all the coefficients of the nine earnings functions were estimated jointly) and by simultaneously introducing the across-equation restrictions implied by the symmetry constraints. The use of annual earnings, instead of the wage rate, facilitates comparison between the results in this paper and those available in the labor demand literature that use the average income share in a given year to

estimate translog equations.[7] The variables held constant in the vector $Z$ include years of schooling, years of labor market experience (age-schooling-6), and years of labor market experience squared.

Table 2 presents the estimated technology parameters. Several findings are worth stressing. First, all immigrant groups have had a negative impact on the earnings of the white native-born population. Thus immigrants, as a group, are substitutes with the single largest demographic group in the labor force. Second, this strong degree of substitutability is *not* evident in the black native-born population. Table 2 provides no evidence that black native-born men have been adversely affected by white or Asian immigrants, and only marginal evidence that black natives and black or Hispanic immigrants are substitutes. Surprisingly, the technological relationship between black natives and white immigrants (who make up over 40 percent of the immigrant population) is one of strong complementarity. Finally, there is no evidence of substitutability between the Hispanic native-born population and the three other native-born groups under analysis (whites, blacks, and Asians). This result resembles the finding obtained by Borjas (1983) in his study of the 1976 Survey of Income and Education.

It is of substantial interest that the results in Table 2 show a technological relationship between black natives and white immigrants different from that between black natives and either Hispanic or black immigrants. In particular, the former relationship indicates complementary inputs, whereas the latter relationships indicate (weakly) substitutable inputs. These findings are consistent with the theoretical expectation that "like" inputs are more substitutable than "unlike" inputs. White immigrants, for instance, tend to originate in Western European countries and have high levels of education. On arrival in the United States these immigrants—unlike black natives—perform relatively well in the

---

[7]The study was replicated using the wage rate as the dependent variable, with similar qualitative results.

IMMIGRANTS, MINORITIES, AND LABOR MARKET COMPETITION    387

*Table 2.* Estimates of Technology Parameters (1980 Census).
(t-ratios in parentheses)

|     | BN | HN | AN | WI | BI | HI | AI | F | K |
|-----|----|----|----|----|----|----|----|---|---|
| WN | −1158.6*<br>(−4.56) | −98.5<br>(−.90) | −120.0<br>(−.93) | −3972.7*<br>(−10.62) | −527.1*<br>(−2.68) | −396.5*<br>(−3.46) | −586.8*<br>(−4.33) | −1370.0*<br>(−5.40) | 1771.5*<br>(7.68) |
| BN |    | −79.2<br>(−.74) | −156.5<br>(−1.37) | 876.2*<br>(2.34) | −287.6<br>(−1.72) | −149.9<br>(−1.44) | −9.9<br>(−.08) | 482.6*<br>(2.24) | 549.4*<br>(7.01) |
| HN |    |    | 179.3<br>(1.29) | −425.4*<br>(−2.45) | −1590.3*<br>(−8.43) | 278.9*<br>(2.66) | 686.4*<br>(4.61) | −212.4*<br>(−2.09) | 247.6*<br>(11.27) |
| AN |    |    |    | 80.6<br>(.42) | −190.8<br>(−.64) | 182.6<br>(1.48) | 319.5<br>(.79) | −86.1<br>(−.58) | 89.9*<br>(3.84) |
| WI |    |    |    |    | 1554.7*<br>(5.32) | −84.4<br>(−.50) | 890.1*<br>(3.85) | 4606.2*<br>(14.72) | 277.3*<br>(2.28) |
| BI |    |    |    |    |    | 129.7<br>(.82) | 108.6<br>(.37) | 639.8*<br>(2.88) | 34.4<br>(1.07) |
| HI |    |    |    |    |    |    | −722.7*<br>(−5.30) | 226.5<br>(1.80) | 235.8<br>(1.80) |
| AI |    |    |    |    |    |    |    | 438.6*<br>(2.82) | 105.0*<br>(4.14) |
| F |    |    |    |    |    |    |    |    | −173.6*<br>(−3.70) |

*Note*: For an explanation of abbreviations, see the text.
*Significant at the 5 percent level.

labor market. Black and Hispanic immigrants, on the other hand, are characterized by low levels of education and—like black natives—do not perform well in the labor market. The finding in Table 2, therefore, implies that the impact of immigration on black natives is likely to shift over time as the skill composition of the immigrant population in the United States changes.

Greater insight into the substantive implications of these technological relationships can be gained by calculating the corresponding elasticities of factor prices, $d \ln r_i/d \ln X_j$, for the relevant technology parameters. Table 3 presents the estimated changes in the earnings of the four native-born male groups as the supplies of the four immigrant groups increase. These cross-elasticities of demand are most revealing for what they do *not* show. In particular, despite the statistical significance of many of the technological parameters, Table 3 does not show these effects to be numerically important. For example, the cross-elasticity of the earnings of white native-born men with respect to the quantity of white foreign-born men is −.025.

This finding implies that a 10 percent increase in the supply of these immigrants decreases white native earnings by less than three-tenths of one percent, and that even a doubling in the number of these immigrants reduces white native earnings by only 2.5 percent.

This remarkable result is evident in each of the 16 elasticities presented in Table 3. None of the elasticities takes on a value exceeding |.03|. Thus, even if some immigrant groups compete with the native-born in the labor market, the numerical impact of this competition is trivial.

It is notable that a similar result was obtained by Grossman (1982). Using a different methodology (estimating translog production functions) and a different data set (the 1970 Census), Grossman estimated that a 10 percent increase in the number of immigrants reduces the native-born wage by between .2 and .3 percent (Grossman 1982:600). The similarity between two sets of findings so different in their derivation strengthens the conclusion that immigrants have not played a major role in the determination of wage levels for native-born men in recent years.

*Table 3.* Elasticities of Factor Prices (1980 Census).

| With Respect to the Quantity of: | The Change in the Wage of: | | | |
|---|---|---|---|---|
| | WN | BN | HN | AN |
| WI | −.025* | .021* | −.015* | .006 |
| | (−10.62) | (2.34) | (−2.45) | (.42) |
| BI | −.001* | −.003 | −.021* | −.005 |
| | (−2.68) | (−1.72) | (−8.43) | (−.64) |
| HI | −.002* | −.004 | .010* | .013 |
| | (−3.46) | (−1.44) | (2.69) | (1.48) |
| AI | −.002* | −.000 | .014* | .013 |
| | (−4.33) | (−.08) | (4.61) | (.79) |

*Note:* For an explanation of abbreviations, see the text.
The t-ratios in parentheses refer to the technological parameter $\gamma_{ij}$.
*Significant at the 5 percent level.

Immigrants, however, have had a sizable impact on the determination of their *own* wage levels. Table 4 presents the set of price elasticities of demand describing what happens to the earnings of immigrant men as the quantities of immigrant men increase. These elasticities, on average, are much larger than the cross-elasticities between native earnings and immigrant supplies. In particular, the own-elasticities presented in Table 4 reveal that increases in the supply of type $i$ immigrants significantly reduce the earnings of those immigrants. For example, a 10 percent increase in the number of white immigrants reduces the earnings of white immigrants by 10.9 percent; a 10 percent increase in the number of black immigrants reduces black immigrant earnings by 5.8 percent; a 10 percent increase in the number of Hispanic immigrants reduces Hispanic immigrant earnings by 13.9 percent; and a 10 percent increase in the number of Asian immigrants reduces Asian immigrant earnings by 7.9 percent.[8]

### Extensions of the Empirical Analysis

### Endogeneity of Supply

The validity of the assumption of inelastic labor supplies that is implicitly used in the estimation of the results in the previous section can be questioned. After all, the wage differentials created across labor markets by the interactions among labor inputs are likely to induce internal migration patterns whereby the groups move to areas in which they are likely to do relatively well. The presence of mobility costs or imperfect information (or both) suggests that the wage differentials do not vanish in the long run and that the correct estimation of (2) requires that the supply of inputs to labor markets be modeled more fully.

To account for the endogeneity of the supply variables, it is assumed that at the SMSA level relative supplies of labor inputs are affected by a vector of socioeconomic characteristics, $A$, describing the SMSA. Hence:

$$(8) \qquad (X_j/X_i)^{1/2} = A\beta + \epsilon$$

[8]One important criticism of these results—as well as of most of the labor demand literature—is that substantive findings are being obtained from across-SMSA correlations between wage levels and relative supplies. If, as is likely, some small groups are concentrated in a relatively few labor markets, "outlying" labor markets may play a relatively large role in the estimation procedure. Borjas (1986a), however, using the 1970 Census, shows that restricting the analysis

to the few SMSAs containing relatively large numbers of minority groups (e.g., blacks or Hispanics) or to SMSAs in a particular region (e.g., the South) does not have a major impact on the estimated demand system.

IMMIGRANTS, MINORITIES, AND LABOR MARKET COMPETITION    389

*Table 4.* Elasticities of Factor Prices Within the Immigrant Population (1980 Census).

| | The Change in the Wage of: | | | |
|---|---|---|---|---|
| *With Respect to the Quantity of:* | *WI* | *BI* | *HI* | *AI* |
| WI | −1.087* | .167* | −.004 | .048* |
| | (−2.35) | (5.32) | (−.50) | (3.85) |
| BI | .015* | −.576 | .002 | .002 |
| | (5.32) | (−1.48) | (.82) | (.37) |
| HI | −.002 | .014 | −1.395* | −.039* |
| | (−.50) | (.82) | (−1.97) | (−5.30) |
| AI | .012* | .007 | −.018* | −.787 |
| | (3.85) | (.37) | (−5.30) | (−1.88) |

*Note*: For an explanation of abbreviations, see the text.
The t-ratios in parentheses refer to the technological parameter $\gamma_{ij}$ for the cross-elasticities, and to $(\gamma_{ii} - r_i)$ for the own-elasticities.
*Significant at the 5 percent level.

The vector $A$ includes the proportions of the labor force employed in each of the one-digit industry groups, the probability of receiving Supplementary Security Income (SSI) assistance (relative to the poverty rate), and the mean level of SSI payments (relative to the mean wage level in the SMSA).[9] The industrial composition of the SMSA is likely to affect supplies, since particular combinations of industrial concentrations will attract individuals with specific skills to the locality. Similarly, the chances of receiving a particular form of public assistance (SSI), *relative* to the SMSA's poverty rate, as well as the "real" levels of that assistance, measure the economic welfare of low income individuals in the SMSA. If the expected value of public assistance payments differs significantly across SMSAs, geographic differences in the location of racial or immigrant groups are likely to arise.

The demand system in (2) was reestimated using two stage least squares, and the resulting estimates are summarized in Table 5. This table parallels the cross-price elasticities presented in Table 3. A comparison of these two tables shows that the

[9]The industry composition variables were calculated from the 1980 Census file, and the public assistance variables were obtained from the 1976 Survey of Income and Education.

qualitative impact of immigrants on the earnings of the native-born is generally unaffected by the estimation procedure (except for the effects on black natives), although the 2SLS cross-price elasticities tend to be slightly larger than the corresponding OLS estimates. Despite the absolute increase in the numerical impact, however, it must be stressed that even the 2SLS elasticities predict numerically small impacts. For example, a 10 percent increase in the number of white immigrants reduces white native-born earnings by .4 percent according to the 2SLS regression and by .25 percent according to the OLS regression. Thus, even though the 2SLS technique roughly doubles the size of the cross-price elasticity, the numerical impact remains trivial.

## The Heterogeneity of Hispanics

In the previous sections, male Hispanics have been disaggregated by nativity status rather than by national origin. There are four major national groups in the U.S. Hispanic population: Mexicans (MX), Puerto Ricans (PR); Cubans (CU); and "other" Hispanics (OS), mostly of Central and South American origin. Previous research (Reimers 1983; Borjas and Tienda 1985) has documented that differences in labor market outcomes across these four Hispanic groups are as large as, if not larger than,

Table 5. Elasticities of Factor Prices (1980 Census),
Adjusted for Endogeneity of Supply.

| With Respect to the Quantity of: | The Change in the Wage of: | | | |
|---|---|---|---|---|
| | WN | BN | HN | AN |
| WI | −.042*<br>(−10.16) | .024<br>(1.61) | −.005*<br>(−3.78) | .030<br>(.86) |
| BI | −.001<br>(−.82) | .005<br>(1.55) | −.017*<br>(−4.19) | −.032*<br>(−2.00) |
| HI | .002<br>(1.11) | .014*<br>(2.91) | .024*<br>(4.19) | .010<br>(.69) |
| AI | −.003<br>(−1.63) | −.007<br>(−1.86) | .025*<br>(4.28) | .020<br>(.54) |

Note: For an explanation of abbreviations, see the text.
The t-ratios in parentheses refer to the technological parameter $\gamma_{ij}$.
*Significant at the 5 percent level.

Table 6. Elasticities of Factor Prices Across Hispanic
and Non-Hispanic Groups (1980 Census).

| With Respect to the Quantity of: | The Change in the Wage of: | | | | | |
|---|---|---|---|---|---|---|
| | WN | BN | AN | WI | BI | AI |
| MX | −.003*<br>(−3.76) | −.007*<br>(−2.19) | −.002<br>(−.28) | −.004<br>(−.94) | −.003<br>(−.19) | −.004<br>(−.69) |
| PR | .000<br>(.18) | .004*<br>(3.90) | −.016<br>(−1.49) | .005*<br>(2.29) | −.056*<br>(−3.47) | .017*<br>(2.32) |
| CU | .001*<br>(2.42) | .004*<br>(3.36) | .010*<br>(2.09) | .006*<br>(2.81) | .024*<br>(2.44) | −.020*<br>(−4.77) |
| OS | −.001*<br>(−2.17) | .004<br>(.41) | .004<br>(.75) | .010*<br>(3.17) | −.134*<br>(−6.59) | −.003<br>(−.38) |

Note: For an explanation of abbreviations, see the text.
The t-ratios in parentheses refer to the technological parameter $\gamma_{ij}$.
*Significant at the 5 percent level.

the differences by nativity status. These findings suggest that an alternative substantively important decomposition of the Hispanic labor force exists. The demand system in (2) was reestimated, using ordinary least squares, after replacing the Hispanic native and Hispanic immigrant group with four Hispanic groups based on national origin. The cross-elasticities of demand between the four Hispanic groups and the other male labor force groups are presented in Table 6.

Several interesting findings are provided by these selected results. First, Mexicans—who make up nearly 60 percent of the male Hispanic population—have had a negative impact on the earnings of both white and black native-born men. This impact, however, is small: a 10 percent increase in the number of Mexicans reduces the earnings of white native-born men by .03 percent and the earnings of black native-born men by .07 percent. Second, Puerto Ricans are substitutable inputs only with black immigrants; there is a complementary or independent relationship between Puerto Ricans and all other native-born male groups. Third, Cubans have not had an adverse impact on the earnings of any of the native-born male groups. In fact, a significant complementary relationship exists between Cuban men and white, black, and

*Table 7.* Elasticities of Factor Prices
Within Hispanic Groups (1980 Census).

| With Respect to the Quantity of: | The Change in the Wage of: | | | |
|---|---|---|---|---|
| | MX | PR | CU | OS |
| MX | −1.275* | .0078* | .003* | .001 |
| | (−2.43) | (5.65) | (2.48) | (.70) |
| PR | .031* | −1.020 | .000 | −.013* |
| | (5.65) | (−1.76) | (.04) | (−3.00) |
| CU | .016* | .000 | .482 | −.004 |
| | (2.48) | (.04) | (1.03) | (−.49) |
| OS | .003 | −.015* | −.002 | −.828 |
| | (.70) | (−3.00) | (−.49) | (−1.89) |

*Note*: For an explanation of abbreviations, see the text.
The t-ratios in parentheses refer to the technological parameter $\gamma_{ij}$ for the cross-elasticities, and to $(\gamma_n - r_i)$ for own-elasticities.
*Significant at the 5 percent level.

Asian native-born men. Interestingly, Cubans are substitutable only with one of the immigrant groups—Asian immigrants. It is of interest to note that Asian immigrants, like Cubans, tend to have above-average success in the labor market.

Despite the statistical significance of these cross effects, their numerical magnitude is small. On the other hand, Table 7 shows that the numerical impact of increases in the supply of the different types of Hispanics on their own wage is much larger. The own price elasticity of demand for the various Hispanic groups ranges around unity (in absolute value) for three of the groups, and is perversely positive but insignificant for the fourth (Cubans). Thus a 10 percent increase in the supply of Mexicans, Puerto Ricans, or other Hispanics will lead to about a 10 percent decrease in the wage of the own group.

## Summary

This study of the extent of labor market competition among immigrants, minorities, and the native-born population has found that, in general, immigrants tend to be substitutes for some labor market groups and complements for others. White native-born men tend to be adversely affected by the increase in immigrant supply, whereas

black native-born men have, if anything, gained slightly from increases in the immigrant supply. All these cross-effects of shifts in immigrant supply on the earnings of native-born men are numerically very small.

On the other hand, increases in the supply of immigrants do have a sizable impact on the earnings of immigrants themselves. An increase of 10 percent in the supply of immigrants reduces the immigrant wage by about 10 percent. Thus, immigrants' main competitors in the labor market are other immigrants.

These results withstand changes in the estimation procedure and disaggregations of Hispanics into national origin groups. Increases in the supply of the various Hispanic groups—Mexicans, Puerto Ricans, Cubans, and other Hispanics—have small effects on the earnings of non-Hispanics, but sizable effects on the earnings of the groups themselves.

Despite these varied results, the empirical study of the impact immigrants have had on the U.S. labor market is still in its infancy. Difficult substantive and technical problems remain to be resolved. Perhaps the most important issue is the modeling of the labor supply decisions of immigrants and native workers. In particular, it is well known that a large fraction of immigrants reside in a relatively small number of labor

392          INDUSTRIAL AND LABOR RELATIONS REVIEW

markets. The factors motivating these internal migration decisions among the foreign-born population need to be specified explicitly in the wage determination process. In addition, since the geographic concentration of immigrants in a small number of labor markets is likely to exaggerate their impact within those labor markets, the native population may respond by initiating its own set of migration flows. If such speculations are correct, it is likely that future research will lead to an increased understanding of the wage determination process for both native- and foreign-born persons.

One finding of this study, tentative though it must be, bears emphasis: namely, the common assumption that immigrants have large effects on native earnings is *not* confirmed by Census data. Even a detailed disaggregation of the immigrant population by racial and ethnic background and of the Hispanic population by national origin fails to reveal a single instance in which cross-effects are large.

**REFERENCES**

**Borjas, George J.**
1986a   "The Demographic Determinants of the Demand for Black Labor." In Richard B. Freeman and Harry J. Holzer, eds., *The Black Youth Employment Crisis*. Chicago: University of Chicago Press, pp. 191–230.
1986b   "The Sensitivity of Labor Demand Functions to Choice of Dependent Variable." *Review of Economics and Statistics*, Vol. 68, No. 1, pp. 58–66.
1985    "Assimilation, Changes in Cohort Quality, and the Earnings of Immigrants." *Journal of Labor Economics*, Vol. 3, No. 4, pp. 463–89.
1983    "The Substitutability of Black, Hispanic and White Labor." *Economic Inquiry*, Vol. 21, No. 1, pp. 93–106.

**Borjas, George J., and Marta Tienda**
1985    *Hispanics in the U.S. Economy*. Orlando, Fla.: Academic Press.

**Chiswick, Barry R.**
1978    "The Effect of Americanization on the Earnings of Foreign-Born Men." *Journal of Political Economy*, Vol. 85, No. 5, pp. 897–922.

**Diewert, W. E.**
1971    "An Application of the Shephard Duality Theorem: A Generalized Leontief Production Function." *Journal of Political Economy*, Vol. 79, No. 3, pp. 481–507.

**Grant, James H.**
1979    "Substitution Among Labor: Labor and Capital in U.S. Manufacturing." Ph.D. diss., Michigan State University.

**Grant, James H., and Daniel S. Hamermesh**
1981    "Labor Market Competition Among Youths, White Women and Others." *Review of Economics and Statistics*, Vol. 63, No. 3, pp. 354–60.

**Griffin, James M.**
1982    "The Approximation Characteristics of Generalized Functional Forms: Results from Pseudo-Data Experiments." *Advances in Applied Microeconomics*, Vol. 3, pp. 3–18.

**Grossman, Jean B.**
1982    "The Substitutability of Natives and Immigrants in Production." *Review of Economics and Statistics*, Vol. 54, No. 4, pp. 596–603.

**Hamermesh, Daniel S.**
1987    "The Demand for Labor in the Long Run." In Orley Ashenfelter and Richard Layard, eds., *Handbook of Labor Economics*. New York: North-Holland.

**Hicks, John**
1970    "Elasticity of Substitution Again: Substitutes and Complements." *Oxford Economic Papers*, Vol. 22, No. 3, pp. 289–96.

**Johnson, George E.**
1980    "The Labor Market Effects of Immigration." *Industrial and Labor Relations Review*, Vol. 33, No. 3, pp. 331–41.

**Reimers, Cordelia W.**
1983    "Labor Market Discrimination Against Hispanic and Black Men." *Review of Economics and Statistics*, Vol. 65, No. 4, pp. 570–79.

**Sato, Ryuzo, and Tetsunori Koizumi**
1973    "On the Elasticities of Substitution and Complementarity." *Oxford Economic Papers*, Vol. 25, No. 1, pp. 44–56.

**Smith, Sharon**
1977    *Equal Pay in the Public Sector: Fact or Fantasy*. Princeton: Princeton University Press.

**Wales, Terence J.**
1977    "On the Flexibility of Functional Forms: An Empirical Approach." *Journal of Econometrics*, Vol. 5, No. 2, pp. 183–93.

# [11]

# THE IMPACT OF THE MARIEL BOATLIFT ON THE MIAMI LABOR MARKET

DAVID CARD*

Using data from the Current Population Survey, this paper describes the effect of the Mariel Boatlift of 1980 on the Miami labor market. The Mariel immigrants increased the Miami labor force by 7%, and the percentage increase in labor supply to less-skilled occupations and industries was even greater because most of the immigrants were relatively unskilled. Nevertheless, the Mariel influx appears to have had virtually no effect on the wages or unemployment rates of less-skilled workers, even among Cubans who had immigrated earlier. The author suggests that the ability of Miami's labor market to rapidly absorb the Mariel immigrants was largely owing to its adjustment to other large waves of immigrants in the two decades before the Mariel Boatlift.

ONE of the chief concerns of immigration policy–makers is the extent to which immigrants depress the labor market opportunities of less-skilled natives. Despite the presumption that an influx of immigrants will substantially reduce native wages, existing empirical studies suggest that the effect is small. (See the survey by Greenwood and McDowell [1986] and studies by Grossman [1982], Borjas [1987], and Lalonde and Topel [1987].) There are two leading explanations for this finding. First, immigrants have, on average, only slightly lower skills than the native population. Thus, econometric studies based on the distribution of the existing stock of immigrants probably understate the effect of unskilled immigration on less-skilled natives. Second, the locational choices of immigrants and natives presumably depend on expected labor market opportunities. Immigrants tend to move to cities where the growth in demand for labor can accommodate their supply. Even if new immigrants cluster in only a few cities (as they do in the United States), inter-city migration of natives will tend to offset the adverse effects of immigration.

These considerations illustrate the difficulty of using the correlation across cities between wages and immigrant densities to measure the effect of immigration on the labor market opportunities of natives. They also underscore the value of a natural experiment that corresponds more closely to an exogenous increase in the supply of immigrants to a particular labor market.

The experiences of the Miami labor market in the aftermath of the Mariel Boatlift form one such experiment. From May to September 1980, some 125,000 Cuban immigrants arrived in Miami on a flotilla of privately chartered boats. Their arrival was the consequence of an unlikely sequence of events culminating in Castro's

* The author is Professor of Economics, Princeton University. He thanks George Borjas, Alan Krueger, Bruce Meyer, and seminar participants at Princeton University for their comments.

A data appendix with copies of the computer programs used to generate the tables in this paper is available from the author at the Industrial Relations Section, Firestone Library, Princeton University, Princeton, NJ 08544.

*Industrial and Labor Relations Review*, Vol. 43, No. 2 (January 1990). © by Cornell University.
0019-7939/90/4302 $01.00

declaration on April 20, 1980, that Cubans wishing to emigrate to the United States were free to leave from the port of Mariel.[1] Fifty percent of the Mariel immigrants settled permanently in Miami. The result was a 7% increase in the labor force of Miami and a 20% increase in the number of Cuban workers in Miami.

This paper summarizes the effects of the Boatlift on the Miami labor market, focusing on wages and unemployment rates of less-skilled workers. The analysis is based on individual micro-data for 1979–85 from the merged outgoing rotation group samples of the Current Population Survey (CPS).

Three features of the Mariel incident and the Census data greatly facilitate the analysis. First, the CPS sample of the Miami metropolitan area is relatively large: roughly 1,200 individuals per month. Second, a comprehensive picture of the Miami labor market in the months just before the Mariel Boatlift is available from the 1980 Census, which was conducted on April 1, 1980. Finally, unlike most other ethnic groups, Cubans are separately identified in the CPS questionnaire. Thus, it is possible to estimate wage rates, unemployment rates, and other economic indicators for both Cubans and non-Cubans in the Miami labor market, and to measure the effects of the Mariel immigration on the two groups separately.

### Overview of the Miami Labor Market Before the Boatlift

For at least a decade prior to the Mariel Boatlift, Miami was the most immigrant-intensive city in the country. Tabulations from the 1980 Census indicate that 35.5% of residents in the Miami Standard Metropolitan Statistical Area (SMSA) were foreign-born,[2] compared to 22.3% in Los Angeles, the city with the next-highest immigrant fraction, and 6.1% nationwide. At the time of the Census, 56% of immigrants in Miami were of Cuban origin. The remaining foreign-born residents, who accounted for 16% of the Miami population, included other Hispanic groups and a broad selection of Caribbean and European nationals.

Miami also has a significant black population. The fraction of black residents was 15.0% in 1970 and had increased to 17.3% by the time of the 1980 Census. The large concentrations of both immigrants and blacks makes Miami ideal for studying the effect of increased immigration on the labor market opportunities of black natives.

Table 1 describes the four major groups in the Miami labor force in 1979: white non-Hispanics; black non-Hispanics; Cubans (foreign-born and native-born); and other Hispanics. For simplicity, I have restricted attention to individuals age 16–61, a group that represents roughly 60% of the Miami population. The fractions of Cubans and blacks in the 16–61 age group are 27.2% and 26.3%, respectively, and the fractions of white non-Hispanics and non-Cuban Hispanics are 34.4% and 11.1%. Overall, 73% of 16–61-year-olds participated in the labor force, with somewhat higher rates among whites and Cubans and lower rates among blacks and other Hispanics. Education levels in Miami are somewhat below the national average: the mean of completed education for 16–61-year-olds in 1979 was 11.8 years in Miami, compared with 12.2 years nationwide.

The occupation distributions in rows 7–17 of Table 1 give a crude indication of the degree of labor market competition among the four groups. Cubans and other Hispanics have very similar occupation distributions, with a higher representation in craft and operative occupations than either whites or blacks. Blacks are more highly concentrated in laborer and service-related occupations, and are significantly under-represented in managerial occupations.

A useful summary measure of the

---

[1] See Masud-Piloto (1988, chaps. 6–7) for an overview of the political developments that led to the Mariel Boatlift.
[2] See U.S. Department of Commerce (1983). The Miami SMSA consists of Dade County, and includes Miami City as well as a number of smaller towns and cities. Throughout this paper, I use "Miami" to refer to this broader geographic region.

*Table 1.* Characteristics of 16–61-Year-Olds in Miami, 1979.

| Characteristic | Whites | Blacks | Cubans | Hispanics | All |
|---|---|---|---|---|---|
| *Characteristics of Population Age 16–61* | | | | | |
| 1. Estimated Number (1000's) | 319.3 | 244.1 | 252.4 | 102.9 | 928.4 |
| 2. Mean Education | 12.8 | 11.4 | 11.0 | 11.6 | 11.8 |
| 3. Percent in Labor Force | 75.6 | 68.3 | 77.2 | 68.8 | 73.1 |
| *Characteristics of Those in Labor Force* | | | | | |
| 4. Estimated Number (1000's) | 241.3 | 166.6 | 194.7 | 70.8 | 678.2 |
| 5. Mean Education | 13.1 | 11.8 | 11.3 | 11.9 | 12.1 |
| 6. Percent Age 16–24 | 21.1 | 24.1 | 22.0 | 26.0 | 22.8 |
| *Occupation Distribution (Percent of Employed)* | | | | | |
| 7. Professional and Technical | 19.1 | 10.9 | 9.5 | 10.1 | 13.2 |
| 8. Managers | 15.7 | 2.8 | 8.6 | 8.1 | 9.4 |
| 9. Sales | 6.2 | 4.4 | 7.8 | 7.6 | 6.5 |
| 10. Clerical | 21.9 | 21.0 | 19.1 | 20.9 | 20.9 |
| 11. Craftsmen | 13.3 | 9.4 | 15.1 | 12.7 | 12.8 |
| 12. Operatives | 4.4 | 8.4 | 19.4 | 16.7 | 11.1 |
| 13. Transportation Operatives | 2.6 | 8.1 | 5.4 | 5.9 | 5.2 |
| 14. Laborers | 5.1 | 10.5 | 4.7 | 4.0 | 6.3 |
| 15. Farm Workers | 1.1 | 0.1 | 0.4 | 0.8 | 0.6 |
| 16. Less-Skilled Service Workers | 5.0 | 13.3 | 6.1 | 10.2 | 8.0 |
| 17. More-Skilled Service Workers | 5.7 | 10.9 | 4.0 | 3.0 | 6.2 |

*Notes:* White and black groups exclude hispanics. Hispanic group includes all hispanics other than Cubans. Less-skilled service workers include cleaning and food service workers. More-skilled service workers include health service, personal service, and protective service workers.

*Source:* Based on samples of employed workers in the outgoing rotation groups of the Current Population Survey in 1979.

overlap in the occupation distributions of the different groups is the average percent increase in labor supply in occupations held by one group that would result from a one percentage point increase in the overall fraction of workers in a second group.[3] This index has the simple form $\sum_j s_{1j} s_{2j} / s_j$, where $s_{1j}$ is the fraction of workers of group 1 in occupation $j$, $s_{2j}$ is the fraction of workers of group 2 in occupation $j$, and $s_j$ is the fraction of all workers in occupation $j$. Based on the distributions in Table 1, an inflow of immigrants resulting in a one percentage point increase in the fraction of Cubans in Miami would lead to a weighted average increase of .95% in the supply of labor to occupations held by whites. Under the same conditions the increase would be .99% for blacks, 1.02% for non-Cuban Hispanics, and 1.06% for Cubans themselves. These calculations suggest that the overlap between the occupational distributions of the four groups is relatively high.

[3] This index is derived in Altonji and Card (1989:15–16).

## The Mariel Immigration

Due to the unauthorized nature of the Boatlift, no exact count of the number of Mariel immigrants is available, and there is little precise information on the characteristics or final destinations of the immigrants. This section summarizes some of the available information, including data from the March 1985 Mobility Supplement to the Current Population Survey, which allows Mariel immigrants to be distinguished from other Cubans.

Most sources estimate the number of Mariel immigrants at between 120,000 and 125,000. A recent Census Bureau report (U.S. Department of Commerce 1988:9) states that 126,000 refugees entered the United States as "Cuban Entrants" (the special immigration status awarded to the Mariel refugees) between April 1980 and June 1981. Based on the settlement pattern of earlier Cubans, it is widely assumed that about one-half of these refugees settled permanently in Miami. The Census Bureau "Experimental County Population Estimates" file shows an increase of 80,500 in the Dade County population between April 1 and July 1 of 1980; 59,800 of these new entrants were age 16–61. My own tabulations from the CPS indicate that the Cuban share of the 16–61 age group increased from 27% in 1979 to 33% in 1981.[4] A similar increase is registered in CPS-based estimates of the Cuban share of the 16–61-year-old labor force, which changed from 37.2% in 1979 to 44.8% in 1981. Assuming that the Cuban share of the labor force would have remained constant between 1979 and 1981 in the absence of the Boatlift, these figures suggest that the Mariel immigration added approximately 45,000 to the Miami labor force—an increase of 7%.

From the first days of the Boatlift, the characteristics of the Mariel immigrants (hereafter referred to as Mariels) have been a subject of controversy. Among those who were permitted to leave Cuba were several hundred inmates of mental hospitals and jails. Many of these individuals were arrested by immigration officials upon their arrival in the United States, and over 1,000 were sent to a special prison facility in Atlanta to await deportation back to Cuba.[5] A similar number were arrested for crimes committed in the United States, and they still await determination of their ultimate immigration status.[6] Contemporary reports indicate that the Mariels included a relatively high fraction of less-skilled workers and a high fraction of individuals with low English ability (*Business Week* 1980).

Although the regular Current Population Survey questionnaire does not distinguish Mariels from other foreign and native-born Cubans, the March 1985 Mobility Supplement survey asked each respondent where he or she lived in March 1980 (one month before the start of the Boatlift). Table 2 presents a descriptive summary of the Cuban population interviewed in this survey, classified by whether the respondent claimed to be living abroad or in the United States five years earlier. The sample sizes, particularly of post-1980 entrants, are small.[7] Nevertheless, these data confirm the general impression that Mariels, on average, have less education, are somewhat younger, and are more likely to be male than other Cubans. The figures in Table 2 also suggest that the Mariels have lower labor force attachment and lower occupational attainment than other Cubans. Mariels are more heavily concentrated in laborer and service occupations, and are less likely to hold sales, clerical, and craft jobs.

The unadjusted wage gap between Mariels and other Cubans is 34%. Part of this differential is clearly attributable to the lower education levels and younger ages of the Mariels. A simple linear regression for the logarithm of average hourly earnings fitted to the sample of Cubans with earnings in 1984 suggests that the Mariels earned 18% lower wages than other Cubans, controlling for education, potential experience, and gender (the standard error of this estimate is .08). This gap presumably reflects the combination of lower language ability and a shorter assimilation time in the United States among the Mariels, as well as any differences in ability or motivation between the earlier and later Cuban immigrants.

### The Effect of the Mariel Immigration on the Miami Labor Market

Observers in Miami at the time of the Boatlift noted the strain caused by the Mariel immigration. The homicide rate

---

[4] These tabulations are presented in greater detail in an earlier version of this paper (Card 1989, Table 2).

[5] See Masud-Piloto (1988:100–103). Under a 1984 agreement a total of 2,700 Mariel immigrants were to be returned to Cuba.

[6] Mariel immigrants were blamed for, and indeed seem to have committed, many crimes in the first few months after the Boatlift. Wilbanks (1984) reported that 38 of the 574 homicides in Miami in 1980 were committed by Mariel immigrants. Disaffected Mariels were involved in 6 airline highjacking attempts in August 1980. See Masud-Piloto (1988:95–96).

[7] The weighted count of all Cubans in the March 1985 CPS who entered the United States after 1980 is 85,800, which is only 69% of the estimated 125,000 Mariel refugees.

*Table 2.* Characteristics of Mariel Immigrants and Other Cubans: Tabulations from March 1985 CPS.

| Characteristic | Mariel Immigrants | All other Cubans |
|---|---|---|
| Educational Attainment (Percent of Population in Each Category): | | |
| No High School | 56.5 | 25.4 |
| Some High School | 9.1 | 13.3 |
| Completed High School | 9.5 | 33.4 |
| Some College | 6.8 | 12.0 |
| Completed College | 18.1 | 15.8 |
| Percent Male | 55.6 | 50.7 |
| Percent Under 30 in 1980 | 38.7 | 29.6 |
| Mean Age in 1980 (Years) | 34.9 | 38.0 |
| Percent in Miami in 1985 | 53.9 | 52.4 |
| Percent Worked in 1984 | 60.6 | 73.4 |
| Mean Log Hourly Earnings | 1.37 | 1.71 |
| Occupation Distribution (Percent Employed in Each Category): | | |
| Professional/Managers | 19.3 | 21.0 |
| Technical | 0.0 | 1.5 |
| Sales | 4.5 | 11.2 |
| Clerical | 2.5 | 13.5 |
| Craftsmen | 9.5 | 19.9 |
| Operatives | 19.1 | 13.8 |
| Transportation Ops. | 3.8 | 4.3 |
| Laborers | 10.8 | 3.3 |
| Farm Workers | 0.0 | 1.8 |
| Less-Skilled Service | 26.0 | 7.4 |
| More-Skilled Service | 4.6 | 2.3 |
| Sample Size | 50 | 528 |
| Weighted Count | 42,300 | 476,900 |

*Note:* The sample consists of all Cubans in the March 1985 Current Population Survey age 21–66 (i.e., age 16–61 in 1980). Mariel immigrants are identified as those Cubans who stated that they lived outside the United States 5 years previously.

increased nearly 50% between 1979 and 1980 (see Wilbanks 1984:142). On the weekend of May 17, 1980, a three-day riot occurred in several black neighborhoods, killing 13. A government-sponsored committee that was set up to investigate the riot identified other long-standing grievances in the black community as its cause, but cited the labor market competition of Cuban refugees as an important background factor (Governor of Florida 1980: 14–15).

Another widely cited indicator of the labor market pressure created by the Mariel influx is the Miami unemployment rate, which rose from 5.0% in April 1980

to 7.1% in July. Over the same period state and national unemployment rates followed a similar pattern, suggesting that the changes in Miami were not solely a response to the Mariel influx. Nevertheless, widespread joblessness of refugees throughout the summer of 1980 contributed to a perception that labor market opportunities for less-skilled natives were threatened by the Mariel immigrants.[8]

Tables 3 and 4 present simple averages of wage rates and unemployment rates for whites, blacks, Cubans, and other Hispanics in the Miami labor market between 1979 and 1985. For comparative purposes, I have assembled similar data for whites, blacks, and Hispanics in four other cities: Atlanta, Los Angeles, Houston, and Tampa–St. Petersburg. These four cities were selected both because they had relatively large populations of blacks and Hispanics and because they exhibited a pattern of economic growth similar to that in Miami over the late 1970s and early 1980s. A comparison of employment growth rates (based on establishment-level data) suggests that economic conditions were very similar in Miami and the average of the four comparison cities between 1976 and 1984.

The wage data in Table 3 reveal several features of the Miami labor market. Perhaps most obvious is that earnings are lower in Miami than in the comparison cities. The differentials in 1979 ranged from 8% for whites to 15% for blacks. More surprising is that real earnings levels of whites in both Miami and the comparison cities were fairly constant between 1979 and 1985. This pattern contrasts with the general decline in real wages in the U.S. economy over this period (see Bound and Johnson 1989:5–6) and underscores the relatively close correspondence between economic conditions in Miami and the comparison cities.

---

[8] For example, a Florida State Employment Service official and a Department of Labor Wage and Hours Division official noted downward pressure on wages and working conditions in the unskilled segment of the Miami labor market (*Business Week* 1980).

*Table 3.* Logarithms of Real Hourly Earnings of Workers Age 16–61 in Miami and Four Comparison Cities, 1979–85.

| Group | 1979 | 1980 | 1981 | 1982 | 1983 | 1984 | 1985 |
|---|---|---|---|---|---|---|---|
| *Miami:* | | | | | | | |
| Whites | 1.85 | 1.83 | 1.85 | 1.82 | 1.82 | 1.82 | 1.82 |
| | (.03) | (.03) | (.03) | (.03) | (.03) | (.03) | (.05) |
| Blacks | 1.59 | 1.55 | 1.61 | 1.48 | 1.48 | 1.57 | 1.60 |
| | (.03) | (.02) | (.03) | (.03) | (.03) | (.03) | (.04) |
| Cubans | 1.58 | 1.54 | 1.51 | 1.49 | 1.49 | 1.53 | 1.49 |
| | (.02) | (.02) | (.02) | (.02) | (.02) | (.03) | (.04) |
| Hispanics | 1.52 | 1.54 | 1.54 | 1.53 | 1.48 | 1.59 | 1.54 |
| | (.04) | (.04) | (.05) | (.05) | (.04) | (.04) | (.06) |
| *Comparison Cities:* | | | | | | | |
| Whites | 1.93 | 1.90 | 1.91 | 1.91 | 1.90 | 1.91 | 1.92 |
| | (.01) | (.01) | (.01) | (.01) | (.01) | (.01) | (.01) |
| Blacks | 1.74 | 1.70 | 1.72 | 1.71 | 1.69 | 1.67 | 1.65 |
| | (.01) | (.02) | (.02) | (.01) | (.02) | (.02) | (.03) |
| Hispanics | 1.65 | 1.63 | 1.61 | 1.61 | 1.58 | 1.60 | 1.58 |
| | (.01) | (.01) | (.01) | (.01) | (.01) | (.01) | (.02) |

*Note:* Entries represent means of log hourly earnings (deflated by the Consumer Price Index—1980 = 100) for workers age 16–61 in Miami and four comparison cities: Atlanta, Houston, Los Angeles, and Tampa–St. Petersburg. See note to Table 1 for definitions of groups.

*Source:* Based on samples of employed workers in the outgoing rotation groups of the Current Population Survey in 1979–85. Due to a change in SMSA coding procedures in 1985, the 1985 sample is based on individuals in outgoing rotation groups for January–June of 1985 only.

In contrast to the pattern for whites, the trends in earnings for nonwhites and Hispanics differ somewhat between Miami and the comparison cities. Black wages in Miami were roughly constant from 1979 to 1981, fell in 1982 and 1983, and rose to their previous level in 1984. Black earnings in the comparison cities, on the other hand, show a steady downward trend between 1979 and 1985. These data provide no evidence of a negative impact of the Mariel immigration on black wages in Miami. The data do suggest a relative downturn in black wages in Miami during 1982–83. It seems likely, however, that this downturn reflects an unusually severe cyclical effect associated with the 1982–83 recession. (I return to this issue in Table 6, below.)

Wage rates for non-Cuban Hispanics in Miami were fairly stable between 1979 and 1985, with only a slight dip in 1983. In contrast, Hispanic wage rates in the comparison cities fell about 6 percentage points over this period. Again, there is no evidence of a negative effect in Miami,

either in the immediate post-Mariel period or over the longer run.

Table 3 does indicate a decline in Cuban wage rates relative to the wage rates of other groups in Miami. Relative to the wages of whites, for example, Cuban wages fell by 6–7 percentage points between 1979 and 1981. Assuming that the wages of earlier Cuban immigrants were constant, this decline is consistent with the addition of 45,000 Mariel workers to the pool of Cubans in the Miami labor force, and with the 34% wage differential between Mariels and other Cubans noted in Table 3. A more thorough analysis of Cuban wages is presented in Table 7, below.

The unemployment rates in Table 4 lead to the same general conclusions as the wage data in Table 3. There is no evidence that the Mariel influx adversely affected the unemployment rate of either whites or blacks. The unemployment rates suggest a severe cyclical downturn in the black labor market in Miami in 1982–83. Black unemployment rates in Miami, which had been

## THE MARIEL BOATLIFT                                        251

*Table 4.* Unemployment Rates of Individuals Age 16–61 in Miami and
Four Comparison Cities, 1979–85.
(Standard Errors in Parentheses)

| Group | 1979 | 1980 | 1981 | 1982 | 1983 | 1984 | 1985 |
|---|---|---|---|---|---|---|---|
| *Miami:* | | | | | | | |
| Whites | 5.1 | 2.5 | 3.9 | 5.2 | 6.7 | 3.6 | 4.9 |
|  | (1.1) | (0.8) | (0.9) | (1.1) | (1.1) | (0.9) | (1.4) |
| Blacks | 8.3 | 5.6 | 9.6 | 16.0 | 18.4 | 14.2 | 7.8 |
|  | (1.7) | (1.3) | (1.8) | (2.3) | (2.5) | (2.3) | (2.3) |
| Cubans | 5.3 | 7.2 | 10.1 | 10.8 | 13.1 | 7.7 | 5.5 |
|  | (1.2) | (1.3) | (1.5) | (1.5) | (1.6) | (1.4) | (1.7) |
| Hispanics | 6.5 | 7.7 | 11.8 | 9.1 | 7.5 | 12.1 | 3.7 |
|  | (2.3) | (2.2) | (3.0) | (2.5) | (2.1) | (2.4) | (1.9) |
| *Comparison Cities:* | | | | | | | |
| Whites | 4.4 | 4.4 | 4.3 | 6.8 | 6.9 | 5.4 | 4.9 |
|  | (0.3) | (0.3) | (0.3) | (0.3) | (0.3) | (0.3) | (0.4) |
| Blacks | 10.3 | 12.6 | 12.6 | 12.7 | 18.4 | 12.1 | 13.3 |
|  | (0.8) | (0.9) | (0.9) | (0.9) | (1.1) | (0.9) | (1.3) |
| Hispanics | 6.3 | 8.7 | 8.3 | 12.1 | 11.8 | 9.8 | 9.3 |
|  | (0.6) | (0.6) | (0.6) | (0.7) | (0.7) | (0.6) | (0.8) |

*Note:* Entries represent means of unemployment indicator variable for individuals age 16–61 in Miami and four comparison cities: Atlanta, Houston, Los Angeles, and Tampa–St. Petersburg. Samples are based on individuals in the labor force. See notes to Table 3 for definitions of groups and data sources.

2–4 points lower than those in the comparison cities from 1979 to 1981, equalled or exceeded those in the comparison cities from 1982 to 1984. The 1985 data indicate a return to the pre-1982 pattern, although the sampling errors are large enough to prevent precise inferences.

Unlike the situation for whites and blacks, there was a sizable increase in Cuban unemployment rates in Miami following the Mariel immigration. Cuban unemployment rates were roughly 3 percentage points higher during 1980–81 than would have been expected on the basis of earlier (and later) patterns. Assuming that the unemployment rates of earlier Cuban immigrants were unaffected by the Mariel influx, this effect is consistent with unemployment rates of around 20% among the Mariels themselves. Although far from conclusive, this simple calculation suggests that the increase in Cuban unemployment rates could easily be explained as a result of the addition of the Mariel refugees to the Cuban population, with little or no effect on earlier immigrants.

The simple averages of wages and unemployment rates in Tables 3 and 4, which combine workers of all ages and education levels, do not directly address the question of whether the Mariel immigration reduced the earnings of less-skilled natives in Miami. A more direct answer is provided by the data in Table 5. In order to identify "less-skilled" workers, I fit a linear regression equation for the logarithm of hourly earnings to workers in the comparison cities. The explanatory variables in this regression included education, potential experience, squared potential experience, indicator variables for each gender and race group, and interactions of the gender-race indicators with potential experience and squared potential experience. I then used the estimated coefficients from this equation to form a predicted wage for each non-Cuban worker in Miami, and sorted the sample from each year into quartiles on the basis of predicted wage rates.

This procedure provides a simple way to identify more- and less-skilled workers in the Miami labor market. Means of actual log wages for each quartile and year are presented in the first four columns of

INDUSTRIAL AND LABOR RELATIONS REVIEW

*Table 5.* Means of Log Wages of Non-Cubans in Miami by Quartile
of Predicted Wages, 1979–85.
(Standard Errors in Parentheses)

| | Mean of Log Wage by Quartile of Predicted Wage | | | | Difference of |
| Year | 1st Quart. | 2nd Quart. | 3rd Quart. | 4th Quart. | Means: 4th – 1st |
|---|---|---|---|---|---|
| 1979 | 1.31 | 1.61 | 1.71 | 2.15 | .84 |
| | (.03) | (.03) | (.03) | (.04) | (.05) |
| 1980 | 1.31 | 1.52 | 1.74 | 2.09 | .77 |
| | (.03) | (.03) | (.03) | (.04) | (.05) |
| 1981 | 1.40 | 1.57 | 1.79 | 2.06 | .66 |
| | (.03) | (.03) | (.03) | (.04) | (.05) |
| 1982 | 1.24 | 1.57 | 1.77 | 2.04 | .80 |
| | (.03) | (.03) | (.03) | (.04) | (.05) |
| 1983 | 1.27 | 1.53 | 1.76 | 2.11 | .84 |
| | (.03) | (.04) | (.03) | (.05) | (.06) |
| 1984 | 1.33 | 1.59 | 1.80 | 2.12 | .79 |
| | (.03) | (.04) | (.04) | (.04) | (.05) |
| 1985 | 1.27 | 1.57 | 1.81 | 2.14 | .87 |
| | (.04) | (.04) | (.04) | (.05) | (.06) |

*Note:* Predicted wage is based on a linear prediction equation for the log wage fitted to individuals in four comparison cities; see text. The sample consists of non-Cubans (male and female, white, black, and Hispanic) between the ages of 16 and 61 with valid wage data in the earnings supplement of the Current Population Survey. Wages are deflated by the Consumer Price Index (1980 = 100).

Table 5. The difference in mean wages between the first and fourth quartiles, which provides an index of the spread in the wage distribution, is presented in the fifth column of the table.

If the Mariel immigration reduced the wages of less-skilled natives, one would expect to observe a decline in the wage of workers in the lowest skill quartile, at least relative to workers in the upper quartile. The actual averages show no evidence of this effect. Apart from the temporary increase in relative wages of workers in the lowest quartile between 1979 and 1981, the distribution of non-Cubans' wages in the Miami labor market was remarkably stable between 1979 and 1985. Taken together with the data in Table 3, these data provide little evidence of a negative effect of the Mariel influx on the earnings of natives.

A final check is provided in Table 6, which contains more detailed information on wages, employment rates, and unemployment rates for blacks in Miami between 1979 and 1985. I separately analyzed the set of all blacks and the set of blacks with less than 12 years of education in order to isolate any stronger effect on the less-skilled segment of the black population. For both groups I calculated the differential in wages between Miami and the comparison cities (both the unadjusted difference in mean log ways and a regression-adjusted differential that controls for education, gender, marital status, part-time status, private/public employment, and potential experience) and the differentials in the employment-population rate and the unemployment rate between Miami and the comparison cities.

As indicated in Table 3, the wage differential for blacks in Miami relative to those in the comparison cities decreased slightly between 1979 and 1981. The differential increased substantially in 1982, but then began a steady downward trend after 1983. By 1985, the wage gap was less than 5% for all black workers, and was actually positive for less-educated blacks. The magnitudes of the regression-adjusted wage differentials are not significantly different from the unadjusted wage differentials, and show no evidence of any effect of the Mariel immigration on black wages.

A similar conclusion emerges from the pattern of differentials in employment-

## THE MARIEL BOATLIFT                                                      253

*Table 6.* Comparison of Wages, Unemployment Rates, and Employment Rates for Blacks in
Miami and Comparison Cities.
(Standard Errors in Parentheses)

| | All Backs | | | | Low-Education Blacks | | | |
|---|---|---|---|---|---|---|---|---|
| | Difference in Log Wages, Miami − Comparison | | Difference in Emp./Unemp., Miami − Comparison | | Difference in Log Wages, Miami − Comparison | | Difference in Emp./Unemp., Miami − Comparison | |
| Year | Actual | Adjusted | Emp. − Pop. Rate | Unemp. Rate | Actual | Adjusted | Emp. − Pop. Rate | Unemp. Rate |
| 1979 | −.15 (.03) | −.12 (.03) | .00 (.03) | −2.0 (1.9) | −.13 (.05) | −.15 (.05) | .03 (.04) | −.8 (3.8) |
| 1980 | −.16 (.03) | −.12 (.03) | .05 (.03) | −7.1 (1.6) | −.07 (.05) | −.07 (.05) | .03 (.04) | −8.2 (3.5) |
| 1981 | −.11 (.03) | −.10 (.03) | .02 (.03) | −3.0 (2.0) | −.05 (.05) | −.11 (.05) | .04 (.04) | −7.7 (4.2) |
| 1982 | −.24 (.03) | −.20 (.03) | −.06 (.03) | 3.3 (2.4) | −.17 (.05) | −.20 (.05) | −.04 (.04) | .6 (4.7) |
| 1983 | −.21 (.03) | −.15 (.03) | −.02 (.03) | .1 (2.7) | −.13 (.06) | −.11 (.05) | .04 (.04) | −3.3 (4.7) |
| 1984 | −.10 (.03) | −.05 (.03) | −.04 (.03) | 2.1 (2.4) | −.04 (.06) | −.03 (.05) | .05 (.04) | .1 (4.7) |
| 1985 | −.05 (.04) | −.01 (.04) | −.06 (.04) | −5.5 (2.6) | .18 (.07) | .09 (.07) | .00 (.06) | −4.7 (5.6) |

*Notes:* Low-education blacks are those with less than 12 years of completed education. Adjusted differences in
log wages between blacks in Miami and comparison cities are obtained from a linear regression model that
includes education, potential experience, and other control variables; see text. Wages are deflated by the
Consumer Price Index (1980 = 100). "Emp.-Pop. Rate" refers to the employment:population ratio. "Unemp.
Rate" refers to the unemployment rate among those in the labor force.

population ratios and unemployment rates.[9]
Among all blacks, there is some evidence
of a relative decline in the employment-
to-population ratio in Miami between 1979
and 1985.[10] This effect seems to have
started in 1982, and is less pronounced
among low-education blacks than among
those with more education. As noted in Ta-

ble 4, the series of unemployment rate differentials indicates a sharp downturn in labor market opportunities for blacks in 1982.
Given the lag between the arrival of the
Mariels and the emergence of this unemployment gap, however, the gap seems
more likely to have resulted from the 1982
recession than from the influx of less-
skilled immigrants.

The effects of the Mariel immigration
on Cuban labor market outcomes are
examined in detail in Table 7. The first
column of the table reproduces the means
of log wages in each year from the third
row of Table 3. The second column gives
predicted log wages of Cubans in Miami,
using estimated coefficients from a regression equation fit to Hispanics in the four
comparison cities. The gap between actual
and predicted wages is presented in the
third column of the table. These series
show that the 9 percentage point decline
in Cuban real wage rates in Miami
between 1979 and 1985 was a result of two

---

[9] I also computed regression-adjusted employment-
population and unemployment gaps using simple
linear probability models. The explanatory power of
the statistical models is so low, however, that the
adjusted differentials are almost identical to the
unadjusted differentials.

[10] Although they are not reported in Table 6, I
have also constructed differentials in the labor force
participation rate between Miami and the comparison cities. For blacks as a whole these show a decline
in relative participation rates in Miami starting in
1982, although the decline is only temporary for the
low-education group. The differential in labor force
participation rates is approximately equal to the
differential in the employment-population rate plus
the differential in the unemployment rate multiplied
by the average labor force participation rate (.7 for
the overall group, .55 for the low-education group).

*Table* 7. Means of Log Wages of Cubans in Miami: Actual and Predicted,
and by Quartile of Predicted Wages.
(Standard Errors in Parentheses)

| Year | Mean of Log Wages Log in Miami | | | Mean of Log Wages by Quartile of Predicted Wages | | | | Mean Log Wage of Cubans Outside Miami | Difference in Cuban Wages, Miami − Rest-of-U.S. | |
|------|--------|--------|---------|------|------|------|------|------|--------|---------|
| | Actual | Pre-dicted | Actual-Pre-dicted | 1st | 2nd | 3rd | 4th | | Actual | Ad-justed |
| 1979 | 1.58 | 1.73 | −.15 | 1.31 | 1.44 | 1.64 | 1.90 | 1.71 | −.13 | −.10 |
| | (.02) | (.02) | (.03) | (.02) | (.03) | (.04) | (.05) | (.04) | (.04) | (.04) |
| 1980 | 1.54 | 1.68 | −.14 | 1.25 | 1.49 | 1.59 | 1.81 | 1.66 | −.12 | −.06 |
| | (.02) | (.02) | (.03) | (.02) | (.05) | (.04) | (.05) | (.03) | (.04) | (.03) |
| 1981 | 1.51 | 1.68 | −.17 | 1.23 | 1.43 | 1.55 | 1.80 | 1.63 | −.13 | −.09 |
| | (.02) | (.02) | (.03) | (.03) | (.03) | (.04) | (.05) | (.03) | (.04) | (.03) |
| 1982 | 1.49 | 1.68 | −.19 | 1.27 | 1.43 | 1.50 | 1.77 | 1.71 | −.22 | −.12 |
| | (.02) | (.02) | (.03) | (.03) | (.04) | (.04) | (.06) | (.03) | (.04) | (.03) |
| 1983 | 1.48 | 1.65 | −.17 | 1.16 | 1.41 | 1.56 | 1.80 | 1.62 | −.14 | −.08 |
| | (.03) | (.02) | (.03) | (.02) | (.04) | (.04) | (.06) | (.03) | (.04) | (.03) |
| 1984 | 1.53 | 1.69 | −.17 | 1.20 | 1.40 | 1.65 | 1.88 | 1.63 | −.10 | −.08 |
| | (.03) | (.02) | (.03) | (.03) | (.04) | (.05) | (.06) | (.03) | (.04) | (.03) |
| 1985 | 1.49 | 1.67 | −.18 | 1.19 | 1.43 | 1.53 | 1.80 | 1.77 | −.27 | −.19 |
| | (.04) | (.03) | (.05) | (.06) | (.06) | (.08) | (.09) | (.06) | (.07) | (.05) |

*Notes:* Predicted wage is based on a linear prediction equation for the log wage fitted to individuals in four comparison cities; see text. Predicted wages for Cubans in Miami are based on coefficients for Hispanics in comparison cities. The adjusted wage gap between Cubans in Miami and Cubans in the rest of the U.S. are obtained from a linear regression model that includes education, potential experience, and other control variables; see text. Wages are deflated by the Consumer Price Index (1980 = 100).

complementary factors: a 6% relative decline in the "quality" of the Cuban labor force in Miami, as measured by the decline in their predicted wages, and a 3 percentage point increase in the quality-adjusted wage gap between Cuban workers in Miami and Hispanic workers in the comparison cities. Two-thirds of the wage decline is therefore attributed to the changing productivity characteristics of the Cuban labor force, and one-third to a decrease in the return to skills for Cubans in the Miami labor market.

The next four columns of Table 7 give the means of log wages for Cuban workers in each quartile of the distribution of predicted wages (using the same prediction equation as was used to form the means in column 2). These means suggest that real wage rates of Cubans in the lowest quartile of the wage distribution declined by 11–12 percentage points between 1979 and 1985. The decline is smaller for workers in the higher quartiles, but there is some variation between

1984 and 1985, and in light of the sampling errors it is difficult to draw precise inferences. The difference between the means of the first and fourth quartiles is 9 percentage points higher in 1984 than 1979, but the gap narrows to only 2 points in 1985. These figures are consistent with a larger decline in earnings at the low end of the Cuban wage distribution after the Mariel immigration, as might be expected from the addition of a large group of relatively unskilled workers to the pool of Cubans. The extent of the decline, however, is not precisely measured.

An alternative method to assess the effect of the Mariel immigration on the earnings of Cubans in the Miami labor market is to compare Cuban wages in Miami to the wages of Cubans elsewhere in the United States. Since the fraction of Mariels in the Cuban labor force is roughly the same inside and outside Miami, this comparison controls for any unobservable differences in skill between

*Globalization and Labour Markets II*

the Mariels and other Cubans (due to language ability, for example).[11] The ninth and tenth columns of Table 7 contain estimates of the wage differential for Cubans in Miami relative to those elsewhere in the country, both unadjusted and adjusted for education, gender, part-time status, private sector/public sector employment, marital status (interacted with gender), and potential experience.

The earnings differentials computed in this way are roughly constant between 1979 and 1984. The 1982 unadjusted wage differential is 10 percentage points larger than earlier or later ones, but the regression-adjusted differential is not significantly different from any of the other differentials. The 1985 data also indicate a slightly higher Cuban wage rate outside Miami. In any case, a comparison of Cuban wages inside and outside the Miami labor market shows no evidence of a widening gap in the years immediately following the Mariel immigration. On the assumption that the Mariel influx had no effect on the wage rates of other Cubans *outside* Miami, this finding suggests that the observed downturn in Cuban wages in Miami can be attributed solely to the "dilution" of the Cuban labor force with less-skilled Mariel workers.

### Interpretation of the Findings

The data in Table 3–7 point to two conclusions. First, the Mariel immigration had essentially no effect on the wages or employment outcomes of non-Cuban workers in the Miami labor market. Second, and perhaps even more surprising, the Mariel immigration had no strong effect on the wages of other Cubans. The observed decline in average Cuban wage rates in Miami after 1980 is no larger than would be expected by simply adding the Mariel immigrants to the pool of Cuban workers, assuming that the Mariels earned

about one-third less than other comparable Cubans (as the March 1985 data suggest). This conclusion is confirmed by a comparison of Cuban wage rates inside and outside Miami, which shows no relative change over the period.

These conclusions lead naturally to the question of how the Miami labor market was able to absorb a 7% increase in the labor force with no adverse effects. One possible answer is that the Mariels displaced other immigrants and natives who would have moved to Miami in the early 1980s had the Boatlift not occurred. Some evidence on this hypothesis is provided by comparing population growth rates in Miami to those in other Florida cities. From 1970 to 1980, the Miami population grew at an annual rate of 2.5% per year while the population of the rest of Florida grew at a rate of 3.9%. After April 1, 1980, the growth rate in Miami slowed to 1.4% per year while that in the rest of the state decreased to 3.4%.[12] The greater slowdown in Miami suggests that the Boatlift may have actually held back long-run population growth in Miami. In fact, the population of Dade county in 1986 was about equal to the pre-Boatlift projection of the University of Florida Bureau of Economic and Business Research under their "low population growth" scenario (see *Florida Statistical Abstract 1981*, Table 1.24).

Nevertheless, data from the March 1985 Current Population Survey suggest that Miami continued to attract new foreign-born immigrants after 1980. A total of 2.7% of all non-Cuban immigrants who arrived in the United States after March 1980 were living in Miami in March 1985. At the time of the 1980 Census, however, only 1.8% of all non-Cuban immigrants in the United States lived in Miami. Thus, Miami attracted "more than its share" of new non-Cuban immigrants to the country in the five-year period after the Mariel immigration. The implication is that the slowdown in the rate of growth of the

---

[11] This proposition is strictly true only if the unobservable differences have a constant proportional effect on all Mariels, independent of the level of observed skills or location choice.

[12] These figures are obtained from U.S. Department of Commerce (1971, Table 32, and 1988, Table 1).

Miami SMSA after June 1980 occurred because of a change in the net migration rate of natives and older cohorts of immigrants, rather than because of a change in the inflow rate of new immigrants. This finding is consistent with the pattern of domestic migration between 1970 and 1980 identified by Filer (1988), who found a strong negative correlation across SMSAs between the net in-migration rate of natives and the in-migration rate of immigrants.

A second explanation for the rapid absorption of the Mariel immigrants is the growth of industries that utilize relatively unskilled labor. Altonji and Card's (1989) tabulations from the 1970 and 1980 Censuses indicate that a small set of industries employ a large fraction of immigrants, and that these industries expanded more rapidly between 1970 and 1980 in cities with large immigrant populations than in other cities. The immigrant-intensive industries identified in their analysis are apparel and textiles, agriculture, furniture, private household services, hotels and motels, eating and drinking establishments, and business services. These are relatively low-wage industries that employ large numbers of semi-skilled operatives and laborers.

A comparison of the industry distributions of employment in Miami and the entire country before and after the Mariel Boatlift shows little change in the relative importance of immigrant-intensive industries in Miami.[13] Nevertheless, these tabulations suggest that the industry distribution in Miami in the late 1970s was well suited to handle an influx of unskilled immigrants. Textile and apparel industries were particularly prominent in Miami, with 5.5% of total employment in these industries as compared to only 2.3% nationwide. Seventy-five percent of workers in textiles and apparel and 45% of workers in other manufacturing industries

were Cubans. Although employment in immigrant-intensive industries did not expand after the Boatlift, and the Cuban share of employment in these industries was relatively stable, the Mariels may have simply replaced earlier cohorts of Cuban immigrants as the latter moved to more desirable jobs.

### Conclusions

The experiences of the Miami labor market in the aftermath of the Mariel Boatlift provide a natural experiment with which to evaluate the effect of unskilled immigration on the labor market opportunities of native workers. The Mariel immigrants increased the labor force of the Miami metropolitan area by 7%. Because most of these immigrants were relatively unskilled, the proportional increase in labor supply to less-skilled occupations and industries was much greater.

Yet, this study shows that the influx of Mariel immigrants had virtually no effect on the wage rates of less-skilled non-Cuban workers. Similarly, there is no evidence of an increase in unemployment among less-skilled blacks or other non-Cuban workers. Rather, the data analysis suggests a remarkably rapid absorption of the Mariel immigrants into the Miami labor force, with negligible effects on other groups. Even among the Cuban population there is no indication that wages or unemployment rates of earlier immigrants were substantially affected by the arrival of the Mariels.

Despite the clear-cut nature of these findings, some caution is required in their interpretation, since the Miami labor market is far from typical of other local labor markets in the United States. Although the arrival of some 60,000 refugees in only a six-month period occasioned problems for the Mariel immigrants, in many respects Miami was better prepared to receive them than any other city. In the two decades before the Mariel Boatlift Miami had absorbed a continuing flow of Cubans, and in the years since the Boatlift it has continued to receive large numbers

---

[13] These tabulations are reported in Card (1989, Table 9). Pre-Boatlift data are based on the 1979 and 1980 March Current Population Surveys. Post-Boatlift data are based on the March 1984 and March 1985 CPS.

of Nicaraguans and other Central Americans. Thus, the Mariel immigration can be seen as part of a long-run pattern that distinguishes Miami from most other American cities.

Two factors that may have been especially important in facilitating the absorption of the Mariel immigrants are related to the distinctive character of the Miami labor market. First, Miami's industry structure was well suited to make use of an influx of unskilled labor. This structure, and particularly the high concentration of textile and apparel industries, evolved over the previous two decades in response to earlier waves of immigrants, and may have allowed the Mariel immigrants to take up unskilled jobs as earlier Cuban immigrants moved to better ones. Second, because of the high concentration of Hispanics in Miami, the lack of English-speaking ability among the Mariels may have had smaller effects than could be expected for other immigrants in other cities.

A final factor in the Mariel immigration is the response of domestic migration. A comparison of Miami growth rates to those in the rest of Florida suggests that the net migration rate of natives and earlier immigrants into the Miami area slowed considerably after the Boatlift. To some extent the Mariels may have displaced other migrants from within the United States who could have been expected to move to Miami.

## REFERENCES

Altonji, Joseph, and David Card. 1989. "The Effects of Immigration on the Labor Market Outcomes of Natives." Princeton University Industrial Relations Section Working Paper Number 256, August.

Borjas, George. 1987. "Immigrants, Minorities, and Labor Market Competition." *Industrial and Labor Relations Review*, Vol. 40 (April), pp. 382–92.

Bound, John, and George Johnson. 1989. "Changes in the Structure of Wages During the 1980's: An Evaluation of Alternative Explanations." National Bureau of Economic Research Working Paper Number 2983, May.

*Business Week*. 1980. "The New Wave of Cubans Is Swamping Miami." No. 2651 (August 25), pp. 86–88.

Card, David. 1989. "The Impact of the Mariel Boatlift on the Miami Labor Market." National Bureau of Economic Research Working Paper Number 3069, August.

Filer, Randall. 1988. "The Impact of Immigrant Arrivals on Migratory Patterns of U.S. Workers." Unpublished manuscript, Hunter College and the Graduate Center, City University of New York, October.

Governor of Florida. 1980. *Report of the Governor's Dade County Citizen's Committee*. Miami.

Greenwood, Michael, and John McDowell. 1984. "The Factor Market Consequences of U.S. Immigration." *Journal of Economic Literature*, Vol. 34 (December), pp. 1738–72.

Grossman, Jean. 1982. "The Substitutability of Natives and Immigrants in Production." *Review of Economics and Statistics*, Vol. 64 (November), pp. 596–603.

Lalonde, Robert, and Robert Topel. 1987. "Labor Market Adjustments to Increased Immigration." Unpublished manuscript, University of Chicago Graduate School of Business, September.

Masud-Piloto, Felix Roberto. 1988. *With Open Arms: Cuban Migration to the United States*. Totowa, N.J.: Rowman & Littlefield.

United States Department of Commerce, Bureau of the Census. 1971. *1970 Census of Population—Number of Inhabitants: United States Summary* (PC1-A1). Washington, D.C.: GPO.

———. 1983. *1980 Census of Population—Characteristics of the Population: Detailed Population Characteristics*. Vol. 1, Chap. D, Part 2, Florida: PC80-1-D11. Washington, D.C.: GPO.

———. 1988. *Current Population Reports—Population Estimates and Projections: United States Population Estimates by Age, Sex, and Race: 1980 to 1987*. Series P-25, No. 1022. Washington, D.C.: GPO, March.

———. 1988. *Current Population Reports—Local Population Estimates: South 1986 Population and 1985 Per Capita Income Estimates for Counties and Incorporated Places*. Series P-26, No. 86-S-SC. Washington, D.C.: GPO, March.

University of Florida Bureau of Economics and Business Research. 1981. *Florida Statistical Abstract*. Gainesville: University Presses of Florida.

Wilbanks, William. 1984. *Murder in Miami: An Analysis of Homicide Patterns and Trends in Dade County, Florida, 1917–1983*. Lanham, Md.: University Press of America.

# [12]

# The Effects of Immigration on the Labor Market Outcomes of Less-skilled Natives

Joseph G. Altonji and David Card

One of the most controversial aspects of immigration policy is the extent to which the arrival of immigrants helps or harms less-skilled natives. Although economists have developed a variety of theoretical models to analyze this question (see, e.g., Johnson 1980a, 1980b; Chiswick 1982; or Borjas 1987), relatively little empirical evidence is available.[1] In this paper, we use variation in the fraction of immigrants across different cities to measure the effects of immigration on the labor market outcomes of less-skilled natives. We assemble information from the 1970 and 1980 Censuses on labor market outcomes of natives in 120 major cities. Information from consecutive Censuses allows us to correlate changes in immigrant fractions with changes in native outcomes within cities—thereby abstracting from differences across cities that might bias a simpler cross-sectional analysis. We also provide a variety of information on the industry distributions of natives and immigrants and analyze the changes in these distributions that have occurred in cities with higher and lower immigrant shares.

In the first section of the paper, we present a simple theoretical model that describes the effects of immigration on the domestic labor market. We assume that the labor market within each city consists of skilled and unskilled workers and that immigration adds workers to both sectors, with relative additions

David Card is professor of economics at Princeton University and a research associate of the National Bureau of Economic Research. Joseph G. Altonji is professor of economics at Northwestern University and a faculty research fellow of the National Bureau of Economic Research.

The authors are grateful to Brain McCall and Sarah Turner for assistance with this research and to the National Bureau of Economic Research, the Center for Urban Affairs and Policy Research, Northwestern University, and the Industrial Relations Section, Princeton University, for research funding. They thank John Abowd, Francine Blau, George Borjas, Gregory DeFreitas, Richard Freeman, Peter Kuhn, and participants in seminars at Columbia University, the University of Minnesota, Princeton University, and the National Bureau of Economic Research for comments on earlier drafts.

depending on the nature of immigrant inflows to the city in question. Our theoretical framework departs from earlier models in two ways. On the one hand, we disaggregate labor along skill lines rather than along the lines of national origin. On the other hand, we allow for demand-side effects associated with increases in the local population and for supply-side effects associated with the possible crowding out of native workers in response to lower wage rates. The model leads to a simple empirical specification in which wage and employment outcomes of less-skilled natives (either in cross section or within cities over time) vary with the share and skill composition of immigrants in the local labor market.

In the second section of the paper, we address the question of whether immigrants and natives within the same city compete in the same labor market. Given the size of immigrant flows during the last two decades, our theoretical analysis implies that large adverse effects on less-skilled natives are unlikely unless increases in immigration lead to proportionately larger increases in the supply of labor to less-skilled jobs. We focus on industry-specific labor markets within cities. We develop a simple index that measures the effect of a given inflow of immigrants on the labor market of natives. We find that a 1 percentage point increase in the share of immigrants in a city generates approximately a 1 percent increase in the supply of labor to industries in which less-skilled natives are employed. The degree of competition between immigrants and less-skilled natives varies somewhat by race and sex group, being highest for black females and lowest for black males. Overall, however, the results suggest that immigrants are not sufficiently concentrated in the industries that employ less-skilled natives to have large effects on the less-skilled native groups.

We go on to investigate whether immigrant inflows have displaced less-skilled natives from certain industries. Here, we compare the industry distributions of less-skilled natives in cities with relatively high and relatively low immigrant densities. We find some evidence that less-skilled natives in high-immigrant cities have moved out of immigrant-intensive industries. We also find that the nationwide trend of falling employment in these industries has been slower in high-immigrant cities, suggesting that the availability of immigrant labor has enabled certain low-wage industries to survive in high-immigrant cities.[2]

In the third section of the paper, we turn to a regression analysis of the relation between immigrant shares (or the change in immigrant shares) and employment outcomes of natives (or the change in these outcomes) across major cities. The results vary somewhat between the cross-sectional and first-difference analyses. We argue, however, that the first-difference analysis is less likely to be contaminated by city-specific factors that affect immigrant densities and native outcomes. The analysis of changes shows no effect of increased immigration on participation or employment rates of less-skilled natives. It does reveal a systematically negative effect on native wages, although the specific estimates depend on the group and on whether we use an instrumental variables procedure to account for the fact that immigration inflows may depend on local labor market conditions. For the four race/sex groups that we consider, the instrumental variables estimates (which we prefer) imply that an inflow of immigrants equal to 1 percent of the population of a standard metropolitan statistical area (SMSA) reduces average weekly earnings of less-skilled natives by about 1.2 percent.[3] The least squares estimates, by comparison, imply a more modest .3 percent reduction.

## 7.1   Analytical Framework

Our framework for analyzing the effect of immigration on the labor market outcomes of less-skilled natives is to view the inflow of immigrants to each city (or, more precisely, SMSA) as an outward shift in the supply of labor. Since we are specifically interested in the effects of immigration on less-skilled natives, we consider a two-sector labor market consisting of skilled and unskilled labor. Within skill categories, we make no distinction between native and immigrant labor or between earlier and later cohorts of immigrants. We assume that the demands for skilled and unskilled labor in each city are decreasing functions of their respective wage rates and that prices of capital and other inputs are exogenous to the local labor market.

This framework contrasts with the one adopted by Borjas (1987), for example, who treats immigrants and natives as separate factors of production and assumes that locally produced output is sold at an exogenous price. In this case, the conventional elasticities of labor demand are undefined since an increase in the wage rate of one type of labor with other factor prices held constant leads to an increase in marginal cost that drives local firms out of business.[4] Given that many of the goods produced within a city are nontraded services, however, and that many others enjoy some degree of imperfect substitutability due to transportation costs, we believe that it is more reasonable to posit the existence of downward-sloping labor demand functions at the local level.

The observation that the demand for labor within a local economy arises in part from the demand for location-specific goods and services implies that a partial equilibrium model of the labor market is potentially misleading. In the extreme case, if *all* output is locally consumed, and if new immigrants arrive in the same skill proportions as the existing labor force, then an influx of immigrants leads to a new equilibrium at the original wage rates, with proportionately higher levels of employment, output, and consumption.[5] More generally, the arrival of new immigrants shifts the demand for city output and hence the demand functions for skilled and unskilled labor. The size of this effect depends on the share of output consumed locally and on the relative skill composition of the existing and immigrating labor forces.

To illustrate these propositions and establish a framework for our empirical analysis, consider an urban economy with two goods: a locally produced good (or service), $Y$, that is consumed locally and exported to other cities and an imported national good.[6] Assume that $Y$ is produced by a competitive industry with a constant-returns-to-scale technology using skilled labor, unskilled labor, and other inputs (capital and/or raw materials) whose prices are exogenous and fixed.[7] Under these conditions, total industry cost (in units of the imported good) is described by a function of the form

$$C(w_s, w_u, Y) = Yc(w_s, w_u),$$

where $w_u$ and $w_s$ represent the real wages of unskilled and skilled labor (in units of the imported good), and $c(\cdot)$ is a unit cost function.[8] Let $q$ represent the unit price of local output (denoted in units of the imported good). The assumptions of constant returns and perfect competition imply that $q = c(w_s, w_u)$.

Demand for $Y$ arises from three sources: local demand from skilled workers, $Y_s$; local demand from unskilled workers, $Y_u$; and export demand from the rest of the economy, $Y_x$. Let $D_s(q, w_s)$ and $D_u(q, w_u)$ represent the per capita demand functions of skilled and unskilled workers, respectively, and let $D_x(q)$ represent the demand function for locally produced output from the rest of the economy. Let $P_s$ and $P_u$ represent the populations of skilled and unskilled workers in the city, and denote the total population by $P = P_s + P_u$. Product market equilibrium requires

(1)        $$Y = P_s \cdot D_s(q, w_s) + P_u \cdot D_u(q, w_u) + D_x(q).$$

Let $L_s(w_s, q)$ and $L_u(w_u, q)$ represent the per capita labor supply functions of skilled and unskilled workers, respectively. Equilibrium in the local labor market requires

(2a)        $$P_s \cdot L_s(w_s, q) = Y \cdot c_1 (w_s, w_u)$$

and

(2b)        $$P_u \cdot L_u(w_u, q) = Y \cdot c_2(w_s, w_u),$$

where $c_1(\cdot)$ and $c_2(\cdot)$ denote the partial derivatives of the unit cost function with respect to unskilled and skilled wage rates, respectively.

Suppose that in an initial equilibrium the fraction of unskilled workers in the local population is $a = P_u/P$. We wish to analyze the effect of an inflow of immigrants of size $\Delta I$. Let $\alpha$ represent the share of unskilled workers in the new group. The effects of an immigrant inflow can be obtained by differentiating equations (1), (2a), and (2b) and making use of the fact that the proportional change in the price of output, $\Delta q/q$, equals the share-weighted sum of the proportional changes in all factor prices.

For simplicity, assume that the cross-elasticities of the output demand and labor supply are zero.[9] Then the proportional changes in skilled and unskilled wage rates satisfy the following pair of equations:

**205**     Immigration and the Labor Market Outcomes of Less-skilled Natives

(3a)        $\lambda_u (\alpha/a) \Delta I/P = (\eta_{uu} - \varepsilon_u)\Delta \log w_u + \eta_{us}\Delta \log w_s$,

(3b)   $\lambda_s [(1-\alpha)/(1-a)] \Delta I/P = \eta_{su}\Delta \log w_u + (\eta_{ss} - \varepsilon_s)\Delta \log w_s$,

where $\eta_{ij}$ is the elasticity of labor demand for skill group $i$ with respect to the
wage of group $j$, $\varepsilon_i$ is the elasticity of labor supply of group $i$, and $\lambda_s$ and $\lambda_u$
are a pair of numbers between zero and one:

$$\lambda_u = (Y - Y_u - k_1 \cdot Y_s) / Y, \quad k_1 = a(1 - \alpha)/[\alpha(1-a)],$$
$$\lambda_s = (Y - k_2 \cdot Y_u - Y_s) / Y, \quad k_2 = \alpha(1-a)/[a(1-\alpha)].$$

The labor demand elasticities in equations (3a) and (3b) are determined by
the conventional Marshall-Hicks formulas:

$$\eta_{ij} = \theta_j(\sigma_{ij} - \gamma),$$

where $\theta_i$ is the share of the value of output paid as wages to skill group $i$, $\sigma_{ij}$
is the partial elasticity of substitution of skill group $i$ with respect to group $j$,
and $\gamma$ is the elasticity of demand for $Y$ with respect to its relative price $q$ (a
weighted average of the elasticities of demand exhibited by consumers in the
local market and those elsewhere in the economy).

The expressions $\lambda_u (\alpha/a)\Delta I/P$ and $\lambda_s [(1 - \alpha)/(1 - a)]\Delta I/P$ in equations
(3a) and (3b) give the effective percentage increases in unskilled and skilled
labor resulting from an inflow of immigrants $\Delta I$. The increases in skilled and
unskilled populations are $\alpha\Delta I$ and $(1 - \alpha)\Delta I$, respectively. The proportional
increases in the populations of unskilled and skilled workers are therefore
$(\alpha/a)\Delta I/P$ and $[(1 - \alpha)/(1 - a)]\Delta I/P$, respectively. The factors $\lambda_u$ and $\lambda_s$
adjust the gross increases in labor supply for the net increases in demand gen-
erated by the new immigrants. If local output is consumed entirely within the
city and immigration is balanced in the sense that $\alpha = a$, then $\lambda_u = \lambda_s = 0$.
Otherwise, the effective increases in labor supply depend on the fraction of
local output sold outside the city and on the imbalance of skill ratios between
the existing and the newly arriving population. In the simple case where
newly arriving immigrants have the same skills as the existing population, $\lambda_u$
$= \lambda_s = Y_x/Y$, the fraction of output exported. If newly arriving immigrants
are less skilled, however, $\lambda_u > Y_x/Y > \lambda_s$, accentuating the effective increase
in unskilled labor supply.

Using equations (3a) and (3b), changes in wages rates can be related to
changes in the fraction of immigrants in the local population ($f$) by noting
that $\Delta f = \Delta(I/P) = (1 - f)\Delta I/P$. In the special case that the demand for
unskilled labor is independent of the wage rate of skilled labor (i.e., $\eta_{us} = 0$),
equation (3a) can be simplified to

(4)
$$\Delta \log w_u = \frac{-\lambda_u}{\varepsilon_u - \eta_{uu}} (\alpha/a)\Delta I/P,$$

$$= \frac{-\lambda_u}{(1 - f) (\varepsilon_u - \eta_{uu})} (\alpha/a)\Delta f,$$

which specializes to the formula derived by Johnson (1980a) when $\lambda_u = 1$ and $\alpha = a.$[10] Our model extends Johnson's earlier analysis in two directions: by allowing for skilled and unskilled workers in the existing and immigrating populations and by accounting in a very simple manner for the effect of added population on the demand for local output.

If the demand for unskilled workers depends on the wage rate of skilled labor (i.e., $\eta_{us} \neq 0$), then the expression for the change in unskilled wage rates takes the more general form

$$(5) \qquad \Delta \log w_u = B_u \Delta I/P,$$

where

$$B_u = \frac{-\lambda_u (\alpha/a) - \lambda_s \dfrac{(1 - \alpha)}{(1 - a)} \eta_{us} / (\varepsilon_s - \eta_{ss})}{(\varepsilon_u - \eta_{uu}) - \eta_{us}\eta_{su} / (\varepsilon_s - \eta_{ss})}.$$

Using the labor supply function, the change in the per capita labor supply of unskilled natives can then be written as

$$(6) \qquad \Delta \log L_u = \varepsilon_u \cdot B_u \Delta I/P.$$

To get some idea of the magnitude of the coefficient $B_u$ relating wage changes to immigrant inflows, suppose that $\alpha = a$, so that $\lambda_u = \lambda_s$. In this case, equation (5) can be rewritten as

$$\Delta \log w_u = \lambda b_u \Delta I/P,$$

where the coefficient $b_u$ ($b_u < 0$) is a function only of the supply and demand elasticities for skilled and unskilled labor, and $\lambda$ equals the fraction of local production exported to other cities. Values of the coefficient $b_u$ corresponding to alternative values of the supply and demand parameters of the model are displayed in table 7.1. The rows of the table present alternative choices for the ratio between the partial elasticity of unskilled labor with respect to nonlabor inputs ($\sigma_{uk}$) and the partial elasticity of skilled labor with respect to nonlabor inputs ($\sigma_{sk}$). The share-weighted average of these two elasticities is constrained to equal .6.[11] The columns of the table present alternative choices for the partial elasticity of substitution between skilled and unskilled labor ($\sigma_{su}$). For each choice of the technological parameters, two values of $b_u$ are reported, corresponding to alternative choices for the elasticities of labor supply: .1 and 1.0. Other parameters in the model are set as follows: the share of skilled labor ($\theta_s$) = .4, the share of unskilled labor ($\theta_u$) = .3, and the elasticity of demand for city output ($\gamma$) = $-2.5$.

The first row of the table presents calculated values of $b_u$ under the assumption that capital is a substitute for unskilled labor and a complement for skilled labor.[12] As Hamermesh (1986, 460–62) has noted in his review of the literature on labor demand, many empirical studies based on the distinction be-

**207**     Immigration and the Labor Market Outcomes of Less-skilled Natives

Table 7.1          Predicted Effect of an Increase in Immigration on Unskilled
                   Wage Rates

| Ratio of Partial Elasticities of Substitution with Capital $(\sigma_{kl}/\sigma_{ku})^a$ | Labor Supply Elasticity $(\varepsilon)^b$ | Partial Elasticity of Substitution of Skilled for Unskilled Labor $(\sigma_{su})$ | | |
|---|---|---|---|---|
| | | .25 | 1.0 | 3.0 |
| 1.  −.25 | .1 | . . . | −.31 | −.42 |
|          | 1.0 | . . . | −.27 | −.30 |
| 2.  0 | .1 | −.27 | −.39 | −.45 |
|       | 1.0 | −.29 | −.30 | −.31 |
| 3.  .5 | .1 | −.42 | −.46 | −.48 |
|        | 1.0 | −.32 | −.33 | −.33 |
| 4.  1.0 | .1 | −.49 | −.49 | −.49 |
|         | 1.0 | −.34 | −.34 | −.34 |

*Note*: For notation and assumptions, see the text.
[a] Share-weighted average of substitution elasticities of skilled and unskilled labor with capital is constrained to equal .6.
[b] Labor supply elasticities of skilled and unskilled workers are constrained to be equal.

tween blue-collar and white-collar workers in manufacturing have confirmed this hypothesis. In contrast, the last row of the table presents values of $b_u$ under the assumption that skilled and unskilled labor are equally substitutable with capital.[13] Despite the wide variation in demand and supply parameters represented in the table, the range of the coefficient $b_u$ is relatively modest: from −.49 to −.27.[14] Under the assumption that immigrants add nothing to the demand for locally produced output (i.e., $\lambda = 1$), these coefficients imply that a 1 percent increase in the population of a city due to an influx of immigrants with the same skill composition as the existing labor force reduces unskilled wages by .3–.5 percent. The implied reduction in the per capita labor supply of natives (and existing immigrants) is proportional to this reduction in wages, multiplied by the elasticity of labor supply. If the elasticity of labor supply is in the range of zero to one, the implied reduction in per capita labor supply of natives is 0–.5 percent.

The magnitude of these predicted effects is dampened by any expansionary effect that immigrants have on the demand for locally produced goods. For example, if one-third of output is consumed locally, then the implied wage effects of a given immigrant inflow are reduced by approximately one-third.[15] Any imbalance in the skill distribution of arriving immigrants, on the other hand, accentuates their effect on the local labor market. In the most extreme case, if newly arriving immigrants are all unskilled and the proportion of skilled workers in the existing labor force is .5, then the predicted value of $b_u$ ranges from −2.0 to −1.0, implying roughly two to three times larger effects on unskilled wage rates.

Our empirical strategy in section 7.3 below is to correlate variation in the share of immigrants in the local labor market with variation in the employ-ment and wage outcomes of less-skilled natives. We interpret the coefficient relating wages to immigrant shares as an estimate of the expression $B_u$ in equa-tion (5) and the coefficient relating employment rates (or participation rates) to immigrant shares as an estimate of the product of $B_u$ and the elasticity of labor supply of unskilled native workers. As the previous discussion makes clear, the value of $B_u$ depends on the nature of immigrant flows to each city and on the characteristics of the demand for output produced in each city. Even ignoring these issues (as we do), it is important to keep in mind the potential endogeneity of immigrant inflows to different cities. If the supply of immigrants is wage elastic, then the covariation across cities between the la-bor market outcomes of natives and the share of immigrants in the labor mar-ket will be a positively biased estimate of the expression $B_u$. In our analysis, we address this issue with an instrumental variables scheme that isolates the component of immigrant inflows associated with the predetermined character-istics of each city.

Before turning to the empirical work, two limitations of the model deserve discussion. First, the model assumes that the existing native population is immobile. However, one might loosely interpret the supply elasticity of na-tives to reflect both labor supply changes of the current population of the city and out-migration (or in-migration) of natives to (or from) other cities.[16] If one interprets the intercity mobility of natives as raising the long-run elasticity of labor supply, then one would conclude that migration by natives in response to immigrant inflows would lower the effect of immigration on wages. It would also lower the effect on per capita labor supply of natives, as measured by a variable such as the employment/population ratio.[17] However, intercity migration would imply spillover effects on wages and employment/population ratios in other cities, which we ignore in our empirical work.

Second, the model assumes that the local labor market clears. Within the model, unemployment can be viewed as depending on the wage rate relative to the benefits of being unemployed. This view is most sensible in the long run. Barriers to wage adjustment (such as binding minimum wage levels or fixed welfare benefits) might be expected to strengthen the effect of an in-crease in immigrants on the employment and unemployment outcomes of na-tives while weakening the effects on wage levels relative to those implied by equations (6) and (7). The employment effects for natives could be especially large if employers of immigrants are less likely to comply with minimum wage laws or to be unionized.[18]

## 7.2   Industry Distributions of Natives and Immigrants

Our empirical analysis is based on the labor market outcomes of less-skilled natives in 120 major SMSAs in the 1970 and 1980 Censuses. We consider four groups of "less-skilled" natives: white males with less than twelve years of completed education; white females with less than thirteen years of completed education; black males with less than thirteen years of completed education; and black females with less than thirteen years of completed education. Our data base consists of samples of each race/sex group drawn from the 1/100 Public Use Sample of the 1970 Census and the 5/100 "A" sample of the 1980 Census. A description of our sampling procedures and information on our procedures for matching SMSA definitions between the 1970 and the 1980 Censuses are provided in Appendices A and B.

Table 7.2 provides an overview of our samples of less-skilled natives. The samples are restricted to individuals between the ages of nineteen and sixty-four who report themselves as not in school during the Census week.[19] Because of the age and education requirements, the average age of our less-skilled native groups is close to 40. The average years of complete schooling is less than eight for white male high school dropouts and between ten and eleven for the other groups.

The labor market outcomes that we consider are the labor force participation rate during the Census week; the employment rate during the Census week (measured for those in the labor force in the Census week); the

**Table 7.2**      **Descriptive Statistics for Native Samples**

| Demographic and Economic Characteristics: | White Male Dropouts | | White Females No College | | Black Males No College | | Black Females No College | |
|---|---|---|---|---|---|---|---|---|
| | 1970 | 1980 | 1970 | 1980 | 1970 | 1980 | 1970 | 1980 |
| 1. Age | 44.3 | 43.5 | 40.9 | 40.8 | 39.1 | 37.4 | 38.7 | 38.3 |
| 2. Education | 8.5 | 8.8 | 10.6 | 11.0 | 9.2 | 10.2 | 9.6 | 10.4 |
| 3. Labor force participation rate ($\times$ 100) | 88.8 | 81.0 | 47.3 | 56.5 | 83.6 | 78.4 | 55.1 | 59.1 |
| 4. Employment rate ($\times$ 100) | 96.0 | 91.1 | 95.6 | 94.0 | 94.4 | 86.9 | 92.6 | 87.9 |
| 5. Employment population rate Census week ($\times$ 100) | 85.2 | 73.7 | 45.2 | 53.3 | 78.9 | 68.3 | 51.1 | 52.1 |
| 6. Employment population rate last year ($\times$ 100) | 91.6 | 82.9 | 54.5 | 61.1 | 86.7 | 78.0 | 60.8 | 60.1 |
| 7. Logarithm of weeks worked last year | 3.81 | 3.75 | 3.57 | 3.60 | 3.77 | 3.69 | 3.58 | 3.60 |
| 8. Logarithm of weekly earnings last year (current $) | 4.95 | 5.52 | 4.26 | 4.96 | 4.61 | 5.29 | 4.03 | 4.90 |
| 9. Sample size | 84,068 | 24,925 | 99,488 | 81,151 | 27,779 | 29,723 | 34,013 | 34,540 |

*Note*: Samples consist of individuals age 16–64 in 120 major SMSAs. Individuals enrolled in school in Census week are excluded. White male dropouts sample includes individuals with less than 12 years of completed education. Samples for other groups include individuals with less than 13 years of completed education. For further information, see App. A.

employment-population ratio in the Census week; the fraction of people who reported working at any time in the previous year (for simplicity, we refer to this as the employment-population ratio last year); and the logarithms of weeks worked and average weekly earnings during the previous year (measured for those individuals who report positive weeks of work and positive earnings in the previous year). Precise definitions of these outcomes are presented in Appendix A.

The model of the previous section treats the market for less-skilled workers within each city as homogeneous. Even within a particular city, however, the market for less-skilled workers may be segmented along industry lines. If immigrants and natives tend to work in different industries, then the first-round effects of new immigration will be mainly concentrated among existing immigrants. If immigrants tend to work in the same industries as a particular subgroup of natives, however, then the effects of immigration on this subgroup of less-skilled natives will be magnified.

Some simple evidence on the correspondence between industry distributions of natives and immigrants is presented in table 7.3. For the ten two-digit industries with the highest immigrant employment shares and the ten industries with the lowest immigrant shares, this table shows the fraction of each of the four less-skilled native groups in the industry in 1980.[20] High-immigrant-share industries include several low-wage manufacturing industries (apparel, leather, furniture, miscellaneous manufacturing, and textiles) as well as low-wage service industries (private household services, hotels and motels, restaurants and bars, and transportation services) and agriculture. Low-immigrant-share industries include the government sector as well as railroads, communications, and several regionally based industries (tobacco, pipelines, coal mining, and oil and gas extraction). A comparison of the second and third columns of the table shows that industries with high or low immigrant shares in 1980 exhibited the same characteristic in 1970, although the immigrant fractions in many industries increased sharply between 1970 and 1980.[21] The immigrant share of total employment in all industries in our sample of 120 cities increased from 6.0 percent in 1970 to 9.6 percent in 1980.[22]

The data in table 7.3 suggest that immigrants are most directly competitive with native women—particularly black women. In fact, the proportion of black females in the ten highest-immigrant-share industries in 1980 was almost as high as the fraction of immigrants in those industries. By comparison, black males are the least concentrated in high-immigrant-share industries and the most heavily concentrated in low-immigrant-share industries.

One way to evaluate the effect of immigration on a particular native group is to calculate the overlap in the industry distribution of the group with the industry distribution of immigrants. Assuming that interindustry mobility costs are large, the effects of immigration on native wages will be directly proportional to the average increase in labor supply to industries in which natives are employed. To formalize this measure, let $S_{Ni}$ represent the share of the native group in the $i$th industry, let $E_i$ represent the initial level of total

**211** Immigration and the Labor Market Outcomes of Less-skilled Natives

Table 7.3      **Distributions of Natives in High- and Low-Immigrant-Share Industries, 1980**

| | % Immigrant 1980 | % Immigrant 1970 | % of All Immigrants in Industry | % of Natives in Industry | | | | |
|---|---|---|---|---|---|---|---|---|
| Industry | | | | All | White Males | White Females | Black Males | Black Females |
| High immigrant share: | | | | | | | | |
| 1. Apparel | 38.4 | 21.1 | 5.1 | 1.3 | .6 | 2.0 | .5 | 2.3 |
| 2. Leather | 27.3 | 14.4 | .6 | .2 | .3 | .3 | .1 | .3 |
| 3. Agriculture, crops | 25.8 | 10.0 | 1.5 | .6 | 1.2 | .4 | .5 | .3 |
| 4. Furniture | 21.0 | 11.0 | 1.0 | .4 | .7 | .4 | .6 | .4 |
| 5. Miscellaneous manufacturing | 20.9 | 10.6 | 2.3 | 1.1 | 1.2 | 1.3 | 1.0 | 1.4 |
| 6. Private household services | 20.2 | 9.5 | 1.4 | .7 | .2 | .8 | .2 | 6.0 |
| 7. Hotels and motels | 18.2 | 10.6 | 2.2 | 1.2 | .7 | 1.7 | 1.2 | 3.5 |
| 8. Transportation services | 15.8 | 11.2 | .5 | .3 | .1 | .4 | .1 | .1 |
| 9. Restaurants and bars | 15.6 | 9.3 | 6.4 | 3.9 | 2.5 | 7.6 | 3.1 | 5.5 |
| 10. Textile mills | 15.6 | 8.8 | .8 | .5 | .7 | .7 | .6 | .8 |
| Total: 10 industries | . . . | . . . | 21.8 | 10.1 | 8.2 | 15.6 | 7.9 | 20.6 |
| Low immigrant share: | | | | | | | | |
| 1. Pipelines | 1.5 | 1.9 | .0 | .0 | .0 | .0 | .0 | .0 |
| 2. Gov't.: justice and public safety | 2.8 | 2.3 | .4 | 1.4 | .9 | .8 | 2.0 | 1.0 |
| 3. Gov't.: revenue and taxation | 2.8 | 3.4 | .1 | .4 | .0 | .5 | .2 | .5 |
| 4. Coal mining | 3.5 | 2.4 | .0 | .1 | .1 | .0 | .1 | .0 |
| 5. Railroads | 3.8 | 3.5 | .3 | .6 | 1.4 | .1 | 1.1 | .2 |
| 6. Tobacco | 3.9 | 1.8 | .0 | .1 | .1 | .1 | .2 | .2 |
| 7. U.S. Post Office | 4.1 | 2.4 | .4 | 1.0 | .9 | .4 | 2.6 | 1.3 |
| 8. Oil and gas extraction | 4.2 | 2.0 | .2 | .4 | .4 | .2 | .2 | .1 |
| 9. Communications | 4.4 | 3.1 | .8 | 1.7 | .5 | 2.1 | 1.1 | 1.9 |
| 10. Gov't.: economic programs | 4.5 | 2.9 | .3 | .6 | .2 | .5 | .9 | .8 |
| Total: 10 industries | . . . | . . . | 2.5 | 6.1 | 4.5 | 4.7 | 8.4 | 6.0 |

*Note*: Based on the industry distributions of 19- to 64-year-olds in 120 major SMSAs in the 1980 Census.
ᵃ All natives include all education groups. Other groups are defined in the note to table 7.2.

employment in industry $i$, and let $\Delta E_i$ represent the increase in labor supply to the $i$th industry associated with the arrival of a fixed number of new immigrants $\Delta E$. The average proportional increase in labor supply experienced by the native group is

$$\sum_i S_{Ni} \frac{\Delta E_i}{E_i}$$

Suppose that new immigrants sort themselves into industries in the same proportions as existing immigrants. Then $\Delta E_i = S_{Ii}\Delta E$, where $S_{Ii}$ is the share of
existing immigrants employed in industry $i$. Finally, $E_i = S_i E$, where $S_i$ is the
share of all workers in industry $i$, and $E$ is level of total employment in the
labor market. Thus, the average proportional increase in labor supply experienced by the native group is $\beta\Delta E/E$, where

$$\beta = \sum_i \frac{S_{Ni}}{S_i} \frac{S_{Ii}}{S_i}$$

This expression reduces to one in the case of a homogeneous labor market, in
which $S_{Ni} = S_{Ii} = S_i$. In a heterogeneous labor market, however, the average
proportional increase in labor supply experienced by a particular native group
may be more or less than $\Delta E/E$, depending on the degree of similarity between the industry distributions of immigrants and the native group.

Estimates of this index of labor market competition are presented in table
7.4 for the four groups of less-skilled natives. We have calculated the index
separately using the 1970 and 1980 industry distributions of natives and immigrants. We have also calculated the index separately over two subsets of
cities: the twenty cities with the highest fraction of less-skilled immigrants in
1980 and the forty cities with the lowest fraction of less-skilled immigrants
in 1980. These cities are identified in Appendix D.

Estimates of the index of labor market competition are very similar using
the 1970 and 1980 industry distributions. The values of the index range from
a low of .85 in 1980 for white males in low-immigrant cities to 1.28 in 1970
for black females and are consistently below one for black males. The results
confirm the impression that black females are in most direct competition with
immigrants, whereas black males are most isolated from immigrant competition. Nevertheless, the values of the index are not far from one for any of the
groups, suggesting that increases in the share of immigrants in the labor market have roughly proportional effects on the labor markets of unskilled natives.[23] The differences in the index between high- and low-immigrant cities
are positive for males and negative for females, suggesting that immigrants
and native males are in more direct contact in high-immigrant cities while
immigrants and native females are in less direct contact. One interpretation of
this finding is that less-skilled native females have been displaced from
immigrant-intensive industries in high-immigrant cities. We explore this hypothesis next.

Evidence on the extent of industry displacement is presented in tables 7.5
and 7.6, which give the cross-sectional and time-series patterns of differences
in the industry distributions of less-skilled natives in high-immigrant and low-
immigrant cities. For ten high-immigrant-share industries and ten major
immigrant-employing industries, table 7.5 displays the relative share of unskilled natives in high- versus low-immigrant cities. Specifically, let $E_{N_i}^H$ and
$E_{N_i}^L$ represent the employment of native group $N$ in industry $i$ in high-
immigrant and low-immigrant cities, respectively. Let $E_i^H$ and $E_i^L$ represent

**213**     Immigration and the Labor Market Outcomes of Less-skilled Natives

Table 7.4     **Estimated Index of Labor Market Competition between Immigrants and Natives**

|                            | All Cities |      | High-Immigrant Cities |      | Low-Immigrant Cities |      |
|----------------------------|------------|------|-----------------------|------|----------------------|------|
| Native Group               | 1970       | 1980 | 1970                  | 1980 | 1970                 | 1980 |
| 1. White male dropouts     | 1.06       | 1.00 | 1.09                  | 1.03 | .99                  | .85  |
| 2. White female no college | 1.09       | 1.08 | 1.05                  | 1.03 | 1.10                 | 1.12 |
| 3. Black males no college  | .94        | .94  | .97                   | .93  | .91                  | .91  |
| 4. Black females no college| 1.24       | 1.15 | 1.28                  | 1.06 | 1.20                 | 1.16 |

*Note*: For definition of index, see the text. High-immigrant cities include 20 SMSAs with highest fraction of less-skilled immigrants. Low-immigrant cities include 40 SMSAs with lowest fraction of less-skilled immigrants.

total employment in industry $i$ in these cities, and let $E_N^H$ and $E_N^L$ represent total employment of the native group in these cities. For each industry and native group, table 7.5 displays the ratio

$$\frac{E_{N_i}^H / E_i^H}{E_{N_i}^L / E_i^L} \div \frac{E_N^H / E^H}{E_N^L / E^L},$$

which represents the relative employment share of natives in the $i$th industry in high- versus low-immigrant cities, divided by the relative shares of natives in total employment in those cities. A value of unity indicates that natives have equal shares of employment in the industry in the two groups of cities, controlling for their relative shares in total employment. A value of less than unity, on the other hand, indicates relative displacement in the high-immigrant-fraction cities.

For most of the high-immigrant-share industries, there is evidence of displacement of natives in the high-immigrant-share cities. The displacement effects are less apparent for white males, with ratios in excess of unity for four industries.[24] For the other three groups, however, relative employment shares in the set of high-immigrant cities are generally less than unity. By comparison, the evidence of displacement of less-skilled natives from the major immigrant-employing industries in the lower panel of table 7.5 is mixed. On balance, these data suggest that the industry displacement of natives is restricted to low-wage service and manufacturing industries and agriculture. As the ratios in the right-hand column of table 7.5 suggest, these industries are generally more important in high-immigrant than low-immigrant cities, although in cross section it is difficult to distinguish alternative explanations for this effect.[25]

Table 7.6 repeats the analysis in table 7.5, taking the ratio of the relative

**Table 7.5**          **Relative Industry Distributions of Natives in High- and Low-Immigrant Cities, 1980**

| Industry | % of All Immigrants in Industry | Relative Share of Native Group: High- vs. Low-Immigrant Cities[a] | | | | High- vs. Low-Immigrant Cities[b] |
|---|---|---|---|---|---|---|
| | | White Males | White Females | Black Males | Black Females | |
| High immigrant share: | | | | | | |
| 1. Apparel | 5.1 | 1.43 | .49 | 1.29 | .44 | 2.64 |
| 2. Leather | .6 | 1.33 | .71 | .62 | .97 | 1.40 |
| 3. Agriculture, crops | 1.5 | .56 | .86 | .84 | .74 | 1.71 |
| 4. Furniture | 1.0 | .64 | .68 | .68 | .36 | .94 |
| 5. Miscellaneous manufacturing | 2.3 | .83 | 1.04 | .65 | .66 | 1.89 |
| 6. Private household services | 1.4 | ... | .65 | .35 | .79 | 1.25 |
| 7. Hotels and motels | 2.2 | 1.42 | .91 | .67 | .54 | 1.25 |
| 8. Transportation services | .5 | .59 | 1.12 | .09 | 1.33 | 2.29 |
| 9. Restaurants and bars | 6.4 | 1.32 | .80 | .95 | .50 | 1.01 |
| 10. Textile mills | .8 | .73 | .77 | 1.22 | .65 | .57 |
| Other major immigrant employers: | | | | | | |
| 1. Hospitals and health services | 8.4 | 1.71 | .89 | 1.48 | 1.07 | .91 |
| 2. Construction | 5.7 | .97 | 1.04 | .83 | .81 | 1.00 |
| 3. Education | 4.5 | .94 | 1.15 | 1.07 | 1.00 | .89 |
| 4. Business services | 3.3 | 1.51 | .81 | 1.18 | .99 | 1.51 |
| 5. Electrical equipment | 3.3 | .75 | 1.13 | .61 | .82 | 1.17 |
| 6. Machinery | 3.2 | .91 | 1.62 | .84 | 1.32 | .68 |
| 7. Transportation equipment | 2.7 | .78 | 1.52 | .74 | .72 | .74 |
| 8. Grocery stores | 2.6 | 1.61 | .89 | 1.89 | .98 | 1.03 |
| 9. Wholesale trade: nondurables | 2.5 | 1.27 | .94 | .96 | 1.33 | 1.17 |
| 10. Food products | 2.1 | .81 | 1.35 | .65 | .70 | .79 |

*Note*: Based on the industry distributions of 19- to 64-year-olds in 120 SMSAs in the 1980 Census. High-immigrant cities include 20 SMSAs with the highest fraction of less-skilled immigrants. Low-immigrant cities include 40 SMSAs with the lowest fraction of less-skilled immigrants.

[a] For each industry and native group, the relative share is the proportion of industry employment contributed by the native group in high-immigrant cities, divided by the same proportion in low-immigrant cities. This ratio is then divided by the ratio of the shares of the native group in total employment in the two groups of cities.

[b] Ratio of industry share of total employment in high-immigrant cities to industry share of total employment in low-immigrant cities.

**215**    Immigration and the Labor Market Outcomes of Less-skilled Natives

Table 7.6    Relative Growth of Employment Shares of Natives in High- and Low-Immigrant Cities, 1970–80

| Industry | Relative Growth of Native Group: High- vs. Low-Immigrant Cities[a] | | | | Relative Growth of Total Employment: High- vs. Low-Immigrant Cities[b] | Growth of Total Employment All Cities[c] |
|---|---|---|---|---|---|---|
| | White Males | White Females | Black Males | Black Females | | |
| High immigrant share: | | | | | | |
| 1. Apparel | 1.73 | .85 | .82 | .39 | 1.30 | .67 |
| 2. Leather | 1.33 | 1.72 | .19 | .43 | 3.10 | .62 |
| 3. Agriculture, crops | .43 | .72 | 1.29 | 1.45 | 1.88 | .95 |
| 4. Furniture | .77 | .88 | 1.26 | 1.59 | 1.06 | .85 |
| 5. Miscellaneous manufacturing | .67 | .91 | .75 | .33 | 1.11 | .96 |
| 6. Private household services | . . . | .72 | .38 | .83 | 1.55 | .52 |
| 7. Hotels and motels | 1.47 | 1.15 | .71 | .72 | .93 | 1.16 |
| 8. Transportation services | .61 | 2.23 | .04 | 2.16 | .68 | 1.39 |
| 9. Restaurants and bars | 1.36 | .97 | .89 | .98 | .94 | 1.05 |
| 10. Textile mills | .94 | .88 | 2.01 | .95 | .82 | .56 |
| Other major immigrant employers: | | | | | | |
| 1. Hospitals and health services | 1.75 | 1.04 | 1.00 | 1.08 | .91 | 1.17 |
| 2. Construction | .89 | .77 | .77 | .72 | 1.13 | 1.03 |
| 3. Education | 1.00 | 1.15 | 1.27 | 1.52 | .82 | .89 |
| 4. Business services | 1.28 | .89 | .56 | .67 | .97 | 1.32 |
| 5. Electrical equipment | .60 | 1.08 | .66 | .64 | 1.38 | .75 |
| 6. Machinery | .79 | 1.05 | .65 | .52 | 1.40 | .93 |
| 7. Transportation equipment | .83 | 1.54 | 1.07 | .87 | 1.11 | .78 |
| 8. Grocery stores | 1.33 | 1.04 | 1.15 | 1.14 | 1.07 | .92 |
| 9. Wholesale trade: nondurables[d] | . . . | . . . | . . . | . . . | . . . | . . . |
| 10. Food products | .75 | 1.09 | .89 | .72 | .93 | .78 |

*Note:* For definitions of high-immigrant and low-immigrant cities, see the note to table 7.5.
[a] For formula, see the text.
[b] Relative ratio of 1980 to 1970 employment totals for industry in high-immigrant vs. low-immigrant cities.
[c] Ratio of 1980 to 1970 employment totals for industry in all cities.
[d] Data for wholesale trade nondurables industry not available.

employment share of natives in 1980 to the relative employment share in 1970. A value of unity for this ratio suggests that natives have maintained their relative share of industry employment, controlling for the relative growth of total employment of natives in the two sets of cities. A value of less than unity, on the other hand, suggests that natives have lost relative share in the industry in high-immigrant versus low-immigrant cities.[26]

The results in table 7.6 are generally consistent with those in table 7.5 and suggest some movement of less-skilled natives out of high-immigrant-share industries in the high-immigrant cities between 1970 and 1980. The fifth column of the table indicates the relative growth of total employment by industry in high- versus low-immigrant-share industries, while the sixth column gives the ratio of total employment in the industry in 1980 in all cities to total employment in all cities in 1980. Although several high-immigrant industries were declining relatively quickly between 1970 and 1980, in most cases the relative decline was slower in high-immigrant cities. This suggests that the availability of immigrant labor may allow certain industries to survive in high-immigrant cities even at the same time as natives continue to exit from these industries.

Our analysis of the industry distributions of immigrants and less-skilled natives suggests three conclusions. First, a 1 percentage point increase in the share of immigrants generates approximately a 1 percent increase in the supply of labor to industries in which less-skilled natives are employed. There is no indication that immigrants and less-skilled natives are concentrated in particular industries in a manner that would greatly accentuate the labor market competition between them or, on the other hand, substantially reduce the degree of labor market competition between them. Second, among the four native groups that we consider, immigrants are most directly competitive with black females and least competitive with black men. Third, differences in industry distributions between high- and low-immigrant cities suggest that natives have been displaced from some low-wage service and manufacturing industries and that these industries have declined less quickly in cities with more immigrants.

## 7.3   An Analysis of the Effects of Immigration on Less-skilled Natives

In this section, we examine the correlation across cities between the labor market outcomes of less-skilled natives and the fraction of immigrants in the city. We present cross-sectional analyses for 1970 and 1980 as well as a first-differenced analysis of changes between 1970 and 1980. Our basic approach is very simple. We regress SMSA averages of the labor market outcome variables for our four race/sex groups against measures of the immigrant fraction in the SMSA and a variety of controls for the characteristics of each city. Before turning to the results of the analysis, however, we first discuss the construction of SMSA means for the outcome variables. We then briefly discuss potential econometric problems with the cross-sectional and first-differenced analyses and offer some comments on the interpretation of our estimates.

### 7.3.1 Construction of SMSA-Level Outcome Measures and Control Variables

The first step in our analysis is to construct SMSA-specific means of the outcome variables that are purged of differences in the observable characteristics of the native population across different cities. Given the limited information collected in the Census, this step amounts to regression adjusting the outcome variables for differences in age and education. Such an adjustment has two potential advantages. First, it should reduce the sampling variation associated with the means of the outcome variables across different cities. Second, it should eliminate any bias arising from correlations between the fraction of immigrants in a city and the age and educational attainment of natives.

For each race/sex group in each of the two Censuses, we regress each of the outcome variables against a full set of SMSA dummies and a flexible function of age and education. Specifically, we include a cubic polynomial in age, a detailed set of dummy variables for different education levels, and a full set of interactions of age and education up to the second order. We then use the estimated SMSA dummies as our regression-adjusted outcome measures.[27]

The explanatory variables in the second step of our analysis include the fraction of immigrants in each SMSA and three additional control variables: the logarithm of SMSA population and SMSA-specific means of age and education for the particular race/sex group under consideration. Although the outcome variables are adjusted for age and education, we found in preliminary work that the mean of adjusted weekly earnings is correlated across cities with the mean of education, particularly for blacks. We have no explanation for this phenomenon, although it may indicate a correlation across cities between the quality and the quantity of education among blacks or possibly a market externality associated with higher levels of education among the less-skilled black population. In any case, we include SMSA-specific means of age and education for the particular race/sex group in all our SMSA-level regressions. These means are calculated directly from our native extracts.

Our measure of the fraction of immigrants in each SMSA is the fraction of foreign-born residents, taken from published tabulations of the 1970 and 1980 Censuses. From the standpoint of the theoretical model, it would be preferable to use the fraction of immigrants in the local labor force. Since our sample sizes for 1970 are too small to provide reliable estimates of the fraction of immigrants in many of the smaller cities, we have relied instead on the published population data. Provided that changes in the immigrant labor force are proportional to changes in the population of immigrants, the use of fraction of immigrants in the population will not affect our results.

### 7.3.2   Econometric Issues

We next turn to a brief discussion of our estimating equations. We focus on three issues: possible sources of bias in the estimating equations; the interpretation of differences between cross-sectional and first-differenced estimates of the effects of immigration; and the use of weighted least squares in the estimation.

Our cross-sectional estimating equations have the form

$$(7) \qquad \hat{Y}_{Nj} = X_{Nj} b + f_j c + e_{Nj},$$

where $\hat{Y}_{Nj}$ is the adjusted labor market outcome for native group $N$ in city $j$, $X_{Nj}$ is a vector of control variables for the race/sex group and city (the mean of age and education for the group and the logarithm of SMSA population), $f_j$ is the fraction of immigrants in the city, and $e_{Nj}$ is a residual term. Similarly, our first-differenced estimating equations have the form

$$(8) \qquad \Delta \hat{Y}_{Nj} = \Delta X_{Nj} b + \Delta f_j c + \Delta e_{Nj},$$

where $\Delta Z_j$ refers to the change in the variable $Z$ in city $j$ between 1970 and 1980.

Depending on the choice of outcome measure $Y$, these equations have the form of equations (5) or (6) derived from our theoretical model. The interpretation of estimates of the coefficient $c$ obtained from equation (7) or (8), however, depends on the nature of the residual terms in these equations. These residuals can be decomposed into two conceptually distinct components: (1) a market-level SMSA effect due to factors other than immigration (e.g., unmeasured characteristics of natives or demand shocks affecting the local economy) and (2) sampling variation arising from the fact that we observe only a sample of natives in each SMSA. Let $Y_{Nj}$ represent the true population value of the outcome variable for natives in city $j$. Then we may decompose $e_{Nj}$ as

$$e_{Nj} = a_{Nj} + \hat{Y}_{Nj} - Y_{Nj},$$

where $a_{Nj}$ represents the SMSA effect due to factors other than immigration, and $\hat{Y}_{Nj} - Y_{Nj}$ is the component of $e_{Nj}$ attributable to sampling variability. Only if $a_{Nj}$ is orthogonal to the fraction of immigrants in the city will estimates of the coefficient $c$ from the cross-sectional regression (7) yield unbiased estimates of $B_u$ or $\varepsilon \cdot B_u$, as described by equation (5) or (6). In the first-differenced specification, the corresponding requirement is that *changes* in the unmeasured SMSA effects be uncorrelated with changes in the fraction of immigrants in the city between 1970 and 1980.

Clearly, the main advantage of the first-differenced analysis is that it eliminates any bias introduced by city-specific fixed effects that are correlated with the fraction of immigrants in a city and the labor market outcomes of natives. Transitory effects (associated with transitory fluctuations in the demand for the output of specific cities, e.g.) will still lead to biases in the differenced analysis if they influence the inflow rate of immigrants. Bartel's (1989) recent analysis suggests that economic conditions have a relatively small effect on the destination city chosen by immigrants. Instead, Bartel's findings suggest that immigrants are mainly attracted to cities with large concentrations of previous immigrants from the same country (see also Greenwood and McDowell 1986). Nevertheless, her research leaves open the possibility that the timing and size of immigrant inflows are affected by economic conditions in particular cities.

We attempt to control for any potential correlation between immigrant inflows and local economic conditions in our first-differenced analysis by an instrumental variables procedure. As suggested by Bartel's (1989) work, we use the fraction of immigrants in a city in 1970 to predict the change in the fraction of immigrants over the following decade.[28] Immigrant inflows are strongly correlated with the initial fraction of immigrants in a city, and these variables are reasonably strong predictors of the change in immigrant fraction.

In comparing the cross-sectional and first-difference results, one should also keep in mind that the first-difference analysis is more likely to capture the short-run effects of immigration, in which the capital stock and the industry/skill composition of labor demand have not had time to adjust fully. The effects of immigration on per capita employment rates and wages may weaken over time as natives move to other cities or to labor market sectors that are less affected by immigrant competition. Dynamic issues are not addressed in our formal model, but we suspect that the short-run effects of immigration on employment of less-skilled natives will be larger than the long-run effects. The relative magnitude of the short-run and long-run effects on wages depend on whether there are barriers to wage adjustments in the short run. In fact, we find that the cross-sectional estimates of the effect of immigration on employment outcomes of natives are *larger* than the differenced estimates, whereas the opposite is true of the estimated effects on wages. This leads us to suspect that the differences between the cross-sectional and the differenced results are primarily due to correlations between city-specific effects and immigrant shares that are eliminated in first-differences rather than to a distinction between long-run and short-run effects.

A final econometric issue arises from the relatively small samples of black natives in many cities, particularly in our 1970 sample. We restrict our cross-sectional and differenced analysis of each race/sex group to the set of cities for which we have at least thirty group members in both 1970 and 1980. Consequently, we work with a set of ninety-one cities for black males, a set of ninety-four cities for black females, and a full set of 120 cities for white men and women. We also use weighted least squares methods to estimate our equations, using the square root of the number of observations for the race/sex group in the city as a weight. In our first-differenced specifications, we use as a weight $(N_{70}^{-1} + N_{80}^{-1})^{-1/2}$, where $N_{70}$ and $N_{80}$ are the number of observations for the native subgroup in the SMSA in 1970 and 1980, respectively.[29] This weighting scheme assumes that the residual $e_{Nj}$ arises mainly from sampling variability associated with the estimated outcome measure. Even controlling for the covariates in our models, however, the labor market outcomes of different race/sex groups are correlated across cities, suggesting the presence of omitted city-specific effects. We have not adjusted our standard errors or estimation procedures to take account of such error components.

### 7.3.3    Empirical Results

To provide an introduction and overview of our results, table 7.7 presents weighted least squares estimates of the effects of immigration on the labor market outcomes of the pooled set of four race/sex groups. The estimated equations include unrestricted intercepts for the four groups as well as group-specific coefficients on the means of age and education. The coefficients on the immigrant share variable and the population variable, however, are restricted to be the same across the four native subgroups.

The cross-sectional results for 1970 show significantly negative effects of an increase in immigrant shares on the labor force participation rates and employment rates of less-skilled natives. The results imply that a 10 percentage point increase in the fraction of immigrants in an SMSA would lead to a reduction in the employment/population ratio of less-skilled natives of roughly 2 percent. The employment rate would also fall by 1 percent, implying an increase in unemployment rates of about 1 percent. Among those who work, average weeks per year would fall by about 2 percent.

**Table 7.7**          **Effects of Immigration on Four Groups of Less-Skilled Natives, Pooled Sample (standard errors in parentheses)**

| Outcome Variable | Cross-sectional | | First-Differenced | |
|---|---|---|---|---|
|  | 1970 | 1980 | 1980–70 | 1980–70 IV[a] |
| 1. Labor force/ | −.173 | −.083 | .080 | −.102 |
| population | (.066) | (.049) | (.083) | (.122) |
| 2. Employment/ | −.240 | −.054 | .404 | .085 |
| population | (.074) | (.060) | (.097) | (.144) |
| 3. Employment/labor | −.109 | .019 | .461 | .231 |
| force | (.036) | (.040) | (.077) | (.113) |
| 4. Fraction worked last | −.161 | −.158 | .090 | −.246 |
| year | (.063) | (.050) | (.084) | (.125) |
| 5. Log weeks worked | −.191 | −.088 | .232 | .142 |
|  | (.078) | (.061) | (.132) | (.193) |
| 6. Log earnings/week | .467 | .018 | −.262 | −1.205 |
|  | (.165) | (.112) | (.228) | (.342) |

*Note*: All equations included subgroup-specific intercepts, the total population in the SMSA, and the average education and age of the subgroup in the SMSA (with subgroup-specific coefficients). The sample size is 424.

[a] Estimated by instrumental variables. The change in the fraction of immigrants in the SMSA is instrumented with the fraction of immigrants in 1970 and its square.

These negative employment effects contrast sharply with the finding that immigration has a positive effect on weekly wages. The estimated coefficient in row 6 implies that a 10 percentage point increase in the immigrant share would lead to a 4.7 percent increase in weekly earnings. Within the context of our model, these results can be reconciled only if the labor supply elasticity of less-skilled natives is negative.[30]

The 1980 cross-sectional results for the various employment outcomes also indicate a negative effect of immigration, although the estimated coefficients are smaller in magnitude than those for 1970. In the 1980 data, however, the estimated effect of immigrant densities on the average weekly earnings of natives is essentially zero. This gives further reason for caution in the interpretation of the 1970 results.

Weighted least squares estimates of the first-differenced specification are presented in the third column of table 7.7. In contrast to the cross-sectional results, these estimates suggest a modest *positive* effect of the fraction of immigrants on the employment outcomes of natives. The estimated effect on earnings per week is negative ($-.267$) but not statistically different from zero.

Instrumental-variables estimates of the first-differenced specification are presented in column 4. These estimates give an ambiguous picture of the effect of immigration on the employment outcomes of natives. A marginally significant positive effect on the employment rate in the Census week is counterbalanced by a marginally significant negative effect on the employment-population ratio last year. Nevertheless, the instrumented first-differenced results indicate a significantly negative effect of immigration on wages. The coefficient is $-1.2$ with a standard error of .242. The more negative effect associated with the instrumental variables estimation scheme is consistent with the hypothesis that the least squares estimate is positively biased by endogenous immigration inflows.

On balance, the pooled data suggest that the effect of immigrant densities on the employment and participation rates of natives is small and potentially zero. If the instrumented first-differenced specification is taken at face value, however, the effect on wages is apparently negative. For the most part, these conclusions carry over to the detailed results for the four subgroups, to which we now turn.

*Results for Individual Race/Sex Groups*

Estimates of the relation between immigrant fractions and the labor market outcomes of black males are presented in table 7.8, which has the same format as table 7.7. As in the pooled analysis, the cross-sectional results for black men suggest a negative correlation between the fraction of immigrants and employment outcomes. In the differenced analysis, however, the relation is much less consistent. Likewise, although the 1970 cross-sectional analysis suggests a positive effect of immigration on black male wages, the 1980 cross-sectional results and the differenced results indicate a negative effect.

222　　Joseph G. Altonji and David Card

Table 7.8　　Effects of Immigration on Black Males with Less than Thirteen Years of Education (standard errors in parentheses)

| Outcome Variable | Cross-sectional | | First-Differenced | |
|---|---|---|---|---|
| | 1970 | 1980 | 1980–70 | 1980–70 IV[a] |
| 1. Labor force/population | −.145 | −.136 | −.040 | −.273 |
| | (.126) | (.084) | (.170) | (.240) |
| 2. Employment/population | −.264 | −.068 | .658 | .285 |
| | (.156) | (.115) | (.234) | (.234) |
| 3. Employment/labor force | −.165 | .046 | .864 | .623 |
| | (.090) | (.098) | (.210) | (.294) |
| 4. Fraction worked last year | −.183 | −.214 | .101 | −.268 |
| | (.100) | (.081) | (.168) | (.168) |
| 5. Log weeks worked | −.154 | −.051 | −.447 | .272 |
| | (.121) | (.111) | (.252) | (.351) |
| 6. Log earnings/week | .736 | −.153 | −.806 | −1.910 |
| | (.346) | (.248) | (.494) | (.706) |

*Note*: All equations include average age and education in the SMSA as well as total population. The sample size is 91.
[a] Estimated by instrumental variables. See the note to table 7.7.

Table 7.9　　Effects of Immigration on White Males with Less than Twelve Years of Education (standard errors in parentheses)

| Outcome Variable | Cross-sectional | | First-Differenced | |
|---|---|---|---|---|
| | 1970 | 1980 | 1980–70 | 1980–70 IV[a] |
| 1. Labor force/population | −.193 | −.079 | .066 | .036 |
| | (.075) | (.083) | (.149) | (.231) |
| 2. Employment/population | −.279 | −.159 | .349 | .109 |
| | (.101) | (.112) | (.186) | (.289) |
| 3. Employment/labor force | −.107 | −.110 | .343 | .086 |
| | (.053) | (.074) | (.134) | (.211) |
| 4. Fraction worked last year | −.151 | −.215 | −.145 | −.609 |
| | (.070) | (.078) | (.136) | (.211) |
| 5. Log weeks worked | −.223 | −.312 | −.018 | −.190 |
| | (.074) | (.106) | (.211) | (.328) |
| 6. Log earnings/week | −.264 | −.178 | −.356 | −1.103 |
| | (.201) | (.212) | (.406) | (.637) |

*Note*: All equations include average age and education in the SMSA as well as total population. The sample size is 120.
[a] Estimated by instrumental variables. See the note to table 7.7.

The results for white male dropouts are presented in table 7.9. These results are very similar to those for black males, although the point estimates of the effects of immigration on wages are somewhat smaller in magnitude. Again, the differenced specifications in particular suggest a negative effect of immigrant densities on native wage rates, while the effects on employment and participation rates are smaller and vary with the precise measure of employment.

The regression results for black females in table 7.10 are of particular interest, given the evidence in section 7.2 that black women are in closer competition with immigrants than the other three groups. Nevertheless, the estimated coefficients for this group are not much different than those for the other groups. The cross-sectional results suggest a small negative effect of immigrant shares on employment outcomes and a modest positive effect on weekly wages. These conclusions are reversed, however, in the first-differenced analysis, which suggests a generally positive effect on employment rates and a negative effect on wage rates. The differenced results for black females are not particularly sensitive to choice of least squares or instrumental variables estimation, although as in previous tables the strongest negative wage effect is obtained by the instrumental variables procedure.

Table 7.11 presents our results for white females. Again, the cross-sectional results for 1970 indicate a negative relation between immigrant shares and employment outcomes, while the differenced analysis indicates much weaker effects. The cross-sectional and first-differenced specifications fit by least squares suggest a positive effect of immigrant shares on wage rates. When the change in immigrant share is instrumented, however, the estimated wage coefficient is negative and consistent with the results for the other native groups.

A check on the wage effects reported for the different native groups in tables 7.7–7.11 is contained in table 7.12. Here, we estimate the same specifications using the wage outcomes of immigrant workers as the dependent variable. We

**Table 7.10**    **Effects of Immigration on Black Females with Less than Thirteen Year of Education (standard errors in parentheses)**

| | Cross-sectional | | First-Differenced | |
|---|---|---|---|---|
| Outcome Variable | 1970 | 1980 | 1980–70 | 1980–70 IV[a] |
| 1. Labor force/population | −.216 | −.063 | −.154 | −.221 |
| | (.179) | (.119) | (.256) | (.357) |
| 2. Employment/ | −.221 | .003 | .149 | .032 |
| population | (.192) | (.128) | (.269) | (.374) |
| 3. Employment/labor | −.037 | .073 | .457 | .320 |
| force | (.105) | (.086) | (.186) | (.259) |
| 4. Fraction worked last | −.165 | −.127 | .054 | −.219 |
| year | (.169) | (.120) | (.272) | (.379) |
| 5. Log weeks worked | −.247 | .143 | .735 | .217 |
| | (.232) | (.143) | (.387) | (.542) |
| 6. Log earnings/week | 1.213 | .533 | −.838 | −1.369 |
| | (.402) | (.236) | (.609) | (.848) |

*Note:* All equations include average age and education in the SMSA as well as total population. The sample size is 94.

[a] Estimated by instrumental variables. See the note to table 7.7.

**Table 7.11**     **Effects of Immigration on White Females with Less than Thirteen Years of Education (standard errors in parentheses)**

| | Cross-sectional | | First-Differenced | |
|---|---|---|---|---|
| Outcome Variable | 1970 | 1980 | 1980–70 | 1980–70 IV[a] |
| 1. Labor force/population | −.037 | .058 | .273 | −.044 |
| | (.144) | (.097) | (.137) | (.207) |
| 2. Employment/population | −.095 | .027 | .420 | −.089 |
| | (.150) | (.105) | (.154) | (.240) |
| 3. Employment/labor | −.132 | −.045 | .306 | −.017 |
| force | (.058) | (.045) | (.125) | (.190) |
| 4. Fraction worked last | −.047 | .005 | .189 | −.162 |
| year | (.145) | (.098) | (.146) | (.222) |
| 5. Log weeks worked | −.094 | −.118 | .133 | .335 |
| | (.170) | (.110) | (.270) | (.399) |
| 6. Log earnings/week | .667 | .397 | .309 | −.955 |
| | (.245) | (.132) | (.430) | (.663) |

*Note*: All equations include average age and education in the SMSA as well as total population. The sample size is 120.
[a] Estimated by instrumental variables. See the note to table 7.7.

**Table 7.12**     **Effects of Immigration on Male Immigrant Wages (standard errors in parentheses)**

| | Cross-sectional | | First-Differenced | |
|---|---|---|---|---|
| Outcome Variable | 1970 | 1980 | 1980–70 | 1980–70 IV[a] |
| 1. Log earnings/week | −.459 | −.741 | −.504 | −.823 |
| (unadjusted) | (.357) | (.181) | (.381) | (.512) |
| 2. Log earnings/week | .116 | −.499 | −.958 | −1.492 |
| (adjusted) | (.302) | (.167) | (.354) | (.481) |

*Note*: Immigrant group includes males age 16–64 not in school in Census week. All equations include average age and education in the SMSA as well as total population. The sample size is 74.
[a] Estimated by instrumental variables. See the note to table 7.7.

use two measures of immigrant wages: the mean of actual log weekly earnings for male immigrants and an adjusted mean that controls for the average levels of age and education of immigrants in each city. The results reveal three findings. First, unadjusted mean earnings of immigrants are more strongly correlated in cross section with the fraction of immigrants than mean earnings that have been adjusted for measured skill attributes. This suggests a negative correlation between the skill level of immigrants and their fraction in the population. Second, as we found for the native groups, the instrumental variables estimate of the first-differenced specification leads to the largest negative estimate of the effect of immigrant densities on wages. Finally, the instrumental variables estimates of the effect of immigrant shares on immigrant wages is very similar to the corresponding estimate for native wages. There is no evidence that immigrants have a stronger negative effect on their own wages than on those of less-skilled natives.

*Other Results*

We estimated many of our least squares models for the 1970, 1980, and differenced samples with a control for the fraction of blacks in the SMSA population. This addition made little difference to the results.

We also reestimated many of our specifications using the fraction of "less-skilled" immigrants in the SMSA population in place of the overall fraction of immigrants in the SMSA population. We defined the fraction of "less-skilled" immigrants as the product of the fraction of immigrants in the SMSA population and the fraction of male immigrants in the SMSA whose predicted earnings are less than the national median for male immigrants (see App. D). The (unweighted) correlation across 120 cities between the "less-skilled" immigrant fraction and the total immigrant fraction is .94 in 1970 and .95 in 1980. The correlation of changes in the two immigrant measures is .82. Perhaps as a result, least squares results using the fraction of less-skilled immigrants are similar to those reported in tables 7.7–7.11. The regression coefficients typically increase in absolute value, reflecting the fact that the scale of the less-skilled immigrant variable is compressed relative to the other variable. It is worth noting that instrumental variables estimates (using the fraction of immigrants in the SMSA in 1970 and its square as instruments) point to a somewhat larger negative effect of the fraction of less-skilled immigrants on the weekly earnings of natives. The coefficients for black males, white males, black females, and white females are $-7.0$, $-4.8$, $-12.9$, and $-12.3$, respectively. These estimates are very imprecise, however, perhaps because the correlation between fraction of immigrants in 1970 and the change in fraction of less-skilled immigrants in the SMSA is only .27.[31]

Finally, we reestimated the 1980 cross-sectional specifications and the first-differenced specifications for each of our labor market outcome variables using the SMSA-specific mean of the corresponding labor market outcome for white males age 31–64 with thirteen or more years of schooling as a control variable. We view this approach, which uses the labor market outcomes of highly skilled workers to control for general labor market conditions within each city, as an alternative to our instrumental variables procedure. It is strictly correct only if, in contrast to the implications of our model, immigration has no effect on more highly educated white males. The results from this alternative procedure are generally similar to our ordinary least squares estimates and suggest smaller negative effects of immigration on less-skilled native wages than the instrumental variables procedure.

## 7.4  Conclusions

This paper presents a variety of evidence on the effects of immigration on the labor market outcomes of less-skilled natives. Working from a simple theoretical model of a local labor market, we show that the effects of immigration can be estimated from the correlations between the fraction of immigrants in a city and the employment and wage outcomes of natives. We go on to compute these correlations using city-specific outcomes for individuals in 120 major SMSAs in the 1970 and 1980 Censuses. We also use the relative industry distributions of immigrants and natives to provide a direct assessment of the degree of labor market competition between them.

Our empirical findings indicate a modest degree of competition between immigrants and less-skilled natives. A comparison of industry distributions shows that an increase in the fraction of immigrants in the labor force translates to an approximately equivalent percentage increase in the supply of labor to industries in which less-skilled natives are employed. Based on this calculation, immigrant inflows of the magnitude observed between 1970 and 1980 generated 1–2 percent increases in labor supply to these industries in most cities. A comparison of the industry distributions of less-skilled natives in high- and low-immigrant-share cities between 1970 and 1980 shows some displacement of natives out of low-wage immigrant-intensive industries.

We find little evidence that inflows of immigrants are associated with large or systematic effects on the employment or unemployment rates of less-skilled natives. Our estimates of the effect of immigration on native wage rates are sensitive to the choice of specification and estimation procedure. When we consider first-differences between 1980 and 1970 and use an instrumental variables estimation procedure to control for endogeneity of immigrant inflows, we find that a 1 percentage point increase in the fraction of immigrants in an SMSA reduces less-skilled native wages by roughly 1.2 percent. The least squares estimates imply a wage reduction of .3 percent. We point out a number of reasons to prefer the instrumental variables procedure, but additional research, perhaps with the 1990 Census, will be required before one can draw strong conclusions about the response of wages to immigration.

# Appendix A
## *Sampling Procedures and Variable Definitions*

### Sampling Procedures

Our 1970 samples are drawn from the 1/100 County Group Public Use Sample based on the 5% version of the 1970 Census questionnaire. The sample universe consists of all individuals age 19–64 currently residing in one of 120 SMSAs. (The samples actually contain 121 SMSAs, but, for comparability with the 1980 Census, Dallas and Fort Worth are considered as one SMSA). As described in the text, our analysis is limited to individuals not currently enrolled in school and in specific race/sex/education and national origin groups from this universe.

Our 1980 samples are drawn from the 5/100 Public Use "A" Sample of the 1980 Census. The sample universe consists of all individuals age 19–64 currently residing in one of 120 SMSAs (adjusted to 1970 boundaries: see App. B). To limit the size of the samples, stratified random samples of individuals meeting the above requirements were drawn by SMSA. Samples of native-born nonblacks (i.e., race coded as white, American Indian, Asian, or other) were drawn to generate approximately twenty-three hundred observations per SMSA for all age/sex/education levels. The samples were then further restricted to two subsets of observations: females with twelve or fewer years of completed education and males with eleven or fewer years of completed education. Samples of native-born blacks were drawn to generate a maximum of 500 observations per SMSA for black females with twelve or fewer years of completed education and 500 observations per SMSA for black males with twelve or fewer years of completed education. One hundred percent samples of foreign-born individuals were taken for all but five large SMSAs, which were sampled with the following probabilities: Chicago, .400; Los Angeles, .170; Miami, .500; New York, .137; and San Francisco, .550.

Labor Market Outcome Variable Definitions

The following labor market outcome variables are defined for all individuals in the sample universe:

- employed in the previous year (P35 = 0 in 1970; P94 = 1 in 1980);
- in the labor force in the Census week (P31 = 1, 2, 4, 5 in 1970; P81 = 1, 2, 4, 5 in 1980);
- employed in the Census reference week (P31 = 1, 2, 4, 5 in 1970; P81 = 1, 2, 4, 5 in 1980).

For individuals in the labor force in the Census week, a fourth variable is defined to be one if the individual was employed in the Census week and zero otherwise.

For individuals who worked in the previous year and who reported strictly positive values for the number of weeks worked in the previous year (P36 = 0–5 in 1970; P95 > 0 in 1980) and earnings in the previous year (P37 = 0–500 in 1970; P101 > 0 in 1980), two additional variables are defined: weeks worked in the previous year and earnings per week in the previous year. For 1980, these variables are constructed directly: weeks worked is measured by variable P95; and earnings per week is measured by P101/P35. (These calculations make no adjustments for allocated responses or truncation of the reported earnings figure.) For 1970, only interval measures of weeks worked and total annual earnings are available. We assigned midpoints of the intervals to the weeks and earnings figures and then constructed earnings per week as the ratio of the assigned values.

## Appendix B
## *Matching SMSA Definitions between 1970 and 1980*

The Public Use Samples of the 1970 Census identify 125 individual SMSAs (see pp. 123–26 of the *Description and Technical Documentation for the Public Use Samples of Basic Records from the 1970 Census*). A total of 120 of these are used in our statistical analysis. Four SMSAs were deleted because of difficulty matching between 1970 and 1980 or because of too small sample sizes: Lorain-Elyria, Ohio; Johnstown, Pennsylvania; San Bernadino–Riverside, California; and Wilkes Barre–Hazelton, Pennsylvania. The Fort Worth SMSA was merged with Dallas (see below).

The Census Bureau publication *Geographic Identification Code Scheme* (1983, 11–17) gives a detailed list of changes in the county-level definitions of SMSAs between 1970 and 1980. In most cases, these changes involve the addition of surrounding counties or parts of these counties to the SMSA. The major exceptions are (1) the combination of Dallas and Fort Worth into a single SMSA; (2) the creation of a separate SMSA consisting of Nassau and Suffolk counties of New York State (formerly part of the New York SMSA); and (3) the reclassification of Bergen County, New Jersey, from the Paterson-Clifton-Passaic SMSA to the New York SMSA.

Our general matching strategy was to redefine 1980 SMSA boundaries to the 1970 boundaries. With only a few exceptions, this involved deleting individuals from the 1980 Census file who resided in counties that were classified as part of the SMSA in 1980 but not in 1970. For example, Montgomery County, New York, was added to the Albany-Schenectady-Troy SMSA in 1973. Individuals in this county were therefore deleted from the 1980 file. County-level information for each household is coded in the variable COGRP (location 6–8 of the household record) of the Public Use "A" Sample of the 1980 Census. County group codes are obtained from the 1980 County Group Equivalence File (1980 Census of Population and Housing, Public Use Micro Data Sample, part 77) and Appendix M of the 1980 Census Public Use Microdata Samples Technical Documentation. In most cases, individual counties are identified by one or more county group codes. For these cases, the deletion is accomplished by specifying the county group code(s) of those counties added to the SMSA after 1970.

In some cases, only parts of a surrounding county group were added to the SMSA. In these cases, we randomly deleted a fraction of individuals from the added county or county group. The fraction of individuals deleted was set equal to the relative population of the part of the county added to the SMSA. Estimates of population for county subgroups were obtained from the 1980 County Group Equivalency File.

In all, a total of forty-nine counties or county subgroups were deleted from the definitions of the 120 SMSAs. Another forty counties or county subgroups were partially deleted. The number of individual records actually affected by these deletion procedures is small. For example, of 244,941 immigrants identified on the 1980 Public Use A Sample using the 1980 SMSA definitions, 2,609 (1.07 percent) were deleted in the change to the 1970 definitions. A copy of the computer instructions that performed the deletions is available from David Card on request.

To account for changes in the classification of Nassau and Suffolk counties in New York State, we added individuals in the Nassau-Suffolk SMSA in 1980 to the New York SMSA sample. To account for the changes in definition of the Paterson-Clifton-Passaic SMSA, we added individuals in the 1980 sample living in Bergen County, New Jersey (classified as part of the New York SMSA in 1980), to the Paterson-Clifton-Passaic SMSA sample and deleted them from the New York SMSA sample. To account for the reclassification of Dallas and Fort Worth into a single SMSA, we combined individuals from the Dallas and Fort Worth SMSAs in the 1970 Census file into a single Dallas–Fort Worth sample. No attempt was made to deal with minor reclassifications affecting the Boston and Providence SMSAs and the Detroit and Flint SMSAs.

# Appendix C
## *Industry Definitions*

### Matching of 1970 and 1980 Three-Digit Codes

Our procedure was to reclassify the three-digit industry codes of individuals in the 1970 Census to 1980 industry codes. The Census Bureau provided us with cross-tabulations of 1970 and 1980 three-digit industry codes for samples of males and females who had been coded under both systems. These cross-tabulations were used to estimate the probability that an individual with a given 1970 code would be classified in a particular industry under the 1980 coding scheme. Using these probabilities, a computer program was developed that reclassifies individuals probabilistically from their 1970 three-digit industry to a particular 1980 three-digit industry. The computer program processes males and females separately. A copy of the program is available from David Card.

### Industry Classifications Used in Tables 7.3–7.6

Using the three-digit industry titles in Appendix H of the Public Use Microdata Samples Technical Documentation, we developed a "two-digit" classification consisting of seventy-six individual industries. (There are 231 separate industries in the 1980 Census industry coding system.) This classification combines many smaller three-digit industries: for example, "agricultural services except horticulture" (industry 020) and "horticultural services" (industry 021). A listing of the computer instructions used to classify three-digit industries into this two-digit system is available from David Card.


# Appendix D
## Classification of High- and Low-Immigrant Cities

In order to determine average immigrant skill levels by SMSA, a regression equation was fit to the log of average weekly earnings for the 1980 sample of male immigrants. The equation included the same flexible function of age and education used to regression adjust native outcomes (see the text description) as well as a set of forty-six country/region dummy variables and their interactions with an indicator variable for having entered the United States after 1970 and a variable representing years in the United States. (Chiswick [1978], Borjas [1985, 1987], and others have shown that country of origin, immigration cohort, and years since immigration affect earnings in the United States.) This equation was then used to assign a predicted wage to each male immigrant. Immigrants with a predicted wage less than the median predicted wage for the entire United States were classified as "low skill." Finally, the fraction of low-

**Table 7D.1**      **Twenty Cities with Highest Fraction of Low-Skill Immigrants**

| City | Fraction Immigrants | Fraction Low-Skill Immigrants |
|------|---------------------|-------------------------------|
| Miami | .36 | .20 |
| El Paso | .21 | .20 |
| Los Angeles | .22 | .16 |
| Salinas | .19 | .16 |
| Jersey City | .24 | .15 |
| Oxnard-Ventura | .13 | .10 |
| New York | .21 | .10 |
| Honolulu | .15 | .10 |
| Paterson | .15 | .09 |
| Fresno | .11 | .09 |
| San Diego | .13 | .08 |
| Anaheim | .13 | .08 |
| Bakersfield | .09 | .08 |
| Stockton | .11 | .08 |
| Santa Barbara | .12 | .07 |
| San Francisco | .16 | .07 |
| San Jose | .14 | .07 |
| Houston | .08 | .06 |
| San Antonio | .07 | .06 |
| Providence | .09 | .06 |

**231**     Immigration and the Labor Market Outcomes of Less-skilled Natives

Table 7D.2             **Forty Cities with Lowest Fraction of Low-Skill Immigrants**

| City | Fraction Immigrants | Fraction Low-Skill Immigrants |
|------|---------------------|-------------------------------|
| Huntington-Ashland, KY | .01 | .00 |
| Chattanooga | .01 | .00 |
| Birmingham | .01 | .00 |
| Knoxville | .01 | .00 |
| York, PA | .01 | .00 |
| Canton | .02 | .00 |
| Jackson, MS | .01 | .00 |
| Cincinnati | .02 | .01 |
| Dayton | .02 | .01 |
| Flint | .03 | .01 |
| Appleton | .02 | .01 |
| Louisville | .01 | .01 |
| St. Louis | .02 | .01 |
| Nashville | .01 | .01 |
| Indianapolis | .02 | .01 |
| Richmond | .02 | .01 |
| Duluth | .03 | .01 |
| Memphis | .01 | .01 |
| Akron | .03 | .01 |
| Greensboro | .01 | .01 |
| South Bend | .03 | .01 |
| Utica-Rome, NY | .04 | .01 |
| Erie, PA | .03 | .01 |
| Pittsburgh | .03 | .01 |
| Harrisburg | .02 | .01 |
| Binghampton | .04 | .01 |
| Greenville | .02 | .01 |
| Peoria | .02 | .01 |
| Wilmington | .03 | .01 |
| Fort Wayne | .02 | .01 |
| Mobile | .01 | .01 |
| Madison | .03 | .01 |
| Lancaster | .02 | .01 |
| Toledo | .03 | .01 |
| Youngstown | .04 | .01 |
| Lansing | .03 | .01 |
| Columbus | .02 | .01 |
| Atlanta | .02 | .01 |
| Minneapolis | .03 | .01 |
| Shreveport | .02 | .01 |

skill immigrants in each SMSA was determined by multiplying the fraction of immigrants in the SMSA by the fraction of immigrants who are classified as low skill. Table 7D.1 lists the twenty cities with the highest fraction of low-skill immigrants. Table 7D.2 lists the forty cities with the lowest fraction of low-skill immigrants.

## Notes

1. Most of the available evidence is summarized by Greenwood and McDowell (1986), General Accounting Office (1988), and Papademetriou et al. (1989). Two studies of particular relevance to ours are Grossman (1982) and Borjas (1987). Lalonde and Topel (in this volume) provide a parallel study to ours, focusing on the effects of recent immigrants on the labor market outcomes of earlier immigrants. Muller and Espenshade (1985) analyze the effect of immigrants on various California cities.

2. A similar conclusion is reached by Kuhn and Wooton (in this volume) and Papademetriou et al. (1989, ch. 4).

3. The average change in the percentage of immigrants between 1970 and 1980 in the 120 SMSAs in our sample is 1.4 and ranges between 0 and 11.4 percent.

4. If the price of output is exogenous, it is more convenient to work with the elasticities of factor prices with respect to factor quantities, holding constant marginal cost. These are usually known as elasticities of complementarity (see, e.g., Hamermesh 1986).

5. This depends, of course, on constant returns to scale and on perfectly elastic supplies of capital and other inputs.

6. In order to avoid the theoretical prediction of factor price equalization across cities, it is necessary to assume that the number of goods produced within a city is less than the number of locally supplied factors. For further discussion of this point, see Kuhn and Wooton (in this volume).

7. We ignore land or any other locally supplied factors.

8. For notational simplicity, we suppress the dependence of $c(\cdot)$ on the prices of nonlabor inputs.

9. In the notation of eqq. (1) and (2), $\partial D_j(q, w_j)/\partial w_j = 0$, and $\partial L_j(w_j, q)/\partial q = 0$, for $j = (u, s)$.

10. Johnson (1980a) makes the further assumption that the elasticity of labor supply among existing immigrants is zero, so that the effective supply elasticity in the market for unskilled labor is $(1 - f_u)\varepsilon$, where $f_u$ is the fraction of immigrants in the existing pool of unskilled workers, and $\varepsilon$ is the labor supply elasticity of natives.

11. That is, $\theta_u\sigma_{uk} + \theta_s\sigma_{sk} = .6(\theta_u + \theta_s)$, where $\theta_j$ represents the value share of labor in the $j$th skill group.

12. No entries are included in the first row under the column for $\sigma_{su} = .25$. In this row of the table, $\sigma_{sk}$ is strongly negative ($-.525$). Thus, skilled and unskilled labor must be relatively strong substitutes (i.e., $\sigma_{su} > .8$) to satisfy the restrictions on the matrix of partial elasticities.

13. If $\sigma_{uk} = \sigma_{sk}$, eq. (5) implies that the value of the coefficient $b_u$ is independent of the substitutability between skilled and unskilled labor.

14. The elasticities of demand for unskilled labor with respect to its own wage rate ($\eta_{uu}$) implied by the parameter choices in table 7.1 range from $-1.0$ (in the lower-left-hand entries of the table) to $-2.6$ (in the upper-right-hand entries of the table).

15. Estimates of the fraction of output produced in a city that is consumed locally are not easily obtained. Roughly 35 percent of consumer expenditures are allocated to personal, health, business, and education services, public utilities, transportation services, and other goods with a high local content.

16. If the immigrants are primarily unskilled, then one might expect out-migration of unskilled natives and in-migration of skilled natives.

17. Filer (1988) shows that the net migration rate of natives to an SMSA between 1975 and 1980 is negatively related to the migration rate of immigrants into the SMSA between 1970 and 1974 and to the migration rate of immigrants into the SMSA be-

tween 1975 and 1980. The negative relation appears to be strongest for low-skilled and less-educated natives.

18. Papademetriou et al. (1989, chap. 4) summarize evidence from a few industry studies suggesting that in some cases immigrant labor has been used to undercut union firms paying higher wages and employing native workers.

19. By "Census week" we mean the week immediately preceding the administration of the Census, for which individuals report their major activity. The Census is administered on 1. April.

20. Our two-digit industry classification is explained in App. C.

21. Of the ten highest-immigrant-share industries in 1980, seven were in the top ten industries by immigrant share in 1970. The rank-order correlation across industries between the 1970 and 1980 immigrant shares is .86.

22. The average fraction of immigrants in the total population in our sample of cities in 1970 was .044 and ranged from .003 to .242. The average fraction of immigrants in the total population in 1980 was .058 and ranged from .008 to .357.

23. It should be pointed out that the index is computed from the industry distribution of existing immigrants and cannot be used to assess the effects of an inflow of immigrants that are much different from the existing stock.

24. The number of white males in private household services is so low that the index cannot be calculated.

25. For example, many high-immigrant-share cities are also major transportation centers (New York, Los Angeles, Miami). This fact may partially explain the relatively high share of the transportation services industry in the high-immigrant-share cities.

26. It is interesting to note that total employment growth rates between 1970 and 1980 for the twenty high-immigrant-share cities and the forty low-immigrant-share cities were virtually identical: the ratio of 1980 to 1970 employment was .92 for the high-immigrant-share cities and .91 for the low-immigrant-share cities. The relative growth rates of less-skilled native employment, however, were somewhat different in the two sets of cities. The relative ratios of 1980 to 1970 employment totals in high-versus low-immigrant cities were .96 for white males, .90 for white females, 1.02 for black males, and .87 for black females.

27. A similar approach is used by Borjas (1987).

28. An alternative strategy is to study the effect of immigrant flows to particular SMSAs that one can identify as exogenous. For example, Card (1990) examines the effect of the Marial boat lift on the Miami labor market and finds little effect on the wages and unemployment rates of less-skilled blacks and other non-Cuban groups. His results for wages are somewhat at variance with the instrumental variables estimates we report below.

29. The instrumental variables estimation of the first-difference equation also uses these weights.

30. The implied per capita labor supply elasticity is roughly minus one. An alternative explanation, which might be consistent with an extended version of the model allowing for heterogeneity within the population of less-skilled natives, is that a downward shift in the wage distribution induced by immigration results in the exit from the labor force of natives with the lowest skill levels. However, given that the decline in the employment population ratio is small, a compositional shift cannot explain the results even if the wages of those who left employment were essentially zero prior to their departure.

31. In contrast, the correlation between the fraction of immigrants in 1970 and the change in fraction of all immigrants in the SMSA is .60. These correlations refer to the unweighted sample of 120 SMSAs.

**234   Joseph G. Altonji and David Card**

# References

Bartel, Ann. 1989. Where do the new U.S. immigrants live? *Journal of Labor Economics* 7 (October):371–91.

Borjas, George. 1985. Assimilation, changes in cohort quality, and earnings of immigrants. *Journal of Labor Economics* 3(October):463–89.

———. 1987. Immigrants, minorities, and labor market competition. *Industrial and Labor Relations Review* 40(April):382–93.

Card, David. 1990. The impact of the Mariel boatlift on the Miami labor market. *Industrial and Labor Relations Review* 43(January):245–57.

Chiswick, Barry. 1982. The impact of immigration on the level and distribution of economic well-being. In *The gateway: U.S. immigration issues and policies,* ed. Barry Chiswick. Washington, D.C.: American Enterprise Institute.

Filer, Randall. 1988. The impact of immigrant arrivals on migratory patterns of native workers. Typescript, Department of Economics, Hunter College-CUNY.

General Accounting Office. 1988. *Illegal aliens: Influence of illegal workers on wages and working conditions of legal workers.* Washington, D.C.: U.S. Government Printing Office.

Greenwood, Michael, and John McDowell. 1986. The factor market consequences of U.S. immigration. *Journal of Economic Literature* 24(December):1738–72.

Grossman, Jean. 1982. The substitutability of natives and immigrants in production. *Review of Economics and Statistics* 64(November):596–603.

Hamermesh, Daniel. 1986. The demand for labor in the long run. In *Handbook of labor economics,* ed. Orley Ashenfelter and Richard Layard. Amsterdam: North-Holland.

Johnson, George. 1980a. The labor market effects of immigration. *Industrial and Labor Relations Review* 33(April):331–41.

———. 1980b. The theory of labor market intervention. *Economica* 47(August): 309–30.

Muller, Thomas, and Thomas Espenshade. 1985. *The fourth wave: California's newest immigrants.* Washington, D.C.: Urban Institute Press.

Papademetriou, Demetrios, et al. 1989. The effects of immigration on the U.S. economy and labor market. U.S. Department of Labor Bureau of International Labor Affairs Immigration Policy and Research Report no. 1, May.

# [13]

## Immigration and Wages: Evidence from the 1980's

### By Kristin F. Butcher and David Card*

More immigrants entered the United States during the past decade than in any comparable period since the 1920's. Among the issues raised by this influx, none is as controversial as its effect on the labor market opportunities of native-born workers. Evidence on the labor market consequences of immigration is limited (see Michael Greenwood and John McDowell, 1986, and George Borjas, 1990). This paper presents new evidence on the effects of immigration, based on changes in the distributions of wages in 24 major cities during the 1980's. Although immigrant inflows are small relative to the populations of most cities, recent immigrants are a significant fraction of less-educated workers in many cities. We therefore concentrate on measuring the effects of immigration at the lower tail of the wage distribution. In particular, we ask whether recent declines in the real earnings of the least-skilled workers in the U.S. economy are related to immigration. Our empirical analysis reveals large differences across cities in the relative growth rates of wages for low- and high-paid workers. Nevertheless, these differences bear little or no relation to the size of immigrant inflows. Our results therefore confirm the findings of earlier studies, based on 1970 and 1980 Census data, that suggest that the labor market consequences of higher immigration are relatively small.

### I. Characteristics of New Immigrants in 1980 and 1985

A standard approach to measuring the labor market effects of immigration is to treat different cities within the United States as distinct labor markets, and to compare labor market outcomes across cities with higher and lower immigrant densities. We

follow this approach here, tracking wages in 24 major cities during the period from 1979 to 1989. Our sample includes the 10 most immigrant-intensive cities identifiable in *Current Population Survey* (*CPS*) microdata files, along with a group of 14 other cities (listed in Table 2). The other cities were selected by a variety of criteria, including stable boundaries, relatively large sample sizes, and a desire for geographic comparability with the high-immigrant cities. We believe that the sample gives a fair picture of the variation in immigrant inflow rates and relative immigrant "quality" across major U.S. cities.

We begin by presenting some simple evidence on the nature of recent immigrant inflows into the United States. The first two columns of Table 1 contain data from the 1980 Census on the characteristics of natives and recent immigrants (i.e., those who immigrated between 1975 and 1980) in the 24 cities in our sample. Recent immigrants are younger, less educated, and more likely to be male than natives (or earlier immigrants). The proportion of Hispanics is also much higher among recent immigrants than in the native population. The education distribution of newly arriving immigrants is relatively disperse: the fraction of college graduates is about the same as in the native population, but close to one-quarter of recent immigrants have less than an elementary education. As a result, recent immigrants make up 17 percent of the population in these cities with 6 or fewer years of schooling, and 10 percent of the population with less than an eighth-grade education.

Columns 3 and 4 of Table 1 present the characteristics of individuals in the March 1985 *CPS*, classified by whether or not the respondent was living in the United States 5 years earlier. Based on responses to a similar question in the 1980 Census, we estimate that 85 percent of those living abroad 5 years ago are immigrants. Demographic differences between the two groups

* Princeton University, Princeton NJ 08544.

TABLE 1—COMPARISON OF RECENT IMMIGRANTS
AND OTHERS IN 24 CITIES,
1980 CENSUS AND MARCH 1985 *CPS*

|  | 1980 Census | | March 1985 CPS | |
|---|---|---|---|---|
|  | (1) | (2) | (3) | (4) |
| Pct of Total | 86.8 | 3.4 | 96.6 | 3.4 |
| Pct Female | 51.4 | 48.2 | 51.5 | 46.5 |
| Mean Age | 37.4 | 31.3 | 37.7 | 31.7 |
| Pct Age 16–24 | 24.7 | 34.4 | 21.7 | 33.0 |
| Pct Hispanic | 5.0 | 39.0 | 11.2 | 36.7 |
| **Education (Years):** | | | | |
| Mean | 12.5 | 10.7 | 12.7 | 11.3 |
| Pct 0–6 | 2.3 | 22.8 | 3.4 | 15.0 |
| Pct 16+ | 18.0 | 17.3 | 22.3 | 21.0 |
| **Work in Previous Year:** | | | | |
| Pct Worked | 71.5 | 59.5 | 71.4 | 60.6 |
| Avg. Log Wage | 1.82 | 1.51 | 2.06 | 1.75 |
| Std. Deviation | 0.66 | 0.66 | 0.66 | 0.64 |

*Note:* Samples contain individuals age 16–68 in 24
cities. Col. (1) contains natives; Col. (2) contains immigrants who entered the United States between 1975
and 1980; Col. (3) contains individuals who were living
in the United States in March 1980; Col. (4) contains
individuals who were living abroad in March 1980.

TABLE 2—CHARACTERISTICS OF 24 MAJOR CITIES

|  | Percent Recent Imms: | | Growth Rate[a] | Wage Gap[b] |
|---|---|---|---|---|
|  | 1980 | 1985 | | |
| New York | 4.4 | 6.0 | 0.4 | 34.5 |
| Los Angeles | 7.7 | 7.3 | 1.8 | 44.5 |
| Chicago | 2.5 | 2.4 | 0.3 | 32.3 |
| Philadelphia | 0.9 | 1.5 | 0.5 | 25.9 |
| Detroit | 0.8 | 0.9 | −0.4 | 15.2 |
| San Fransisco | 4.3 | 4.1 | 1.3 | 27.5 |
| Washington, D.C. | 2.8 | 3.8 | 1.6 | 27.7 |
| Baltimore | 0.7 | 1.6 | 0.7 | 26.6 |
| Houston | 3.3 | 3.5 | 2.4 | 32.2 |
| Minneapolis | 1.1 | 0.9 | 1.3 | 3.4 |
| Dallas | 1.7 | 4.7 | 3.4 | 31.6 |
| Seattle | 1.9 | 2.5 | 1.6 | 24.3 |
| Anaheim | 4.8 | 3.9 | 2.0 | 44.2 |
| Milwaukee | 0.6 | 3.3 | −0.1 | 19.4 |
| Atlanta | 0.7 | 2.4 | 3.1 | 17.1 |
| San Diego | 4.0 | 3.9 | 2.9 | 34.8 |
| Miami | 6.1 | 8.7 | 1.4 | 30.8 |
| Denver | 1.4 | 0.9 | 2.0 | 9.2 |
| Riverside, CA | 1.9 | 4.4 | 4.4 | 22.2 |
| San Jose | 4.4 | 3.6 | 1.3 | 20.7 |
| New Orleans | 1.3 | 2.1 | 0.7 | 14.5 |
| Tampa | 0.7 | 5.1 | 2.8 | 21.7 |
| Portland | 1.5 | 1.6 | 0.8 | 14.2 |
| Sacramento | 1.7 | 3.2 | 2.8 | 17.0 |

[a]Annual percentage growth rate in population
1980–87.
[b]1980 wage gap between recent immigrants and
native born.

are consistent with the differences between
recent immigrants and others in the 1980
Census. The 30 percent wage gap between
the new arrivals and other workers is also
very similar to the gap between recent immigrants and others in 1980. We conclude
from these comparisons that the relative
"quality" of arriving immigrant cohorts was
relatively stable between 1975 and 1985.

## II. Immigration to Specific Cities

From this general overview we turn to a
specific examination of the nature of immigrant flows to each of the 24 cities in our
data set. Table 2 provides information on
the percent of "recent immigrants" in each
city in 1980 and 1985, together with data on
the overall population growth rate between
1980 and 1987, and the wage gap between
recent immigrants and natives in 1980. Two
important features of U.S. immigration are
highlighted in the table. First, recent immigrants are highly concentrated in only a few
cities. Three cities (New York, Los Angeles,
and Miami) accounted for 51 percent of
recent immigrants in both 1980 and 1985.
Second, there is substantial variation across

cities in the composition of recent immigrant inflows. As a general rule, the quality
of recent immigrants, measured by their
wage gap relative to native workers, is lower
in cities with higher inflow rate. A key correlate of both inflow rates and the relative
wage of recent immigrants is the fraction of
Hispanic immigrants, which ranges from under 10 percent in Detroit, Minneapolis,
Seattle, and Portland to over one-half in
cities in California and Texas.

An important feature of immigration to a
local labor market is its effect on population
growth. A natural assumption is that an
inflow of new immigrants generates a proportional increase in the labor force and
population of a city. Recent research by
Randall Filer (1990), however, suggests that
the intercity migration decisions of native
workers are highly sensitive to immigrant
inflows. Indeed, Filer's analysis of population movements between 1975 and 1980 im-

plies that immigrant arrivals are almost completely offset by native outflows.

There is some evidence of offsetting out-migration in Table 2, particularly for the high-immigrant cities of New York, Los Angeles, and Miami. All three cities had large immigrant inflows but relatively modest growth rate during the 1980's. In the absence of out-migration, an increase in the fraction of new immigrants will raise the population growth rate of a city point-for-point. Therefore, if native inflow rates are independent of immigration rates, population growth rates should be linearly related to immigration inflow rates, with a slope of 1.0. In fact, the slope of a regression line fitted to all 24 cities in our data set is 1.04 (with a standard error of 0.54). When a similar regression is fit to the subset of observations that excludes New York, Los Angeles, and Miami, however, the estimated slope is much higher (2.76, with a standard error of 0.67). This regression accounts for about one-half of the variation in growth rates in the subset of 21 cities. From this evidence we conclude that native in-migration flows during the 1980's were actually *positively* correlated with inflows of recent immigrants to all but the 3 most immigrant-intensive cities.

One explanation for the difference between the highest-immigrant cities and other major cities is based on the composition of immigrant inflows. Between 1980 and 1985, over one-half million Cuban and Southeast Asian refugees arrived in the United States (Frederick Hollmann, 1990, Table V). Most of the Cubans, and perhaps one-half of the Asians, settled in either New York, Los Angeles, or Miami. To the extent that the refugees were drawn to these cities by cultural and ethnic ties, their location decisions may have been less sensitive to local labor market conditions than the decisions of other newly arriving immigrants. It should be pointed out, however, that New York and Los Angeles had large immigrant inflows during the 1970's and grew more slowly than most other U.S. cities between 1970 and 1980. The experiences of these two cities during the 1980's were therefore in keeping with earlier trends. What is appar-

ently different between the 1970's and 1980's is the emergence of a positive relation between immigration and overall population growth among other cities.

## III. Immigration and Wages

Table 3 turns to an examination of wage outcomes in different cities during the past decade. The data are taken from merged files of the 12 monthly *Current Population Surveys* administered in 1979, 1980, 1988, and 1989, and pertain to hourly wage rates (for hourly rated workers) or the ratio of average weekly earnings to average weekly hours (for salaried workers). For each city and each year, we have calculated the 10th and 90th percentiles of the log wage distribution. The first two columns of Table 3 represent (unweighted) averages of the 1979 and 1980 percentiles, and the second two columns represent changes from the 1979–80 average to the 1988–89 average.

TABLE 3—LEVELS AND CHANGES IN PERCENTILES OF LOG WAGES IN 24 CITIES: 1979–80 TO 1988–89

| | Percentiles in 1979–80 | | Changes from 1979–80 to 1988–89 | |
|---|---|---|---|---|
| | 10th | 90th | 10th | 90th |
| New York | 1.14 | 2.39 | 0.47 | 0.67 |
| Los Angeles | 1.14 | 2.46 | 0.34 | 0.56 |
| Chicago | 1.18 | 2.50 | 0.30 | 0.48 |
| Philadelphia | 1.12 | 2.38 | 0.44 | 0.59 |
| Detroit | 1.13 | 2.51 | 0.29 | 0.46 |
| San Fransisco | 1.26 | 2.56 | 0.35 | 0.56 |
| Washington, D.C. | 1.18 | 2.69 | 0.43 | 0.41 |
| Baltimore | 1.12 | 2.39 | 0.36 | 0.54 |
| Houston | 1.14 | 2.45 | 0.22 | 0.52 |
| Minneapolis | 1.15 | 2.47 | 0.39 | 0.50 |
| Dallas | 1.14 | 2.35 | 0.28 | 0.58 |
| Seattle | 1.27 | 2.50 | 0.29 | 0.49 |
| Anaheim | 1.14 | 2.55 | 0.40 | 0.50 |
| Milwaukee | 1.12 | 2.39 | 0.30 | 0.46 |
| Atlanta | 1.12 | 2.40 | 0.39 | 0.58 |
| San Diego | 1.12 | 2.44 | 0.36 | 0.52 |
| Miami | 1.10 | 2.20 | 0.29 | 0.63 |
| Denver | 1.15 | 2.50 | 0.29 | 0.45 |
| Riverside, CA | 1.12 | 2.41 | 0.37 | 0.58 |
| San Jose | 1.25 | 2.63 | 0.40 | 0.58 |
| New Orleans | 1.13 | 2.36 | 0.19 | 0.49 |
| Tampa | 1.10 | 2.17 | 0.29 | 0.59 |
| Portland | 1.19 | 2.46 | 0.29 | 0.44 |
| Sacramento | 1.12 | 2.46 | 0.43 | 0.48 |

The distribution of hourly wages in each city is approximately lognormal, although the distributions contain prominent "spikes" at points like $3.00, $5.00, and $10.00 per hour. The spread between the 10th and the 90th percentile of log wages in any city tends to be strictly proportional to the estimated standard deviation, as is the case for a normal distribution.

The 1979–80 data reveal sharp differences across cities in both the level and dispersion in wages. Interestingly, there is less variation across cities in the 10th percentile of wages than in wages at the middle or upper end of the earnings distribution. This is apparently due to the restraining effect of the minimum wage, that served as the 10th percentile of wages in many cities in 1979 and 1980. One implication of a binding national wage floor is that the dispersion of wages within a city is highly correlated with the average level of wages. In 1979–80, this pattern is clearly present in the data. Despite the differences in mean log wages across cities, however, 97 percent of the overall variation in individual wages for workers in our sample of cities is within-city variation.

Intercity differences in the 10th percentile of wages in 1979–80 are uncorrelated with differences in the fraction of recent immigrants (or total immigrants) in the city. Wages at the upper end of the earnings distribution are weakly negatively related to the fraction of recent immigrants, but weakly positively related to the overall fraction of immigrants. These small and unsystematic correlations are consistent with findings in the previous literature. Looking across cities in 1979–80, there is no evidence of any effect of immigration on the level of wages.

Changes in the distribution of wages over the last decade also show considerable intercity variation. Mean log wages in most cities grew at roughly the same rate as the Consumer Price Index (CPI), which rose 44 percent between 1979–80 and 1988–89. Mean log wages in Detroit, Houston, and New Orleans, however, grew much more slowly than average consumer prices, while those in New York grew faster. As shown in the third and fourth columns of Table 3,

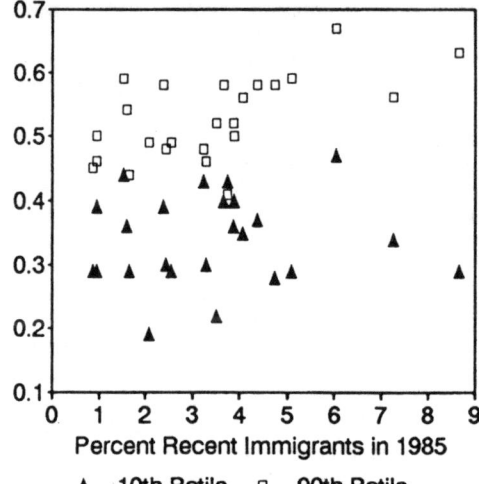

FIGURE 1. IMMIGRATION AND CHANGE IN WAGE DECILES IN 24 MAJOR CITIES, 1979–80 TO 1988–89

there are significant differences across cities in the relative growth of the 10th and 90th percentiles of wages (and in the corresponding change in the standard deviation of wages). In every city except Washington, D.C., wage rates in the upper tail of the earnings distribution grew more quickly than those in the lower tail. Thus, the growth in wage inequality during the 1980's (Chinhui Juhn et al., 1989) was almost entirely due to an increase in the within-city variance.

The rise in wage inequality over the 1980's was greater in cities with relatively bigger immigrant inflows. This is illustrated in Figure 1, which plots the changes in the 10th and 90th percentiles of wages for each city against the fraction of recent immigrants in 1985. Contrary to our expectations, however, the data suggest that higher immigration is associated with more rapid increases in the 90th percentile of wages, rather than with any relative decline in the 10th percentile of wages.

One explanation for the pattern of the data in Figure 1 is that the cost of living rose more rapidly in cities with larger immigrant inflows, and that these increases in prices lead to wage increases for high-wage workers. To test this possibility we constructed wage changes relative to city-specific cost-of-living indexes, which are available from the Bureau of Labor Statistics for most of the cities in our sample. As hypothesized, the change in the city-specific cost of living is positively correlated with the fraction of recent immigrants in 1985. Adjusting for changes in the local cost of living, the change in the 90th percentile of wages is still positively related to the fraction of recent immigrants, but the regression coefficient is halved and falls to statistical insignificance. Similarly, an adjustment for the local cost of living causes the regression coefficient relating the change in the 10th percentile of wages to the fraction of recent immigrants in 1985 to become (slightly) negative. Thus, adjusting for city-specific changes in the cost of living, we find less evidence of a positive correlation between immigration rates and the growth of high-skilled wages, and more evidence of a negative correlation between immigration and the growth of low-skilled wages. Neither of these correlations, however, is large or statistically significant.

We have also calculated the effect of higher immigration on the various percentiles of the wage distribution, controlling for such factors as the overall population growth rate, the fraction of immigrants initially living in each city, and the initial level of wages in the city. In no case do we find a large or statistically significant effect of immigration on the rate of increase of wages for the least-skilled workers.

## IV. Conclusions

We believe that the evidence we have assembled for the 1980's confirms the conclusions from earlier studies of 1970 and 1980 Census data. In particular, we find little indication of an adverse wage effect of immigration, either cross sectionally or within cities over time. Even for workers at the 10th percentile of the wage distribution there is no evidence of a significant decline in wages in response to immigrant inflows. The one important difference that emerges between our analysis and earlier studies is the finding of a positive link between immigrant inflows and net native migration. During the 1980's, rapidly growing cities in Texas, Florida, and California attracted both native and newly arriving immigrant workers. This configuration is quite different from the pattern of offsetting immigrant and native population inflows identified by Filer in earlier data.

## REFERENCES

**Borjas, George,** *Friends or Strangers: The Impact of Immigrants on the U.S. Economy,* New York: Basic Books, 1990.

**Filer, Randall K.,** "The Impact of Immigrant Arrivals in Migratory Patterns of Native Workers," in R. Freeman and G. Borjas, eds., *U.S. Immigration: Destinations and Sources,* Chicago: University of Chicago Press, 1990.

**Greenwood, Michael and McDowell, John,** "The Factor Market Consequences of U.S. Immigration," *Journal of Economic Literature,* December 1986, *24,* 1738–72.

**Hollmann, Frederick W.,** "United States Population Estimates, by Age, Sex, Race, and Hispanic Origin: 1980 to 1988," *Current Population Reports,* Series P-25, No. 1045, Washington: USGPO, 1990.

**Juhn, Chinhui, Murphy, Kevin M., and Pierce, Brooks W.,** "Wage Inequality and the Rise in Returns to Skill," unpublished manuscript, University of Chicago Graduate School of Business, 1989.

# [14]

## Immigrants in the American Labor Market: Quality, Assimilation, and Distributional Effects

*By* ROBERT J. LALONDE AND ROBERT H. TOPEL*

Immigration to the United States during the 1970's and 1980's was greater than in any decade since the 1920's. Simultaneously, the proportion of immigrants arriving from Europe or English-speaking countries declined dramatically from 46 percent in the 1960's to only 13 percent in the 1980's. These changes in the pace and composition of immigrant flows have raised three main concerns that have dominated recent literature and policy discussions. First, are recent immigrants less prepared to succeed in the U.S. labor market than their predecessors? The typical new immigrant may bring skills (including language, culture, and educational attainment) that are less attuned to the American market. Further, this decline in immigrant "quality" may have been magnified by immigration reforms of the 1960's, that gave less weight to individuals' skills in admission decisions. Thus average immigrant quality may have also declined *within* ethnic groups. Second, do new immigrants recover from their initial earnings disadvantage? As a policy issue, if new immigrants do not assimilate, the increased immigrant flows may place additional burdens on public welfare systems, while exacerbating other social problems associated with persistent poverty.

The third concern is the distributional impact of immigration on natives' welfare. To the extent that immigrant and native skills are substitutable, increased immigration may reduce natives' earnings and employment prospects. In fact, the 1970's and 1980's were periods of declining real wages and rising unemployment among less-skilled

American workers. These facts have motivated policy proposals and legislation designed to curtail the entry of low-wage immigrants to the United States, while giving greater emphasis to skill-based criteria in admissions decisions.

This paper provides evidence on immigrants' performance and impact in the U.S. labor market. We document that new immigrants do bring fewer marketable skills to the United States than did earlier cohorts, and that changes in the source countries of recent immigrants account for all of this decline in immigrant "quality." We find no important evidence that quality has declined *within* immigrant ethnic groups. We also show that immigrants assimilate rapidly in the U.S. market (10 years of U.S. experience offsets most of the earnings disadvantage of new immigrants), and that assimilation is more rapid for groups who start with lower initial wages.

These findings imply that immigrants' long-run earnings potential is similar to that of ethnically similar natives. In this sense, we think that fears about declining immigrant quality have been exaggerated. We present additional evidence that increased immigration has had a negligible impact on U.S. workers' wages and employment prospects. Taken together, these results suggest that recent changes in the rate and composition of immigration will not have serious long-run effects on the U.S. labor market.

### I. Changes in Immigrant Quality

Recent studies (see George Borjas, 1985; Barry Chiswick, 1986) indicate a decline in the labor market skills of recent immigrants to the United States. There are two possible sources for this decline. First, non-European immigrants may arrive with fewer skills. Second, even absent changes in source

*University of Chicago, Chicago, IL 60637, and NBER. We gratefully acknowledge the support of the Alfred P. Sloan Foundation and the National Science Foundation. Topel's work was supported by the William Ladany Faculty Research Fund at the Graduate School of Business, University of Chicago.

TABLE 1—DIFFERENCES IN WAGES AND
SCHOOLING FOR RECENT IMMIGRANTS AND NATIVES

| Immigrant Group Years in U.S. | Wage Relative to Natives | | |
|---|---|---|---|
| | 1970 | | 1980 |
| | (1) | (2)[b] | (3) |
| **A: Immigrants' Relative Log Weekly Wages**[a] | | | |
| All: | | | |
| 1–5 | −.20 | −.35 | −.35 |
| 6–10 | −.06 | −.25 | −.21 |
| 11–15 | 0 | −.14 | −.14 |
| European: | | | |
| 1–5 | 0 | − | −.02 |
| 6–10 | .07 | − | −.06 |
| 11–15 | .07 | − | 0 |
| Asian: | | | |
| 1–5 | −.09 | − | −.22 |
| 6–10 | .09 | − | −.04 |
| 11–15 | .11 | − | .15 |
| Mexican: | | | |
| 1–5 | −.68 | − | −.69 |
| 6–10 | −.49 | − | −.59 |
| 11–15 | −.34 | − | −.48 |

| **B: Immigrants' Years of Completed Schooling**[c] | | |
|---|---|---|
| | 1970 | 1980 |
| All Immigrants: | 10.8 | 11.6 |
| Europeans | 10.9 | 12.1 |
| Asians | 14.4 | 14.3 |
| Mexicans | 6.4 | 7.0 |
| Natives | 11.6 | 12.7 |

*Source*: Calculations from 1970 and 1980 Census.

[a]Average differences between log weekly wages of immigrants and natives with comparable labor market experience.

[b]The wage differentials in this column are weighted by the 1980 distributions of immigrant shares and native education.

[c]Average years of completed schooling among immigrants with 0–10 years in the United States and native male labor force participants.

countries, average productivity may decline *within* immigrant groups when changes in laws and incentives favor the entry of less-skilled individuals.

To address the question of declining immigrant quality, Table 1 compares recent immigrants' and natives' earnings and education in the 1970 and 1980 Censuses. In 1970, the average new immigrant arrived in the United States with 10.8 years of completed schooling, and earned about 20 percent less than natives with similar labor market experience (col. 1). Between 1970

and 1980, new immigrants' schooling increased overall, but declined relative to natives. Simultaneously, new immigrants' earnings disadvantage rose by an additional 15 points, to 35 percent (col. 3). In this sense, the average (relative) "quality" of new immigrants declined during the decade, even though average schooling levels suggest no decline in quality *within* immigrant groups.

The evidence in Table 1 suggests that change in source countries and changes in average years of native schooling may account for the decline in relative immigrant earnings. To test that proposition, we recalculated the relative earnings of 1970 immigrants, but we weighted each immigrant group by the group's relative share among new immigrants in 1980. We also reweighted natives' earnings to reflect their 1980 distribution of completed schooling. The calculations show that if the distribution of immigrants across source countries had been the same in 1970 as in 1980, and if educational attainment of U.S. workers had been the same in 1970 as in 1980, the relative earnings of immigrants in 1970 would have been at their 1980 level. For example, persons in the United States less than 5 years in 1970 would have earned 35 percent less than comparable natives, which is identical to the 1980 earnings gap. This indicates that the main factor affecting the relative earnings of new immigrants is simply where they come from. There is no evidence of declining quality *within* immigrant ethnic groups.

## II. Assimilation of Immigrants

The evidence in Table 1 suggests that average immigrant quality (as measured by earning capacity) declined in the 1970's. Since Asia and Latin America remained the most important sources of (legal and illegal) immigration during the 1980's, there is little doubt that the decline in the earning capacity of new immigrants has continued. But since immigrants assimilate with time in the United States, the decline in new immigrants' *initial* earning capacity overstates the long-term decline in immigrant quality. Further, those groups with the largest initial earnings disadvantage assimilate the most. Thus an increase in the shares of Asians and Hispanics among new immigrants reduces new immigrants' relative earnings, but increases the average rate of assimilation.

These points are also demonstrated in Table 1. The cohort of immigrants who arrived in the United States between 1965 and 1969 (1–5 years in the United States in 1970) earned 20 percent less than comparable natives in 1969. By 1979, that cohort had been in the United States for 11–15 years and they earned 14 percent less than comparable natives, so relative earnings grew by 7 percent over the decade. This growth is the average of assimilation rates within immigrant groups. The table shows that assimilation is much larger among Asians and Hispanics than among Europeans, who were the largest immigrant group in 1970. Europeans who arrived between 1965 and 1969 experienced no relative earnings growth at all during the 1970's, but they also started from parity in 1969. By comparison, Asians and Mexicans experienced relative earnings growth of 24 and 20 percent over the decade, respectively. Since Asians and Mexicans accounted for vastly larger proportions of new immigrants in the 1970's and 1980's, the rate of convergence between immigrant and native earnings will be correspondingly larger than in the past.

Rapid earnings growth does not mean that assimilation eliminates the earnings gap between immigrants and natives. Nor should we expect the gap to be eliminated, since there are important earnings differentials among *natives* of different ethnic backgrounds. To illustrate, column 1 of Table 2 reports estimated wage differentials among natives of various ancestry, based on cross-sectional data from the 1980 Census. Since these estimates control for the usual list of observable background characteristics, the reported values are approximate percentage differentials between the earnings of the indicated ethnic group and European-Americans with the same observable characteristics. As the table shows, a typical Mexican-American earns about 11 percent less than a comparable European, while an Asian-American earns about 7 percent less.

TABLE 2—RATES OF IMMIGRANT ASSIMILATION

| Ethnic Group | (1) | (2) | (3) | (4) | (5) |
|---|---|---|---|---|---|
| Europeans | – | −.05 | .09 | .08 | .08 |
|  |  | (.02) | (.02) | (.03) | (.03) |
| Asians | −.07 | −.33 | .24 | .25 | .24 |
|  | (.03) | (.02) | (.03) | (.03) | (.09) |
| Middle Easterners | .06 | −.40 | .28 | .29 | .42 |
|  | (.05) | (.06) | (.07) | (.07) | (.20) |
| Mexicans | −.11 | −.22 | .17 | .22 | .21 |
|  | (.02) | (.02) | (.03) | (.03) | (.09) |
| Other Latin American and Caribbean | −.20 | −.22 | .23 | .24 | .19 |
|  | (.03) | (.03) | (.03) | (.03) | (.09) |

*Source*: Calculations using 1970 and 1980 U.S. Census Microdata files and our paper (1991b, Table 5).

*Note*: Col. (1) = log wage differences for ethnic natives; Col. (2) = initial gap with ethnic natives; the rates of assimilation in cols. (3), (4), and (5) are relative to: Col. (3) ethnic natives 1980 cross section; Col. (4) old immigrants 1980 Cross Section; Col. (5) old immigrants 1970–80 panel.

Estimates control for years of completed schooling, a quartic in experience, and interactions between schooling and experience. Additional controls do not affect the results. Assimilation rates estimate the effect of the first 10 years' U.S. experience on wages, measured relative to observationally identical ethnic natives and ethnic immigrants who have been in the U.S. for more than 30 years. Standard errors are in parentheses.

In our view, these estimates suggest that the relevant question is not whether immigrants catch up with the modal native (who has European ancestry), but rather whether they catch up to natives of similar ancestry to their own.

To frame this question more precisely, consider the following decomposition of the regression-adjusted wage differential between immigrants from arrival cohort $i$ in census year $t$ and natives of similar ethnicity:

$$(1) \qquad \varepsilon_{it} = a_{it} + b_{it} + u_i,$$

where the parameters $a_{it}$ represent the average level of accumulated, U.S.-specific, human capital embodied in members of arrival cohort $i$ during year $t = 1970$ or $t = 1980$. Assimilation occurs when the relative human capital of an immigrant cohort rises with time spent in the United States, $a_{it} < a_{i,t+10}$. Identification of this from estimates of $\varepsilon_{it}$ is complicated by the appearance of $b_{it}$, that represents the impact of aggregate labor market conditions on immigrant cohort $i$'s earnings, and by $u_i$, that represents the cohort-average value of other unobserved factors (immigrant "quality") that affect productivity. Based on (1), two possible estimators of immigrant assimilation are possible. From a single cross section, say $t = 1980$, we can estimate the effect of 10 years residence in the United States by comparing the relative earnings of persons who arrived between 1975 and 1979 ($i = 75$) to the earnings of similar immigrants who arrived between 1965 and 1969 ($i = 65$):

$$(2) \quad \varepsilon_{65,80} - \varepsilon_{75,80} = a_{65,80} - a_{75,80} + b_{65,80}$$
$$- b_{75,80} + u_{65} - u_{75}.$$

This provides unbiased estimates of assimilation only if ($i$) there are no time effects on relative earnings of the two cohorts, $E(b_{65,t} - b_{75,t}) = 0$, and ($ii$) the cohorts have the same average talent, $E(u_{65} - u_{75}) = 0$. For example, when the average quality of successive immigrant cohorts declines, $u_{65} > u_{75}$, equation (2) will overstate the rate of immigrant assimilation. This issue underlies Borjas's 1985 criticism of Chiswick's 1978 estimates of assimilation.

The alternative to (2) is to form a quasi panel by following the wage growth of a single cohort between the 1970 and 1980 Censuses. For the cohort that arrived between 1965 and 1969, this estimate is

$$(3) \quad \varepsilon_{65,80} - \varepsilon_{65,70} = a_{65,80} - a_{65,70}$$
$$+ b_{65,80} - b_{65,70}.$$

This estimator of assimilation will be unbiased if aggregate market conditions do not change the cohort's relative earning power, $E(b_{65,80} - b_{65,70}) = 0$. Our estimates of (3) use earlier immigrants and natives of the same ethnicity as recent immigrants as normalizing groups. If recent immigrants' human capital substitutes for that of ethnically similar earlier immigrants or natives, the identifying condition is likely to be satisfied.

As shown by Table 2, both estimates of assimilation indicate that most of new immigrants' earnings disadvantage is eliminated after only 10 years' experience in the U.S. labor market. Column 2 shows the initial difference in log weekly wages between immigrants who arrived between 1975 and 1979 and natives of the same ethnicity. New immigrants' wages typically start out well below those of natives. But the data show that this earnings disadvantage rapidly narrows. Column 3 and 4 show estimates of 10 years' assimilation, based on applying (2) to cross-sectional data from the 1980 Census. Although the two sets of estimates rely on different normalizing groups, they nevertheless indicate rapid and nearly identical rates of immigrant assimilation. Both estimates indicate that Asian immigrants will overcome 75 percent ($= .24/.32$) of their original wage shortfall after 10 years in the United States. Other groups show similar patterns of strong assimilation. Notice that the largest wage gains occur for groups with the largest initial wage gap.

These estimates are subject to the criticism that immigrant quality may have fallen over time within ethnic groups. That decline would cause (2) to overstate the rate of assimilation. Although our estimates in Table 1 showed no evidence of declining immigrant quality within ethnic groups, the "panel" estimator in (3) avoids this concern by following the earning growth of a fixed cohort over time. As shown in column 5, panel estimates confirm that declining immigrant quality within ethnic groups is not an important issue: estimates of assimilation are large, and they are nearly identical to the cross-sectional estimates shown in column 4. We conclude that immigrants assimilate rapidly in the U.S. labor market.

### III. The Effects of Increased Immigration on Wages and Employment

Immigrant flows accounted for only about 5 percent of growth in aggregate labor supply during the 1970's and 1980's. At this level of aggregation it is difficult to argue that immigration had important effects on natives' wages and employment prospects.

Yet immigration is heavily concentrated in certain geographic areas and among certain skill groups. For example, during the 1970's immigrants accounted for nearly two-thirds of labor force growth in Los Angeles, and over one-third of growth in Miami. This concentration raises the possibility of significant distributional effects on some natives' wages, at least in the short run. In light of these facts, we have argued elsewhere (1991a) that the largest impact of immigration on wages and employment must be for individuals who are good substitutes for new immigrants in terms of both location and skills. In our analysis, these individuals are other current and past immigrants of similar ethnicity, as well as less-skilled natives located in areas that have experienced large immigration flows.

As shown by Table 3, our estimates indicate that increased immigration has had relatively small effects on recent immigrants', and on young black and Hispanic natives', wages and earnings. The econometric framework for isolating these effects is spelled out in our 1991a paper. Briefly, the estimates are derived by comparing the *relative* wages of the indicated groups among SMSAs with varying amounts of immigration, while controlling for a host of background characteristics. As above, there are two approaches to estimating these effects. The first column of Table 3 shows estimates derived from cross-sectional data in the 1980 Census, while the second column shows panel estimates derived from relative wage *changes* within SMSAs with varying immigration flows during the 1970's.

Several aspects of these results are noteworthy. First, even the largest of the crowding effects we estimate is small. For example, as shown in panel A, a 100 percent increase in the rate of new immigration (0-5 years since entry) to the typical SMSA reduces the wages of new immigrants by only 2.4 percent. Second, the wage penalty for membership in a large immigration cohort is smaller for immigrants who have been in the United States longer. This suggests that as immigrants assimilate they "melt" into the U.S. labor market by becoming better substitutes for natives. This is

TABLE 3—THE EFFECTS ON WEEKLY WAGES OF A 100 PERCENT INCREASE IN THE SIZE OF AN IMMIGRATION COHORT

| Years Since Immigration | Source | |
|---|---|---|
| | 1980 Cross Section | 1970–80 Panel |
| **A: Own Effects on Immigrants** | | |
| 1–5 | −.024 | −.024 |
| | (.008) | (.010) |
| 6–10 | −.026 | −.025 |
| | (.008) | (.010) |
| 11–15 | −.009 | −.006 |
| | (.011) | (.009) |
| 16–20 | .010 | .019 |
| | (.013) | (.012) |
| 21–30 | .019 | −.007 |
| | (.010) | (.010) |

| **B: Cross Effects on Young Natives** | Wages | Annual Earnings |
|---|---|---|
| Blacks | −.007 | −.004 |
| | (.004) | (.006) |
| Hispanics | .005 | .010 |
| | (.007) | (.007) |

*Source*: Our paper (1991a, Tables 6.7 (col. 2), 6.10B, col. (2) and (4), 6.12, col. (2)), and accompanying text.

*Notes*: Estimates reflect the change in log earnings or weekly wages for the indicated group, relative to immigrants in an SMSA who had been in the United States 30 years or more. Effects on natives refer to the impact of a change in post-1965 immigration on black or Hispanic earnings. The characteristics controlled for are years of schooling, potential experience, marital status, number of children, disability status, race and ethnicity, occupation, and industry.

important, since it implies that immigration's effects on natives, who by definition are fully assimilated, are likely to be negligible. This point is confirmed in panel B of Table 3, where we report estimated effects of new immigration on the wages of young native black and Hispanic men, whose skills may be most substitutable for those of immigrants. These effects are smaller than the direct effects in panel A, and we regard them as economically negligible.

The foregoing estimates reflect immigration's impact on wages, leaving open the possibility that there are larger effects on employment and unemployment. One way of testing this possibility is to replicate the preceding analysis, but replacing log weekly wages with log annual earnings (wages times weeks worked). Our 1991a paper shows that the estimates in panel A are virtually unchanged by this procedure, which implies that all of immigration's impact on earnings comes through its effect on wages; weeks of employment are unaffected. Over all, we have been unable to adduce any evidence of important distributional effects of immigration on wages and employment.

## IV. Conclusion

At a time when new immigrants are entering the United States in the largest numbers in recent history, wages and employment prospects of less-skilled Americans have fallen dramatically. At the same time, new immigrants' earnings have fallen, raising questions about the long-term quality of new immigrant waves. It is tempting to see a connection between these facts and to advocate changes in policies that affect the quantity and quality of new immigrants to the United States.

Our evidence suggests that these policy concerns are exaggerated. It is true that immigrant quality, as measured by initial earnings, has declined as source countries have shifted toward Asia and Latin America. But these immigrants assimilate rapidly, and our result suggests that their long-run earning potential will be much like ethnically similar natives. Thus the long-run impact on productivity and income distribution will be much smaller than indicated by the initial earnings data. Further, although it is true that immigration has small effects

on equilibrium wages, virtually all of this burden falls on immigrants themselves. Labor market effects for nonimmigrants are negligible. Taken together, these results suggest that any adverse effects of current immigration flows on the U.S. labor market and on native welfare will be small.

## REFERENCES

Borjas, George, "Assimilation, Changes in Cohort Quality, and the Earnings of Immigrants," *Journal of Labour Economics*, October 1985, *4*, 463–89.

_____, *Friends or Strangers: The Impact of Immigrants on the U.S. Economy*, New York: Basic Books, 1990.

Chiswick, Barry, "The Effect of Americanization of the Earnings of Foreign-Born Men," *Journal of Political Economy*, October 1978, *86*, 897–921.

_____, "Is the New Immigration Less Skilled than the Old?," *Journal of Labor Economics*, April 1986, *4*, 168–92.

LaLonde, Robert and Topel, Robert H., (1991a) "Labor Market Adjustments to Increased Immigration," in R. Freeman, ed., *Immigration, Trade, and the Labor Market*, Chicago: University of Chicago Press, 1991.

_____ and _____, (1991b) "The Assimilation of Immigrants in the United States: Immigrant Quality and the Changing Price of Skills," in *The Determinants and Effects of Immigration on the U.S. and Source Economies*, Chicago: University of Chicago Press, 1991, forthcoming.

# [15]

GEORGE J. BORJAS
*Harvard University*

RICHARD B. FREEMAN
*Harvard University*

LAWRENCE F. KATZ
*Harvard University*

## How Much Do Immigration and Trade Affect Labor Market Outcomes?

IMMIGRATION AND TRADE—particularly with less developed countries (LDCs)—have become more significant to the U.S. economy since the 1960s than they were earlier in the postwar period. The number of immigrants relative to native-born workers has risen; an increasing proportion of immigrants come from less developed countries; and a disproportionate number of immigrants have relatively little schooling. The ratio of exports and imports to GDP has risen as well, and an increasing proportion of imports have come from less developed countries. Immigration and trade have thus increased the effective labor supply of less skilled workers in the United States, with potential consequences for relative wages and employment.

To what extent might the economic woes of less skilled and low-paid American workers be attributed to changes in trade or immigration? To what extent have immigration and trade benefited other Americans?

These questions have spurred considerable debate in recent years. Some analysts stress the potentially adverse distributional effects of immigration and trade on low-income Americans. Others stress their potentially positive effects on the economy. Standard models suggest

We are grateful to John Abowd, John DiNardo, Robert Lawrence, and Matthew Slaughter for helpful suggestions; to Marianne Bertrand, Alida Castillo-Freeman, and Gabriel Hanz for excellent research assistance; to Howard Shatz and Kenneth Troske for providing some of the data used in the paper; and to the National Science Foundation for research support.

1

that both immigration and trade alter national output *and* the distribution of income through the same mechanism—by increasing the nation's implicit supply of relatively scarce factors of production—so that their benefits and distributional costs are intrinsically related. While there is empirical evidence that trade may have more far-reaching benefits on economic performance, and one could argue that immigration may have positive or negative effects on the aggregate economy through economies or diseconomies of scale, trade and immigration are still likely to affect *relative* economic outcomes.[1] Factors for which immigration and trade are good substitutes will lose relative to factors that are complementary.[2]

This paper provides new estimates of the impact of immigration and trade on the U.S. labor market, taking account of the extensive debate that has developed since our earlier work.[3] We first review the dimensions of immigration and trade flows to the United States since the 1960s. Then we examine the relation between economic outcomes for native workers and immigrant flows to regional labor markets. We next use the aggregate "factor proportions approach" to simulate the impact of immigration and trade on national supplies of labor by skill under different counterfactuals. We also consider Adrian Wood's controversial claim that using input coefficients for the appropriate import-competing activities leads to much larger trade effects than we, or others, have estimated.[4] We then use the factor proportions approach to examine the contributions of immigration and trade to recent changes in U.S. educational wage differentials and attempt to provide a broader assessment of the impact of immigration on the incomes of U.S. natives. Finally, we offer some concluding thoughts.

Our major findings are as follows:

—Immigration does not have a consistent, discernible effect on area

1. On the beneficial effects of openness to trade on national economic performance, see Frankel and Romer (1996) and Sachs and Warner (1995).

2. This will be true unless essentially no unskilled American works in import-competing activities (because U.S. firms have shifted production to utterly different products) or competes with immigrants in the labor market (because all immigrants have skills that complement those of natives). With a fixed linear homogeneous production function, if trade or immigration raises GDP a lot, there will necessarily be large effects on the distribution of income (and small effects if GDP is raised slightly).

3. Borjas, Freeman, and Katz (1992).

4. Wood (1994, 1995).

economic outcomes; other regional factors dominate the ups and downs of area economies.

—The location decisions of the native population respond to immigration; the native flow to the primary immigrant-receiving state, California, has been greatly reduced by the influx of immigrants since 1970.

—Immigration has had a marked adverse impact on the economic status of the least skilled U.S. workers (high school dropouts and those in the bottom 20 percent of the wage distribution).

—Trade has had small effects on the overall implicit labor supply of the less skilled. However, the trade effect is larger if one assumes that economic activities displaced by imports employ technologies comparable to the least skilled plants in U.S. manufacturing industries.

These are not the final words on the effects of immigration and trade on the job market. We do not explore all of the possible avenues by which these flows influence labor market outcomes. For instance, we do not estimate the extent to which immigrants may take jobs that no native would take and so may overstate the effect of immigration on the less skilled.[5] Nor do we explore the potential effects of trade on native outcomes that occur entirely through prices (with no observed change in trade quantities), and thus we may understate the distributional effects of trade on outcomes.

### The Two Shocks

The starting point for our analysis is the significant increase in immigration and trade that has occurred in the United States since the 1960s. While neither immigration nor trade flows are entirely exogenous shocks to the U.S. job market, the huge changes in recent years have come primarily from developments that are unrelated to contemporaneous labor market conditions in the United States. On the immigration side, the major impetus for the increased flow of legal immigration from less developed countries were the 1965 Amendments to

---

5. Hamermesh (1997) contrasts the quality of jobs held by immigrants and by natives and finds little support for this claim, so we doubt that this is a major consideration in assessing the effect of immigration.

4                    *Brookings Papers on Economic Activity, 1:1997*

**Table 1. The Foreign-Born Population of the United States and Its National Origins, 1960–96**

Units as indicated

|  | Foreign-born population | | | | |
|---|---|---|---|---|---|
| Item | 1960 | 1970 | 1980 | 1990 | 1996 |
| In millions | 9.7 | 9.7 | 14.1 | 19.8 | 24.6 |
| As percentage of entire population | 5.4 | 4.8 | 6.2 | 7.9 | 9.3 |
| Distribution by origin[a] | | | | | |
| Canada and Europe | 84 | 68 | 43 | 26 | . . . |
| Caribbean and Latin America | 9 | 19 | 31 | 43 | . . . |
| Asia | 5 | 9 | 18 | 25 | . . . |
| Other | 2 | 4 | 8 | 6 | . . . |

Source: Authors' calculations. Data for 1960 are from U.S. Bureau of the Census, *Historical Statistics of the United States, Colonial Times to 1870*, vol. 1 (Department of Commerce, 1975). Data for 1970–90 are from *Statistical Abstract of the United States* (various years). Data for 1996 are from the Census Bureau and are available on the bureau's worldwide web page.

a. Percent.

the Immigration and Nationality Act.[6] Illegal immigration has also responded to policy developments (such as the ending of the *bracero*, or guest worker, program in 1964), but probably depends more on the huge wage differential between Mexico and the United States than on U.S. labor market developments.[7] On the trade side, the worldwide movement toward more open trade, the increased productivity of workers in LDCs, the entry of China into the world economy, and changes in exchange rates have altered trade flows, irrespective of changes in the U.S. labor market.

## Immigration

Immigration began to surge not long after the enactment of the 1965 amendments, reversing a long downward trend in the foreign-born share of the U.S. population. Table 1 quantifies these patterns. In 1960, 5.4 percent of the population was foreign-born; in 1970, the foreign-born share bottomed out at 4.8 percent. Between 1970 and 1996, the number of foreign-born persons increased by 15 million, raising the foreign-

6. Borjas (1990, chap. 2) provides a brief summary of the policy changes initiated by the 1965 legislation.

7. In particular, the illegal flow has certainly not been motivated by rising real wages for less skilled workers in the United States. Those wages have fallen in recent years. Hanson and Spilimbergo (1997) show that illegal immigration from Mexico (as proxied by border apprehensions) is particularly sensitive to labor market conditions in Mexico.

*George J. Borjas, Richard B. Freeman, and Lawrence F. Katz*       5

**Figure 1. Percentage of Adult Population that Was Foreign Born, 1950–90[a]**

Percent

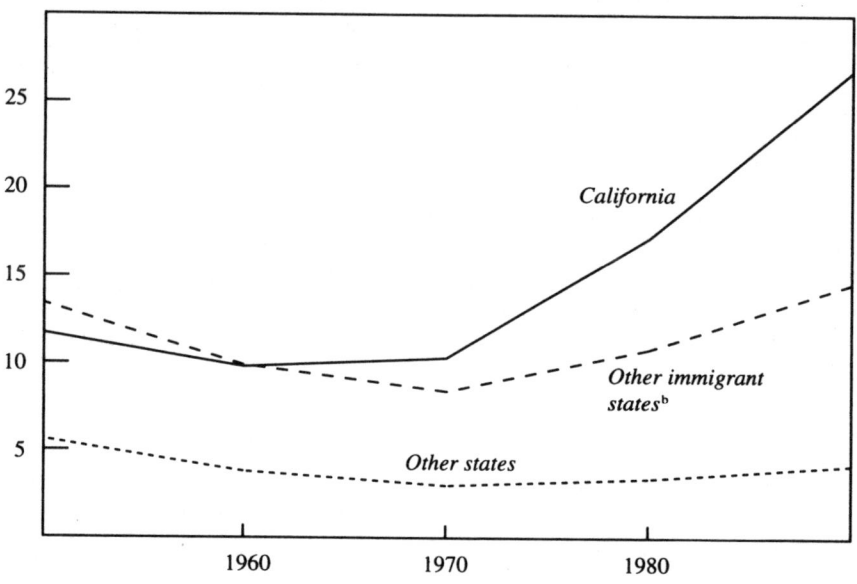

Source: Authors' calculations based on data from the census Public Use Microdata Sample (PUMS) (various years); see table 2 below for details.
a. Adults are aged eighteen to sixty-four.
b. New York, New Jersey, Illinois, Florida, and Texas.

born share of the U.S. population to 7.9 percent in 1990 and 9.3 percent in 1996. During this period, the proportion of immigrants from LDCs was rising.

Historically, immigrants have clustered in a small number of geographic areas, and this concentration has increased over time. In 1960, 60 percent of immigrants lived in one of the six main immigrant-receiving states: California, New York, Texas, Florida, New Jersey, and Illinois. By 1990, 75 percent of immigrants lived in these states, and over 33 percent lived in California alone. This geographic concentration reflects the propensity of immigrants to enter the United States through a limited number of gateway cities or states and spread out slowly to other areas of the country in subsequent years.[8] Figure 1 illustrates the impact of the immigrant supply shock on the percent of

8. Bartel (1989).

the adult population (aged eighteen to sixty-four) that was foreign-born in California, in other immigrant-receiving states, and in the rest of the country over the period 1950–90. Before 1970, the foreign-born share was stable or declining in each region. Between 1970 and 1990, this share almost tripled in California (rising from 10.3 percent to 26.8 percent), almost doubled in the other immigrant-receiving states (from 8.4 to 14.6 percent), and rose slightly in the rest of the country (from 3.0 to 4.2 percent).

The effect of immigration on native labor depends critically on the distribution of skills between immigrants and natives. If the skill distribution of immigrants matches that of natives, immigration will not affect the relative supply of skills and thus will not change the structure of wages. By contrast, if immigrants are less skilled than natives, immigration will shift the distribution of income toward the more skilled, and conversely if immigrants are more skilled than natives.

Table 2 compares the distributions of years of schooling for immigrants and natives in the United States and in California for 1990 and 1995, and also reports the immigrant contribution to the labor supply of workers with different years of schooling. The distribution of immigrants by educational attainment is more dispersed than that of natives. A disproportionately high number of immigrants have fewer than nine years of schooling, but also, a disproportionately high number have more than sixteen years of schooling. On average, however, immigrants have fewer years of schooling than natives—a difference that has grown over the past two decades, as the mean years of schooling in the immigrant population increased less rapidly than the mean years of schooling of natives. As a result, the immigrant contribution to the supply of skills has become increasingly concentrated in the lower educational categories. By 1995, one-half of workers with fewer than nine years of schooling and one-third of workers with fewer than twelve years of schooling were immigrants.

In 1995, over 30 percent of the working-age population in California was foreign-born; consequently, one can learn much by comparing California's experience with that of other states. California has an exceptionally large less educated immigrant population that stands in contrast to the high number of well-educated natives. The lower panel of table 2 shows that by 1995, 90 percent of Californians with fewer

*George J. Borjas, Richard B. Freeman, and Lawrence F. Katz*          7

**Table 2. Distribution of Natives and Immigrants by Educational Attainment, United States and California, 1990 and 1995**

Percent

| Region and years of schooling | 1990 census data | | | 1995 CPS data | | |
|---|---|---|---|---|---|---|
| | Natives | Immigrants | Immigrant share in skill group | Natives | Immigrants | Immigrant share in skill group |
| *United States* | | | | | | |
| Fewer than 9 | 4.2 | 22.4 | 36.9 | 2.8 | 22.6 | 49.6 |
| 9 to 11 | 14.0 | 16.0 | 11.1 | 9.9 | 12.3 | 13.1 |
| 12 | 32.0 | 20.1 | 6.4 | 34.6 | 24.8 | 8.0 |
| 13 to 15 | 29.5 | 21.1 | 7.2 | 30.0 | 19.0 | 7.1 |
| 16 | 13.8 | 12.0 | 8.6 | 15.7 | 13.5 | 9.4 |
| More than 16 | 6.6 | 8.4 | 12.1 | 7.1 | 7.8 | 11.7 |
| *California* | | | | | | |
| Fewer than 9 | 2.2 | 28.6 | 82.6 | 1.5 | 30.3 | 90.1 |
| 9 to 11 | 11.9 | 17.4 | 34.8 | 7.7 | 14.3 | 44.6 |
| 12 | 24.0 | 16.7 | 20.3 | 26.8 | 21.7 | 26.1 |
| 13 to 15 | 37.5 | 20.5 | 16.7 | 37.9 | 17.6 | 16.8 |
| 16 | 16.4 | 11.0 | 19.7 | 17.7 | 11.2 | 21.7 |
| More than 16 | 7.9 | 5.8 | 21.2 | 8.5 | 5.0 | 20.3 |

Source: Authors' calculations. Data for 1990 are from the Census Bureau's Public Use Microdata Sample. Data for 1995 are from the Merged Outgoing Rotation Group (MORG) files from the Census Bureau's Current Population Survey (CPS). Throughout the paper, the authors use census and CPS data released in electronic form by the Census Bureau.

a. First two columns under each data set give, for the United States and California, the percentage of native-born persons or immigrants, aged eighteen to sixty-four, who have the given number of years of schooling. Third column under each data set gives the percentage of persons with the given educational attainment who are immigrants. Immigrants are those born abroad who are noncitizens or naturalized citizens. All others are natives.

than nine years of schooling and 68 percent of those with fewer than twelve years of schooling were foreign-born.[9]

Table 3 examines the distribution of immigrants and natives by occupation and industry. The first two columns of data report the percent distribution of native and immigrant workers among occupations and industries nationwide. If immigrants were randomly distributed by occupation and industry, the figures in these two columns would be

9. It is worth emphasizing that the U.S. labor market does not value natives and immigrants with the same educational attainment identically. In fact, the 1990 census indicates that there is roughly a 0.10 log point gap between the earnings of natives and immigrants with the same number of years of schooling. As a result, simple head counts of immigrants will exaggerate their contribution to labor supply. A more accurate picture is obtained by counting immigrants and natives in terms of efficiency units. Below, we calculate the contributions that ''equivalent'' immigrants make to labor supply.

**Table 3. Representation of Immigrants, by Occupation and Industry, 1995[a]**

Percent, except as indicated

| Occupation or industry | U.S. distribution by occupation or industry | | | Percentage of workers who are immigrants | |
|---|---|---|---|---|---|
| | Immigrants | Natives | Ratio of immigrant to native distribution[b] | United States | California |
| **Occupation** | | | | | |
| Managerial and professional specialty | 21.2 | 28.2 | 0.75 | 7.6 | 16.5 |
| Technical and related support | 2.5 | 3.2 | 0.78 | 7.7 | 20.2 |
| Sales | 9.4 | 12.1 | 0.76 | 7.9 | 19.8 |
| Administrative support, including clerical | 9.7 | 15.4 | 0.63 | 6.4 | 18.2 |
| Precision, production, craft, repair | 11.7 | 11.0 | 1.06 | 10.5 | 29.5 |
| Operators, fabricators | 14.9 | 10.5 | 1.42 | 13.5 | 49.5 |
| Handlers, equipment cleaners, helpers, laborers | 5.7 | 4.2 | 1.36 | 12.9 | 40.3 |
| Private household | 2.1 | 0.5 | 4.20 | 31.5 | 63.7 |
| Service, excluding private household | 17.4 | 12.5 | 1.39 | 13.3 | 35.3 |
| Farming, forestry, fishing | 5.4 | 2.5 | 2.16 | 19.4 | 70.7 |
| **Industry** | | | | | |
| Agriculture | 5.0 | 2.3 | 2.17 | 19.0 | 68.3 |
| Mining | 0.3 | 0.6 | 0.50 | 5.1 | 19.4 |
| Construction | 6.4 | 6.6 | 0.97 | 9.7 | 24.4 |
| Manufacturing | 20.2 | 16.2 | 1.24 | 12.0 | 41.3 |
| Transport, communication, utilities | 5.3 | 7.2 | 0.74 | 7.5 | 19.0 |
| Wholesale trade | 4.4 | 3.9 | 1.13 | 11.0 | 30.4 |
| Retail trade | 17.7 | 16.5 | 1.07 | 10.5 | 29.4 |
| Finance, insurance, real estate | 5.0 | 6.3 | 0.81 | 7.9 | 19.3 |
| Services | 33.4 | 35.1 | 0.95 | 9.5 | 22.7 |
| Government | 2.3 | 5.2 | 0.44 | 4.5 | 11.4 |

Source: Authors' calculations based on data from the 1995 CPS. MORG file.
a. See table 2. note a for definition of immigrants.
b. Fist column divided by second column.

roughly the same. They are not. As the ratios of the immigrant share to the native share in the third column show, immigrants are more concentrated in lower skill occupations than natives and work in a different set of industries. There are relatively more immigrants working in farming occupations, in service jobs, as private household workers, and as operators and fabricators. There are relatively more immigrants in agriculture, in manufacturing, and in wholesale and retail trade. Immigrants are less likely than natives to work in white collar jobs—such as managerial and professional specialties, administrative support, sales and technical support—and are especially underrepresented in government jobs. In part these differences are due to lower educational attainment, but some of them cannot be so easily explained.

The last two columns of table 3 record the proportion of immigrants in different occupations and industries, for the United States and for California. The figures for the entire country provide another way of showing the concentration of immigrants in low-skill occupations and selected industries. The figures for California emphasize the importance of immigration in that state's economy. In some occupations, such as farming, private household, and operators and fabricators, about half or more of California's work force consists of immigrants. In 1995, immigrants made up 68.3 percent of its agricultural work force and 41.3 percent of its manufacturing work force. These numbers suggest that immigration may have affected the industrial structure of California. Between 1970 and 1990, the proportion of workers employed in immigrant-intensive industries fell by only 4.1 percentage points (8 percent) in California, as compared with an 8.6 percentage point (16 percent) decline in nonimmigrant states, and a 9.4 percentage point (20 percent) decline in the other immigrant-receiving states.[10] The fraction of California's workers employed in the private household industry fell less than in other states, and the fraction employed in apparel and accessories rose in California but declined elsewhere. To the extent that the industries spurred by immigration compete with similar industries located elsewhere in the country (as might be the case for manufacturing and, possibly, agriculture), the observed change in industry mix pro-

---

10. We define immigrant-intensive industries as those with a larger share of immigrants than the national average immigrant share of total employment; these comprise personal services (including private household services), agriculture, business and repair services, retail trade, and manufacturing.

vides yet another potential means by which the effects of immigration are diffused across the country.

Finally, while many immigrants work in manufacturing, many also work in nontraded sectors. The significant immigrant representation in services and retail trade highlights a critical difference between the potential effects of trade and of immigration on native workers. Less skilled natives can escape trade competition with low-paid workers overseas by specializing in the production of nontraded goods; the local sales clerk must live in the United States to deal with customers. Indeed, when no American competes with the Chinese in producing low-cost children's toys, increased imports of those toys benefit even less skilled Americans. But there is no such ''cone of diversification'' escape that allows native workers to avoid competition from immigrants. Immigrants can just as easily work in nontraded goods and services as in the traded goods sector.

### Trade

The upper panel of figure 2 shows that the most widely used measure of trade, the ratio of exports plus imports to GDP, increased markedly from 1970 to 1980, stabilized in the 1980s, and has risen since 1990.[11] While much of the growth in the 1970s was trade between the United States and other advanced countries, the share of imports from LDCs (defined in this figure as all nonindustrial countries, exclusive of the petroleum producing countries) has increased continuously since the 1970s, accelerating in the 1990s.[12] The bottom panel of figure 2 shows that the ratio of imports from LDCs to U.S. GDP rose from 0.023 in 1980 to 0.028 in 1990 and to 0.041 in 1996. Nearly 40 percent of U.S.

11. The ratio $(EX + IM)$/GDP exaggerates the relative magnitude of trade, because $EX$ (exports) and $IM$ (imports) are measured in terms of sales, while GDP is a value-added concept. Sales are roughly twice GDP, so that a consistent indicator of the magnitude of trade in terms of the traded proportion of sales would be about half of $(EX + IM)$/GDP. Since the ratio of sales to GDP has not changed much over time, the growth of $(EX + IM)$/GDP roughly tracks the growth of $(EX + IM)$/sales.

12. We classify countries on the basis of their level of economic development when the implicit supply shock began, in the 1970s or 1980s. As a result, Japan is classified as an industrial nation, but the four ''tigers'' (Korea, Singapore, Hong Kong, and Taiwan) are classified as LDCs. On the questions of whether to treat Japan in the 1960s as advanced and whether to treat some of the tigers as advanced economies today, see Sachs and Shatz (1994).

*George J. Borjas, Richard B. Freeman, and Lawrence F. Katz*     11

**Figure 2. Growing Openness and LDC Trade, 1970–96**[a]

Ratio

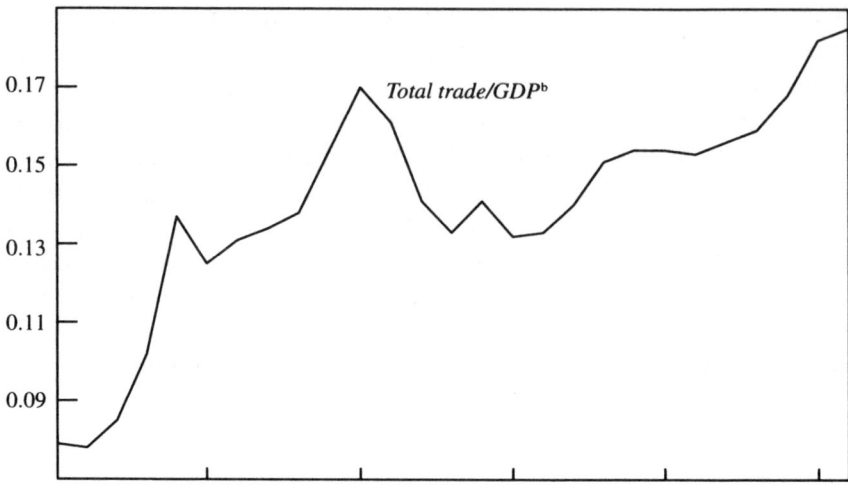

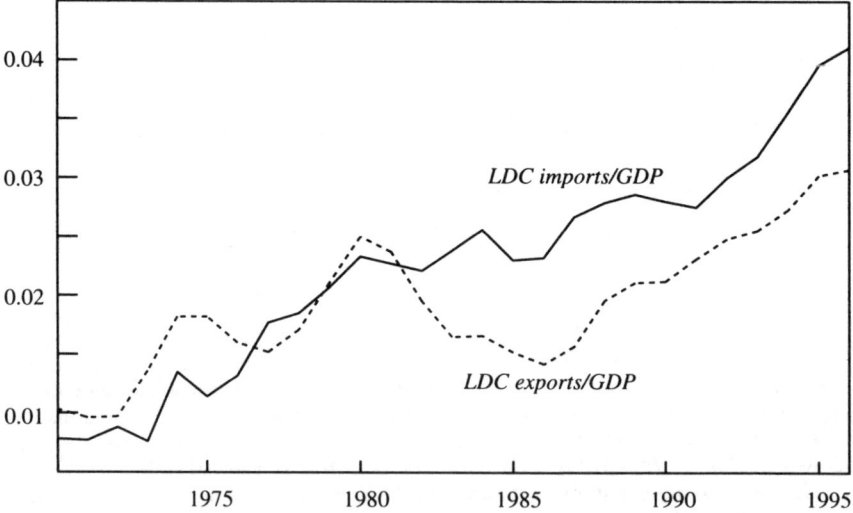

Source: Authors' calculations based on data from the *Economic Report of the President, 1997.*
a. LDC trade flows include those with trading partners other than Canada, Japan, Australia, New Zealand, South Africa, members of the Organization of Petroleum Exporting Countries, and the countries of western Europe.
b. Exports plus imports divided by GDP.

imports came from LDCs in 1996, and the largest trade deficit was with China, whose goods made up 6 percent of imports.

The effect of imports and exports on workers depends on the characteristics of workers in those industries affected by trade. If import-intensive industries disproportionately use less skilled workers and export-intensive industries disproportionately use more skilled workers, trade will shift the distribution of income from the less skilled to the more skilled.[13] Table 4 shows how the average characteristics of workers in American manufacturing industries in 1990 differed along trade lines calculated in two different ways. The lines listed as import- or export-weighted averages weight the characteristics of workers in each industry by the ratio of imports (or exports) to sales times the employment in the industry. The lines listed as high export or import intensity are obtained by ranking manufacturing industries by the ratio of exports or imports to sales, and then selecting off the top of the list until 10 percent of the manufacturing labor force is represented. The figures given for LDC import or export intensity are calculated in a similar manner, using LDC imports and exports to weight or categorize industries. For the rest of the economy, we differentiate between agriculture, which is a major exporter, and ''all other'' industries: services, trade, and government. Despite the growing international trade in services, the ''all other'' category can be roughly viewed as the nontraded sector for the purpose of comparison with manufacturing.

The table shows that in the manufacturing sector, the workers most affected by imports are disproportionately immigrants, women, blacks, and the less educated; whereas those most affected by exports are disproportionately native-born, nonblack, and educated men. Moreover, the wages of workers in the top 10 percent of importing industries were 0.53 log point below the wages of those in the top 10 percent of export industries, and the wages of the ''average'' import worker were 0.15 log point less than those of the average export worker. Classified by imports and exports with LDCs alone, the skill (wage) composition of the import-affected workers and the skill composition of the export-affected workers differ even more.

Looking beyond the manufacturing sector, however, the picture is

13. Trefler (1993) discusses the difficulties involved in calculating relative factor proportions.

**Table 4. Demographic Composition of the U.S. Work Force, by Industry, 1990**

Percent, except as indicated

| Industry[a] | Immigrants | Women | Blacks | High school dropouts | College graduates | Log wage index[b] |
|---|---|---|---|---|---|---|
| All industries | 9.1 | 41.3 | 10.0 | 14.6 | 24.8 | 0.00 |
| Manufacturing | 10.1 | 31.7 | 10.1 | 20.6 | 16.6 | 0.08 |
| High import intensity | 19.7 | 55.8 | 10.9 | 28.8 | 15.6 | -0.14 |
| Import-weighted average | 12.5 | 38.1 | 10.0 | 22.5 | 15.9 | 0.04 |
| High export intensity | 8.8 | 25.7 | 6.8 | 9.7 | 30.7 | 0.39 |
| Export-weighted average | 9.8 | 29.5 | 8.8 | 17.0 | 20.5 | 0.19 |
| High LDC import intensity | 19.9 | 58.2 | 11.2 | 29.7 | 15.1 | -0.17 |
| LDC import–weighted average | 15.7 | 48.5 | 10.7 | 27.2 | 13.8 | -0.09 |
| High LDC export intensity | 11.1 | 34.0 | 6.9 | 14.4 | 22.4 | 0.20 |
| LDC export–weighted average | 10.1 | 30.3 | 8.8 | 17.5 | 19.8 | 0.17 |
| Agriculture | 12.7 | 17.9 | 4.7 | 29.5 | 13.1 | -0.49 |
| All other[c] | 8.7 | 44.7 | 10.1 | 12.7 | 27.1 | -0.01 |

Source: Authors' calculations. Data on imports and exports by industry are compiled by Robert Feenstra and are available on the worldwide web page of the National Bureau of Economic Research (NBER). Data on LDC imports and exports are from Sachs and Shatz (1994). Data on industry shipments are from the NBER Productivity Database, also available on the NBER's worldwide web page. Industry data on immigrants, women, and educational attainments are from the 1990 census PUMS. Data on blacks and on wages are averages of 1989-91 data from CPS MORG files.

a. Aggregations based on data at the three-digit level. High import or export intensity industries are obtained by ranking industries by the ratio of imports or exports to total shipments and then selecting industries off the top of the list until 10 percent of the manufacturing labor force is represented. LDC imports and exports are, respectively, those from and to less developed countries. Weighted averages weight each industry by employment times the import or export intensity ratio.

b. Log of hourly wage index constructed so that U.S. average log wage = 0.

c. Nonmanufacturing, nonagricultural.

more complex. Agriculture uses low-wage male workers to a greater extent than even the top 10 percent of importing industries in manufacturing. In the heterogeneous "all other" category, the proportion of women exceeds that in the average import sector; and the proportion of college graduates exceeds that in the average export sector. The different composition of the labor force in exporting and importing industries has two implications for trade-based explanations of changes in the U.S. job market. First, the fact that women are disproportionately concentrated in industries that import from LDCs suggests that LDC trade should have affected women more adversely than men. But rates of pay and employment for women have risen since 1970. The evidence thus suggests that there is something wrong with models in which the traded goods sector determines wages for women throughout the economy. The expansion of the "all other" category, which disproportionately employs women, can explain this seeming paradox in a more general model of wage determination. Second, the large and increasing difference between the skill mix of the top and bottom importing and exporting industries raises the possibility that trade may have particular adverse effects on the economic position of some less skilled workers.[14]

### The Impact of Immigration: Area Studies

Suppose (1) that immigrant flows are uncorrelated with economic conditions in an area; and (2) that natives do not alter decisions about location or capital investment in response to immigration. Then comparing native outcomes or changes in outcomes between areas of more immigration and areas of less would offer a good way to isolate the impact of immigration on natives.[15] Put differently, one knows that immigrants flock to California. Why not just compare labor market

14. While table 4 shows data for 1990, we have also calculated the equivalent data for 1980; we find that the differentiation between the top 10 percent of import and export sectors increased between 1980 and 1990. One reason for this finding is that LDCs were more dominant in the high–import intensity sectors in 1990 than in 1980. Another is that the automobile industry (a large high-wage industry) was a more significant importer in 1980 than in 1990.

15. Grossman (1982) represents the first application of this approach. Her finding of a near zero correlation between native wages and immigrant penetration in a local labor market has been confirmed by most studies in this literature.

*George J. Borjas, Richard B. Freeman, and Lawrence F. Katz*          15

outcomes in California to the outcomes observed in the rest of the country?

The problem with contrasting native outcomes between immigrant-intensive areas and nonimmigrant areas is that neither proposition 1 nor 2 appears to be valid for the United States. The cities or states where immigrants cluster have done well in some periods and poorly in others, producing a potentially spurious correlation between immigration and area outcomes. For reasons that are probably unrelated to immigration, California is a high-wage state. As a result, immigration will appear to improve native economic opportunities in a cross-section dominated by California. To avoid this spurious cross-sectional spatial correlation, most analysts relate the *change* in the economic position of natives in an area over time to the *change* in the number of immigrants.[16] But a state's economy also fluctuates over time for reasons that are independent of immigration, creating the possibility of spurious longitudinal correlations as well. When California's economy booms, there will be a positive correlation between immigration and the economic position of natives; in a recession, the correlation will be negative. Elsewhere, we report that the time-varying conditions of individual states lead to unstable estimates of immigrant effects on native outcomes.[17] If one had perfect measures of how economic conditions change within a state and affect relative wages across skill groups, one would be able to control for those conditions and isolate the effect of immigration. Such measures, however, are not available.

Another problem with area analysis is that natives may adjust to the immediate impact of immigration in an area by moving their labor or capital to other localities until native wages and returns to capital are equalized across areas. For example, a large immigrant flow arriving in Los Angeles might well result in fewer unskilled workers from Mississippi or Michigan moving to California and a reallocation of capital from those states to California. A comparison of the wage of less skilled natives between California and other states, therefore, might show little difference because the effects of immigration were diffused around the economy, not because immigration had no economic effects.

16. See, for example, Altonji and Card (1991); LaLonde and Topel (1991), and Schoeni (1996).
17. Borjas, Freeman, and Katz (1996).

*Regional Differences in Native Wages and Employment*

We examine the link between immigration and native outcomes across areas for the periods 1960–70, 1970–80, and 1980–90, using data extracts from the 1960, 1970, 1980, and 1990 Public Use Microdata Samples (PUMS) of the decennial census. The extracts include all persons aged eighteen to sixty-four (as of the census year) who do not live in group quarters. In the 1960 and 1970 censuses, the data extracts are a 1 percent random sample of the population. In 1980 and 1990, the immigrant extracts form a 5 percent random sample and the native extracts form a 1 percent random sample. We define a person as an immigrant if he or she was born abroad and is either a noncitizen or a naturalized citizen; all other persons are classified as natives. Because immigrants are concentrated in particular educational groups, we examine the impact of immigration on the labor market outcomes of natives in five educational categories, or "skill groups": fewer than nine years of schooling, nine to eleven years, twelve years, thirteen to fifteen years, and at least sixteen years.

The labor market is likely to respond to supply shocks with price and quantity adjustments. Our measures of labor market outcomes are log weekly earnings and log annual earnings from the previous calendar year and the probability of working during the census week. The analysis of the employment probability uses all the observations in our data, while the analysis of weekly or annual earnings uses the subsample of persons who worked for pay at some time in the year preceding the census, were not self-employed, and were working in the civilian sector.

The geographic scope of the labor market in question can affect estimates of the impact of immigration. Studies of a small geographic area are more likely to miss effects of immigration than studies of large areas because native migration and capital responses may diffuse those effects in small areas. We use three alternative definitions of the geographic area: metropolitan areas, states, and census regions. An advantage of using states or regions as the geographic unit is that data at these levels are available for the entire period 1960–90. We limit the analysis of metropolitan areas to the 1980 and 1990 censuses, across which 236 metropolitan areas can be matched. The 1970 census PUMS identifies far fewer metropolitan areas and the 1960 PUMS does not identify any.

We use age-adjusted measures of labor market outcomes, estimated separately for male and female U.S. natives. We purge our data of age effects in the following way. Let $y_{ijkt}$ be the labor market outcome for person $i$, residing in area $j$, belonging to skill group $k$, in census year $t$; and let $Z_{ijkt}$ be a vector of dummy variables indicating whether the worker is aged eighteen to twenty-four, twenty-five to thirty-four, thirty-five to forty-four, forty-five to fifty-four, or fifty-five to sixty-four. Finally, let $r_{jkt}$ be a fixed effect giving the age-adjusted "average" labor market outcome experienced by a native who lives in area $j$ and belongs to skill group $k$ in year $t$. We then estimate the following regression separately for each native group based on sex and education in each census year:

(1)                         $y_{ijkt} = Z_{ijkt}\beta_{kt} + r_{jkt} + u_{ijkt},$

where $u_{ijkt}$ is the error term, assumed uncorrelated with the independent variables in the model. The age-adjusted measures of outcomes are given by the fixed effects $r$, evaluated at the mean age distribution of the native sample from the pooled 1970, 1980, and 1990 censuses.

We use the estimated fixed effects $r$ to calculate first difference estimates of changes in the labor market outcome for each sex-education group. We define the change in outcome for a particular sex-education group in a particular region as

(2)                         $\Delta r_{jkt} = r_{jkt} - r_{j,k,t-10}.$

Table 5 summarizes the key patterns in our data, in terms of regression coefficients linking changes in wages or immigration from one decade to the next. The first and third rows report the results of regressing the change in age-adjusted log weekly earnings in the 1980s for a state-education cell on the change in log weekly earnings in the 1970s for the same state-education cell.[18] The regression includes a vector of education fixed effects; by including these, we isolate the secular correlation in wage growth within an educational group. The results reveal a strong *negative* relation in wage growth by state between the two periods. The coefficient in the male regression is $-1$, implying a complete reversal in the ranking of states by wage growth between the 1970s

18. The wage growth regressions are weighted by $(n_x\, n_y)/(n_x + n_y)$, where $n_t$ gives the sample size in year $t$, and $x$ and $y$ are the years spanned by the period defining the dependent variable.

**Table 5. State Cross-Section Autoregressions Estimating Changes in Native Earnings Growth and Immigrant Flows between Census Decades[a]**

| Sample | Dependent variable | Independent variable | Coefficient | $R^2$ |
|--------|--------------------|--------------------|-------------|-------|
| Males | Wage growth, 1980–90 | Wage growth, 1970–80 | −1.052 (0.068) | 0.640 |
| | Wage growth, 1970–80 | Wage growth, 1960–70 | 0.002 (0.084) | 0.149 |
| Females | Wage growth, 1980–90 | Wage growth, 1970–80 | −0.591 (0.073) | 0.438 |
| | Wage growth, 1970–80 | Wage growth, 1960–70 | 0.179 (0.058) | 0.456 |
| All persons | Immigrant supply change, 1980–90 | Immigrant supply change, 1970–80 | 1.498 (0.054) | 0.753 |
| | Immigrant supply change, 1970–80 | Immigrant supply change, 1960–70 | 1.251 (0.098) | 0.500 |

Source: Authors' calculations based on data from the census PUMS (various years).

a. Wage growth is defined as the log change in age-adjusted weekly earnings: $r_{jkt} - r_{j,k,t-10}$, from equation 2 in the text, where $j$ represents one of the fifty states or the District of Columbia and $k$ represents one of the five skill groups described in the text. Change in the immigrant supply, from equation 3 in the text, is $(M_{jkt} - M_{j,k,t-10})/N_{j,k,t-10}$, where $M_{jk}$ and $N_{jk}$ are the number of immigrants and natives, respectively, in the given state and skill group. Regressions include fixed effects identifying each skill group. Standard errors are shown in parentheses. Each regression contains 255 observations.

and the 1980s. Figure 3, which compares rates of growth of wages by state in the census data, illustrates this striking pattern.[19]

When we obtained this result, we initially wondered if it might largely reflect measurement error; the log of the 1980 weekly wage enters each side of the regression equation with opposite sign. This is not the case. We estimate an analogous regression using 1970–80 wage growth as the dependent variable and 1960–70 wage growth as the independent variable. This regression, reported in the second and fourth rows of table 5 and illustrated in figure 3, shows no correlation in wage growth for men between the two decades and a positive correlation for women.[20] We next wondered whether the result was due to some pe-

19. The figure "aggregates" the data across skill groups in a state by weighting the wages of workers with different levels of schooling by the national proportion of workers in each educational group.

20. Although the regional structure of wage growth changed over the period, the correlation matrix in wage levels indicates that these are strongly and positively correlated over time. Every single element in the wage level correlation matrix, for both men and women, over the period 1960–90 exceeds 0.91, where the matrix of correlation coefficients is weighted by the sample size in the state-education cell in the 1990 census.

*George J. Borjas, Richard B. Freeman, and Lawrence F. Katz*          19

**Figure 3. The Changing Regional Wage Structure**[a]

Change in log earnings, 1980–90[b]

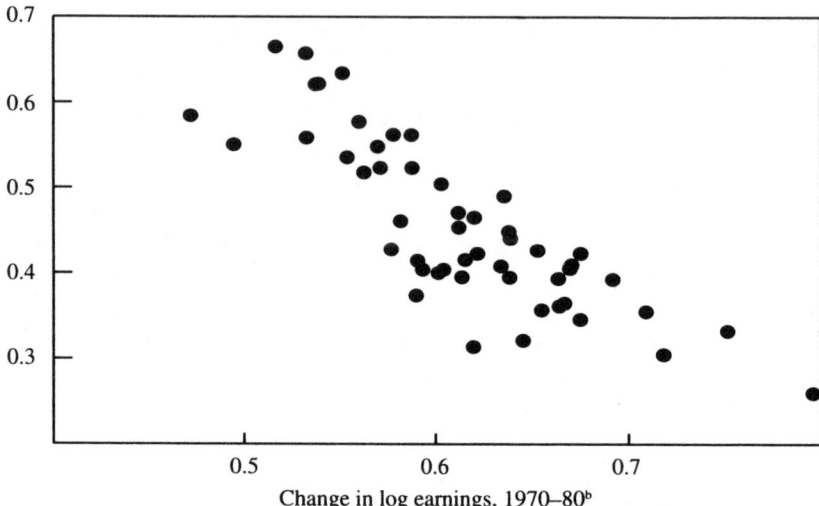

Change in log earnings, 1970–80[b]

Change in log earnings, 1970–80[b]

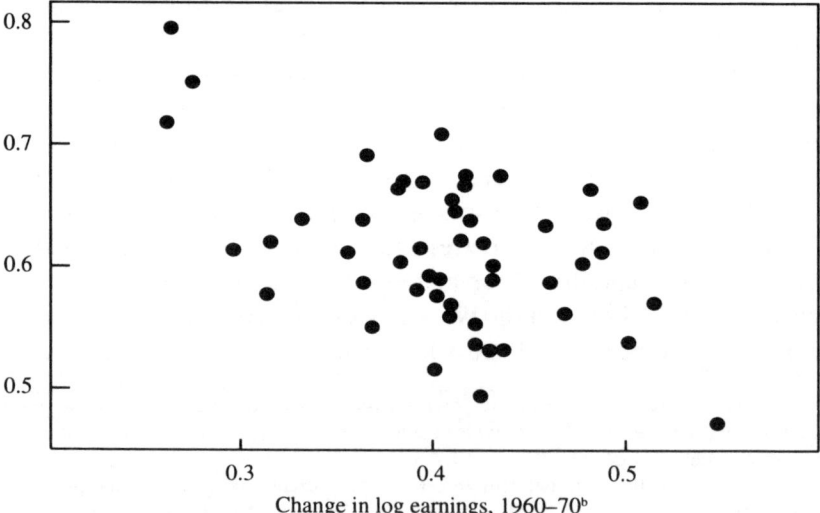

Change in log earnings, 1960–70[b]

Source: Authors' calculations based on data from the census PUMS (various years).
a. Each plotted point represents one of the fifty states or the District of Columbia.
b. Δln weekly earnings of natives aged eighteen to sixty-four.

culiarity in the census data. However, we reestimated these regressions using establishment data on average log weekly wages for workers covered by each state's unemployment insurance system and again found a strong negative correlation between wage growth by state in the 1970s and in the 1980s.

The fact that the high–wage growth states of the 1970s became low–wage growth states in the 1980s has a crucial implication for any analysis that exploits spatial differences to infer the effects of immigration on native outcomes. Since the states that received large numbers of immigrants in the 1970s also received large numbers of immigrants in the 1980s, the reversal of wage growth among states implies a reversal in the sign of the correlation between changes in wages and in immigration by state. As a result, one's inferences about the impact of immigration will almost certainly differ according to the period analyzed.

Formally, let $M_{jkt}$ be the number of immigrants (both male and female) who live in region $j$ and belong to skill group $k$ in census year $t$, and let $N_{jkt}$ be the number of (male and female) natives in that region and skill group. We define the change in labor supply due to immigration during the decade that ends in year $t$ as

$$(3) \qquad \Delta m_{jkt} = \frac{M_{jkt} - M_{j.k.t-10}}{N_{j.k.t-10}}.$$

The fifth row of table 5 reports the results of regressing the change in the immigrant supply over 1980–90 on the change in the immigrant supply over 1970–80, including a vector of education fixed effects to isolate changes within educational groups. The regression shows a strong positive correlation between the growth of immigrants in a state in the 1970s and the growth of immigrants in that state in the 1980s. In the sixth row, we lag the regression by one decade; the correlation in supply shocks between the 1960s and the 1970s is also positive and is almost as strong.

The data thus indicate that immigration induced large supply shocks in the same states in the 1970s and in the 1980s. But they also show that the states that experienced high wage growth in the 1970s experienced low wage growth in the 1980s. The result is a reversal in the sign of the correlation between changes in immigration by state and changes in wages. The correlation between $\Delta m$ and $\Delta r$ by state switches from $-0.19$ in 1970–80 to 0.34 in 1980–90 for men, and from $-0.18$ to

*George J. Borjas, Richard B. Freeman, and Lawrence F. Katz*        21

0.44 for women. Studies that calculate spatial correlations between wage growth and immigrant supply shocks will not be able to obtain consistently negative or positive effects across different censuses unless they can control for the forces that caused the regional wage structure to change so dramatically over time. These unobserved structural forces are so strong that a consistent impact of immigration, if such exists, probably cannot be detected in an analysis of interarea differences.

In view of this observation, it is not surprising that our analysis of regional differences in wage trends show little systematic evidence that the immigrant supply shock had an impact on the weekly earnings of natives. For simplicity, we divide the country into three regions: California, the other five states that receive large numbers of immigrants (New York, Texas, Florida, New Jersey, and Illinois), and the remainder of the country.

Table 6 reports log weekly earnings in each of these regions for natives in each educational group relative to natives with exactly twelve years of education in the given region, from 1960 to 1990.[21] For almost every educational group, the pattern of wage differentials moves similarly in California, the other immigrant-receiving states, and the nonimmigrant states. Consider, for example, native men who have between nine and eleven years of schooling. In 1990, this group made up 14.0 percent of native adults. Native men in this educational group who lived in California earned 0.08 log point less than natives with a high school diploma in 1960 and 0.19 log point less in 1990. Their counterparts in the other immigrant-receiving states earned 0.12 log point less than natives with a high school diploma in 1960 and 0.24 log point less in 1990. The trend in the relative wage of this skill group was similar in the states that had few immigrants: $-0.13$ log point in 1960 and $-0.24$ log point in 1990. Thus from 1960 to 1990, the relative wage of this less skilled group of native men declined by about 0.11 log point in each of the regions, even though the immigrant shock to California was disproportionately less skilled. The natural "difference-in-difference" estimate of the immigrant wage effect—the wage growth of California's natives less the wage growth of natives in the nonimmigrant states—suggests that immigration did not affect native wage

21. The fixed effects for the aggregated regions are obtained by "adding up" $r_{jkt}$ over the states in the region, with each state's observation weighted by the number of working natives in that state in the given census year.

**Table 6. Relative Log Weekly Earnings of Natives by Skill Group, 1960–90**

Log index[a]

| | | Males | | | Females | | |
|---|---|---|---|---|---|---|---|
| Years of schooling | Year | California | Other immigrant states[b] | Other states | California | Other immigrant states[b] | Other states |
| Fewer than 9 | 1960 | −0.215 | −0.344 | −0.383 | −0.357 | −0.395 | −0.510 |
| | 1970 | −0.193 | −0.345 | −0.359 | −0.336 | −0.331 | −0.384 |
| | 1980 | −0.194 | −0.359 | −0.361 | −0.163 | −0.271 | −0.268 |
| | 1990 | −0.331 | −0.366 | −0.343 | −0.208 | −0.374 | −0.285 |
| 9 to 11 | 1960 | −0.084 | −0.120 | −0.128 | −0.196 | −0.216 | −0.247 |
| | 1970 | −0.111 | −0.175 | −0.175 | −0.208 | −0.220 | −0.220 |
| | 1980 | −0.176 | −0.212 | −0.219 | −0.207 | −0.204 | −0.186 |
| | 1990 | −0.187 | −0.235 | −0.239 | −0.215 | −0.239 | −0.218 |
| 13 to 15 | 1960 | 0.059 | 0.081 | 0.085 | 0.043 | 0.115 | 0.129 |
| | 1970 | 0.061 | 0.081 | 0.077 | 0.091 | 0.134 | 0.112 |
| | 1980 | 0.052 | 0.062 | 0.046 | 0.068 | 0.113 | 0.097 |
| | 1990 | 0.089 | 0.100 | 0.083 | 0.127 | 0.153 | 0.156 |
| 16 or more | 1960 | 0.271 | 0.308 | 0.305 | 0.439 | 0.510 | 0.544 |
| | 1970 | 0.313 | 0.374 | 0.334 | 0.500 | 0.565 | 0.589 |
| | 1980 | 0.280 | 0.322 | 0.262 | 0.362 | 0.446 | 0.428 |
| | 1990 | 0.414 | 0.463 | 0.410 | 0.513 | 0.579 | 0.558 |

Source: Authors' calculations based on data from the census PUMS (various years).

a. Log of index constructed so that log earnings of natives with exactly twelve years of schooling = 0 in each sample year and region.

b. New York, New Jersey, Illinois, Florida, and Texas.

differentials. The one exception to this pattern is native men who have less than nine years of schooling, which is an extremely small group.

The raw data thus suggest that it is extremely difficult to obtain consistent estimates of the labor market effects of immigration from spatial correlations. Our efforts to find such effects support this inference. Consider the regression model

$$(4) \qquad \Delta r_{jkt} = \alpha_t + \beta_t \, \Delta m_{jkt} + v_j + \tau_k + u_{jkt},$$

where $v_j$ is a fixed effect indicating the group's area of residence and $\tau_k$ is a fixed effect indicating the group's educational attainment. The education fixed effects net out any change occurring in the national market for workers with that level of education, while the area fixed effects net out the impact of the level of state economic activity on all natives residing in that state. They represent our best effort to control for factors unrelated to immigration that might affect outcomes across groups and states.

We measure the immigration supply shock as the change in the size of the immigrant population relative to the native population at the beginning of the decade (see equation 3). This measure differs from the first difference in the foreign-born share of the work force that is used in many area studies of immigration. It avoids the potential endogeneity of the immigration variable due to the possibility that the native population at the end of the decade depends on immigration, and also the potential endogeneity of labor force participation (of both immigrants and natives) to the immigrant supply shock.[22] Finally, we use the supply shock in the specific educational group as the measure of immigrant penetration. This variable helps us to better capture the "own" effects in the data.[23]

Table 7 presents our estimates of the coefficient β, from the 1960–90 census data. There is a great deal of variation in the estimated coefficients by scope of geographic area, sex, and time period, making it difficult to draw any robust generalization about the effects of immigration on labor market outcomes.[24] Consider, for example, the relationship between immigration and the employment probability for native men. The regression coefficients for the 1980s suggest that immigrant supply shocks lead to lower employment for native workers, and that this effect becomes more negative, the greater the scope of the geographic area. At the regional level, the regressions suggest that a 10 percentage point increase in the relative number of immigrants re-

22. We replicated the regression analysis using counts of workers, with little change in the underlying results.

23. Although it seems as if the specification in equation 4 ignores cross-effects between various types of immigrant workers and natives, the regressions do include area fixed effects. These fixed effects partly control for the supply shock attributable to the total immigrant flow into an area. We also experimented with alternative specifications of the regressions that allowed for an "own effect" as well as some cross-effects. However, the correlation between the own supply shock and the total supply shock is typically above 0.7, so that the data do not allow a reliable estimation of a more general model.

24. In Borjas, Freeman, and Katz (1996) we note that analysis of native wage growth in the 1980s shows that the spatial correlation became more negative as the geographic area under consideration was expanded. Table 7, however, indicates that the negative correlation between the regression coefficients and the scope of the geographic area disappears in earlier decades, in particular, in the 1960s.

**Table 7. Estimating the Impact of Immigration on Native Earnings and Employment, First Difference Regressions[a]**

| Dependent variable and geographic scope | Coefficient on immigration variable | | | | | |
|---|---|---|---|---|---|---|
| | Males | | | Females | | |
| | 1980–90 | 1970–80 | 1960–70 | 1980–90 | 1970–80 | 1960–70 |
| **Log weekly earnings** | | | | | | |
| Regions | -0.126 (0.082) | 0.008 (0.107) | 0.813 (0.145) | 0.015 (0.041) | 0.377 (0.241) | 1.130 (0.338) |
| States | -0.103 (0.057) | 0.071 (0.075) | 0.591 (0.107) | -0.022 (0.035) | 0.373 (0.141) | 0.203 (0.206) |
| Metropolitan areas | -0.061 (0.030) | … | … | 0.014 (0.031) | … | … |
| **Log annual earnings** | | | | | | |
| Regions | -0.174 (0.087) | -0.003 (0.139) | 0.855 (0.177) | 0.066 (0.068) | 0.191 (0.299) | 1.075 (0.425) |
| States | -0.110 (0.056) | 0.066 (0.092) | 0.674 (0.118) | 0.006 (0.056) | 0.303 (0.156) | 0.829 (0.268) |
| Metropolitan areas | -0.054 (0.037) | … | … | 0.024 (0.040) | … | … |
| **Employment rate** | | | | | | |
| Regions | -0.045 (0.012) | 0.127 (0.059) | -0.159 (0.044) | 0.028 (0.013) | 0.123 (0.119) | 0.142 (0.059) |
| States | -0.025 (0.008) | 0.079 (0.049) | -0.063 (0.031) | 0.010 (0.011) | 0.110 (0.094) | 0.187 (0.054) |
| Metropolitan areas | -0.011 (0.013) | … | … | -0.003 (0.008) | … | … |

Source: Authors' calculations based on data from the census PUMS (various years).

a. The dependent variable, for each specification, is the change (over the given decade) in the given labor market outcome (age-adjusted log earnings or employment rate) for natives in a given region, state, or metropolitan area $j$ and given skill group $k$. The independent variable is the contemporaneous change in the relative immigrant supply, $(M_{jk,t} - M_{jk,t-10})/N_{jk,t-10}$, where $M_{jk}$ and $N_{jk}$ are the number of immigrants and natives, respectively, in area $j$ and skill group $k$. Regression equations, which are estimates of equation 4 in the text, include a constant term and fixed effects identifying each area and skill group. Standard errors are shown in parentheses.

duces the employment-to-population ratio of natives by about 0.45
percentage point. But this coefficient is implausibly large and positive
in the 1970s and implausibly large and negative in the 1960s. The data
also reveal little consistency in the results for weekly and annual earnings, or for men and women.

One way to interpret the inconsistent spatial correlations between
changes in native outcomes and immigration over the period 1960–90
is that the economic impact of immigration on native labor market
outcomes simply changes over time or differs by sex. That is, we have
the ''right'' estimates, but they vary a great deal. We do not believe
that this is so. If it were, the historical record would provide virtually
no information about the future effects of immigration or of changes in
immigration policy on native outcomes.

Our interpretation of the results in table 7 is that the spatial correlation between changes in native outcomes and immigration do not, in
fact, measure what we want them to measure. The inconsistency in the
signs of the correlations over time provides little information about the
structural impact of immigration on the native labor market. Our finding
that the pattern of regional wage changes has shifted dramatically over
time—while the same regions keep receiving immigrants—suggests
that unobserved factors are driving the evolution of the regional wage
structure, that these factors have little to do with immigration, and that
they dominate the data. The one valid inference from an analysis of
spatial correlations is that immigration is not a major determinant of
the regional structure of labor market outcomes for natives.

### Immigration and Native Internal Migration

The fact that immigration is not consistently related to regional labor
market outcomes for natives raises the question of why immigration
effects are so weak at the regional level, despite the striking geographic
clustering of immigrants. One hypothesis is that the immigration effect
is diffused through the internal migration flows of native workers or
capital. Previous research has focused on labor flows, without reaching
a clear consensus of findings. Some studies find that metropolitan areas
where immigrants cluster had lower rates of native in-migration and
higher rates of native out-migration in the 1970s.[25] David Card reports

25. See, for example, Filer (1992) and White and Hunter (1993).

that the unexpected arrival of 120,000 *Marielitos* in Miami in 1980 did not raise the city's population growth over the next five years relative to demographic predictions made before the Mariel boatlift.[26] Consistent with these studies, William Frey and Kao-Lee Liaw find a strong negative correlation between immigration and the net migration rates of natives in the 1990 census.[27] By contrast, in a later study Card reports a slight positive correlation between the rate of growth in the number of native workers and the rate of growth in the number of immigrant workers by metropolitan area, over the period 1985–90.[28] Therefore it remains in question whether native internal migration is an important mechanism for diffusing the effects of immigration nationwide.

We address this issue by examining the population trends of natives and immigrants aged eighteen to sixty-four, by state, using decennial census data from 1950 to 1990.[29] We analyze data at the state level because the state of residence is the one measure of native location decisions that is available in each of these data sets. As with wage outcomes, it is instructive to compare population trends in California, other immigrant-receiving states, and nonimmigrant states. Table 8 reports the proportions of the total population, of natives, and of immigrants living in these areas from 1950 to 1990. As shown above, large-scale immigration to the United States resumed around 1970 and has continued since. Hence by contrasting changes in the residential location of the native population before and after 1970, one can assess the effects of immigration on native location decisions.[30] The period of analysis thus spans *both* the preimmigration pattern of internal migration (the "pretreatment period") and the postimmigration adjustments (the "treatment period").

The data reveal one important fact: up to 1970, the share of natives who lived in the major immigrant-receiving state, California, was rising rapidly; since 1970, the share of natives living in California has barely changed. Between 1950 and 1970 the fraction of natives who lived in California rose by 2.7 percentage points (39 percent): between 1950

26. Card (1990).
27. Frey (1995a, 1995b); Frey and Liaw (1996).
28. Card (1997).
29. We use the sample of persons who do not reside in group quarters.
30. The data clearly indicate that the migration patterns of the U.S. population (as opposed to cross-state differences in fertility and death rates) dominate shifts in population across states; see Blanchard and Katz (1992).

**Table 8. Distribution of Native and Immigrant Populations, by Region, 1950–90[a]**
Percent

| Year | Entire population | | | Natives | | | Immigrants | | |
|---|---|---|---|---|---|---|---|---|---|
| | California | Other immigrant states[b] | Other states | California | Other immigrant states[b] | Other states | California | Other immigrant states[b] | Other states |
| 1950 | 7.2 | 26.9 | 65.9 | 6.9 | 25.4 | 67.7 | 10.4 | 44.4 | 45.2 |
| 1960 | 8.9 | 27.3 | 63.7 | 8.6 | 26.2 | 65.2 | 14.6 | 44.9 | 40.6 |
| 1970 | 10.2 | 27.1 | 62.7 | 9.6 | 26.2 | 64.2 | 20.1 | 43.8 | 36.0 |
| 1980 | 10.9 | 26.7 | 62.4 | 9.7 | 25.6 | 64.8 | 27.2 | 41.9 | 30.9 |
| 1990 | 12.4 | 27.0 | 60.7 | 10.0 | 25.5 | 64.4 | 33.8 | 40.0 | 26.1 |

Source: Authors' calculations based on data from the census PUMS (various years).
a. Sample includes individuals aged eighteen to sixty-four and not living in group quarters.
b. New York, New Jersey, Illinois, Florida, and Texas.

and 1960 it increased from 6.9 to 8.6 percent and between 1960 and
1970 it increased from 8.6 to 9.6 percent. In contrast, the fraction of
natives living in California rose by only 0.1 percentage point from 1970
to 1980 and by just 0.3 point from 1980 to 1990, a cumulative increase
of 0.4 point (4.2 percent).

If California's share of the total U.S. population had also stabilized
between 1970 and 1990, one would perhaps conclude that the state had
reached some equilibrium steady-state share of the population. But
California's share rose from 10.2 percent in 1970 to 12.4 percent in
1990: a 2.2 percentage point (22 percent) increase. In fact, California
shifted from growth based on native migration to growth based on
immigrants. If the share of the native population in California had
increased in the 1970s and 1980s at the same rate as in the 1950s and
1960s, 12.3 percent of natives would have lived in California in 1990.[31]
An extrapolation of the pre-1970 demographic trends—that is, before
the immigrant supply shock—accurately predicts the state's share of
the entire U.S. population in 1990.[32] Figure 4 shows that the data point
for California (like the points for each of the other immigrant-receiving
states) lies close to the regression line linking the population growth
rate in 1970–90 to that in 1950–70. This finding suggests that the
increasing number of immigrants who chose to settle in California
displaced the native net migration that would otherwise have occurred
and thus diffused the economic effects of immigration from California
to the rest of the country.

We formalize this insight with a simple regression model. We define the simple annualized population growth rate contributions for
natives, $\Delta n_j(t, t')$, and immigrants, $\Delta m_j(t, t')$, as

(5) $$\Delta n_j(t, t') = \frac{N_{jt'} - N_{jt}}{L_{jt}} \div (t' - t)$$

and

---

31. Extrapolating the trend over 1950–70 to this later period implies that the native
share would have grown by 2.7 percentage points between 1970 and 1990. Admittedly,
this simple exercise assumes away the nonlinearities that may exist in the rate of change
in California's population share.

32. Evidence provided by Blanchard and Katz (1992) presages this finding: their
figure 1 shows that California lies on the regression line linking the rate of employment
growth in 1970–90 to that in 1950–70.

**Figure 4. Actual versus Predicted State Population Growth Rates, 1970–90[a]**

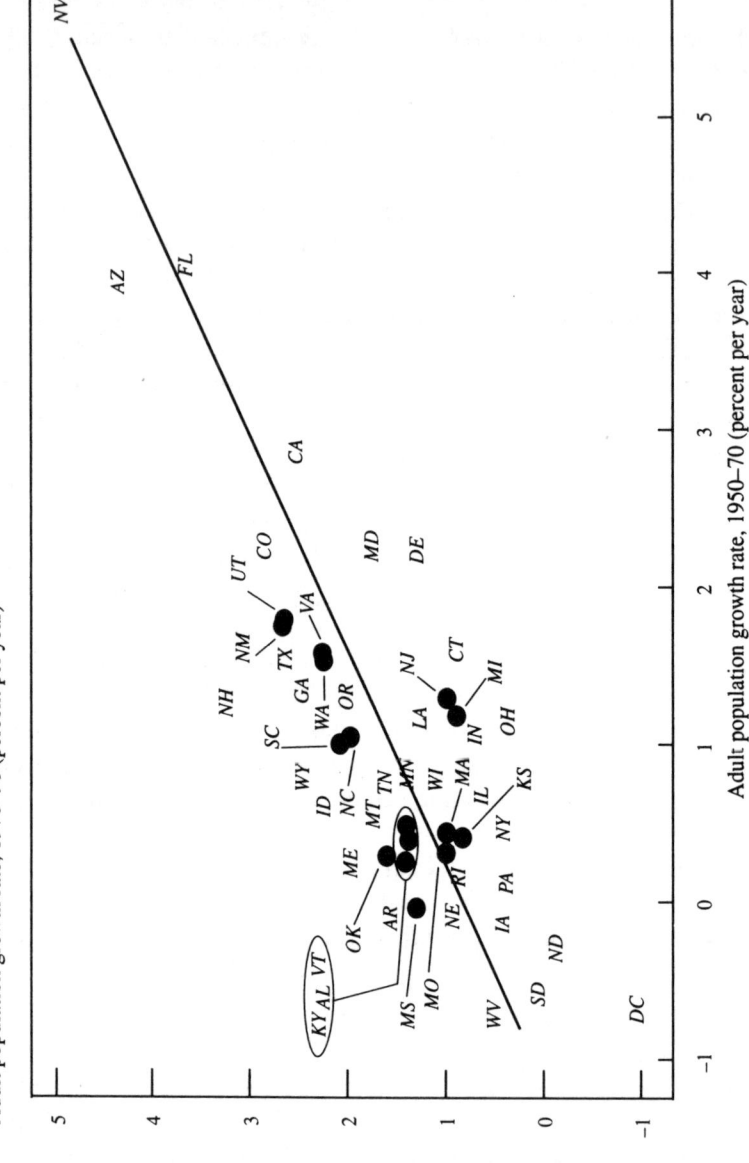

Source: Authors' calculations based on data from the census PUMS (various years).
a. Observations for the fifty states plus the District of Columbia are labeled by postal codes. The least squares line shown is given by $y = 0.75x + 0.86$, $R^2 = 0.68$.

**Table 9. Estimating the Response of State Native Population Flows to State Immigrant Population Flows**[a]

|  | Double differences | |
|---|---|---|
| *First differences,* *1970–90* | *1970–90* *minus* *1960–70* | *1970–90* *minus* *1950–70* |
| 0.777 | −0.756 | −1.673 |
| (0.311) | (0.278) | (0.285) |

Source: Authors' calculations based on data from the census PUMS (various years).

a. For first differences specification, dependent variable is the average annual contribution of native population growth to overall population growth in each state; independent variable is the contribution of immigrant population growth. For double difference specifications, the changes in these average annual contributions (between periods given) are used as variables. For details, see equations 7 (first differences) and 8 (double differences) in the text. Sample comprises the fifty states plus the District of Columbia, except for the final column, which excludes Alaska and Hawaii. Standard errors are shown in parentheses.

(6) $$\Delta m_j(t,\ t') = \frac{M_{jt'} - M_{jt}}{L_{jt}} \div (t' - t),$$

where $N_{jt}$ gives the number of natives living in state $j$ in year $t$, $M_{jt}$ gives the respective number of immigrants, and $L_{jt} = N_{jt} + M_{jt}$. We then estimate the following first difference regression model:

(7) $$\Delta n_j(70,\ 90) = a + b\ \Delta m_j(70,\ 90) + e_j,$$

where "70" and "90" indicate the census years 1970 and 1990, respectively, and $e_j$ is the stochastic error. This regression links the annual growth rate of natives in a state to the growth rate of immigrants in that state, both relative to the state's total population in the base year, 1970. Because the dependent and independent variables are scaled by the same factor, the coefficient $b$ measures the impact of an additional immigrant arriving in the state between 1970 and 1990 on the change in the number of natives living in that state during that period.

The sample contains fifty-one observations (for each state plus the District of Columbia). The first column in table 9 reports the estimated coefficient $b$.[33] The data reveal a positive and significant relation between immigration by state and change in the size of the native population. Does this positive coefficient imply that natives do not respond to immigration in their location decisions, or perhaps even respond by

33. All the first difference models estimated in this section are weighted by the factor $(n_x n_y)/(n_x + n_y)$, where $n_t$ gives the sample size in year $t$, and $x$ and $y$ are the years spanned by the period defining the dependent variable. We also estimated the models separately for men and women, with little change in the results.

moving *to* areas penetrated by immigrants? How can one reconcile these results with the fact that native migration to the major immigrant-receiving state, California, effectively ended around 1970?

The key difference between the regression model in equation 7 and our earlier tabulations is that the first difference regression compares population growth among states with different levels of immigration in 1970–90, rather than native migration in a given state before and after the immigrant supply shock. The regression estimated in the first column of table 9 implicitly assumes that each state would have had the same rate of native population growth in the absence of immigration, so that California and Vermont were on the same population growth path. But if each state had its own growth path prior to immigration, and that growth path would have continued absent immigration, the regression gives a misleading inference about the effects of immigration. To isolate the impact of immigration on the net migration of native workers, one needs a difference-in-difference comparison of how a given state's population grows before and after the immigrant supply shock. The following double difference model provides such a comparison:

$$(8) \quad \Delta n_j(70, 90) - \Delta n_j(60, 70)$$

$$= \alpha + \beta \left[ \Delta m_j(70, 90) - \Delta m_j(60, 70) \right] + v_j,$$

where the coefficient $\beta$ measures the impact of an increase in the number of immigrants on the number of natives, relative to the "preexisting conditions" in the state. A useful interpretation of the double difference in equation 8 is that it imposes a particular structure on the state's fixed effect—the rate of population growth that the state was experiencing before the immigrant supply shock.

The second column of table 9 reports the coefficient from the double difference model, using the state's population growth from 1960 to 1970 as the counterfactual control.[34] Controlling for the state's pre-1970 population growth path changes the sign of the effect of immigration on native net migration from positive to negative. In fact, the estimated $\beta$ suggests considerable displacement (the coefficient is not significantly different from $-1$).

---

34. The double difference models are weighted by $(n_x n_y n_z)/(n_x n_z + 4 n_x n_z + n_x n_y)$, where $n_t$ gives the sample size in year $t$, $x$ and $z$ are the years that span the period defining the dependent variable (with $z > y > x$).

The regression coefficient presented in the second column essentially reiterates the descriptive results presented in table 8. The negative coefficient reflects the facts that California experienced the largest immigrant supply shock and that its native population share stopped growing when the supply shock began. The third column of the table reestimates the double difference model using the annualized population growth rate over 1950–70 to control for conditions in the state before the immigrant supply shock. This regression yields an even more negative coefficient—indeed, it seems too negative, because it is larger than one in absolute value. This "excess sensitivity" is probably a functional form issue. It is unclear whether, in the absence of an immigration shock, California's share of the native population would have grown at the rapid rate of 1.4 percentage points per decade that prevailed over 1950–70. The only term in the regression that would capture this possible nonlinearity is the change in the rate of growth of the immigrant population.

Table 9 demonstrates that the sign of the impact of immigration on the growth of the native population depends critically on the counterfactual implicit or explicit in a particular regression model. While the data support the inclusion of a lagged native population growth rate in the model linking native net migration to immigration, this is not the reason why we prefer this model.[35] Selection of a model depends not simply on statistical results, but on the economic relevance of the counterfactual that it poses. We contrast native growth rates before and after the immigrant supply shock because this comparison may provide a plausible answer to the question of what would have happened to the native population if immigration had remained at pre-1970 levels; that is, the growth path that would have been observed if the immigrant supply shock had never occurred.

---

35. The double difference regression in equation 8 imposes two restrictions on the coefficients. In particular, the coefficient on the 1960–70 native growth rate is unity and the coefficient of the 1960–70 immigrant growth rate is equal, but of opposite sign, to the coefficient on the 1970–90 immigrant growth rate. The unrestricted regression is

$$\Delta n_j(70, 90) = 0.988 \,\Delta n_j(60, 70) - 1.218 \,\Delta m_j(70, 90) + 3.310 \,\Delta m_j(60, 70),$$
$$\qquad\qquad\quad (0.167) \qquad\qquad (0.333) \qquad\qquad\quad (0.925)$$

where the regression includes a constant term and standard errors are in parentheses. The restriction on the native coefficient is satisfied by the data, whereas the restriction on the immigrant coefficients is rejected (with a $t$ statistic of 2.68).

*George J. Borjas, Richard B. Freeman, and Lawrence F. Katz*          33

**Table 10. Distribution of Regional Adult Populations by Educational Attainment, 1950–90**[a]

Percent

| Region and year | Years of schooling | | | | |
| | Fewer than 9 | 9 to 11 | 12 | 13 to 15 | 16 or more |
|---|---|---|---|---|---|
| California | | | | | |
| 1950 | 26.8 | 20.5 | 31.8 | 13.2 | 7.7 |
| 1960 | 20.9 | 21.8 | 32.6 | 15.0 | 9.7 |
| 1970 | 12.5 | 17.8 | 36.6 | 19.9 | 13.2 |
| 1980 | 9.6 | 13.2 | 34.2 | 24.8 | 18.3 |
| 1990 | 9.3 | 13.4 | 22.0 | 33.0 | 22.3 |
| Other immigrant states[b] | | | | | |
| 1950 | 39.8 | 20.6 | 25.1 | 7.8 | 6.7 |
| 1960 | 30.5 | 22.8 | 28.3 | 9.9 | 8.4 |
| 1970 | 19.1 | 21.2 | 35.1 | 12.9 | 11.6 |
| 1980 | 11.0 | 16.1 | 37.7 | 18.4 | 16.8 |
| 1990 | 6.6 | 14.2 | 29.2 | 28.1 | 21.8 |
| Other states | | | | | |
| 1950 | 42.6 | 20.0 | 24.0 | 7.9 | 5.4 |
| 1960 | 32.6 | 21.4 | 29.6 | 9.2 | 7.2 |
| 1970 | 19.7 | 20.8 | 37.2 | 12.1 | 10.2 |
| 1980 | 10.5 | 16.4 | 40.8 | 17.3 | 15.0 |
| 1990 | 5.0 | 14.3 | 33.3 | 28.0 | 19.4 |
| United States | | | | | |
| 1950 | 40.7 | 20.2 | 24.9 | 8.2 | 5.9 |
| 1960 | 31.0 | 21.8 | 29.5 | 9.9 | 7.7 |
| 1970 | 18.8 | 20.6 | 36.6 | 13.1 | 10.9 |
| 1980 | 10.5 | 16.0 | 39.2 | 18.4 | 15.9 |
| 1990 | 6.0 | 14.2 | 30.8 | 28.6 | 20.4 |

Source: Authors' calculations based on data from the census PUMS (various years).
a. Sample includes individuals aged eighteen to sixty-four and not living in group quarters.
b. New York, New Jersey, Illinois, Florida, and Texas.

## Does Immigration Change Factor Proportions within a State?

The migration response of natives would completely diffuse the adverse effect of the immigrant supply shock on local labor markets if the native flows of particular skill groups counterbalanced the immigrant shock and left the relative factor proportions within a state unchanged. We now investigate whether this was, in fact, the case.

We begin by classifying workers according to the five educational groups defined above. Table 10 reports the trends in the factor shares of these skill groups in each of our three areas and in the United States as a whole. It therefore summarizes what happens to the relative supply of the skill groups in these regions as a result of both immigration and the internal migration flows of natives. There has been substantial convergence in the regional distribution of skills over 1950–90. At the beginning of the period, California had relatively few persons who lacked a high school diploma; in 1950, 47.3 percent of California's adult population had less than twelve years of schooling, as compared with 62.6 percent in the states without a strong immigrant presence. By 1990, 22.7 percent of California's population was in this educational group, as compared with 19.3 percent for the nonimmigrant states. California's share of less educated workers declined less rapidly than shares in the rest of the nation, both before and after the immigration shock. From being much more educated than the rest of the nation before 1970, the population of California has changed to a bimodal distribution, with a modestly larger share of both those with less than a high school degree and those with at least a college degree. Table 10 raises the question of whether the educational distribution of the populations of immigrant-receiving states moved closer to that of the rest of the country because of increased unskilled immigration or because of preexisting forces leading toward convergence in educational distributions across regions.

We formalize the analysis by estimating regression models designed to measure how the factor proportion of the various skill groups changed within a state over the period 1950–90. We define the change in factor proportions for skill group $k$ in state $j$ as

$$(9) \qquad \Delta p_{jk}(t, t') = \frac{L_{jkt'}}{L_{jt'}} - \frac{L_{jkt}}{L_{jt}},$$

where $L_{jkt}$ gives the number of persons in state $j$ belonging to skill group $k$ at time $t$, and $L_{jt}$ gives the total number of persons living in the state. We define the immigrant contribution to the change in factor proportions over the period as

$$(10) \qquad \Delta \widetilde{m}_{jk}(t, t') = \frac{M_{jkt'}}{L_{jt'}} - \frac{M_{jkt}}{L_{jt}}.$$

Consider the regression model

$$(11) \qquad \Delta p_{jk}(70, 90) = c + d\, \Delta \widetilde{m}_{jk}(70, 90) + v_j + \tau_k + e_{jk},$$

*George J. Borjas, Richard B. Freeman, and Lawrence F. Katz*          35

where $v_j$ is a fixed effect indicating the state of residence and $\tau_k$ is a fixed effect indicating educational attainment. The empirical evidence presented in the previous section indicates that the growth rate of the total population in the state is essentially unrelated to immigration. This implies that one can treat the variable $\Delta \tilde{m}_{jk}(70, 90)$ as exogenous, despite the fact that the right-hand side includes a measure of $L_{j,90}$. The state fixed effect helps to define the immigrant supply shock in terms of within-state deviations, so that the coefficient $d$ measures how factor proportions change within a state when a particular skill group experiences a supply shock.[36] The coefficient $d$ has the interpretation

$$(12) \qquad\qquad d = \frac{L_{j,k,90} - \gamma L_{j,k,70}}{M_{j,k,90} - \gamma M_{j,k,70}},$$

where $\gamma$ equals $L_{j,90}/L_{j,70}$, the state's population growth between 1970 and 1990.[37] If the state's population had not changed over the period ($\gamma$ equal to one), the coefficient $d$ would simply measure the change in the size of the population associated with the entry of an additional immigrant in that educational group ($\Delta L_{jk}/\Delta M_{jk}$). If there were no migration response in the native population, the coefficient $d$ would then be one, while if native migration completely offset the immigrant supply shock, the coefficient would be zero. In fact, the state's population did increase over the period, for reasons independent of immigration. Consequently the coefficient $d$ measures the impact of an additional immigrant on the total population relative to what would be expected if all groups had experienced neutral growth (at the rate $\gamma$) over the period 1970–90.

Table 11 reports the estimated coefficient $d$ for a variety of regression specifications. The first row estimates the first difference model given by equation 11. The coefficient reported in the first column of data

---

36. If there were only two skill groups in the population, $u$ and $s$, the fixed effect model of equation 11 would be numerically equivalent to the regression

$$\Delta p_{ju}(70, 90) - \Delta p_{js}(70, 90) = (\tau_u - \tau_s) + d\,[\Delta \tilde{m}_{ju}(70, 90)$$
$$- \Delta \tilde{m}_{js}(70, 90)] + (e_{ju} - e_{js}),$$

so that the regression would simply estimate how the difference in immigrant supply shocks between the two groups affects the factor proportions within the state.

37. In particular, note that $\Delta p_{jk}(t, t') = (L_{jkt'} - \gamma L_{jkt})/L_{jt'}$ and that $\Delta \tilde{m}_{jk}(t, t') = (M_{jkt'} - \gamma M_{jkt})/L_{jt'}$.

**Table 11. Estimating the Impact of Immigration on State Factor Proportions, 1970–90[a]**

| Skill grouping and specification | Actual population counts | | Efficiency unit counts | |
|---|---|---|---|---|
| | No initial conditions control | With initial conditions control | No initial conditions control | With initial conditions control |
| *Five skill groups[b]* | | | | |
| First differences[c] | 2.772 | 2.654 | 2.172 | 1.956 |
| | (1.247) | (0.767) | (1.129) | (0.458) |
| Double differences[d] | 0.721 | −0.093 | 0.626 | −0.254 |
| | (0.284) | (0.285) | (0.271) | (0.261) |
| *High school dropouts and all others* | | | | |
| First differences[c] | 1.004 | 1.256 | 0.904 | 1.002 |
| | (1.649) | (0.655) | (1.673) | (0.463) |
| Double differences[f] | 1.224 | −0.320 | 0.496 | −0.336 |
| | (0.703) | (0.469) | (0.330) | (0.298) |

Source: Authors' calculations based on data from the census PUMS (various years).

a. For first difference equations, dependent variable is the change over the period 1970–90 in the proportion of people in state $j$ who fall in skill group $k$ [$\Delta p_{jk}(70,90)$]; independent variable is the immigrant contribution to this change in factor proportions [$\Delta \tilde{m}_{jk}(70,90)$]. Double difference equations take the changes in these variables between the periods 1950–70 and 1970–90. Equations are estimated both by using actual populations counts and by using efficiency unit counts, which weigh each person by the typical wage of a person with the same characteristics in 1980. Where indicated, equations control for initial own-group factor proportions as measured in 1950. All equations include fixed effects identifying each region and skill group. Standard errors are shown in parentheses.

b. Fewer than nine years of schooling, ten to eleven years, twelve years, thirteen to fifteen years, and sixteen or more years.

c. $N = 255$.

d. $N = 245$.

e. $N = 102$.

f. $N = 98$.

*George J. Borjas, Richard B. Freeman, and Lawrence F. Katz*          37

suggests that $d$ is strongly positive. An additional immigrant in a given skill group raises the total number of persons in that skill group by 2.8.[38] But we have argued that a more useful counterfactual exercise is to compare the growth rate of a particular skill group before and after the immigrant supply shock. This suggests the alternative double difference regression specification

(13)   $\Delta p_{jk}(70, 90) - \Delta p_{jk}(50, 70)$

$$= \alpha + \delta \left[\Delta \widetilde{m}_{jk}(70, 90) - \Delta \widetilde{m}_{jk}(50, 70)\right] + v_j + \tau_k + e_{jk}.$$

The second row of table 11 shows that the estimated $\delta$ is 0.72. This implies, at most, a moderate native response to immigration within a skill group, indicating that immigration does alter factor proportions within a state.

Our discussion of the raw data describing trends in the differences of skill distributions between geographic regions, as shown in table 10, suggests that the regression models of equations 11 and 13 ignore a factor that played a key role over the period 1950–90: the convergence of skill distributions across states. This process was in operation before the immigrant supply shock began. To control for the convergence, we add to the regression model a variable giving the fraction of the state's adult population that belonged to educational group $k$ in 1950: $L_{j,k,50}/L_{j,50}$. The resulting coefficients from the expanded specification are reported in the second column of table 11.[39] The inclusion of this "initial conditions" variable does not affect the estimated migration effect in the single difference model, but does reduce the impact of immigration on the total supply of workers in a given skill group to zero in the double difference model. In other words, when one controls for the state's preexisting conditions (both in terms of the initial skill distribution and the rate at which this distribution was changing before 1970), the evidence suggests that immigration does not alter the factor proportions of skill groups within a state.

---

38. Card (1997) also reports a positive correlation between the number of immigrants in a particular skill group who entered a local labor market and the number of similarly skilled natives who chose to reside in that labor market in the period 1985–90.

39. The coefficient of the 1950 factor proportion has a strong negative effect in all the models estimated in this section, suggesting the importance of convergence in educational levels across states.

The last two rows of table 11 report the regression results when we redefine skill groups by aggregating to the two groups whose factor proportions are most sensitive to immigration: workers with less than a high school education and workers with at least a high school education. The single difference models consistently yield a strong positive correlation between immigration and changes in factor proportions within these aggregated skill groups, but this positive effect vanishes when we control for the pre-1970 growth rates of the skill groups in the state and for the convergence process.

Finally, we convert the population counts into efficiency units by weighting each person by the relative wage of a person who has similar observed characteristics (that is, sex, age, education, and nationality) in the base period 1980.[40] Calculating supply shifts in terms of efficiency units yields a better measure of changes in the supplies of particular skill groups than the simple population counts used throughout our analysis. We use these efficiency unit counts to reestimate the various specifications; the last two columns of table 11 show that our regression results are not affected.

In sum, the answer to whether immigration affects factor proportions within a state appears to depend on how one specifies the counterfactual of what would have happened absent immigration. Under our preferred specification—which controls for the initial level and past change in state skill distributions—the evidence shows that much of the adverse impact of immigration on the economic opportunities of workers in areas directly affected by the immigrant supply shock was diffused across the country, as native migration flows responded to local influxes of immigrants.[41]

40. We divide the labor force aged eighteen to sixty-four into 280 distinct groups based on sex-age-education-nationality cells (2 sex groups $\times$ 5 age groups $\times$ 4 education groups $\times$ 7 nationality groups = 280 cells). The age groups are eighteen to twenty-four, twenty-five to thirty-four, thirty-five to forty-four, forty-five to fifty-four, and fifty-five to sixty-four; the educational groups are fewer than twelve years of schooling, twelve years, thirteen to fifteen years, and sixteen plus years; and the nationality groups are black U.S. natives, nonblack U.S. natives, Mexican immigrants, other Latin American immigrants, European immigrants, Asian immigrants, and other immigrants. We then calculate the average hourly wage for full-time workers in each cell using the 1980 census PUMS and weight individuals by the estimated average wage for their sex-age-education-nationality cell in 1980.

41. An alternative way to examine the effects of immigration would be to look at

*George J. Borjas, Richard B. Freeman, and Lawrence F. Katz*          39

## The Aggregate Factor Proportions Approach

Trade theorists have long recognized that trade and immigration (and international capital flows) are potentially substitute ways for a country to make use of factors that are scarce within its borders.[42] Nevertheless, empirical studies of trade and immigration have proceeded independently. To the extent that trade and immigration are substitute means of altering effective national factor proportions, it is incorrect to analyze them separately. Examining how changes in trade affect U.S. workers without recognizing that in the absence of trade there will be increased economic incentives for greater immigration (or capital flows) will likely overstate the effects of trade. Examining how immigration affects U.S. workers without recognizing that reduced levels of immigration will create incentives for greater trade (and capital flows) will likely overstate the economic effects of immigration.

In earlier work, we tried to remedy this problem by analyzing how trade and immigration *together* alter the nation's endowments of labor skills.[43] The basic idea of our aggregate factor proportions approach is to compare the nation's actual supplies of skilled and unskilled labor to those it would have had at different levels of immigration or trade; and then to assess the relative wage consequences of these immigration- or trade-induced changes in factor supplies, where the effective factor endowment of a given skill group is the sum of the number of native workers, the number of immigrants, and the number of workers "em-

wages or employment on an occupational basis. Complaints by groups of mathematicians and software engineers about immigrant competition and the American Medical Association's proposal to restrict foreign supply of medical personnel show that native workers in these areas perceive considerable competition from foreign-born workers. There is, however, a major problem in using occupations as a unit of observation over the period covered by the immigration shock: the Census Bureau implemented a major reclassification of occupations between the 1970 and 1980 censuses (U.S. Bureau of the Census, 1989). Our own exploratory work relating occupational earnings to immigrant intensities suggests that empirical results are sensitive to the concordance among the occupations over the period. In our view, an occupations-based approach merits further study as an alternative to the spatial correlations approach, bearing in mind this basic problem. For an insightful study using occupations as the unit of analysis, see Friedberg (1996), who uses data on the occupational distribution of recent Russian immigrants to Israel before and after immigration to examine effects of immigration on Israeli natives.

42. See Mundell (1957) for this view of trade and immigration.
43. Borjas, Freeman, and Katz (1992, 1996).

bodied'' in net imports. We estimate the latter using fixed coefficient factor content calculations.

In its simplest form, our analysis uses a constant elasticity of substitution (CES) aggregate production function with two inputs: skilled labor ($s$) and unskilled labor ($u$). We postulate that relative wages are determined by the intersection of an inelastic (predetermined) short-run relative labor supply function and a downward-sloping relative labor demand function derived from the CES. In this framework, skilled wages relative to unskilled wages in year $t$, $w_{st}/w_{ut}$, will depend on the relative labor supplies in year $t$, $x_{st}/x_{ut}$, and the level of relative labor demand, so that

$$(14) \qquad \ln \frac{w_{st}}{w_{ut}} = \frac{1}{\sigma} \left( D_t - \ln \frac{x_{st}}{x_{ut}} \right),$$

where $\sigma$ is the aggregate elasticity of substitution between skilled and unskilled workers and $D_t$ indexes log relative demand shifts for skilled workers.[44] The impact of a given change in relative skill supplies depends inversely on the magnitude of $\sigma$.

As noted, the national (implicit) supply of skill group $k$ at time $t$ has three components: native workers ($N_{kt}$), immigrant workers ($M_{kt}$), and the effective supply of workers of type $k$ contained in net trade flows ($T_{kt}$):

$$(15) \qquad x_{kt} = N_{kt} + M_{kt} + T_{kt} = N_{kt} \left( 1 + \frac{M_{kt} + T_{kt}}{N_{kt}} \right).$$

The log relative supply of skilled workers is affected by the skill composition of the native work force and the relative contributions of immigration and trade to the supplies of skilled and unskilled workers:

$$(16) \qquad \ln \frac{x_{st}}{x_{ut}} = \ln \frac{N_{st}}{N_{ut}} + \ln \left( 1 + \frac{M_{st} + T_{st}}{N_{st}} \right) - \ln \left( 1 + \frac{M_{ut} + T_{ut}}{N_{ut}} \right).$$

44. The aggregate elasticity of substitution ($\sigma$) reflects not only technical substitution possibilities in production at the firm or industry level, but also consumer substitution possibilities across goods and services. The appropriate value of $\sigma$ for assessing how aggregate changes in relative skill supplies affect relative wages is likely to be substantially larger than the elasticity of substitution in production of skilled and unskilled workers for a representative firm or industry.

We assume that the stock of immigrants at time $t$ is predetermined relative to trade flows. Thus the separate contributions of immigration and trade to the log relative supply of skilled workers, $\ln(x_{st}/x_{ut})$, are given by

$$(17) \quad \text{immigration contribution} = \ln\left(1 + \frac{M_{st}}{N_{st}}\right) - \ln\left(1 + \frac{M_{ut}}{N_{ut}}\right)$$

and

$$(18) \quad \text{trade contribution} = \ln\left(1 + \frac{T_{st}}{L_{st}}\right) - \ln\left(1 + \frac{T_{ut}}{L_{ut}}\right),$$

where $L_{kt} = N_{kt} + M_{kt}$ is the direct labor supply of group $k$ (both native- and foreign-born).

To use equations 14, 17, and 18 to assess how immigration and trade affect the wages of more skilled natives relative to those of less skilled natives, we need the following information: the change in the number of immigrants relative to natives with different levels of skill; the implicit change in skill supplies embodied in trade; and an estimate of the responsiveness of relative wages to relative skill supplies $(1/\sigma)$. We also need to aggregate heterogeneous workers into our aggregates of skilled and of unskilled labor. Since the aggregate factor proportions approach simulates what might have happened to the labor market under different immigration and trade scenarios, we must also carefully specify the counterfactual under consideration.

### When Are Factor Contents Useful?

Under what conditions will this framework provide useful insight into the effects of immigration and trade on the labor market? The first condition is that changes in national relative skill supplies affect national relative wages. If the world economy were sufficiently integrated to create factor price equalization among countries, then relative labor supply conditions in the world would enter the wage determination equation.[45] Neither national demand nor national supply conditions

45. For this argument in relation to the world economy, see Leamer (1996a); and in relation to the Organisation for Economic Co-operation and Development, see Davis (1996) and Krugman (1995a).

would affect relative wages, except to the extent they changed relative demand and supply within the world economy. But a large body of empirical evidence shows that national economic conditions *do* affect relative wages by skill and education. Many time-series studies of the United States find that increases in the (detrended) relative supply of more educated workers are negatively related to changes in the relative wages of more educated workers.[46] Similar correlations have been found for many other countries, including Britain, Canada, South Korea, and Sweden.[47] Canada and the United States have sufficiently separate labor markets that differences in the rates of growth of the relative supply of college-educated workers from the 1970s to the 1980s help to explain the much larger growth in the college–high school wage differential in the United States during the 1980s.[48] More generally, research indicates that levels and changes in relative pay by skill across countries depend substantially on national wage-setting institutions and relative skill supplies.[49]

The second condition is that one can define skill categories to distinguish which groups of immigrants and natives are substitutes or complements. The standard assumption is that persons with the same number of years of schooling are perfect substitutes and those with different levels of schooling are imperfect substitutes (possibly, complements). But immigrants earn less than natives with the same schooling, so perhaps they should be viewed as substitutes for natives with modestly lower education. A sizable number of immigrants have less than nine years of schooling, which could make them complements even for native high school dropouts with nine to eleven years of schooling. And some immigrants work in specialized areas where they may complement natives with similar skills—for example, as language teachers or owners of specialty restaurants.

Determining which groups of immigrants compete with which groups of natives is not a trivial issue. If one uses years of schooling to define skill categories, one obtains different pictures of immigrant effects on factor proportions depending on where one cuts the schooling distri-

46. Freeman (1975); Katz and Murphy (1992); Murphy and Welch (1992).
47. On these countries respectively, see Schmitt (1995), Freeman and Needels (1993), Kim and Topel (1995), and Edin and Holmlund (1995).
48. Freeman and Needels (1993).
49. See, for example, Blau and Kahn (1996) and Freeman and Katz (1994).

*George J. Borjas, Richard B. Freeman, and Lawrence F. Katz*        43

bution. We deal with this problem by specifying competing native groups based both on alternative educational groupings and on the position of immigrants in the native earnings distribution.

The third condition is that the estimate of the effect of trade on national skill proportions captures the full impact of trade on wages. This is a contentious and difficult issue, on which trade economists have divergent views. Some believe that factor content analyses are essentially meaningless; others regard them as a valid measure of potential trade effects on the labor market for modest trade shocks relative to a well-defined baseline scenario. Some argue that all the information needed to assess the effects of trade on the labor market is contained in the prices of traded goods, which have magnified effects on wages, and that actual trade flows are irrelevant. Little did we realize when we wrote our 1992 paper using factor content analysis that the field would become such a battle zone.[50]

There are circumstances under which factor content analyses are justifiable in standard trade models. If one begins with autarky and then allows for trade, and trade is a modest proportion of the national economy, the change in national factor endowments due to the factor content of trade measures the pressure of trade for changes in relative wages.[51] In this scenario, as in our model, the fall of trade barriers creates a flow of tradables whose factor content times the reciprocal of the appropriate elasticity of substitution produces the implied effect of the opening of trade on relative wages.

But there are also circumstances under which the flows of traded goods may bear little or no relation to the pressure from trade on wages. As an extreme case, suppose that an LDC firm begins producing souvenirs of the Empire State building and informs souvenir stands that it can provide products at lower prices than U.S. producers. The souvenir stands will then inform American manufacturers that they have to meet the new price to keep their business. The U.S. firms, in turn, will tell their workers that the firms can stay in business only if the workers take a pay cut. If the workers accept the cut, the U.S. firms will maintain

50. On the problems with factor content analyses, see Leamer (1996b) and Deardorff and Hakura (1994); on their validity, see Deardorff and Staiger (1988), Krugman (1995b), Sachs and Shatz (1994), and Wood (1994, 1995); and on the irrelevance of actual trade flows, see Bhagwati and Dehejia (1994).

51. Deardorff and Staiger (1988); Krugman (1995b).

their hold on the souvenir market, with no new trade flows. But the threat of trade (like the threat of entry in a contestable market) will have reduced wages in the United States. In this example, the only "footprint" of trade is the change in the relative price of souvenirs. This is, in stark form, the argument that trade flows do not accurately reflect trade pressures on the labor market.

This model is difficult to assess empirically, and there have been only limited efforts to do so.[52] The analyst must show, first, that the domestic relative price of goods produced by the less skilled has fallen; and second, that this price change is due to the "unobservable" threat of trade rather than some other factor (for example, differences in sectoral rates of technological change or, as in the 1980s, a fall in the real value of the minimum wage). If foreign goods are imperfect substitutes for U.S.–made goods in the same sector, the analyst must assess the degree of substitutability. In a world in which product and labor demand curves in traded goods are not perfectly elastic at the "going world price" and in which native workers in the traded goods sector may earn some economic rents, trade may also alter the wage structure by making demand curves more elastic and squeezing those rents.[53] Moreover, the model implies that labor skill ratios fall within sectors, as firms substitute toward the low-skill workers displaced from import-competing industries—which is contrary to the observed rise in those ratios.[54] While the price-side model may be hard to estimate, it does suggest that factor content analyses that infer the effect of trade on implicit national factor endowments from observed trade flows are likely to understate the impact of trade on relative wages.[55]

There is yet another area of controversy in factor content analysis. The standard analysis estimates the labor supply embodied in traded goods using current average unit labor coefficients for different skill categories from import-competing and export-producing sectors in the

52. See, for example, Sachs and Shatz (1994), Krueger (1997), and Baldwin and Cain (1997).

53. On the elasticity of demand curves, see Rodrik (1997); on the squeezing of rents, see Borjas and Ramey (1995).

54. See Lawrence and Slaughter (1993), Berman, Bound, and Griliches (1994), and Autor, Katz, and Krueger (1997).

55. Baldwin and Cain (1997) provide a useful examination of the evidence on price effects and find similar modest impacts of trade on U.S. relative wages using both the price and factor content approaches.

George J. Borjas, Richard B. Freeman, and Lawrence F. Katz         45

home economy.[56] But Adrian Wood argues that one should not use unit labor coefficients from current advanced country production relations when assessing the factor content of imports from LDCs to advanced industrial nations.[57] One reason is that within every sector there is a wide distribution of labor input coefficients, reflecting differences in skill intensities of employment, differences in labor productivity, and differentiated products. If LDC trade has driven out the most unskilled labor–intensive modes of production from an import-competing industry, current average labor input coefficients will understate the effect of LDC trade in augmenting the effective supply of less skilled workers in advanced nations. The appropriate labor input coefficients are those for the marginal technologies and products that would expand in import-competing sectors absent this trade. Wood also argues that firms may alter their technologies or input coefficients in response to trade pressures.

We are sympathetic to Wood's argument. As he emphasizes, there is substantial heterogeneity in the relative utilization of less skilled workers (that is, high school dropouts) across plants. Tabulations from the Worker-Establishment Characteristic Database (WECD), an employer-employee matched database for U.S. manufacturing in 1990 compiled by the U.S. Bureau of the Census, show substantial differences in the educational composition of the work force within detailed manufacturing industries.[58] Within the typical three-digit industry, the employment share of high school dropouts in the bottom quarter of plants, ranked by average worker education, is 2.4 times the industry average (0.40 versus 0.17).[59] Mark Doms, Timothy Dunne, and Kenneth Troske find that establishments with less educated workers are much less likely to use new technologies than those with more skilled workers in the same industry. J. Bradford Jensen and Troske find that in most four-digit manufacturing industries in 1992, the ninetieth percentile plant (ranked by labor productivity) had labor productivity that was over three times that of the tenth percentile plant.[60] If LDC imports

56. See, for example, Sachs and Shatz (1994).
57. Wood (1994, 1995).
58. We are grateful to Kenneth Troske for these tabulations. The WECD is documented and described in Troske (1995) and Doms, Dunne, and Troske (1997).
59. The bottom quarter of plants, in terms of average worker education, employ 15 percent of all workers in the typical industry.
60. Doms, Dunne, and Troske (1997); Jensen and Troske (1997).

affect the less skilled and lower productivity segment of a three-digit industry, then the actual increment to the implicit supply of low-skilled workers from such trade flows could easily be three times larger than the estimates based on current average industry skill shares and labor productivity levels.

To address this issue, Wood takes input coefficients from LDCs and adjusts them for relative wages in the United States or western Europe to approximate marginal input coefficients and assumes that, absent trade, technologies would not improve in the traded goods sector. Elsewhere, we use input coefficients averaged over an earlier period (1967–87), but do not examine the sensitivity of results to alternative assumptions.[61] In the present study, we use U.S. input coefficients (skill shares) from past years (1970, 1980, 1990) and carefully specify our assumptions about the technology for producing import-competing and other goods and product demand responses.

### The Facts to Be Explained

It is well documented that educational wage differentials and overall wage inequality have greatly increased in the United States since the late 1970s. Most estimates of changes in educational wage differentials are based on samples containing both U.S. natives and immigrants.[62] Since recent immigrants typically earn less than U.S. natives with the same level of education, the disproportionately growing share of immigrants among less educated workers in the United States means that the usual estimates may overstate changes in relative wages by education for U.S. natives. To assess the contributions of immigration- and trade-induced changes in relative labor supplies on the relative wages of U.S. natives requires estimates of changes in educational wage differentials for U.S. natives alone.

Table 12 presents estimates for three measures of educational wage differentials for natives between 1960 and 1995. The differentials are derived from cross-section regressions of log hourly earnings on five education dummies (zero to eight years of schooling, nine to eleven years, thirteen to fifteen years, sixteen years, and seventeen plus years,

61. Borjas, Freeman, and Katz (1992).
62. See, for example, Bound and Johnson (1992) and Mishel, Bernstein, and Schmitt (1997).

George J. Borjas, Richard B. Freeman, and Lawrence F. Katz     47

**Table 12. Native Log Wage Differentials, by Educational Attainment, 1960–95**[a]
Log point difference

| Year | College graduate relative to high school graduate[b] | College or more relative to high school graduate[c] | High school or more relative to high school dropout[d] |
|------|------|------|------|
| 1960 | 0.319 | 0.317 | 0.280 |
| 1970 | 0.362 | 0.374 | 0.312 |
| 1980 | 0.279 | 0.304 | 0.301 |
| 1990 | 0.412 | 0.458 | 0.374 |
| 1995 | 0.420 | 0.495 | 0.410 |

Source: Authors' calculations. Wage data for 1960–90 actually refer to 1959, 1969, 1979, and 1989 and are from the census PUMS. Wages for 1995 are extrapolated from the 1990 census PUMS, using observed changes between the February 1990 CPS and the 1995 CPS. MORG file.

a. Wages are hourly earnings of full-time native wage and salary workers aged eighteen to sixty-four, adjusted for age, sex, race, and region, as described in the text.

b. Log wage of natives with exactly sixteen years of schooling less that of natives with exactly twelve years.

c. Log wage of natives with sixteen or more years of schooling less that of natives with exactly twelve years.

d. Log wage of natives with twelve or more years of schooling less that of natives with fewer than twelve years.

with twelve years as the base group), a quartic in age, a female dummy, a nonwhite dummy, and three region dummies. Our samples comprise native full-time workers aged eighteen to sixty-four, from the 1960, 1970, 1980, and 1990 census PUMSs and the Merged Outgoing Rotation Group (MORG) file of the 1995 Current Population Survey (CPS) from the Bureau of Labor Statistics. The first column of table 12 displays the log wage gap between workers with exactly sixteen years of schooling (college graduates) and those with exactly twelve years of schooling (high school graduates). The second column expands the college group to include those with advanced degrees. Both measures of the college–high school wage differential expand modestly in the 1960s, contract in the 1970s, and increase substantially in the 1980s. The growth rate in the college–high school wage gap slows down from 1990 to 1995, but the increase over this period remains sizable when those with advanced degrees are included in the college group. The time pattern of changes in the college–high school wage gap for natives is quite similar to estimates for the overall U.S. work force, using samples that include both immigrants and natives.[63]

The last column of table 12 examines the wage of native high school dropouts relative to that of natives with at least twelve years of schooling. High school dropouts are the group most likely to be adversely

63. See, for example, Autor, Katz, and Krueger (1997).

affected by the recent growth of less skilled immigration and trade with LDCs. The relative earnings of native high school dropouts declined by 0.073 log point from 1980 to 1990 and continued to decline at the same rate in the early 1990s.

Note that there has been a decline in the relative wages of less educated workers since 1980, even though the relative supply (of both natives and immigrants) has continued to decline. Table 13 documents changes in the educational composition of direct U.S. labor input (natives plus immigrants), measured in full-time equivalents (or total hours worked), from 1960 to 1995.[64] Although the share of high school dropouts has declined consistently and the share of college equivalents has grown throughout the past thirty-five years, the rate of growth of the relative supply of more educated workers accelerated in the 1970s and decelerated in the 1980s. The slower growth of the relative supply of skills may help to explain the quite different outcomes for relative wages by education in the 1970s and in the 1980s and 1990s illustrated in table 12.

To examine the impact of the supply shifts induced by trade and immigration on native relative wages, we aggregate workers into skill groups in two ways. First, following David Autor, Katz, and Alan Krueger and also George Johnson, we aggregate the labor force into high school equivalents (all workers with twelve or fewer years of schooling and one-half of those with some college education) and college equivalents (all workers with at least a college degree and one-half of those with some college education).[65] Katz and Kevin Murphy show

64. Changes introduced in the 1990 census to the educational attainment question make it difficult to assess accurately changes in relative education supplies over the 1980s using the public use samples of the 1980 and 1990 censuses. The CPS continued to use the old question ("highest grade attended and completed") through 1991. Thus the 1980 and 1990 CPS, MORG files have consistent education coding and can be used to measure changes in relative supplies by educational group. The February 1990 CPS asked individuals about educational attainment with both the new and the old questions. We estimate changes from 1990 to 1995 using the February 1990 CPS and the 1995 CPS, MORG file. Changes from 1990 to 1995 should be interpreted with some caution, because the complete overhaul of the CPS in 1994, with the shift to computer-assisted interviewing, implies the possibility of unknown differences in responses to education questions. We use the coding scheme suggested by Jaeger (1997) for the new census and CPS education codes, classifying workers indicating twelve years of schooling but no degree as high school graduates. The data appendix of Autor, Katz, and Krueger (1997) provides additional information on these issues of data comparability.

65. Autor, Katz, and Krueger (1997); Johnson (1997a).

**Table 13. Distribution of U.S. Workers by Educational Attainment, 1960–95**

Percent

| | | Full-time equivalent employment shares[a] | | | | | |
|---|---|---|---|---|---|---|---|
| *Year* | *Data source* | *High school dropouts*[b] | *High school graduates*[c] | *Some college*[d] | *College graduates*[e] | *College equivalents*[f] | *High school or more*[g] |
| *Levels* | | | | | | | |
| 1960 | Census | 49.5 | 27.7 | 12.2 | 10.6 | 16.7 | ... |
| 1970 | Census | 35.9 | 34.7 | 15.6 | 13.8 | 21.6 | ... |
| 1980 | Census | 20.7 | 36.1 | 22.8 | 20.4 | 31.8 | ... |
| 1980 | CPS, MORG | 19.1 | 38.0 | 22.0 | 20.9 | 31.9 | ... |
| 1990 | CPS, MORG | 12.7 | 36.2 | 25.1 | 26.1 | 38.6 | ... |
| 1990 | Census | 11.4 | 33.0 | 30.2 | 25.4 | 40.6 | ... |
| 1990 | CPS, February | 11.5 | 36.8 | 25.2 | 26.5 | 39.1 | ... |
| 1995 | CPS, MORG | 9.0 | 33.7 | 29.4 | 27.9 | 42.6 | ... |
| *Changes in log relative employment*[h] | | | | | | | |
| 1960–70 | Census | ... | ... | ... | ... | 3.19 | 5.62 |
| 1970–80 | Census | ... | ... | ... | ... | 5.26 | 7.61 |
| 1980–90 | CPS, MORG | ... | ... | ... | ... | 2.94 | 4.86 |
| 1990–95 | CPS, February to MORG | ... | ... | ... | ... | 2.94 | 5.41 |

Source: Autor, Katz, and Krueger (1997, table 1).

a. Hours worked by workers (natives and immigrants) in given skill group as proportion of all hours worked.

b. Fewer than twelve years of schooling.

c. Exactly twelve years of schooling.

d. Thirteen to fifteen years of schooling.

e. Sixteen or more years of schooling.

f. All those with sixteen or more years of schooling plus half of those with some college.

g. Twelve or more years of schooling.

h. Average annual log changes ( × 100) in relative full-time equivalent employment shares.

that detrended changes in the supplies of similar aggregates of college equivalents relative to high school equivalents do a reasonable job of explaining changes in a broad measure of the college–high school wage differentials such as that presented in the second column of table 12.[66] They estimate a version of equation 14 and find the elasticity of the relative wage of college graduates to changes in the relative supply of college equivalents is approximately $-0.709$ (implying an economy-wide estimate of the elasticity of substitution between college equivalents and high school equivalents, $\sigma$, of 1.41). Thus we calculate immigration- and trade-induced changes in the relative supplies of college and high school equivalents and examine the implied relative wage effects using the Katz-Murphy estimate of the wage elasticity.

Second, we divide the labor force into high school dropouts and all other workers and use an estimated wage elasticity for the response of the relative wage of dropouts to their relative supply of $-0.322$, from time-series estimates covering the period 1963–87 that we report in an earlier study.[67]

We address compositional changes within our broad educational groups by adjusting the changes in hours by skill group into efficiency units, by weighting each individual's hours by the average wage of an individual with similar observed characteristics (that is, sex, age, education, and nationality) in a base period (1980).[68]

### The Effect of Immigration on Relative Labor Supplies

Table 14 shows our estimates of the contribution of immigration to labor supply in efficiency units by broad educational groups from 1960 to 1995. The first two columns display the immigrant-to-native effi-

66. Katz and Murphy (1992).
67. Borjas, Freeman, and Katz (1992).
68. Katz and Murphy (1992) provide a justification for this efficiency units approach to aggregation in measuring how relative supply and demand shifts affect relative wages by skill group. In the present study, we divide the labor force aged eighteen to sixty-four into 280 distinct groups based on sex-age-education-nationality cells (2 sex groups × 5 age groups × 4 education groups × 7 nationality groups = 280 cells). We calculate the average hourly wage for full-time workers in each cell using the 1 percent random sample from the 1980 census PUMS for natives and 5 percent random sample from the 1980 census PUMS for immigrants. Thus we weight each individual's annual hours of work by the estimated average wage for their sex-age-education-nationality cell in 1980. See note 40 for more details on the definition of the groups.

**Table 14. Immigrant Contribution to Labor Supply, by Educational Attainment, 1960–95**

Ratio

| Sample and year | Immigrant-to-native ratio[a] | | | | | |
|---|---|---|---|---|---|---|
| | High school dropouts versus graduates | | | High school versus college equivalents | | |
| | Dropouts[b] | Graduates[c] | Log gap[d] | High school[e] | College[f] | Log gap[d] |
| **All immigrants** | | | | | | |
| 1960 | 0.088 | 0.051 | 0.035 | 0.068 | 0.061 | 0.007 |
| 1970 | 0.069 | 0.046 | 0.022 | 0.051 | 0.059 | −0.007 |
| 1980 | 0.109 | 0.058 | 0.047 | 0.063 | 0.073 | −0.009 |
| 1990 | 0.242 | 0.079 | 0.141 | 0.094 | 0.090 | 0.004 |
| 1995 | 0.383 | 0.083 | 0.244 | 0.107 | 0.090 | 0.015 |
| **Post-1979 immigrants[g]** | | | | | | |
| 1995 | 0.207 | 0.041 | 0.149 | 0.056 | 0.043 | 0.013 |

Source: Authors' calculations. Data for 1960–90 are from the census PUMS (various years); and for 1995, from the 1995 CPS, MORG file.
a. Ratios are in efficiency units, which weigh each worker by hours worked times the typical wage of a worker of the same age, sex, nationality, and education in 1980.
b. Fewer than twelve years of schooling.
c. At least twelve years of schooling.
d. $\ln(1 + M_{st}/N_{st}) - \ln(1 + M_{ut}/N_{ut})$, where $M$ and $N$ are, respectively, immigrant and native workers (in efficiency units), and $u$ and $s$ refer, respectively, to the lesser and greater of the two categories of educational attainment being compared.
e. All of those with twelve or fewer years of schooling plus half of those with some college.
f. All of those with sixteen or more years of schooling plus half of those with some college.
g. Immigrants who arrived before 1980 are treated as natives.

ciency unit ratios $(M/N)$ for high school dropouts and those with at least twelve years of schooling. The third column follows equation 17 in presenting the immigration contribution to the log supply of dropouts relative to more educated workers. The estimates for all immigrants in table 14 show the growing contribution of immigration to the supply of high school dropouts, especially since 1980; the ratio of immigrants to natives among dropouts increased from 0.109 in 1980 to 0.383 in 1995.[69] These changes reflect both the rapid decline of the share of native labor force participants who are dropouts and the increased immigration since 1980, while there was little decline in the share of immigrant workers who have less than twelve years of schooling.

Some of the growth shown in table 14 in the immigrant contribution to the relative supply of dropouts since 1980 would have occurred even if immigration had been cut off in 1980. This is because of differences in the age structure of less educated immigrants and natives in 1980. To determine the effect on the labor supply by education of those immigrants who entered after 1979, in the last row of table 14 we treat all immigrants living in the United States before 1980 as natives. Post-1979 immigrants increased the relative supply of dropouts in 1995 by 0.149 log point, which is 0.048 log point smaller than the 0.197 log point increase from 1980 to 1995 shown in the upper panel of the table.

With our preferred relative wage elasticity for dropouts of $-0.322$, the estimates in the first three columns of table 14 imply that the immigrant contribution to the relative supply of dropouts can explain a change in the wage of dropouts relative to that of nondropouts of be-

69. The Census Bureau switched its approach to adjusting sampling weights by age, sex, race or Hispanic origin, and state starting with the implementation of the revised CPS survey in 1994. Barry Edmonston has pointed out to us, in personal communication, that demographers have raised concerns that the official sampling weights may underweight the Asian and American Indian populations by 30 percent or more in the 1995 CPS. Since Asians are disproportionately immigrants, and more educated than the typical immigrant, our tabulations of immigrant employment and efficiency unit shares from the 1995 CPS, MORG file may slightly overestimate the relative contribution of immigrants to less educated skill groups in comparison with more educated skill groups. We checked the sensitivity of all our findings from the 1995 CPS increasing the relative weights of Asians and American Indians in the sample by 30 percent. The effects of this adjustment are modest in every case and lead to no substantive changes in our conclusions. For example, the log relative supply contribution of immigrants to dropouts declines from 0.244 to 0.243 and the log relative supply contribution of immigrants to high school equivalents declines from 0.015 to 0.012, when the 1995 CPS sample is reweighted in this manner.

tween $-0.048$ and $-0.063$ log point from 1980 to 1995. Thus the factor proportions approach, treating immigrant and native efficiency units within the dropout and graduate skill categories as perfect substitutes, implies that immigration-induced changes in labor supply may account for 44 to 58 percent of the 0.109 log point decline in the relative earnings of dropouts over this period.

The last three columns of table 14 reveal only modest effects of immigration on the supply of high school equivalents relative to college equivalents. Since the education distribution of immigrants is bimodal—many have less than twelve years of schooling and many have college and advanced degrees—the effect of immigration on relative skill supplies is greatly diminished when one aggregates workers into high school and college equivalent workers. The estimate for all immigrants puts the immigration impact on the relative supply of high school equivalents at 0.024 log point from 1980 to 1995. The estimate for post-1979 immigrants indicates that these expanded the relative supply of high school equivalents by 0.013 log point in 1995. Using our preferred relative wage elasticity of $-0.709$, we estimate that the contribution of immigration to changes in the college–high school wage differential from 1980 to 1995 ranges from 0.009 to 0.017 log point; or 5 to 9 percent of the actual 0.191 log point increase in the college–high school wage differential for U.S. natives over this period.

We conclude that the immigrant-induced increases in relative labor supply are strongly concentrated on U.S. workers with fewer than twelve years of schooling and that the slowdown in the rate of decline of the relative supply of dropouts due to unskilled immigration may explain a sizable fraction of the decline in the earnings of dropouts relative to those with twelve or more years of schooling over the period 1980–95. In contrast, the immigrant supply contribution for a broader group of less educated workers is too small to account for even 10 percent of the sharp growth in the college–high school wage differential during this period.

In our assessment of the immigrant contribution to changes in skill supplies, we classify workers into skill groups by years of schooling. Under this approach, the impact of less skilled immigration on the relative supply of less educated natives is magnified by the rapidly declining share of high school dropouts in the native labor force. But low-wage and less skilled immigrants may compete with a broader group of low-wage natives than native high school dropouts. As an alternative way to measure immigrant-induced changes in labor market competition, we classify workers into skill groups based on their hourly wages rather than level of education. We sort workers by wages in each year (1980, 1990, and 1995) and define skill groups by percentile cut-off points in the native wage distribution.[70] We focus on two aggregation schemes: (a) workers with wages above and below the twentieth percentile of the native wage distribution (since the share of dropouts in the labor force in 1980, when the large immigration shock began, was approximately 20 percent); and (b) workers with wages above and below the sixtieth percentile of the native wage distribution (a group close in size to high school equivalents in 1980). Immigrant contributions to the relative supply of these two groups are determined by the difference in the ratio of immigrants to natives above and below the cut-off point in the native wage distribution defining the low- and high-skill aggregates. Thus we compare how the growth of immigration differentially affects fixed shares of low- and high-wage natives.

Table 15 presents our estimates of immigrant-induced supply shifts by skill groups defined by percentiles of the native wage distribution. It indicates that immigrants are increasingly concentrated in the lower parts of the native wage distribution. For all immigrants, the table shows that the log relative supply contribution of immigrants to the bottom 20 percent of natives relative to the upper 80 percent increased from 0.030 log point to 0.130 log point between 1980 and 1995. The lower panel shows that immigrants who arrived since 1980 expanded the relative supply of the bottom 20 percent of native workers in 1995 by a similar amount, 0.094 log point. Comparing these results with those in table 14, we conclude that the post-1979 immigration relative supply increment to less-skilled labor is modestly lower when measured relative to a fixed share of low-wage natives rather than relative to the declining share of high school dropouts. The contribution of recent immigrants to the relative supply of workers earning wages below the sixtieth native percentile is actually somewhat larger than the immigrant

---

70. Specifically, we adjust wages for differences in sex, age, and region. For each year, we run a regression of log hourly wages of U.S. natives on a quartic in age, a female dummy, an interaction of age and the female dummy, and three region dummies. We then sort both natives and immigrants by their adjusted log hourly wages (actual log hourly wage less the predicted wage from this native wage regression).

**Table 15. Immigrant Contribution to the Labor Supply, by Wage Group, 1980–95**

Ratio

| | Immigrant-to-native ratio[a] | | | | | |
|---|---|---|---|---|---|---|
| | Twentieth percentile wage cut | | | Sixtieth percentile wage cut | | |
| *Sample and year* | *Bottom 20 percent* | *Top 80 percent* | *Log gap*[b] | *Bottom 60 percent* | *Top 40 percent* | *Log gap*[b] |
| All immigrants | | | | | | |
| 1980 | 0.094 | 0.062 | 0.030 | 0.075 | 0.058 | 0.016 |
| 1990 | 0.149 | 0.085 | 0.057 | 0.110 | 0.079 | 0.028 |
| 1995 | 0.229 | 0.079 | 0.130 | 0.136 | 0.069 | 0.060 |
| Post-1979 immigrants[c] | | | | | | |
| 1995 | 0.145 | 0.042 | 0.094 | 0.084 | 0.032 | 0.049 |

Source: Authors' calculations. Data for 1980–90 are from the census PUMS (various years); and for 1995, from the 1995 CPS, MORG file.

a. Ratio is hours worked by immigrants divided by hours worked by natives. Wage groups sort workers on the basis of whether their adjusted wages are above or below the wage received by natives in the given percentile of the adjusted wage distribution for natives. Wages are adjusted for age, sex, and region.

b. $\ln(1 + M_{nl}/N_{nl}) - \ln(1 + M_{sl}/N_{sl})$, where $M$ and $N$ are, respectively, the number of immigrant and native worker-hours, and $n$ and $s$ refer, respectively, to those in the lower and higher wage groups being compared.

c. Immigrants who arrived before 1980 are treated as natives.

effect on the relative supply of high school equivalents, since a disproportionate number of college-educated immigrants earn relatively low
wages.

Both the educational group and wage group approaches to measuring
the effects of immigrants on relative skill supplies may overstate the
effects of immigrant competition on low-skill natives. If immigrants
and natives with similar education, or wages, or both operate in partially
segmented labor markets, changes in immigrant supply may have little
impact on native wages. The growing share of immigrants in the lower
part of the native wage distribution may reflect declining labor market
conditions due to immigrant crowding into a segmented immigrant labor
market, rather than increased competition for low-wage natives. It is
difficult to assess this alternative hypothesis within our framework.
However, David Jaeger presents some aggregate and metropolitan area–
level data from the 1980 and 1990 censuses indicating that changes in
the relative supply of immigrants to natives within sex-education groups
have little effect on the immigrant-native wage gap for a given group.[71]
This evidence suggests that immigrants and natives may be nearly perfect substitutes in production within broad educational groups (as we
assume in our education-based approach).

### The Effect of LDC Trade on Implicit Relative Labor Supplies

We next examine the extent to which increased trade between the
United States and less developed countries has implicitly augmented
the relative supply of less skilled workers in the U.S. labor market.
The growth of such trade has accelerated in the 1990s, with LDC
imports as a percentage of GDP rising from 2.3 percent in 1980 to 2.8
percent in 1990 and to 4.1 percent in 1996. Trade in manufactures with
less developed countries has the potential to affect less skilled U.S.
workers adversely, since, as illustrated in table 4, LDC imports are
concentrated in industries that disproportionately employ less educated
workers and exports to LDCs are found in industries that are much more
skill intensive. If the impact of LDC trade is concentrated on industries
disproportionately employing high school dropouts, and if the appropriate skill coefficients to assess the effects of such trade on the nation's
factor proportions differ greatly from the average skill coefficients used

71. Jaeger (1995).

in most factor content studies, LDC trade may have a significant effect on the least skilled workers, whose relative wages have been falling sharply.[72]

We examine the implications of eliminating trade with LDCs in manufactures, using equation 18 under different assumptions concerning the skill-intensity and productivity of U.S. production that would replace LDC imports. We first follow the standard practice of estimating the labor supply embodied in both LDC and developed country trade flows in a given year, using that year's average unit labor coefficients for different skill groups of U.S. production in the three-digit manufacturing industries in which the imports and exports arise. More precisely, we estimate the implicit labor supply (in efficiency units) of skill group $k$ embodied in trade in manufactures in year $t$ as

$$(20) \qquad T_{kt} = \sum_l e_{klt} L_{lt} \frac{TR_{lt}}{S_{lt}},$$

where $e_{klt}$ is the proportion of group $k$ (in labor efficiency units) in industry $l$ in year $t$; $L_{lt}$ is the total labor efficiency units used in industry $l$ in year $t$; and $TR_{lt}/S_{lt}$ is the ratio of imports less exports to shipments for industry $l$ in year $t$. The proportional impact of trade on the labor supply of skill group $k$ in year $t$ is then given by $T_{kt}/L_{kt}$, where $L_{kt}$ is the total efficiency units of group $k$ (both natives and immigrants) employed in the aggregate U.S. labor market in year $t$.[73]

We examine imports by source country and exports by receiving country for manufactures measured at the three-digit industry level. We classify western European countries (except Greece and Portugal), Australia, New Zealand, Japan, and Canada as developed countries and we include U.S. trade flows with all other countries in the LDC trade flow aggregate.

Table 16 shows the effect of LDC and developed country trade on

---

72. Thus analyses that aggregate workers into categories such as high school and college equivalents or production and nonproduction workers and assume that LDC imports displace domestic production at average current sectoral factor ratios (for example, Sachs and Shatz, 1994; Krugman, 1995a; and Lawrence, 1996) may understate the impact of LDC trade on the smaller but highly exposed group of least skilled workers (that is, high school dropouts).

73. Since overall U.S. trade and trade with LDCs in manufactures are not balanced, we implicitly assume that any scale (aggregate demand) effects of trade deficits have skill-neutral effects on labor demand.

**Table 16. Implicit Contribution of Trade to Labor Supply, by Skill Group, 1980–90[a]**

Ratio

| Year and trading partners[c] | Ratio of trade-embodied labor to total labor[b] | | | | | |
| --- | --- | --- | --- | --- | --- | --- |
| | High school dropouts versus graduates | | | High school versus college equivalents | | |
| | Dropouts[d] | Graduates[c] | Log gap[f] | High school[g] | College[h] | Log gap[f] |
| 1980 | | | | | | |
| LDCs | 0.0012 | −0.0026 | 0.0038 | −0.0014 | −0.0027 | 0.0013 |
| Developed countries | 0.0043 | 0.0012 | 0.0031 | 0.0029 | −0.0003 | 0.0032 |
| 1990 | | | | | | |
| LDCs | 0.0135 | 0.0031 | 0.0103 | 0.0068 | 0.0016 | 0.0052 |
| Developed countries | 0.0054 | 0.0023 | 0.0031 | 0.0044 | 0.0007 | 0.0037 |

Source: Authors' calculations. Data on skill group shares and industry employment are from the census PUMS (various years); and on industry shipments, from the NBER Productivity Database. Also (see note a) Sachs and Shatz (1994) and Autor, Krueger, and Katz (1997).

a. Imports (by country of origin) and exports (by receiving country) in manufactures are allocated to a consistent set of set of three-digit Census of Population industries, using trade flow data from Sachs and Shatz and industry code concordances from Autor, Katz, and Krueger. 1980 trade flows by country and industry are proxied by 1978 trade flows.

b. Estimated as $T_{kt}/L_{kt}$, where $T_{kt}$, trade-embodied labor, is $T_{kt} = \sum_i e_{kit} L_{it}(TR_{it}/S_{it})$; $e_{kit}$ is the fraction of all workers in industry $i$ at time $t$ who fall in skill group $k$; $L$ represents total labor; and $TR/S$ is the ratio of imports less exports to shipments. Labor is measured in efficiency units, which weight each worker by hours worked times the typical wage of a worker of the same age, sex, nationality, and education in 1980.

c. Developed country trade includes trade with western Europe (except Greece and Portugal), Australia, New Zealand, Japan, and Canada. LDC trade includes all other trade flows.

d. Fewer than twelve years of schooling.

e. At least twelve years of schooling.

f. $\ln(1 + T_{ut}/L_{ut}) - \ln(1 + T_{st}/L_{st})$, where $u$ and $s$ refer, respectively, to the lesser and the greater of the two categories of educational attainment being compared.

g. All of those with twelve or fewer years of schooling plus half of those with some college.

h. All of those with sixteen or more years of schooling plus half of those with some college.

labor supply by education in 1980 and 1990, using the contemporary average unit labor coefficients and following the approach of equation 18. The implicit relative labor supply effects of trade are quite small in 1980 and increase only modestly (0.007 log point) from 1980 to 1990. There is no noticeable change in the impact of trade with developed countries on relative labor supplies in this period. We therefore conclude that it is likely that any possible "action" in trade's impacts on different skill groups in the United States will be found in the growing trade with LDCs—specifically, in the surge of 1990–95—and will only be substantial if LDC trade displaces activities that use less skilled labor much more intensively than is reflected in contemporary industry average labor skill coefficients.

Table 17 presents estimates of the implicit effect of LDC trade on labor supply by skill in 1980, 1990, and 1995, under three alternative counterfactuals: "low," "middle," and "high". In all three counterfactuals, we assume that the reduction in domestic production from the elimination of exports to LDCs would occur at contemporary industry average skill shares and labor productivity. Andrew Bernard and Jensen document that exporting plants are more productive and employ a substantially larger share of more skilled (nonproduction) workers, on average, than other plants within the same four-digit industry.[74] The marginal production affected by reductions in exports is likely to be that of plants in the lower part of the skill and labor productivity distribution of exporting plants. The average skill shares and productivity in the industry may be a reasonable proxy for these marginal exporting plants. The low counterfactual follows table 16 in assuming that imports and exports both embody labor supply at contemporary industry average skill intensities and productivity. The middle counterfactual assumes that the implicit labor efficiency units from LDC imports in each three-digit industry are replaced by domestic production using production methods lagged by ten to fifteen years, which typically utilize a larger share of less educated labor than contemporary industry average skill shares. The high counterfactual assumes that domestic production replaces LDC imports by using average industry skill shares and labor productivity from 1970 (before the growth of LDC imports in manufactures), and that consumers have inelastic demand for the goods, so

74. Bernard and Jensen (1995).

**Table 17. Implicit Contribution of LDC Trade to Labor Supply, Alternative Counterfactuals, 1980–95[a]**

Ratio

| Year and counterfactual[k] | Ratio of LDC trade-embodied labor to total labor[b] | | | | | |
| | High school dropouts versus graduates | | | High school versus college equivalents | | |
| | Dropouts[d] | Graduates[c] | Log gap[f] | High school[g] | College[h] | Log gap[i] |
| --- | --- | --- | --- | --- | --- | --- |
| **1980** | | | | | | |
| Low | 0.0012 | −0.0026 | 0.0038 | −0.0014 | −0.0027 | 0.0013 |
| Middle | 0.0060 | −0.0036 | 0.0096 | −0.0008 | −0.0038 | 0.0030 |
| High | 0.0094 | −0.0022 | 0.0116 | 0.0013 | −0.0028 | 0.0041 |
| **1990** | | | | | | |
| Low | 0.0135 | 0.0031 | 0.0103 | 0.0068 | 0.0016 | 0.0052 |
| Middle | 0.0235 | 0.0019 | 0.0213 | 0.0093 | −0.0012 | 0.0105 |
| High | 0.0824 | 0.0199 | 0.0595 | 0.0395 | 0.0095 | 0.0293 |
| **1995** | | | | | | |
| Low | 0.0253 | 0.0040 | 0.0210 | 0.0110 | 0.0014 | 0.0095 |
| Middle | 0.0416 | 0.0022 | 0.0386 | 0.0149 | −0.0022 | 0.0169 |
| High | 0.1372 | 0.0273 | 0.1016 | 0.0609 | 0.0163 | 0.0429 |

Source: Authors' calculations for 1980 and 1990 are based on the data used for table 16. For 1995, imports-to-sales ratios by industry equal 1990 imports-to-sales ratios times 1.413 (the ratio of the LDC imports–to–GDP ratio in 1995 to the same ratio in 1990); and exports-to-sales ratios are 1990 ratios multiplied by 1.415. to adjust for growth in the LDC exports–to–GDP ratio from 1990 to 1995. Data on skill group shares and industry employment for 1995 are from the 1995 CPS, MORG file.

a. See table 16, note c for definition of LDC trade, and also note a.

b. Estimated as $T_{It}/L_{t}$. where $T_{It}$ trade-embodied labor. is $TM_{It} - TX_{It}$. $TM_{It}$ is $\sum_{I}c_{Ibt}b_{It}(IM_{It}/S_{It})$. where $c_{Ibt}$ is the fraction of all workers in industry $I$ in base year $b$ who fall in skill group $k$; $p_{It}$ is the productivity adjustment taken as part of the counterfactual; $L$ represents labor, in efficiency units; $IM$ is imports; and $S$ is shipments. $TX_{It}$ is $\sum_{I}c_{Ibt}b_{It}(EX_{It}/S_{It})$. where $EX$ is exports.

c. The "low" counterfactuals use contemporary skill shares and productivity for both imports and exports as in table 16 for 1990 and 1980, but assume 1990 factor ratios for imports in 1995. The "middle" counterfactuals allocate efficiency units in imports in industry $I$ in year $t$. $L_{It}(IM_{It}/S_{It})$. to skill groups using 1980 average skill shares in that industry ($b = 1980$) for 1980 and 1995. and 1970 average skill shares ($b = 1970$) for 1980. Thus $p_{It} = 1$ in the middle counterfactuals. The "high" counterfactual allocates imports in industry $I$ to skill groups using 1970 average skill shares in $I$ ($b = 1970$) and adjusts upward the total efficiency units used to replace imports in order to keep output constant. assuming no productivity growth from the base year to $t$. Thus $p_{It} = (L_{It}/Q_{It}/(L_{It}/Q_{It}))$ in the high counterfactuals. All counterfactuals use contemporary average skill shares and productivity for industry $I$.

d. Fewer than twelve years of schooling.

e. At least twelve years of schooling.

f. $\ln(1 + T_{st}/L_{st}) - \ln(1 + T_{ut}/L_{ut})$. where $u$ and $s$ refer. respectively. to the lesser and the greater of the two categories of educational attainment being compared.

g. All of those with twelve or fewer years of schooling plus half of those with some college.

h. All of those with sixteen or more years of schooling plus half of those with some college.

that the increase in domestic output to replace imports equals the real output contained in imports. The assumptions of no technological progress since 1970 and inelastic consumer demand are extreme. We believe that the middle counterfactual is the most realistic of the three.

The estimates of the impact on relative labor supplies of LDC trade under the middle and high counterfactuals in table 17 suggest much greater effects of the growth of LDC trade on educational wage differentials than does the assumption that LDC trade displaces domestic output at current average unit labor input coefficients. The middle and high counterfactuals imply that LDC trade augmented the relative supply of dropouts by 0.04 to 0.10 log point in 1995.[75] Under these assumptions, the elimination of LDC trade in 1995 would have increased the relative wage of dropouts by 0.012 to 0.033 log point, given our assumed relative wage elasticity of $-0.322$. The effects are larger than in table 16, but still modest, for the supply of high school equivalents relative to college equivalents under our preferred middle counterfactual.

## Summarizing the Contributions of Immigration and Trade

Table 18 summarizes our aggregate factor proportions estimates of the contributions of the post-1979 immigration and LDC trade shocks to changes in educational wage differentials from 1980 to 1995, under different assumptions about the responsiveness of relative wages to changes in relative skill supplies. We examine the counterfactual of cutting off all immigration and all growth in trade flows with LDCs in January 1, 1980. Thus we present the implied wage effects of 1995 changes in skill supplies of immigrants who arrived after 1979 and of the implicit labor supplies embodied in the change in LDC trade flows between 1980 and 1995.

75. Our estimates of the effects of LDC trade on the implicit relative supply of high school dropouts in 1990 under the high counterfactual are roughly similar to Wood's (1995) estimates of the impact of LDC trade on unskilled workers for the same year, using adjusted LDC–based labor input coefficients. Wood estimates that LDC trade reduced the demand for skilled relative to unskilled workers in manufactures by 21.5 percent (0.20 log point). If we normalize our implicit labor supply effects of LDC trade in 1990 by labor efficiency units by skill group in manufacturing, rather than in the entire economy, we obtain an relative labor supply increasing effect (and relative labor demand decreasing effect) for high school dropouts of 18 percent (0.165 log point).

**Table 18. Estimated Contributions of Immigration and LDC Trade to Growth in Log Wage Differentials, 1980–95[a]**

Log points, except as indicated

| | Wage comparison | | | | | |
|---|---|---|---|---|---|---|
| | High school graduates versus dropouts | | | College versus high school graduates | | |
| Item | | | | | | |
| Assumed wage elasticity | −0.2 | −0.322 | −0.4 | −0.5 | −0.709 | −1 |
| Actual change, 1980–95 | 0.109 | 0.109 | 0.109 | 0.191 | 0.191 | 0.191 |
| Estimated contribution | | | | | | |
| Post-1979 immigration | 0.030 | 0.048 | 0.060 | 0.007 | 0.009 | 0.013 |
| LDC trade | 0.006 | 0.009 | 0.012 | 0.007 | 0.010 | 0.014 |
| Immigration plus trade | 0.036 | 0.057 | 0.072 | 0.014 | 0.019 | 0.027 |
| Percent contribution[b] | | | | | | |
| Post-1979 immigration | 27 | 44 | 55 | 3 | 5 | 7 |
| LDC trade | 6 | 8 | 11 | 4 | 5 | 7 |
| Immigration plus trade | 33 | 52 | 66 | 7 | 10 | 14 |

Source: Authors' calculations based on model described in text. Actual changes in log wage differentials are from table 12. Contribution of post-1979 immigration to labor supply is from table 14. Contribution of LDC trade to labor supply is a difference over 1980–95, from table 17, using the middle counterfactual.

a. Wage differentials are measured as differences in adjusted log wages, as described in the text. Actual change in differentials is expressed in log points, as are individual contributions.

b. Log point contribution of item as percentage of actual log point change, 1980–95.

This table highlights the fact that immigration has a much larger impact on U.S. native high school dropouts than does LDC trade. The impact of post-1979 immigrants on relative skill supplies can explain a 0.030 to 0.060 log point decline (27 to 55 percent of the actual decline) in the relative wages of high school dropouts over 1980–95, depending on the wage elasticity chosen. Increased LDC trade, under our preferred middle counterfactual and the −0.322 wage elasticity, explains less than 10 percent of the declining relative wage of dropouts. The table also shows that immigration and LDC trade have similar, relatively modest effects on the college–high school wage differential. In combination, they probably account for no more than 10 percent of the large, 0.191 log point increase in this differential from 1980 to 1995.

This paper asks how much immigration and trade affect labor market outcomes. Our answer is that the impact of increased immigration and LDC trade on the labor market does not explain much of the increase in the college wage premium or overall wage inequality in the United States. Other factors—such as an acceleration of skill-biased technological change, a slowdown in the growth of the relative supply of college graduates, and institutional changes in the labor market—are probably more important than immigration and trade in explaining the widening of the U.S. wage structure since the late 1970s. But the concentration of immigration and trade at the lower end of the skill distribution does explain an important part of the decline in the relative wage of high school dropouts. The reason is that a disproportionate share of immigrants has less than a high school education, and a disproportionate and rising share of imports is from sectors that employ such workers. Moreover, as in our earlier work, we find that immigration has a larger impact on less educated workers than does trade.[76]

### Toward a Full Accounting of the Effects of Immigration

In standard models of immigration and trade, the income losses of natives who compete with immigrants or with imports are more than matched by the income gains of natives whose skills or capital complement those of immigrants or of imports. How large might these effects be? Since capital is a likely beneficiary of immigration, we take a step toward a fuller accounting of the distributional effects of immigration by extending our two-input (skilled and unskilled labor) model to incorporate capital as a third factor. We use this extended model to simulate the distributional and efficiency impacts of the post-1979 immigration flow and to check whether the conclusion that immigration explains much of the declining relative wage of high school dropouts holds up in such a framework.[77]

Suppose that one can represent the U.S. economy by an aggregate production function $f[K, bN, (1 - b)N]$, where $K$ is capital, $N$ gives the number of workers, and $b$ gives the fraction of workers who are skilled. We assume that the production function has constant returns to scale and that natives own the capital stock. Then in a preimmigration regime, the national income accruing to native workers is

$$(20) \qquad Q_N = f_k K + f_s b N + f_U (1 - b) N,$$

76. Borjas, Freeman, and Katz (1992).

77. We concentrate on immigration both because our analysis suggests that the distributional effects of immigration are larger than those of trade and because the persistent trade imbalances and large volume of intraindustry trade mean that a full accounting of trade's effects would take us far beyond the labor market focus of this paper.

where $f_i$ is the marginal product of input $i$, and $S$ and $U$ represent skilled and unskilled labor, respectively. The total increase in national income accruing to natives when the United States admits $M$ immigrants equals

$$(21) \qquad \Delta Q_N = \left( K\, \frac{\partial f_K}{\partial M} + bN\, \frac{\partial f_S}{\partial M} + (1-b)N\, \frac{\partial f_U}{\partial M} \right) M.$$

Assume that a fraction $\beta$ of immigrants are skilled. Suppose, initially, that capital is infinitely elastic, so that $\partial f_K/\partial M$ is zero. Then if $\beta$ equals $b$, immigration does not alter the relative factor ratio in the United States and natives neither lose nor gain from immigration ($\Delta Q_N$ is zero because all the terms in equation 21 vanish). Because the price of capital is fixed, immigration can only affect native incomes when $\beta$ does not equal $b$. The United States has been admitting immigrants who, on average, are less skilled than native workers. Thus $\beta$ is less than $b$, and there are both gains and losses from immigration; the winners are the skilled workers and the losers are the unskilled workers. The net gain to natives, however, is positive.[78]

Some studies of immigration assume that the capital stock (rather than the price of capital) is fixed. In this case, there would be a net gain to the United States from immigration, even when $\beta$ equaled $b$. The gains would accrue to native-owned capital. In terms of equation 21, $K\,\partial f_K/\partial M$ would be positive, and the gains to skilled and unskilled workers would depend on the own effects of shifts in supply, as well as on the cross-effects among the three inputs.

Equation 21 can be evaluated numerically if one makes assumptions about the responsiveness of factor prices to an increase in immigrant labor supply. We simulate the model in this equation by using the two polar assumptions about capital and a set of assumptions about the responsiveness of factor prices to immigration. In particular, let $\epsilon_{ij}$ be the factor price elasticity $\partial \ln f_i/\partial \ln X_j$, where $X_j$ is the quantity of input $j$. Daniel Hamermesh surveys an extensive literature that attempts to estimate these elasticities.[79] We used a variety of assumptions about these elasticities from the range that he provides. The simulation pre-

78. Borjas (1995) discusses the economic benefits from immigration using this framework and presents a more detailed discussion of the algebra underlying the simulations presented below.
79. Hamermesh (1993).

*George J. Borjas, Richard B. Freeman, and Lawrence F. Katz*        65

**Table 19. Simulated Costs and Benefits of Post-1979 Immigration**[a]

| Item | Holding price of capital fixed | Holding capital stock fixed |
|---|---|---|
| Percent change in earnings | | |
|   Capital | . . . | 6.50 |
|   Skilled native workers | 0.35 | −2.49 |
|   Unskilled native workers | −4.64 | −4.57 |
| Percent change in skilled-to-unskilled earnings ratio | 4.99 | 2.08 |
| Percent change in total native earnings | 0.05 | 0.13 |
| Dollar GDP gain, assuming $7 trillion GDP | 3.5 billion | 9.1 billion |

Source: Authors' calculations based on model described in text. Data on factor GDP shares are from Autor, Katz, and Krueger (1997, table A1).

a. Changes relative to counterfactual of no immigration after 1979.

sented below uses estimates from the upper end of this range. Simulations based on smaller estimates yield both miniscule benefits and miniscule costs of immigration. In particular, we assume that $\epsilon_{ss} = -1.5$, $\epsilon_{UU} = -0.8$, and $\epsilon_{SU} = 0.05$.[80] This assumption builds capital-skill complementarity into the calculations.

The simulation requires estimates of the parameters $b$ and $\beta$, as well as of the share of income accruing to each of the factors. We estimate these parameters from the 1995 CPS, MORG files. We define skilled workers as those having at least a high school education and unskilled workers as high school dropouts. The 1995 CPS then implies that $b$ is 0.91 and $\beta$ is 0.68 for immigrants who entered after 1979. We make the standard assumption that the labor share of income (for all workers) is 0.7. Using data from the study by Autor, Katz, and Krueger, we estimate that the skilled worker share of GDP is 0.661 and that of unskilled workers is 0.039.[81] Finally, we need an estimate of the immigrant supply shock. The 1995 CPS implies that post-1979 immigrants increased labor supply, in terms of full-time equivalent workers, by 5.5 percent.

Table 19 reports the simulation results, using both polar assumptions about capital. The first column of data gives the results when we assume that the price of capital is fixed (so that capital adjusts completely to the entry of immigrants). In this case, unskilled workers suffer a 4.6

80. These assumptions determine all the other elasticities in the model, because of the mathematical property that the relevant weighted average of factor price elasticities is zero.

81. Autor, Katz, and Krueger (1997, table A1).

percent decline in earnings, whereas skilled workers gain about 0.4 percent. This produces a change in the relative wage of these two groups of 5.0 percent, the same magnitude as estimated in our middle case in table 18. This redistribution generates a net gain for the U.S. economy of 0.05 percent of GDP, or roughly $3.5 billion per year in a $7 trillion economy. The second column gives the results when we assume that the capital stock is fixed. In this case, the main beneficiary of immigration is native-owned capital. The capitalists experience a 6.5 percent increase in income, while both skilled and unskilled workers suffer losses: 2.5 percent and 4.6 percent, respectively. The wage of skilled relative to unskilled workers changes by 2.1 percent. The net gain to the economy is 0.13 percent, which roughly translates into $9.1 billion a year. The simulation therefore reveals that the economic gains from immigration are small in such a massive economy.[82]

It is worth emphasizing that this simulation assumes that all workers within a given skill group are perfect substitutes. A more general analysis would take into account complementarities that might exist between some immigrants (such as those with fewer than nine years of schooling or those with specialized training) and some native workers. Such complementarities would increase the gains to the U.S. economy from immigration. A more complete model would also allow for gains from increased product variety associated with immigration. But our estimates may also overstate the "true" gain because they ignore the possibility that trade would substitute for immigration if fewer immigrants had entered the country. The bottom line from our simulations is that the economic impact of immigration is mainly redistributional and primarily affects a small group of the least educated U.S. native workers.

## Conclusions

In the past two or three decades there has been a substantial growth in immigration and trade between the United States and the less developed countries. The large flow of less educated immigrants from LDCs and the rapid growth in U.S. imports of LDC manufactured goods has

82. Johnson (1997b) concludes from a similar but more detailed analysis that the effects of immigration on the national economy are even smaller than our estimates.

increased the effective supply of less educated labor relative to more educated labor in the United States. This, in turn, has raised questions about the potential contribution of trade and immigration to the rise in the wage differential between more and less educated workers.

Determining the effects of immigration and trade on economic outcomes is difficult. It is difficult because immigration and trade may have an effect on national labor market outcomes without greatly affecting relative outcomes in the regions most immediately touched by trade flows or immigrant flows. It is also difficult because many other factors affect the U.S. job market; without adequate controls for those factors, the influence of immigration or trade can be hard to discern in a given body of data. And, most important, it is difficult because one must specify a realistic counterfactual of how the economy would have developed, how native labor would have acted, and how firms would have produced goods, in the absence of the relevant immigration or trade flows. These counterfactuals, in turn, require good estimates of the magnitudes of various economic parameters.

In this paper, we try to specify appropriate counterfactuals and to quantify the potential effects of immigration and trade with different estimated or postulated parameters. We conclude that the effects of immigration and trade flows on relative skill supplies have not been substantial enough to account for more than a small proportion of the overall widening of the wage structure over the past fifteen years and have played only a modest role in the expansion of the college–high school wage differential in the United States. Under various plausible specifications, the main adverse effect of immigration and trade on U.S. native outcomes falls on workers with less than a high school education: the combined effects of immigration and trade may explain half of the decline of the relative wages of high school dropouts since 1980. Immigration has a particularly large impact on the outcomes for these workers because the flow of less educated immigrants into the country has been substantial; immigration increased the relative supply of workers with less than a high school degree by 15 to 20 percent over the period 1980–95. Increased trade from LDCs appears to have been much less important than immigration for the relative earnings of low-wage U.S. workers.

# References

Altonji, Joseph G., and David E. Card. 1991. "The Effects of Immigration on the Labor Market Outcomes of Less-Skilled Natives." In *Immigration, Trade, and the Labor Market*, edited by John M. Abowd and Richard B. Freeman. University of Chicago Press.

Autor, David H., Lawrence F. Katz, and Alan B. Krueger. 1997. "Computing Inequality: Have Computers Changed the Labor Market?" Working Paper 5956. Cambridge, Mass.: National Bureau of Economic Research (March).

Baldwin, Robert E., and Glen G. Cain. 1997. "Shifts in U.S. Relative Wages: The Role of Trade, Technology, and Factor Endowments." Working Paper 5934. Cambridge, Mass.: National Bureau of Economic Research (February).

Bartel, Ann P. 1989. "Where Do the New U.S. Immigrants Live?" *Journal of Labor Economics* 7(4): 371–91.

Berman, Eli, John Bound, and Zvi Griliches. 1994. "Changes in the Demand for Skilled Labor within U.S. Manufacturing: Evidence from the Annual Survey of Manufactures." *Quarterly Journal of Economics* 109(2): 367–97.

Bernard, Andrew B., and J. Bradford Jensen. 1995. "Exporters, Jobs, and Wages in U.S. Manufacturing: 1976–1987." *BPEA, Microeconomics, 1995*, 67–119.

Bhagwati, Jagdish, and Vivek H. Dehejia. 1994. "Freer Trade and Wages of the Unskilled—Is Marx Striking Again?" In *Trade and Wages: Leveling Wages Down?*, edited by Jagdish Bhagwati and Marvin H. Kosters. Washington: American Enterprise Institute.

Blanchard, Olivier Jean, and Lawrence F. Katz. 1992. "Regional Evolutions." *BPEA*, 1:1992, 1–75.

Blau, Francine D., and Lawrence M. Kahn. 1996. "International Differences in Male Wage Inequality: Institutions versus Market Forces." *Journal of Political Economy* 104(4): 791–836.

Borjas, George J. 1990. *Friends or Strangers: The Impact of Immigrants on the U.S. Economy*. Basic Books.

———. 1994. "The Economics of Immigration." *Journal of Economic Literature* 32(4): 1667–717.

———. 1995. "The Economic Benefits from Immigration." *Journal of Economic Perspectives* 9(2): 3–22.

Borjas, George J., Richard B. Freeman, and Lawrence F. Katz. 1992. "On the Labor Market Effects of Immigration and Trade." In *Immigration and the Work Force: Economic Consequences for the United States and Source Areas*, edited by George J. Borjas and Richard B. Freeman. University of Chicago Press.

*George J. Borjas, Richard B. Freeman, and Lawrence F. Katz*          87

————. 1996. "Searching for the Effect of Immigration on the Labor Market." *American Economic Review, Papers and Proceedings* 86(2): 246–51.

Borjas, George J., and Valerie A. Ramey. 1995. "Foreign Competition, Market Power, and Wage Inequality." *Quarterly Journal of Economics* 110(4): 1075–110.

Bound, John, and George Johnson. 1992. "Changes in the Structure of Wages in the 1980's: An Evaluation of Alternative Explanations." *American Economic Review* 82(3): 371–92.

Butcher, Kristin F., and David E. Card. 1991. "Immigration and Wages: Evidence from the 1980's." *American Economic Review, Papers and Proceedings* 81(2): 292–96.

Butcher, Kristin F., and John DiNardo. 1997. "The Immigrant and Native-Born Wage Distributions: Evidence from United States Censuses." Unpublished paper. Boston University and University of California, Irvine (June).

Card, David E. 1990. "The Impact of the Mariel Boatlift on the Miami Labor Market." *Industrial and Labor Relations Review* 43(2): 245–57.

————. 1997. "Immigrant Inflows, Native Outflows, and the Local Labor Market Impacts of Higher Immigration," Working Paper 5927. Cambridge, Mass.: National Bureau of Economic Research (February).

Davis, Donald R. 1996. "Does European Unemployment Prop Up American Wages?" Working Paper 5620. Cambridge, Mass.: National Bureau of Economic Research (June).

Deardorff, Alan V, and Dalia S. Hakura. 1994. "Trade and Wages—What are the Questions?" In *Trade and Wages: Leveling Wages Down?*, edited by Jagdish Bhagwati and Marvin H. Kosters. Washington: American Enterprise Institute.

Deardorff, Alan V., and Robert W. Staiger. 1988. "An Interpretation of the Factor Content of Trade." *Journal of International Economics* 24(1–2): 93–107.

Doms, Mark, Timothy Dunne, and Kenneth R. Troske. 1997. "Workers, Wages, and Technology." *Quarterly Journal of Economics* 112(1): 253–90.

Edin, Per-Anders, and Bertil Holmlund. 1995. "The Swedish Wage Structure: The Rise and Fall of Solidarity Wage Policy?" In *Differences and Changes in Wage Structures*, edited by Richard B. Freeman and Lawrence F. Katz. University of Chicago Press.

Filer, Randall K. 1992. "The Effect of Immigrant Arrivals on Migratory Patterns of Native Workers." In *Immigration and the Work Force: Economic Consequences for the United States and Source Areas*, edited by George J. Borjas and Richard B. Freeman. University of Chicago Press.

Fortin, Nicole, and Thomas Lemieux. 1996. "Rank Regression, Wage Distributions, and the Gender Gap." CRDE Working Paper 1096. University of Montreal (April).

Frankel, Jeffrey A., and David Romer. 1996. "Trade and Growth: An Empirical Investigation." Working Paper 5476. Cambridge, Mass.: National Bureau of Economic Research (March).

Freeman, Richard B. 1975. "Overinvestment in College Training?" *Journal of Human Resources* 10(3): 287–311.

Freeman, Richard B., and Lawrence F. Katz. 1994. "Rising Wage Inequality: The United States vs. Other Advanced Countries." In *Working Under Different Rules*, edited by Richard B. Freeman. Russell Sage Foundation.

Freeman, Richard B., and Karen Needels. 1993. "Skill Differentials in Canada in an Era of Rising Labor Market Inequality." In *Small Differences That Matter: Labor Markets and Income Maintenance in Canada and the United States*, edited by David E. Card and Richard B. Freeman. University of Chicago Press.

Frey, William H. 1994. "The New White Flight." *American Demographics* 16(4): 40–48.

———. 1995a. "Immigration and Internal Migration 'Flight' from U.S. Metropolitan Areas: Toward a New Demographic Balkanisation." *Urban Studies* 32(4–5): 733–57.

———. 1995b. "Immigration Impacts on Internal Migration of the Poor: 1990 Census Evidence for U.S. States." *International Journal of Population Geography* 1: 51–67.

Frey, William H., and Kao-Lee Liaw. 1996. "The Impact of Recent Immigration on Population Redistribution within the United States." Research Report 96-376. University of Michigan, Population Studies Center (December).

Friedberg, Rachel M. 1996. "The Impact of Mass Migration on the Israeli Labor Market." Unpublished paper. Brown University (November).

Grossman, Jean Baldwin. 1982. "The Substitutability of Natives and Immigrants in Production." *Review of Economics and Statistics* 64(4): 596–603.

Hamermesh, Daniel S. 1993. *Labor Demand*. Princeton University Press.

———. 1997. "Immigration and the Quality of Jobs." Unpublished paper. University of Texas (February).

Hanson, Gordon H., and Antonio Spilimbergo. 1997. "Illegal Immigration, Border Enforcement, and Relative Wages: Evidence from Apprehensions at the U.S.–Mexico Border." Unpublished paper. University of Texas (March).

Jaeger, David A. 1995. "Skill Differences and the Effect of Immigrants on the Wages of Natives." Unpublished paper. U.S. Bureau of Labor Statistics (November).

———. 1997. "Reconciling the Old and New Census Bureau Education Questions: Recommendations for Researchers." *Journal of Business and Economic Statistics* 15(3): 300–09.

Jensen, J. Bradford, and Kenneth R. Troske. 1997. "Increasing Wage Disper-

*George J. Borjas, Richard B. Freeman, and Lawrence F. Katz*      89

sion in U.S. Manufacturing: Plant-Level Evidence on the Role of Trade and Technology.'' Paper prepared for the Council on Foreign Relations Study Group on Global Trade and Wages (March).

Johnson, George E. 1997a. ''Changes in Earnings Inequality: The Role of Demand Shifts.'' *Journal of Economic Perspectives* 11(2): 41–54.

———. 1997b. ''Estimation of the Impact of Immigration on the Distribution of Income Among Minorities and Others.'' Unpublished paper. University of Michigan (February).

Katz, Lawrence F., and Kevin M. Murphy. 1992. ''Changes in Relative Wages, 1963–1987: Supply and Demand Factors.'' *Quarterly Journal of Economics* 107(1): 35–78.

Kim, Dae-Il, and Robert H. Topel. 1995. ''Labor Markets and Economic Growth: Lessons from Korea's Industrialization, 1970–1990.'' In *Differences and Changes in Wage Structures*, edited by Richard B. Freeman and Lawrence F. Katz. University of Chicago Press.

Krueger, Alan B. 1997. ''Labor Market Shifts and the Price Puzzle Revisited.'' Working Paper 5924. Cambridge, Mass.: National Bureau of Economic Research (February).

Krugman, Paul R. 1995a. ''Growing World Trade: Causes and Consequences.'' *BPEA, 1:1995*, 327–77.

———. 1995b. ''Technology, Trade, and Factor Prices.'' Working Paper 5355. Cambridge, Mass.: National Bureau of Economic Research (November).

LaLonde, Robert J., and Robert H. Topel. 1991. ''Labor Market Adjustments to Increased Immigration.'' In *Immigration, Trade, and the Labor Market*, edited by John M. Abowd and Richard B. Freeman. University of Chicago Press.

Lawrence, Robert Z. 1996. *Single World, Divided Nations? International Trade and OECD Labor Markets*. Paris: Brookings and Organisation for Economic Co-operation and Development.

Lawrence, Robert Z., and Matthew J. Slaughter. 1993. ''International Trade and American Wages in the 1980s: Giant Sucking Sound or Small Hiccup?'' *BPEA, Microeconomics 2:1993*, 161–226.

Leamer, Edward E. 1996a. ''In Search of Stolper-Samuelson Effects on U.S. Wages.'' Working Paper 5427. Cambridge, Mass.: National Bureau of Economic Research (January).

———. 1996b. ''What's the Use of Factor Contents?'' Working Paper 5448. Cambridge, Mass.: National Bureau of Economic Research (February).

Mishel, Lawrence, Jared Bernstein, and John Schmitt. 1997. *The State of Working America, 1996–97*. Armonk, N.Y.: M. E. Sharpe.

Mundell, Robert A. 1957. ''International Trade and Factor Mobility.'' *American Economic Review* 47(3): 321–35.

Murphy, Kevin M., and Finis Welch. 1992. "The Structure of Wages." *Quarterly Journal of Economics* 107(1): 285–326.

Rodrik, Dani. 1997. *Has Globalization Gone Too Far?* Washington: Institute for International Economics.

Sachs, Jeffrey D., and Howard J. Shatz. 1994. "Trade and Jobs in U.S. Manufacturing." *BPEA, 1:1994*, 1–84.

Sachs, Jeffrey D., and Andrew Warner. 1995. "Economic Reform and the Process of Global Integration." *BPEA, 1:1995*, 1–118.

Schmitt, John. 1995. "The Changing Structure of Male Earnings in Britain, 1974–1988." In *Differences and Changes in Wage Structures*, edited by Richard B. Freeman and Lawrence F. Katz. University of Chicago Press.

Schoeni, Robert F. 1996. "The Effect of Immigrants on the Employment and Wages of Native Workers: Evidence from the 1970s and 1980s." Unpublished paper. RAND (February).

Trefler, Daniel. 1993. "International Factor Price Differences: Leontief Was Right!" *Journal of Political Economy* 101(6): 961–87.

Troske, Kenneth R. 1995. "The Worker Establishment Characteristics Database." Research Paper 95-10. U.S. Bureau of the Census, Center for Economic Studies (June).

U.S. Bureau of the Census. 1989. "The Relationship between the 1970 and 1980 Industry and Occupation Classification Systems" Technical Paper 59. Department of Commerce (February).

White, Michael J., and Lori M. Hunter. 1993. "The Migratory Response of Native-Born Workers to the Presence of Immigrants in the Labor Market." Working Paper 93-08. Brown University, Population Studies and Training Center (July).

Wood, Adrian. 1994. *North-South Trade, Employment, and Inequality: Changing Fortunes in a Skill-Driven World*. Oxford: Clarendon Press.

———. 1995. "How Trade Hurt Unskilled Workers." *Journal of Economic Perspectives* 9(3): 57–80.

# [16]

ELSEVIER

Labour Economics 4 (1997) 1–28

LABOUR
ECONOMICS

# The factor-market consequences of unskilled immigration to the United States

Michael J. Greenwood [a], Gary L. Hunt [b], Ulrich Kohli [c,*]

[a] *University of Colorado, Boulder, CO, USA*
[b] *University of Maine, Orono, ME, USA*
[c] *University of Geneva, 102 Boulevard Carl-Vogt, 1211 Geneva, Switzerland*

Received 19 October 1994; revised 15 August 1996

## Abstract

This paper applies the production-theory approach to migration to assess the wage and employment effects of unskilled immigration to the United States. Native labour and foreign-born labour are disaggregated into four skill categories. Together with capital, this adds up to nine inputs. The data are cross section for 121 metropolitan areas. Both an aggregate cost function and a production function are estimated. The functional form that we use is the Symmetric Normalized Quadratic Semiflexible function. Special attention is devoted to required curvature conditions which have frequently been violated in previous work. Elasticity estimates are reported for alternative settings, including for the short run when we view domestic factor prices as given and the long run when we treat them as flexible. The results indicate that an increase of unskilled immigration has a small – but statistically significant – negative effect on low- and medium-skill native workers.

*JEL classification:* F22; J23; E23; C51

*Keywords:* Immigration; Skill levels; Production theory; Semiflexible functional forms; Curvature conditions

---

* Corresponding author.

2     *M.J. Greenwood et al. / Labour Economics 4 (1997) 1–28*

## 1. Introduction

Does immigration of unskilled labour threaten the employment opportunities and the earnings of native workers? This question, which has long worried policymakers and the public alike, has recently been examined by Altonji and Card (1991), LaLonde and Topel (1991), and Rivera-Batiz and Sechzer (1991), among others. The question of the factor market consequences of immigration is a major issue in the debate about international economic integration. Thus, the North-American Free Trade Agreement (NAFTA) has greatly increased U.S. access to the Mexican labour market. Similarly, in Europe, fears have been expressed about the economic impact of immigration since international labour mobility is an important ingredient of the Single Market Act, and European Union membership may be extended to many low-wage East-European nations in the not too distant future.

One line of research which has proved useful to answer this and related questions is what has become known as the production theory approach to immigration. This approach, pioneered by Baldwin-Grossman (1982), views foreign-born workers as an input to the technology: they are used together with native labour and domestic capital to produce aggregate output. The question that then arises is whether immigrants are substitutes or complements for native workers; [1] see Greenwood et al. (1996) for recent evidence for the United States. [2] It is sometimes argued that the treatment of native workers and immigrants as different factors of production is rather arbitrary, and that it may be more sensible to disaggregate labour according to skills (Rivera-Batiz and Sechzer, 1991). On the other hand, a case can be made that even if it were possible to control for the level of work experience and education, immigrants are not perfect substitutes for domestic workers given that immigrants are self-selected and that they bring along country-specific skills, whereas domestic workers have a better knowledge of local conditions, customs, and language (Borjas, 1985; Chiswick, 1986). We believe that these arguments are not contradictory, and we therefore disaggregate labour both on the basis of origins and on the basis of skills. Thus, in the empirical part of this paper, we distinguish between native and foreign-born workers, and we allow for four levels of skills within each group. Together with capital, this yields a total of nine inputs. The production structure that we consider here is therefore much more detailed and much larger than in any previous study.

---

[1] For a review of alternative channels by which immigration can affect domestic markets, see Greenwood and McDowell (1986), Greenwood (1994), and Greenwood and Hunt (1995).

[2] The emphasis of our earlier paper is on the choice of functional forms and curvature conditions. Furthermore, we adopt essentially the same disaggregation of labour as Baldwin-Grossman (1982): natives, nonrecent immigrants, and recent immigrants. The model is thus much smaller than the one presented here, and no direct attempt is made to disaggregate labour according to skills.

*M.J. Greenwood et al / Labour Economics 4 (1997) 1–28*                    3

While we have already referred, rather loosely, to the concepts of substitution and complementarity, these must be defined with great care, and it appears that this has not always been the case in the literature. Some of the available evidence is in terms of Allen–Uzawa elasticities of substitution, and some of it is by way of Hicksian elasticities of complementarity. The passage from one set of elasticities to the other is not trivial, which makes comparisons between studies difficult at best, and meaningless at worst. We will report estimates of both sets of elasticities to avoid any ambiguity. Moreover, we will propose yet a third set that is well suited to assess the short-run effects of unskilled immigration when the rental prices of the other factors are rigid.

Some authors have argued that much of the evidence derived from the production theory approach to immigration is inconclusive, most effects being very close to zero (Chiswick et al., 1992). However, small does not mean statistically insignificant, and we therefore report t-values for all estimates of Allen–Uzawa elasticities of substitution, Hicksian elasticities of complementarity, and the related price and quantity effects.

As soon as the number of inputs exceeds two, simple and well-known functional forms such as the Cobb–Douglas and the CES are inappropriate representations of an arbitrary production function since they severely restrict the substitution possibilities allowed for by the technology. Thus, much of the empirical work based on the production theory approach to immigration is conducted with the help of flexible functional forms. [3] We will conform to the same tendency, selecting the Symmetric Normalized Quadratic functional form. This function is particularly well suited for the job at hand for at least two reasons. First, unlike most other functional forms, it allows concavity to be imposed globally without interfering with flexibility. Curvature conditions are often violated in empirical work, even in the context of much smaller models. [4] Yet these conditions are part of the theoretical framework, and they must be met for the estimates to make any economic sense. Given the large size of the model that we specify, there is little chance that curvature conditions would be met at the outset which makes it necessary to impose them. Second, precisely because of that large size, it turns out that full flexibility is not needed. The Symmetric Normalized Quadratic functional form makes it possible to test for a reduction in flexibility, thereby allowing for large savings in terms of the number of parameters and yielding potentially more efficient estimates. The paper provides one of the first applications of the concept of semiflexibility introduced by Diewert and Wales (1988).

---

[3] Thus Baldwin-Grossman (1982), and Rivera-Batiz and Sechzer (1991) use the Translog; Bean et al. (1988) use the Generalized-Leontief.

[4] Thus, a little known fact about the widely cited Baldwin-Grossman (1982) study is that her estimated production function fails to be concave; this point is also made by Chiswick (1989). Similarly, the estimates reported by Borjas (1983), and by Bean et al. (1988) are not compatible with well-behaved production functions.

The remainder of this paper is set out as follows. Section 2 briefly reviews the description of the technology by means of the aggregate production and cost functions. The Symmetric Normalized Quadratic functional form, the question of curvature conditions, and the concept of semiflexibility are discussed in Section 3. Section 4 gives an account of the construction of the data. Our main empirical results are contained in Sections 5 and 6. A further discussion of our results in the context of NAFTA can be found in Section 7, and Section 8 concludes.

## 2. Representation of the technology

Assume that production requires $J$ inputs; let $x \equiv [x_j]$ and $w \equiv [w_j]$ be the vectors of input quantities and prices, respectively, and let $y$ and $p$ denote the quantity and the price of aggregate output. The aggregate production function is given by

$$y = f(x). \tag{1}$$

We assume that $f(\cdot)$ is increasing, linearly homogeneous, and quasiconcave. The first-order conditions for cost minimization require

$$w_j = w_j(p, x) = p\partial f(x)/\partial x_j, \quad j = 1, \ldots, J. \tag{2}$$

The substitution and complementarity possibilities allowed for by the technology can be described by a set of Hicksian elasticities of complementarity, $\Psi \equiv [\psi_{jk}]$, defined as [5]

$$\psi_{jk} \equiv f(x)f_{jk}(x)/[f_j(x)f_k(x)], \quad j, k = 1, \ldots, J, \tag{3}$$

where $f_j(xx)/\partial x_j$ and $f_{jk}(x) \equiv \partial^2 f(x)/(\partial x_j \partial x_k)$ for short. The Hicksian elasticities of complementarity are defined for given input quantities and a given price of output; $\psi_{jk}$ is positive if inputs $j$ and $k$ are q-complements, to use the Hicks (1970) terminology, and negative if they are q-substitutes. The same substitution and complementarity relationships can be described more intuitively by the quantity elasticities of inverse demands. Let $H \equiv [\eta_{jk}]$, where

$$\eta_{jk} \equiv \partial \ln[w_j(p, x)]/\partial \ln(x_j), \quad j, k = 1, \ldots, J. \tag{4}$$

These elasticities indicate the impact of a change in the input mix on factor rental prices. Making use of Eqs. (2) and (3) and of the linear homogeneity of $f(x)$, it is apparent that the elements of $H$ can be calculated from $\Psi$ directly:

$$\eta_{jk} = \psi_{jk} s_k, \quad j, k = 1, \ldots, J, \tag{5}$$

$s_k$ being the share of input $k$ in total costs, $s_k \equiv x_k w_k/(\Sigma w_j x_j)$.

---

[5] See Sato and Koizumi (1973) and Syrquin and Hollender (1982), for instance.

*M.J. Greenwood et al. / Labour Economics 4 (1997) 1–28*                    5

As an alternative to production function (1), and since cost minimization and constant returns to scale are assumed, the technology can be described by the following unit cost function:

$$c(w) \equiv \min_{x} \left\{ \sum_j w_j x_j : f(x) \geq 1 \right\}. \tag{6}$$

Cost function (6) is linearly homogeneous in input prices, and given the assumptions made on $f(\cdot)$, it is also nondecreasing and quasiconcave; Diewert (1974). Moreover, under competitive conditions, unit cost equals $p$. The demand for input $j$ can then be derived by differentiation; Shephard (1953):

$$x_j = x_j(w, y) = y \partial c(w) / \partial w_j, \quad j = 1, \ldots, J. \tag{7}$$

The description of the technology by the cost function makes it easy to derive the set of Allen–Uzawa elasticities of substitution, $\Sigma \equiv [\sigma_{jk}]$; indeed, as shown by Uzawa (1962),

$$\sigma_{jk} = c(w) c_{jk}(w) / \left[ c_j(w) c_k(w) \right], \quad j, k = 1, \ldots, J, \tag{8}$$

where $c_j(w) \equiv \partial c(w) / \partial w_j$ and $c_{jk}(w) \equiv \partial^2 c(w) / (\partial w_j \partial w_k)$. These elasticities are defined for given input prices and a given level of output. Inputs $j$ and $k$ are substitutes in the Allen–Uzawa sense if $\sigma_{jk} \geq 0$, and they are complements otherwise. It is also useful to define the partial price elasticities of input demands:

$$\epsilon_{jk} \equiv \partial \ln \left[ x_j(y, w) \right] / \partial \ln(w_k), \quad j, k = 1, \ldots, J. \tag{9}$$

Making use of (7) and (8), it is evident that these can be calculated from $\Sigma$ directly:

$$\epsilon_{jk} = \sigma_{jk} s_k, \quad j, k = 1, \ldots, J. \tag{10}$$

While both the Hicksian and the Allen–Uzawa elasticities give an adequate description of the substitution possibilities inherent to the technology, they describe fundamentally different experiments, since $x$ and $p$ are exogenous in the former case and endogenous in the latter case, while the reverse treatment applies to $w$ and $y$. The passage from one set of elasticities to the other is not trivial. If the number of inputs exceeds two, inputs $j$ and $k$ could be Hicksian q-complements, and yet nothing can be said out of hand as to whether they are Allen–Uzawa substitutes or complements. It is therefore crucial to be very precise as to what variables are being held constant when two inputs are described as being complements or substitutes. In what follows, we will report empirical estimates of both sets of elasticities. For this purpose, both production function (1) and cost function (6) will be estimated. [6]

---

[6] It is often possible to derive one set of elasticities from the other, essentially by inverting a bordered Hessian matrix; see Kohli (1991). However, this is not possible here since the Hessians of the cost and production functions turn out to be of less than full rank; see Section 3 for additional details.

## 3. Functional form, concavity, and semiflexibility

We use the Symmetric Normalized Quadratic functional form introduced by Diewert and Wales (1987). In the cost function context, it is as follows:

$$p = \tfrac{1}{2}\Sigma\Sigma a_{jk}w_j w_k/(\Sigma\alpha_j w_j) + \Sigma c_j w_j, \tag{11}$$

where $a_{jk} = a_{kj}$, and $\Sigma a_{jk} = 0$. The $\alpha_j$'s are nonnegative and predetermined subject to the condition $\Sigma\alpha_j = 1$. This functional form is flexible at the point of normalization of the data; it is necessarily homogeneous of degree one in prices, and it is globally concave if and only if $A \equiv [a_{jk}]$ is negative semi-definite. Given that $\Sigma a_{jk} = 0$, $A$ is at most of rank $J - 1$. Let $\tilde{A}$ be the matrix obtained by deleting the last row and the last column of $A$. Exploiting a result by Lau (1978), Diewert and Wales (1987) have shown that $\tilde{A}$ can be forced to be negative semi-definite by using the reparameterization of Wiley et al. (1973). Thus, one sets $\tilde{A} = -TT'$, where $T \equiv [\tau_{mn}]$ is a lower triangular matrix.

As indicated by Eq. (7), the input demand functions, relative to output, are obtained by differentiation:

$$x_j/y = \Sigma a_{jk}w_k/(\Sigma\alpha_k w_k) - \tfrac{1}{2}\alpha_j\Sigma\Sigma a_{km}w_k w_m/(\Sigma\alpha_k w_k)^2 + c_j. \tag{12}$$

The same functional form is used for the production function which is therefore written as

$$y = \tfrac{1}{2}\Sigma\Sigma b_{jk} x_j x_k/(\Sigma\beta_j x_j) + \Sigma d_j x_j, \tag{13}$$

where $b_{jk} = b_{kj}$, $\Sigma b_{jk} = 0$, and $\Sigma\beta_j = 1$. This function is globally concave if and only if $B \equiv [b_{jk}]$ is negative semi-definite. This can again be imposed by the reparameterization of Wiley et al. (1973). As to the inverse input demand functions (the marginal product conditions), they are as follows:

$$w_j/p = \Sigma b_{jk} x_k/(\Sigma\beta_k x_k) - \tfrac{1}{2}\beta_j\Sigma\Sigma b_{km} x_k x_m/(\Sigma\beta_k x_k)^2 + d_j. \tag{14}$$

One difficulty with flexible functional forms is that their number of parameters increases very rapidly with the number of inputs. Even if one assumes linear homogeneity, the number of parameters in a $N$-input model is equal to $N + (N-1)N/2$. Thus, if $N = 2$, the number of parameters is 3; if $N = 4$, there are 10 parameters, and if $N = 8$, the number of parameters rises to 36; if $N = 16$, the number of parameters jumps to 136. This may lead to serious problems of multicollinearity and it may lead to inefficient estimates. One way around this problem has been suggested by Diewert and Wales (1988), who introduce the concept of K-flexibility, or semiflexibility. A functional form $g(z)$ is said to be semiflexible at some point $z^*$ if it has enough free parameters for $g(z^*)$, its gradient $\nabla g(z^*)$, and its Hessian $\nabla^2 g(z^*)$ to attain arbitrary values, provided that

$\nabla^2 g(z^*)$ is restricted to have rank $K < N$. A semiflexible functional form therefore has less parameters than a flexible one, and, although it is not flexible, it does not impose any obvious a priori restrictions on the size or the signs of the elasticities of substitution or complementarity.

The concept of semiflexibility rests on some new results obtained by Diewert and Wales (1988). They show that any semi-definite $N \times N$ matrix of rank $K$, [7] where $K$ is less than the maximal possible rank $N$, has a $K$-column triangular decomposition. This means that $T \equiv [\tau_{mn}]$ is now such that $\tau_{mn} = 0$ for $1 \leq m < n \leq N$ and for $n = K + 1, \ldots, N$. Thus, $T$ now is defined as a lower triangular $N$ by $N$ matrix which has zeros in its last $N - K$ columns. Note that $T$ now has only $N(N + 1)/2 - (N - K)(N - K + 1)/2$ free parameters. This may mean a substantial reduction in the number of parameters to be estimated. Thus, if $N = 8$ and $K = 3$, the number of free parameters is 21, as opposed to 36 in the unrestricted case. This reparameterization applied to $-\tilde{A}$ in Eq. (11), and its counterpart $-\tilde{B}$ in Eq. (13), yields the K-flexible, or semiflexible, versions of the Symmetric Normalized Quadratic cost and production functions.

## 4. Data

A key requirement of this study is to classify foreign-born and native workers by skill level. One way to accomplish this is to organize individuals according to their reported occupation. Since we use U.S. Census data, this grouping could have been based on the occupation reported by the individual. However, we chose not to follow this approach because it entails a number of potentially arbitrary assignments of occupations to one skill category or another. Individual earnings have a systematic and a random component. Our method of distinguishing native and foreign-born skill classes focuses on the systematic component. Rather than grouping individuals based on their actual 1979 earnings as reported in 1980, which would have implicitly included both the systematic and random components of earnings, we used an estimated human capital function to develop a prediction, or expectation, of the individual's earnings, given his or her personal characteristics. A standard earnings function was estimated for both the foreign-born and the natives. [8] The earnings regressions were estimated with microdata from two random samples, each of approximately 10,000 individuals, drawn from the 1980 Public Use Microdata Sample (PUMS) of the U.S. Census. One sample was made up of foreign-born persons, and the other of natives. The wide variation that exists in immigrant concentrations across the United States provides the rationale for using cross-sectional data on Standard Metropolitan Statistical Areas (SMSAs) to

---

[7] $N$ is equal to $J - 1$ in the case of $\tilde{A}$.

[8] These results are available from the authors on request.

estimate the model described above. [9] Each of the 121 SMSAs used in this study is represented in each sample. The foreign-born sample consists of 20 percent of the relevant population of foreign-born persons enumerated in each SMSA.

The two regressions were then used to generate expected earnings for each individual in both the foreign-born and the native samples. Based on the national distribution of expected earnings of native workers, the native sample was then divided into quartiles as follows: (1) high earnings: expected earnings greater than $18,572; (2) medium-high earnings: expected earnings between $13,226 and $18,572; (3) medium-low earnings: expected earnings between $7,685 and $13,226; and (4), low earnings: expected earnings less than $7,685. The foreign-born were classified according to exactly the same scheme. In the work that follows, we refer to native labour and foreign-born labour as high-skill, medium-skill, low-skill and unskilled. Thus, for any given SMSA, when we refer to high-skill native or foreign-born labour, we mean the respective number of individuals with expected 1979 earnings greater than $18,572.

Nominal output data on a value-added basis have been compiled by the Bureau of Economic Analysis (BEA) in the form of gross regional product data at the state level, but not at the SMSA level. Our strategy is to estimate SMSA level nominal output by sharing down state level nominal output to the area level using SMSA and state personal income data by major industry division. Specifically, nominal output for the 121 SMSAs was formed in the following way. Let nominal output (thousands of dollars) for each of the areas be stacked in a $121 \times 1$ vector $Y$. The following steps were undertaken to create $Y$:

$$Y = \operatorname{diag}\left[ C_1 / C_2 \right) D' \right], \tag{15}$$

where $"/"$ indicates Hadamard, or element-by-element, division, and $C_1$ is a $121 \times 10$ matrix of 1980 Gross State Product defined for 121 areas and 10 major industry divisions (BEA, 1986); $C_2$ is a $121 \times 10$ matrix of 1980 state earnings, again for 121 areas and 10 major industry divisions (BEA, 1986); $D$, finally, is a $121 \times 10$ matrix of 1980 earnings defined for the same 121 areas and 10 major industry divisions (BEA, 1983). Data in $C_1$ and $C_2$ are the data for the states in which the 121 areas are located.

As far as capital services are concerned, we begin by calculating the user cost of capital ($w_9$):

$$w_9 = \gamma \cdot \tau, \tag{16}$$

where $\gamma$ is the 1980 nominal value of the user cost of capital for the U.S. as a

---

[9] For example, 40.9 percent of Miami's 1980 population was foreign-born, which was the highest fraction among the SMSAs. Other SMSAs with high proportions were Jersey City (26.9 percent), Los Angeles (23.9 percent), New York (23.2 percent), and El Paso (22.4 percent), but a number of SMSAs had below 10.0 percent of their population foreign-born, with several midwestern areas below 2.0 percent.

*M.J. Greenwood et al. / Labour Economics 4 (1997) 1–28*					9

whole and $\tau$ is a $121 \times 1$ vector of SMSA user costs of capital relative to the U.S. value incorporating local tax structure features. As for output, the area's relative user cost of capital is the value for the state in which the area is located; $w_9$ is a $121 \times 1$ vector. The source of the $\tau$ vector is Regional Economic Models, Inc. The U.S. value of the user cost of capital was computed by the Jorgensonian formula:

$$\gamma = \{[1 - k - uz][(1 - u)r + \delta] p_K\}/(1 - u), \tag{17}$$

where $k$ is the investment tax credit, $u$ is the combined federal and state marginal tax rate on capital income (inclusive of local deductibility), $z$ is the present value of one dollar's worth of depreciation allowances, $r$ is the financial cost of capital, $\delta$ is the economic depreciation rate, and $p_K$ is the implicit deflator for investment output. All data are weighted averages of structures and equipment. Capital income from each area is obtained by subtracting labour income from nominal output. The quantity of capital services ($x_9$) is then calculated implicitly by deflating capital income by its rental price ($w_9$).

We also require an index of real output (real value added). Let $x_j^h$ and $w_j^h$ be the quantity and the price of input $j$ in region $h$. We first define $\tilde{w}_j$ as the mean price of input $j$ across all regions:

$$\tilde{w}_j \equiv \left(\sum_h w_j^h x_j^h\right) \bigg/ \left(\sum_h x_j^h\right). \tag{18}$$

We next define $s_j^h$ as the value added share of input $j$ in region $h$:

$$s_j^h \equiv w_j^h x_j^h \bigg/ \left(\sum_j w_j^h x_j^h\right). \tag{19}$$

We also define $\tilde{s}_j$ as the mean value added share of input $j$, that is the share of input $j$ in the total of the value added by all regions:

$$\tilde{s}_j \equiv \left(\sum_h w_j^h x_j^h\right) \bigg/ \left(\sum_h \sum_j w_j^h x_j^h\right). \tag{20}$$

The price of output in region $h$ ($p^h$) is then calculated as a Tornqvist price index, where the prices in region $h$ are compared to the corresponding mean prices:

$$p^h = \exp\left[\sum_j \tfrac{1}{2}\left(s_j^h + \tilde{s}_j\right) \ln\left(w_j^h / \tilde{w}_j\right)\right]. \tag{21}$$

Finally, the quantity of real value added in region $h$ is obtained implicitly as

$$y^h = \left(\sum_j w_j^h x_j^h\right) \bigg/ p^h. \tag{22}$$

Table 1 reports means, standard deviations, and minimum and maximum values

Table 1
Labour shares: Summary statistics (percentages) [a]

|  |  | Mean | St. dev. | Minimum | Maximum |
|---|---|---|---|---|---|
| (i) Quantity shares |  |  |  |  |  |
| 1. | Hi-S natives | 22.51 | 3.17 | 12.67 | 28.81 |
| 2. | Me-S natives | 23.84 | 2.44 | 14.43 | 29.47 |
| 3. | Lo-S natives | 23.14 | 2.38 | 15.55 | 28.25 |
| 4. | Un-S natives | 24.62 | 2.94 | 16.45 | 31.04 |
| 5. | Hi-S foreign-born | 0.76 | 0.56 | 0.05 | 3.05 |
| 6. | Me-S foreign-born | 1.48 | 1.46 | 0.19 | 10.47 |
| 7. | Lo-S foreign-born | 1.86 | 2.05 | 0.18 | 13.21 |
| 8. | Un-S foreign-born | 1.79 | 2.29 | 0.15 | 14.17 |
|  | Labor, total | 100.00 |  |  |  |
| (ii) Value shares |  |  |  |  |  |
| 1. | Hi-S natives | 43.50 | 4.83 | 25.84 | 53.53 |
| 2. | Me-S natives | 26.62 | 3.06 | 16.60 | 35.03 |
| 3. | Lo-S natives | 16.78 | 2.59 | 12.41 | 24.01 |
| 4. | Un-S natives | 7.45 | 1.53 | 4.78 | 11.82 |
| 5. | Hi-S foreign-born | 1.73 | 1.17 | 0.16 | 6.26 |
| 6. | Me-S foreign-born | 1.81 | 1.78 | 0.13 | 12.24 |
| 7. | Lo-S foreign-born | 1.45 | 1.72 | 0.10 | 10.98 |
| 8. | Un-S foreign-born | 0.66 | 1.00 | 0.04 | 6.13 |
|  | Labor, total | 100.00 |  |  |  |

[a] Hi-S: high-skilled; Me-S: medium-skilled; Lo-S: low-skilled; Un-S: unskilled.

of the various labour shares, both in quantity terms and in value terms. One sees that immigrants make up about ten percent of the U.S. labour force; in income terms, their share is close to five percent. Unskilled immigrants make up less than two percent of the total labour force; their income share amounts to about 0.6 percent. These numbers vary substantially from SMSA to SMSA, however. Thus, the proportion of unskilled foreign-born workers is as small as 0.15 percent in Utica-Rome, and as large as 10.3 percent in Oxnard, and even 14.2 percent in Miami.

## 5. Estimation results

We assume that systems (2) and (7) are exact, except for errors in optimization. In each case we specify a vector of additive disturbances which we assume to be identically distributed normal random vectors with mean vector zero. The models are then estimated by using an iterative version of the Zellner (1962) method for seemingly unrelated regressor equations as implemented in SHAZAM, version 7.0 (White, 1978); this method is numerically equivalent to maximum likelihood. We have 1089 observations (nine equations times 121 regions) to estimate a maximum of 45 unknown parameters.

*M.J. Greenwood et al. / Labour Economics 4 (1997) 1–28*          11

Our estimation method does not make allowance for possible problems due to errors in measurement, and this must be kept in mind when interpreting the results. It is particularly our measures of value added and the capital stock at the SMSA level which are likely to be subject to such errors since both are computed from data available at the state level only, although the industry mix of each SMSA is taken into account. This assumes that each industry is homogeneous across SMSAs within each state. There are at least two sources of potential biases which might invalidate this assumption. Thus, the contribution of capital could be underestimated in large urban areas where the price of land is higher; in other words, the share of capital could be underestimated in large SMSAs, and overestimated in small ones. A second source of bias which can arise, but which operates in the opposite direction, results from the fact that some of the industries considered here, such as manufacturing and services, are quite heterogeneous. There is evidence that firms intensive in skilled labor tend to locate in large urban areas which tend to offer more amenities likely to attract highly educated people. To the extent that these industries are relatively less capital intensive, the share of capital could well be overestimated in large urban areas. Thus, we find that these two sources of biases tend to offset each other, although it is impossible to tell which effect might dominate. Given that our employment and wage data are drawn directly from the U.S. Census, and that these should be much less prone to large and systematic biases, the errors in measurement are most likely to affect the estimates of the cross terms between capital and the different types of labour. The emphasis of this paper is on the impact of unskilled immigrants on the employment and income of other labour categories; the corresponding cross terms are much less likely to be affected by the errors in measurement problems described above.

We begin our econometric work by focusing on the cost function. We started by estimating the rigid ($K = 0$) version of the model, after having set the $\alpha_j$'s to the sample mean cost shares of the corresponding inputs. We then reestimated the model, setting $K$ to larger and larger values; it quickly became apparent that there is no gain in going beyond the $K = 3$ semiflexible model: any additional flexibility does not lead to any increases in the value of the likelihood function; [10] we therefore report in Table 2 parameter estimates for the $K = 3$ version of the model.

---

[10] This is compatible with the findings of Kohli (1994). The logarithms of the likelihood functions are as follows: 4145.059 ($K = 0$), 4213.749 ($K = 1$), 4233.831 ($K = 2$), and 4236.269 ($K \geq 3$). Thus, the hypothesis $K = 3$, conditional on $K > 3$, cannot be rejected at any level of significance. Although the hypothesis $K = 2$, conditional on $K = 3$, cannot be rejected at conventional levels of significance either, we proceed with the $K = 3$ version of the model to avoid any risk of type-II errors. For comparison purposes, we also estimated a CES cost function, with global concavity imposed. This produces an estimate of the Allen–Uzawa elasticity of substitution which is numerically very close to zero, with a logarithm of the likelihood function of 4145.059, that is the same value as for the $K = 0$ version of the Symmetric Normalized Quadratic functional form.

Table 2
Cost function: Symmetric normalized quadratic semiflexible functional form ($K = 3$) – parameter estimates [a]

| | | | | | |
|---|---|---|---|---|---|
| $\tau_{11}$ | 0.35255 | (12.48) | $\tau_{21}$ | 0.21548 | (12.16) |
| $\tau_{31}$ | 0.11916 | (7.72) | $\tau_{41}$ | 0.06413 | (6.11) |
| $\tau_{51}$ | -0.02239 | (-2.86) | $\tau_{61}$ | -0.02409 | (-2.35) |
| $\tau_{71}$ | -0.01363 | (-1.54) | $\tau_{81}$ | -0.00299 | (-0.60) |
| $\tau_{22}$ | -0.09956 | (-2.96) | $\tau_{32}$ | -0.08061 | (-2.27) |
| $\tau_{42}$ | 0.09200 | (2.85) | $\tau_{52}$ | 0.02276 | (1.53) |
| $\tau_{62}$ | 0.03446 | (2.05) | $\tau_{72}$ | 0.04139 | (4.36) |
| $\tau_{82}$ | 0.01392 | (1.82) | $\tau_{33}$ | 0.07001 | (1.93) |
| $\tau_{43}$ | -0.06540 | (-1.38) | $\tau_{53}$ | 0.02791 | (2.47) |
| $\tau_{63}$ | 0.03141 | (1.98) | $\tau_{73}$ | -0.00044 | (-0.03) |
| $\tau_{83}$ | 0.00912 | (1.08) | $c_1$ | 0.20521 | (52.32) |
| $c_2$ | 0.12163 | (57.59) | $c_3$ | 0.07768 | (54.88) |
| $c_4$ | 0.03382 | (52.65) | $c_5$ | 0.00868 | (15.02) |
| $c_6$ | 0.00913 | (11.40) | $c_7$ | 0.00725 | (9.67) |
| $c_8$ | 0.00324 | (7.91) | $c_9$ | 0.53269 | (80.05) |

[a] Asymptotic-$t$ values in parentheses. The subscripts are as follows: 1. native labour, high-skill ($x_1$); 2. native labour, medium-skill ($x_2$); 3. native labour, low-skill ($x_3$); 4. native labour, unskilled ($x_4$); 5. foreign-born labour, high-skill ($x_5$); 6. foreign-born labour, medium-skill ($x_6$); 7. foreign-born labour, low-skill ($x_7$); 8. foreign-born labour, unskilled ($x_8$); 9. capital ($x_9$).

This model has 30 free parameters. The estimated function is necessarily globally concave, and we verified that monotonicity is satisfied for all observations.

Estimates of Allen–Uzawa elasticities of substitution at the sample mean are shown in Table 3. The corresponding asymptotic $t$-values are also reported. [11] Many of these elasticities are estimated with a fair degree of precision, with well over half the $t$-values in excess of two in absolute terms. We find that all four categories of native labour tend to be Allen–Uzawa complements for each other (the only exception involves unskilled and low skilled labour). Moreover, all four categories of native labour are Allen–Uzawa substitutes for capital, and generally also for immigrant labour (the only exceptions again involve unskilled native labour which is found to be an Allen–Uzawa complement for unskilled and low-skill immigrant labour. Without exceptions, all four categories of foreign-born labour are Allen–Uzawa complements for each other as well as for capital. These

---

[11] To compute these t-values, one obviously needs the variances of the corresponding elasticity estimates. These are calculated as follows. Elasticity $\sigma_{jk}$ can be written as $\sigma_{jk} = \phi^{jk}(\Theta, w)$ where $\Theta$ is the vector of estimated parameters (the $\tau_{jk}$'s and the $c_j$'s) and $w$ is the vector of exogenous input prices. Note that function $\phi^{jk}(\cdot)$ is highly nonlinear. A linear approximation of the variance of $\sigma_{jk}$ can be obtained as $\phi_{\Theta}^{jk}(\Theta, w)'$ Cov$(\Theta)\phi_{\Theta}^{jk}(\Theta, w)$ where $\phi_{\Theta}^{jk}(\cdot)$ is the vector of partial derivatives of $\phi^{jk}(\cdot)$ with respect to the components of $\Theta$ – $\phi_{\Theta}^{jk}(\cdot)$ is the gradient of $\phi^{jk}(\cdot)$ with respect to $\Theta$ – and Cov$(\Theta)$ is the estimated variance–covariance matrix of the components of $\Theta$. The procedure is exactly the same for the other elasticity estimates and accompanying $t$-values reported in this paper.

M.J. Greenwood et al. / Labour Economics 4 (1997) 1–28　　　　　13

Table 3
Allen-Uzawa elasticities of substitution at the sample mean ($\sigma_{jk} \equiv cc_{jk}/(c_j c_k)$) [a]

|            | $k=1$   | $k=2$   | $k=3$   | $k=4$    | $k=5$    | $k=6$    | $k=7$    | $k=8$    | $k=9$   |
|------------|---------|---------|---------|----------|----------|----------|----------|----------|---------|
| $\sigma_{1k}$ | -2.950  | -3.042  | -2.634  | -3.256   | 4.426    | 4.533    | 3.229    | 1.581    | 2.218   |
|            | (-5.73) | (-7.58) | (-7.28) | (-6.30)  | (3.08)   | (2.43)   | (1.58)   | (0.61)   | (8.12)  |
| $\sigma_{2k}$ |         | -3.806  | -3.565  | -1.132   | 6.708    | 7.764    | 8.001    | 5.139    | 2.250   |
|            |         | (-6.42) | (-6.41) | (-1.34)  | (3.47)   | (3.21)   | (2.82)   | (1.42)   | (8.90)  |
| $\sigma_{3k}$ |         |         | -4.240  | 1.656    | 3.775    | 4.864    | 8.860    | 3.327    | 2.056   |
|            |         |         | (-4.14) | (1.42)   | (1.73)   | (1.79)   | (3.04)   | (0.87)   | (7.04)  |
| $\sigma_{4k}$ |         |         |         | -14.728  | 3.972    | 1.388    | -12.081  | -4.483   | 2.309   |
|            |         |         |         | (-5.74)  | (1.47)   | (0.39)   | (-2.81)  | (-0.67)  | (7.04)  |
| $\sigma_{5k}$ |         |         |         |          | -23.828  | -27.747  | -19.607  | -22.635  | -2.771  |
|            |         |         |         |          | (-2.09)  | (-2.29)  | (-1.67)  | (-1.61)  | (-2.75) |
| $\sigma_{6k}$ |         |         |         |          |          | -33.057  | -26.307  | -28.287  | -2.768  |
|            |         |         |         |          |          | (-2.01)  | (-1.72)  | (-1.52)  | (-2.15) |
| $\sigma_{7k}$ |         |         |         |          |          |          | -36.133  | -26.040  | -2.175  |
|            |         |         |         |          |          |          | (-2.07)  | (-1.34)  | (-1.50) |
| $\sigma_{8k}$ |         |         |         |          |          |          |          | -27.131  | -0.610  |
|            |         |         |         |          |          |          |          | (-1.04)  | (-0.33) |
| $\sigma_{9k}$ |         |         |         |          |          |          |          |          | -1.689  |
|            |         |         |         |          |          |          |          |          | (-9.68) |

[a] These values are based on the estimates of Table 2; the subscripts are as defined at the bottom of that table.

results largely confirm those obtained by Greenwood et al. (1996), particularly if we think of recent immigrants as being mostly unskilled.

Table 4 contains some summary statistics showing the variations of the $\sigma_{jk}$'s across SMSAs: mean, standard deviation, as well as minimum and maximum values. It appears that these variations, due to differences in relative prices, are not very pronounced. In particular, there are no instances of sign reversals.

We next turn to the estimates of the price elasticities of input demand at the sample mean. They are shown together with their asymptotic $t$-values in Table 5. Their signs are the same as those of the Allen–Uzawa elasticities, but their magnitudes are easier to interpret. Of considerable interest are the estimates in columns 5 to 8: they indicate the impact of changes in the wage rates of foreign-born workers on the demand for all inputs. Thus, a reduction in the implicit rental price of unskilled and low-skill immigrant workers, which might come about from greater access to the Mexican labour market, would increase the demand for capital, the demand for all categories of immigrants, and the demand for unskilled native workers. It would, however, have an adverse effect on the demand for skilled native workers. Note, however, that only about half of these effects are statistically significant at the ten-percent level for an appropriate two-tail test; moreover, they tend to be very weak. In fact, the largest elasticities that appear in this table tend to relate to own price effects or to involve capital and highly skilled native labour.

Table 4
Allen-Uzawa elasticities of substitution–summary statistics [a]

|  | Mean | St. dev. | Minimum | Maximum |
|---|---|---|---|---|
| $\sigma_{11}$ | -2.797 | 0.382 | -4.358 | -1.910 |
| $\sigma_{12}$ | -2.886 | 0.412 | -4.580 | -1.938 |
| $\sigma_{13}$ | -2.511 | 0.310 | -3.743 | -1.773 |
| $\sigma_{14}$ | -3.065 | 0.472 | -4.991 | -2.018 |
| $\sigma_{15}$ | 4.574 | 0.563 | 3.521 | 6.996 |
| $\sigma_{16}$ | 4.697 | 0.703 | 3.402 | 7.502 |
| $\sigma_{17}$ | 3.205 | 0.421 | 2.351 | 4.584 |
| $\sigma_{18}$ | 1.487 | 0.255 | 0.952 | 2.077 |
| $\sigma_{19}$ | 2.180 | 0.084 | 1.944 | 2.483 |
| $\sigma_{22}$ | -3.603 | 0.581 | -6.033 | -2.308 |
| $\sigma_{23}$ | -3.385 | 0.498 | -5.418 | -2.251 |
| $\sigma_{24}$ | -1.104 | 0.044 | -1.182 | -0.935 |
| $\sigma_{25}$ | 6.935 | 0.732 | 5.643 | 10.396 |
| $\sigma_{26}$ | 8.045 | 1.034 | 6.211 | 12.591 |
| $\sigma_{27}$ | 7.986 | 0.793 | 6.373 | 10.628 |
| $\sigma_{28}$ | 4.941 | 0.549 | 3.774 | 6.258 |
| $\sigma_{29}$ | 2.216 | 0.110 | 1.932 | 2.571 |
| $\sigma_{33}$ | -4.027 | 0.585 | -6.381 | -2.692 |
| $\sigma_{34}$ | 1.478 | 0.500 | 0.505 | 3.722 |
| $\sigma_{35}$ | 3.937 | 0.514 | 3.064 | 6.232 |
| $\sigma_{36}$ | 5.082 | 0.766 | 3.766 | 8.368 |
| $\sigma_{37}$ | 8.904 | 0.911 | 7.065 | 11.938 |
| $\sigma_{38}$ | 3.206 | 0.383 | 2.382 | 4.205 |
| $\sigma_{39}$ | 2.039 | 0.074 | 1.860 | 2.238 |
| $\sigma_{44}$ | -13.587 | 3.091 | -26.938 | -7.582 |
| $\sigma_{45}$ | 4.058 | 0.579 | 2.922 | 5.966 |
| $\sigma_{46}$ | 1.411 | 0.320 | 0.799 | 2.429 |
| $\sigma_{47}$ | -12.080 | 1.558 | -17.176 | -9.088 |
| $\sigma_{48}$ | -4.378 | 0.423 | -5.472 | -3.481 |
| $\sigma_{49}$ | 2.241 | 0.177 | 1.823 | 2.876 |
| $\sigma_{55}$ | -29.212 | 11.710 | -105.190 | -12.624 |
| $\sigma_{56}$ | -34.290 | 14.635 | -129.080 | -14.521 |
| $\sigma_{57}$ | -22.975 | 7.691 | -63.478 | -11.100 |
| $\sigma_{58}$ | -25.436 | 7.209 | -58.831 | -14.435 |
| $\sigma_{59}$ | -3.000 | 0.468 | -5.351 | -2.022 |
| $\sigma_{66}$ | -41.214 | 18.740 | -162.100 | -17.084 |
| $\sigma_{67}$ | -31.126 | 11.353 | -90.499 | -14.623 |
| $\sigma_{68}$ | -32.021 | 9.945 | -77.530 | -17.809 |
| $\sigma_{69}$ | -3.000 | 0.497 | -5.498 | -2.016 |
| $\sigma_{77}$ | -41.066 | 13.071 | -89.314 | -21.236 |
| $\sigma_{78}$ | -28.263 | 7.251 | -51.172 | -17.414 |
| $\sigma_{79}$ | -2.267 | 0.232 | -3.020 | -1.734 |
| $\sigma_{88}$ | -28.323 | 6.121 | -49.779 | -17.873 |
| $\sigma_{89}$ | -0.564 | 0.100 | -0.738 | -0.132 |
| $\sigma_{99}$ | -1.737 | 0.096 | -2.023 | -1.431 |

[a] These values are based on the estimates of Table 2; the subscripts are as defined at the bottom of that table.

Table 5
Price elasticity estimates at the sample mean ($\epsilon_{jk} \equiv \partial \ln[x_j(y, \mathbf{w})]/\partial \ln(w_k)$) [a]

|  | $k = 1$ | $k = 2$ | $k = 3$ | $k = 4$ | $k = 5$ | $k = 6$ | $k = 7$ | $k = 8$ | $k = 9$ |
|---|---|---|---|---|---|---|---|---|---|
| $\epsilon_{1k}$ | -0.606 | -0.370 | -0.205 | -0.110 | 0.038 | 0.041 | 0.023 | 0.005 | 1.182 |
|  | (-6.00) | (-7.99) | (-7.68) | (-6.57) | (2.96) | (2.33) | (1.52) | (0.60) | (7.87) |
| $\epsilon_{2k}$ | -0.625 | -0.463 | -0.277 | -0.038 | 0.058 | 0.071 | 0.058 | 0.017 | 1.199 |
|  | (-7.98) | (-6.64) | (-6.65) | (-1.34) | (3.43) | (3.19) | (2.77) | (1.39) | (8.66) |
| $\epsilon_{3k}$ | -0.541 | -0.434 | -0.330 | 0.056 | 0.033 | 0.044 | 0.064 | 0.011 | 1.096 |
|  | (-7.52) | (-6.59) | (-4.23) | (1.41) | (1.71) | (1.77) | (3.02) | (0.86) | (6.92) |
| $\epsilon_{4k}$ | -0.669 | -0.138 | 0.129 | -0.498 | 0.035 | 0.013 | -0.088 | -0.015 | 1.231 |
|  | (-6.38) | (-1.34) | (1.41) | (-5.87) | (1.46) | (0.38) | (-3.07) | (-0.68) | (6.97) |
| $\epsilon_{5k}$ | 0.909 | 0.816 | 0.293 | 0.134 | -0.207 | -0.253 | -0.142 | -0.073 | -1.477 |
|  | (3.08) | (3.47) | (1.74) | (1.47) | (-2.17) | (-2.43) | (-1.72) | (-1.66) | (-2.75) |
| $\epsilon_{6k}$ | 0.931 | 0.945 | 0.378 | 0.047 | -0.241 | -0.302 | -0.191 | -0.092 | -1.475 |
|  | (2.42) | (3.20) | (1.79) | (0.39) | (-2.41) | (-2.14) | (-1.80) | (-1.59) | (-2.16) |
| $\epsilon_{7k}$ | 0.663 | 0.974 | 0.689 | -0.409 | -0.170 | -0.240 | -0.262 | -0.085 | -1.160 |
|  | (1.57) | (2.81) | (3.03) | (-2.81) | (-1.71) | (-1.79) | (-2.24) | (-1.39) | (-1.50) |
| $\epsilon_{8k}$ | 0.325 | 0.625 | 0.259 | -0.152 | -0.197 | -0.258 | -0.189 | -0.088 | -0.325 |
|  | (0.61) | (1.42) | (0.87) | (-0.67) | (-1.65) | (-1.57) | (-1.39) | (-1.07) | (-0.33) |
| $\epsilon_{9k}$ | 0.455 | 0.274 | 0.160 | 0.078 | -0.024 | -0.025 | -0.016 | -0.002 | -0.900 |
|  | (8.48) | (9.25) | (7.36) | (7.43) | (-2.62) | (-2.06) | (-1.44) | (-0.33) | (-9.55) |

[a] These values are based on the estimates of Table 2; the subscripts are as defined at the bottom of that table.

While Allen–Uzawa elasticities of substitution and price elasticities of input demand are familiar concepts, and they are of undeniable interest, it is often argued that they are not very useful if one tries to assess the impact of immigration on the income of domestic factors of production. Indeed, assuming full employment, it is the Hicksian elasticities of complementarity that are the most relevant. Consequently we now turn to the estimates of the production function. Parameter values for the $K = 3$ semiflexible version are shown in Table 6, where the $\beta_j$'s are set to the value-added shares at the sample mean. We again find that nothing is gained by increasing the value of $K$ beyond 3, [12] and we verified that monotonicity is satisfied over the observed range of quantities and prices. Estimates of Hicksian elasticities of complementarity are shown in Table 7. It is apparent that native labour is a q-complement for capital, irrespective of skills, whereas foreign-born labour, with the exception of unskilled workers, is a q-substitute for capital. There is evidence of q-substitutability between medium-skill and low-skill

---

[12] The logarithms of the likelihood functions are as follows: 4700.419 ($K = 0$), 4777.254 ($K = 1$), 4791.492 ($K = 2$), and 4793.460 ($K \geq 3$). As a comparison, we also estimated a CES production function; this produces an estimate of the Hicksian elasticity of complementarity of 0.029; although the CES and the Symmetric Normalized Quadratic models are not nested, it is revealing that the logarithm of the likelihood function for the CES is 4705.002, which is barely more than for the $K = 0$ version of the Symmetric Normalized Quadratic.

Table 6
Production function: Symmetric normalized quadratic semiflexible functional form ($K = 3$) – parameter estimates [a]

| $\tau_{11}$ | -0.11009 | (-10.14) | $\tau_{21}$ | 0.00939 | (0.59) |
|---|---|---|---|---|---|
| $\tau_{31}$ | 0.00490 | (0.48) | $\tau_{41}$ | -0.06117 | (-8.59) |
| $\tau_{51}$ | 0.02282 | (3.19) | $\tau_{61}$ | 0.00789 | (1.55) |
| $\tau_{71}$ | -0.00557 | (-1.24) | $\tau_{81}$ | 0.00038 | (0.12) |
| $\tau_{22}$ | 0.05891 | (4.16) | $\tau_{32}$ | 0.07162 | (5.76) |
| $\tau_{42}$ | -0.03166 | (-2.20) | $\tau_{52}$ | -0.00093 | (-0.09) |
| $\tau_{62}$ | 0.00031 | (0.04) | $\tau_{72}$ | -0.00913 | (-1.41) |
| $\tau_{82}$ | 0.00836 | (1.80) | $\tau_{33}$ | 0.02796 | (0.97) |
| $\tau_{43}$ | -0.03127 | (-1.63) | $\tau_{53}$ | -0.02614 | (-2.65) |
| $\tau_{63}$ | -0.00958 | (-1.00) | $\tau_{73}$ | 0.00212 | (0.22) |
| $\tau_{83}$ | 0.00770 | (1.31) | $d_1$ | 0.19748 | (181.10) |
| $d_2$ | 0.11482 | (168.86) | $d_3$ | 0.07306 | (180.48) |
| $d_4$ | 0.03182 | (125.87) | $d_5$ | 0.01115 | (30.57) |
| $d_6$ | 0.01216 | (50.77) | $d_7$ | 0.00942 | (45.21) |
| $d_8$ | 0.00387 | (33.08) | $d_9$ | 0.54750 | (331.89) |

[a] Asymptotic-$t$ values in parentheses. The subscripts are as defined at the bottom of Table 2.

Table 7
Hicksian elasticities of complementarity at the sample mean ($\psi_{jk} \equiv ff_{jk}/(f_j f_k)$) [a]

| | $k = 1$ | $k = 2$ | $k = 3$ | $k = 4$ | $k = 5$ | $k = 6$ | $k = 7$ | $k = 8$ | $k = 9$ |
|---|---|---|---|---|---|---|---|---|---|
| $\psi_{1k}$ | -0.311 | 0.046 | 0.037 | -1.073 | 1.143 | 0.362 | -0.330 | 0.055 | 0.134 |
| | (-5.14) | (0.57) | (0.47) | (-6.75) | (2.71) | (1.53) | (-1.25) | (0.12) | (7.70) |
| $\psi_{2k}$ | | -0.270 | -0.509 | 0.669 | -0.125 | -0.066 | 0.547 | -1.117 | 0.072 |
| | | (-1.87) | (-4.08) | (1.97) | (-0.20) | (-0.19) | (1.42) | (-1.61) | (2.84) |
| $\psi_{3k}$ | | | -1.113 | 1.482 | 0.842 | 0.233 | 0.905 | -2.888 | 0.138 |
| | | | (-3.77) | (3.09) | (1.15) | (0.36) | (1.17) | (-2.59) | (5.74) |
| $\psi_{4k}$ | | | | -5.660 | 1.551 | 0.499 | -1.883 | 4.298 | 0.337 |
| | | | | (-5.28) | (1.12) | (0.37) | (-1.14) | (1.75) | (9.55) |
| $\psi_{5k}$ | | | | | -9.703 | -3.177 | 1.658 | 4.647 | -0.382 |
| | | | | | (-1.69) | (-1.67) | (0.63) | (1.16) | (-2.67) |
| $\psi_{6k}$ | | | | | | -1.044 | 0.586 | 1.451 | -0.109 |
| | | | | | | (-0.72) | (0.47) | (0.63) | (-1.29) |
| $\psi_{7k}$ | | | | | | | -1.342 | 1.707 | -0.043 |
| | | | | | | | (-0.74) | (0.56) | (-0.50) |
| $\psi_{8k}$ | | | | | | | | -8.639 | 0.255 |
| | | | | | | | | (-1.36) | (1.94) |
| $\psi_{9k}$ | | | | | | | | | -0.092 |
| | | | | | | | | | (-9.40) |

[a] These values are based on the estimates of Table 6; the subscripts are as defined at the bottom of Table 2.

*M.J. Greenwood et al. / Labour Economics 4 (1997) 1–28*                    17

Table 8
Hicksian elasticities of complementarity–summary statistics [a]

|  | Mean | St. dev. | Minimum | Maximum |
|---|---|---|---|---|
| $\psi_{11}$ | -0.288 | 0.039 | -0.399 | -0.201 |
| $\psi_{12}$ | 0.065 | 0.038 | -0.047 | 0.140 |
| $\psi_{13}$ | 0.069 | 0.055 | -0.083 | 0.192 |
| $\psi_{14}$ | -1.072 | 0.006 | -1.078 | -1.036 |
| $\psi_{15}$ | 1.031 | 0.168 | 0.717 | 1.857 |
| $\psi_{16}$ | 0.347 | 0.016 | 0.308 | 0.398 |
| $\psi_{17}$ | -0.317 | 0.021 | -0.403 | -0.280 |
| $\psi_{18}$ | 0.121 | 0.102 | -0.145 | 0.429 |
| $\psi_{19}$ | 0.136 | 0.010 | 0.079 | 0.149 |
| $\psi_{22}$ | -0.265 | 0.018 | -0.306 | -0.214 |
| $\psi_{23}$ | -0.499 | 0.020 | -0.540 | -0.435 |
| $\psi_{24}$ | 0.744 | 0.137 | 0.393 | 1.045 |
| $\psi_{25}$ | -0.177 | 0.082 | -0.318 | 0.241 |
| $\psi_{26}$ | -0.086 | 0.023 | -0.137 | 0.006 |
| $\psi_{27}$ | 0.552 | 0.021 | 0.441 | 0.582 |
| $\psi_{28}$ | -1.112 | 0.007 | -1.131 | -1.086 |
| $\psi_{29}$ | 0.062 | 0.012 | 0.026 | 0.090 |
| $\psi_{33}$ | -1.113 | 0.005 | -1.120 | -1.087 |
| $\psi_{34}$ | 1.623 | 0.239 | 1.005 | 2.176 |
| $\psi_{35}$ | 0.744 | 0.151 | 0.473 | 1.514 |
| $\psi_{36}$ | 0.218 | 0.021 | 0.181 | 0.295 |
| $\psi_{37}$ | 0.931 | 0.045 | 0.717 | 0.989 |
| $\psi_{38}$ | -2.985 | 0.168 | -3.564 | -2.527 |
| $\psi_{39}$ | 0.138 | 0.013 | 0.104 | 0.179 |
| $\psi_{44}$ | -6.067 | 0.705 | -7.721 | -4.312 |
| $\psi_{45}$ | 1.470 | 0.133 | 1.183 | 2.075 |
| $\psi_{46}$ | 0.520 | 0.069 | 0.377 | 0.669 |
| $\psi_{47}$ | -1.915 | 0.059 | -2.024 | -1.699 |
| $\psi_{48}$ | 4.767 | 0.706 | 2.905 | 6.558 |
| $\psi_{49}$ | 0.373 | 0.072 | 0.167 | 0.521 |
| $\psi_{55}$ | -8.734 | 1.824 | -19.125 | -5.918 |
| $\psi_{56}$ | -2.993 | 0.291 | -4.396 | -2.447 |
| $\psi_{57}$ | 1.492 | 0.270 | 0.970 | 2.680 |
| $\psi_{58}$ | 4.469 | 0.323 | 3.961 | 6.084 |
| $\psi_{59}$ | -0.421 | 0.070 | -0.532 | -0.061 |
| $\psi_{66}$ | -1.039 | 0.007 | -1.046 | -1.013 |
| $\psi_{67}$ | 0.548 | 0.057 | 0.396 | 0.662 |
| $\psi_{68}$ | 1.481 | 0.091 | 1.270 | 1.863 |
| $\psi_{69}$ | -0.139 | 0.042 | -0.232 | 0.011 |
| $\psi_{77}$ | -1.339 | 0.013 | -1.358 | -1.296 |
| $\psi_{78}$ | 1.822 | 0.166 | 1.229 | 2.268 |
| $\psi_{79}$ | -0.053 | 0.027 | -0.131 | -0.004 |
| $\psi_{88}$ | -9.288 | 1.037 | -13.196 | -6.707 |
| $\psi_{89}$ | 0.287 | 0.059 | 0.120 | 0.501 |
| $\psi_{99}$ | -0.112 | 0.033 | -0.190 | -0.041 |

[a] These values are based on the estimates of Table 6; the subscripts are as defined at the bottom of Table 2.

native workers, and between high-skill and medium-skill immigrants. Within the native group, we also find that unskilled labour acts as a q-complement for low- and medium-skill workers. The links between the native and the foreign-born groups are rather weak. One exception concerns unskilled immigrants, who are found to be strong q-substitutes for low- and medium-skill native workers, and q-complements for unskilled U.S.-born workers.

Summary statistics pertaining to the Hicksian elasticities of complementarity are reported in Table 8. It appears that some of the elasticities vary a fair bit across SMSAs, with even some sign reversals in several cases. Thus, $\psi_{12}$ and $\psi_{13}$, which are positive at the mean of the sample, are negative for several observations, indicating that all categories of skilled native labour are q-substitutes in some areas, including Miami, New York, New Orleans, Houston, Los Angeles, and San Francisco. These are precisely among the urban centers where much of the recent immigration has taken place. [13]

The impact of changes in input quantities on factor rental prices can best be assessed with the help of the quantity elasticities of inverse input demands shown in Table 9. Of particular interest are the estimates in columns 5 to 8 that show the effect of exogenous changes in the number of immigrants. Thus it is apparent that an exogenous increase in number of foreign-born unskilled workers would not only depress their own wage rate, but it would also lead to a reduction in the remuneration of low- and medium-skill native workers. The effects are strongest in Miami, Jersey City, Salinas, El Paso, and Oxnard, all of which have substantial immigrant concentrations, and they are weakest in Little Rock, which has a very low concentration. The impact on highly skilled native workers is almost nil at the mean of the sample, but it is negative in several SMSAs, particularly in Miami, Los Angeles, New York, San Francisco, San Jose, and Houston. Skilled immigrants and capital, on the other hand, would benefit from increased unskilled immigration, as would unskilled natives. Note, however, that all these effects are very small, and often not statistically significant.

## 6. The short-run impact of unskilled immigration

The estimates shown in Table 9 adequately assess the long-run impact of immigration, once factor rental prices have had time to adjust and full employment has been restored. It is of interest, however, to assess the short-run impact of unskilled immigration. We view the short run as being characterized by a given stock of capital, a given price of output, a given number of unskilled foreign-born

---

[13] See LaLonde and Topel (1991) and Butcher and Card (1991).

M.J. Greenwood et al. / Labour Economics 4 (1997) 1–28

Table 9
Quantity elasticity estimates at the sample mean ($\eta_{jk} \equiv \ln[w_j(p, x)]/\ln(x_k)$) [a]

|  | $k = 1$ | $k = 2$ | $k = 3$ | $k = 4$ | $k = 5$ | $k = 6$ | $k = 7$ | $k = 8$ | $k = 9$ |
|---|---|---|---|---|---|---|---|---|---|
| $\eta_{1k}$ | -0.061 | 0.005 | 0.003 | -0.034 | 0.013 | 0.004 | -0.003 | 0.000 | 0.073 |
|  | (-5.11) | (0.57) | (0.47) | (-6.72) | (2.80) | (1.54) | (-1.23) | (0.12) | (7.73) |
| $\eta_{2k}$ | 0.009 | -0.031 | -0.037 | 0.021 | -0.001 | -0.001 | 0.005 | -0.004 | 0.039 |
|  | (0.57) | (-1.87) | (-4.08) | (1.98) | (-0.20) | (-0.19) | (1.42) | (-1.61) | (2.85) |
| $\eta_{3k}$ | 0.007 | -0.058 | -0.081 | 0.047 | 0.009 | 0.003 | 0.009 | -0.011 | 0.076 |
|  | (0.47) | (-4.07) | (-3.77) | (3.09) | (1.16) | (0.36) | (1.17) | (-2.58) | (5.75) |
| $\eta_{4k}$ | -0.212 | 0.077 | 0.108 | -0.180 | 0.017 | 0.006 | -0.018 | 0.017 | 0.184 |
|  | (-6.74) | (1.98) | (3.10) | (-5.27) | (1.12) | (0.37) | (-1.14) | (1.75) | (9.60) |
| $\eta_{5k}$ | 0.225 | -0.143 | 0.061 | 0.049 | -0.108 | -0.039 | 0.156 | 0.018 | -0.209 |
|  | (2.70) | (-0.20) | (1.15) | (1.12) | (-1.73) | (-1.69) | (0.63) | (1.14) | (-2.67) |
| $\eta_{6k}$ | 0.071 | -0.008 | 0.017 | 0.016 | -0.035 | -0.013 | 0.006 | 0.006 | -0.060 |
|  | (1.53) | (-0.19) | (0.36) | (0.37) | (-1.67) | (-0.73) | (0.47) | (0.63) | (-1.29) |
| $\eta_{7k}$ | 0.065 | 0.063 | 0.066 | -0.060 | 0.018 | 0.007 | -0.013 | 0.007 | -0.023 |
|  | (-1.25) | (1.42) | (1.16) | (-1.14) | (0.63) | (0.47) | (-0.74) | (0.56) | (-0.50) |
| $\eta_{8k}$ | 0.011 | -0.128 | -0.211 | 0.137 | 0.052 | 0.018 | 0.016 | -0.033 | 0.139 |
|  | (0.12) | (-1.61) | (-2.58) | (1.75) | (1.17) | (0.64) | (0.56) | (-1.35) | (1.94) |
| $\eta_{9k}$ | 0.026 | 0.008 | 0.010 | 0.011 | -0.004 | -0.001 | -0.000 | 0.001 | -0.050 |
|  | (7.63) | (2.83) | (5.69) | (9.36) | (-2.73) | (-1.30) | (-0.50) | (1.92) | (-9.47) |

[a] These values are based on the estimates of Table 6; the subscripts are as defined at the bottom of Table 2.

workers, and given rental prices for the remaining categories of labour. [14] Thus, in the short run, increased unskilled immigration may lead to changes in the demands of all other types of labour, native as well as foreign-born. We thus seek to obtain a set of elasticities ($\mu_{jk}$) that are defined for given wage rates for native workers and skilled immigrants, a given amount of unskilled immigrant labour, a given stock of capital, and a given price of output:

$$\mu_{jk} \equiv \partial \ln\left[ h_j(w_1, w_2, w_3, w_4, w_5, w_6, w_7; x_8, x_9; p) \right] / \partial \ln(z_k), \qquad (23)$$

where $h_j \in \{x_1, x_2, x_3, x_4, x_5, x_6, x_7; w_8, w_9; y\}$ and $z_k \in$

---

[14] Our assumption of factor price exogeneity in the short run in metropolitan labour markets in the U.S. is consistent with the findings of wage rigidity over a sample of two years recently reported by Holzer (1991) and Holzer and Montgomery (1993). Their evidence supports quantity adjustments in the short run. On the other hand, the evidence reported by Topel (1986) and Adams (1985) indicates some short-run factor price flexibility. The evidence reported by Marston (1985) on the rapidity of adjustment of metropolitan labour markets in the United States is also consistent with quantity adjustments over a period of up to one year, but these adjustments occur through rapid migration responses and are interpreted by Marston as equilibrating adjustments rather than short-run adjustments. Because of this aspect of his analysis and because his estimates of the speed of adjustment are much faster than any others reported in the literature (e.g. Treyz et al., 1993), our assumptions are most appropriate in the context of the results reported by Holzer (1991) and Holzer and Montgomery (1993).

Table 10

Short-run effects of an increase in unskilled immigration (values at the sample mean) [a]

$\mu_{jk} \equiv \ln[h_j(w_1, w_2, w_3, w_4, w_5, w_6, w_7; x_8, x_9; p)]/\ln(z_k)$;

$h_j \in \{x_1, x_2, x_3, x_4, x_5, x_6, x_7; w_8, w_9; y\}$, $z_k \in \{w_1, w_2, w_3, w_4, w_5, w_6, w_7; x_8, x_9; p\}$.

|  | $z_k = w_1$ | $z_k = w_2$ | $z_k = w_3$ | $z_k = w_4$ | $z_k = w_5$ | $z_k = w_6$ | $z_k = w_7$ | $z_k = x_8$ | $z_k = x_9$ | $z_k = p$ |
|---|---|---|---|---|---|---|---|---|---|---|
| $\mu_{1k}$ | -1.842 | -1.133 | -0.669 | -0.304 | 0.040 | 0.046 | 0.022 | 0.062 | 0.938 | 3.840 |
| $\mu_{2k}$ | -1.912 | -1.202 | -0.742 | -0.267 | 0.036 | 0.044 | 0.033 | -0.066 | 1.066 | 4.009 |
| $\mu_{3k}$ | -1.768 | -1.162 | -0.780 | -0.151 | 0.023 | 0.034 | 0.052 | -0.007 | 1.007 | 3.752 |
| $\mu_{4k}$ | -1.845 | -0.961 | -0.346 | -0.636 | 0.076 | 0.071 | -0.049 | 0.285 | 0.715 | 3.690 |
| $\mu_{5k}$ | 0.943 | 0.507 | 0.206 | 0.295 | -0.035 | -0.034 | 0.019 | 0.759 | 0.241 | -1.901 |
| $\mu_{6k}$ | 1.036 | 0.590 | 0.288 | 0.262 | -0.032 | -0.033 | 0.007 | 0.964 | 0.036 | -2.118 |
| $\mu_{7k}$ | 0.626 | 0.560 | 0.553 | -0.230 | 0.022 | 0.009 | -0.079 | 0.904 | 0.096 | -1.461 |
| $\mu_{8k}$ | -3.932 | 2.458 | 0.167 | -2.972 | -2.031 | -2.710 | -2.018 | -11.158 | 11.158 | 12.038 |
| $\mu_{9k}$ | -0.361 | -0.243 | -0.147 | -0.045 | -0.004 | -0.001 | -0.001 | 0.068 | -0.068 | 1.803 |
| $\mu_{yk}$ | -0.788 | -0.488 | -0.292 | -0.125 | 0.017 | 0.019 | 0.011 | 0.039 | 0.961 | 1.647 |

[a] These values are based on the estimates of Table 2; the subscripts are as defined at the bottom of that table.

$\{w_1, w_2, w_3, w_4, w_5, w_6, w_7; x_8, x_9; p\}$. Such elasticities can easily be derived from our cost function estimates. Indeed, the comparative statics of that model can be described as follows:

$$\begin{bmatrix} \hat{x}_a \\ \hat{x}_b \\ \hat{p} \end{bmatrix} = \begin{bmatrix} E_{aa} & E_{ab} & u_a \\ E_{ba} & E_{bb} & u_b \\ s'_a & s'_b & 0 \end{bmatrix} \begin{bmatrix} \hat{w}_a \\ \hat{w}_b \\ \hat{y} \end{bmatrix}, \tag{24}$$

where the hats ( ˆ ) indicate relative changes; $x_a$ and $x_b$ consist of the first seven and the last two components of $x$, respectively; $w_a$ and $w_b$ are similarly defined; $s_a$ and $s_b$ are vectors containing the first seven and the last two cost shares, respectively; $u_a$ and $u_b$ are, the seven-dimensional and the two-dimensional unit vectors; $E_{aa}$, $E_{ab}$, $E_{ba}$, and $E_{bb}$ are the parts of elasticity matrix $E \equiv [\epsilon_{jk}]$ accordingly defined. It is then a simple matter to solve (24) for $\hat{x}_a$, $\hat{w}_b$, and $\hat{y}$ as functions of $\hat{w}_a$, $\hat{x}_b$, and $\hat{p}$. [15]

We report in Table 10 sample-mean estimates of the $\mu_{jk}$'s obtained in this fashion. We observe that a one-percent increase in unskilled immigration ($x_8$) would reduce employment of low- to medium-skill native workers by approximately 0.01 percent and 0.07 percent, respectively. It would actually enhance the employment opportunities of all other workers, and it would lead to an increase in

---

[15] Given the nonlinearities of the inversion procedure, however, it is rather inconvenient to calculate standard errors; this is why none are reported in Table 10.

*M.J. Greenwood et al. / Labour Economics 4 (1997) 1–28*                    21

the rental price of capital. It would, however, severely depress the wage rate of unskilled immigrants.

It is apparent from the estimates in Table 10 that the short-run demand for native labour mostly depends on the wage rates of U.S.-born workers, and on the available amount of capital. The wages of skilled immigrants and the number of unskilled foreign-born workers have relatively little influence. Regarding the role of the capital stock, one notes its importance in determining the demand for native labour, whereas the elasticities of the demand for skilled foreign labour with respect to capital ($\mu_{59}$, $\mu_{69}$, and $\mu_{79}$) are all three close to zero. If one considers that skilled foreign-born workers largely consist of nonrecent immigrants, these findings confirm the results of Greenwood et al. (1996).

## 7. NAFTA and unskilled immigration to the United States

NAFTA is likely to have an effect, both in the short run and in the long run, on migration within North America. NAFTA is basically a free trade agreement between Canada, the United States, and Mexico, and it allows for the free movement of goods and services of North-American origin at the producer level. It is likely to have an effect on the relative prices of goods and services, and on factor rental prices. These changes, in turn, will impact on migration between the three countries.

Our model is a partial equilibrium model that focuses exclusively on the United States and that abstracts from trade matters. As such, it cannot be expected to make a prediction as to the likely effects of NAFTA on U.S. immigration. However, it is possible to use the evidence available elsewhere in the literature to come up with a range of possible outcomes. Our econometric estimates can then be used to assess the likely short-run and long-run consequences for employment and income distribution within the United States.

Because our emphasis is on unskilled immigration, we focus our analysis on Mexico and the United States. It is safe to assume that Mexico is relatively abundant in unskilled labour compared to the United States. Under these circumstances, the reduction and removal of barriers to trade implemented under NAFTA will tend to reduce the gap in real wages for unskilled workers between the two countries. Consequently, in the long run, less pressure will exist for migration from Mexico to the United States. Because of the relative size of the U.S. economy, this reduction in the wage gap will be achieved chiefly by way of an increase in the Mexican wage rate. It is unlikely, however, that factor price equalization will be complete as a result of freer trade under NAFTA for several reasons. First, factor-price equalization generally requires that production be nonjoint, a very restrictive assumption. Second, it only holds for countries with similar relative factor endowments, which clearly does not apply at the present to Mexico and the United States. Third, transportation costs and the existence of numerous distortions in goods as well as in factor markets, on both sides of the border, will prevent goods and factor prices from equalizing. Fourth, some specialization in production seems unavoidable due to the relatively small size of the Mexican economy and the existence of nontraded goods. It therefore seems likely that NAFTA will reduce Mexican immigration to the United States, but not eliminate it.

This analysis is confirmed by Hinojosa-Ojeda and Robinson (1992) who present an extensive review of computable general equilibrium (CGE) model estimates of the relative wage effects from NAFTA. Their conclusions are summarized in the following excerpt.

> "The International Trade Commission (ITC) model, which is the most stylized and closest to standard trade theory, does yield a fall in the wage of unskilled labor in the United States, and a rise in Mexico, after trade liberalization. On the U.S. side, however, the effect is tiny. This empirical result is robust and is replicated in all the CGE models." (p. 93)

Using a different methodology for estimating real wage gap changes, Hill and Mendez (1984) report reductions of 6 to 18 percent in the U.S.–Mexican real wage gap from an elimination of all barriers to trade by both countries. Their corresponding estimates of the decrease in Mexican–U.S. immigration lies between 9 and 35 percent.

In contrast to the relatively small effects characterizing the CGE literature, Leamer (1993) presents an analysis in which the effects are rather large. Although the basis of his analysis is standard trade theory, as is the case of the CGE models, he develops a scenario in which Mexico becomes large. U.S. protection is increased vis-à-vis the rest of the world (ROW) and Mexico's productivity quickly rises to OECD levels. Mexico grows very rapidly by capturing an increasingly large share of U.S. markets as trade is diverted from the ROW to Mexico. Under this 'large Mexico' scenario, Leamer finds that the reduction in the unskilled real wage gap could be quite substantial, perhaps as large as 15 percent.

Hill and Mendez (1984) report that the range of immigration elasticities with respect to relative real wages is 0.5 to 2.0. Using these estimates in conjunction with Leamer's findings, one might predict a drop in unskilled immigration to the United States as large as 30 percent; this figure would be substantially less if based on the CGE analyses.

While most studies conclude that NAFTA will reduce the unskilled real wage gap between the United States and Mexico, some authors have pointed out that the opposite might well take place in the short to medium run. Hinojosa-Ojeda and McCleery (1992) develop a two-country stylized dynamic CGE model with which they analyze the effects of 'NAFTA-like' policy changes and other developments on the Mexican and U.S. economies. Immigration is treated explicitly and is related to the utility of Mexicans remaining in Mexico or migrating to the United

*M.J. Greenwood et al. / Labour Economics 4 (1997) 1–28*                    23

States. Real wages in the low-wage sectors of both countries and Mexicans' nonpecuniary benefits from living in Mexico affect utility. A key aspect of their model for immigration is the delineation of the low-wage sector. In Mexico, it is essentially subsistence agriculture. In the United States, it is nontraded, local services (e.g., janitorial services, gardening, restaurant services, maid services). The high-wage sectors in both countries produce tradeables. Free trade increases the demand for unskilled labour in the United States as the positive effects on the skill-intensive tradeables sector induce increased demand for nontradeables. In Mexico, a prolonged adjustment period combined with relatively high labour force growth reduces the growth of real wages for unskilled labour. Under these circumstances, the real wage gap for unskilled labour rises between the United States and Mexico, thereby stimulating increased immigration for a lengthy period of time. The simulations conducted by Hinojosa-Ojeda and McCleery indicate about a two percentage point increase in Mexican immigration to the United States per year under their 'NAFTA-like' scenario. This continues for 15 to 20 years. The cumulated increase is therefore 35 to 50 percent. A reversal of this immigration pattern does occur eventually, when growth in Mexican demand for unskilled labour finally exceeds labour force growth.

The hypothesis of a temporary increase of unskilled immigration from Mexico – a 'migration hump' to use the terminology of Martin (1993) – is also supported by the experience of countries such as Italy, Spain, and South Korea where rapid economic growth actually encouraged more outmigration in the short run. As economic conditions improve, more migration occurs, in part because labour is released from agriculture as modernization takes place when capital is substituted for labour. Strong network ties already exist between Mexico and the United States, linking individuals in Mexico with potential jobs in the United States; Massey (1988). The CGE models noted above, where they have a migration component, predict a short-run increase of about 75,000 to 100,000 migrants from Mexico to the United States annually; Levy and van Wijnbergen (1992), and Robinson et al. (1993).

One might add that the hypothesis of a temporary increase in the supply of unskilled foreign-born workers is relevant even if unskilled immigration to the United States were to fall. That is, by making it easier for U.S. firms to locate in Mexico, and thus to have a much wider access to unskilled Mexican labour, it is as if NAFTA lead to an increase in the pool of unskilled foreign-born workers. This would be true even if no Mexican worker were actually to cross the border.

Based on these various considerations, the range of potential outcomes for Mexican unskilled immigration to the United States under NAFTA is clearly very wide: from a decrease of about one third to an increase of more than one third over a period of a couple of decades. Using the 1990 U.S. Census of Population Public Use Microdata Sample (PUMS) B (1%) files, estimates of the skill distribution of foreign-born workers in the United States were made following the methodology used to obtain the 1980 skill data on which our econometric

24     *M.J. Greenwood et al. / Labour Economics 4 (1997) 1–28*

Table 11

Real income consequences of a large increase in the supply of unskilled foreign-born workers (shock minus control, percentage points) [a]

| | USA | Tucson | El Paso | Oxnard |
|---|---|---|---|---|
| 1. Hi-S natives | 0.0045 | 0.0106 | 0.0085 | 0.0759 |
| 2. Me-S natives | -0.0861 | -0.0673 | -0.3302 | -0.2727 |
| 3. Lo-S natives | -0.2229 | -0.1825 | -0.8345 | -0.8024 |
| 4. Un-S natives | 0.3323 | 0.3292 | 1.2339 | 1.4885 |
| 5. Hi-S foreign-born | 0.3593 | 0.2464 | 1.3303 | 1.0798 |
| 6. Me-S foreign-born | 0.1123 | 0.0873 | 0.4126 | 0.4039 |
| 7. Lo-S foreign-born | 0.1322 | 0.1133 | 0.5103 | 0.4893 |
| 8. Un-S foreign-born | -0.6671 | -0.5711 | -2.4539 | -2.6964 |
| 9. Capital | 0.0200 | 0.0169 | 0.0720 | 0.0895 |

[a] These values are based on the estimates of Table 6; they are obtained by simulating the model, assuming a 20% increase in the supply of unskilled foreign-born workers.

estimates are based. These estimates indicate that Mexicans represent about 60 percent of the unskilled foreign-born labour in the United States in 1990. The comparable figures for states where Mexican immigrants are relatively concentrated are: nearly 70 percent in California, and nearly 80 percent in Arizona and Texas. A one third change in the flow of Mexican unskilled immigration therefore translates, in the long run, into a change of approximately one fifth in the stock of unskilled foreign-born labour on a national basis. In the cases of Arizona, Texas, and California, the changes are on the order of one fourth. In the short run, the stock effects would clearly be much smaller.

The estimates of the quantity elasticities given in Table 9 could be used the assess the long-run consequences of a 20 percent increase in the stock of unskilled immigrants. However, one must remember that these figures are point estimates, and thus they are valid for small changes only. A 20 percent change can hardly be viewed as small, and thus, given the nonlinearities of the model, the use of these point elasticities might be misleading. It seems preferable therefore to assess the consequences of this rather large shock by simulating the model. The estimates in Table 11 report the income effects (shock minus control, in percentage terms) for a 20 percent increase in the stock of unskilled immigrants; the figures for three representative SMSAs where the concentration of Mexican immigrants is rather large are also shown.

One sees that, nationwide, the shock depresses the wages of low skilled natives by about two tenths of one percent. This effect is of about the same size in Tucson, but it is nearly four times as large in El Paso and in Oxnard. The negative effect on medium-skilled natives is less than one tenth of one percent on average, but it is more than three times as large in El Paso and in Oxnard. Unskilled native workers benefit by about three tenth of one percent on average, but the gains would be much larger in Oxnard (1.5%) and El Paso (1.2%). Unskilled immigrant workers who previously entered the United States are hurt the most, losing about two thirds of one percent of their income on average; once again, the effect would substantially larger in Oxnard (2.7%) and El Paso (2.5%). The return on capital improves slightly in all SMSAs.

The above results apply to NAFTA-induced increases in unskilled immigration consistent with the scenario developed by Hinojosa-Ojeda and McCleery (1992). For the scenario of NAFTA-induced reductions in unskilled immigration consistent with the scenario developed by Leamer (1993), the results are largely symmetric. The large changes in Mexican unskilled immigration induced by NAFTA under either scenario produce only small wage effects on natives and foreign-born workers in the United States.

## 8. Conclusions

The production structure that we have estimated, by counting nine inputs, is larger than anything that has been contemplated in previous studies. As a result, our estimates are more detailed than those previously obtained. In spite of the unprecedented size of the model, the use of the Symmetric Normalized Quadratic functional form has enabled us to guarantee that no violations of curvature conditions occur, a problem that has plagued much of the earlier empirical work using the production theory approach. Moreover, we have innovated by using a semiflexible representation of the technology, and we have shown that the resulting reduction in flexibility is not incompatible with the data.

While some of our empirical evidence is inconclusive, and many of the effects that we uncovered are small, the pessimism that is sometimes expressed towards the production-theory approach does not seem to be justified. Indeed, even small effects may be statistically significant. By computing the relevant standard errors, we have been able to show at high levels of statistical confidence that native skilled workers are Allen–Uzawa complements for each other and Allen–Uzawa substitutes for capital and for skilled immigrant labour, whereas foreign-born workers tend to be Allen–Uzawa complements for each other and for capital. Capital is also found to be a Hicksian q-complement for all forms of native labour, while it is a Hicksian q-substitute for skilled immigrants. In any case, the fact that some of the cross effects cannot be pinpointed with great precision should not be used as a pretext to use the CES functional form, since any type of Allen–Uzawa complementarity and Hicksian substitution is then ruled out. Indeed, the CES function, which is so often favored in theoretical work, performs very poorly when confronted with the data.

Our results confirm the conclusions of earlier studies, namely that immigration of unskilled workers does not lead to large changes in income distribution and employment opportunities. [16] An inflow of unskilled foreign-born workers would, in the short run, lead to a reduction in the demand for low- to medium-skill native workers, and, in the long run, would reduce their earnings. However, these effects are very small. Not surprisingly, it is the unskilled immigrants themselves who would bear the bulk of the adjustment in the form of a reduction in their own wages. All other factors of production tend to benefit from increased unskilled immigration, although these effects are often not significant and they do vary across SMSAs, thus giving credit to the often expressed view that the consequences of international labour mobility are not uniform across the country.

It was beyond the scope of the paper to predict the immigration effects of NAFTA. In fact, there is much disagreement among the profession as to the likely impact of NAFTA on unskilled immigration in the short run. One view that seems to predominate is that it is immigration from Mexico is likely to fall in the very long run; however, rapid economic growth in Mexico could produce a migration hump in the shorter run. In any case, taking the estimates of other authors as to the likely effects of NAFTA on immigration flows and using our econometric results, we can conclude that the income distribution effects of immigration under NAFTA would be minimal, and that the short-run employment effects would be negligible. It is only if wages failed to adjust in the long run that a change in the number of foreign-born workers would eventually lead to large employment effects. The only group that is affected by unskilled immigration in a significant way, in the short run as well as in the long run, consists of prior unskilled immigrants.

## Acknowledgements

We are grateful to two anonymous referees for their comments and suggestions on an earlier draft. This work was partially supported by the U.S. Department of Labor, contract J-9-K-9-0074, and the Swiss National Science Foundation, grant #12-36328.92.

## References

Adams, James D., 1985, Permanent differences in unemployment and permanent wage differentials, Quarterly Journal of Economics 100, 29–56.
Altonji, Joseph G. and David Card, 1991, The effects of immigration on the labor market outcomes of less-skilled natives, In: John M. Abowd and Richard B. Freeman, eds., Immigration, trade, and the labor market (University of Chicago Press, Chicago, IL).

---

[16] One exception is a recent study by Borjas et al. (1992) who argue that these effects could be much larger than usually recognized. However, their calculations are based on estimates drawn from different studies, and they include the direct labour content of foreign trade. For these reasons, comparisons of their results with other findings are problematic.

*M.J. Greenwood et al. / Labour Economics 4 (1997) 1–28*                    27

Baldwin-Grossman, Jean, 1982, The substitutability of natives and immigrants in production, Review of Economics and Statistics 64, 596–603.

Bean, Frank D., B. Lindsay Lowell and Lowell J. Taylor, 1988, Undocumented Mexican immigrants and the earnings of other workers in the United States, Demography 25, 35–52.

Borjas, George J., 1983, The substitutability of Black, Hispanic and White labor, Economic Inquiry 21, 93–106.

Borjas, George J., 1985, Assimilation, changes in cohort quality, and the earnings of immigrants, Journal of Labor Economics 3, 463–489.

Borjas, George J., Richard B. Freeman, and Lawrence F. Katz, 1992, On the labor market effects of immigration and trade, In: George J. Borjas and Richard B. Freeman, eds., Immigration and the work force: Economic consequences for the United States and source areas (The University of Chicago Press, Chicago, IL).

BEA (Bureau of Economic Analysis), 1983, Local area personal income, Vol. 1, Summary, 1976–81 (U.S. Government Printing Office, Washington, DC).

BEA (Bureau of Economic Analysis), 1986, Local area personal income, Vol. 1, Summary, 1979–84 (U.S. Government Printing Office, Washington, DC).

Butcher, Kristin F. and David Card, 1991, Immigration and wages: Evidence from the 1980s, American Economic Review, Papers and Proceedings, 81, 292–296.

Chiswick, Barry R., 1986, Is the new immigration less skilled than the old?, Journal of Labor Economics 4, 168–192.

Chiswick, Carmel U., 1989, The impact of immigration on the human capital of natives, Journal of Labor Economics 7, 464–486.

Chiswick, Carmel U., Barry R. Chiswick and Georgios Karras, 1992, The impact of immigrants on the macroeconomy, Carnegie-Rochester Conference Series on Public Policy 37, 279–316.

Diewert, W. Erwin, 1974, Applications of duality theory, In: Michael D. Intriligator and David A. Kendrick, eds., Frontiers of quantitative economics, Vol. 2 (North-Holland, Amsterdam).

Diewert, W. Erwin and Terence J. Wales, 1987, Flexible functional forms and global curvature conditions, Econometrica 55, 43–68.

Diewert, W. Erwin and Terence J. Wales, 1988, A normalized quadratic semiflexible functional form, Journal of Econometrics 37, 327–342.

Greenwood, Michael J., 1994, Potential channels of immigrant influence on the economy of the receiving country, Papers in Regional Science 73, 211–240.

Greenwood, Michael J. and Gary L. Hunt, 1995, Economic effects of immigrants on native and foreign-born workers: Complementarity, substitutability, and other channels of influence, Southern Economic Journal 61, 1076–1097.

Greenwood, Michael J., Gary L. Hunt and Ulrich Kohli, 1996, The short-run and long-run factor-market consequences of recent immigration to the United States, Journal of Regional Science 36, 43–66.

Greenwood, Michael J. and John M. McDowell, 1986, The factor market consequences of U.S. immigration, Journal of Economic Literature 24, 1738–1772.

Hicks, John R., 1970, Elasticity of substitution again: Substitutes and complements, Oxford Economic Papers 22, 289–296.

Hill, John K. and Jose A. Mendez, 1984, The effect of commercial policy on international migration flows: The case of the United States and Mexico, Journal of International Economics 17, 41–53.

Hinojosa-Ojeda, Raul A. and Robert K. McCleery, 1992, U.S.–Mexico interdependence, social pacts, and policy perspectives: A computable general equilibrium approach, In: Jorge A. Bustemante, Clark W. Reynolds and Raul A. Hinojosa-Ojeda, eds., U.S.–Mexico relations (Stanford University Press, Stanford, CA).

Hinojosa-Ojeda, Raul A. and Sherman Robinson, 1992, Labor issues in a North American free trade area, In: Nora Lustig, Barry P. Bosworth, and Robert Z. Lawrence, eds., North American free trade (The Brookings Institution, Washington, DC).

Holzer, Harry J., 1991, Employment, unemployment and demand shifts in local labor markets, Review of Economics and Statistics 73, 25–32.

Holzer, Harry J. and Edward B. Montgomery, 1993, Asymmetries and rigidities in wage adjustments by firms, Review of Economics and Statistics 75, 397–408.

Kohli, Ulrich, 1991, Technology, duality, and foreign trade (University of Michigan Press, Ann Arbor, MI).

Kohli, Ulrich, 1994, Canadian imports and exports by origin and destination: A semi-flexible approach, Canadian Journal of Economics 27, 580–603.

LaLonde, Robert J. and Robert H. Topel, 1991, Labor market adjustments to increased immigration, In: John M. Abowd and Richard B. Freeman, eds., Immigration, trade, and the labor market (University of Chicago Press, Chicago, IL).

Lau, Lawrence J., 1978, Testing and imposing monotonicity, convexity, and quasiconvexity constraints, In: Melvyn Fuss and Daniel McFadden, eds., Production economics: A dual approach to theory and applications, Vol. 1 (North-Holland, Amsterdam).

Leamer, Edward E., 1993, Wage effects of a U.S.–Mexican free trade agreement, In: Peter M. Garber, ed., The Mexico–U.S. free trade agreement (M.I.T. Press, Cambridge, MA).

Levy, Santiago and Sweder van Wijnbergen, 1992, Mexico and the free trade agreement between Mexico and the United States, The World Bank Economic Review 4, 481–502.

Marston, Stephen T., 1985, Two views of the geographic distribution of unemployment, Quarterly Journal of Economics 100, 57–79.

Martin, Philip L., 1993, Trade and migration: NAFTA and agriculture (Institute for International Economics, Washington, DC).

Massey, Douglas S., 1988, Economic development and international migration in comparative perspective, Population and Development Review 14, 383–413.

Rivera-Batiz, Francisco L. and Selig L. Sechzer, 1991, Substitution and complementarity between immigrant and native labor in the United States, In: Francisco L. Rivera-Batiz, Selig L. Sechzer and Ira N. Gans, eds., U.S. immigration policy reform in the 1980s: A preliminary assessment (Praeger, New York, NY).

Robinson, Sherman, Mary E. Burfisher, Raul Hinojosa-Ojeda and Karen E. Thierfelder, 1993, Agricultural policies and migration in a U.S.–Mexico free trade area: A computable general equilibrium analysis, Journal of Policy Modeling 15, 673–701.

Sato, Ryuzo and Tetsunori Koizumi, 1973, On the elasticities of substitution and complementarity, Oxford Economic Papers 25, 44–56.

Shephard, Ronald W., 1953, Cost and production functions (Princeton University Press, Princeton, NJ).

Syrquin, Moshe and Gideon Hollender, 1982, Elasticities of substitution and complementarity: The general case, Oxford Economic Papers 34, 515–519.

Topel, Robert H., 1986, Local labor markets, Journal of Political Economy 94, S111–S143.

Treyz, George I., Dan S. Rickman, Gary L. Hunt and Michael J. Greenwood, 1993, The dynamics of U.S. internal migration, Review of Economics and Statistics 75, 209–214.

Uzawa, Hirofumi, 1962, Production functions with constant elasticities of substitution, Review of Economic Studies 23, 101–108.

White, Kenneth J., 1978, A general computer program for econometric methods: SHAZAM, Econometrica 46, 239–240.

Wiley, D.E., W.H. Schmidt and W.J. Bramble, 1973, Studies of a class of covariance structure models, Journal of the American Statistical Association 68, 317–323.

Zellner, Arnold, 1962, An efficient method of estimating seemingly unrelated regressions and tests for aggregation bias, Journal of the American Statistical Association 57, 348–368.

# [17]

*Journal of Economic Perspectives—Volume 9, Number 2—Spring 1995—Pages 23–44*

# The Impact of Immigrants on Host Country Wages, Employment and Growth

Rachel M. Friedberg and Jennifer Hunt

Immigration is a contentious issue in the industrialized nations of the world. This is true not merely in traditional receiving countries, such as the United States, Canada and Australia, but in recent decades also in Europe, which historically experienced net emigration. In Europe, for example, support has risen in recent years for virulently anti-immigrant political parties, such as the National Front in France, the National Alliance in Italy, and the Republikaner in Germany. The debate has a particularly interesting twist in those countries most of whose residents are themselves descendants of immigrants. The inscription on the Statue of Liberty exhorts the world to "give me your tired, your poor, your huddled masses yearning to breathe free . . . ." Yet there has always been a tension between this open-door philosophy and fear of the economic and social impact of the next wave of immigrants.

Many of the key issues in the debate on immigration policy are economic. Most attention has been paid to the potential adverse effect on the labor market outcomes of native-born workers: immigrants may compete with native-born workers in the labor market, displacing them in employment or bidding down wages. Less attention has been devoted to the possible benefits of immigration. Immigrants may complement some native factors in production, which would lead to these factors benefiting from immigration, and overall welfare may rise. Another question less commonly asked is how immigration influences growth in per capita income. Cases in which it would be interesting to understand this link include the role of immigration in creating the large internal American

■ *Rachel M. Friedberg is Assistant Professor of Economics, Brown University, Providence, Rhode Island. Jennifer Hunt is Assistant Professor of Economics, Yale University, New Haven, Connecticut. Both are Faculty Research Fellows at the National Bureau of Economic Research, Cambridge, Massachusetts.*

*Table 1*
**Immigrants as a Percentage of the Population**

|  | 1981 | 1991 |
|---|---|---|
| Australia | 20.6 | 22.7 |
| Austria | 3.9 | 6.6 |
| Belgium | 9.0 | 9.2 |
| Canada | 16.1 | 15.6 |
| Denmark | 2.0 | 3.3 |
| Finland | .3 | .7 |
| France | 6.8 | 6.3 |
| West Germany | 7.5 | 8.2 |
| Italy | .6 | 1.5 |
| Luxembourg | 26.1 | 28.4 |
| Netherlands | 3.8 | 4.8 |
| Norway | 2.1 | 3.5 |
| Spain | .5 | .9 |
| Sweden | 5.0 | 5.7 |
| Switzerland | 14.3 | 17.1 |
| United Kingdom | 2.8 | 3.1 |
| United States | 6.2 | 7.9 |

*Note:* Later year is 1990 for France, West Germany, Luxembourg, and the U.S. Earlier year is 1986 for Canada, 1982 for France, 1984 for the UK and 1980 for the U.S. People are classified as immigrants on the basis of nativity or citizenship, depending on the country.
*Source:* OECD, *Trends in International Migration* (1994).

market in the late nineteenth and early twentieth century; the effect of immigration back to Germany after World War II; and the current mass migration to Israel. The connection between immigration and growth is likely to depend upon the circumstances of the receiving economy and the characteristics of the immigrant inflow.

Immigration policy varies considerably from country to country. The United States allows in large numbers, most of whom enter based on their family ties with earlier immigrants already in the country. In Canada and Australia, entry is based much more on skill qualifications. All people born in the United States, even those born to illegal immigrant parents, are automatically granted citizenship. In Germany and Switzerland, even the children of people who have lived in those countries for decades may not be considered citizens of the country.

Until recently, little detailed empirical work has been done on the impact of immigrants on the receiving economy. This paper discusses the recent theoretical and empirical research on immigration's impact on the income growth and labor market outcomes of natives.

*Figure 1*
**Immigrant Flows to the United States**

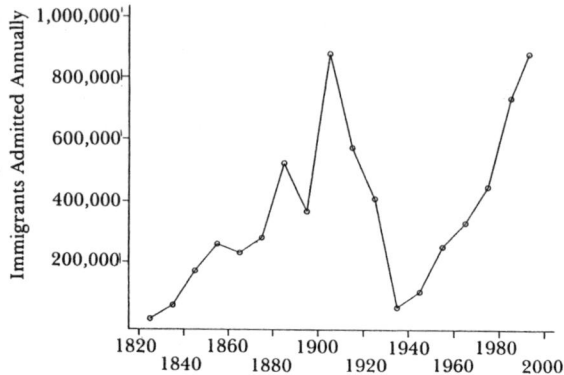

*Note:* Excludes immigrants legalized under the Immigration Reform and Control Act of 1986.
*Source:* U.S. Immigration and Naturalization Service, *Statistical Yearbook* (1994) and the U.S. Bureau of the Census, *Statistical Abstract of the United States* (1994).

## Immigration Facts

Before focusing on particular questions, the size of international migration flows should be put in perspective. Approximately 100 million people in the world live in a country other than their own. Between 1975 and 1980, approximately 5 million people migrated from one country to another. Two-thirds of immigration in that period was to a handful of host countries: the United States, Canada and Australia.

Most of the research on the impact of immigration has been on the developed countries. Table 1 shows immigrants as a fraction of the population in selected OECD countries in 1981 and 1991. Luxembourg, Australia, Switzerland and Canada have notably high proportions of foreigners (over 15 percent). Other countries with significant immigrant shares are Belgium, West Germany and the United States (7–10 percent).

The United States has had one of the largest increases in the fraction foreign-born, rising from 4.7 percent in 1970 to 7.9 percent in 1990. Figure 1 shows inflows to the United States since the 1820s. Immigration peaked in the beginning of this century, with massive flows from southern and eastern Europe. In absolute numbers, immigration is once again returning to those historic levels. As shown in Figure 2, however, the immigration rate (defined as

*Figure 2*
**Immigration Rates to the United States**

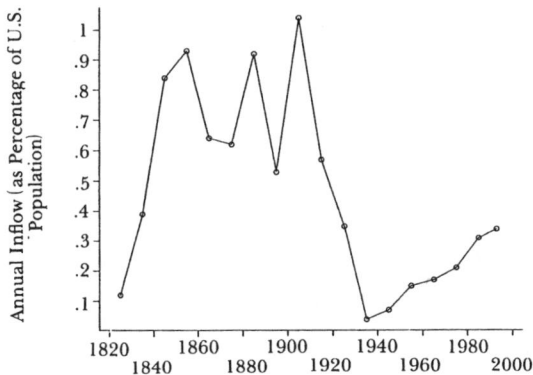

*Note:* Excludes immigrants legalized under the Immigration Reform and Control Act of 1986.
*Source:* U.S. Immigration and Naturalization Service, *Statistical Yearbook* (1994) and U.S. Bureau of the Census, *Statistical Abstract of the United States* (1994).

inflows as a percent of the U.S. population) is relatively low in comparison. Still, immigration is an increasingly important component of population growth in the United States, rising from 13 percent of growth in the 1960s, to 19 percent in the 1970s, and to 25 percent in the 1980s.

The country composition of immigration to the United States has changed greatly over time, partly due to the dramatic change in entry policy brought about by the Immigration and Nationality Act amendments of 1965, which abolished the national origins quota system in place since the 1920s. As seen in Table 2, in the 1950s, over half of all immigrants came from Europe. Currently, fewer than one in five immigrants is European. Almost 40 percent of recent immigrants are from Asia (especially Southeast Asia), and a roughly equal number originate in Mexico, the Caribbean and Latin America.[1] Most immigrants, therefore, come from countries that are poorer and less educated than the United States. Table 2 also shows the share of 1980s immigrants from each region who have less than a high school education. The source country composition of immigration has shifted toward countries whose immigrants have less education. Forty-one percent of all new adult immigrants do not possess a high school diploma, in comparison to 23 percent of natives. It is interesting to note that the educational distribution of immigrants is relatively bimodal: although the average level of schooling possessed by immigrants is lower than natives', 24 percent of new immigrants to the United States are

---

[1] In the 1980s, the share of Mexicans alone was as high as 22.6 percent.

Table 2

**Source Country and Educational Composition of U.S. Immigration**

|  | 1951–60 | 1993 | % less than high school |
|---|---|---|---|
| Europe | 52.7 | 18.3 | 19.3 |
| Asia | 6.1 | 38.2 | 26.4 |
| Canada | 15.0 | 2.6 | 14.0 |
| Mexico | 11.9 | 14.0 | 76.1 |
| South and | | | |
| Other America | 12.7 | 23.3 | 48.4 |
| Africa | .6 | 2.8 | 12.5 |
| Other | 1.0 | .7 | 23.8 |

*Note:* "% less than high school" is the percentage of people who immigrated to the United States in 1980–90 who were aged 25 or older in 1990 and did not possess a high school degree.

*Source:* U.S. Immigration and Naturalization Service, *Statistical Yearbook of the INS 1993* (1994), U.S. Bureau of the Census, *The Foreign-Born Population of the United States, 1990 Census of Population* (1993a).

college graduates, compared to 20.3 percent of natives. The low level of education possessed by many immigrants has important implications for their potential impact on the U.S. economy.

A small percentage of immigrants to the United States entered or have remained in the country illegally (Warren and Passel, 1987; Chiswick, 1988; and Borjas, Freeman, and Lang, 1991). The flow of illegals has been estimated to be between 200,000 to 300,000 per year, compared to a legal flow of about 900,000 per year. The illegal immigrant population was estimated at around 3.4 million in 1992 (equal to 1.3 percent of the U.S. population), when the stock of foreign-born in the United States was about 21 million (equal to 8.2 percent of the U.S. population). About 40 percent of the illegals have come to the United States from Mexico.

Undocumented immigrants tend to concentrate in certain cities, industries and occupations. For example, it is estimated that 43 percent of all illegal aliens live in the state of California, a state in which 21.7 percent of the population is foreign-born, and illegal immigrants comprise 4.7 percent. California recently voted into law the controversial Proposition 187, which would make illegal aliens ineligible for public health and education services. Another third of the illegal immigrant population lives in New York, Texas and Florida. The greater concentration of undocumented workers will make their impact less diffuse than that of legal immigrants. The effect of illegal immigration may also be qualitatively different from that of legal immigration, since illegal workers are constrained in the types of jobs they can take. Empirical study of the effect of illegal immigration on the labor market is, of course, hampered by the difficulty in obtaining data on their presence in the labor market, conditions of employment and so on.

A key factor determining the impact of immigration on the receiving economy is how many immigrants remain permanently in their host countries and how many eventually return to their countries of origin. It is very difficult to obtain data on remigration, but it has been estimated that roughly one in four immigrants to the United States eventually returns permanently to his or her country of origin.[2] In addition to the rate of remigration, the question of who returns is also important for understanding the long-term impact of immigration. Return migration may be dominated by people who fail to do well in the United States, give up and return home, or by those who are most successful. In this way, selective remigration may magnify or mitigate the initial impact of immigration.

## Theoretical Impact of Immigrants on Native Factors of Production

Theoretical predictions of the impact of immigration on the wages of natives depend upon the model used. The most important modelling decisions are whether the host economy is open or closed to international trade and the degree of substitutability between immigrants and natives.

In a closed economy model, immigrants will lower the price of factors with which they are perfect substitutes, have an ambiguous effect on the price of factors with which they are imperfect substitutes and raise the price of factors with which they are complements. For example, consider an economy where production takes place using capital and skilled labor, which are complementary, and unskilled labor, which is a substitute for the other two factors. If immigration of unskilled workers occurs, the wage of unskilled workers will fall, while the effect on the return to capital and the skilled wage will be ambiguous. The fall in the unskilled wage will induce employers to substitute away from capital and skilled labor to unskilled labor. However, since the greater supply of unskilled labor means that optimal output is now higher, this scale effect will induce employers to use more of all inputs. If the immigrants are skilled, they will lower the skilled wage, causing an ambiguous effect on the unskilled wage, due once again to competing substitution and scale effects. However, the fall in the skilled wage and the rise in skilled employment will lead to increased demand for the complementary factor, capital, and hence an increase in the return to capital.

[2] Warren and Kraly (1985) and the Immigration and Naturalization Service (1994) estimate a remigration rate of 31 percent for all immigrants during 1901–90 and 22 percent for those who arrived between 1981–90.

Immigration will lower the wage more if immigrants are prepared to work for less than natives, as seems plausible in the case of illegal immigrants, for example. An influx of such immigrants not only shifts labor supply, but makes it more elastic.

In the most commonly employed open economy model, the Heckscher-Ohlin model, the results are quite different. If technology is assumed to be the same across countries, trade will be driven by factor endowments, and factor price equalization occurs if countries' factor endowments are not too different. In this situation, immigration will cause production of the more labor-intensive good to increase, but factor prices will remain unchanged. In an open economy, the adjustment may be thought of as occurring through the labor embodied in traded goods: immigration will cause the country to compensate by exporting more (or importing less) labor as embodied in goods.

Notice that if factor price equalization obtains, there is no (economic) reason for migration to occur between countries. An explanation for migration from poor to rich countries in the context of this model could be that rich countries have tariffs on goods that make intensive use of unskilled labor, in an attempt to raise the domestic wage of unskilled labor above the world level. If labor is mobile, however, immigration of unskilled labor from abroad will occur until the wage of such labor returns to the world level (by which point the country will be specialized in the production of the good that makes intensive use of unskilled labor). Once the country is specialized, the impact of immigration will have effects similar to those of the closed economy case. If immigration is restricted—as it is in reality—the wage could remain above the world level for some time. Notice, however, that if capital is internationally mobile, factor price equalization should occur even if tariffs and restrictions on labor mobility are present.

A model of trade and factor flows that captures many realistic features is one in which countries have very different endowments of factors, and factor price equalization might not occur even with free trade; rather, countries will specialize in production, instead of each producing all goods. Thus, countries with a large labor endowment will produce a more labor-intensive mix of goods than countries with a large capital endowment. The resulting cross-country differences in wages could then generate migration. In this case, the impact of a labor influx will then depend upon its size: a large enough inflow will force the country to move to a more labor-intensive mix of products, which will lower the wage (and increase the return to capital). Enough migration (or capital movement) will once more eliminate wage differentials. On the other hand, a small inflow will not affect wages, as the country will increase production of its relatively labor-intensive goods and sell more of those goods on the world market, and thus factor price equalization will be achieved through trade.[3]

---

[3]If technologies are allowed to differ across countries, as in Markusen (1983), factors will flow toward the country that has an absolute advantage in their use.

If the country receiving immigrants is a large one, the increase in output of labor-intensive goods spurred by immigration will reduce the world prices of those goods. This may reduce the wage, even under conditions where factor price equalization would hold for a small country.

Any changes in wages of native groups will be accompanied by changes in native employment or hours worked. In the example of unskilled immigration to a closed economy, although total employment of unskilled workers (including immigrants) will increase, the fall in the unskilled wage will cause some natives to leave the labor force or reduce their hours, and the employment rate (or labor force participation rate) of natives may fall. Conversely, the employment rate of any group whose wage rises as a result of immigration is likely to increase.

These models do not directly predict that unemployment will result from immigration, yet they do predict movements of factors between production sectors of different factor intensity (even in models with factor price equalization), and to the extent that job matching and capital movement do not occur instantaneously, unemployment will result in the short run even for natives. The job search problem will of course be more acute for the immigrants themselves, all of whom must find new jobs. In the closed economy model, which predicts an adjustment of the wage, unemployment could result if the wage is made rigid by institutional arrangements. This is particularly likely in the European setting, in countries where union contracts apply to most workers. In such a case, the adjustment to immigration will come through unemployment rather than through reduced wages.

Models that do admit equilibrium unemployment include the efficiency wage model of Shapiro and Stiglitz (1984). In that model, firms cannot perfectly observe workers' level of effort, and so to elicit higher productivity, they need to build in an incentive for workers not to shirk. Equilibrium unemployment serves as that worker discipline device. Workers who are caught shirking are fired, so the fear of becoming unemployed induces workers to put forth effort, as long as the wage is sufficiently high. In equilibrium then, wages are negatively related to the unemployment rate.

In this model, an influx of immigrants increases the size of the labor force, which allows firms to lower the wage and raise employment. However, the lower wage must be accompanied by a rise in the unemployment rate to maintain workers' incentive not to shirk. How the rise in unemployment is distributed across natives and immigrants is an empirical question.

## Empirical Approaches to Evaluating Labor Market Responses

### Cross-Section Differencing

Most approaches to measuring the impact of immigration on the labor market outcomes of natives have used as a starting point the idea that one can look at a cross-section of cities or regions in a country and use variations in immigrant density to identify the effect of immigrants on the outcome of interest. For example, one might look at the proportion of immigrants in many cities and the level of wages in those cities. A possible difficulty with this approach follows from the discussion of open economies: in the presence of free trade within the recipient country, along with capital mobility or labor mobility, factor price equalization is likely to obtain. In this case, even if immigrants affect native wages at the national level, an uneven distribution of immigrants across the country may not result (in the long run) in cross-section wage differences, as wages may be equalized by flows in goods or factors. It appears likely, however, that regional wage differentials may appear in the short term as the result of supply or demand shocks.

Another important consideration is the fact that immigrants may choose where to settle in the receiving country. Immigrants, likely to be the most mobile of workers, will probably move to those regions whose demand shocks have led to higher wages. Because of this endogeneity, a naive econometrician might conclude that greater immigrant density leads to higher wages. In fact, if one plots the mean 1990 wage and salary income of the 30 largest Standard Metropolitan Statistical Areas (SMSAs) in the United States against the fraction of those cities' population that is foreign-born, as in Figure 3, one finds that cities with higher immigrant densities also have higher mean incomes. The correlation between these two variables is 0.37.

If immigrants choose their location based upon the level of the wage, but not on foreseen rises in it, the endogencity problem may be circumvented by using data from two or more time periods. The change in immigrant density will not be affected by the change in the local wage, and any correlation between those two changes will be attributable to the effect of a change in immigrant density on the change in the wage. Differencing also eliminates location-specific effects that do not vary over time and offers the advantage of focusing more on the short term by looking at the effect of immigrant flows rather than stocks. However, if immigrants choose locations with growing wages, a spurious positive correlation between immigrants and wages will still be present in the differenced estimation.

In an example of differenced estimation, Goldin (1994) exploits U.S. cross-city variation using several sources of data from the period 1890–1923. She examines the effect of changes in the number of foreign-born as a fraction of city population on changes in wages in different occupations and industries, matching the city-level wage data with information on immigrant density taken from the nearest Censuses of Population. For some subperiods and groups, the effects are positive or zero, but the most common result is that a 1 percentage point increase in the fraction of the population that is foreign-born reduces wages from 1.0–1.6 percent. Some of Goldin's results may be affected by the "composition" problem, common to many papers in this literature: city-level wages are a composite of the wages of immigrants and natives in that location. Therefore, if immigrants earn less than natives, cities with higher proportions of immigrants will have lower average wages, even if immigrants have no

*Figure 3*
**Earnings and Immigrant Densities in the 30 Largest SMSAs**

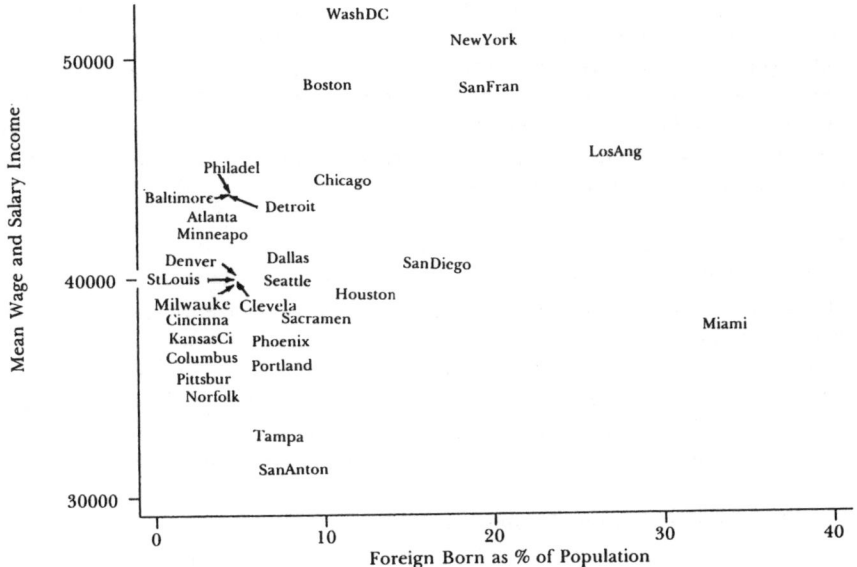

*Note:* Income numbers are at the household level.
*Source:* U.S. Bureau of the Census (1993b).

negative impact on the native wage. Without being able to distinguish native from immigrant earnings, it is not possible to sort out between these two alternatives.

In a cross-section study of more recent data, LaLonde and Topel (1991) examine levels and changes in immigrant density across U.S. cities (SMSAs), but analyze individual-level census data on males from 1970 and 1980, and allow different waves of immigrants to have different effects. The use of individual-level data reduces the simultaneity problem, because it is possible to control for many of the characteristics that might cause people to move to growing areas. It also allows city-specific effects to be controlled for, even in an undifferenced cross-section. However, the problem remains that flows of goods or people may diffuse the effects of immigration and render them imperceptible to cross-section analysis.

Lalonde and Topel (1991) focus upon the effect of different immigrant cohorts on each other, reasoning that since immigrants will affect each other more than they affect natives, any effect found can be viewed as an upper bound on the impact of immigrants on native groups. The largest effect found is the impact of male immigrants who have been in the United States for five or fewer years on their own group: the preferred estimates suggest that increasing the fraction of such immigrants in the labor force by 10 percent reduces their wages by about 0.3 percent. If young blacks and Hispanics are included as groups in this analysis, their wages are found to be insignificantly affected by the number of immigrants (the point estimates are similar to the inter-immigrant group effects). The results are not sensitive to whether annual or weekly wages are used, which leads the authors to conclude that time without a job, measured either by unemployment or by exiting the labor force, is not an important factor. These findings suggest that the labor market impact of immigrants is not a cause for concern.

**Instrumental Variables**

The next step in sophistication is to find "instruments" for the change in immigrant density. If a variable can be found that is sufficiently correlated with the change in immigrant density, but does not directly influence the outcome variables, one can use the instrumental variables technique to remove the bias due to immigrant choice of regions with improving outcomes. If the instrumental variable is also uncorrelated with omitted information on trade flows and the mobility of native labor and capital, the bias due to their omission will also be remedied.

The challenge is to find a suitable instrument. As one example, Altonji and Card (1991) use the stock of immigrants in 1970 as an instrument for the change in the fraction of foreign-born individuals in the population from 1970 to 1980. Their logic is that in this period, new immigrants tended to move to places where similar immigrants already resided (Bartel, 1989) and that this initial concentration of immigrants does not directly influence the outcome variables. They try to explain changes in wages and unemployment across SMSAs from 1970 to 1980, controlling for changes in average age and education in each metropolitan area. The analysis focuses on the less-skilled native groups one would expect to be most negatively affected by immigration: white male high school dropouts, and black and white females and black males with high school education or less. The results suggest that immigrants had an unexpected *negative* effect on unemployment in the census week. They also had a negative effect on the fraction of the population who worked in the previous year and on weekly earnings in the previous year. No significant impact was found on the labor force participation rate or the employment to population ratio in the census week or the number of weeks worked in the previous year. The magnitudes of the coefficients imply that a 1 percentage point increase in the percent of foreign-born in a city reduces the unemployment rate by 0.23 percentage points; reduces the number who worked in the previous year by 0.25 percentage points; and reduces wages of unskilled natives by 1.2 percent, at most.

Along with those of Goldin (1994), the Altonji and Card (1991) wage results are among the most negative found by studies with an important cross-section dimension. The instrumental variables technique should eliminate positive bias caused by immigrants moving to areas with growing wages, as well as bias toward zero due to factor price equalization across the country. This may explain why Altonji and Card arrive at a more negative figure than most papers that do not use instrumental variables. To compare their results to those of other studies, it is necessary to convert the wage coefficient into an elasticity: for a city whose foreign population share increases from 7 to 8 percent (a 14 percent increase), the wage is predicted to fall by 1.2 percent. Hence, in their results, a 10 percent increase in foreign share implies a 0.86 percent fall in wages (weekly earnings).

It is interesting to put these instrumental variables results into perspective by comparing them with related results on the expansion of the U.S. workforce with the labor force entry of the post–World War II baby-boom generation. Welch (1979) studies the effect of generational crowding on wages. He finds that for white male high school dropouts, an age cohort which is 10 percent larger will have 0.8–1.8 percent lower weekly earnings, which is similar to the immigrant crowding effect. However, Welch also finds that the effect of a large age cohort on annual earnings is about 2.5 percent, which implies that an important part of the effect of crowding comes through less employment, together with the lower wages. By contrast, Altonji and Card (1991) find that immigration has either a small or positive effect on employment. Taken together, these results imply that the overall adverse impact of immigration is smaller than that of generational crowding. Welch calculates that the baby boom was responsible for a 12 percent drop in the wages of high school dropouts from 1967–1975. To induce the same wage reduction would require a 140 percent (or 10 percentage point) increase in the immigrant share, using Altonji and Card's estimate.

Another perspective on the size of these results is what they imply for changes in immigration policy. According to these estimates, had the United States increased by 10 percent the number of immigrants admitted in the 1980s, the immigrant density would have been 0.25 percentage points (or 4 percent) higher than it was at the end of the decade, and U.S. wages would have been 0.4 percent lower as a result. As another example, if there were no illegal immigrants in California, the wage level would be 2.0–5.5 percent higher.[4]

Comparative studies across countries shed light on whether these results from the United States hold in other labor market settings. In their study of the West German labor market, Pischke and Velling (1994) apply the technique

---

[4] Measuring immigration's impact in California is problematic because the density of immigrants is so much higher there than the U.S. average on which most estimates of the wage elasticity are based. The distinction between percent changes and percentage point changes becomes important here.

developed in Altonji and Card to German data for 1985 and 1989. It is interesting to note that they also find no significant detrimental effects of immigrants on employment, unemployment or wages. This accords with the evidence from the United States discussed so far.


### Production Functions

A less common use of cross-section data has been to estimate a production function to compute elasticities of substitution between immigrants and natives, which allows computation of the effect of immigrants on other factor prices. Jean Grossman (1982) carries out such a study, based on the estimation of a trans-log production function using 1970 data across SMSAs. Grossman finds significant effects of immigrants on natives, with magnitudes suggesting that a 10 percent increase in the number of employed immigrants would reduce native wages by 1 percent. In this model, it should be noted that natives are not distinguished by skill.


### Factor Price Equalization Considerations

The literature relying primarily on cross-section data thus finds modest effects of immigrants on natives' labor market outcomes. However, as already discussed, the results of these studies are likely to be biased toward zero if instrumenting has not successfully dealt with the immigrants' location decision. Also, such cross-section studies are likely to be biased toward zero if the effects of immigration are spread evenly across an economy by factor price equalization, which is the issue confronted in this section.

The question of whether factor price equalization holds within a country is difficult. Different regions do appear to have product mixes that vary in how intensively they use different factors, yet the resulting wage differentials should vanish in the presence of labor or capital mobility. If mobility costs are postulated, it is possible that wage differentials could exist in the steady state. Yet even under this scenario, relative wages across regions will be less sensitive to immigration than the national wage, assuming domestic regions are more open to each other than the national economy is to other countries.

Some empirical evidence is available to assess the extent and speed of factor price equalization. For the United States, Blanchard and Katz (1992) document that wage differentials caused by a demand shock of 1 percent to employment growth in a particular state appear to linger for up to 10 years, and unemployment and labor force participation differentials for about 6 years. In a parallel study of Europe, Decressin and Fatàs (1995) find that unemployment and labor force participation are perturbed for about 4 years by region-specific shocks (they do not analyze wages). These studies suggest that it is reasonable to seek the impact of immigration by using cross-section data on regions, and that the bias toward zero due to factor price equalization may be small.

Some cautionary evidence is provided by Filer (1992) and White and Hunter (1993), whose studies of the 1970s show that internal migrants in the United States avoided those areas where immigrants were arriving from abroad. This can be seen as a mechanism through which factor price equalization could occur. Although the skill composition of internal migrants may be different from that of immigrants from abroad, internal migrants presumably have a qualitatively similar effect on wages. Failing to take into account the fact that net internal migration to a region falls in response to immigration from abroad will lead to underestimates of the effect of immigration on wages in cross-section studies. This is because a reduction in net migration to high-immigration areas will keep wages there higher than they would otherwise have been. The bias caused by the omission of internal migration may be remedied by suitable instrumental variables, and may therefore be less of an issue in the Altonji and Card (1991) estimation than in the LaLonde and Topel (1991) estimation. More recent work on internal migration has failed to confirm the offsetting effect found in the earlier analyses,[5] but it nevertheless underscores the importance of instrumenting for the immigrant density.

In summary, it is probably reasonable to assume that factor price equalization is not so rapid or complete as to render cross-section analysis of immigration useless. However, it remains important to use instrumental variables to capture the impact of immigration, both to take into account the choice of location by immigrants and also the possibility of compensating flows of factors and goods.

**Natural Experiments**

A number of studies examining "natural experiments" in immigration are able to shed light on the importance of biases in cross-section analysis. These studies seek episodes where the timing and location of immigration may be politically rather than economically motivated, which reduces the problem of immigrants choosing locations based on their labor market conditions. For example, Card (1990) examines the impact of the Cubans who increased Miami's population by about 7 percent in the May 1980 Mariel boatlift. The timing of this influx was politically determined, and the arrival location was to some extent exogenous, due to Miami's proximity to Cuba (although not all the Mariels remained in Miami). It is thus reasonable to examine the evolution of variables of interest in the period immediately following the boatlift, comparing

---

[5]For examples, see Butcher and Card (1991) and White and Liang (1994), using U.S. data from the 1980s, and Pischke and Velling (1994) using data from Germany.

the outcomes with those in similar cities and ascribing differences in patterns to the arrival of the Mariels.[6]

Using yearly data from the Current Population Survey, Card (1990) considers wages, employment rates and unemployment rates for unskilled whites and blacks, for non-Cuban Hispanics and for Cubans. Only Cubans appear to have been negatively affected. The observed pattern for Cubans, however, seems consistent with the idea that their relative decline was a compositional effect, caused by the addition of the Mariels, who (as is known from a 1985 survey) earned less and had higher unemployment than other Cubans. Card finds that population growth in Miami slowed, however, and he speculates that other migration to Miami may have been reduced in response to the boatlift. Since Card examines yearly data, however, any type of factor price equalization adjustment must have happened very quickly.

In another natural experiment, Hunt (1992) examines the repatriation to France of Algerians of European origin prompted by Algerian independence in 1962. This influx of skilled labor increased the French labor force by 1.6 percent. Its timing was exogenous, and the location of the repatriates determined to a large extent by climate (and proximity to port of arrival). In a differenced cross-section analysis for the years 1962 and 1968, Hunt uses as instrumental variables the temperature of the region and the stock of pre-1962 repatriates. She finds that a 1 percentage point increase in the repatriate share of the labor force reduced the wage of a region by at most 0.8 percent (zero in some specifications) and raised the unemployment rate of natives by 0.2 percentage points. It also turned out that other immigrants from abroad were more likely to move to areas with more repatriates, and this effect offset the reduction in internal migration to these areas caused by lower wages and higher unemployment.

A final example along these lines is the return of Portuguese colonialists from Africa after a Marxist revolution in 1974, studied by Carrington and deLima (1994). They use a time-series specification, comparisons with Spain and a cross-section across the twelve provinces of Portugal. They find that their results are very sensitive to the approach taken. On the whole, the natural experiment literature adds to the evidence suggesting a limited impact of immigrants on natives.

### Time Series

The use of time-series data at a national level avoids any bias toward zero due to factor price equalization and endogenous regional choice of immigrants,

---

[6]This kind of analysis is not possible in general, because only the census provides information on birthplace, rather than simply ethnicity.

but introduces a different bias toward zero: immigrants will tend to come to a country at times when labor market outcomes are favorable. An additional difficulty is that of modelling the movement of wages over a long time period. In an example of pure time-series analysis, Pope and Withers (1993) find no negative effects of immigration on Australian natives over the period 1861–1981. In their study, they use the labor market characteristics of sending countries and transport costs to Australia as instrumental variables for the migration rates.

**Wage Inequality Literature**

A series of recent papers motivated by rising inequality has estimated elasticities similar to or smaller than the Altonji and Card and Goldin estimates, but in a context that suggests immigration may have economically important effects. These papers use the yearly data from the Current Population Survey to estimate how the relative supplies of different educational groups affect their relative wages. Such studies have used both time-series and regional cross-section analysis. A calculation is then made as to the contribution of immigrants to the increase in the relative supply of the least-educated group in the 1980s and, hence, to the relative decline of the wage of the less skilled. To compare the results with those discussed so far, we must assume that the increase in inequality comes entirely from a fall in the wage of the less skilled. The elasticities calculated using this assumption will thus overstate the negative impact of immigration on the absolute wage of the unskilled.

Borjas, Freeman, and Katz (1992) use time-series data for the United States from 1967–1987. Their results suggest that immigration accounted for one-quarter of the 10 percent decline in the relative earnings of high school dropouts from 1980–1988, a period when immigrants as a proportion of the labor force rose from 6.9 percent to 9.3 percent. This means a 1 percentage point increase in the proportion of immigrants reduces the absolute wage of dropouts by at most 1.2 percent, the same magnitude calculated by Altonji and Card.

Borjas and Ramey (1993) look at relative wages in a panel of 44 SMSAs from 1977–1991, using data from the Current Population Survey. Their estimates suggest that a 1 percentage point increase in fraction foreign-born reduces the wage of high school dropouts relative to college graduates by 0.6 percent. This is half as large as the Altonji and Card estimate.

Greater reliance on time-series data avoids the biases present in the cross-section estimation toward finding no effect of immigration (like the problems involving immigrant choice of location and factor price equalization discussed earlier). It seems likely, however, that data constraints cause the estimates in the wage inequality literature to overstate immigration's impact on native wages. One reason is the composition problem: the results confound the negative impact with the purely mechanical negative effect on the average unskilled wage of adding unskilled immigrants, whose earnings are below the unskilled native average. The method also constrains the effect on relative wages of increasing the supply of unskilled workers to be the same, whether the increase is due to natives or immigrants, but since unskilled natives are probably better substitutes for each other than are unskilled immigrants, the elasticity estimated will be larger than the true elasticity for unskilled immigrants.[7] Both of these problems arise due to data constraints, since the immigrant density can be calculated from the CPS only for certain years. Notice that if foreign-born high school dropouts earn 20 percent less than native dropouts, the increase in their number from 1980–1988 would be expected to reduce the average dropout wage by 1.5 percent just due to the composition effect, and this magnitude is large compared to the total impact of 2.5 percent ascribed to immigration in Borjas, Freeman, and Katz (1992).

The wage inequality literature thus points to an upper bound on the negative effect of immigration on wages similar to that of the cross-section literature, but suggests the true effect is considerably smaller. The upper bound would suggest that immigration had a significant role to play in the rise in inequality in the 1980s.

## Immigration and Growth

Labor economists interested in migration have focused empirically upon labor market outcomes such as wages and employment. They have typically assumed an economy with an aggregate production technology displaying constant returns to scale. Macroeconomists and international economists have paid some attention to the question of the influence of migration on (per capita) growth, which may be particularly interesting in the context of increasing returns to scale. Of course, growth would then feed back into the variables traditionally in the domain of labor economists. While recent theoretical work has made strides toward explaining the possible links between immigration and growth, only a few empirical studies have been conducted, and no clear picture has emerged from these.

A simple theoretical analysis can be based on a modified Solow (1956) growth model. Production is a function of labor and human capital, which are internationally mobile, and physical capital, which is not. Assume there is no

---

[7]Borjas and Ramey (1993) recognize this problem, and they include the percentage foreign-born explicitly on the right-hand side of their regression, which avoids constraining the impact of natives to be the same as that of immigrants. However, their foreign-born variable is constructed by interpolating between the 1970 and 1980 censuses and the 1989 CPS, and the time-series variation is thus to a large extent a trend.

trade between countries.[8] A country receives immigrants if it has a higher ratio of physical capital to labor, which implies a higher wage rate. Immigrants are assumed to bring no physical capital with them, but they do bring human capital and will bring more human capital if the ratio of physical capital to human capital is high. In such a model, the key to the impact of immigration is whether immigrants bring enough human capital to offset their dilution of physical capital in the receiving economy. If immigrants have little human capital, their impact is akin to that of faster population growth in slowing per capita growth. If immigrant human capital levels are higher than natives' by a sufficient amount, growth will be speeded up.[9]

Obviously, these models have their limitations. They view economies as closed except to immigrants and the human capital they carry. They also tend to imply that in the long run everyone lives in one country. Braun (1992) extends the models to allow for perfect physical capital mobility and introduces the concept of a natural resource that is subject to congestion. People and capital will move to places well endowed with this resource or with better technologies, but this migration will not continue forever, due to the increasing congestion of the natural resource.

When the assumption of constant returns to scale production is replaced with that of increasing returns to scale, the results are transformed. Brezis and Krugman (1993) formalize this in a free trade model where the country receiving immigrants can borrow and lend at the world interest rate. In this case, if (exogenous) immigration occurs, output will increase more than proportionately, which implies a rise in the rate of return to capital as well as an increase in the wage. Since the interest rate must equal the world rate, however, the capital-to-labor ratio will rise in response, further increasing the wage. Since a higher quantity of labor results in a higher wage in these models, the receiving country's aggregate labor demand curve becomes upward sloping.

The theoretical models generally predict that a migrant will move either to a country with a higher wage or a country where the expected stream of wages is higher. But if higher immigration can help create the higher wages that make that immigration attractive in the first place, then there is simultaneity between growth and migration that will be difficult to disentangle empirically. A paper that tackles this issue is that by Barro and Sala-i-Martin (1992). They include migration in an equation regressing growth in per capita income on the level of per capita income (and other variables) for Japanese and American regions in different time periods. In this context, the coefficient on the level of income indicates the rate of convergence between regions (which one could

---

[8]Some readers may recognize this as a human capital-augmented Solow-Swan model. The theoretical discussion of growth in this section draws heavily on Barro and Sala-i-Martin (1995).

[9]These results are little altered by moving to a Ramsey growth model, which allows the savings rate to be endogenous. For details, again see Barro and Sala-i-Martin (1995).

view as recovery from shocks or as short-term growth). The impact of migration on growth may be judged in two ways: by the way in which including a migration variable affects the estimated convergence coefficient and also by the actual coefficient on migration, which can be interpreted as the effect of migration on long-term growth. For both Japan and the United States, adding migration to the convergence regression raises the convergence coefficient slightly and yields a positive coefficient on migration. For the United States, this coefficient suggests that a 1 percentage point higher net migration rate is associated with a 0.1 percent higher growth rate.

If measures of temperature and population density of the region (the latter proxying for housing costs or, possibly, the congestable resource of Braun's model) are used as instrumental variables for migration, the coefficient becomes insignificant for both the United States and Japan (and the convergence coefficient is virtually unchanged). The point estimate suggests that a 1 percentage point rise in the net migration rate raises long-term growth by 0.01 percent for the United States, and by 0.04 percent for Japan. The authors conclude that migration has little effect on growth, but the results may be due to weak instruments.

A puzzle arises when the work of Barro and Sala-i-Martin (1992) is compared with that of Blanchard and Katz (1992), whose study of the U.S. states concludes that migration is the major labor market response to state-specific shocks to employment growth. The very different framework in which Blanchard and Katz study the question makes comparisons difficult, however. They estimate a system of equations for employment growth, participation rates and unemployment. Their results reveal that after a shock to employment growth in a state, participation and unemployment rates eventually return to their pre-shock levels. Employment returns to its old growth rate but no higher, which implies that employment is permanently lower than it would have been in the absence of the shock. Since participation and unemployment rates are back at their old levels, the lower employment must be due to emigration from the state. This picture suggests that migration is a very important equilibrating mechanism for recovery from shocks to a state, which is at odds with the Barro and Sala-i-Martin results.

There are few papers which can be appealed to for a resolution of this puzzle in the U.S. data. In a study of migration among the OECD countries, Dolado, Goria, and Ichino (1993) contribute to our understanding of the question by performing structural estimation of the Solow-based model described above, using national panel data. Net migration is instrumented using lagged values of migration, savings rates, schooling rates and population density. The coefficient on the migration variable is not reported, but in their approach, adding migration reduces the convergence coefficient. Although they refer to migration in a different setting, these results are more in accordance with the Blanchard and Katz (1992) finding.

As outlined in the theoretical discussion, the expected results depend upon the human capital level of the migrants compared to the natives. Dolado, Goria, and Ichino document that immigrants to OECD countries have lower human capital than natives. Borjas, Bronars, and Trejo (1992) demonstrate that the Roy model captures self-selection among internal migrants in the United States: wage compression at home encourages the skilled to emigrate, while wage dispersion attracts the skilled. Immigrants move to where their skills are best rewarded, and thus relative immigrant quality will depend on the wage dispersion in the receiving region. Migrant quality has not been explicitly accounted for thus far in the internal migration and growth literature. It is conceivable that doing so might help resolve the puzzle of U.S. internal migration.

## Conclusion

Despite the popular belief that immigrants have a large adverse impact on the wages and employment opportunities of the native-born population, the literature on this question does not provide much support for this conclusion. Economic theory is equivocal, and empirical estimates in a variety of settings and using a variety of approaches have shown that the effect of immigration on the labor market outcomes of natives is small. There is no evidence of economically significant reductions in native employment. Most empirical analysis of the United States and other countries finds that a 10 percent increase in the fraction of immigrants in the population reduces native wages by at most 1 percent. Even those natives who should be the closest substitutes with immigrant labor have not been found to suffer significantly as a result of increased immigration. The upper bound on the wage impact is large enough to explain one-quarter of the rise in inequality in the United States in the 1980s, but the true effect is probably considerably smaller.

The theoretical literature on immigration and economic growth suggests that the impact of immigrants on natives' income growth depends crucially on the human capital levels of the immigrants. Empirical research on this question has yielded conflicting answers, and more work on this issue is needed.

■ *We thank Joseph Altonji, Andrea Ichino, Lawrence Katz, Xavier Sala-i-Martin, James Morsink, T. N. Srinivasan and David Weil for helpful discussions, and Edward Lee for able research assistance.*

# References

**Altonji, Joseph, and David Card,** "The Effects of Immigration on the Labor Market Outcomes of Less-skilled Natives." In Abowd, J., and R. Freeman, eds., *Immigration, Trade and the Labor Market.* Chicago: University of Chicago Press, 1991, pp. 201–34.

**Barro, Robert, and Xavier Sala-i-Martin,** "Regional Growth and Migration: A Japan-United States Comparison," *Journal of the International and Japanese Economies,* December 1992, *6,* 312–46.

**Barro, Robert, and Xavier Sala-i-Martin,** *Economic Growth.* New York: McGraw Hill, 1995.

**Bartel, Ann,** "Where Do the New U.S. Immigrants Live?," *Journal of Labor Economics,* October 1989, 7, 371–91.

**Blanchard, Olivier, and Lawrence Katz,** "Regional Evolutions," *Brookings Papers on Economic Activity,* 1992, *1,* 1–61.

**Borjas, George, Stephen Bronars, and Stephen Trejo,** "Self-Selection and Internal Migration in the United States," *Journal of Urban Economics,* September 1992, *32,* 159–85.

**Borjas, George, Richard Freeman, and Lawrence Katz,** "On the Labor Market Impacts of Immigration and Trade." In Borjas, G., and R. Freeman, eds., *Immigration and the Work Force: Economic Consequences for the United States and Source Areas.* Chicago: University of Chicago Press, 1992, pp. 213–44.

**Borjas, George, Richard Freeman, and Kevin Lang,** "Undocumented Mexican-Born Workers in the United States: How Many? How Permanent?" In Abowd, J., and R. Freeman, eds., *Immigration, Trade, and the Labor Market.* Chicago: University of Chicago Press, 1991, pp. 77–100.

**Borjas, George, and Valerie Ramey,** "Foreign Competition, Market Power and Wage Inequality: Theory and Evidence." NBER Working Paper 4556, 1993.

**Braun, Juan,** "Migration and Economic Growth," working paper, Harvard University, 1992.

**Brezis, Elise, and Paul Krugman,** "Immigration, Investment and Real Wages." NBER Working Paper 4563, 1993.

**Butcher, Kristin, and David Card,** "Immigration and Wages: Evidence from the 1980s," *American Economic Review,* May 1991, *81,* 292–96.

**Card, David,** "The Impact of the Mariel Boatlift on the Miami Labor Market," *Industrial and Labor Relations Review,* January 1990, *43,* 245–57.

**Carrington, William, and Pedro deLima,** "Large-Scale Immigration and Labor Markets: An Analysis of the Retornados and Their Impact on Portugal," working paper, Johns Hopkins University, 1994.

**Chiswick, Barry,** *The Gateway: U.S. Immigration Issues and Policies.* Washington, D.C.: American Enterprise Institute, 1982.

**Chiswick, Barry,** *Illegal Aliens: Their Employment and Employers.* Kalamazoo, Mich.: W. E. Upjohn Institute for Employment Research, 1988.

**Decressin, Jörg, and Antonio Fatàs,** "Regional Labour Market Dynamics in Europe," *European Economic Review,* forthcoming, 1995.

**Dolado, Juan, Alessandra Goria, and Andrea Ichino,** "Immigration, Human Capital and Growth in the Host Country," working paper, Fondazione ENI Enrico Mattei, 1993.

**Filer, Randall,** "The Impact of Immigrant Arrivals on Migratory Patterns of Native Workers." In Borjas, G., and R. Freeman, eds., *Immigration and the Work Force: Economic Consequences for the United States and Source Areas.* Chicago: University of Chicago Press, 1992, pp. 245–70.

**Goldin, Claudia,** "The Political Economy of Immigration Restriction in the United States, 1890–1921." In Goldin, C., and G. Libecap, eds., *The Regulated Economy: A Historical Approach to Political Economy.* Chicago: University of Chicago Press, 1994, pp. 223–57.

**Grossman, Jean,** "The Substitutability of Natives and Immigrants in Production," *Review of Economics and Statistics,* November 1982, *64,* 596–603.

**Hunt, Jennifer,** "The Impact of the 1962 Repatriates from Algeria on the French Labor Market," *Industrial and Labor Relations Review,* April 1992, *45,* 556–72.

**Jasso, Guillermina, and Mark Rosenzweig,** *The New Chosen People: Immigrants in the United States.* New York: Russell Sage Foundation, 1990.

**LaLonde, Robert, and Robert Topel,** "Labor Market Adjustments to Increased Immigration." In Abowd, J., and R. Freeman, eds., *Immigration, Trade and the Labor Market.* Chicago: University of Chicago Press, 1991, pp. 167–200.

**Markusen, James,** "Factor Movements and Commodity Trade as Complements," *Journal* *of International Economics*, May 1983, *14*, 341–56.

**Organization for Economic Cooperation and Development,** *Trends in International Migration* (*SOPEMI Annual Report* 1993). Paris: OECD, 1994.

**Pischke, Jörn-Steffen, and Johannes Velling,** "Wage and Employment Effects of Immigration to Germany: An Analysis Based on Local Markets," working paper, MIT, 1994.

**Pope, David, and Glenn Withers,** "Do Migrants Rob Jobs? Lessons of Australian History, 1861–1991," *Journal of Economic History*, December 1993, *53*, 719–42.

**Shapiro, Carl, and Joseph Stiglitz,** "Equilibrium Unemployment as a Discipline Device," *American Economic Review*, June 1984, *74*, 433–44.

**Simon, Julian,** *The Economic Consequences of Immigration*. Cambridge, Mass.: Basil Blackwell, 1989.

**Solow, Robert,** "A Contribution to the Theory of Economic Growth," *Quarterly Journal of Economics*, February 1956, *70*, 65–94.

**U.S. Bureau of the Census,** *General Social and Economic Characteristics, 1980 Census of Population*. Washington, D.C.: Government Printing Office, 1983.

**U.S. Bureau of the Census,** *The Foreign-Born Population of the United States, 1990 Census of Population*. Washington, D.C.: Government Printing Office, 1993a.

**U.S. Bureau of the Census,** *General Social and Economic Characteristics, 1990 Census of Population*. Washington, D.C.: Government Printing Office, 1993b.

**U.S. Bureau of the Census,** *Statistical Abstract of the United States 1994*. Washington, D.C.: Government Printing Office, 1994.

**U.S. Immigration and Naturalization Service,** *Statistical Yearbook of the Immigration and Naturalization Service 1993*. Washington, D.C.: Government Printing Office, 1994.

**Warren, Robert, and Ellen Percy Kraly,** "The Elusive Exodus: Emigration from the United States." *Population Trends and Public Policy Occasional Paper*. No. 8. Washington, D.C.: Population Reference Bureau, March 1985.

**Warren, Robert, and Jeffrey Passel,** "A Count of the Uncountable: Estimates of Undocumented Aliens Counted in the 1980 U.S. Census," *Demography*, August, 1987, *24*, 375–93.

**Welch, Finis,** "Effects of Cohort Size on Earnings: The Baby Boom Babies' Financial Bust," *Journal of Political Economy*, October 1979, *87*, S65–S97.

**White, Michael J., and Lori Hunter,** "The Migratory Response of Native-Born Workers to the Presence of Immigrants in the Labor Market." Brown University PSTC Working Paper 93–08, July 1993.

**White, Michael J., and Zai Liang,** "The Effect of Immigration on the Internal Migration of the Native Born Population, 1981–90," mimeo, Brown University, 1994.

# Part III
# FDI and Labour Markets

# [18]

*The Economic Journal*, **107** (*November*), 1787–1797. © Royal Economic Society 1997. Published by Blackwell Publishers, 108 Cowley Road, Oxford OX4 1JF, UK and 350 Main Street, Malden, MA 02148, USA.

## FOREIGN DIRECT INVESTMENT AND EMPLOYMENT: HOME COUNTRY EXPERIENCE IN THE UNITED STATES AND SWEDEN*

*Magnus Blomström, Gunnar Fors and Robert E. Lipsey*

We compare the relation between foreign affiliate production and parent employment in US manufacturing multinationals with that in Swedish firms. US multinationals appear to have allocated some of their more labour-intensive operations selling in world markets to affiliates in developing countries, reducing the labour intensity in their home production. Swedish multinationals produce relatively little in developing countries and most of that has been for sale within host countries with import-substituting trade regimes. The great majority of Swedish affiliate production is in high-income countries, the United States and Europe, and is associated with more employment, particularly blue-collar employment, in the parent companies. The small Swedish-owned production that does take place in developing countries is also associated with more white-collar employment at home. The effects on white-collar employment within the Swedish firms have grown smaller and weaker over time.

### I. INTRODUCTION

Most countries have been engaged in extensive internal debates over the role of multinational corporations (MNCs) in their economies. Inward investment has been feared as a source of foreign influence, or even control, and of competition with local entrepreneurs, but also welcomed for its promise of superior technology and employment opportunities, and the hope that it would substitute for imports and perhaps increase exports. Outward investment has been opposed in home countries as substituting for exports and reducing domestic capital investment and job creation, but it has been defended as necessary for the growth and prosperity of home-based firms in the contest for world-wide markets. The policy-making of both host and home countries of multinationals, however, has suffered from uncertainty about the effects of investment.

In this paper we analyse some effects of foreign production on the demand for labour by home-country parent firms as a consequence of their decisions to allocate different types of production to different types of host countries. We abstract here from any effects of foreign production on the amount of home production by displacement of or additions to exports, a subject we and others have dealt with extensively elsewhere. Controlling for the value of home production, we concentrate on the issue of factor proportions in home operations, asking whether production abroad tends to raise or lower the labour intensity of home production, or its skill intensity. If the home country is a high labour cost country, one could imagine that firms would seek to place

* This paper is part of the NBER's research program in International Trade and Investment. We thank the participants at a session of the *Royal Economic Society Annual Conference*, March 1997, and an anonymous referee for valuable comments. We are indebted to IUI and the US Department of Commerce for the use of their data and especially to Dale Shannon for help with the analysis. Financial support from HSFR, and the Marianne and Marcus Wallenberg Foundation is gratefully acknowledged.

in their foreign affiliates those labour-intensive operations, either products or stages of production, that are so integral to the firm's strategy that they must remain under the parent's control (other labour-intensive products could be purchased from local firms in low labour cost countries).

We do not have much information on the skill distribution of home-country employment by MNCs (none for the United States and only a breakdown into white-collar and blue-collar workers for Sweden), but we can try to draw some inferences from examining the association with parent employment separately for affiliates in developed and developing countries. A negative association of parent employment per unit of output with developing country production would suggest an allocation of labour-intensive production to low-wage countries. A positive association would suggest either an allocation of labour-intensive production to the parent or a need for supervisory or other non-production employment at home for each addition to foreign production.

We have analysed cross-sections here, assuming in our interpretations that differences among firms, or differences among firms within industries, represent choices by firms as to how to organise their world-wide production, and not only, or mainly, differences in firm characteristics that dictate the extent of foreign production. For a government deciding whether to encourage or discourage foreign production by its country's firms, it may not matter. If foreign production is associated with, for example, less employment of unskilled workers at home for a given amount of home production, a policy of encouragement of foreign investment will tend to shift the home demand for labour away from unskilled workers. That will be true whether the policy enlarges the role of the type of firm that invests abroad, relative to other types of firms, without causing any changes in firm allocations of production, or whether it encourages individual firms to alter the allocation of their production between home and foreign locations.

## II. EARLIER WORK ON HOME-COUNTRY EFFECTS

Probably the most extensively studied aspect of home-country effects has been whether production by foreign affiliates of a home country's firms is a 'substitute' or a 'complement' to home-country production by the parent firms or by other home-country firms (see Blomström and Kokko, 1994 for a survey). The difficulty in these studies is the lack of convincing counterfactual situations. What would have happened in the absence of affiliate production? Would the parent have supplied, by exporting, the markets now served by affiliates? Or would the markets now served by affiliates' production or by some combination of affiliate and home-country production have been lost to the parent firm, as was assumed in the Reddaway (1967, 1968) reports for the United Kingdom?

Evidence from studies of US trade has suggested either a positive relationship or no relationship between US-owned production in a market and exports to that market by the parent firms and by US firms in general (see e.g. Blomström *et al.* 1988). It has also found negative relationships between US-owned production and exports to the host country from other sources. A positive relation was found across firms between production abroad and firm exports to the world, suggesting that such production had not been at the expense of firm exports to third countries (Lipsey and Weiss, 1981, 1984).

Studies of Swedish firms have reported some more mixed results, with a long period of findings of positive relationships (see e.g. Swedenborg, 1979) and some more recent reports of negative ones, particularly in third-country markets (Svensson, 1996).

The main reason for positive relationships is the role of FDI in the rivalry for markets. The reason for the ambiguity of the results of most of these studies is that they do not take account of a firm's most important motivation for producing in a market: the chance to increase its market share or even the size of the market itself or to defend its existing market share. Such a study would require data on the size of particular product markets in host countries, a difficult enterprise that has been undertaken for only a few products and countries.

Other aspects of home-country effects that have been studied include the competition between home and foreign markets for an MNC's capital resources, internal or financed from outside, the extent to which expansion of offshore production by US multinationals reduces labour demand at home, and the relation of foreign production to home-country wage levels. On the first topic, a study for a few US firms indicated that home and foreign investment were not independent, and that an increase in plant and equipment investment in foreign operation caused a decrease at home because it raised the firm's cost of capital (Stevens and Lipsey, 1992). Brainard and Riker (1997) have recently concluded that foreign affiliate employment by US multinationals only modestly substitutes for US parent employment at the margin. They find a much stronger substitution among workers in US foreign affiliates located in different low-wage host countries. Finally, US wage studies have suggested a positive relationship across firms between foreign activity and home-country wage levels (Kravis and Lipsey, 1988). That relationship may reflect an allocation of low-skill activities to foreign operations, but it is difficult to disentangle that effect from the influence in the opposite direction of high parent-firm skill levels in permitting the firm to operate abroad or in making such operations profitable.

## III. FOREIGN PRODUCTION AND PARENT EMPLOYMENT

*Results for US firms*

We present here some simple descriptive equations showing the relationship, within manufacturing firms, between foreign production (proxied by affiliate net sales) and employment in the parent firms, given the level of parent production.[1] This relationship, for the United States in 1989, is described in equation 1 (*t*-values in parentheses).

[1] Data on US multinationals are from the individual firm reports underlying US Department of Commerce (1992), which is a census of US foreign direct investment in 1989. Since these data are confidential, the calculations reported here were carried out within the Bureau of Economic Analysis of the US Department of Commerce.

$$PEMP = 1,455 + 6 \cdot 00 \, PNS - 1 \cdot 16 \, ANS \quad \bar{R}^2 = 0 \cdot 87$$

$$(5 \cdot 2) \quad (52 \cdot 3) \quad (6 \cdot 1) \quad \text{No. obs.} = 1,104 \tag{1}$$

where PEMP = employment in parent firm $i$, PNS = sales of parent firm $i$ minus imports from its foreign affiliates and ANS = sales of all foreign affiliates of parent firm $i$ minus affiliate imports from the United States.

The estimation results for equation 1, relating absolute amounts of foreign output to absolute numbers of employees, suggest that more foreign output means fewer employees at home for a given level of home output. Our interpretation of this result is that larger foreign affiliate production is associated with an allocation of the more labour-intensive portions of the firm's output to the foreign operations, and more capital-intensive portions to home operations. Therefore, a given amount of home production will involve lower home employment, the larger is the amount of the firm's foreign output.

Given the crudeness of the parent employment–sales relationship, we worried that the apparent effect of affiliate production might be spurious. That could happen if there were an association of affiliate production with residuals from the parent relationship. If, for example, additions to production for large parents had lower labour requirements than those for small parents, because there were scale economies, and if larger parents also owned more foreign production than smaller ones, there would be a negative correlation between affiliate production and parent employment, but we would be attributing the effects of scale economies to the foreign production. To test for this possibility, we added a squared parent net sales, or scale, coefficient to the equation, as in equation 2.

$$PEMP = 1,400 + 6 \cdot 05 \, PNS - 0 \cdot 000012 \, (PNS)^2 - 1 \cdot 15 \, ANS \quad \bar{R}^2 = 0 \cdot 86$$

$$(4 \cdot 57) \quad (40 \cdot 3) \quad (0 \cdot 6) \quad (5 \cdot 9) \quad \text{No. obs.} = 1,104 \tag{2}$$

There is only an indication of scale economies, but the squared PNS term is not significant and the coefficient for affiliate net sales is hardly affected.

If the negative coefficient for affiliate employment represents allocation of labour-intensive production to low-wage countries, it should be production in such countries that affects parent employment. When we divide foreign production into production in developed (DC) and developing (LDC) countries, we have the results in equation 3 below.

$$PEMP = 1,594 + 6 \cdot 18 \, PNS - 0 \cdot 184 \, ANSDC - 12 \cdot 1 \, ANSLDC \quad \bar{R}^2 = 0 \cdot 87$$

$$(5 \cdot 6) \quad (54 \cdot 2) \quad (0 \cdot 8) \quad (8 \cdot 6) \quad \text{No. obs.} = 1,104 \tag{3}$$

where ANSDC = affiliate net sales in developed countries and ANSLDC = Affiliate net sales in developing countries. These results confirm that the negative effect on parent employment comes from the allocation of labour-intensive production stages to affiliates located in developing countries.

We can summarise the US results as saying that each additional million dollars of parent net sales adds about six employees to the parent labour force but, given the parent sales level, each additional million dollars of affiliate net sales is associated with firms having one fewer employee. However, affiliate production in developing countries has a much stronger effect on parent employment. Substituting a million dollars of affiliate net sales in developing countries for a million dollars in parent sales is associated with a reduction in parent employment by 18. Even adding a million dollars of output at home and a similar amount in developing countries would be associated with a decline in home employment.

*Results for Swedish firms*

For Sweden, we have access to the individual firm reports from six surveys of Swedish foreign direct investment,[2] spanning the period 1970–94. Thus, here we are also able to compare the results over time.

The Swedish experience seems to differ from that of the United States. In the cross-section regressions for Swedish MNCs, the coefficients for ANS are positive and significantly different from zero for each separate year (see Table 1). This suggests that, given the level of sales by the parent, MNCs with more sales abroad will also have higher employment in the parent company. This may indicate that MNCs with more activities abroad need, e.g., additional supervisory, management, marketing, and R&D personnel in the parent company, in order to coordinate and support the activities in foreign affiliates. In 1990, for example, the estimated coefficient for ANS equals 0·18, suggesting that an increase in affiliate net sales of around 5–6 million SEK (approximately 1 million US$) is associated with having one more employee in the parent company.[3] Thus, there is no evidence that production abroad by Swedish firms involves the allocation of labour-intensive operations to affiliates.

Although the coefficient for ANS is positive and significant each year in the Swedish regressions, the results indicate that the slope of the relationship between parent employment and affiliate sales has decreased since the 1970s. The coefficient for ANS was 0·35 in 1970 compared with 0·04 in 1994. Thus, it appears that foreign expansion in more recent times does not require the same extent of support functions in the parent company as before. Another explanation for the change over time may be that the positive association between PEMP and ANS has more recently been offset by negative reallocation effects of foreign expansion on parent employment. It is, of course, possible that we have both positive and negative effects of foreign expansion on PEMP at the same time, and that the net effect, which has been positive during the entire period 1970–94, is now close to zero.

In sharp contrast to the US multinationals, production by Swedish MNCs in both developed and developing countries seems to have a positive effect on parent employment (see Table 1). Both affiliate net sales in developed countries (ANSDC) and affiliate net sales in less developed countries (ANSLDC) are positively related to parent employment throughout the period. The changes over time that we found for the overall effect of foreign sales become less clear

Table 1

*OLS Regression Results for Swedish Parent Employment*

| Year | PNS | ANS | ANSDC | ANSLDC | adj. $R^2$ |
|------|-----|-----|-------|--------|-----------|
| 1970 ($N = 91$) | 1·67*** (32·65) | 0·35*** (4·63) | — | — | 0·96 |
| | 1·66*** (33·39) | — | 0·21** (2·26) | 2·07*** (3·13) | 0·96 |
| 1974 ($N = 105$) | 1·53*** (38·42) | 0·38*** (5·18) | — | — | 0·97 |
| | 1·51*** (40·88) | — | 0·16* (1·81) | 2·76*** (4·54) | 0·97 |
| 1978 ($N = 111$) | 1·34*** (38·32) | 0·31*** (5·32) | — | — | 0·97 |
| | 1·31*** (39·03) | — | 0·23*** (3·96) | 1·46*** (4·71) | 0·97 |
| 1986 ($N = 105$) | 0·91*** (32·36) | 0·22*** (6·94) | — | — | 0·98 |
| | 0·89*** (29·56) | — | 0·20*** (5·82) | 1·20** (2·61) | 0·98 |
| 1990 ($N = 117$) | 0·86*** (22·91) | 0·18*** (6·27) | — | — | 0·94 |
| | 0·83*** (19·83) | — | 0·17*** (5·86) | 0·93** (2·38) | 0·94 |
| 1994 ($N = 108$) | 0·67*** (27·65) | 0·040** (2·09) | — | — | 0·95 |
| | 0·61*** (25·61) | — | 0·021 (1·23) | 1·26*** (5·68) | 0·96 |

*Notes:* *t*-values in parentheses. ***, **, * indicate significance at the 1, 5 and 10 % significance level, respectively, using a two-sided *t*-test. Nine different industry dummies are included in all regressions. Results for intercepts and dummies are not shown. Sales figures are in million 1990 SEK. The deflator used is Swedish manufacturing PPI. PNS, Parent net sales (parent sales minus imports from foreign affiliates); ANS, affiliate net sales (affiliate sales minus imports from the Swedish parent); ANSDC, affiliate net sales developed countries; ANSLDC, affiliate net sales less developed countries.

when we separate between DCs and LDCs, although the non-significant coefficient for ANSDC might indicate a smaller association between parent employment and DC affiliate sales in more recent times.

Apparently, the decrease in the ANS coefficient is related to the affiliate sales in developed countries (where the Swedish MNCs have most of their affiliate sales). The estimated coefficient for ANSLDC is at a much higher level than that of ANSDC for each year, suggesting that, on the margin, an increase in affiliate net sales in LDCs is associated with a larger addition to parent employment than a corresponding increase in affiliate net sales in a developed country.

[2] The Swedish data are from the Industriens Utredningsinstitut (IUI) of Stockholm. The IUI has completed six surveys of Swedish firms' activities abroad. These surveys cover virtually all Swedish multinationals in manufacturing and are in general comparable to the US data.

[3] The addition of a squared PNS term in the Swedish regressions did not change the results with respect to ANS.

Table 2

*OLS Regression Results for Swedish White-collar Parent Employment*

| Year | PNS | ANS | ANSDC | ANSLDC | adj. $R^2$ |
|------|-----|-----|-------|--------|-----------|
| 1970 ($N = 91$) | 0·58*** (22·46) | 0·067* (1·79) | — | — | 0·91 |
| | 0·57*** (23·25) | — | −0·017 (−0·39) | 1·09*** (3·34) | 0·92 |
| 1974 ($N = 105$) | 0·52*** (25·55) | 0·063* (1·68) | — | — | 0·92 |
| | 0·51*** (28·89) | — | −0·086** (−2·04) | 1·68*** (5·77) | 0·94 |
| 1978 ($N = 71$) | 0·66*** (19·49) | −0·023 (−0·71) | — | — | 0·92 |
| | 0·63*** (21·71) | — | −0·082*** (−2·86) | 0·94*** (5·18) | 0·95 |
| 1994 ($N = 106$) | 0·33*** (13·88) | −0·0092 (−0·49) | — | — | 0·82 |
| | 0·30*** (11·61) | — | −0·020 (−1·06) | 0·60** (2·51) | 0·83 |

*Notes:* See Table 1.

## White- and blue-collar parent employment

In addition to the overall effect of foreign production on home-country labour, foreign activities by MNCs may also have effects on the composition of labour at home. The Swedish data allow us to break parent employment into white-collar and blue-collar workers, which we will use as proxies for skilled and unskilled workers, respectively. While this is far from an exact measure of skill levels, its rough usefulness is confirmed by the fact that the average wage for white-collar employees in Swedish manufacturing is 50 % higher than the average for blue-collar workers. Furthermore, while we have no data on wages for blue- and white-collar workers in Swedish multinationals, the IUI data show that the wage level in parent companies is strongly and positively related to the share of white-collar workers in the companies. This analysis is not possible with the US data.

Table 2 reports the results from the Swedish regressions using white-collar parent employment (WPEMP) as the dependent variable, and Table 3 the results using blue-collar parent employment (BPEMP) as the dependent variable. Our findings suggest that Swedish firms' foreign activities are positively and significantly related only to parent blue-collar employment. In the case of white-collar parent employment we find a weak positive association in 1970 and 1974, but no effect after that. This seems somewhat paradoxical, since it is reasonable to expect that it is the demand for skilled labour (supervision, management, marketing, and R&D) that should increase in the parent company as MNCs expand abroad, rather than unskilled labour. However, although it is not possible to impose any causal relationship here, the results indicate that those Swedish MNCs that expanded abroad, also

Table 3

*OLS Regression Results for Swedish Blue-collar Parent Employment*

| Year | PNS | ANS | ANS.DC | ANS.LDC | adj. $R^2$ |
|------|-----|-----|--------|---------|-----------|
| 1970 (N = 91) | 1·10*** (30·01) | 0·28*** (5·25) | — | — | 0·95 |
|  | 1·09*** (30·00) | — | 0·22*** (3·35) | 0·98** (2·03) | 0·95 |
| 1974 (N = 105) | 1·01*** (35·49) | 0·32*** (6·04) | — | — | 0·96 |
|  | 1·00*** (35·59) | — | 0·25*** (3·66) | 1·08** (2·34) | 0·96 |
| 1978 (N = 71) | 0·85*** (11·56) | 0·29*** (4·11) | — | — | 0·88 |
|  | 0·85*** (11·16) | — | 0·29*** (3·80) | 0·24 (0·50) | 0·88 |
| 1994 (N = 106) | 0·34*** (24·00) | 0·047*** (4·08) | — | — | 0·94 |
|  | 0·31*** (21·96) | — | 0·035*** (3·34) | 0·70*** (5·24) | 0·95 |

*Notes:* See Table 1.

increased the number of blue-collar workers at home, while not changing white-collar employment. This could be an indication that skilled based production stages in Swedish multinationals are increasingly located abroad, while the unskilled production stages are retained and expanded in Sweden.

The different effects on white- and blue-collar workers came out more clearly when we separated affiliate net sales by the location of affiliates (see Tables 2 and 3). In the blue-collar equation, the estimated coefficients for ANSDC are positive and strongly significant for every year, while in the white-collar regressions, the coefficients for ANSDC are negative for all years, although only significantly different from zero for 1974 and 1978. This suggests that foreign expansion by Swedish MNCs in developed countries is positively associated with the parents' employment of blue-collar workers, and negatively associated with (or not associated with) the number of white-collar workers in the parent. On the other hand, the coefficients for ANSLDC are positive and significant in both the white- and blue-collar regressions, suggesting that expansion in LDCs is associated with increases in both kinds of employment in the parent company. Hence, in the case of affiliates located in LDCs, there seems to be some support for the proposition that more white-collar workers are required in the parent company to coordinate and support the MNCs' activities.

### IV. CONCLUSIONS

We have found that in US firms, larger foreign production is associated with smaller parent employment, given the size of parent production. When the variable measuring foreign production is divided between developed and developing countries, the impact on parent employment is traced to the production in developing countries. Our interpretation of these relationships is that the implied lower labour intensity of home production in the presence of higher foreign production reflects a strategy on the part of investing firms of allocating labour-intensive portions of their output or labour-intensive stages of production to affiliates in low-wage countries. The affiliates then supply such products or such elements of the final product to the United States and, mostly, to the rest of the world. The alternative interpretation of these relationships, that it reflects the tendency of the most efficient firms at home to invest the most abroad, would not explain why it is the production in developing countries, and not that in developed countries, that is associated with lower employment for a given level of home production.[4] We attribute the strategy mainly to the high price of unskilled labour in the United States, reflecting nominal wage levels and, possibly, more restrictive labour standards than in developing host countries.

Swedish parents, on the other hand, employ more labour at home, given the size of home production, when they produce more abroad, and that effect is particularly large for production in developing countries. It, thus, appears that there is little allocation of labour-intensive production to low-wage countries within the Swedish firms, and that the labour effect we observe reflects the need for supervisory and other auxiliary employment within the parent associated with production abroad, especially in developing countries.

The contrast between the two countries' firms suggests a difference in investment strategy, and that explanation is supported by the evidence. US firms produce much more of their foreign output in developing countries, about 20 % in 1994, compared with only 7 % among Swedish firms. The geographical distribution in LDCs is also different, with the US firms producing much more in Asia and the Swedish firms mainly in Latin America. While the Swedish affiliates located in developing countries appear to be largely import substituting, exporting hardly any of their output, US affiliates are considerably more oriented towards world markets, exporting a third of their production in 1994. Thus, the US affiliates in developing countries appear to be much more a part of an allocation of the MNCs' production for world-wide markets to take advantage of factor price differences.

When we divide the Swedish parent employment into white-collar and blue-collar employees we find that additions to total parent employment associated with foreign production are mainly among blue-collar workers. However, if we distinguish between affiliate production in developed and developing countries, we find the latter associated with higher parent white-collar employment, as we would expect from the hypothesis that developing country operations require parent supervision.

---

[4] Our cross-section analysis does not, of course, prove causality, in the sense that, of two identical firms, one assigned by chance to produce only at home and the other assigned to produce one million dollars of goods abroad, the one producing abroad will end up with fewer home employees (the United States) or more home employees (Sweden). A limited test of the opposite causation, that the firms that are more efficient at home, or more capital intensive at home, tend to invest more abroad, is performed at the industry level by including industry dummies in the Swedish equations without obliterating the relationship. The possibility remains that there are such effects within industries, at the firm level.

Blue-collar employment is positively related to both developed and developing country production. The association with developed country production seems to imply an allocation of blue-collar employment to Sweden and of white-collar employment to foreign affiliates, perhaps partly reflecting the extensive acquisitions by Swedish firms in the United States and Europe where blue-collar workers are expensive. However, that hypothesis leaves unexplained the high positive coefficients for developing country affiliate production in equations for Swedish parent blue-collar employment. The reason for these results may not be substantive, but may be a reflection of the small numbers of Swedish firms with developing country affiliates.

A possible explanation of the difference in strategies between Swedish and US multinationals is that it reflects the difference in comparative advantage between the two home locations, as revealed by the composition of their trade with each other. More than half of Sweden's imports from the United States are from R&D-intensive sectors and only a quarter from sectors intensive in skilled labour, while almost 60 % of Sweden's exports to the United States are from skilled-labour-intensive sectors, with large employment of technicians and skilled manual workers, and only 17 % from R&D-intensive sectors. If the country specialisations run that way, it would be logical for Swedish multinationals to place the skilled-labour-intensive parts of their production at home and the R&D-intensive parts in the United States or other countries more suited than Sweden to such production. The same logic would persuade US multinationals to concentrate their R&D-intensive production at home (Blomström, Lipsey and Ohlsson, 1990).

*Stockholm School of Economics and NBER*                    MAGNUS BLOMSTRÖM

*Research Institute of Industrial Economics and Stockholm School of Economics*
                                                            GUNNAR FORS

*City University of New York and NBER*                    ROBERT E. LIPSEY

REFERENCES

Baldwin, Robert E. (1988). *Trade Policy Issues and Empirical Analysis*. Chicago: University of Chicago Press.
Blomström, Magnus and Kokko, Ari (1994). 'Home country effects of foreign direct investment: Sweden.' In Globerman (1994), pp. 341–64.
Blomström, Magnus, Lipsey, Robert E. and Kulchycky, Ksenia (1988). 'U.S. and Swedish direct investments and exports.' In Baldwin (1988), pp. 254–7.
Blomström, Magnus, Lipsey, Robert E. and Ohlsson, Lennart (1990). 'What do rich countries trade with each other? R&D and the composition of U.S. and Swedish trade.' *Banca Nazionale del Lavoro Quarterly Review*, No. 173, pp. 215–35.
Brainard, S. Lael and Riker, D. A. (1997). 'Are U.S. multinationals exporting U.S. jobs?' NBER Working Paper 5958, Cambridge, MA: NBER, March.
Globerman, Steven (1994). *Canadian-Based Multinationals*. The Industry Canada Research Series, Vol 4. Calgary: University of Calgary Press.
Kravis, Irving B. and Lipsey, Robert E. (1988). 'The effect of multinational firms' foreign operations on their domestic employment.' NBER Working Paper 2760, Cambridge, MA: NBER, November.
Lipsey, Robert E. and Weiss, Merle Y. (1981). 'Foreign production and exports in manufacturing industries.' *Review of Economics and Statistics*, vol. 63, no. 4, pp. 488–94.
Lipsey, Robert E. and Weiss, Merle Y. (1984). 'Foreign production and exports of individual firms.' *Review of Economics and Statistics*, vol. 64, no. 2, pp. 304–8.

Reddaway, W. B. (1967). *Effects of UK Direct Investments Overseas: An Interim Report*. Cambridge: Cambridge University, Dept. of Applied Economics, Occasional Papers: 12.

Reddaway, W. B. (1968). *Effects of UK Direct Investments Overseas: Final Report*. Cambridge: Cambridge University, Dept. of Applied Economics, Occasional Papers: 15.

Stevens, Guy and Lipsey, Robert E. (1992). 'Interactions between domestic and foreign investment.' *Journal of International Money and Finance*, vol. 11, no. 1, pp. 40–62.

Svensson, R. (1996). 'Effects of overseas production on home country exports: evidence based on Swedish multinationals.' *Weltwirtschaftliches Archiv*, Band 132, Heft 2, pp. 304–29.

Swedenborg, Birgitta (1979). *The Multinational Operations of Swedish Firms: An Analysis of Determinants and Effects*. Stockholm: Industriens Utredningsinstitut.

U.S. Department of Commerce (1992). *U.S. Direct Investment Abroad: 1989 Benchmark Survey, Final Results*. Washington, D.C.: Bureau of Economic Analysis, U.S. Department of Commerce.

# [19]

# Are US Multinationals Exporting US Jobs?

*S. Lael Brainard and David A. Riker**

**Abstract**

Many allege that multinationals are 'exporting' US jobs when they expand operations abroad. This paper investigates the extent to which expansion of offshore production by US multinationals reduces labor demand at home and at other offshore locations, using a panel on US multinationals and their foreign affiliates between 1983 and 1992. The results suggest that foreign affiliate employment substitutes modestly at the margins for US parent employment. There is much stronger substitution between workers at affiliates in alternative low-wage locations. In contrast, activities performed by affiliates at locations with different workforce skill levels in the same region appear to be complements. The results suggest a vertical division of activities among countries with different workforce skill levels, where workers in developing countries compete with each other to perform the activities most sensitive to labor costs. When wages in developing countries, such as Mexico, fall 10 per cent, US parent employment falls 0.17 per cent, while affiliates in other developing countries, such as Malaysia, lay off 1.6 per cent of their workforce.

## 1 Introduction

Several prominent labor organizations undertook an intense political campaign to oppose the North American Free Trade Agreement (NAFTA) on the grounds that it would encourage the relocation of US plants south of the border, substituting cheap Mexican workers for costly US workers. This is only the latest instance of recurring allegations that offshore production is

* We are grateful to Andrew Bernard, Ernie Berndt, Larry Katz, Ed Leamer, Steve Pischke, Matt Slaughter, and Bill Zeile for helpful comments, to the Division of International Investment at the Bureau of Economic Analysis for assistance with the data, and to the National Science Foundation for support under grant SES-9223462 and a graduate fellowship. The authors take sole responsibility for the use and interpretation of the data, and for any errors therein. This paper is part of NBER's research program in International Trade and Investment. Any opinions expressed are those of the authors and not those of the National Bureau of Economic Research.

tantamount to exporting US jobs. These allegations receive substantial support from economic theory. The dominant economic models explain multinational expansion as a means of exploiting labor cost differences, predicting that foreign direct investment (FDI) should flow from advanced industrial countries to developing countries. However, this is at odds with casual empiricism – in recent years more than 80 per cent of FDI has been directed at industrialized countries (Graham and Krugman, 1990).[1]

To this point, there has been no attempt to investigate the relationship between offshore production and domestic parent employment directly. This research makes a first attempt. The treatment of multinationals formalized by Caves (1982) and subsequent researchers suggests that the firm is the appropriate unit of analysis because of the importance of firm-specific proprietary assets. We use a detailed firm-level panel on US foreign affiliates and parents spanning the period 1983–92 to examine the response of employment within multinationals across different plant locations to changes in relative local wages.

The paper first briefly describes the data set and empirical regularities. We note that employment has increased most in countries where wages have increased most relative to the wages paid by the parent in the United States, contrary to the labor competition story. We also note that casual examination of the data does not provide strong evidence of offsetting employment changes within firms between plants.

We then go on to link the changing distribution of employment within firms to relative labor costs by estimating elasticities of substitution of multinational labor demand across different plant locations. We jointly estimate the labor demand equations for different plants within a firm that derive from a translog cost function. This estimation strategy in effect allows for the possibilities that each firm has a global production function and that workers in different locations are imperfectly substitutable because of different attributes or adjustment costs.

We employ various aggregations of the affiliate locations to distinguish the level of development, geographic proximity, and industry value added. The analysis confirms that labor employed by affiliates overseas substitutes at the margins for labor employed by parents at home, but the degree of substitution between parents is small. In contrast, there is strong substitution between workers at affiliates in different developing countries, suggesting there is a vertical separation of activities to take advantage of wage differentials, with workers in developing countries performing the activities that are most sensitive to labor costs. The story that US jobs are 'exported' to low-cost production sites is supplanted by the suggestion that employment shifting takes place predominantly between offshore affiliates in less developed countries. Moreover, the estimates suggest that the activities performed by labor employed in countries at different levels of development within the western hemisphere are complementary, and labor substitution between countries at different levels of development within the eastern hemisphere is weak. This suggests a vertical decomposition of production activities between industrialized and developing country affiliates within each hemisphere.

The pattern of price elasticities reinforces the conclusions drawn from the employment elasticities. Although employment at affiliates in developing countries is very sensitive to wages in other developing countries, parent employment responds very little when foreign affiliate wages fall.

## 2  Related Literature

Although this paper is the first to estimate the elasticity of substitution within firms between overseas affiliate employment and US parent employment directly, several papers have investigated related questions. Using data from 1966 and 1970, Lipsey, Kravis, and Roldan (1982) show that the labor intensity of affiliate production exceeds that of parent production and is greatest for affiliates in developing countries. They also show that labor intensity is negatively correlated with the destination market wage. These conclusions are consistent with our finding that employment at affiliates in developing countries appears most sensitive to wage competition from other locations.

Slaughter (1993) compares industry-level affiliate employment to US manufacturing employment in 1977 and 1989 for production and nonproduction workers. The aggregates yield no support to claims that expansion by US multinationals overseas was an important cause of the reduced demand for production workers at home over the 1980s. While total US manufacturing employment shrank 10 per cent between 1979 and 1989, total overseas affiliate employment shrank 14 per cent. Further, while production employment declined 15 per cent between 1979 and 1989 in the US, overseas affiliate employment declined even more – by 21 per cent. Using a similar approach, Lawrence (1994) confirms these findings. In work closely related to ours, Slaughter (1995) uses a translog cost function approach to estimate substitution between total overseas affiliate employment, total industry-wide domestic employment, and an aggregate of US industry-wide capital and overseas affiliate capital for the periods 1977 and 1982 to 1989. He finds that domestic industry employment and overseas affiliate employment are complementary, but only weakly related.

## 3  Conceptual Approach

The growing number and importance of multinational firms suggests an important international link in labor demands related to but conceptually separate from trade. This paper examines whether multinationals' labor demands across locations are related, either through technological synergy (a vertical division of production across locations) or through common product demand (a horizontal division). To the extent that either of these conditions holds, multinationals would be expected to shift production and employment across borders to minimize costs in response to changes in relative production costs. For example, an appreciation of the dollar would imply an increase in relative US wages and an accompanying shift of production offshore.

Below, we use estimation procedures developed in the literature on multifactor (for example, capital and labor) demands to estimate the relationship between overseas affiliate employment and US employment by treating them as distinct factors of production. We analyze labor demand within firms across plant locations, by fitting a firm-level global cost function specified in terms of relative wages (which are taken as exogenous). Two aspects of this estimation strategy deserve particular attention. First, each multinational is permitted to have a single production function across all its plant locations. Second, workers employed in different locations are treated as potentially differentiated in skills or quality. This estimation strategy is designed to impose as little structure as possible on the relationship between labor employed by the parent at home and by foreign affiliates in different countries.

We assume the supply of labor is nationally segmented by immigration restrictions and highly elastic (reflecting the conventional assumption of competitive labor markets). In contrast, the demand for labor is linked across countries by firms that produce in a number of countries (as well as by international trade in goods). Foreign investment by multinationals is treated as a flow of firm-specific proprietary advantages across borders, for example in the form of trademarks, product or process designs, or marketing networks.

In the extreme case where labor is perfectly substitutable across plants in different countries, we would expect the cost-minimizing firm to shift all employment and production to the lowest-cost location. However, there are a number of frictions that may impede this type of wage-chasing employment reallocation: the distribution of skills might vary across locations, there may be considerable fixed costs or adjustment costs associated with plant capacity, and there may be proximity considerations that impede trade such as tariffs, local content requirements, or transport costs.

The estimation approach is designed to measure the extent to which labor substitution across locations diverges from the frictionless case. It focuses on wage-induced marginal shifts in labor demand among the firms' existing production locations, taking as given the international configuration of plant capacity.[2] In effect, we treat labor in different countries as separate factors and estimate substitution among them, assuming nationally segmented labor supplies and location-specific plant capacity.

In principle, it would be possible to include a separate equation for the firm's labor demand in each of the countries in which affiliates potentially operate. However, this would be intractable, since there is a daunting multiplicity of possible affiliate configurations with a data set covering 90 countries. Even if it were tractable, it is not clear that estimating a cross-elasticity for every pair of locations would be illuminating. Instead, we aggregate labor across subsets of countries that share certain economic characteristics related to the frictions discussed above.[3]

In aggregating across plant locations, the literature on multinationals suggests that the following distinctions are particularly salient:[4]

- *Geography:* There is a clear distinction in the multinational literature between vertical expansion across borders for purposes of access to low-cost factors of production and horizontal expansion across borders for purposes of market access (Brainard, 1993a). Multinationals are more likely to expand for purposes of market access when transport costs and trade barriers are high. The less tradeable are intermediate and final goods, the lower is labor substitution between affiliates likely to be. Conversely, production should be more 'footloose' among geographically proximate countries the more distance restricts international trade. We would expect to see more vertical decomposition of activities in markets that are located close to each other, and more horizontal decomposition in markets that are located farther away, all else being equal. We therefore distinguish between affiliates that are located close to parents in the western hemisphere (defined as the Americas), and affiliates located in the more distant eastern hemisphere (defined as the rest of the world).[5]

- *Factor supplies/development:* Since the distribution of skills and other factors varies across countries, the average attributes of the labor force are likely to differ across locations, reducing the degree of substitution. To the extent that multinationals locate each stage of production in the country with the most favorable relative factor costs, we would expect to see more substitution between countries with similar factor proportions. We differentiate between affiliates located in advanced industrial countries and those located in developing countries as a way of proxying differences in the relative supply of skills.[6] Below, we follow a common tradition in trade estimation of proxying factor proportion differences by per capita income differences.[7]

## 4   Data and Empirical Regularities

This study uses firm-level data from the *Annual Survey of U.S. Direct Investment Abroad*, which is administered on a mandatory basis and audited by the Bureau of Economic Analysis (BEA).[8] The data set is a three-dimensional panel, in which each firm's production activities in up to 90 countries are tracked over a ten-year period ending in 1992, yielding approximately 70 000 firm–country–time observations. We include all firms whose parent industry is in the manufacturing sector. The panel includes data on an annual basis for each reported affiliate and parent on employment, employee compensation, exports, sales, location, and a three-digit industry identifier.[9] Because the data are business confidential, this is the first time this panel has been subjected to formal econometric analysis.

To this data set we append economic development rankings of countries from the *World Development Report* (World Bank, 1989) (based on per capita income) and measures of average industry wages by country from the Bureau of Labor Statistics (BLS).

*Changes in Employment Shares over Time*

Before presenting the formal econometric estimates, we first examine a number of simple firm-level relationships between labor allocation and wages across locations. Figure 1 shows how the allocation of employment within US multinationals (averaged across firms) has evolved across locations over time. Employment at affiliates in the eastern hemisphere has expanded from 23 per cent of total firm employment in 1983 to 28 per cent in 1992. It consistently exceeds employment at affiliates in the western hemisphere, which has risen only marginally to 15 per cent in 1992. There is less contrast between the change in employment in developing and advanced industrial countries. The share of employment at affiliates in advanced industrialized countries has expanded over the decade from 21 to 24 per cent of total firm employment, while the share at affiliates in developing countries has expanded similarly, rising from 18 to 20 per cent of employment.

Over the same time period, the average multinational has reduced the share of total employment at the US parent from 61 to 56 per cent. Aggregating across firms, employment by US multinationals in the United States has declined similarly as a share of total US manufacturing employment over the 1980s, from roughly half to 45 per cent (not shown). Thus, the popular perception that US multinationals have expanded their overseas employment at the expense of domestic employment is supported by the evidence on average within-firm shares of employment. However, contrary to conventional wisdom, much of the growth abroad has occurred in advanced industrial countries, especially outside the western hemisphere.

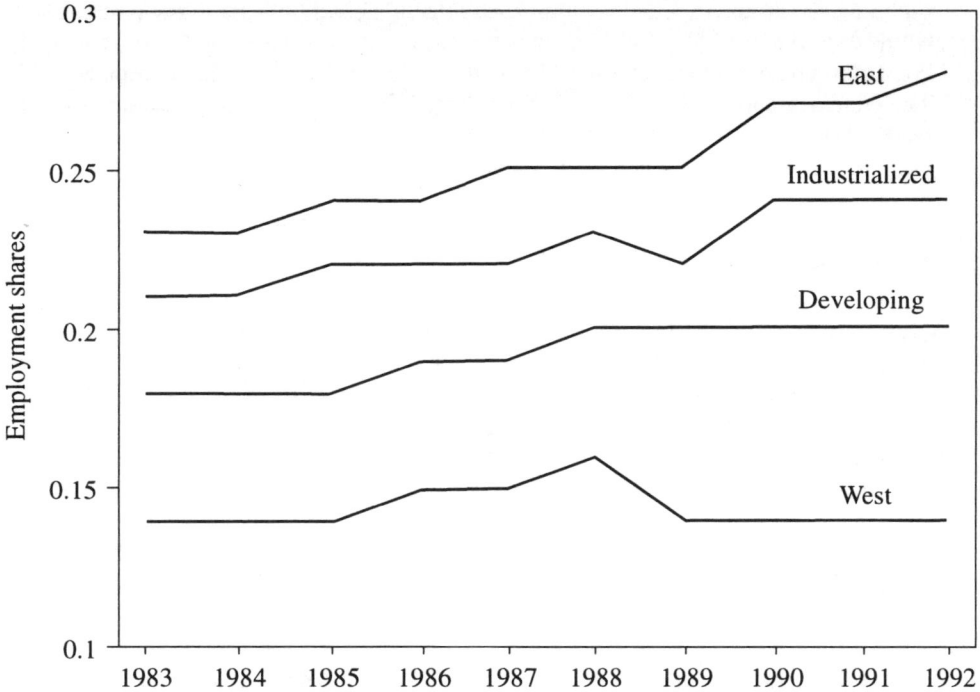

*Figure 1    Affiliate employment shares (average within firm shares)*

*Relative Wage Developments*

Corresponding changes in relative wages[10] are portrayed in Figure 2. While the ratio of wages paid by affiliates in developing countries to parent wages has remained remarkably flat at roughly 30 per cent over the decade, the ratio of wages in advanced industrial countries has risen substantially, reaching over 90 per cent by 1992. Similarly, the relative wage at affiliates in the eastern hemisphere has risen from slightly over half to 80 per cent, while the relative wages of affiliates in the western hemisphere have remained relatively flat around 50 per cent (mainly reflecting an expansion of employment in developing country affiliates relative to Canada).

Together, Figures 1 and 2 suggest the rather surprising conclusion that employment has expanded most in precisely those areas where the relative wage has also grown the most and is closest to wages in the United States. However, the timing differs somewhat: while most of the relative wage expansion occurred during the period of dollar depreciation, 1985 to 1988, much of the employment expansion occurred in the early and late 1980s. Furthermore, simple correlations between averages of employment shares and relative wages across firms may be misleading because they do not address either the correlation within firms or the multilateral nature of the firms' employment allocation decisions.

*Distribution of Employment across Locations*

Next we shed some light on substitution among labor employed in different locations by

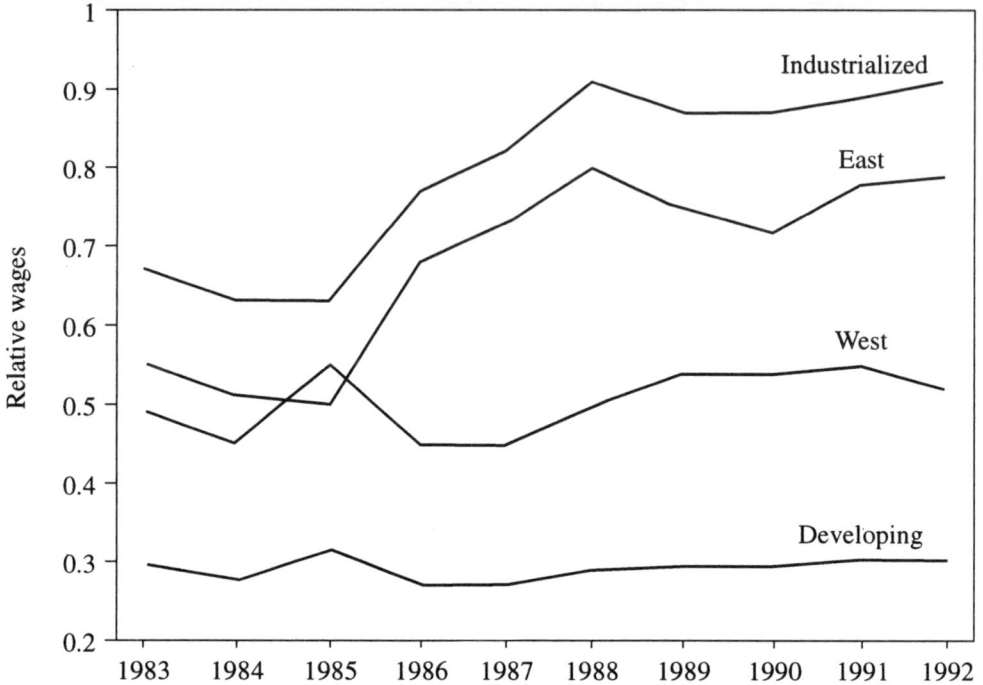

*Figure 2    Affiliate wages relative to parent wages (average within firm relative wages)*

examining the degree to which employment changes at particular locations within multinationals have been offset by opposite changes at other locations. Table 1 examines bilateral employment change offsets within firms. The histogram presented in panel (a) compares employment changes at parent locations with employment changes aggregated across all affiliates within firms. Over a quarter of the observations entail large, complementary expansions of roughly equal magnitudes by both affiliates and parents. Roughly one-eighth of the observations entail small expansions of affiliate employment offset by small contractions of similar magnitudes at the parent.

Panel (b) matches employment changes across all affiliates in advanced industrial countries with changes across affiliates in developing countries. Here, roughly one-eighth of the observations evidenced small complementary expansions of roughly equal magnitudes in both types of affiliates, while one-ninth of the observations evidenced complementary expansions with relatively greater expansion across developing country affiliates. Another one-sixth of the observations evidenced small expansions in developing country locations offset by contractions in industrialized country affiliates.

Panel (c) compares affiliates in the western and eastern hemispheres. Here again, the changes are fairly evenly spread. Over one-fifth of the firms evidenced complementary expansions in the west and the east of equal magnitudes and one-tenth evidenced sizeable contractions in both eastern and western hemispheres; another one-twelfth evidenced small contractions in the east offset by comparable expansion in the west.

*Table 1  Employment offset histograms*

(a) Parent vs. affiliate offsets

|  | Parent | | | |
| | Layoffs | | Hires | |
|  | Over 200 | 0–200 | 0–200 | Over 200 |
|---|---|---|---|---|
| Affiliates | | | | |
| Hires | | | | |
| Over 150 | 6.0 | 7.8 | 4.9 | 26.6 |
| 0–150 | 3.8 | 11.5 | 6.8 | 4.7 |
| Layoffs | | | | |
| 0–150 | 3.3 | 6.5 | 4.0 | 2.9 |
| Over 150 | 6.0 | 1.4 | 1.1 | 2.9 |

(b) Industrialized vs. developing country affiliate offsets

|  | Industrialized | | | |
| | Layoffs | | Hires | |
|  | Over 80 | 0–80 | 0–80 | Over 80 |
|---|---|---|---|---|
| Developing | | | | |
| Hires | | | | |
| Over 200 | 6.8 | 2.5 | 2.0 | 9.6 |
| 0–200 | 8.9 | 8.5 | 12.9 | 10.6 |
| Layoffs | | | | |
| 0–200 | 6.7 | 4.6 | 4.3 | 5.2 |
| Over 200 | 9.1 | 1.8 | 1.7 | 5.0 |

(c) Western vs. eastern affiliate offsets

|  | Western | | | |
| | Layoffs | | Hires | |
|  | Over 80 | 0–80 | 0–80 | Over 80 |
|---|---|---|---|---|
| Eastern | | | | |
| Hires | | | | |
| Over 200 | 4.6 | 3.1 | 4.0 | 10.4 |
| 0–200 | 4.7 | 5.2 | 12.4 | 6.5 |
| Layoffs | | | | |
| 0–200 | 5.4 | 4.4 | 7.9 | 4.8 |
| Over 200 | 11.1 | 3.2 | 3.5 | 7.1 |

*Note*:  Tables report distribution of offsetting employment changes on average within firms.

Table 1 suggests that most changes have entailed complementary expansions across different types of locations. In addition, a number of firms have experienced small offsetting reallocations of labor from parents to affiliates and within affiliates from the eastern hemisphere to the western hemisphere, and from advanced industrial locations to developing locations.

The conclusion that the degree of one-for-one *quantity shifting* across borders is relatively low at the firm level is consistent with conclusions based on aggregate data (Lawrence, 1994; Slaughter, 1993; Lipsey, 1994). However, it is a big leap to conclude from these quantity movements that the price responsiveness of employment across locations within firms is low. Even when we observe similar expansion across all sites, there may be considerable *shifting of shares* in response to price movements. Moreover, simple ratios can shed little light on allocations across a multiplicity of potential sites. Such subtleties motivate our estimation of multifactor demand relationships.

## 5  Methodology

The most widely used methodology for estimating multi-factor demands is to fit the factor demand equations that derive from the cost function.[11] The 'translog' form of the cost function initially proposed by Christenson et al. (1973) has been applied extensively in estimating both macro and microeconomic production relationships. It is essentially a second-order log-linear approximation to an unspecified general cost function. Its popularity stems from its generality: the functional form imposes few restrictions on factor substitution.

By Shepard's Lemma, differentiation of the cost functions with respect to the $n$ factor prices yields $n$ factor demands, which are typically converted to the following system of $n$ linear equations (Hamermesh, 1993; Berndt and Wood, 1978):

$$S_{ft}^{(n \times 1)} = \alpha^{(n \times 1)} + \beta^{(n \times n)} W_{ft}^{(n \times 1)} + \Gamma^{(n \times n)} K_f^{(n \times 1)} + \varepsilon_{ft}^{(n \times 1)} \tag{1}$$

$S$ is a vector of cost shares. It is expressed as a linear function of a vector of constants, $\alpha$, the coefficient matrix, $\beta$, multiplied by the $(n \times 1)$ factor price vector (in logs), a vector of firm fixed effects, $K$, and a vector of residuals, $\varepsilon$, satisfying the standard assumptions for seemingly unrelated estimation ($SUR$). An output term can also be added on the right hand side to allow for variable returns to scale. The only restriction that is imposed in the estimates below is symmetry of the $\beta$ matrix, which follows from the assumption of a twice differentiable global cost function.

The size of the system, $n$, depends on the aggregation of affiliates across countries. The elements of the factor price vector are composed of the log geometric weighted average of compensation per employee (weighting by relative employment) across each subset of locations. In the estimates below, we report three levels of disaggregation, partitioning the affiliates into one, two, and four subsets along the economic dimensions discussed above.

We take advantage of the multidimensional nature of our panel data to control for firm and year fixed effects. Thus, reported estimates are based on 'within firm' estimation. Although firm fixed effects might capture a variety of possible heterogeneities among firms' international production relationships, we have a particular interpretation in mind. This interpretation follows Berndt and Hesse (1986), who propose a variant to the standard translog called a variable or short-run cost function, where the stocks of relatively fixed factors such as physical capital are included in the share equations in lieu of the price of capital. We effectively estimate labor substitution among locations conditional on the capital stock, assuming that capacity adjustment is not an important option during the short time horizons under consideration. This assumes that the relatively fixed configuration of multinational plant capacity across locations could have a significant role in bounding wage-chasing labor substitution across borders. The firm fixed effects are used to capture firm-specific plant configurations.[12] When instead we control for plant capacity directly, using BEA data on plant and equipment expenditures, the results are robust.

We also experimented with various formulations of the wage measure to take into account possible lags in the adjustment of labor across locations (including current wages, one-year lagged wages, two- and three-year moving average wages, and predicted wages). The general pattern across coefficients is relatively stable across different formulations. We report results using a two-year moving average wage in the equations below.

From the *SUR* estimates of the $\beta$ matrix, we construct Allen partial cross-elasticities of substitution, $ES_{ij}$, and price elasticities, $PE_{ij}$, using the following formulae, respectively:

$$\hat{ES}_{ij} = 1 + \frac{\hat{\beta}_{ij}}{S_i S_j} \qquad \hat{PE}_{ij} = \frac{\hat{\beta}_{ij} + S_i S_j}{S_i}$$

Although the $\beta$ are constrained to be constant across the sample by pooling assumptions implicit in the specification, the cost shares vary by firm and over time. We follow the translog estimation approach of Anderson and Thursby (1986) in using the mean shares of the actual data, rather than the fitted shares, a common alternative. For each of the Allen cross-partials, we report confidence (half) intervals. We used both Delta Method and bootstrap resampling techniques in estimating the half-intervals.[13] The results were similar, so we report only the bootstrapped estimates.

We also check whether substitution relationships vary with industry value added on the presumption that this might be correlated with the labor intensity of production. We separate the firms into two groups based on the value added of their production.[14] The translog is estimated separately for the high value added and low value added firms; this approach imposes pooling restrictions, whereby the slope terms, $\beta$, as well as the intercepts, $\alpha$, are allowed to vary by industry grouping.

The translog estimation approach effectively imposes the hypothesis that factor demands are linked across borders. If there were no linkage between factor demands, it would not imply a testable set of restrictions on the estimated $\beta$ matrix, since the left-hand side of the equation system is the cost shares. Therefore, we ran a preliminary set of hypothesis tests, regressing labor demand (in levels rather than shares) in each location or aggregation of locations against 'local' and 'offshore' wages. We were able to reject the null hypothesis that factor demands are not linked across borders at a very high level of significance.

The BEA panel data set measures total employment at each location, aggregating across various types of labor, and compensation per employee, averaging across various types of labor.[15] By treating different types of labor as a composite factor of production, we run the risk of finding spurious substitution relationships that actually reflect differences in the composition of labor. For instance, if affiliates add production workers to a fixed core of white collar workers as they expand production, then employment expansion may lead to a declining composite wage even if the underlying wages for each type of worker do not change.[16] In this case, we would see a negative correlation between employment and firm-level wages for reasons other than labor substitution.

Therefore, we estimated the equations reported below by both substituting BLS industry wages for BEA firm wages directly, and using the BLS industry wages to serve as instrumental variables for BEA firm wages. The estimates based on BLS industry wages yield similar results in terms of the relative size and significance of substitution between various locations, but generally magnify the estimated substitution between parents and affiliates relative to that between affiliates.

## 6   Elasticities of Substitution across Affiliates

We next turn to the elasticity estimates. Panel (a) of Table 2 presents elasticities derived from the simplest formulation of equation (1), which aggregates across all affiliates. The cross-elasticity of substitution between parents and all affiliates, $ES_{pa}$, is slightly below one, implying that labor abroad substitutes one-for-one for parent labor. When the sample is split into high value added and low value added industries, as in the second and third rows of panel (a), the elasticity does not change. The parent, $ES_{pp}$, and affiliate, $ES_{aa}$, own-elasticities are negative as predicted (not reported).

Panel (b) in Table 2 splits the affiliate locations into two groups based on their level of per capita income, which is used to proxy relative skill endowments. The cross-elasticity between the parents and both the subset of affiliates located in developing countries, $ES_{pl}$, and the subset located in industrialized countries, $ES_{ph}$, drops below one. Substitution is markedly higher between affiliates in different countries, $ES_{hl}$. This suggests that the activities undertaken by affiliates in more and less developed economies are more similar than those undertaken by parents and either type of affiliates.

Separate equations are estimated for firms in low and high value-added industries in the second and third rows. The finding that substitution is much stronger between labor at different affiliates than between parents and either type of affiliate is particularly pronounced for low value added industries. This is consistent with the presumption that the greater less-skilled labor intensity of production activities in low value-added industries makes them more sensitive to labor costs.

Panel (c) of Table 2 splits the set of affiliates along geographical rather than development lines to reflect proximity differences. Affiliate locations are divided into western and eastern hemispheres. Similar results were obtained using a split between countries adjacent to the United States and other countries.[17]

The results suggest that proximity has little effect on substitution between parents and affiliates. The cross-elasticities of substitution between parents and both types of affiliates are below one. In addition, the cross-elasticity with eastern hemisphere affiliates, $ES_{pe}$, is slightly larger than that with affiliates in the same hemisphere, consistent with greater vertical differentiation in the hemisphere closer to the parent. Similar to the development breakdown, the cross-elasticity between affiliates in different hemispheres, $ES_{we}$, is significantly higher

*Table 2   Elasticities of substitution*

(a)   All affiliates

| Sample | ES(pa) | No. of obs. |
|---|---|---|
| All firms | 0.95 | 10 435 |
| | (0.047) | |
| High value added | 0.969 | 4 642 |
| industries | (0.065) | |
| Low value added | 0.955 | 4 895 |
| industries | (0.071) | |

(b)   Affiliates divided by development

| Sample | ES(ph) | ES(pl) | ES(hl) | No. of obs. |
|---|---|---|---|---|
| All firms | 0.656 | 0.863 | 2.024 | 4 024 |
| | (0.047) | (0.098) | (0.267) | |
| High value added | 0.786 | 1.06 | 1.56 | 2 281 |
| industries | (0.063) | (0.148) | (0.336) | |
| Low value added | 0.557 | 0.743 | 2.53 | 1 493 |
| industries | (0.080) | (0.142) | (0.446) | |

(c)   Affiliates divided by region

| Sample | ES(pw) | ES(pe) | ES(we) | No. of obs. |
|---|---|---|---|---|
| All firms | 0.623 | 0.816 | 1.910 | 4 605 |
| | (0.060) | (0.049) | (0.172) | |
| High value added | 0.788 | 1.12 | 2.09 | 2 492 |
| industries | (0.085) | (0.066) | (0.222) | |
| Low value added | 0.421 | 0.588 | 1.63 | 1 794 |
| industries | (0.095) | (0.789) | (0.288) | |

*Note*:   Tables report Allen cross-partial elasticities of substitution derived from translog cost functions. Firm and year fixed effects are included. Confidence intervals are reported in parentheses. The own elasticities (which are not reported here) are all negative. Notation is as follows: $p$ represents parent; $a$ represents affiliate; $h$ refers to industrialized country affiliates; $l$ refers to less developed country affiliates; $w$ refers to western hemisphere affiliates; and $e$ refers to eastern hemisphere affiliates.

than that between parents and either type of affiliate. This suggests, as above, that affiliates tend to perform activities that are more similar to each other than to parent activities, and that the differentiation is somewhat greater for affiliates located in the same hemisphere.

We next examine the pattern of substitution more closely by further dividing the groups of affiliate locations. In Table 3, we investigate relationships among affiliates in different industrial

*Table 3    Elasticities of substitution: affiliates divided by development and region (1486 observations)*

(a)   Cross-partial elasticities of substitution

| Parent–affiliate | | | | | | Between affiliates | | | |
| --- | --- | --- | --- | --- | --- | --- | --- | --- | --- |
| *p/hw* | *p/he* | *p/lw* | *p/le* | *h/h* | *w/w* | *e/e* | *l/l* | *hw/le* | *he/lw* |
| 0.303 | 0.708 | 0.475 | 0.532 | 1.35 | −1.73 | 0.943 | 5.26 | 5.73 | 2.46 |
| (0.142) | (0.105) | (0.174) | (0.604) | (0.428) | (1.30) | (0.590) | (1.72) | (1.72) | (0.553) |

(b)   Price elasticities of substitution

| Parent response to affiliate | | | | | | Between affiliates | | | |
| --- | --- | --- | --- | --- | --- | --- | --- | --- | --- |
| *p/hw* | *p/he* | *p/lw* | *p/le* | *hw/he* | *wh/wl* | *eh/el* | *lw/le* | *hw/le* | *he/lw* |
| 0.011 | 0.125 | 0.015 | 0.009 | 0.239 | −0.053 | 0.015 | 0.086 | 0.093 | 0.076 |

| Affiliate response to parent | | | | | | Between affiliates | | | |
| --- | --- | --- | --- | --- | --- | --- | --- | --- | --- |
| *hw/p* | *he/p* | *lw/p* | *le/p* | *he/hw* | *wl/wh* | *el/eh* | *le/lw* | *le/hw* | *le/hw* |
| 0.224 | 0.524 | 0.351 | 0.393 | 0.049 | −0.063 | 0.167 | 0.162 | 0.210 | 0.090 |

(c)   Number of affiliate observations

| Total | *hw* | *he* | *lw* | *le* |
| --- | --- | --- | --- | --- |
| 66 301 | 8 349 | 35 956 | 12 966 | 9 030 |

*Note*:    Tables report Allen cross-partial elasticities of substitution derived from translog cost functions and the associated price elasticities; a price elasticity represented as *a/b* refers to the elasticity of employment in location *a* in response to a wage change in location *b*. Firm and year fixed effects are included. Confidence intervals are reported in parentheses. The own elasticities (which are not reported here) are all negative. Notation is as follows: *p* represents parent; *h* refers to industrialized country affiliates; *l* refers to less developed country affiliates; *w* refers to western hemisphere affiliates; and *e* refers to eastern hemisphere affiliates.

countries and separately among different developing countries by dividing each development group by location. And similarly, we investigate relationships among affiliates in countries at different levels of development within each hemisphere.

The results in Table 3 suggest that labor substitution is strongest between affiliates at similar levels of development. The elasticity of substitution between affiliates in different developing countries, $ES_{ll}$, is particularly high. Substitution is lower among labor in different industrial countries, $ES_{hh}$, but still above unity.

In contrast, there is complementarity or negligible substitution between locations at different levels of development within the same hemisphere. Within the western hemisphere, the activities performed by labor in industrial countries is complementary to the activities performed by labor in developing countries, $ES_{ww} < 0$, suggesting a vertical separation of activities. And although there is substitution between countries at different levels of development within the eastern hemisphere, $ES_{ee}$, it is weak (below unity).

The cross-elasticity between parents and all types of affiliates is positive but well below one, suggesting weak substitution. Moreover, similarly to Table 2, substitution between parents and affiliates in industrialized countries in the eastern hemisphere, $ES_{phe}$, is marginally greater than substitution between parents and affiliates in industrialized countries in the western hemisphere, suggesting a greater vertical separation of activities among locations that are proximate to the parent.

The results suggest that the expansion of employment in a developing country in the western hemisphere such as Brazil threatens parent employment in the United States much less than it does labor at affiliates in developing countries in Asia. And it actually raises employment at affiliates in advanced industrial countries in the same hemisphere, such as Canada. Labor at parent locations in the United States competes only on the margins with labor at affiliates in developing countries, suggesting a strong vertical separation of activities and possibly quality differentials. At the same time, there is intense competition between labor employed in different developing countries. In contrast, there appears to be a strong vertical separation of activities, and hence low substitution or even complementarity, between locations at different development levels within each hemisphere.

The cross-elasticities of substitution between affiliates in locations at different income levels across hemispheres, $ES_{helw}$ and $ES_{hwle}$, are more difficult to interpret. Both are large and statistically significant. This result may simply be an artefact of the aggregation choice. Almost all of the 'developing' category in the eastern hemisphere are middle-income countries, whereas almost all of the 'developing' category in the western hemisphere are low-income countries.

*Robustness*

As described above, we solve the zero demands problem by aggregating across locations into economically meaningful groupings. However, even after aggregating, some firms do not employ workers in more than one location. The equations estimated above cover only those firms that have employment in all included categories. (It is worth noting that a majority of the firms in the sample do not have any affiliates in less developed countries.) Thus, for instance, the equations that estimate cross-elasticities between affiliates at the same level of development across hemispheres only include firms that have at least one affiliate each in a less developed eastern hemisphere country, a less developed western hemisphere location, an industrialized western hemisphere location, and an industrialized eastern hemisphere location. We checked whether this estimation was robust by running similar equations for the excluded subsets of firms that have no affiliates in one or more of these four categories. Both the size and significance of the cross-elasticities were remarkably similar across firm configurations, so we do not report those results separately.

Following the production function literature, we included controls for scale both at the level of the plant and the firm. In both cases, as long as firm fixed effects are included, the results are essentially unchanged (although the fit of the equations improves), so we do not report the results here. In short, the firm fixed effects fully capture any effects of scale on the cross-elasticities of substitution.

The BEA data are comprised of a subset of firms that is surveyed every year and a second subset that is surveyed only in benchmark years and estimated by BEA statisticians in other years. We performed the estimations for both the full sample and the subsample of firms that are surveyed every year to ensure that the sampling techniques do not in some way bias the results. The results were essentially the same, so we report only the full sample results above.

Linear homogeneity of the cost function is often assumed in translog production function estimation. In the equations reported above, imposing this restriction occasionally changes the absolute size of the coefficients moderately, but rarely affects the relative size of the coefficients. Thus, we do not report the results for the linear homogeneity restriction. Moreover, we do not see a compelling economic rationale for imposing such a restriction in this setting.


## 7  Conclusion

Our estimates suggest that labor in the United States does compete at the margins with labor abroad via multinational production. But substitution between labor employed by parents in the United States and affiliates abroad is low. Labor substitution is far greater between affiliates in countries at similar levels of development.[18]

The greatest degree of competition is between labor in different developing countries, particularly in low value added industries. Labor at affiliates in industrialized countries similarly competes with labor at affiliates in other industrialized countries, but to a more moderate degree. In contrast, affiliate workers in countries at different levels of development within the western hemisphere appear to be complements, while affiliates at different levels of development within the eastern hemisphere are only weakly related.

The results suggest there is a vertical separation of activities to take advantage of wage differentials, with affiliates in developing countries performing the activities that are most sensitive to labor costs. This supports findings by Lipsey et al. (1982) that factor intensities vary with relative wages among locations. The results further suggest that the activities of affiliates in countries at different levels of development may be complementary, especially in the hemisphere closer to the parent. Subsequent research focusing exclusively on affiliates, and using a more general estimation approach, confirms that complementarity characterizes affiliates in countries at different levels of development more broadly (Riker and Brainard, 1997). In addition, western hemisphere affiliates appear to compete with parent labor somewhat less than do eastern hemisphere affiliates, consistent with greater vertical differentiation within the western hemisphere.

Price elasticities tell a similar story. Although employment at affiliates in developing countries is very sensitive to wage variation in other developing countries, parent employment responds very little to variations in affiliate wages, and affiliate employment actually expands when wages in countries at a different level of development fall. For example, US parent employment falls one-sixth of one per cent when wages in developing countries in the western hemisphere, such as Mexico, fall 10 per cent. At the same time, affiliates in other developing countries, such as Malaysia, lay off 1.6 per cent of their workforce, and affiliates in high-income countries in the same hemisphere (Canada) actually expand employment by 0.5 per cent.

# Notes

1.  Formal investigations also suggest that multinational activity is more likely between countries the greater are their similarities in factor proportions and per capita income, contrary to both the dominant economic models and popular perceptions (Brainard, 1993b).
2.  It is important to note that the data set permits us only to estimate marginal shifts in employment and production across locations. The establishment of new plants is difficult to discern in the data.
3.  Restricting the country dimension of the data transforms the firms' configurations in a way that permits us to pool across firms in fitting a common specification. Otherwise, we would face the problem of 'zero demands' that arises in multifactor demand estimation when pooling over a sample of firms that use a different set of factors rather than different quantities of the same set of factors.
4.  See Markusen (1995).
5.  We experimented with other geographical splits that are described in greater detail below.
6.  The country rankings are taken from the *World Development Report* (World Bank, 1989). The 'high income' category is taken directly from the *World Development Report*, while our 'low income' category combines low and middle-income economies.
7.  In subsequent work, Riker and Brainard (1996) instead classify locations according to the average educational attainment of the population, with similar results.
8.  Due to the business-confidential status of the firm-level data, the data are not available from the authors of this study.
9.  US parents are required to report this data for any affiliates whose sales exceed $15 million.
10. Unless otherwise noted, the term wages refers to the BEA measure of compensation per employee.
11. The cost function approach has several advantages over a production function approach that are detailed in Berndt (1981) and Hamermesh (1993). For a detailed discussion of the literature, see Hammermesh (1993).
12. A fixed effects estimator is preferable to a random effects estimator, since the sample is essentially the entire population, and we do not claim to draw inferences outside the sample (Greene, 1990).
13. Bootstrap estimates were based on one hundred resamplings from the empirical distribution of the fined residuals. We thank P.O. Gourinchas for suggesting this approach.
14. The categorization is based on a ranking of parent industry value added, defined as the ratio of gross margins to employment.
15. The BEA data distinguish production and nonproduction workers for benchmark survey years (1982, 1989), but this data is unavailable at the firm level.
16. We thank Mike Piore and Steve Pischke for raising these issues.
17. When, instead, a three-way split between Asia, Europe, and the western hemisphere is used, substitution between Asian affiliates and parents looks similar to that between western hemisphere affiliates and parents, and larger than that between European affiliates and parents. There is also strong substitution between Asian affiliates and western hemisphere affiliates, but only weak substitution between the western hemisphere and Europe, and complementarity between Asian and European affiliates. Combining Asia and Europe moderates these relationships because of this distinction.
18. In interpreting these results, it is important to keep in mind that parents employ many more workers than do affiliates in aggregate, and that affiliate employment is heavily concentrated in industrialized countries, particularly in the eastern hemisphere.

# References

Anderson, Richard G. and Jerry Thursby (1986), 'Confidence Intervals for Elasticities Estimators in Translog Models,' *Review of Economics and Statistics*, **68**, 647–56.
Berndt, Ernst (1981), 'Modelling the Simultaneous Demand for Factors of Production,' in Zmira Hornstein et al., (eds), *The Economics of the Labor Market*, London: Her Majesty's Stationery Office.

Berndt, Ernst and Mohammed Khaled (1979), 'Parametric Productivity Measurement and Choice Among Flexible Functional Forms,' *Journal of Political Economy*, **87** (6), 1220–45.

Berndt, Ernst and Dieter Hesse (1986), 'Measuring and Assessing Capacity Utilization in the Manufacturing Sectors of Nine OECD Countries,' *European Economic Review*, **30**, 961–89.

Berndt, Ernst and David Wood (1979), 'Engineering and Econometric Interpretations of Energy-Capital Complementarity,' *American Economic Review*, **69** (3), 342–54.

Brainard, S. Lael (1993a), 'An Empirical Assessment of the Factor Proportions Explanation of Multinational Sales,' National Bureau of Economic Research Working Paper No. 4583, Cambridge, MA.

Brainard, S. Lael (1993b), 'An Empirical Assessment of the Proximity–Concentration Tradeoff between Multinational Sales and Trade,' forthcoming in *American Economic Review*.

Brainard, S. Lael (1997), 'An Empirical Assessment of the Proximity–Concentration Tradeoff between Multinational Sales and Trade,' *American Economic Review*, September.

Bureau of Labor Statistics, Foreign Labor Statistics, *Unpublished Hourly Compensation Costs for Production Workers in Manufacturing, 29 Countries or Areas, 40 Manufacturing Industries*, 1979 and 1986–92.

Caves, Richard (1982), *Multinational Enterprise and Economic Analysis*, Cambridge: Cambridge University Press.

Christenson, Laurits, Dale Jorgenson, and Lawrence Lau (1973), 'Transcendental Logarithmic Production Frontiers,' *Review of Economics and Statistics*, **55**, 28–45.

Graham, Edward and Paul Krugman (1990), *Foreign Direct Investment in the US*, Washington, DC: International Institute of Economics.

Greene, William H. (1990), *Econometric Analysis*, New York: Macmillan.

Hamermesh, Daniel (1993), *Labor Demand*, Princeton: Princeton University Press.

Lawrence, Robert (1995), 'Trade, Multinationals, and Labor,' National Bureau of Economic Research Working Paper no. 4836, Cambridge, MA.

Lipsey, Robert (1994), 'Outward Direct Investment and the US Economy,' National Bureau of Economic Research Working Paper No. 4691, December.

Lipsey, Robert, Irving Kravis, and Romualdo Roldan (1982), 'Do Multinational Firms Adapt Factor Proportions to Relative Factor Prices?' in Anne Krueger (ed.), *Trade and Employment in Developing Countries: Factor Supply and Substitution*, Chicago: University of Chicago Press.

Markusen, James (1995), 'The Boundaries of Multinational Enterprises and the Theory of International Trade,' *Journal of Economic Perspectives*, **9**, 169–90.

Riker, David A. and S. Lael Brainard (1997), 'US Multinationals and Competition with Low Wage Countries', National Bureau of Economic Research Working Paper No. 5959.

Slaughter, Matt (1993), 'International Trade, Multinational Corporations, and American Wage Divergence in the 1980s,' mimeo, MIT.

Slaughter, Matt (1995), 'Multinational Corporations, Outsourcing, and American Wage Divergence,' National Bureau of Economic Research Working Paper No. 5253, Cambridge, MA.

US Department of Commerce, Bureau of Economic Analysis (1983–1992), *Annual Survey of US Direct Investment Abroad*.

World Bank (1989), *World Development Report*, New York; Oxford; Toronto and Melbourne: Oxford University Press for the World Bank.

# [20]

## THE IMPACT OF OUTSOURCING AND HIGH-TECHNOLOGY CAPITAL ON WAGES: ESTIMATES FOR THE UNITED STATES, 1979–1990*

### Robert C. Feenstra and Gordon H. Hanson

We estimate the relative influence of trade versus technology on wages in a "large-country" setting, where technological change affects product prices. Trade is measured by the foreign outsourcing of intermediate inputs, while technological change is measured by expenditures on high-technology capital such as computers. The estimation procedure we develop, which modifies the conventional "price regression," is able to distinguish whether product price changes are due to factor-biased versus sector-biased technology shifts. In our base specification we find that computers explain about 35 percent of the increase in the relative wage of nonproduction workers, while outsourcing explains 15 percent; both of these effects are higher in other specifications.

## I. Introduction

The recent economic performance of less-skilled workers in industrial countries is an important policy topic and the subject of intense academic attention. During the 1980s and 1990s the wages of low-skilled workers have fallen relative to those of high-skilled workers. In the United States the earnings of the low-skilled have also declined in real terms. The two most widely cited explanations for the rise in wage inequality are skill-biased technical change and trade with low-wage countries. Of these two, technical change due to the use of computers is often believed to be the dominant explanation.

The goal of this paper is to develop a new methodology and estimate the impact of trade and technology on wages, for the United States over the period 1979–1990. We will measure trade by the foreign outsourcing of intermediate inputs,[1] while we will

* The authors thank James Anderson, Robert Baldwin, Alan Deardorff, James Harrigan, Lawrence Katz, Edward Leamer, David Richardson, and Matthew Slaughter for very useful comments. Financial support from the National Science Foundation is gratefully acknowledged.

1. Foreign outsourcing was first considered by Lawrence and Slaughter [1993] and more recently by Feenstra and Hanson [1996a, 1996b]. Lawrence and Slaughter [1993] and Berman, Bound, and Griliches [1994] argue that the amount of outsourcing from the United States is too small to explain the change in wages, but this was due to the narrow measure of outsourcing that they used (see Feenstra and Hanson [1996a], pp. 106–107). We will be using a measure of outsourcing constructed as in Feenstra and Hanson [1996b], which is estimated imports of intermediate inputs into each industry. This measure may also miss aspects of outsourcing, such as the use of computer programmers in India for products otherwise manufactured in the United States. Leamer [1998] introduces

*The Quarterly Journal of Economics,* August 1999

measure potential technical change by the shift toward high-technology capital such as computers. The starting point for our analysis is a popular method to predict wage changes under zero-profits: a regression of the *change* in industry prices on the *level* of factor cost-shares in that industry, where the estimated coefficients are interpreted as the predicted change in factor-prices that are consistent with the movement in product prices. This "price regression" was first used by Baldwin and Hilton [1984], and more recently by Leamer [1994, 1998], Baldwin and Cain [1997], and Krueger [1997]. In contrast to existing literature, we argue that when fully specified, this regression becomes an *identity* and cannot offer any prediction of the implied changes in factor prices, other than that which actually occurred.

To move beyond this stalemate, we shall modify the conventional price regression using a two-stage estimation procedure. First, we examine how changes in structural variables, such as foreign outsourcing and high-technology capital, affect industry prices and productivity. By treating industry prices (and productivity) as endogenous, we allow for a large-open-economy setting. From these first-stage results, we decompose price and productivity changes into portions that are attributable to each structural variable. Second, using a modified version of the price regression, we use the decomposed price and productivity changes from the first stage to estimate the change in primary factor prices that is attributable to each structural variable separately. The results indicate how much of the observed rise in wage inequality is attributable to foreign outsourcing or high-technology capital. While we focus on these two explanations, the methodology we develop is quite general and could be used to examine the relationship between factor prices and many types of changes in production techniques.

Our approach may help resolve an apparent conflict in the literature over whether it is the factor bias or the sector bias of technological changes that matters for wages.[2] Krugman [2000] and Leamer [1998, 2000] have debated this point, with Krugman arguing that factor bias is important in a closed or large open economy, and Leamer arguing that sector bias is all that matters

---

the broader term "delocalization" to indicate the many ways that pieces of the research/production/marketing processes can be moved offshore.

2. See Haskel and Slaughter [1998] and Kahn and Lim [1998] for evidence on the sector-bias of technical change and Berman, Bound, and Machin [1997] for international evidence on skill-biased technical change.

in a small open economy (or even with log-linear pass-through from productivity to prices). To resolve this, we need to have an indication of which setting is empirically relevant. This will turn out to be a by-product of our analysis, since our first-stage regression can distinguish between sector-biased and factor-biased technological changes: *both of* these changes affect industry prices, but (with Cobb-Douglas preferences) only the factor-biased changes will have an impact on wages and prices *over and above* their impact on productivity. Thus, in a regression of industry prices on total factor productivity, a test for the presence of additional structural variables can be interpreted as a test for nonneutral technological change (conditional on finding complete pass-through from productivity to prices).

The specification of our model is derived in Sections II and III; while the data are discussed in Section IV, and empirical results are presented in Section V. In our empirical results, we begin by examining the impact of foreign outsourcing and alternative measures of high-technology capital on the relative demand for skilled labor. This allows comparison with existing literature and our later results. We then consider two specifications to explain industry changes in prices and productivity. In the first, we assume that the structural variables enter linearly as independent variables. In that case we find that computers explain about 35 percent of the increase in the relative wage of nonproduction workers, while outsourcing explains 15 percent. In the second specification we allow for interactions between the structural variables and quantities of primary factors, which is a more direct method to control for the contribution of the structural variables to nonneutral technological change. We then find that foreign outsourcing explains about 40 percent of the increase in the relative nonproduction wage, whereas computer expenditures can explain 75 percent of this increase. Our conclusions are discussed further in Section VI.

## II. PRICE REGRESSION

The first step in our empirical specification is derive the "price regression" that has been used by Baldwin and Hilton [1984], Leamer [1994, 1998], Baldwin and Cain [1997], and Krueger [1997]. While the exact specification that is estimated varies across different studies (see Slaughter [1998] for a survey), the typical regression has the change in industry product prices as a dependent variable and industry factor cost shares as independent variables, with total factor productivity sometimes included as a regressor. Following the terminology in Leamer [1998], the coefficients on the factor cost shares are interpreted as the change in factor prices that are *mandated by* the change in product prices and, possibly, productivity.

The standard method to derive the price regression is to totally differentiate the zero-profit condition for each industry. That is, we treat the product prices as changing due to (unspecified) market forces, leading to an implied change in equilibrium factor prices. Expressing this in first-differences, the relationship is

$$(1) \qquad \Delta \ln p_{it}^{VA} = -TFP_{it} + \tfrac{1}{2}(s_{it-1} + s_{it})' \Delta \ln w_{it},$$

where $p_{it}^{VA}$ denotes the value-added price in industry $i = 1, \dots, N$, $TFP_{it}$ denotes total factor productivity, $w_{it}$ denotes the vector of primary factor prices in industry $i$, and $s_{it-1}$ and $s_{it}$ are the primary factor cost-shares that are averaged over the two periods.[3] The ability of (1) to hold in the data will depend on the measure of total factor productivity that is used. In particular, the *dual* Tornqvist index of TFP [Caves, Christensen, and Diewert 1982a, 1982b] is defined as the difference between the log change in industry prices, and the cost-shared weighted change in factor prices. Using this particular measure of productivity, (1) clearly holds as an *identity*, as we assume. It is perhaps more common to work with the primal Tornqvist index of TFP, which equals the log change of output minus the share-weighted growth of inputs. While the primal and dual measures are not equal in general, their difference is extremely small in our sample.[4]

In order to move from equation (1) to the price regression, as it is conventionally applied, we treat $\Delta \ln w_{it}$ as a random variable over industries $i$ and denote its mean value by $\omega_t$. Then using this

---

3. The value-added price is constructed as $\Delta \ln p_{it}^{VA} \equiv [\Delta \ln p_{it} - \tfrac{1}{2}(r_{it-1} + r_{it})' \Delta \ln p_t]/[\Sigma_{j=1}^{N} \tfrac{1}{2}(r_{ijt-1} + r_{jit})]$, where $r_{ijt}$ is the cost-share of intermediate input $j$ used in the production of industry $i = 1, \dots, N$. We impose the assumption of perfect competition, so that revenue equals costs, and the cost-shares are measured by the revenue shares. Hall [1988] and Domowitz, Hubbard, and Petersen [1988] suggest that imperfect competition may bias standard measures of total factor productivity and that one should account for this bias by introducing controls for price-marginal cost markups. In our empirical analysis we find that introducing such controls (output-capital ratios) has little effect on parameter estimates.

4. The primal measure of TFP is defined as the growth of value-added minus the weighted average growth of primary factors. It has a correlation of 0.999 with the dual measure of TFP defined by (2), for 1979–1990.

notation in (1), we readily obtain

(2) $$\Delta \ln p_{it}^{VA} = -TFP_{it} + \tfrac{1}{2}(s_{it-1} + s_{it})'\omega_t + e_{it},$$

where the final term appearing on the right is

(3) $$e_{it} \equiv \tfrac{1}{2}(s_{it-1} + s_{it})'(\Delta \ln w_{it} - \omega_{it}).$$

This term equals the average deviation of industry-specific factor-price changes from their mean levels. We refer to the magnitude in (3) as the "change in wage differentials," since it reflects the change in the industry-specific wages for labor (and rental price of capital) in relation to their manufacturing-wide levels. This term is usually excluded from estimation of the price regression and hence implicitly treated as an error term. The change in wage differentials can be measured with available data, however, and we shall explicitly account for its presence in our work.

There are two general sources of variation in factor prices across industries, leading to interindustry wage differentials: unobserved variation in factor quality and industry-specific rents. There is extensive empirical literature on interindustry differences in wages, much of which is devoted to ascertaining their source (e.g., Krueger and Summers [1988], Murphy and Topel [1990], and Gibbons and Katz [1992]). Since we examine long-run changes in factor prices in an environment where factors are assumed to be perfectly mobile across industries, we prefer to interpret interindustry factor-price variation as resulting from variation in *factor quality* across industries, which is consistent with the neoclassical trade model that is the foundation for our analysis. Under this assumption, the effective wages paid by industries—after accounting for quality differences—are properly measured by the manufacturing-wide wages, or $\omega_t$. It follows that the *effective total factor productivity* is measured by

(4) $$ETFP_{it} \equiv TFP_{it} - e_{it}.$$

Combining (4) and (2), we obtain an alternative version of the price regression that incorporates the interindustry wage differentials:

(2') $$\Delta \ln p_{it}^{VA} = -ETFP_{it} + \tfrac{1}{2}(s_{it-1} + s_{it})'\omega_t.$$

What is exceptional about the price regression in (2') is that by *including* effective TFP as a variable in (2), the regression will fit exactly because it is an identity. That is, if we run (2') as a regression, then the estimated (or mandated) change in factor prices necessarily equals the *actual* change $\omega_t$. The reason that other studies have not obtained this result is because the specification of the price regression is not exactly the same as in $(2')$, as we shall illustrate now.

In Table I we report results from estimating $(2')$ using data from the NBER Productivity Database [Bartelsman and Gray 1996], which contains the value of industry prices, shipments, input usage, and factor prices for four-digit SIC manufacturing industries over the period 1958–1991. There are 450 four-digit SIC industries in the United States. We exclude three industries (SIC 2067, 2794, 3483) due to missing data on materials pur-

TABLE I
DEPENDENT VARIABLE—LOG CHANGE IN INDUSTRY PRICE, 1979–1990

|  | (1) | (2) | (3) | (4) | (5) |
|---|---|---|---|---|---|
| Effective TFP | −1.000 | −1.000 | | | |
|  | (0.007) | (0.0006) | | | |
| TFP | | | −0.963 | −0.753 | |
|  | | | (0.070) | (0.075) | |
| Production cost-share | 4.680 | 4.700 | 3.063 | 2.428 | 3.605 |
|  | (0.016) | (0.012) | (1.222) | (1.162) | (1.885) |
| Nonproduction cost-share | 5.482 | 5.443 | 2.295 | 4.086 | 6.202 |
|  | (0.019) | (0.031) | (1.430) | (1.722) | (4.036) |
| Capital cost-share | 3.953 | 3.972 | 7.888 | 8.058 | 9.535 |
|  | (0.008) | (0.015) | (0.781) | (0.941) | (2.187) |
| Materials cost-share times change in materials price | | 0.997 | 1.00* | 1.00* | 1.219 |
|  | | (0.002) | | | (0.247) |
| Energy cost-share times change in energy price | | 0.996 | 1.00* | 1.00* | −0.930 |
|  | | (0.006) | | | (0.915) |
| constant | | 0.0101 | −0.705 | −0.825 | −1.929 |
|  | | (0.005) | (0.301) | (0.293) | (0.915) |
| $R^2$ | 0.999 | 0.999 | 0.896 | 0.806 | 0.429 |
| N | 447 | 447 | 447 | 446 | 446 |
|  | | | | | [omitting computers] |

Standard errors are in parentheses. All regressions omit three industries with missing data on materials purchases or prices (SIC 2067, 2794, 3483) and are weighted by the industry share of total manufacturing shipments, averaged over the first and last period.
In column (1) the dependent variable is the log change in the industry value-added price and factor cost shares sum to one across primary factors. Effective TFP equals primal TFP minus the change in wage differentials. In columns (2)–(5) the dependent variable is the log change in the gross industry price, and the factor cost shares sum to one across all factors. The materials cost share is multiplied by the log change in the materials price; the energy cost share is treated similarly. Column (2) includes effective TFP as a regressor; column (3) replaces effective TFP with primal TFP; column (4) drops the computer industry (SIC 3573) from the sample; and column (5) also drops the computer industry from the sample and drops TFP as a regressor.
* These coefficients are constrained at unity.

chases or prices.[5] The value-added price is constructed as a log-difference over the period 1979–1990, divided by the number of years in each period to obtain an annualized difference. We use the primal measure of TFP, expressed as an annualized difference. The other independent variables are the average cost-shares (over the first and last year for the period) for production labor, nonproduction labor, and capital. The mean values for these and other variables are shown in Table II.[6]

The regression shown in the first column of Table I includes effective TFP and the average factor-shares. The estimated coefficients can be compared with the annual average changes in the prices of production labor, nonproduction labor, and capital for 1979–1990 shown at the top of Table II. The estimated coefficients are extremely close to the actual factor price changes reported in Table II, and the regression fits nearly perfectly (when we replace effective TFP constructed from the primal with effective TFP constructed from the dual, the regression fits exactly). The wage of nonproduction labor rises faster than that of production labor, indicating an increase in wage inequality during the 1980s.

In order to compare this near-identity with the price regression as it appears in the literature, it is useful to consider another version of (2') where we explicitly introduce the prices of intermediate inputs on the right-hand side, rather than incorporating them into the value-added prices on the left. This again will produce a near identity, but it will prepare us for estimating mandated factor-price changes similar to those found by others. Leamer [1998] includes the materials term on the left, while constraining its coefficient at unity, while Krueger [1997] allows the coefficient to be estimated. We will experiment with both approaches, although our results do not exactly reproduce those of Leamer or Krueger due to differences in the sample and other features.[7] In the second column of Table I, we introduce the

5. There are data on aggregate material purchases for some of these industries, but not on detailed material purchases from individual industries, which we would need in order to construct an estimate of imported intermediate inputs. Since we are forced to exclude these industries in later regressions in which we use foreign outsourcing as an independent variable, for the sake of consistency we also exclude them from the regressions in Table I.

6. Mean price changes for a primary factor are weighted by the average industry share of payments to that factor, which is done to produce means that will replicate the estimated coefficients in the identity in (2') (which are estimated with these implicit weights).

7. In order for (2') to fit as an identity, the capital share that is used must be constructed as a residual, by subtracting the payments to all other factors from the value of shipments. This means that the price of capital being used is the ex post

materials cost share multiplied by its log-change in price over 1979–1990, and similarly for energy, as independent variables. In addition, all variables in the regression are reweighted so that the cost shares over *all factors* sum to unity. This contrasts with regression (1), where the cost shares over just the primary factors sum to unity (that is, the primary factor cost shares are shares of value added).[8] This reweighting has no effect on an identity, of course, and regression (2) continues to fit nearly perfectly. The reweighting does have an impact on the rest of the results in Table I.

In regression (3) we replace effective TFP with primal TFP, so that the change in wage differentials is effectively *excluded* from the price regression, while keeping the coefficients on materials and energy at unity. This approximates the specification in Leamer [1998]. We have now moved from an identity to a regression equation in which the goal is to estimate the changes in factor prices that are warranted by changes in product prices and productivity. The coefficient estimates suggest that the wage of production labor rose faster than nonproduction labor over the period 1979–1990, or that wage inequality *decreased,* which is consistent with Leamer's [1998] findings. What this result indicates is that the omitted variable—the change in wage differentials—is positively correlated with the production labor cost-share (it is also positively correlated with the capital share). Alternatively, in regression (4) we omit the computer industry (SIC 3573) from the sample (following Sachs and Shatz [1994]). In this case the original pattern of wage coefficients is restored, showing that wage inequality *increased.* Finally, in regression (5) we continue to omit the computer industry and also drop TFP as a regressor, while estimating the coefficients on materials and energy (following Krueger [1997]). Then the coefficient estimates showing rising wage inequality are preserved, which is consistent with Krueger's [1997] results, although the magnitude of the effect is exaggerated.

The point of Table I is to show that estimates from the conventional price regression are extremely sensitive to its exact specification (particularly what measure of TFP to include), but that when it is *fully specified* (using effective TFP) it becomes an

---

rate of return. In contrast, Leamer [1998] constructs a capital share using an assumed uniform rate of return on capital across all industries.

8. This is done to be consistent with the definition of the value-added price as the difference between the gross output price and materials prices times materials cost shares (see note 3).

identity. The results obtained when some variable is omitted depend, in the standard way, on the correlation between the omitted and included variables, and this is the only reason for the coefficients obtained to not equal the observed change in wages. This leads to the obvious question of whether the price regression should be used at all to infer wage changes. We believe that such inference can still be made, by modifying the price regression as discussed in the next section.

## III. ENDOGENIZING PRICES AND PRODUCTIVITY

The price regression in (2′) summarizes how value-added prices and productivity comove with primary factor prices, given factor intensities (the average factor cost shares). In order to transform the identity in (2′) into an analytical device through which we can map changes in trade and technology into factor price changes, we must first disentangle the features that contribute to changes in value-added prices and productivity. We propose to examine how changes in a series of structural variables, such as foreign outsourcing and the purchase of high-technology capital, influence value-added prices and effective productivity, and then, using (2′), examine how the changes in value-added prices and productivity implied by the structural variables influence factor prices. Our methodology has two stages. First, we regress changes in effective productivity and value-added prices on the structural variables. Second, using the first-stage estimation results and the price regression, we decompose changes in primary factor prices into portions that are attributable to each structural variable. We begin by describing the mechanics of the estimation and then, building on trade and production theory, provide a conceptual foundation for our regressions.

The impact of structural variables on effective productivity is modeled as

$$(5) \qquad ETFP_{it} = \alpha' \Delta z_{it} + \epsilon_{it},$$

where $z_{it}$ is a $(K \times 1)$ vector of structural variables, $\alpha$ is a $(K \times 1)$ vector of coefficients, and $\epsilon_{it}$ is a disturbance term that captures all other shocks to productivity, which is assumed orthogonal to $z_{it}$. Krugman [2000] argues persuasively that changes in productivity are "passed-through" to industry prices, either because the country in question is large in world markets or because the technology shocks are common across countries. Then the change in effective productivity has a further impact on prices as modeled by

$$(6) \qquad \Delta \ln p_{it}^{VA} = \lambda ETFP_{it} + \beta' \Delta z_{it} + v_{it},$$

where $\lambda$ is the pass-through coefficient (we expect $\lambda \leq 0$), $\beta$ is a $(K \times 1)$ vector of coefficients, and $v_{it}$ is another error term. It is significant that in (6) we allow the structural variables $z_{it}$ to have a *direct* impact $\beta$ on prices, over and above the *indirect* impact via productivity. The need to include this direct impact will be explained below.

Combining (5) and (6), the total impact of the structural variables on value-added prices and productivity in a large-country setting, can be summarized by the following regression:

$$(7) \qquad \Delta \ln p_{it}^{VA} + ETFP_{it} = \gamma' \Delta z_{it} + \eta_{it},$$

where $\gamma = (1 + \lambda)\alpha + \beta$, and $\eta_{it} = (1 + \lambda)\epsilon_{it} + v_{it}$. We will regard (6) as a first-stage regression, which allows us to decompose the total change in value-added prices and effective *TFP* into those components due to each structural variable, namely $\gamma_k \Delta z_{itk}$, where $\gamma_k$ is the $k$th element of $\gamma$ and $\Delta z_{itk}$ is the $k$th element of $\Delta z_{it}$.

As a second-stage, we regress this *component* of the change in price and productivity on the factor-shares, thereby obtaining a predicted wage change due to that structural component. The second-stage regressions for each structural variable $k$ are

$$(8) \qquad \gamma_k \Delta z_{itk} = \delta_k'(s_{it-1} + s_{it})/2 + u_{ikt}.$$

The coefficients $\delta_k$ obtained from these regressions are interpreted as the change in primary factor prices that are explained by structural variable $k$. In other words, the regression coefficients in (8) can be seen as the changes in primary factor prices that would have occurred if changes in structural variable had been the only source of changes in value-added prices and productivity. Thus, (8) is a modified version of the price regression in (2'), in which we attempt to estimate the contribution of each structural variable to the average change in primary factor prices. We perform the regression for each structural variable separately.

This essentially completes the description of our methodology, but we should provide further justification for the use of high-technology capital and outsourcing as structural variables. The idea that high-technology capital impacts productivity is the subject of a large literature (e.g., Berndt and Morrison [1995], Morrison [1997] and Morrison and Siegel [1996]). Similar to that literature, what we have in mind is not the contribution of these

OUTSOURCING AND HIGH-TECHNOLOGY CAPITAL          **917**

equipment purchases to the overall capital stock, but to changes in actual production techniques. Doms, Dunne, and Troske [1997] examine the correlation between the usage of automation technologies and the structure of employment and wages at the plant level, which is a direct treatment of how the adoption of redundant innovations influences production techniques. They focus on whether automation techniques have a *nonneutral* effect on relative demand for production and nonproduction workers. Our approach is at a more aggregate level, using industry measures of expenditure on computers and other technology-intensive equipment, but we also expect that high-technology capital may contribute to a nonneutral shift in productivity.

It is less obvious that foreign (or domestic) outsourcing should also have an impact on measured productivity, although this is implied by the model developed in Feenstra and Hanson [1996a, 1997]. There we consider a good produced in multiple stages of production. These different stages need not take place in a single country, and of course, the more unskilled-labor-intensive stages will be done in the country with lower relative wages for unskilled labor: the transfer of these activities abroad is what we call foreign outsourcing. The activities remaining at home can be aggregated into a production function. With a change in underlying parameters (such as factor endowments at home or abroad, or trade policies), the range of activities done abroad can change. The outsourced activities can be thought of as new intermediate inputs, which will shift the entire production function for activities done at home, and therefore show up in the industry aggregate production function as a change in total factor productivity.[9] This will generally be a nonneutral shift, as outsourcing often takes the form of moving unskilled activities to low-wage countries, thus increasing the relative demand for skilled labor at home.

The presence of nonneutral technological progress implies that the structural variables must enter *directly* into equation (6),

---

9. If we observed the full range of activities that constitute production, we could account for outsourcing directly by examining the process through which production stages are divided across countries. Manufacturing data, however, are typically aggregated over production activities at the industry (or sectoral) level. Thus, the effects of outsourcing can only be observed through their effects on average factor intensities in an industry. When outsourcing raises the average skill intensity of production in U. S. industries, its effects mimic those of industry-specific, skill-biased technological change. For this reason, outsourcing and the adoption of new technologies may have observationally equivalent effects on total factor productivity.

in addition to their indirect impact via productivity. This can be understood as follows. Suppose that technology shocks are common across countries, so that we can treat the determination of factor prices as in a closed economy [Krugman 1995]. Further assume that preferences are Cobb-Douglas. The initial equilibrium is illustrated by point $A$ in Figure I, where we illustrate the zero-profit conditions $p_i = c_i(w,r)$ in two industries $i = 1,2$, where $w$ denotes the wage of unskilled labor and $r$ denotes the wage of skilled labor. The relative demand for unskilled labor is given by the slope of each isocost curve, so the diagram shows the case where industry 1 is skilled-labor intensive.

Initially, consider the case of *neutral* technological progress in industry 1. This is illustrated by the outward shift of the isocost

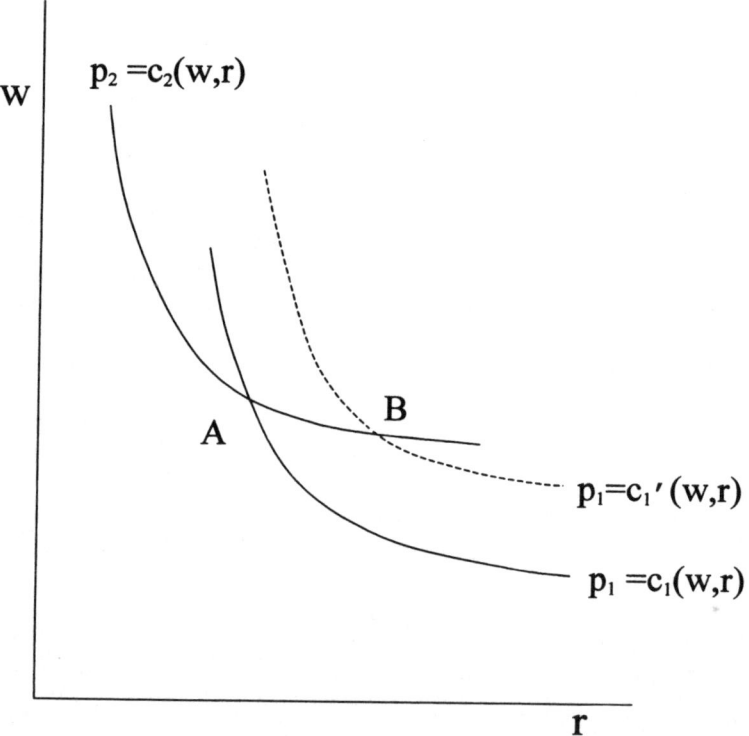

FIGURE I
Hicks-Neutral Technological Progress

line in industry 1 to $p_1 = c_1(w,r)$. In the absence of any change in product prices, the wages would now be determined at point $B$, where there has been an increase in the relative wage of skilled labor. There would also be an increase in the output $y_1$, by exactly the amount of the neutral technological progress. With Cobb-Douglas preferences, this would imply an equal and offsetting drop in $p_1$, which means that the isocost line for industry 1 would shift *back* to its original location, and the factor prices would again be determined at point $A$. This illustrates the general result that, with Cobb-Douglas preferences, the determination of factor prices is *independent* of any Hicks-neutral progress in either industry [Krugman 1995]. In terms of equation (6) we would have $\lambda = -1$ as prices move in an equal and offsetting manner with neutral technological progress, and since there is no further change in prices, then $\beta = 0$.

We contrast this result with the case of skill-biased technological progress, shown in Figure II. This would shift the isocost line for industry 1 out in a clockwise fashion to $p_1 = c_1(w,r)$. Continuing to assume Cobb-Douglas preferences, suppose that $p_1$ drops in an equal and offsetting fashion, so that the isocost line shifts back inwards (equiproportionally) to the *dashed* line through point $A$. In the absence of any factor movement between the industries, output $y_2$ would be unaffected, and output $y_1$ would increase by the same percentage that $p_1$ has decreased. This means that the goods market is in equilibrium. However, the factor markets are definitely *not* in equilibrium, because there has been an increase in the relative demand for skilled labor in industry 1 (and no change in this demand within industry 2). This will lead to an increase in the relative wage of skilled labor, and therefore, an increase in the relative price of good 1. As a result, there will be a further shifting of the isocost lines for both goods (e.g., the isocost line for good 1 will shift outwards and that for good 2 will shift inwards), and the equilibrium will be established at a position such as $C$.[10] The crucial point to recognize is that even for a closed economy with Cobb-Douglas preferences and $\lambda = -1$ in equation (6), there will

---

10. The complete set of relations between nonneutral progress parameters and relative factor prices, depending on the elasticities of substitution in demand and in production, has been worked out by Xu [1998], and the CES and Cobb-Douglas cases have been considered by Bound and Johnson [1992, Appendix] and Katz and Autor [1999], respectively. Unfortunately, there does not appear to be a convenient closed-form solution to show how the change in product prices in (6) depends on the nonneutral progress parameters.

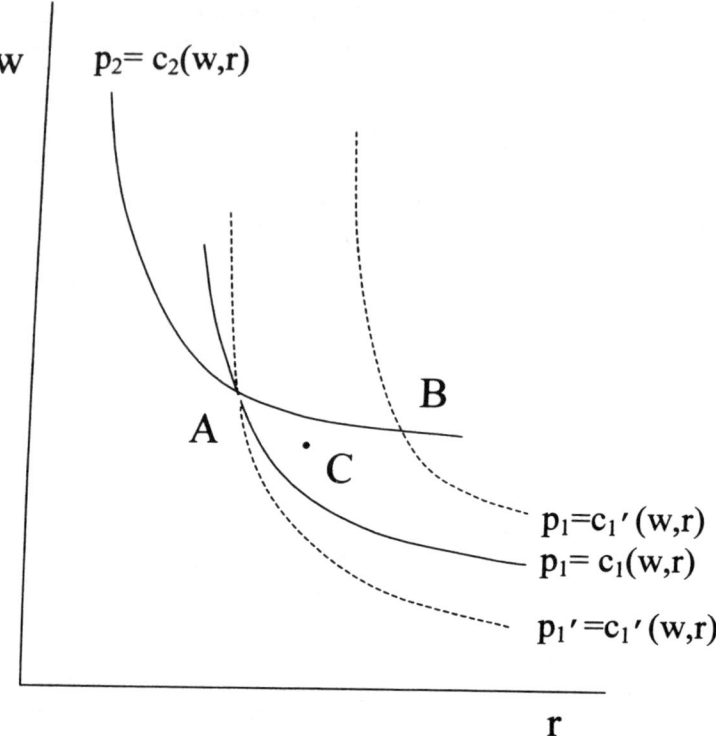

FIGURE II
Skill-Biased Technological Progress

be a *further feedback effect of the nonneutral progress on the goods prices,* so that $\beta \neq 0$ in (6).[11]

Our argument above provides a rationale for the structural variables to linearly affect productivity in (5), and to have a *further* impact on value-added prices in equation (6) when the technological change is nonneutral. Empirically, if we find $\lambda = -1$ and $\beta \neq 0$, then we can interpret this as evidence that the technological progress is nonneutral. It can be noted here that the presence of additional structural variables in (6) (i.e., $\beta \neq 0$) is

---

11. This effect will only be enhanced when considering technological shocks across countries. For example, outsourcing could plausibly be correlated with changes in world prices even beyond its impact on TFP in the domestic industry, meaning that this variable should appear independently in the price equation (6).

precisely how our framework differs from Leamer [1998], who allowed for the pass-through of productivity to prices (i.e., $\lambda \neq 0$), but *did not* allow for other structural variables to affect prices. Leamer argues that even with pass-through from productivity to prices, only the *sectoral* impact of technological change is important. This result relies on his assumption that the pass-through relation between productivity and prices *does not* include any direct impact of structural variables on prices. As we have argued, in order to incorporate *nonneutral* technological shifts, then the additional structural regressors must be included in (6).

A further way to check for evidence of nonneutral technological change would be to include *interaction terms* between the structural variables and the quantities of primary factors, within equations (5)–(7). Such a specification could be derived explicitly from a translog production function, in which the coefficients on the interaction terms would indicate the magnitude of nonneutral technological change.[12] Following this logic, the first-stage regression in (7) could be respecified as

$$(7') \quad \Delta \ln p_{it}^{VA} + ETFP_{it} = \gamma' \Delta z_{it} + \tfrac{1}{2} \Delta z'_{it} A'(\ln x_{it-1} + \ln x_{it}) + \epsilon_{it},$$

where $x_{it}$ is the $(M \times 1)$ vector of primary factor quantities, and $A$ is an $(M \times K)$ matrix of coefficients measuring their interaction with each structural variable in affecting productivity and price. For example, a positive coefficient on the interaction between nonproduction labor and high-technology capital would indicate a complementary relationship between these in increasing productivity.

We could then use the estimated coefficients from the first-stage regression $(7')$ to decompose the change in value-added prices plus productivity into the portions attributable to each structural variable $k$, namely, $\gamma_k \Delta z_{itk} + \tfrac{1}{2} \Delta z_{itk} A_k (\ln x_{it-1} + \ln x_{it})$, where $\gamma_k$ is the $k$th element of $\gamma$ and $A_k$ is the $k$th column of $A$. Finally, we replace the dependent variable in (8) with these magnitudes, and perform the second-stage regression,

$$(8') \quad \gamma_k \Delta z_{itk} + \tfrac{1}{2} \Delta z_{itk} A'_k (\ln x_{it-1} + \ln x_{it}) = \delta'_k (s_{it-t} + s_{it})/2 + u_{itk}.$$

We again interpret the regression coefficients $\delta_k$ from this second-stage regression as the estimated changes in factor prices that are attributable to each structural variable $k$.

---

12. In an earlier draft of the paper, we derived such a specification explicitly. These results are available on request.

## IV. DATA AND PRELIMINARY REGRESSIONS

We shall apply the estimation technique described in equations (7) and (8), or (7') and (8'), to U. S. manufacturing industries for the period 1979–1990, which corresponds to the most recent period between business cycle peaks in the U. S. economy. The data we use are from the NBER Productivity Database [Bartelsman and Gray 1996], as summarized in Table II. The quantity of capital is constructed by Bartelsman and Gray from real investment in assets types, using a perpetual inventory method. We then calculate the price of capital by dividing the payments to capital in each industry (which equals value of shipments less payments to labor and materials) by the quantity of capital; this yields the ex post rental price of capital. There are 450 four-digit SIC industries in the United States; we exclude three industries (SIC 2067, 2794, 3483) due to missing data on materials purchases needed to estimate foreign outsourcing.

Movements in labor earnings and factor cost shares in Table II illustrate the rise in wage inequality that occurred during the 1980s. We also show data for 1972–1979, the previous interval between business cycle peaks, to provide a basis of comparison. During the period 1979–1990 the wages of nonproduction workers increased by 5.44 percent per year, while the wages of production workers increased by only 4.71 percent, so that the wages of nonproduction relative to production workers rose by an average of 0.72 percent per year.[13] Partly as a result of these wage movements, the share of production wages in total shipments declined over the two decades (falling from 12.6 percent to 10.3 percent), while the share of nonproduction wages in total shipments remained nearly constant. Looking at other factor prices, the dramatic increase in energy prices during the 1970s contributed to an increase in the share of energy in total costs, which was reversed during the 1980s as energy prices declined in relative terms.

The rise in total factor productivity from the 1970s to the 1980s is apparent in the lower portion of Table II. Also shown are

---

13. The increase in the wage of nonproduction workers relative to the wage of production workers as reported in the Annual Survey of Manufactures is only a small part of the total increase in wage inequality between more- and less-skilled workers that occurred during the 1980s. See Katz and Murphy [1992] for a discussion. While there are problems with using the production/nonproduction classification as a proxy for skill [Leamer 1994], there is evidence suggesting that in practice the classification shows similar trends as using skill categories [Berman, Bound, and Griliches 1994; Sachs and Shatz 1994].

OUTSOURCING AND HIGH-TECHNOLOGY CAPITAL        923

TABLE II
SUMMARY STATISTICS

| | 1972–1979 | | 1979–1990 | |
|---|---|---|---|---|
| | Average (percent) | Annual change | Average (percent) | Annual change |
| Change in log factor prices: | | | | |
| Production labor | | 7.666 | | 4.714 |
| Nonproduction labor | | 7.207 | | 5.437 |
| Capital | | 8.187 | | 3.954 |
| Materials | | 9.664 | | 3.485 |
| Energy | | 15.732 | | 3.250 |
| Factor cost-shares: | | | | |
| Production labor | 12.55 | −0.303 | 10.31 | −0.156 |
| Nonproduction labor | 6.68 | −0.139 | 6.54 | 0.002 |
| Capital | 24.92 | −0.001 | 27.16 | 0.262 |
| Materials | 50.72 | 0.170 | 49.08 | −0.261 |
| Energy | 2.02 | 0.113 | 2.23 | −0.023 |
| Other variables: | | | | |
| TFP (primal) | | 0.279 | | 0.467 |
| TFP (dual) | | 0.275 | | 0.467 |
| Outsourcing (broad) | 6.31 | 0.303 | 9.67 | 0.363 |
| Outsourcing (narrow) | 2.67 | 0.127 | 4.40 | 0.203 |
| Difference | 3.64 | 0.177 | 5.27 | 0.160 |
| *Using capital services (ex post rental prices):* | | | | |
| High-tech share | 7.75 | 0.125 | 10.20 | 0.326 |
| Computer share | 4.68 | −0.143 | 5.34 | 0.198 |
| Difference | 3.07 | 0.267 | 4.86 | 0.128 |
| *Using capital services (ex ante rental prices):* | | | | |
| High-tech share | 5.45 | 0.115 | 7.23 | 0.218 |
| Computer share | 3.03 | −0.047 | 3.21 | 0.053 |
| Difference | 2.42 | 0.162 | 4.02 | 0.164 |
| *Using computer investment:* | | | | |
| Computer share | 1.86 | — | 3.75 | — |

Averages are computed over the first and last year of each period (except for the computer investment share which is from 1977 for the 1972–1979 period and the average over 1982 and 1987 for the 1979–1990 period), while changes are measured as an average annual change (the change in log factor prices is the annual average change × 100). Both averages and changes are weighted by the industry share of total manufacturing shipments, except for primary factors, which are weighted by the industry share of total manufacturing payments to that factor. All variables are computed over 447 four-digit SIC industries (excluding SIC 2067, 2794, and 3483), except the High-tech share and Computer share, which are computed over two-digit SIC industries. Those two variables are from the Bureau of Labor Statistics, as used in Berndt, Morrison, and Rosenblum [1992] and Morrison [1997].

*Variable definitions:*

Outsourcing (broad) = (imported intermediate inputs)/(total nonenergy intermediates) × 100

Outsourcing (narrow) = (imported intermediate inputs in the same two-digit industry as buyer)/(total nonenergy intermediates) × 100

High-tech share = (high-technology capital)/(total capital) × 100

Computer share = (computer equipment)/(total capital) × 100

Computer investment share = (computer investment)/(total investment) × 100

the changes in the exogenous regressors that form the $z_{it}$ vector. The structural changes that we identify are the extent of foreign outsourcing, measured as the share of imported intermediate inputs in total costs and the share of high-technology capital in the total capital stock. For each variable we will consider several different versions. To measure foreign outsourcing, we combine data on imports of final goods with data on total input purchases. Feenstra [1996, 1997] provides data on total U. S. imports and exports by four-digit SIC manufacturing industry for the period 1972–1994.[14] We combine the trade data with data on material purchases from the *Census of Manufactures*. The *Census* data, which are the raw data used to construct input-output tables, show the value of intermediate inputs that each four-digit manufacturing industry purchased from every other manufacturing industry. For each industry $i$ we measure imported intermediate inputs as

(9) $\sum_{j}$ [input purchases of good $j$ by industry $i$]

$$* \left[ \frac{\text{imports of good } j}{\text{consumption of good } j} \right],$$

where (apparent) consumption of good $j$ is measured as shipments + imports − exports. Expressing imported intermediate inputs relative to total expenditure on nonenergy intermediates in each industry, we obtain the first, *broad* measure of foreign outsourcing. When averaged over all industries, this variable increased from 5.3 percent in 1972 to 7.3 percent in 1979 and 12.1 percent in 1990.

A second measure of outsourcing is obtained by restricting attention to those inputs that are purchased from the same two-digit SIC industry as the good being produced. The idea behind this measure is that foreign outsourcing represents the transfer overseas of production activities that could have been done by that company within the United States. We do not normally think of, say, the import of steel by a U. S. automobile producer as outsourcing. But it is common to consider the purchase of automobile parts by that company as outsourcing, especially if the parts were formerly made by the same company, or at least purchased in the United States. This idea is captured

14. The import and export data are available from Robert Feenstra over the Internet at www.nber.org.

by restricting the four-digit industry subscripts $i$ and $j$ in (9) to be within the same two-digit SIC industry. The resulting measure of imported intermediate inputs is again expressed relative to total expenditure on nonenergy intermediates in each industry, to obtain the second, *narrow* measure of outsourcing. When averaged, this variable increased from 2.2 percent in 1972 to 3.1 percent in 1979 and 5.7 percent in 1990.

Also reported in Table II is the *difference* between the broad and narrow measures of outsourcing, which represents the intermediate inputs from outside the two-digit purchasing industry that are sourced from abroad. Since we feel that the narrow measure—from within the same two-digit industry—best captures the idea of outsourcing, we will often enter the narrow measure and the difference between the broad and narrow as separate variables.

The data we use for high-technology capital are from the Bureau of Labor Statistics (BLS) and have been used by Berndt and Morrison [1995] and Morrison [1997].[15] These data distinguish capital by asset type for two-digit SIC manufacturing industries. The BLS first calculates real investment by asset type in each industry in each year by deflating industry asset purchases (e.g., expenditures on office equipment) by the relevant price index (e.g., the producer price index for office equipment). It then applies a perpetual inventory method to calculate the "productive stock" of each asset type in each industry in each year. Ex post rental prices for each asset are calculated as in Hall and Jorgenson [1967], and reflect the internal rate of return in each industry and capital gains on each asset. By summing the ex post rental prices times the productive stocks of all assets, we obtain the total payments to capital in each industry (equal to value of shipments less payments to labor and materials).

An alternative to the BLS measure of ex post rental prices is an ex ante measure of rental prices used by Berndt and Morrison, which reflects a "safe" rate of return (the Moody rate of Baa bonds) and excludes capital gains on each asset.[16] Summing the ex ante

15. These data are used by the BLS in their multifactor productivity calculations, as discussed in Harper, Berndt, and Wood [1989]. We thank Catherine Morrison and Don Siegel for providing us with these data.
16. The ex ante rental prices we use are the same as those used by Berndt and Morrison [1995] and Morrison [1997]. The formula for these rental prices is given by equation (29) in Harper, Berndt, and Wood [1989], where the Moody rate for Baa bonds is used to measure the ex ante interest rate and the capital gains term is excluded.

rental prices times the productive stocks of all assets does not yield the observed payments to capital in each industry. Nevertheless, the ex ante rental prices might be preferred precisely because they reflect neither capital gains on the assets nor the internal rate of return in the industry.

Berndt and Morrison define high-technology capital to include office, computing, and accounting machinery; communications equipment; science and engineering instruments; and photocopy and related equipment. The share of this equipment in total capital gives us the variable denoted by the *high-tech share.* To calculate the share, we take the ratio of the capital stocks multiplied by the ex post rental prices, which gives a measure of the share of capital services attributable to high-technology equipment, as shown in Table II. This broad measure increases from 7.3 percent in 1972 to 8.3 percent in 1979, and 12.2 percent in 1990. It can also be measured more narrowly to include only the share of office, computing, and accounting machinery in the capital stock, which gives us the *computer share.* This variable is 5.2 percent of capital services in 1972 and 4.2 percent in 1979, and then increases to 6.5 percent in 1990. We will also make use of the *difference* between the high-tech share and the computer share, which represents the fraction of capital services derived from various high-technology assets *other than* office, computing, and accounting machinery.

As an alternative to using ex post rental prices to calculate the services of computers and other high-technology capital, we consider using ex ante rental prices. By this measure, the share of high-technology capital in capital services is 5.0 percent in 1972, 5.9 percent in 1979, and 8.6 percent in 1990, while the share of computers in capital services is 3.2 percent in 1972, 2.9 percent in 1979, and 3.6 percent in 1990. Evidently, the computer share calculated with ex ante rental prices increases much less over 1979–1990 than does the computer share calculated with ex post rental prices.

A third measure of computer expenditures can be taken from the *Census,* which asked firms to report what fraction of investment was devoted to computer purchases in 1977, 1982, and 1987. This variable has been used by Berman, Bound and Griliches [1994] and also by Autor, Katz, and Krueger [1998].[17] The numerator and denominator of this variable are both investment

17. We thank Lawrence Katz for providing us with this variable.

flows, making the ratio difficult to interpret. We will make use of this variable in our sensitivity analysis, as an alternative to the BLS computer share.

Before applying our two-stage estimation procedure, we report in Table III regressions of the share of the total industry

TABLE III
DEPENDENT VARIABLE—CHANGE IN NONPRODUCTION WAGE SHARE, 1979–1990

|  | (1) Mean | (2) Regression | (3) Regression | (4) Regression | (5) Contribution |
|---|---|---|---|---|---|
| $\Delta \ln (K/Y)$ | 0.706 | 0.042 (0.014) | 0.041 (0.014) | 0.033 (0.012) | 6.0–7.7% |
| $\Delta \ln (Y)$ | 1.541 | 0.018 (0.008) | 0.016 (0.008) | 0.007 (0.009) | 2.7–7.1% |
| Outsourcing (narrow) | 0.223 | 0.246 (0.169) | 0.265 (0.175) | 0.193 (0.166) | 11.0–15.2% |
| Outsourcing (difference) | 0.200 | 0.121 (0.046) | 0.154 (0.050) | 0.038 (0.054) | 2.0–7.9% |
| *Capital services (ex post rental prices):* |  |  |  |  |  |
| Computer share | 0.251 | 0.206 (0.102) |  |  | 13.3% |
| High-tech share (difference) | 0.144 | −0.039 (0.129) |  |  | — |
| *Capital services (ex ante rental prices):* |  |  |  |  |  |
| Computer share | 0.070 |  | 0.421 (0.171) |  | 7.6% |
| High-tech share (difference) | 0.166 |  | 0.014 (0.072) |  | 0.6% |
| *Computer investment:* |  |  |  |  |  |
| Computer share | 6.561 |  |  | 0.019 (0.007) | 31.5% |
| High-tech share (ex post rental prices) | 0.395 |  |  | 0.052 (0.051) | 5.3% |
| constant |  | 0.207 (0.042) | 0.214 (0.039) | 0.161 (0.040) | 41.5–55.0% |
| $R^2$ |  | 0.163 | 0.165 | 0.200 |  |
| N |  | 447 | 447 | 447 |  |

The mean of the dependent variable equals 0.389. Standard errors (in parentheses) are robust to heteroskedasticity and correlation in the errors within two-digit industries. The first column shows mean values of the dependent and independent variables for 1979–1990. All regressions and means are computed over 447 four-digit SIC industries and are weighted by the average industry share of the manufacturing wage bill. $\Delta \ln (K/Y)$ is the average annual change in the log capital-shipments ratio, and $\Delta \ln (Y)$ is the average annual change in log real shipments. The outsourcing variables and the computer and high-technology shares are in annual changes and are defined in Table II and the text.

wage bill going to nonproduction workers on the structural variables and some control variables. This regression is very similar to that used by Berman, Bound, and Griliches [1994]; Autor, Katz, and Krueger [1998]; and Feenstra and Hanson [1996a], and allows a direct comparison with those papers. The regressions are run cross-sectionally over the four-digit SIC industries, and include changes in the shipments of each industry and the capital/shipments ratio as controls. The outsourcing variables and the computer and high-tech shares (but not the *Census* computer investment share) are all measured as annual changes.

In column (1) of Table III we report the mean values of the dependent and independent variables for 1979–1990. Since these means are weighted by the industry share of the total manufacturing wage bill, they differ somewhat from those reported in Table II. Following this, we report the regression coefficients in columns (2)–(4), where each regression uses alternative measures of the computer and high-technology variables. In all the regressions we see that the narrow definition of outsourcing has a positive impact on the nonproduction share of the wage bill, as does the computer share and computer investment share. Remaining outsourcing occurring outside of the same two-digit industry has a positive, though smaller, impact on the nonproduction wage share, while the remaining expenditures on high-technology capital are small and insignificant (and in one case negative).

By multiplying the regression coefficients by the mean values for the change in each variable, we obtain the contributions shown in column (5). Of the total annual average change in the nonproduction wage share of 0.39 percent, these contributions show the percentage of that shift due to each of the independent variables. We see that total outsourcing (the narrow measure and the difference) accounts for 13–23 percent of the shift toward nonproduction labor, which is in line with other estimates using slightly different data.[18] The results for computers differ quite dramatically across the specifications. Using capital services at ex post rental prices means that computers plus other expenditures on high-technology capital account for 13 percent of the shift toward nonproduction labor; using capital services as ex ante rental prices means that that these variables can explain only 8 percent

18. See Feenstra and Hanson [1996b] and the "Errata" to those results, available on request.

of this shift; and using the computer investment share and the high-technology capital share means that these variables can account for 32 percent of this shift. We will be interested in comparing these results (qualitatively) with what is obtained when we estimate factor-prices change attributable to the different structural variables.

## V. ESTIMATION RESULTS

The estimation procedure we develop has two stages. First, we estimate the impact of structural variables such as foreign outsourcing, computers, and other high-technology capital on changes in value-added prices plus effective productivity, using either the linear specification in (7) or the specification with interaction terms in (7'). We then use the estimated coefficients from this first-stage regression to calculate the portion of changes in value-added prices plus productivity that is attributable to each structural variable. Second, we separately regress each of these components on average factor shares, as in (8) or (8'), to obtain estimates of the changes in factor prices that are attributable to each structural variable. The estimation is performed by pooling over the 450 U. S. manufacturing industries at the four-digit SIC level for the periods 1979–1990, excluding the three industries (SIC 2067, 2794, 3483) for which detailed materials data needed to construct outsourcing are unavailable. All variables are constructed as differences or averages within this period.

The first-stage regression of value-added prices plus effective TFP on the structural variables is a reduced form, which combines equations (5) and (6). This specification imposes the assumption that the structural variables affect value-added prices over and above their impact on TFP. To justify our approach, we first regress valued-added prices on effective TFP and the structural variables. The structural variables are jointly statistically significant (at the 1 percent level) in this regression, which, following the discussion in Section III, suggests that the structural variables contribute to nonneutral shifts in technology. The estimated pass-through coefficient of effective TFP to value-added prices ($\lambda$ in equation (6)) is $-1.01$ (standard error of 0.01).[19] It is difficult to interpret this coefficient, however, since effective TFP is certainly

---

19. Excluding the structural variables from the regression, the estimated pass-through coefficient is $-1.00$.

correlated with value-added prices by its construction (see (2)), making the OLS estimate biased toward $-1$. In principle, one could use instrumental variables to obtain consistent estimates of the pass-through coefficient, but the best candidate instruments we have for TFP are the structural variables, which are invalid given that they are correlated with value-added prices, independent of their correlation with effective TFP.[20] Thus, we cannot improve upon the OLS estimate of $-1.01$ between productivity and prices, although we can conclude that the structural variables enter this relation independently. As argued in Section III, the appearance of these structural variables can be interpreted as evidence of nonneutral technological progress (conditional on the pass-through coefficient being $-1$). The fact that we are not able to obtain a consistent estimate of the pass-through coefficient does not hinder our analysis, since by summing (5) and (6), we can estimate the combined equation (7) where the pass-through coefficient does not explicitly appear.

There are three additional estimation issues to be addressed. First, two of the structural variables, the computer share and the high-tech share, are only available at the two-digit level. That these variables do not vary across four-digit industries within a two-digit industry raises the possibility that the errors in (7) or (7′) will be correlated within two-digit groups [Moulton 1986]. We control for this by allowing the errors in (7) and (7′) to be correlated across four-digit industries within each two-digit industry, where we continue to assume that the errors are uncorrelated across two-digit groups.

Second, the dependent variable in (8) and (8′), which is the contribution of each structural variable to changes in share-weighted factor price changes, is constructed using regression coefficients from the estimation of either (7) or (7′). For a given structural variable, the same estimated coefficients are embodied in the dependent variable of each industry, which implies that, by construction, the disturbance terms in (8) and (8′) will be correlated across observations. We adjust the standard errors of the estimated factor-price changes in (8) and (8′) to reflect this

---

20. To verify this, we regressed value-added prices on effective TFP, using the structural variables as instruments. In a test of overidentifying restrictions on the instruments [Newey 1985], we reject the null hypothesis that the instruments are uncorrelated with the error term at any reasonable level of significance.

covariance structure in the errors. Details of the correction procedure are available on request from the authors.[21]

Third, in equation (7') average log factor quantities appear as regressors, interacted with the structural variables. It is natural to imagine that shocks to value-added prices or productivity would influence factor employments, in which case the factor quantities would be correlated with the disturbance terms and OLS coefficient estimates would be inconsistent. Since we lack good instruments for factor quantities, there is no obvious solution to the potential endogeneity problem. It is thus important to interpret the coefficient estimates with care.

*V.A. Linear Decomposition*

Initially, we make use of the assumed linear relation between value-added prices plus effective TFP and the structural variables, as in (7). These estimation results from this first-stage regression are shown in Table IV, where each column refers to an alternative measure of the high-technology and computer capital shares. From the discussion in Section III, we expect the structural variables to positively affect productivity and to have a positive effect on the dependent variable overall. This is confirmed for all variables that are significantly estimated. Narrow outsourcing is significant in most specifications, while broad outsourcing is less so. Computers are also significant, but not other high-technology capital. It can also be noted that the constant term picks up all nominal changes that are common across factor prices, so the portions explained by each structural variable can be viewed as real changes.

The second-stage of the estimation is to decompose the dependent variable from (7) into that part explained by each structural variable, and then use these components as the dependent variables in (8), where the independent variables are the average shares of primary factors in the industries over 1979–1990. These regressions are shown in Table V, and the coefficients are interpreted as predicted factor-price changes due to each

---

21. A further issue is that if industries are imperfectly competitive, then the measure of total factor productivity is biased because the capital share includes pure profits [Hall 1988]. In unreported results, we controlled for this by including the log change in the output-capital ratio as a regressor in (7) and (7') [Domowitz, Hubbard, and Peterson 1988]. Since this and other control variables (lagged total factor productivity, sectoral dummy variables) have little impact on the coefficient estimates, we report regression results for (7) and (7') with no additional controls included.

TABLE IV

DEPENDENT VARIABLE—CHANGE IN VALUE-ADDED PRICES PLUS EFFECTIVE TFP,
1979–1990

|  | (1) | (2) | (3) |
|---|---|---|---|
| Independent variables: | | | |
| Outsourcing (narrow) | 0.064 | 0.080 | 0.040 |
|  | (0.031) | (0.035) | (0.030) |
| Outsourcing (difference) | 0.079 | 0.113 | 0.035 |
|  | (0.047) | (0.044) | (0.049) |
| *Capital services (ex post rental prices):* | | | |
| Computer share | 0.167 | | |
|  | (0.066) | | |
| High-tech share (difference) | 0.076 | | |
|  | (0.072) | | |
| *Capital services (ex ante rental prices):* | | | |
| Computer share | | 0.192 | |
|  | | (0.108) | |
| High-tech share (difference) | | −0.048 | |
|  | | (0.082) | |
| *Computer investment:* | | | |
| Computer share | | | 0.008 |
|  | | | (0.004) |
| High-tech share (ex post rental prices) | | | 0.093 |
|  | | | (0.049) |
| constant | 4.263 | 4.294 | 4.244 |
|  | (0.032) | (0.039) | (0.033) |
| $R^2$ | 0.153 | 0.109 | 0.213 |
| N | 447 | 447 | 447 |

All estimation is over four-digit SIC industries, and equations are weighted by the average industry share of manufacturing shipments. Standard errors (in parentheses) are robust to heteroskedasticity and correlation in the errors within two-digit industry groups. The dependent variable is the log change in value-added prices plus effective TFP (primal total factor productivity minus the change in wage differentials). The outsourcing variables and the computer and high-technology shares are all measured as annual changes; the computer investment share is measured as the average over 1982 and 1987. All variables are defined in Table II and the text.

structural variable. In Table V we report the results using the high-technology and computer shares computed with ex post rental prices, while in Table VI we will show how the results are affected by using alternative measures of high-tech capital.

Consider the coefficient estimates in regression (1) of Table V. Foreign outsourcing measured narrowly (within its two-digit industry) is estimated to have increased the (real) nonproduction wage by 0.10 percent annually over 1979–1990, with a small effect on the production labor wage. Outsourcing outside the two–digit industry in regression (2) increased the nonproduction wage by

TABLE V
ESTIMATED FACTOR-PRICE CHANGES—1979–1990

| Dependent variable, Change in share-weighted factor prices explained by: | Outsourcing *(narrow)* (1) | Outsourcing *(difference)* (2) | Computer *share* (3) | High-tech *share (difference)* (4) |
|---|---|---|---|---|
| *Mean of dependent variable* | 0.014 | 0.013 | 0.031 | 0.008 |
| Independent variables: | | | | |
| Production labor share | −0.010 | 0.020 | −0.005 | 0.026 |
| | (0.009) | (0.014) | (0.012) | (0.025) |
| Nonproduction labor share | 0.099 | 0.063 | 0.248 | 0.007 |
| | (0.049) | (0.039) | (0.100) | (0.004) |
| Capital share | 0.002 | −0.001 | 0.001 | 0.004 |
| | (0.003) | (0.003) | (0.004) | (0.004) |
| $R^2$ | 0.256 | 0.227 | 0.505 | 0.310 |
| N | 447 | 447 | 447 | 447 |

Coefficient estimates used to construct the dependent variable are those from column (1) of Table IV. Standard errors are in parentheses and are calculated as described in the text to account for cross-observation correlation in the disturbances that arises from the construction of the dependent variable. Observations are by four-digit SIC industry. All regressions are weighted by the average industry share of total manufacturing shipments.

0.06 percent annually, while raising the production wage by 0.02 percent annually. Taking the difference between the estimates for nonproduction and production labor, outsourcing in the same two-digit industry led to an increase in the relative wage of nonproduction labor of 0.11 percent annually; outsourcing outside the two-digit industry also raised the relative nonproduction wage, but insignificantly. These estimates are shown in the first row of Table VI, and can be compared with the actual increase in nonproduction relative to production wages of 0.72 percent per year over 1979–1990, from Table II. Hence, our initial estimates suggest that outsourcing can account for about 15 percent of the observed increase in the relative wage of nonproduction labor, or somewhat more if we incorporate the imprecise estimates from broad outsourcing.

In column (3) of Table V we report the same coefficients for computers. The estimates indicate that computers led to an increase in the wage of nonproduction labor by 0.25 percent annually (standard error of 0.10), with no impact on the production wage. This coefficient is also shown on the first row of Table VI, and indicates that computers can explain about 35 percent of the observed increase in the relative wage of nonproduction labor.

TABLE VI

ESTIMATED RISE IN WAGE INEQUALITY—ALTERNATIVE MEASURES OF
HIGH-TECHNOLOGY CAPITAL

| Dependent variable, Change in value-added prices plus TFP explained by: | Outsourcing (narrow) | Outsourcing (difference) | Computer share | High-tech share (difference) |
|---|---|---|---|---|
| (1) *Using BLS capital services (ex post rental prices) for computer share and high-tech share:* | | | | |
| Difference between non-prod. and prod. share | 0.108 (0.055) | 0.042 (0.030) | 0.252 (0.103) | −0.019 (0.017) |
| (2) *Using BLS capital services (ex ante rental prices) for computer share and high-tech share:* | | | | |
| Difference between non-prod. and prod. share | 0.136 (0.063) | 0.061 (0.036) | 0.143 (0.082) | −0.003 (n.a.) |
| (3) *Using Census investment flow for computer share and BLS capital services (ex post rental prices) for high-tech share:* | | | | |
| Difference between non-prod. and prod. share | 0.069 (0.051) | 0.018 (n.a.) | 0.591 (0.326) | 0.118 (0.064) |

Coefficients shown are the difference between the estimated impact of each dependent variable on the wages of nonproduction labor and the wages of production labor. The row number identifies the column number in Table IV from which coefficient estimates are taken to construct the dependent variable. Standard errors are in parentheses and are calculated as described in the text to account for cross-observation correlation in the disturbances that arises from the construction of the dependent variable. If this method fails to give a positive value for the estimated variance, then "n.a." is reported. Observations are by four-digit SIC industry. All regressions are weighted by the average industry share of total manufacturing shipments.

a. The High-tech share is not measured as a difference from the computer share (i.e., it includes all high-tech capital) when using the *Census* measure of the computer share.

High-technology capital in regression (4) of Table V has no impact at all.

To examine the robustness of these results, we checked alternative measures of high–technology capital, with results reported in the remainder of Table VI. Specification (2) uses the high-technology and computer shares constructed using ex ante rental prices. In this case the implied changes in the relative wage of nonproduction labor due to narrow outsourcing are slightly larger, as are the effects of broad outsourcing which are again imprecisely estimated. Conversely, the impact of computers is reduced and now insignificant as compared with using the ex post rental prices. This is similar to what we found in Table III, where the impact of computers is nearly twice as large when using ex post rather than ex ante rental prices. Specification (3) in Table VI uses the computer investment share from the *Census,* and in that case the impact of computers on the relative wage of nonproduction labor is the largest, and can account for most of the increase in the relative nonproduction wage. The largest impact of computers in the labor demand regressions reported in Table III was also obtained using the *Census* investment measure, qualitatively similar to the results in specification (3).

## V.B. Decomposition with Interactions

Our results above have relied on the assumed linear relation between value-added price changes plus productivity and the structural variables, as in (7). As an alternative we make use of the specification in (7′), which also includes interaction terms between the four structural variables and average log quantities for primary factors. This regression is reported in Table VII where we use the high-technology and computer shares constructed with the ex post rental prices.

We argued in Section III that positive coefficients on the interaction terms could be interpreted as *complementary* relationships between that structural variable and primary factor in affecting productivity. By this interpretation the positive and significant coefficients obtained for the interactions of outsourcing (narrow), computers and the remaining high-tech share with nonproduction labor seem sensible. That these variables also have negative interactions with capital, however, is harder to rationalize. Note that the primary factor quantities included in the interaction terms should be properly treated as endogenous variables. Since we do not have suitable instruments for these, we have not corrected for the endogeneity, which may be leading to bias in the coefficient estimates.

From this regression we decompose the dependent variable into those components due to each structural variable, and use these components as dependent variables in the second-stage regressions. The independent variables are the average cost-shares for primary factors. The results for the second-stage regressions are shown in Table VIII, where specification (1) uses the ex post rental prices in constructing the high-tech and computer shares, as in Table VII. We see that outsourcing measured within its own two-digit industry now has a larger effect on the relative wage of nonproduction labor, increasing it by 0.51 percent annually. This is offset, however, by outsourcing measured outside of its two-digit industry, which has the reverse effect. By summing these two coefficients, we find that overall

TABLE VII

DEPENDENT VARIABLE—CHANGE IN VALUE-ADDED PRICES PLUS EFFECTIVE TFP,
1979–1990

| Independent variables: | | | |
|---|---|---|---|
| | | *Nonproduction labor interacted with:* | |
| Outsourcing (narrow) | 0.666 | Outsourcing (narrow) | 0.116 |
| | (0.131) | | (0.033) |
| Outsourcing (difference) | −0.248 | Outsourcing (difference) | −0.092 |
| | (0.229) | | (0.041) |
| Computer share | 0.282 | Computer share | 0.080 |
| | (0.233) | | (0.038) |
| High-tech share (difference) | 1.168 | High-tech share (difference) | −0.023 |
| | (0.307) | | (0.050) |
| *Production labor interacted with:* | | *Capital interacted with:* | |
| Outsourcing (narrow) | −0.002 | Outsourcing (narrow) | −0.113 |
| | (0.042) | | (0.031) |
| Outsourcing (difference) | 0.156 | Outsourcing (difference) | −0.014 |
| | (0.057) | | (0.035) |
| Computer share | 0.026 | Computer share | −0.054 |
| | (0.047) | | (0.041) |
| High-tech share (difference) | 0.302 | High-tech share (difference) | −0.291 |
| | (0.094) | | (0.084) |
| Constant | 4.259 | N | 447 |
| | (0.027) | $R^2$ | 0.115 |

The computer share and the high-tech share are measured using BLS capital services (ex post rental prices). All estimation is over four-digit SIC industries, and the regression is weighted by the average industry share of manufacturing shipments. Standard errors (in parentheses) are robust to heteroskedasticity and correlation in the errors within two-digit industry groups. The dependent variable is the log change in value-added prices plus effective TFP (primal total factor productivity minus the change in wage differentials). The outsourcing variables and the computer and high-technology shares are all measured as annual average changes; factor levels are measured as average log quantities for 1979 and 1990.

outsourcing increases the relative wage of nonproduction labor by 0.29 percent annually, or about 40 percent of its actual increase.

Turning to computers in specification (1), these expenditures lead to an increase in the relative nonproduction wage of 0.56, which is equivalent to 75 percent of the increase. In the other specifications reported in Table VIII, the use of computer expenditures measured with ex ante rental prices in (2) leads to a smaller role of computers and a much larger role for outsourcing. Conversely, the use of the *Census* computer investment share in (3) enables computers to explain all the observed increase in the relative nonproduction wage, whereas outsourcing has a smaller effect, with broad outsourcing more than offsetting the impact of the narrow measure. Again, these differences from our benchmark

TABLE VIII
ESTIMATED RISE IN WAGE INEQUALITY–ALTERNATIVE MEASURES OF
HIGH-TECHNOLOGY CAPITAL

| Dependent variable, Change in value-added prices plus TFP explained by: | Outsourcing (narrow) | Outsourcing (difference) | Computer share | High-tech share (difference) |
|---|---|---|---|---|
| *(1) Using BLS capital services (ex post rental prices) for computer share and high-tech share:* | | | | |
| Difference between non-prod. and prod. share | 0.507 (0.137) | −0.220 (0.089) | 0.557 (0.161) | −0.014 (0.080) |
| *(2) Using BLS capital services (ex ante rental prices) for computer share and high-tech share:* | | | | |
| Difference between non-prod. and prod. share | 0.578 (0.130) | −0.018 (0.055) | 0.155 (0.083) | 0.012 (0.116) |
| *(3) Using Census investment flow for computer share and BLS capital services (ex post rental prices) for high-tech share:* | | | | |
| Difference between non-prod. and prod. share | 0.253 (0.169) | −0.263 (0.106) | 0.703 (0.288) | 0.169 (0.248) |

Coefficients shown are the difference between the estimated impact of each dependent variable on the wages of nonproduction labor and the wages of production labor. The dependent variables for the regression results reported in row (1) are constructed using coefficient estimates from Table VII. Dependent variables for the regression results reported in rows (2) and (3) are constructed using coefficient estimates from regressions similar to that in Table VII, in which the indicated measures of high-technology capital are used as independent variables. Standard errors are in parentheses and are calculated as described in the text to account for cross-observation correlation in the disturbances that arises from the construction of the dependent variable. Observations are by four-digit SIC industry. All regressions are weighted by the average industry share of total manufacturing shipments.

a. The high-tech share is not measured as a difference from the computer share (i.e., it includes all high-tech capital) when using the *Census* measure of the computer share.

specification in (1) are qualitatively similar to what we found from the labor demand regression in Table III.

## VI. CONCLUSIONS

Our goal in this paper has been to estimate the relative influence of trade versus technology on wages, under a "large-country" assumption. To achieve this, we have reinterpreted the conventional price regression as an identity, and then introduced structural variables that have an effect on industry productivity and prices. The structural variables were first introduced in a simple linear specification, and then including interaction terms with factor quantities. The reinterpretation of the price regression is the methodological contribution of the paper.

Our empirical results support the idea that both foreign outsourcing and expenditures on computers have played a role in the increase of the relative wage for nonproduction workers, with the latter variable having an impact that is twice as large as the former in the specifications using ex post rental prices to measure the computer share. By way of contrast, using ex ante rental prices to measure the computer share leads to a smaller impact of computers on the nonproduction wage, and a larger role for outsourcing. Using the *Census* investment share for computers leads to the largest impact for computers and a minimal role for outsourcing. The sensitivity of the results to the exact measure of the computer share is an empirical contribution of the paper, which carries over to other techniques, such as estimating the effects of trade and technology on labor demand.

DEPARTMENT OF ECONOMICS, UNIVERSITY OF CALIFORNIA, DAVIS;
AND NATIONAL BUREAU OF ECONOMIC RESEARCH
DEPARTMENT OF ECONOMICS AND SCHOOL OF BUSINESS ADMINISTRATION, UNIVERSITY
OF MICHIGAN; AND NATIONAL BUREAU OF ECONOMIC RESEARCH

## REFERENCES

Autor, David, Lawrence F. Katz, and Alan B. Krueger, "Computing Inequality: Have Computers Changed the Labor Market?" *Quarterly Journal of Economics,* CXIII (1998), 1169–1214.
Baldwin, Robert E., and Glen G. Cain, "Shifts in U. S. Relative Wages: The Role of Trade, Technology and Factor Endowments," NBER Working Paper No. 5934, 1997.
Baldwin, Robert E. and R. S. Hilton, "A Technique for Indicating Comparative Costs and Predicting Changes in Trade Ratios," *Review of Economics and Statistics,* LXVI (1984), 105–110.
Bartelsman, Eric J., and Wayne Gray, "The NBER Manufacturing Productivity Database," NBER Technical Working Paper No. 205, 1996.
Berman, Eli, John Bound, and Zvi Griliches, "Changes in the Demand for Skilled Labor within U. S. Manufacturing: Evidence from the Annual Survey of Manufactures," *Quarterly Journal of Economics,* CIX (1994), 367–398.
Berman, Eli, John Bound, and Stephen Machin, "Implications of Skill-Biased Technological Change: International Evidence," NBER Working Paper No. 6166, 1997.
Berndt, Ernst R., Catherine J. Morrison, and Larry S. Rosenblum, "High-Tech Capital Formation and Labor Composition in U. S. Manufacturing Industries: An Exploratory Analysis," NBER Working Paper No. 4010, 1992.
Berndt, Ernst R., and Catherine J. Morrison, "High-Tech Capital Formation and Labor Composition in U. S. Manufacturing Industries: An Exploratory Analysis," *Journal of Econometrics,* LXV (1995), 9–43.
Bound, John, and George Johnson, "Changes in the Structure of Wages in the 1980s: An Evaluation of Alternative Explanations," *American Economic Review,* LXXXII (1992), 371–392.
Caves, D. W., Laurits R. Christensen, and W. Erwin Diewert, "The Economic Theory of Index Numbers and the Measurement of Input, Output and Productivity," *Econometrica,* L (1982a), 1393–1414.
Caves, D. W., Laurits R. Christensen, and W. Erwin Diewert, "Multilateral Comparisons of Output, Input, and Productivity Using Superlative Index Numbers," *Economic Journal,* XCII (1982b), 73–86.

Domowitz, Ian, R. Glenn Hubbard, and Bruce C. Petersen, "Market Structure and Cyclical Fluctuations in U. S. Manufacturing." *Review of Economics and Statistics,* LXIX (1988), 55–66.

Doms, Mark, Timothy Dunne, and Kenneth R. Troske, "Workers, Wages, and Technology," *Quarterly Journal of Economics,* CXII (1997), 253–290.

Feenstra, Robert C., "U. S. Imports, 1972–1994: Data and Concordances," NBER Working Paper No. 5515, 1996.

——, "U. S. Exports, 1972–1994, with State Exports and Other U. S. Data," NBER Working Paper No. 5990, 1997.

Feenstra, Robert C., and Gordon H. Hanson, "Foreign Investment, Outsourcing and Relative Wages," in R. C. Feenstra, G. M. Grossman, and D. A. Irwin, eds., *Political Economy of Trade Policy: Essays in Honor of Jagdish Bhagwati* (Cambridge: MIT Press, 1996a), pp. 89–127.

Feenstra, Robert C., and Gordon H. Hanson, "Globalization, Outsourcing, and Wage Inequality," *American Economic Review,* LXXXVI (1996b), 240–245.

Feenstra, Robert C., and Gordon H. Hanson, "Foreign Direct Investment and Relative Wages: Evidence from Mexico's Maquiladoras," *Journal of International Economics,* XLII (1997), 371–394.

Gibbons, Robert, and Lawrence Katz, "Does Unmeasured Ability Explain Inter-Industry Wage Differentials?" *Review of Economic Studies,* LIX (1992), 515–535.

Hall, Robert E., "The Relation between Price and Marginal Cost in U. S. Industry," *Journal of Political Economy,* XCVI (1988), 921–947.

Hall, Robert E., and Dale W. Jorgenson, "Tax Policy and Investment Behavior," *American Economic Review,* LVII (1967), 391–414.

Harper, Michael J., Ernst R. Berndt, and David O. Wood, "Rates of Return and Capital Aggregation Using Alternative Rental Prices," in Dale W. Jorgenson and Ralph Landau, eds., *Technology and Capital Formation* (Cambridge: MIT Press, 1989), pp. 331–372.

Haskel, Jonathan, and Matthew Slaughter, "Does the Sector Bias of Technical Change Explain Changing Wage Inequality?" NBER Working Paper No. 6565, 1998.

Kahn, James, and Jong-Soo Lim, "Skilled-Labor Augmenting Technical Progress in U. S. Manufacturing," mimeo, New York Federal Reserve Bank, 1998.

Katz, Lawrence F., and David Autor, "Changes in the Wage Structure and Earnings Inequality," in David Card and Orley Ashenfelter, eds., *Handbook of Labor Economics* (Amsterdam: North-Holland, 1999), forthcoming.

Katz, Lawrence F., and Kevin M. Murphy, "Changes in Relative Wages, 1963–1987: Supply and Demand Factors," *Quarterly Journal of Economics,* CVII (1992), 35–78.

Krueger, Alan B., "Labor Market Shifts and the Price Puzzle Revisited," NBER Working Paper No. 5924, 1997.

Krueger, Alan B., and Lawrence Summers, "Efficiency Wages and the Inter-Industry Wage Structure," *Econometrica,* LVI (1988), 269–293.

Krugman, Paul, "Technology, Trade, and Factor Prices," *Journal of International Economics,* (2000), forthcoming.

Lawrence, Robert Z., and Matthew J. Slaughter, "International Trade and American Wages in the 1980s: Giant Sucking Sound or Small Hiccup?" *Brooking Papers on Economic Activity: Microeconomics,* 2 (1993), 161–211.

Leamer, Edward E., "Trade, Wages and Revolving Door Ideas," NBER Working Paper No. 4716, 1994.

——, "In Search of Stolper-Samuelson Linkages between International Trade and Lower Wages," in Susan M. Collins, ed., *Imports, Exports, and the American Worker* (Washington, DC: Brookings Institution Press, 1998), pp. 141–203.

——, "What's the Use of Factor Contents?" *Journal of International Economics,* L (2000), forthcoming.

Morrison, Catherine, "Assessing the Productivity of Information Technology Equipment in U. S. Manufacturing Industries," *Review of Economics and Statistics,* LXXIX (1997), 471–481.

Morrison, Catherine, and Donald Siegel, "The Impacts of Technology, Trade and Outsourcing on Employment and Labor Composition," mimeo, 1996.

Moulton, Brent R., "Random Group Effects and the Precision of Regression Estimates," *Journal of Econometrics,* XXXII (1986), 385–397.

Murphy, Kevin M., and Robert H. Topel, "Efficiency Wages Reconsidered: Theory and Evidence," in Yoram Weiss and G. Fishelson, eds., *Advances in the Theory and Measurement of Unemployment* (London: Macmillan, 1990), pp. 204–242.
Newey, Whitney, "Generalized Method of Moments Specification Testing," *Journal of Econometrics,* XXIX (1985), 229–256.
Sachs, Jeffrey D., and Howard J. Shatz, "Trade and Jobs in U. S. Manufacturing," *Brookings Papers on Economic Activity,* 1 (1994), 1–84.
Slaughter, Matthew, "What Are the Results of Product Price Studies and What Can We Learn from Their Differences?" NBER Working Paper No. 6591, 1998.
Xu, Bin, "Factor Bias, Sector Bias, and the Effects of Technical Progress on Relative Wages," University of Florida, mimeo, 1998.

# [21]

# Trade, Multinationals and Labor

*Robert Z. Lawrence*

## Abstract

This paper summarizes and extends previous research on the relationship between low-wage international competition and wage perfonnance in the Developed Countries in the 1980s. The first section argues that poor average US wage performance reflects slow domestic productivity growth rather than international competition. The second section presents evidence which rejects the view that Stolper–Samuelson effects are important in the US, Germany and Japan. In all three countries, neither the wholesale nor the import prices of unskilled labor-intensive products have experienced relative declines. At the same time, despite the rise in relative skilled worker wages, in the US, over the 1980s, the ratio of non-production to production workers grew faster than in the 1960s and 1970s. This suggests that technological change in US manufacturing was particularly biased in favor of white collar workers.

The third section explores the employment and wage behavior in US multinational parents and their foreign-owned manufacturing affiliates between 1977 and 1989. Overall the data point to the dominant impact of a commonly shared technological change rather than the impact of trade and increased international sourcing. Developments at home and abroad were remarkably similar. Employment fell, both in US parents and in affiliates in developed countries and grew only modestly in developing countries. In foreign affiliates in both developed and developing countries, the relative compensation of non-production workers increased and the ratio of production to non-production workers fell. While US parent sourcing from overseas affiliates grew rapidly, the increase accounted for only a small share of total sales. The final section discusses the issue of international labor standards.

## Trade, Multinationals and Labor

The theory of international trade suggests that free trade will raise national income. It does not, however, suggest that the incomes of *all* factors of production will rise. Indeed, Stolper and Samuelson (1941) showed that the removal of import barriers could lower the income of the factor of production used relatively intensively in the production of imported products. If OECD imports are produced using unskilled labor relatively intensively, therefore, freer trade could actually reduce the wages of unskilled workers.

In a second noteworthy application, trade theory also predicts that trade can lead to 'factor price equalization.' Under certain highly restrictive assumptions – in particular that competitive conditions prevail and that technological capabilities are uniform worldwide in both traded and non-traded goods – returns to factors would be equalized around the world.

In principle, these theoretical results were highly relevant to US circumstances during the golden era of the postwar period (1950–73). Over this period, the US economy reduced its trade barriers and expanded its trade with 'low-wage' nations in Europe, Japan and the developing world.[1] Nonetheless, the theory did not excite much attention among US policymakers because real wages in the United States rose steadily and wage differentials between skilled and unskilled workers actually narrowed. Indeed, over the 1970s, although the US economy became considerably more open – trade doubled as a share of gross national product (GNP) – the premium earned by educated workers actually declined.

In the 1980s, however, the US experience was different. Real wages stagnated and relative wages became more dispersed. In 1973, real hourly earnings of non-supervisory workers measured in 1982 dollars by the Consumer Price Index (CPI) were $8.55. By 1992 they had actually *declined* to $7.43 – a level that had been achieved in the late 1960s. Had earnings increased at their earlier pace, they would have risen by 40 per cent to over $12. Or consider real hourly compensation, a more comprehensive measure of the payments to labor because it includes fringe benefits as well as earnings. Between 1973 and 1991, real hourly compensation rose by only 5 per cent. However if one measures labor's income growth, it clearly has slumped since 1973.

A second ominous development in the American economy has accompanied this slump: a dramatic increase in the inequality of earnings based on education, experience and occupation. Bound and Johnson (1992) found that between 1979 and 1988 the ratio of the average wage of a college graduate to the average wage of a high school graduate rose by 15 per cent. Davis (1992) found that between 1979 and 1987 the ratio of weekly earnings of males in their forties to weekly earnings of males in their twenties rose by 25 per cent. The Employment Cost Index indicates that between December 1979 and December 1992 the growth of compensation and earnings of white collar occupations exceeded those of blue collar occupations by 7.9 and 10.9 per cent respectively. However one distinguishes the skilled from the unskilled, the sharp rise in wage inequality between the two in the 1980s is clear.

In the 1980s, European wage performance differed from that in the United States in one crucial respect – typically real wages grew by 1 to 2 per cent annually. In some countries however, increased inequality is also evident. According to the OECD *Employment Outlook* (OECD, 1993), in the UK there was a substantial increase in the ratio of earnings of the highest (90th) to lowest (10th) percentile.[2] Modest increases in this measure of dispersion also occurred in France, the Netherlands and Sweden, but in Italy and other Nordic countries no change was discernable while, in Germany, low-wage workers (those in the bottom decile) actually experienced relatively more rapid growth than those in the top. Data are also available for some of these countries on wage changes by level of schooling. The premium increased in the 1980s for all countries surveyed beside Japan (where it was unchanged) and the Netherlands (where it fell). Age–earnings profiles increased for all countries in the sample besides Sweden. I have also obtained data on the ratio of wages of manual to non-manual workers in several major European countries (EuroStat, 1992). These give a different picture for Germany, showing that between 1978 and 1988 the ratio of manual to non-manual wages fell by 8.1 per cent. They declined by 3 per cent in Italy but actually rose in Belgium and Denmark.

The OECD (1993) argues that the qualitative similarity in these changes suggests 'pervasive economic factors are at work.' An important issue in Europe, however, is the degree to which institutional and regulatory factors repressed wage adjustments and instead raised unemployment. The OECD notes that 'those countries which did not experience an increase in dispersion over the 1980s, Denmark, Finland, Germany, Italy and Norway, are countries where national institutions have a particularly strong influence on wage setting.'

What *has* distinguished European labor market performance has been high levels of unemployment, particularly of workers out of jobs for more than twelve months. In 1991 for example, such workers accounted for just 6.3 per cent of the unemployed in the United States, but in Germany, France, the United Kingdom and Italy the share was typically about 40 per cent. A second feature is that European employment growth has been virtually confined to the public sector.

Also striking in Europe has been the relative decline in the employment of manual workers in industry in general and manufacturing in particular. EuroStat (1992) data indicate that, between 1978 and 1988, the decline in the ratio of industrial employment of manual to non-manual workers in Germany (–16.1 per cent) and Ireland (–15.1 per cent) was similar to the decline in the ratio of production to non-production workers in US manufacturing (–18.5 per cent); while declines (in the ratio of manual to non-manual workers) were about twice as large in French (–26.8 per cent), Danish (–27.7 per cent) and Italian (–30.4 per cent) manufacturing. The data certainly suggest a trade-off between wage flexibility and employment opportunities.

In both Europe and the United States, alarms have been sounded about the role of trade in this poor labor market performance. In the United States, the debate over the North American Free Trade Agreement (NAFTA) crystallized concerns over wage performance that are best captured by Ross Perot's allusion to the 'giant sucking sound' of jobs as they move southward. One of the major concerns about NAFTA was the impetus it provided for what many in the United States see as a major phenomenon – that of 'runaway plants' – the relocation by multinationals to low-wage countries. In Europe, while the absorption of low-wage countries such as Spain, Portugal and Greece into the EC proceeded fairly smoothly during the growth phase in the late 1980s, the recessionary environment of the 1990s has sparked similar fears of 'delocalization,' that is, that firms are relocating to low-wage countries.

The concerns about international competition in the labor market have been voiced not simply in terms of wages but also with regard to the regulatory environment that governs employment. In Europe, an important aspect of creating the single market has been the 'social dimension' – the effort to ensure that minimum labor standards prevail throughout the European Union. In France, a furor was raised by the shift of the Hoover Corporation from France to Scotland, purportedly attracted by both lower wage costs and lower labor standards. In the European debate about freer trade with Eastern Europe and Asia, concerns have been raised not simply about low wages but about 'social dumping,' that is, the downward competitive pressures that are allegedly placed on labor standards as a result of trade. In the United States, concerns about workers' rights have increasingly been reflected in US international trade legislation. Indeed both France and the US have proposed that workers' rights occupy an important role in the post-Uruguay Round agenda.

From the standpoint of the developing economies, these concerns could not have appeared at a worse moment. Since the mid-1980s, these economies have almost universally shifted toward export-oriented, 'market-friendly' policies which are implicitly predicated on the assumption that global markets are available. Similarly, progress in the reconstruction of Eastern Europe and the economies of the former Soviet Union depends critically on their ability to gain access to the markets of the EC.

But is trade in general, and with developing countries in particular, really responsible for the poor labor market performance in developed economies? What role has been played by employment and sourcing shifts within multinationals, and what role should changes in labor standards play in addressing these concerns? These are three questions I will discuss in this paper.

The US experience is perhaps the most suitable for detailed analysis. US wages are generally more flexible than those in other countries, and as indicated in Figure 1, compared with the EC and Japan, the US share of apparent consumption of manufactured goods imported from developing countries is higher and has risen more rapidly over the 1980s. In addition, the United States remains the world's largest multinational investor. In the first section of this paper, therefore, I will consider the impact of trade on average US wage behavior. In the second section, I will concentrate on relative wage behavior in the United States although I will introduce evidence from Germany and Japan. I will argue that the role of trade has been surprisingly small. In the third section I will introduce evidence on wages and employment in

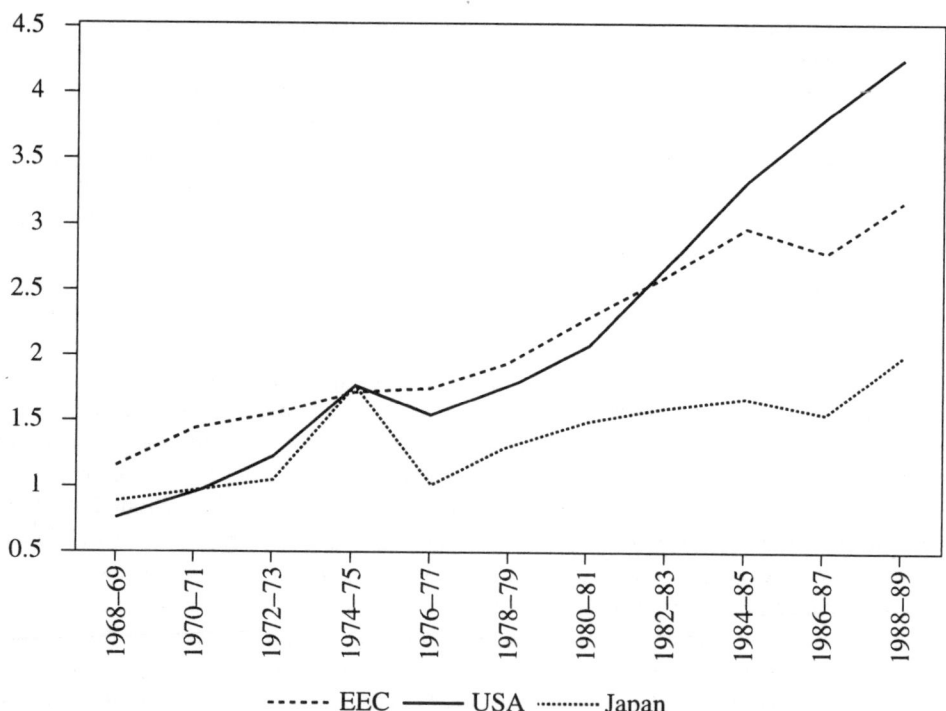

*Figure 1   Manufactured imports from LDCs (share in apparent consumption)*

US multinationals both at home and abroad. These data indicate remarkably similar changes taking place in US multinationals worldwide – a finding that is strongly suggestive that technology rather than trade is exercising a dominant influence. They also indicate that employment growth within US foreign affiliates abroad has been too small to be viewed as having displaced large numbers of jobs in the United States. The same is true of the growth in value added sourced from abroad. In the final section, I consider the issue of labor standards. At a multilateral level, some agreement on basic minimum labor standards could be helpful, both in allaying concerns about the denial of elementary human rights and in limiting the scope for opportunistic protectionist actions. Beyond these minimum standards, however, there are strong reasons for permitting national diversity.

## I  Average Wages

### Measuring Compensation

Before explaining average US wage behavior it is necessary to clarify how wages are measured. The most commonly cited statistic – real average hourly earnings of production workers – shows a *decline* of almost 11 per cent between 1979 and 1991. By contrast, a second commonly cited series – real hourly compensation in the business sector – shows an *increase* of 1.5 per cent over the same period. These series differ because (a) the average hourly earnings series samples only production or non-supervisory workers while the hourly compensation series includes all persons engaged in work (including the self employed); and (b) the hourly earnings series reflects only wages while the compensation measure includes employers' contributions for social insurance and private benefit plans (including retirement and medical care). Both differences are important, and the series have diverged because (a) the wages of production workers have risen more slowly than those of non-production workers; and (b) for all workers, fringe benefits have increased more rapidly than wages. The remainder of this section focuses on the aggregate compensation measure.

### International Factors

Several economists have ascribed the poor average growth in US wages over the 1980s to international factors. Thurow has argued that slow growth in US manufacturing employment due to the trade deficit in manufactured goods is to blame. Leamer (1991) claims that increased capital formation abroad is leading inevitably to 'wage equalization' in which American wage rates converge with those in other countries. According to Leamer, this convergence is not benign because it entails not simply a rise in foreign wage levels but also a decline in average American wage levels. Johnson and Stafford (1993) argue that the erosion of high returns from American technological leadership has been the principle source of the slow rise in American real wages since 1973. However, a careful reading of the data supports none of these views.

It is easy to reject the claim that poor average US wage performance reflects the loss of high-wage manufacturing jobs because of US trade performance. Between 1981 and 1991, the US trade balance in manufactured goods did decline significantly – from a surplus of $18 billion to a deficit of $47 billion. But this shift was not large enough to provide much of an explanation for average wages in the economy as a whole. In 1991, the trade deficit was equal to about 5 per cent of value added in manufacturing. Average hourly earnings in manufacturing were 8.2 per cent higher than those in the private sector generally (average weekly earnings were 29 per cent higher). Since manufacturing accounted for 17 per cent of total employment, shifting an additional (.05 × 17) 0.85 per cent of employment to manufacturing would have raised average hourly and weekly wages by 0.07 and 0.25 per cent respectively – an amount scarcely large enough to explain the poor wage performance of the 1980s.

*Assessing Compensation Performance*

Before turning to the other explanations based on trade it is useful to examine the behavior of US compensation more closely. As a first approximation, we expect changes in real compensation to match the change in output per worker. Since growth of output per worker in the US did slow down dramatically after 1973, it is reasonable to expect that real compensation would decline in parallel. However, the data suggest that real compensation failed to match even the slow improvement in average labor productivity growth.

As Figure 2 indicates, between 1973 and 1979, average real compensation (average hourly compensation deflated by the CPI for urban consumers) increased in line with output per hour in the US business sector. However, from 1979 to 1991, the two trends diverged markedly.

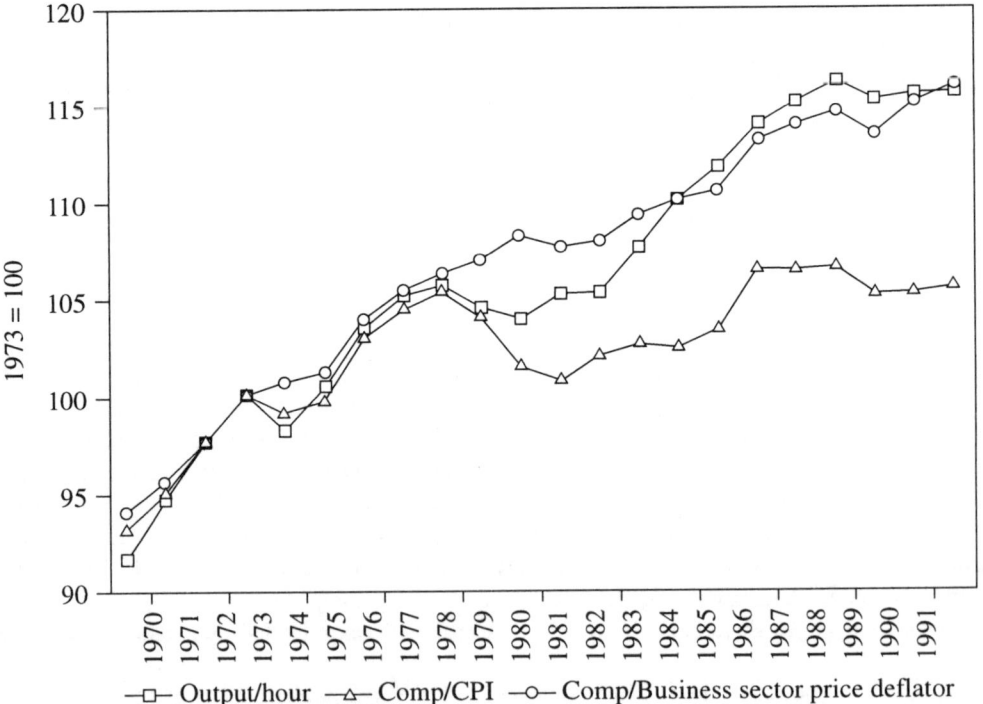

*Figure 2  Output per hour and real hourly compensation*

While output per worker grew by 10.5 per cent – already a very slow pace by historical standards – real hourly compensation grew by only 1.5 per cent.

This divergence could in principle be explained by a shift in incomes from wages to profits. However, in 1991, the share of total compensation in the value added by the business sector was 65.6 per cent – less than one percentage point lower than it was in 1979 (see Table 1). If we deflate nominal compensation by production prices rather than consumption prices, we see that workers in the 1980s were basically compensated for the growth in output per worker. If workers had chosen to consume the products they actually produced, they could have raised their real compensation by as much as the improvement in productivity growth. This finding is

*Table 1    Measures of productivity and compensation*

| Year | Earnings /CPI (1) | Comp /CPI (2) | Output /Hour (3) | Comp /POut (4) | Comp /POut-I (5) | Comp/ CPI-Sh (6) | FWTOT (7) | Comp Share (8) | GDP87/ Hours (9) |
|---|---|---|---|---|---|---|---|---|---|
| 1970 | 98.0 | 89.4 | 87.5 | 88.5 | 86.1 | 88.1 | 126.5 | 67.0 | 89.3 |
| 1971 | 100.4 | 91.2 | 90.4 | 89.7 | 86.9 | 89.8 | 124.2 | 65.7 | 92.5 |
| 1972 | 104.3 | 93.9 | 93.2 | 91.8 | 89.4 | 92.7 | 120.0 | 65.2 | 93.9 |
| 1973 | 104.5 | 96.1 | 95.6 | 94.0 | 91.6 | 94.4 | 116.9 | 65.1 | 95.4 |
| 1974 | 101.4 | 95.1 | 93.9 | 94.3 | 92.0 | 93.2 | 107.1 | 66.5 | 94.7 |
| 1975 | 99.1 | 95.8 | 96.0 | 94.3 | 92.9 | 94.1 | 106.9 | 65.0 | 97.9 |
| 1976 | 100.7 | 98.8 | 98.8 | 97.3 | 96.0 | 96.9 | 107.3 | 65.2 | 100.0 |
| 1977 | 102.1 | 100.3 | 100.5 | 98.7 | 98.0 | 98.4 | 103.8 | 65.0 | 100.7 |
| 1978 | 102.7 | 101.4 | 101.1 | 99.4 | 99.2 | 100.3 | 102.0 | 65.1 | 100.6 |
| 1979 | 100.0 | 100.0 | 100.0 | 100.0 | 100.0 | 100.0 | 100.0 | 66.2 | 100.0 |
| 1980 | 95.2 | 97.5 | 99.3 | 101.0 | 100.8 | 99.2 | 91.7 | 67.3 | 100.4 |
| 1981 | 93.9 | 96.8 | 100.5 | 100.4 | 101.0 | 98.9 | 93.9 | 66.1 | 101.5 |
| 1982 | 93.8 | 98.0 | 100.7 | 102.1 | 102.1 | 100.6 | 97.6 | 67.1 | 101.8 |
| 1983 | 94.9 | 98.5 | 102.9 | 102.4 | 101.1 | 100.5 | 101.5 | 65.9 | 103.9 |
| 1984 | 94.3 | 98.4 | 105.3 | 102.6 | 101.5 | 100.7 | 104.4 | 64.5 | 104.4 |
| 1985 | 93.8 | 99.3 | 106.8 | 103.7 | 101.9 | 102.2 | 105.7 | 64.3 | 105.4 |
| 1986 | 94.1 | 102.4 | 109.0 | 106.6 | 104.7 | 106.2 | 107.6 | 64.7 | 107.8 |
| 1987 | 93.2 | 102.3 | 110.1 | 107.5 | 105.4 | 106.4 | 102.5 | 64.6 | 107.8 |
| 1988 | 92.4 | 102.4 | 111.1 | 108.2 | 105.9 | 106.8 | 102.7 | 64.5 | 108.4 |
| 1989 | 91.8 | 101.0 | 110.2 | 107.1 | 104.5 | 105.3 | 102.0 | 64.3 | 108.4 |
| 1990 | 90.3 | 101.1 | 110.5 | 108.8 | 105.6 | 105.4 | 100.2 | 65.2 | 109.2 |
| 1991 | 89.4 | 101.4 | 110.5 | 109.5 | 105.1 | 105.8 | 101.5 | 65.6 | 110.4 |

*Notes*:
Earnings = Average hourly earnings
CPI = CPI for all urban consumers
Comp = Average hourly compensation
CPI-Sh = CPI minus shelter component
CompShare = share of compensation in
  business output value added

Output = Business sector output (excludes housing)
POut = Deflator for output
POut-I = Deflator for output minus investment
FWTOT = Ratio of fixed weight price index of exports of
  goods and services to price index of imports
Hours = Hours worked in business sector

inconsistent with Leamer's (1992) argument that international competition is bringing US wages down to foreign levels. *If Leamer was correct, we would expect to see real product wages growing more slowly than productivity.*[3]

The wage gap illustrated in Figure 2 is thus almost totally due to a discrepancy between the production and the consumption wage. When nominal compensation is deflated by a *production* price index (in this case the business sector GNP deflator) rather than by the *consumer* price index, this 'production wage' closely tracks the growth in output per worker from 1979 to 1991.

Apparently, the prices of the products that workers consume have risen more rapidly than those which they produce. Three major differences in the composition of the deflators for production and consumption compensation merit attention: first, investment goods. The consumer price index which is used to measure real earnings does not, of course, reflect the prices of investment goods. The prices of the most rapidly growing investment goods, computers, have declined precipitously. Simply subtracting gross domestic investment from business sector output provides a measure of consumption goods output. The implicit deflator from this series suggests that between 1979 and 1991, real compensation in terms of consumer goods increased by 5.1 per cent (versus 1.5 per cent using the CPI-U). Thus about half of the shortfall between product and consumption compensation can be explained by the relative price decline in investment goods.

A second major compositional difference between the CPI and the business sector output used in measuring productivity is housing. Output of owner-occupied housing is not included in the business sector output measure used by the Bureau of Labor Statistics (BLS) to estimate business sector productivity growth. However, the price of shelter is a major component of the consumer price index. Between 1979 and 1991, the index of shelter prices increased by 17 per cent more rapidly than the rest of the CPI. If we deflate hourly compensation by the CPI minus shelter, we obtain an estimated increase in real compensation between 1979 and 1991 of 5.8 per cent – which is similar to the estimate using the business deflator minus investment goods.

The third major difference between production and consumption prices involves the goods and services that enter international trade. If the production wage increases match domestic productivity growth as they appear to have done, the level of real compensation will depend on the impact of import prices on total consumer price inflation. This impact can be picked up by the terms of trade, the ratio of export to import prices. The broadest measure of the terms of trade – using the GDP deflators for exports and imports of goods and services shows an improvement of 5.2 per cent, while the fixed-weight price measures show an increase of 1.5 per cent. This finding is inconsistent with the view of Johnson and Stafford (1993) that an erosion of the rents from US technological leadership explains the slow growth in US wages over this period. If this were the case, the international buying power of US workers (as captured by the ratio of import to domestic wages) would have risen more slowly than their ability to produce domestically produced goods.

In sum, the evidence indicates that had American workers chosen to consume the products they produced, their real compensation would have increased by about 10 per cent over the 1980s – about as much as output per worker in the business sector. However, real wage growth lagged behind productivity growth for two main reasons: (a) much of the productivity growth occurred in industries producing capital goods such as computers, which workers do not generally buy, and (b) because of increases in the relative price of housing (which workers consume but do not produce). International trade played no role in this poor average wage growth. Over the 1980s, the prices of US exports actually rose more rapidly than the prices of the goods the United States imports.

It is noteworthy that the slowdown in US productivity growth has been centered in the services sectors, most of which are *not* exposed to international competition. Productivity growth did slump throughout the economy between 1973 and 1979, but, since 1979, both multifactor and labor productivity in manufacturing have returned to their post-war pace. By contrast, productivity in the rest of the business sector has stagnated. Indeed, between 1979 and 1988, according to the Bureau of Labor Statistics, almost *all* productivity improvements, estimated on a multifactor productivity basis, took place in manufacturing. Similarly there was a substantial divergence between the growth of GDP per worker in the economy as a whole and in manufacturing. If demand for manufactured goods has an elasticity of less than one, faster relative productivity in manufacturing will lead to a decline in manufacturing employment.

## II  Trade and Wage Inequality

Other analysts have suggested that trade (or globalization) helps explain the growing *inequality* in US wages. Reich (1991) has argued that global competition has bifurcated American workers – and thereby American society – into two groups: high-earning 'symbolic analysts' whose talents are rewarded by globalization and the mass of ordinary production workers whose earnings are depressed by it. And referring to growing wage disparity, Murphy and Welch (1991) found a correspondence between the patterns of wage growth and durable goods performance and conclude that 'the evolving pattern of international trade is perhaps a primary cause of recent wage changes.'

### Factor Composition and Quantity of Trade

Studies which have tried to quantify the relationships more precisely, however, have generally concluded that the impact of trade is small. In particular, Borjas et al. (1992: 237) estimate the quantities of educated and uneducated labor embodied in US manufactured goods exports and imports. They concluded that trade flows explained at most 15 per cent (that is, 1.9 percentage points) of the 12.4 per cent increase between 1980 and 1988 in the earnings differential between college-educated workers and their high school-educated counterparts. Moreover, given the decline in the manufactured goods trade deficit from $106 billion in 1988 to $47 billion in 1991, their method would attribute to trade less than one percentage point of the disparity in relative wage growth by that time (in 1993 the deficit had increased again, to $91.5 billion).

When one considers with whom America trades, it is not surprising that estimates of the factor supplies embodied in US manufacturing trade indicate relatively small effects on wages. In 1990, for example, 70 per cent of America's manufacturing imports came from OECD countries – countries with endowments and wage levels very similar to America's.[4] US imports from developing countries did increase rapidly over the decade, but again what needs to be born in mind is the magnitude. In 1990, for example, these imports amounted to $115.8 billion or 2.1 per cent of US GNP versus 1.2 per cent in 1981.[5] It is hard to see how a change of this magnitude – less than one per cent of GNP – could have a large impact on the overall labor market.[6] In a recent study, for example, Sachs and Shatz (1994) estimate that trade with developing countries reduced US manufacturing employment by 5.7 per cent between 1978 and 1990 – a number equal to about one per cent of employment overall.

Wood (1991, 1994) has challenged this methodology on the grounds that the use of the labor intensity measures using developed country production data assumes that imports and domestic products are similar products. Wood argues, on the contrary, that goods imported from developing countries are not close substitutes for those produced in developed countries and are, therefore, far more labor intensive. Thus, he objects to the use of input coefficients from developed countries to estimate the job content of imports. Wood argues instead that the input coefficients of developing countries (with some adjustments) should be used. Moreover, he argues that this problem exists not only for direct manufacturing inputs but also for indirect inputs from other sectors. In addition, he maintains it holds for both goods and services imports. Taking all these factors into account leads him to conclude that the employment and, thus, wage impact is larger than conventional estimates suggest, although he still finds that the effect of the trade of the North with the South is 'much smaller than is popularly supposed.'

But take an extreme version of Wood's hypothesis. Suppose *all* the growth in US imports over the 1980s reflects imports of products that were *not* produced in the United States in 1980 at all. Had imports from developing countries not increased, therefore, Americans would have spent their money on *other* domestic (and imported) products. This counterfactual of the Wood hypothesis suggests that imports may have displaced products which were not unusually labor intensive.

If Wood is correct, as Sachs and Shatz (1994) note, industries in which trade with developing countries have a growing share should record unusually rapid increases in skill intensity as the more unskilled-labor intensive activities move offshore. In fact, Sachs and Shatz do not find unusually large increases in the skill intensity of low-skill sectors.[7]

*Prices*

In any case, there is a problem in using ex post trade flows to make these calculations. Such flows do not necessarily capture the effect of price pressures that operate through trade.[8] If international competition forced US workers to lower their wages, for example, domestic firms might be able to prevent imports from rising. By examining only trade flows, as these calculations do, we would conclude that trade had no impact on wages. In principle, therefore, even if trade flows are small, changes in traded goods prices could have large effects on the prices (and thus factor returns) of domestically produced substitutes. As Bhagwati (1991) has emphasized, relative price changes are the critical intervening variable in the chain of causation from trade to factor prices.

Some studies have estimated the impact of changes in traded goods prices on wages in particular industries. Ravenga (1992) finds statistically significant effects although she estimates the impact on wages to be much smaller than the impact on employment. While this analysis is informative, it is really testing for the effect of trade on returns to industry-specific human capital rather than the general attributes such as education which are of interest here. To do this it is necessary to explore general equilibrium effects.

If trade lowered the relative wages of unskilled workers, according to the Stolper–Samuelson theorem, we would expect to see a decline in the relative price of goods which are produced using unskilled labor relatively intensively. In Lawrence and Slaughter (1993), however, we find that over the 1980s the relative import and export prices of non-skilled labor-intensive goods actually increased slightly. In addition, Lawrence and Slaughter also noted that if trade was the operative factor we would expect to see a contraction in labor-intensive industries, but we would also expect to see that the remaining sectors taking advantage of this labor by using unskilled labor relatively more intensively. In fact, we note that throughout US manufacturing there has been a pervasive upward shift in the ratio of skilled to non-skilled labor. Our conclusion, therefore, is that the simple Stolper–Samuelson process due to trade does not provide an adequate account of the growing wage inequality. Instead, we interpret the evidence as consistent with a bias in manufacturing technology towards the more intensive use of skilled labor. Our conclusion is supported by Berman et al. (1992) and Bound and Johnson (1992) who find that trade played basically no role in America's wage changes in the 1980s and ascribe these changes to technological change and changes in unmeasured labor quality. I should stress, however, that our paper was designed to examine the role of trade and not, directly, to provide evidence on technological change. Moreover since we only examined data for the manufacturing sector, we could not resolve the role played by technology or other factors in economy-wide wage behavior. In addition, I should stress that we did not argue that evidence of an increase in the ratio of skilled to non-skilled workers by itself would constitute sufficient basis to reject the claim that Stolper–Samuelson effects were reducing the wages of unskilled workers. For this purpose the price evidence is crucial.

As might have been anticipated, given its surprising conclusions, our work has been attacked by several authors. First, Leamer has argued that our use of production and non-production workers as proxies for skill levels is misleading because non-production workers include low-skill occupations such as secretaries while production workers could be supervisors with considerable skill. However, as Sachs and Shatz (1994) and Bound et al. (1992) show quite convincingly, this measure actually does fairly well in tracking other measures of skill. Moreover, the evidence indicates that in US manufacturing the rapid increase in non-production workers was actually concentrated in the more highly educated professional and managerial categories. Between 1983 and 1990, for example, manufacturing employment of managers and administrators increased by 25.9 per cent, professionals by 12.9 per cent, while employment of non-sales white-collar workers actually declined by 3.0 per cent.

Cepii (1994) argues that our finding of a rapid increase in the ratio of skilled to unskilled workers simply reflects the fact that the relative supply of skilled workers increased rapidly in the 1980s. But, as reported in Table 2, the shift we find occurred within most industries and not only in the aggregate. As we know from the Rybcynski Theorem, *given product prices* changes in relative factor supplies affect relative product supplies rather than relative factor use. Thus given product prices an increase in the supply of skilled workers raises the supply of skill-intensive goods but does not change the ratios of skilled and unskilled workers employed in each industry. Moreover, if this relative supply was important in changing relative product prices it should have been associated with a *decline* in the relative wages of skilled workers – exactly the opposite of what happened. The fact that manufacturers are using more skilled labor despite its relatively higher price strongly supports the hypothesis that technological change in manufacturing played a role in the wage change.

Sachs and Shatz (1994) raise questions about our use of the price data. In particular, they argue that computer prices should not be included in the sample. When they drop computers,

*Table 2*    *Changes in ratio of production to non-production workers*

| | Production worker employment to non-production worker employment | | | | |
| | Weighted average ratios | | | Decomposition of Change (a) | |
| Year | Value | Change | Change (%) | Between industries | Within industries (%) |
|------|-------|--------|------------|--------------------|------------------------|
| 1959 | 3.23 | – | – | – | – |
| 1969 | 3.00 | (0.22) | −6.91 | 25.1 | 74.9 |
| 1979 | 2.79 | (0.22) | −7.23 | −5.9 | 105.9 |
| 1989 | 2.27 | (0.51) | −18.47 | 30.3 | 69.7 |
| Change over entire period | – | (0.95) | −29.6 | −50.6 | 150.6 |

*Note*:   (a) Based on the following standard decomposing formula: Total Change (industry $x$) = change in employment share × mean prod:nonprod. ratio in period) + (change in prod:nonprod. ratio × mean employment share for period).

*Source*: NBER Databank.

they obtain a negative but statistically insignificant relationship between import price changes and skill intensity, and they note that the size of the effect is small. Similarly, if computer price changes are omitted, instead of rising slightly, the ratio of manufacturing producer prices weighted by production worker employment to prices weighted by non-production workers falls slightly. While we would agree that computer prices are difficult to measure, we are not convinced that this sector should be given no weight at all in the explanation.

Sachs and Shatz also claim on the basis of their regressions omitting the computer industry that there was a negative relationship between total factor productivity growth and skill intensity. They conclude 'TFP growth was less on average in high-skilled than low-skilled industries' and argue, therefore, that technological change was therefore causing wage differentials to narrow rather than widen. Again, the impact of the computer industry is important. In Lawrence and Slaughter (1993), we found that, including computers, the gap between weighted averages of high-skilled and low-skilled productivity growth was positive and thus concluded the impact was the opposite.

## Additional Evidence

I have now undertaken similar investigations of the price behavior of both German and Japanese imports and producer prices. While not as desegregated as the US, these data tell the same story. As shown in Table 3 when price changes over the decade of the 1980s are regressed against the ratio of unskilled to skilled employment they indicate a *positive* rather than negative relationship (that is statistically significant in the case of wholesale prices but not import prices). Similarly, as shown in Table 4, for both countries when industry wholesale and import prices are weighted by production worker shares they show larger increases (or smaller declines) than when weighted by non-production workers. Questions might be raised since these data reflect industrial classification systems which include refined petroleum as a manufactured

*Table 3    Regressions of price changes on ratios of production to non-production workers in
Japan and Germany*

(a)  Wholesale prices (1980–90)

| Regression | Dep. Variable | Constant | JP/NP | GM/NM | R-square | F-stat | No. Obs. |
|---|---|---|---|---|---|---|---|
| 1 | %WP | −14.407<br>(−1.982) | 5.919<br>(1.851) | | 0.1599 | 3.43 | 20 |
| 2 | %WP | −11.197<br>(−1.109) | | 11.896<br>(2.871) | 0.3547 | 8.24 | 17 |

(b)  Import prices (1980–90)

| Regression | Dep. Variable | Constant | JP/NP | GM/NM | R-square | F-stat | No. Obs. |
|---|---|---|---|---|---|---|---|
| 1 | %MP | −29.906<br>(−2.248) | 6.653<br>(1.137) | | 0.067 | 1.29 | 20 |
| 2 | %MP | 6.399<br>(0.789) | | 3.12<br>(1.012) | 0.045 | 1.02 | 24 |

*Notes*:
Industry data generally corresponds to SITC 2-digit classification.
%WP = Per cent change in wholesale prices.
%MP = Per cent change in import prices.
JP/NP = Japanese ratio of production to non-production workers.
GM/NM = German ratio of manual to non-manual workers.

*Sources*:
Eurostat Labour Costs 1988: Principal results. v1. CECA-CEE-CEEA, Luxembourg, 1992.
Ministry of Labour (Japan). December 1989 Survey.
Statistisches Bundesamt Wiesbaden. Reihe 8: Preise und Preisindizes fuer die Ein- und Ausfuhr. 1980, 1985, 1990.
Statistisches Bundesamt Wiesbaden. Reihe 6: Index der Grosshandelsverkaufpreise. 1980, 1985, 1990.
Research and Statistics Department, Bank of Japan. Price Indexes Annual. 1980, 1985, 1990.

product. In addition there are the usual issues relating to the inclusion of computers. However, as reported in Table 4 for the weighted averages, dropping these observations does not affect the results.

In the case of Germany, I was also able to obtain unit value data which could be matched with industry data at a more desegregated level. Again the data indicate no decline in the relative price of manual-worker-intensive products.

Mishel and Bernstein (1994) question whether the shift towards the relatively more intensive use of skilled labor in the 1980s is any greater than it was in earlier decades. In Lawrence and Slaughter (1993) we provided a chart which shows an acceleration in the 1980s. I can report here additional evidence that supports our view. The shift towards the more intensive use of non-production in the 1980s was both larger and more pervasive than in the 1970s and 1960s

*Table 4     Employment-weighted percentage changes in wholesale and import prices for Japan and Germany (1980–1990)*

| | Percentage Change | |
|---|---|---|
| | Wholesale prices | Import prices |
| *Japan* | | |
| All manufacturing industries | | |
| Non-production weights | −5.60 | −18.23 |
| Production weights | −3.90 | −17.29 |
| Difference (Prod − NonProd) | 1.70 | 0.94 |
| w/o office machines | | |
| Non-production weights | −7.09 | −18.69 |
| Production weights | −4.72 | −17.50 |
| Difference | 2.37 | 1.19 |
| w/o petroleum products | | |
| Non-production weights | −5.49 | −18.02 |
| Production weights | −3.84 | −17.19 |
| Difference | 1.65 | 0.83 |
| w/o office mach./petroleum prod. | | |
| Non-production weights | −6.98 | −18.45 |
| Production weights | −4.66 | −17.39 |
| Difference | 2.32 | 1.06 |
| *Germany* | | |
| All manufacturing industries | | |
| Non-manual weights | 23.98 | 15.24 |
| Manual weights | 26.03 | 17.07 |
| Difference (Man − NonMan) | 2.05 | 1.83 |
| w/o office machines | | |
| Non-manual weights | 24.79 | 15.38 |
| Manual weights | 26.21 | 17.11 |
| Difference | 1.42 | 1.73 |
| w/o petroleum products | | |
| Non-manual weights | 24.15 | 15.55 |
| Manual weights | 26.11 | 17.20 |
| Difference | 1.96 | 1.65 |
| w/o office mach/petroleum prod. | | |
| Non-manual weights | 24.97 | 15.70 |
| Manual weights | 26.28 | 17.24 |
| Difference | 1.31 | 1.54 |

*Notes*:
Non-production and non-manual weights weigh each industry's price change by that industry's share of total manufacturing employment of non-production and non-manual labor. Production and manual weights weigh each industry's price change by that industry's share of total manufacturing employment of production and manual labor. Industry data generally correspond to SITC 2-digit classification.

(see Table 2).[9] The ratio of production to non-production workers decreased in 87 per cent of the three digit SIC codes in the 1980s compared with 78 per cent in the 1970s and 62 per cent in the 1960s. In addition the average decrease was 18.47 per cent in the 1980s compared with 6.9 and 7.23 per cent in the 1960s and 1970s respectively. Of course an increase on the manufacturing average could reflect either a change in the mix of industries or in the ratio within industries. As Table 2 indicates both factors were at work. However, 69.7 per cent of the shift occurred within industries. Since this shift occurred despite the fact that relative wages of non-production workers actually increased, it appears to be strongly suggestive of a skilled labor using technological shift that was concentrated in the skill-intensive sector of manufacturing.

Mishel and Bernstein (1994) also raise the question of whether this change in skill intensity should be described as technological change. In particular they find an absence of evidence indicating an association with investment and other hard measures of technical change such as R&D, capital accumulation and computerization and stress the importance of distinguishing developments in manufacturing from those in the rest of the economy.

I believe both the points they make are important. First, if this evidence is correct, those arguing for a major role for technology must apply a broader interpretation that includes new labor–management relations and work organization. Second, I believe that the divergent productivity performance between the manufacturing and services sectors in the United States is a major structural feature of the US economy in the 1980s. Historically, relative productivity growth was faster in goods than in services. But this difference has widened in the 1980s when almost all the improvements in total factor productivity in the business sector were confined to manufacturing. If the demand for manufacturing goods is inelastic, relatively rapid increases in manufacturing productivity will reduce the demand for workers in manufactured goods. With no bias in this change, since production workers are relatively intensively employed in manufacturing, this will reduce the demand for production workers. In combination with a shift within manufacturing towards production worker saving technical change concentrated in non-production worker sectors, the impact on relative wages could be considerable.

There remains the issue of whether technological change itself has been affected by trade. It is noteworthy that, while US productivity growth in manufacturing recovered in the 1980s, it did not exceed the pace it achieved prior to 1973. This could reflect a spur from international competition offsetting a more general slowdown or it could simply reflect a return to previous performance. More generally, the links between trade pressures and productivity growth have not been adequately explored. However, since the relative price of unskilled labor has been declining, we might expect the endogenous response of technology to be a substitution towards rather than away from using unskilled labor.

Finally, an alternative interpretation of the rising ratio of non-production to production workers is that it represents increased foreign outsourcing. Indeed if the production labor-intensive activities were moved abroad this, rather than a change in technology, could explain the rise in the ratio of non-production to production workers found in US manufacturing. If this was the case we would expect to find smaller shifts within industries. However, in Lawrence and Slaughter (1993) we found the shifts as pervasive at the 4-digit SIC level as at the 3-digit level. Moreover, Berman et al. (1992) note that according to the 1987 Census of Manufacturing very little of materials outsourced came from the same SIC 3-digit industry as the establishment itself. This conclusion is also supported by the evidence on multinationals introduced below.

### III   US Multinationals

As reported in Table 5, US firms with foreign operations have not contributed to employment growth within the United States over the past decade – a remarkable result given the rise of about 30 per cent in US employment over the past decade.[10] These firms are particularly important in the US manufacturing sector – indeed they account for more than half of all manufacturing employment. However, between 1977 and 1989, their manufacturing employment in the US fell 14 per cent (from 11 to 10.13 million) – considerably faster than the drop of 1.2 per cent in overall manufacturing employment over the same period.

This sluggish employment growth in US multinationals has been attributed by many Americans to the impact of their foreign operations. It is widely perceived in the US that many of the jobs formerly in these firms have moved abroad. Drawn by low labor costs and low labor standards, multinational corporations (MNCs) are seen as having relocated their production towards low-wage countries. In particular, the jobs of blue-collar workers are viewed as vulnerable to this development. Such international outsourcing could, in principle, provide an alternative explanation of the widespread decline in *both* relative blue-collar wages and in the ratio of blue to white-collar workers employed in US manufacturing.

The data on US multinational activity are collected in extensive and comprehensive benchmark surveys by the Bureau of Economic Analysis (BEA) in 1977 and 1989. These data provide an unusually comprehensive view of developments worldwide in an important group of actors. The data, however, should be treated with care, particularly because the aggregate level at which I will report them here could conceal important compositional changes by country and industry. In addition, all activities of each firm are ascribed to a single industry, which could lead to misclassification of some activity.

If outsourcing is important, the decline in blue-collar intensity in the US should be associated with an increase in blue-collar intensity abroad. In addition, as viewed through the eyes of the Stolper–Samuelson paradigm, if developing countries lower their trade barriers and increase their specialization in unskilled labor-intensive products, in developing countries, the relative wages of production workers should rise, while in developed countries they should fall. In addition, we might expect to see an important increase in the share of sales by foreign affiliates going to the United States. On the other hand, if global changes in technology were dominant, we should see *parallel* increases in the ratio of blue to white-collar employment in the US and in the rest of the world and similar movements in wages.

Employment and compensation data for US multinationals are reported in Table 5. Several features are noteworthy. In 1989, US manufacturing multinationals employed over 13.3 million people, about a quarter of whom were in their foreign affiliates. The data suggest that overall multinationals are not necessarily attracted abroad simply by cheap labor – indeed only about a third of US MNC affiliate manufacturing employment is in developing countries. Nonetheless, within developing countries, MNCs do use production workers relatively more intensively than in developed countries and on average production workers are paid about half rather than three-quarters the compensation of non-production workers. It is noteworthy that the ratio of production to non-production workers in developing countries in 1989 of 1.7 was very similar to the ratios in Europe and Canada of 1.6 and 1.76 respectively in 1977.

There is a widespread view that since both technology and capital are increasingly mobile, productivity is as high in US multinationals abroad as in the United States. If this is the case,

*Table 5* US Multinationals

| | Total 1977 | Total 1989 | Total Change (%) | Employment figures (000's) — Production workers 1977 | Production workers 1989 | Production workers Change (%) | Nonproduction workers 1977 | Nonproduction workers 1989 | Nonproduction workers Change (%) | Employment ratios — Prod. workers emp./Nonprod. worker emp. 1977 | 1989 | Change (%) | Compensation ratios (c) — Prod. workers comp./Nonprod. worker comp. 1977 | 1989 | Change (%) |
|---|---|---|---|---|---|---|---|---|---|---|---|---|---|---|---|
| **United States (a)** | | | | | | | | | | | | | | | |
| Total (b) | 67344 | 90644 | 34.6 | 55179 | 73474 | 33.2 | 12165 | 17170 | 41.1 | 4.54 | 4.28 | -5.7 | (c) | (c) | -6.8 |
| Manufacturing | 19682 | 19425 | -1.3 | 14135 | 13257 | -6.2 | 5547 | 6169 | 11.2 | 2.55 | 2.15 | -15.7 | na | na | – |
| **Multinationals (d)** | | | | | | | | | | | | | | | |
| Total | 18885 | 18765 | -0.6 | na | na | – | na | na | – | na | na | – | na | na | – |
| Manufacturing | 11775 | 10127 | -14.0 | 7257 | na | – | 4518 | na | – | 1.61 | na | – | 0.78 | na | – |
| **Foreign Affiliates (e)** | | | | | | | | | | | | | | | |
| Majority-owned manufacturing affiliates in developed countries | 2754 | 2167 | -21.3 | 1695 | 1196 | -29.5 | 1059 | 971 | -8.3 | 1.60 | 1.23 | -23.1 | 0.75 | 0.66 | -10.8 |
| Canada | 562 | 455 | -19.2 | 358 | 274 | -23.5 | 204 | 181 | -11.5 | 1.76 | 1.52 | -13.6 | 0.86 | 0.81 | -5.2 |
| Europe | 1951 | 1509 | -22.6 | 1202 | 828 | -31.1 | 749 | 681 | -9.1 | 1.60 | 1.22 | -24.2 | 0.70 | 0.63 | -10.0 |
| Japan | 40 | 75 | 86.6 | 14 | 23 | 62.0 | 26 | 52 | 99.7 | 0.53 | 0.43 | -18.9 | 0.75 | 0.69 | -8.5 |
| Australia–New Zealand–S. Afr. | 201 | 129 | -35.8 | 122 | 71 | -41.3 | 80 | 58 | -27.4 | 1.53 | 1.23 | -19.1 | 0.78 | 0.68 | -12.5 |
| Developing countries | 1019 | 1079 | 5.9 | 675 | 679 | 0.6 | 344 | 400 | 16.4 | 1.96 | 1.70 | -13.6 | 0.47 | 0.41 | -12.8 |
| Total | 3773 | 3247 | -14.0 | 2371 | 1875 | -20.9 | 1403 | 1371 | -2.2 | 1.69 | 1.37 | -19.1 | 0.68 | 0.59 | -14.2 |
| **Majority-owned manufacturing affiliates in:** | | | | | | | | | | | | | | | |
| Food & kindred products | 377 | 308 | -18.5 | 248 | 184 | -25.9 | 129 | 124 | -4.2 | 1.93 | 1.49 | -22.7 | 0.57 | 0.62 | 9.8 |
| Textile products & apparel | 102 | 82 | -19.5 | 80 | 59 | -27.2 | 21 | 23 | 9.3 | 3.78 | 2.52 | -33.3 | 0.47 | 0.59 | 23.7 |
| Chemical & allied products | 464 | 475 | 2.2 | 233 | 227 | -2.5 | 231 | 247 | 6.9 | 1.01 | 0.92 | -8.8 | 0.71 | 0.64 | -9.1 |
| Primary and fabricated metals | 229 | 179 | -21.9 | 158 | 117 | -26.1 | 71 | 62 | -12.5 | 2.23 | 1.88 | -15.6 | 0.80 | 0.73 | -9.4 |
| Machinery, except electrical | 523 | 508 | -2.9 | 270 | 254 | -6.0 | 253 | 254 | 0.4 | 1.07 | 1.00 | -6.4 | 0.61 | 0.59 | -3.9 |
| Electric & electronic equipment | 629 | 455 | -27.7 | 422 | 288 | -31.8 | 207 | 167 | -19.3 | 2.03 | 1.72 | -15.5 | 0.56 | 0.54 | -4.3 |
| Transportation equipment | 740 | 597 | -19.4 | 507 | 365 | -28.0 | 233 | 231 | -0.9 | 2.17 | 1.58 | -27.3 | 0.97 | 0.61 | -37.2 |
| Other manufacturing | 709 | 645 | -9.0 | 452 | 382 | -15.5 | 257 | 263 | 2.3 | 1.76 | 1.45 | -17.4 | 0.75 | 0.59 | -21.0 |
| Total | 3773 | 3247 | -14.0 | 2371 | 1875 | -20.9 | 1403 | 1371 | -2.2 | 1.69 | 1.37 | -19.1 | 0.68 | 0.59 | -14.2 |

*Notes:*
(a) Labor force totals according to the US Department of Labor's *Employment, Hours, and Earnings, United States, 1909–90*, Volume 1.
(b) Figures for private nonfarm establishments. The total nonfarm figures are: 1977 – 82.471 million; 1989 – 108.413 million.
(c) The compensation ratio for total US employment is a comparison of the white-collar/blue-collar cost indices in 1977 and 1989 as published by the Bureau of Labor Statistics.
(d) According to and based on US Department of Commerce publications: *1977 US Direct Investment Abroad; 1989 US Direct Investment Abroad.* Information is for nonbank US parents of nonbank US affiliates.
(e) Classified by industry of affiliate. According to the Department of Commerce publications referenced above.

we might expect to see lower wages per worker but similar levels of output per worker. As reported in Table 6, measured in current US dollars, output per employee in developing countries in 1989 was actually about 40.3 per cent of output per employee in developed countries. By contrast compensation per employee averaged 28.5 per cent of US levels (production workers received 22.7 per cent the compensation of their US counterparts, non-production workers 37 per cent, while non-wage income per worker was 49.7 per cent of US levels). Since MNCs actually contribute their capital in the form of know-how it should be expected that the share of non-wage income will be higher in their foreign operations. Moreover, these data certainly dispel the notion of similar productivity levels in developed and developing countries.

*Table 6    US manufacturing foreign affiliates: output and employment (data for 1989)*

|  | Output ($ millions) | Employees | Comp. per worker $ | Net income per worker $ | Output per worker $ |
|---|---|---|---|---|---|
| **Developed countries** | | | | | |
| All workers | 143 244 | 2 167 300 | 33 028 | 12 587 | 66 093 |
| Production workers | – | 1 196 100 | 26 943 | – | – |
| Non-production workers | – | 971 200 | 40 523 | – | – |
| **Developing countries** | | | | | |
| All workers | 28 764 | 1 079 400 | 9 404 | 6 250 | 26 648 |
| Production workers | – | 679 200 | 6 110 | – | – |
| Non-production workers | – | 400 200 | 14 955 | – | – |

Ratio of developing to developed countries for:

| Compensation per worker | |
|---|---|
| All workers | 0.28 |
| Production workers | 0.23 |
| Non-production workers | 0.37 |
| Gross product per worker | 0.40 |
| Net income per worker | 0.50 |

*Sources*:
US Department of Commerce Publications – *US Direct Investment Abroad 1989 Benchmark Survey*, and *Survey of Current Business*, February 1994.

Consider, now, changes in the data between 1977 and 1989 reported in Table 5. These do not support the common perception that overseas employment in US-owned manufacturing foreign affiliates has increased. Indeed, employment in the majority-owned manufacturing foreign affiliates of US MNCs actually declined by 14 per cent — a decline similar to that experienced in their US parents. This decline was mainly due to shrinkage in the European operations of US MNCs where total employment fell by 23 per cent and production worker employment plunged by 31 per cent. Employment growth in US manufacturing MNCs in developing countries was more robust. Between 1977 and 1989 an increase of 5.9 per cent was recorded. However, the overall magnitude of employment in these US foreign affiliates is relatively small. The aggregate rise in employment was just 60 000. This employment growth is small when compared with the drop of 1.7 million that occurred in US manufacturing parents over the same period and the 0.5 million drop that occurred in manufacturing foreign affiliates over the same period. The overall share of developing countries in the employment of US majority-owned foreign manufacturing affiliates increased from just 27 to 34 per cent and their share in the worldwide employment of manufacturing MNCs (that is, in both US parents and foreign affiliates) increased from just 6.8 to 8.1 per cent.

What about production worker employment in these affiliates? Of the 60 000 growth in employment overall, only 4000 occurred in the employment of production workers. As estimated by Slaughter (1994), declines in production worker employment occurred in Europe (–370 700), Central and South America excluding Mexico (–75 300) and South East Asia (–6100). In Mexico, production worker employment increased by 80 900. In Asian countries, while increases were recorded, they were surprisingly small: Malaysia (15 600). Singapore (10 400), South Korea (3900) and Thailand (11 700). Therefore, there is little evidence that on balance large numbers of production worker jobs are shifting within US multinationals away from the US towards the developing countries.

The ratio of production to non-production workers employed in US manufacturing operations worldwide has fallen precipitously. Indeed the declines are of similar magnitude in US manufacturing parents (–15.7 per cent) and in their affiliates in developing countries (–13.6 per cent). The declines were particularly large in Europe (–24.2 per cent) and in Australia, South Africa and New Zealand (–19.1 per cent). Only in Mexico did the ratio increase. There were also declines in this ratio in most major industries. According to Slaughter (1994) who estimated these changes at a 3-digit level, three industries were exceptional and did experience both rising foreign employment in production workers and falling ratios of non-production to production workers. These were tobacco products (+4,000, –15.7 per cent), a subset of chemicals products (SIC 285, 288, and 289) (+10 900, –25.4 per cent) and computers and office equipment (+37 500 and –27.4 per cent).

As I noted above, if the Stolper–Samuelson story was dominant, we would expect to see the relative wages of production workers moving in opposite directions in developed and developing countries. Instead, what we see is that, on the contrary, relative wages of production workers have fallen worldwide. *Together the picture that emerges appears to be far more consistent with the notion of a common shift in technology rather than of expanding trade. Worldwide, we see a rise in the relative employment of non-production workers despite the increase in their relative wage.*

## *1989–91*

More recent data, which reflect the relatively earlier occurrence of recession in the United States, show that overseas employment in US MNCs was more robust than in US parents. Between 1989 and 1991, US-based employment in multinational parents declined by 5.1 per cent (987 000). By contrast, employment in majority-owned manufacturing affiliates increased by 50 700 – 1.6 per cent. It would be erroneous to assume a causal connection between these developments, but even if one were to make such a connection less than 10 per cent of US employment loss could be accounted for by jobs that were transferred abroad.

*Outsourcing*

Technological change also appears to be reducing the growth prospects of very large firms. Increasingly, large US firms are downsizing and slimming down to only those core activities which are essential to their operations – less vital activities are performed in smaller and more flexible suppliers. Figure 3 gives a picture of the quantitative importance of various forms of outsourcing. As might be expected for a period in which the US trade deficit increased, between 1982 and 1989 there was a rapid increase in the purchases of manufactured goods by US-based MNCs from their foreign affiliates. This increased from $25 billion in 1982 to $61.2 billion in 1989. Purchases from unaffiliated foreigners increased even more rapidly from $16.1 billion to $45.3 billion. While the increase has been rapid, these imports still represent only a small share of the total sales of US MNC parents, increasing from 4.1 per cent in 1982 to 6.8 per cent in 1989.[11] Moreover, these numbers refer to purchases from both developed and developing countries.[12] Manufactured imports from *developing* countries were roughly a third of these shares. These effects are thus simply too small to have employment and wage shifts of the size they are alleged to have.[13] Overall value added within US multinational parents fell from 41.6 per cent of sales in 1982 to 37.6 per cent in 1989. Of this 4 point shift almost 1.2 points represented a rise in domestic outsourcing and 2.8 per cent outsourcing from abroad.

The slimming down that is evident in US parents is even more striking in the behavior of their foreign manufacturing affiliates. Between 1982 and 1989 value added within these operations declined from 37.5 to 33.7 per cent of sales of which almost all represented a rise in inputs sourced abroad rather than in the United States. The data for 1991 suggest that this trend has continued with the share of value added performed in house in affiliates declining to 30.6 per cent. The share of inputs sourced by foreign affiliates from their US parents and other US sources has remained fairly constant over this period.[14]

## IV   Labor Standards and Deeper Integration

In most OECD countries, the government has an extensive role in the labor market. It commonly regulates work hours and the cost of overtime, mandates vacations and holidays and sick leave, sets minimum wages; restricts child and forced labor; ensures non-discrimination; provides unemployment, disability and retirement income insurance and, in many countries, health insurance; and sets conditions for hiring and firing, unionization and collective bargaining.

By and large, nations have taken these actions independently, although a voluntary set of international standards has been agreed to at the International Labor Organization (ILO), and the General Agreement on Tariffs and Trade (GATT) does contain a fairly narrow prohibition on trade in goods made with prison labor.[15] Nonetheless, efforts to bring these issues to the international policy arena have been present in both the United States and the European Union. As early as 1953, the United States proposed adding a labor standards article to GATT, and it pushed unsuccessfully for the inclusion of labor standards in the Tokyo and Uruguay Rounds. The US has also tried to induce foreign compliance with worker rights in other aspects of its trade policy. Since the mid-1980s, the US Congress has passed a series of laws that directly link preferential trade and investment benefits to respect for basic worker rights.[16] In Section 301 and Super 301 of the Omnibus Trade Act of 1988, the 'systematic denial of internationally

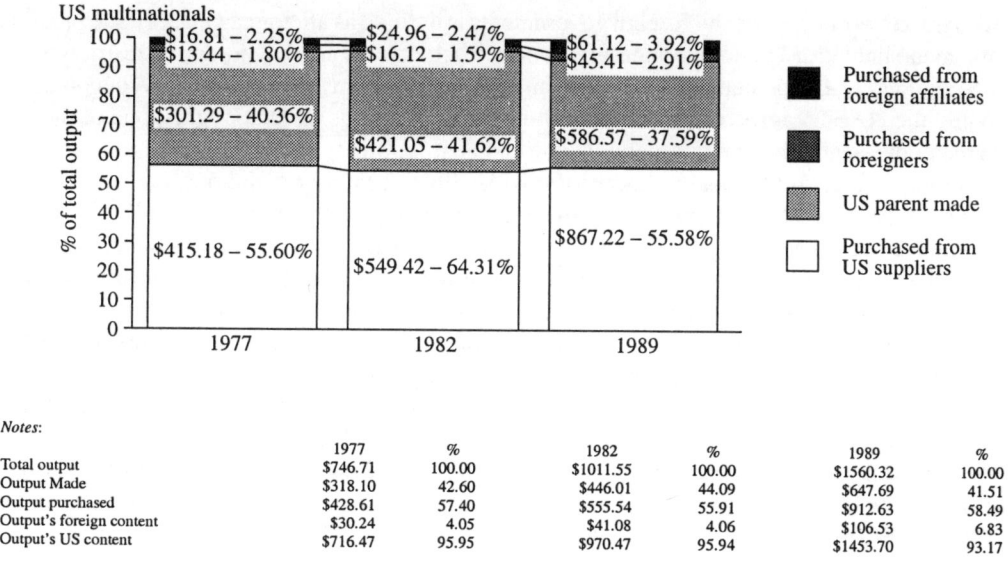

**Notes:**

|                          | 1977     | %      | 1982      | %      | 1989      | %      |
|--------------------------|----------|--------|-----------|--------|-----------|--------|
| Total output             | $746.71  | 100.00 | $1011.55  | 100.00 | $1560.32  | 100.00 |
| Output Made              | $318.10  | 42.60  | $446.01   | 44.09  | $647.69   | 41.51  |
| Output purchased         | $428.61  | 57.40  | $555.54   | 55.91  | $912.63   | 58.49  |
| Output's foreign content | $30.24   | 4.05   | $41.08    | 4.06   | $106.53   | 6.83   |
| Output's US content      | $716.47  | 95.95  | $970.47   | 95.94  | $1453.70  | 93.17  |

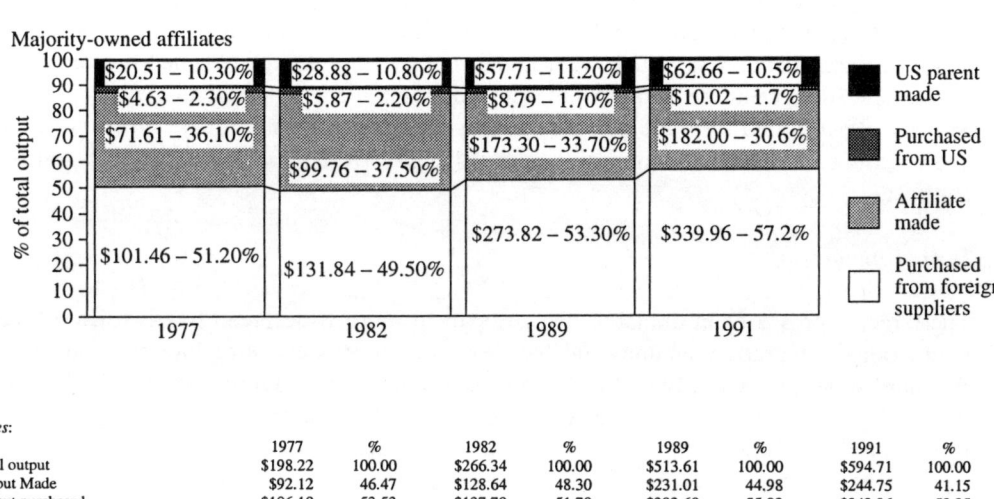

**Notes:**

|                          | 1977     | %      | 1982     | %      | 1989     | %      | 1991     | %      |
|--------------------------|----------|--------|----------|--------|----------|--------|----------|--------|
| Total output             | $198.22  | 100.00 | $266.34  | 100.00 | $513.61  | 100.00 | $594.71  | 100.00 |
| Output Made              | $92.12   | 46.47  | $128.64  | 48.30  | $231.01  | 44.98  | $244.75  | 41.15  |
| Output purchased         | $106.10  | 53.53  | $137.70  | 51.70  | $282.60  | 55.02  | $349.96  | 58.85  |
| Output's foreign content | $173.07  | 87.31  | $231.59  | 86.95  | $447.11  | 87.05  | $87.77   | 14.76  |
| Output's US content      | $25.15   | 12.69  | $34.75   | 13.05  | $66.49   | 12.95  | $12.22   | 2.05   |

*Source*: Based on information provided by The Department of Commerce's Bureau of Economic Analysis, *Survey of Current Business*, 1994.

*Figure 3   Sourcing comparison for US multinationals and their majority-owned affiliates (manufacturing only; all dollars in billions*

recognized worker rights' by foreign governments is defined as an 'unreasonable trade practice' and made liable for US countermeasures where 'such denials cause a burden or restrictions on US commerce.' Labor standards were also an important issue in the recent NAFTA negotiations. While the NAFTA agreement itself did not include provisions on labor rights, one of the side agreements established an international enforcement regime for alleged violations of national minimum wage, child labor, and occupational health and safety regulations, and an oversight and evaluation mechanism (without enforcement powers) for other labor issues.[17]

The US focus has been on achieving 'minimal standards.' By contrast, measures within the European Community have been considerably more extensive. In 1956, according to Steil (1994), French officials argued that social legislation in Europe should be harmonized in conjunction with the reduction of tariff protection to 'make apparent to the workers the link that must exist between the common market's establishment and higher standards of living.' More recently, European countries who fail to provide their workers with 'adequate social protection' are widely viewed as guilty of 'social dumping.' Britain, for example, was accused of social dumping when Hoover moved from Burgundy, France to Scotland. Within Europe, efforts have been made to raise labor standards to prevent such 'dumping.' On 9 December 1989, all EC members besides Britain agreed to the 'Social Charter' that covers an extensive set of worker's rights.[18] The European Commission has also been active in implementing this Charter.[19]

At a multilateral level, however, there are increasing calls for moving beyond the voluntary standards of the ILO and the GATT's prohibition on forced labor (Collingsworth et al., 1994). The United States tried to ensure that discussions on labor standards would take place in the new World Trade Organization (WTO). French leaders have been vocal in calling for European action against other nations with lower standards of social protection. Prime Minister Balladur has demanded that Europe be protected from 'foreign traders with different values.' President Mitterrand has called for trade sanctions against nations with 'inadequate social protection,' and outgoing European Community President Jacques Delors has called for a 'global social contract.'

*Deeper Integration*

These recent pressures in the labor area are part of more widespread trends toward 'deeper international integration' as domestic policies come under increasing international scrutiny. By contrast most post-war liberalization efforts have involved shallow integration. They have aimed at: (a) removing national barriers to the entry of goods and capital; and (b) providing foreign products and investors with the *same* treatment accorded to their domestic counterparts. But they have not tried to constrain the domestic policies of sovereign nations.[20]

Are the calls for international labor standards justifiable? It is useful to distinguish conceptually three types of effects that labor policies might have: (a) those that are purely local; (b) those that operate on international markets through market spillovers; and (c) those that operate on international markets through direct spillovers.[21]

(a) LOCAL EFFECTS
Where nations effectively control their borders and prevent migration, most labor standards will either be confined to local effects or operate through market channels to affect international

trade and investment flows. In fact, despite the widespread perception that such policies have repercussions on trade and investment flows, there are many cases in which government intervention in the labor market will have purely local impacts.

First, policies such as sick leave, maternity leave and family leave are usually financed by payroll taxes. It is often assumed that such taxes on labor raise employment costs thereby affecting resource allocation. However, unless all elements of the compensation package, including wages, are subject to minimum standards, when such standards are imposed, employers can adjust other elements of the package to keep their total costs from rising substantially. Indeed, the evidence suggests that in general the supply of labor is fairly inelastic and that over the long run most payroll taxes are born by labor (OECD, 1993). This implies that such taxes result in lower wages rather than higher compensation costs.[22]

Second, many labor measures actually reflect decisions which might have been taken in the marketplace anyway and are thus not binding constraints. This could be the case with rules about work hours and vacation and minimum wages. In addition, in many countries compliance with binding measures is low and enforcement is weak. Under some circumstances evasion takes the form of employment in the informal sector.[23]

These considerations are important since they remind us that the basic presumption that differences in labor standards will affect trade and investment flows is not necessarily valid.

(b) MARKET SPILLOVERS

In practice, however, many labor market policies will not be perfectly neutral. Indeed, their impact can be quite subtle. Ehrenberg (1994) gives the example of payroll taxes with ceilings, which can shift demand towards more highly-paid workers. Similarly, some employment standards are not all fully shiftable, for example, a binding minimum wage, or child labor laws. If the value employees place on health and safety benefits are less than the employers' costs of complying only part of the costs will be shifted.

In general, therefore, groups seeking to raise labor standards will find their case becomes more difficult, the higher the costs they impose on society. It should therefore come as no surprise that such groups will be against trade, particularly of the kind which is with trading partners which have very different preferences. However, if labor standards reflect the legitimate preferences of a particular nation, it is unclear why others should be entitled to impose their views.

The traditional theory of international trade demonstrates that when costs differ, countries gain from free trade by specializing along the lines of comparative advantage. When Ricardo invoked the principle of comparative advantage, he referred to productive differences that were due to climate (or technology).[24] But in stating his theory, Ricardo could as easily have ascribed the productive differences between nations to the 'social climate' as to the physical climate and his conclusions would have been unchanged: *taking climatic conditions as given,* free trade will maximize global welfare.

The choices of sovereign nation states are reflected in part in their rules and regulations. These regulatory decisions influence relative costs and thus patterns of comparative advantage. Given diversity of national conditions and regulatory preferences, therefore, it will be optimal for nations to have *different* regulations and norms. A strictly level playing field or a common set of standards would be inappropriate.

From this standpoint, therefore, the playing field of international competition will and should never be strictly level. Competition between firms based in different nations can never be fair in the same way as competition between firms based in the same economy. Both traditional determinants of costs such as relative factor endowments, technology and tastes and social determinants of costs such as regulations, institutions and government policies should affect competitive performance. Thus firms producing labor-intensive products *should* find it easier to operate in economies in which labor is more abundant and less costly. Similarly, firms producing in economies with lenient and less costly labor standards *should* find it easier to produce with labor-intensive production methods. If, for example, relatively unsafe activities shift away from countries that place a higher value on safe workplaces towards those with a lower value, global welfare will be enhanced.

In the light of this paradigm, therefore, those seeking more 'level playing fields' based on constraining domestic economic policies simply fail to understand that the benefits of international trade come from allowing nations to be different, rather than requiring them to be similar.

As with most paradigms, however, this view of the world rests on some basic assumptions. If these assumptions are violated, however, free trade may not be globally optimal. In particular, two assumptions are crucial. The first is that the world consists of perfectly functioning, competitive markets – that is, that there are no international market failures. And the second is the normative proposition that no constraints should be imposed on sovereign national choices (an assumption analogous to consumer sovereignty).

The assumption of competitive global markets is important because it rules out the use of strategic labor standard policies, that is, policies designed not only to achieve a given impact on the labor market but also on the nation's terms of trade. As Brown et al. (1993) demonstrate, with market power a labor standard could operate like an optimal tariff and shift the terms of trade. For example, South Africa could raise the price and reduce the supply of gold in the world by raising safety standards in its gold mines.[25] In the presence of this potential, international controls on standard setting might be required.

In the real world, however, most labor standard policy decisions are not motivated by terms of trade considerations and accusations of the use of labor standards for such purposes are rare. Indeed, exporters of labor-intensive products are actually likely to have lower standards and importers higher standards because concerns about employment tend to dominate those of maximizing aggregate national income.

The assumption that nations should be completely free to impose whatever policies they choose may also be questioned. Some have tried to advocate tougher international labor standards on the grounds that these have positive economic effects. These include the alleged labor-income raising effects of capital–labor substitution, productivity enhancement effects of workforce harmony brought about by increased worker participation and the notion that a more equal distribution of income is necessary to stimulate consumer spending (Collingsworth et al., 1994). But the existence of these effects are controversial and, in any case, it is unclear why firms and/or nations should be forced to take actions which are in their own interest.

Instead, the more compelling assaults on complete national sovereignty are based on (a) the notion that there exist basic universal human rights and (b) the 'psychological externalities' which occur when citizens of one country find practices in other countries morally reprehensible. But to what degree and under what circumstances should nations in one country try to change the behavior of others through measures involving trade?

In some cases, the policies in poor countries which offend the sensibilities of those in rich nations actually result from different income levels (that is, income effects) rather than different preferences or values. Thus those in extreme poverty may permit activities which under other circumstances they themselves would regard as abhorrent, for example, child labor or a lack of pollution controls.

The long-run solution to these problems is clearly to raise incomes. Indeed, refusing to trade with such nations could actually retard rather than improve their abilities to provide worker rights. In the short run, however, some of these conflicts can be dealt with through explicit compensation schemes and subsidies. For example, the EC has a set of social funds which allow poorer countries to meet the labor and social standards applied by more affluent members. Similarly, 'debt for nature' swaps allow richer nations to support environmental activities in poorer countries.

In other cases, countries may trade off their adherence to particular practices by obtaining concessions in other areas, for example, in the Uruguay Round some developing countries agreed to the introduction of intellectual property rules in return for increased access in textiles and agriculture. The NAFTA provides another example in which Mexico signed a (side) agreement on labor standards in return for preferential market access. As already noted, the United States has conditioned access to preferential arrangements such as Generalized System of Preferences (GSP) on adherence to basic labor standards.

Where sufficient compensation is not forthcoming, however, there is danger in trying to impose such standards under conditions in which they may damage economic growth. Moreover, there will remain cases in which divergent practices reflect divergent beliefs about the desirability of such standards so that compensation will not be possible, for example, the conflicts between the United States and the Soviet Union over Jewish emigration and those between the United States and China over human rights. Under these circumstances free trade may be difficult to obtain, and indeed, by revealed preference both nations may be better off without such trade.

Trade intervention is of course not the only means of responding to labor measures found to be reprehensible in other nations. An alternative might be insistence on labelling (for example, 'made with union workers', or 'made using ecologically sound standards') that would allow private citizens to exercise their preferences.

On the other hand, where nations actually agree on basic standards, international agreements can help make such standards more credible domestically and reduce the opportunity costs of imposing them alone. In addition, the presence of a reasonable set of mutually agreed minimum standards could help reduce the ability for political interests to exploit these concerns opportunistically for protectionist purposes.

*Direct Spillovers*

Labor market regulations and programs in one country may directly affect conditions in a second country through induced labor flows. Immigration creates problems, for example, when workers from one country can receive benefits but not pay the costs of such benefits in a second. Under these circumstances, since the spillovers are not simply pecuniary, the case for an increased harmonization (or mutual recognition) of policies is considerably stronger. It is thus perhaps not surprising that as it perfects its internal labor market, the European Union has moved to implement more extensive sets of common standards.

In sum, in general there is a strong case for allowing individual nations a wide scope for differentiation in applying labor standards, particularly when the costs and benefits of such standards are fully borne by the nation itself. Even where these standards do affect others through market forces, in principle, given diverse social preferences, the existence of diverse standards will raise global welfare. There is, however, a case for international standards where: (a) there is a strong danger that nations would act strategically in their absence; (b) nations can agree on what those standards should be; and/or (c) nations share a common labor market. Where the failure to maintain certain standards impinges on notions of fundamental human rights they are more difficult to deal with. One solution is to induce poor nations to comply by offering them compensation. A second is to use labelling and other forms of moral suasion. The denial of trading opportunities should probably come only as a last resort and only in the most egregious cases.

## *A Race to the Bottom?*

If labor market policies do not affect total labor costs, there is no reason to believe there will be economic pressures for a convergence of standards. In addition, if these standards reflect choices that nations are willing to make, they will not be changed even if they do have allocative consequences. As Ehrenberg (1994) has pointed out, there are noteworthy differences in minimum wages, occupational standards, and other labor standards across the 50 states of the United States – indeed prior to the early 1970s, the United States did not have national occupational health and safety standards.

## Concluding Comments

International trade enhances potential national welfare. It frees up resources to be put to alternative uses in which they are more productive. However, a necessary condition for these benefits to be realized, is that these resources do not remain unemployed. In several labor markets, particularly in Europe, the loss of a job is viewed with considerable anxiety. The result is that increased trade, or technological progress, is seen as a threat rather than an opportunity.

In this paper, however, I have shown that there is considerable empirical evidence that the sources of poor labor market performance, particularly in the US, are essentially domestic. They reflect ongoing technological shocks that would be present even if the US economy was closed. The role of developing country imports and the sourcing activities of US multinationals both remain too small to account for a significant share of the relative wage changes that have occurred in the US. This evidence suggests that neither international differences in wage rates nor in labor standards are the major factors in OECD labor market behavior that many believe them to be.

These findings suggest the major challenges to policy are: (a) to educate the public on the nature of the changes; (b) to emphasize the need for worker training and education to take advantage of the opportunities new technologies afford; and (c) to develop measures such as earned-income tax credits which redress earnings inequality while preserving and increasing wage flexibility.

Where nations share a common consensus on labor standards, as most do with respect to minimum standards, there is probably merit in reinforcing the credibility of domestic policies through international agreement. International agreement might also help to define the terms of the debate and thus limit the ability of particular interests to obtain trade protection. Nonetheless, there are also gains to be had in allowing considerable scope for the application of different policies, particularly where effects are either borne locally or operate only through international markets. Nations that share a common labor market because of free immigration flows might find a greater interest in increased harmonization, although even in this case, as the US experience indicates, a considerable diversity in standards and practices can be sustained within a single market.

## Notes

1. In 1950, compensation in Germany and the United Kingdom was 13 and 17 per cent of those in the United States, respectively. Today, Mexican wages are about 12 per cent of US levels.
2. This result is also found by Katz et al. (1992).
3. In addition to arguing that trade has reduced average US wage rates, Leamer (1991) argues that trade has lowered the relative wages of unskilled workers. This claim will be discussed below.
4. In 1980, hourly compensation in other OECD countries was 83 per cent of US levels; this dropped to 64 per cent by 1985 but then increased to 103 per cent by 1990.
5. Imports of manufactured goods into the EC in 88/89 amounted to $89 billion – less than 2 per cent of GNP.
6. US exports to developing countries have also grown rapidly. Over the 1980s the US trade *deficit* in manufactured goods trade with developing countries swung by $45.55 billion or 8/10th of a per cent of GDP.
7. Wood also argues that the pressures from international competition could spur technological change that is particularly rapid in labor intensive products. The evidence on this question is somewhat more supportive of Wood: as shown by Lawrence and Slaughter (1993: figure 10) there is a positive slope to a regression of total factor productivity against the ratio of production to non-production workers. Leamer (1994) and Sachs and Shatz (1994) report similar results.
8. Deardorff and Staiger (1988) demonstrate the conditions under which this methodology is appropriate. It is necessary that both preferences and production technology are Cobb–Douglas.
9. Though perhaps not larger than in the 1950s. Sachs and Shatz (1994) show a rapid increase between 1947 and 1960.
10. In 1989, total non-bank MNC employment in the United States was 18.8 million – about the same as the 18.9 million in 1977.
11. Gross product in US manufacturing was $647 billion in 1982 and $1004.6 billion in 1989.
12. Sales of US foreign affiliates of manufactured goods from developing countries to all US purchasers increased from $7.5 billion in 1982 to about $20 billion in 1989.
13. The BEA reaches similar conclusions. In the *Survey of Current Business July 1993* they compared employment patterns in high and low-wage countries over the period 1982 to 1991. The low-wage share of Majority Owned Foreign Affiliate (MOFA) employment increased by 3 percentage points to 34 per cent. Between 1982 and 1989 they find that the domestic content of US parents' output in manufacturing decreased from 96 to 93 per cent.
14. Slaughter (1994) produces evidence that foreign and US labor are actually price complements rather than substitutes. A one per cent drop in foreign wages tends to raise home employment by nearly 0.1 per cent.
15. The original charter of the International Trade Organization (ITO) in 1948 contained a section on labor rights although it was never ratified by the US congress for other reasons.
16. Eligibility under the Caribbean Basin Economic Recovery Act of 1983, the GSP (Generalized System

of Preferences) in 1984, the Overseas Private Investment Corporation (OPIC) in 1985, and 1987
US participation in Multilateral Investment Guarantee Agency have all been conditioned on adherence
to ILO standards on worker rights which include the rights to associate and bargain collectively, the
banning of forced or compulsory or child labor, the provision of reasonable conditions for worker
health and safety and the existence of a national mechanism for determining a generally applicable
minimum wage.

17.  Conspicuous by its absence, and an important reason for the opposition of organized US labor to the
NAFTA were rights of association, organizing and bargaining.

18.  These include rights to freedom of movement; employment and remuneration; the improvement of
living and working conditions – the right to social protection; the right to freedom of association
and collective bargaining; the right to vocational training; the right of men and women to equal
treatment; the right to information, consultation and participation; the right to health and safety in
the workplace; the protection of children and adolescents in employment; the protection of elderly
persons; and protection of persons with disabilities.

19.  The Single European Act allows social policy measures relating to the health and safety of workers
to be adopted by qualified majority, while requiring unanimity in other areas of social policy. The
Commission has accordingly defined a working-time directive (which requires a maximum 48 hour
week and 4 week annual paid vacation) as a 'health and safety' measure. Of course, in Europe a key
quid pro quo to members with lower wage levels is access to the cohesion fund.

20.  Measures for deeper integration do not necessarily involve harmonization of standards or policies.
In some cases 'mutual-recognition' might suffice.

21.  I owe this classification scheme to Richard Cooper's analysis of global environmental policies. See
Cooper (1993).

22.  Actually some labor standards may actually increase the supply of labor and enhance productivity.
Thus a safer workplace may raise workforce participation and the increased unionization and worker
participation in decision making could increase productivity.

23.  Ehrenberg notes that the substantial differences in benefit levels which prevail across the United
States indicates that even within an integrated market there is considerable scope for exercising
local preferences. Maximum weekly Unemployment Insurance (UI) varies from $154 in Nebraska
to $468 in Massachusetts.

24.  These explanations for trade have been so widely invoked that it is sometimes treated as a major
'refutation' of the principle of comparative advantage when it is discovered that institutions and
policies can also affect comparative advantage so that comparative advantage can actually be 'created'
by governments.

25.  Exporting countries have incentives to set standards too high globally because they receive this
secondary terms of trade benefit. Importing countries would do the opposite. This counterintuitive
result implies that labor intensive exporters should set standards too high (see Brown et al. (1993)).

## References

Berman, Eli, John Bound and Zvi Griliches (1994), 'Changes in the Demand for Skilled Labor Within
US Manufacturing Industries: Evidence from the Annual Survey of Manufacturing', *Quarterly Journal
of Economics*, **109** (2), May, 367–97.

Bhagwati, Jagdish (1991), 'Free Traders and Free Immigrationists: Strangers or Friends?', Russell Sage
Foundation, Working Paper No. 20, April.

Borjas, George J., Richard Freeman and Lawrence F. Katz (1992), 'On the Labor Market Effects of
Immigration & Trade', Harvard Institute of Economic Research Discussion Paper No. 1556, Harvard
University, June.

Bound, John and George Johnson (1992), 'Changes in the Structure of Wages in the 1980s: An Evaluation
of Alternative Explanations', *American Economic Review*, **82**, June, 371–92.

Brown, Drusilla K., Alan V. Deardorff and Robert M. Stern (1993), 'International Labor Standards and
Trade: A Theoretical Analysis', *Research Forum on International Economics*, University of Michigan

Discussion Paper No. 333, July.

Centre d'etudes Prospectives et d'Informations (1994), *Le Lettre Du Cepii*, February.

Collingsworth, Terry, J. William Goold and Pharis J. Harvey (1994), 'Time for a New Global Deal', *Foreign Affairs*, Jan/Feb.

Cooper, Richard N. (1993), 'Natural Resources and Environmental Policies', mimeo, Brookings Project on Integrating National Economies.

Davis, Steven J. (1992), 'Cross-Country Patterns of Change in Relative Wages', in Olivier Blanchard and Stanley Fischer (eds), *1992 Macroeconomics Annual*, Cambridge, MA: National Bureau of Economic Research.

Deardorff, Alan and Robert Staiger (1988), 'An Interpretation of the Factor Content of Trade', *Journal of International Economics*, **24**, February, 93–107.

EuroStat (1992), *Labor Costs 1988: Principal Results*, Luxembourg: EC.

Ehrenberg, Ronald G. (1994), *Labor Markets and Integrating National Economies*, Washington, DC: Brookings.

Gullickson, William (1992), 'Multifactor Productivity in Manufacturing, 1984–88', *Monthly Labor Review*, October.

Johnson, George E. and Frank P. Stafford (1993), 'International Competition and Real Wages', paper presented at American Economic Association Meetings, 5–7 January.

Katz, Lawrence F., Gary W. Loveman and David G. Blanchflower (1992), 'A Comparison of Changes in the Structure of Wages in Four OECD Countries', Cambridge, MA: National Bureau for Economic Research.

Lawrence, Robert Z. and Matthew Slaughter (1993), 'Trade and US Wages in the 1980s: Giant Sucking Sound or Small Hiccup?', *Brookings Papers on Economic Activity: Microeconomics*, 161–210.

Leamer, Edward (1991), 'Effects of a US–Mexico Free Trade Agreement', paper presented at Brown University; also NBER Discussion Paper.

Leamer, Edward (1994), 'Trade, Wages and Revolving Door Ideas', National Bureau of Economic Research Working Paper No. 4716, Cambridge, MA.

Mishel, Lawrence and Jared Bernstein (1994), 'Is the Technology Black Box Empty? An Empirical Examination of the Impact of Technology on Wage Inequality and Employment Structure', mimeo, Economic Policy Institute.

Murphy, K. and F. Welch (1991), 'The Role of International Trade in Wage Differences', in M. Kosters (ed.), *Workers and their Wages*, Washington: American Enterprise Institute.

OECD (1993), *Employment Outlook*, July.

Ravenga, Ana L. (1992), 'Exporting Jobs? The Impact of Import Competition on Employment and Wages in US Manufacturing', *Quarterly Journal of Economics*, **107** (1), February, 255–82.

Reich, Robert B. (1991), *The Work of Nations*, New York: Alfred A. Knopf.

Sachs, Jeffery and Howard Shatz (1994), 'Trade and Jobs in US Manufacturing', *Brookings Papers on Economic Activity*, **1**.

Slaughter, Matthew J. (1994), 'International Trade, Multinational Corporations and American Wages', PhD Dissertation, MIT Economics Department.

Steil, B. (1994) ' "Social Correctness" Is the New Protectionism', *Foreign Affairs*, Jan/Feb, **73** (1), 14–20.

Stolper, Wolfgang and Paul A. Samuelson (1941), 'Protection and Real Wages', *Review of Economic Studies*, November, 58–73.

Wood, Adrian (1991), 'How much does Trade with the South Affect Workers in the North?', *World Bank Research Observer*, **6** (1), Jan, 19–36.

Wood, Adrian (1994), *North–South Trade, Employment and Inequality*, Oxford: Clarendon Press.

# [22]

Review of International Economics 5(4), 435–451, 1997

# The Role of Multinational Firms in the Wage-Gap Debate

*James R. Markusen and Anthony J. Venables\**

## Abstract

The observation of an increase in the ratio of skilled to unskilled wages in the high-income countries and in some cases in low/middle-income countries has led to considerable discussion and controversy as to its cause. Virtually none of the analyses have considered a role for multinational investment in explaining the wage-gap phenomenon. This paper adapts the authors' earlier work to consider what role multinationals might play in factor markets. It identifies circumstances under which investment liberalization is likely to raise the wage gap in both the skilled-labor abundant and the unskilled-labor abundant country.

## 1. Introduction

The observation of a rising gap between the wages of skilled and unskilled workers in the United States and rising unemployment in Europe has generated considerable controversy and debate as to the causes of this phenomenon. A more liberal world trading and investment regime is an immediate suspect insofar as the Heckscher–Ohlin model predicts that liberalization should help a country's abundant factor (skilled labor in the USA and Europe) and harm its scarce factor. Some find evidence to support this relationship, notably Wood (1994) and Leamer (1993, 1994, 1996a,b). Others have argued by indirect logic that trade is not to blame, including Lawrence and Slaughter (1993), Krugman and Lawrence (1993), and Krugman (1995). There is a deplorable tendency to simply say that "technical change" is the culprit when some other cause is dismissed, without ever attempting to measure or estimate anything to do with technology.

Despite the fact that we now have a substantial literature on trade with industrial-organization effects (sometimes called the "new trade theory"), almost none of these IO variables have been discussed in this debate. The purpose of this paper is to provide a theoretical analysis of the wage-gap problem by introducing key elements of the new trade theory into the debate. In particular, we will focus on the role of multinational firms and how they may contribute or fail to contribute to the empirical observations on wages. One motivation for doing so is that the late 1970s and 1980s, which was the period of growth in the wage gap in the USA, was also a period (begun after 1973) of tremendous growth in direct investment.[1]

The model quite deliberately resembles a standard Heckscher–Ohlin type trade model with two countries ($h$ and $f$), two goods ($X$ and $Y$), and two factors ($S$ and $L$). The factors will be called skilled and unskilled labor respectively, although it may be more useful to think of the $L$ as a "composite" of unskilled labor and physical capital.

\* Markusen: University of Colorado, Boulder, CO 80309, USA, and NBER-CEPR. Tel: 303-492-0748; Fax: 492-8960; Email: markusen@colorado.edu. Venables: London School of Economics, Houghton Street, London WC2A 2AE, UK, and CEPR. Tel: 44-171-955-7294; Fax: 955-7595; Email: venables@lse.ac.uk. This paper was prepared for the conference "International Trade and Factor Movements between Distorted Economies," held at the University of Konstanz, 4–6 July 1996. We thank all the conference participants, and Albert Schweinberger in particular for comments and suggestions.

*Y* is a competitive sector producing with constant returns to scale. *X* is an increasing-returns, imperfectly-competitive sector. *X* production is composed of three conceptually distinct activities. First, there are firm-level fixed costs using skilled labor (e.g., R&D). Second, plant-level fixed costs use a mix of skilled and unskilled labor. Third, final production requires only unskilled labor (again, it may be useful to think of unskilled labor as a composite of unskilled labor and physical capital). A firm in the *X* sector may serve the other country by exports (then referred to as a national firm) or by building a branch plant (becoming a multinational firm). Shipping costs between markets are in units of unskilled labor.

Factor intensities are crucial to the results of the paper. While our assumptions may seem quantitatively rather arbitrary, we feel that they are qualitatively well grounded in extensive empirical work.[2] We assume that integrated *X* production is skilled-labor intensive relative to *Y* production. Within the *X* sector, firm-level fixed costs are more skilled-labor intensive than plant-level fixed costs which are more skilled-labor intensive than final production. Final production is more skilled-labor intensive than *Y* production. Multinational firms are more skilled-labor intensive than national firms, for a given total output, because the former require additional skilled labor for branch plants, while the latter require additional unskilled labor for shipping costs. These factor-intensive rankings, beginning with the most skilled-labor intensive, are summarized as:

> [firm-level fixed costs] > [plant-level fixed costs] > [integrated *X* production]
> > [branch plant *X* production] > [*Y* production]
>
> [multinational firms] > [national firms] (at common output scale).

One other aspect of factor intensities that is important to the results involves firm scale. An increase in firm scale makes the firm less skilled-labor intensive overall as skilled-labor intensive R&D activities are spread over a larger output. Some readers may find this property of the model counter-empirical. While it is reasonable to suppose that firms become more physical-capital intensive at higher production levels, we know of no empirical evidence or logical argument to suggest that they become more skilled-labor intensive at higher scale. Our assumption is capturing the notion that there are indivisibilities in certain knowledge-intensive activities such as R&D, management, and marketing, logically implying lower skilled-labor intensity at higher scale. In any case, only one of the principal results relies on this property, and we will be careful to point out when it is needed.

The term "firm type" will denote a headquarters location and a number of plants for a given firm. Four firm types are permitted in the model. Firm types $n_h$ and $n_f$ are single-plant national firms with their headquarters and plants in countries *h* and *f* respectively. Firm types $m_h$ and $m_f$ are two-plant multinational firms with their headquarters in countries *h* and *f* respectively. The set of firm types active in equilibrium is referred to as the "regime."

After characterizing the equilibrium regime as a function of country characteristics and trade costs, several results are derived. First, we show how international differences in factor prices depend on country characteristics for a given world endowment of the factors. Results indicate that convergence in relative sizes and endowments will lead to increases in the skilled–unskilled wage ratio in the skilled-labor abundant country. Convergence in country size leads to an increase in the wage ratio in both countries, as multinational firms displace national firms.

Second, investment liberalization (allowing firms to exploit their firm-specific capital abroad) increases the wage gap in the skilled-labor abundant country, and increases the gap in both countries when they differ significantly in relative endowments.

Third, the effects of falling trade costs are complex. Falling trade costs can harm skilled labor in two ways. First, it may replace more skilled-labor intensive multinational firms with less-skilled-labor intensive national firms. Second, it can lead to firm-scale increases which lower the skilled-labor intensity of the $X$ sector at constant factor prices. Results indicate that falling trade costs harm skilled labor in the skilled-labor abundant country unless the two countries are very different in size. In the latter situation, the wage gap can rise in both countries, but for reasons that have nothing to do with multinationals.[3]

Fourth, growth in the world economy (exogenous growth in factor supplies) also has complex effects. Growth favors skilled labor to the extent that more skilled-labor intensive multinational firms displace less-skilled-labor intensive national firms. But growth also brings a firm-scale effect of the type just noted which may harm skilled labor. Results confirm the tension between the two effects. If multinational firms dominate in the initial equilibrium, then the scale effect dominates and the wage gap tends to fall in both countries. If national firms dominate in the initial equilibrium, the regime-shifting effect tends to dominate following growth, with the wage gap increasing in the skilled-labor abundant country which becomes the headquarters of new multinational firms.

Results suggest testable hypotheses for future empirical work. In particular, the wage gap in skilled-labor abundant countries is likely to increase as (1) countries become more similar in relative endowments and size, (2) investment restrictions in the world economy are liberalized and, if national firms are relatively dominant initially, (3) the world economy grows. The wage gap may rise in the initially unskilled-labor abundant country at the same time if (1) countries become more similar in size, or (2) investment restrictions are liberalized.[4] Falling trade costs alone are predicted to lower the return to skilled labor in the skilled-labor abundant country and possibly lower it in both countries.

## 2. Model Structure

As noted above the model has two countries ($h$ and $f$) producing two homogeneous goods, $Y$ and $X$. There are two factors of production, $L$ (unskilled labor), and $S$ (skilled labor). $L$ and $S$ are mobile between industries but internationally immobile. $Y$ will be used as *numéraire* throughout the paper.

Subscripts ($i, j$) will be used to denote the countries ($f, h$). The output of $Y$ in country $i$ is a CES function, identical in both countries. The production function for $Y$ is

$$Y_i = \left( aL_{iy}^{\varepsilon} + (1-a)S_{iy}^{\varepsilon} \right)^{1/\varepsilon}, \quad i = h, f. \tag{1}$$

where $L_{iy}$ and $S_{iy}$ are the unskilled and skilled labor used in the $Y$ sector in country $i$. The elasticity of substitution ($1/(1-\varepsilon)$) is set at 5.0 in the simulation runs reported later in the paper.

Superscripts ($n, m$) will be used to designate a variable as referring to national firms and multinational firms respectively. ($m_i, n_i$) will also be used to indicate the number of active $m$ firms and $n$ firms based in country $i$. It should always be clear from the context what is being represented (e.g., $n_i$ as a variable in an equation always refers to the number of national firms in country $i$).

In order to enter $X$ production with one plant, a firm must incur a fixed cost in units of skilled labor, denoted $F$, and a fixed cost in units of unskilled labor, $G$: national-firm fixed costs are thus $L_i = G$, $S_i = F$.

A two-plant multinational headquartered in country $i$ incurs additional fixed costs in both countries. These include both skilled and unskilled labor costs in the branch-plant in country $j$, and additional skilled-labor costs in the source country $i$. Total fixed costs for a two-plant multinational headquartered in country $i$ are:

$$L_i = G, \quad L_j = \beta G, \quad S_i = F + \gamma F, \quad S_j = \delta F, \quad 1 \geq \beta > (\gamma + \delta).$$

The inequality on the right expresses the assumptions that the second plant is more unskilled-labor intensive than the first, and that there are multiplant economies of scale arising from the joint-input nature of knowledge capital. $\gamma$ can be thought of as a technology-transfer cost. Later in the paper our central-case uses $\beta = 0.75$, $(\gamma + \delta) = 0.5$ ($\gamma = 0.1$, $\delta = 0.4$). The second plant thus requires 75% more unskilled labor than the first plant (all drawn from the host country) and 50% more skilled labor (10% from the source country and 40% from the host country).[5]

Marginal factor requirements are constant in units of unskilled labor. $X_{ij}^n$ denotes the sales in country $j$ of a national firm based in country $i$. Let $w_i$ and $v_i$ denote the prices of unskilled labor and skilled labor respectively in country $i$. A national firm undertakes all its production in its base country, so the cost function of one national firm in country $i$ is given by

$$w_i L_i^n + v_i S_i^n = w_i \left[ c X_{ii}^n + (c + \tau) X_{ij}^n + G \right] + v_i F, \quad i, j = h, f, \quad i \neq j, \tag{2}$$

where $c$ is the constant marginal production cost. $c$, $F$, and $G$ are identical across countries. $\tau$ is the amount of unskilled labor needed to transport one unit of $X$ from country $i$ to country $j$, which we assume to be the same in both directions.

A multinational based in country $i$ has sales in country $j$ of $X_{ij}^m$. It operates one plant in each country incurring fixed costs $(G_i, (1 + \gamma)F_i)$ in its base country, and fixed costs $(\beta G_j, \delta F_j)$ in country $j$. Sales are met entirely from local production, not trade. $L_{ij}^m$ ($S_{ij}^m$) denotes a country $i$ multinational firm's demand for unskilled (skilled) labor in country $j$. A firm type $m_i$ thus has a cost function

$$w_i L_{ii}^m + w_j L_{ij}^m + v_i S_{ii}^m + v_j S_{ij}^m = w_i \left[ c X_{ii}^m + G \right] + w_j \left[ c X_{ij}^m + \beta G \right] + v_i (1 + \gamma) F + v_j \delta F. \tag{3}$$

In our calibration, multinational firms are generally more skilled-labor intensive than national firms, using more skilled labor for branch-plant fixed costs versus the additional unskilled labor for transport costs used by national firms. This depends, however, on firm scale.[6]

Let $\bar{L}_i$ and $\bar{S}_i$ denote the total labor endowments of country $i$. Adding labor demand from $n_i$ national firms, $m_i$ multinationals based in country $i$, and $m_j$ multinationals based in country $j$, gives country $i$ factor market clearing:

$$\bar{L}_i = L_{iy} + n_i L_i^n + m_i L_{ii}^m + m_j L_{ji}^m,$$
$$\bar{S}_i = S_{iy} + n_i S_i^n + m_i S_{ii}^m + m_j S_{ji}^m. \tag{4}$$

In equilibrium, the $X$ sector makes no profits so country $i$ income, denoted $M_i$, is

$$M_i = w_i \bar{L}_i + v_i \bar{S}_i, \quad i = h, f. \tag{5}$$

$p_i$ denotes the price of $X$ in country $i$, and $X_{ic}$ and $Y_{ic}$ denote the consumption of $X$ and $Y$. Utility of the representative consumer in each country is Cobb–Douglas,

$$U_i = X_{ic}^{\alpha} Y_{ic}^{1-\alpha}, \quad X_{ic} \equiv n_i X_{ii}^n + n_j X_{ji}^n + m_i X_{ii}^m + m_j X_{ji}^m, \tag{6}$$

giving demands

$$X_{ic} = \alpha M_i / p_i, \quad Y_{ic} = (1-\alpha) M_i. \tag{7}$$

Equilibrium in the $X$ sector is determined by pricing equations (marginal revenue equals marginal cost) and free-entry conditions. We denote proportional markups of price over marginal cost by $e_{ij}^k$, $(k = n, m)$; so, for example, $e_{ji}^m$ is the markup of a country $j$ multinational in market $i$. Pricing equations of national and multinational firms in each market are (written in complementary-slackness form with associated variables in brackets):

$$p_i(1 - e_{ii}^n) \le w_i c \qquad (X_{ii}^n), \tag{8}$$

$$p_j(1 - e_{ij}^n) \le w_i(c + \tau) \quad (X_{ij}^n), \tag{9}$$

$$p_i(1 - e_{ii}^m) \le w_i c \qquad (X_{ii}^m), \tag{10}$$

$$p_j(1 - e_{ij}^m) \le w_j c \qquad (X_{ij}^m). \tag{11}$$

In a Cournot model with homogeneous products, the optimal markup formula is given by the firm's market share divided by the Marshallian price elasticity of demand in that market. In our model, the price elasticity is one (see equation (7)), reducing the firm's markup to its market share. This gives (also using demand equations (7)):

$$e_{ij}^k = \frac{X_{ij}^k}{X_{jc}} = \frac{p_j X_{ij}^k}{\alpha M_j}, \quad k = n, m, \quad i, j = h, f. \tag{12}$$

There are four zero-profit conditions corresponding to the numbers of the four firm types. Given equations (8)–(11), zero profits can be written as the requirement that markup revenues equal fixed costs:

$$p_h e_{hh}^n X_{hh}^n + p_f e_{hf}^n X_{hf}^n \le w_h G + v_h F \qquad (n_h), \tag{13}$$

$$p_f e_{ff}^n X_{ff}^n + p_h e_{fh}^n X_{fh}^n \le w_f G + v_f F \qquad (n_f), \tag{14}$$

$$p_h e_{hh}^m X_{hh}^m + p_f e_{hf}^m X_{hf}^m \le w_h G + v_h(1 + \gamma)F + w_f \beta G + v_f \delta F \qquad (m_h), \tag{15}$$

$$p_f e_{ff}^m X_{ff}^m + p_h e_{fh}^m X_{fh}^m \le w_f G + v_f(1 + \gamma)F + w_h \beta G + v_h \delta F \qquad (m_f). \tag{16}$$

To summarize the $X$ sector in the model, the eight inequalities (8)–(11) are associated with the eight output levels (two each for four firm types), the eight equations in (12) are associated with the eight markups, and the four inequalities in (13)–(16) are associated with the number of firms of each type. Additionally goods prices are given by (7), income levels from (5) and factor prices from factor market clearing equation (4) together with labor demand from the $Y$ sector.

The model is quite complex and inherently involves inequalities making traditional analytical, comparative-statics methods of limited value. The problems introduced by inequalities are compounded by the fact that we have four different production activities ($Y$, $X$-sector output, national-firm fixed costs, multinational-firm fixed costs), all using factors in different proportions. We will therefore analyze the model numerically, using Rutherford's (1994) nonlinear complementarity solver (now a subsystem of GAMS).

440    *James Markusen and Anthony Venables*

Readers interested in a more analytical development of the theory are referred to Markusen and Venables (1995, 1996b). In those papers, we are able to make good analytical progress either through the use of partial-equilibrium assumptions and/or the assumption that all *X*-sector activities use factors in the same proportions.

## 3. Equilibrium Regime and Factor Prices in Relation to Country Characteristics

Figure 1 presents qualitative information on the equilibrium regime in relation to country characteristics (relative size and relative endowments) for transport costs $\tau =$ 0.15 (*c* is normalized at $c = 1$). Figure 1 is an Edgeworth box with the total world endowment of skilled labor on the vertical axis and the total world endowment of unskilled labor on the horizontal axis. Country *h*'s endowment is measured from the southwest (SW) corner and that of country *f* from the northeast (NE) corner. Any point in the box constitutes a division of the total world endowment between the two countries. For future reference we note that, owing to scaling, the factor-price ratio through the center of the box is quite steep, so basically at any point to the left of column 10, country *f* has the larger total income and, symmetrically, country *h* has the larger income to the right of column 10.

Because the results are rather complex, simplified versions of Figure 1 are presented in Figure 2. In the top panel of Figure 2, we plot the areas of Figure 1 in which type-$n_h$ and type-$n_f$ firms are active, ignoring types-$m_h$ and $m_f$ firms. The bottom panel of Figure 2 does the opposite, plotting areas where types-$m_h$ and $m_f$ firms are active, ignoring national firms. National firms are always active in equilibrium when the countries are

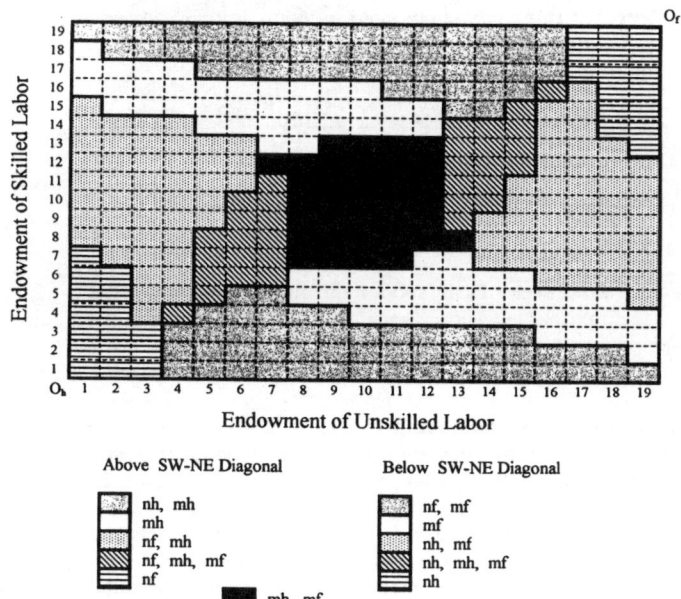

*Figure 1. Production Regime with Transport Costs, $\tau = 0.15$*

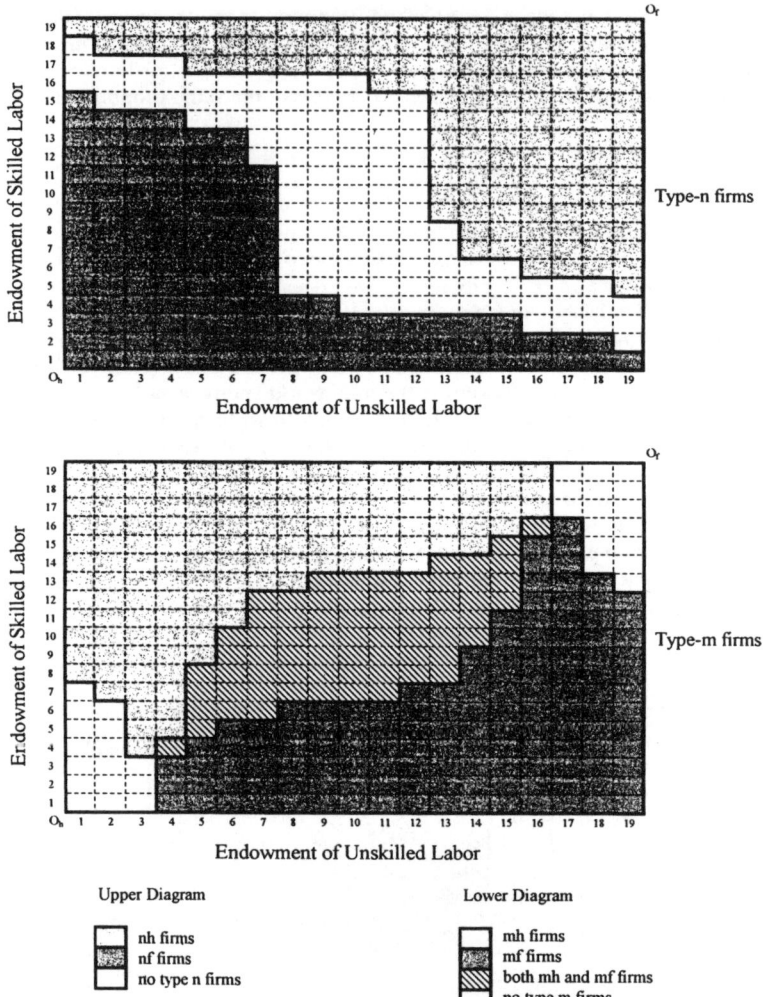

*Figure 2. Regions of type-n and type-m firms, $\tau = 0.15$*

very different in size or very different in relative endowments (top panel). National firms are the only firms active in equilibrium when the countries are extremely different in size (inferred from the bottom panel).

Multinational firms are the only firms active in equilibrium in the center of the box and in the area around the NW–SE diagonal of the factor box where one country is relatively small but relatively well endowed with skilled labor.

The patterns in the two panels of Figure 2 are quite different. For single-plant national firms $n_h$ and $n_f$, both relative endowments and market size are determinants of "comparative advantage." A large domestic market creates what is generally referred

442   *James Markusen and Anthony Venables*

to as a "home market advantage" in the trade and industrial-organization literature. With increasing returns to scale and Cournot competition, a large domestic market favors firms located in that market and equilibrium tends to be characterized by firms concentrating in the larger country more than in proportion to the country-size differences. If only relative endowments mattered, the region of type-$n_h$ firms in the top panel of Figure 2 would lie above the SW–NE diagonal. If only country size mattered, all those points would lie to the right of column 10. In fact, we see that a combination of size and relative endowments determines equilibrium.

The pattern of multinational firms, types-$m_h$ and $m_f$, on the other hand, is related much more closely to relative endowments, and not to country size. When the countries differ significantly in relative endowments, all type-$m$ firms that do exist are located in the skilled-labor abundant country. Country size does not influence much whether we have type-$m_h$ or type-$m_f$ firms since they both have plants in both countries. The dominant type will depend on which country has the lower price for skilled labor, which in turn depends on relative endowments (of course, labor costs are endogenous, a point to which we will return shortly). However, both type-$m$ firms become uncompetitive with national firms located in the larger country when the countries are very different in size. If one country has a very large internal market, a national firm located in that market benefits from high sales in that market, and incurs transport costs on only a small volume of sales to the small country. A multinational firm is disadvantaged by having to maintain a costly plant in the small market.

In section 4, we will consider the effects of falling trade costs or investment liberalization, in the latter case beginning from an equilibrium in which multinationals are initially banned from entering. With reference to Figure 2, the effect of lowering trade costs is to expand the two shaded regions in the top panel toward one another. Eventually they intersect, creating regions of "duopoly" competition between type-$n_h$ and type-$n_f$ firms reminiscent of the "new trade theory." In the lower panel, the shaded and hatched regions shrink toward the center, with multinational firms disappearing entirely as $\tau$ approaches zero.

The effect of a prohibitive investment ban is essentially to change Figure 1 into the top panel of Figure 2, except that the two shaded regions of types-$n_h$ and $n_f$ firms fill the entire parameter space and overlap somewhat in the middle.

Figure 3 plots the real wage of skilled labor (the wage divided by the commodity price index) for the equilibria shown in Figures 1 and 2.[7] There is considerable "Heckscher–Ohlin" quality to this diagram. In the center, there is a region of factor-price equalization. To the northwest of this central region, country $h$, the skilled-labor abundant country, has a lower wage for skilled labor than country $f$. The opposite is true to the southeast of the central region. The principal qualitative difference between this diagram and a Heckscher–Ohlin case lies in the points surrounding the SW–NE diagonal. In a HO model (and its extensions for single-plant monopolistic competition in Helpman and Krugman (1985)), these would also be points of factor-price equalization.

In our model, movements along the SW–NE diagonal away from the central region generate regime switches. National firms enter as countries become significantly different in size. Referring back to our earlier discussion of factor intensities, this regime shift is a shift from more skilled-labor intensive multinational firms to less skilled-labor intensive national firms. Aggregate demand for skilled labor falls at constant factor prices, and in general equilibrium the real wage of skilled labor falls in both countries.

Figure 3 provides an interesting thought experiment about changes in factor price as

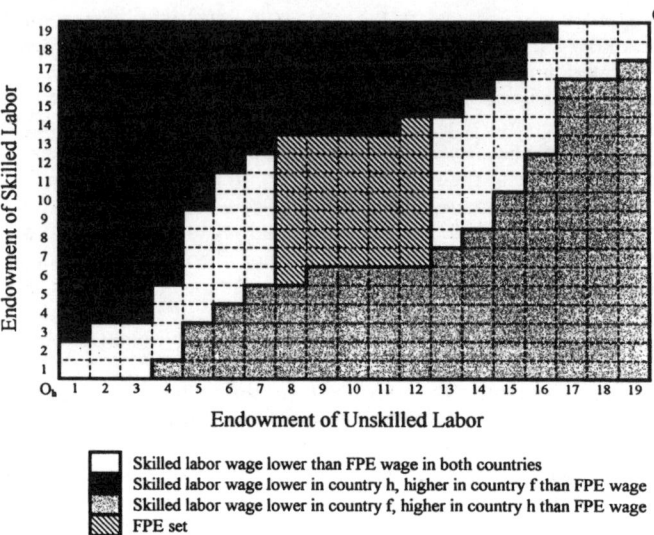

*Figure 3. Real Wage of Skilled Labor, $\tau = 0.15$*

countries become more similar in size and in relative endowments, holding the total world supply of factors fixed.[8] If the countries converge in size, the real wage of skilled labor and the skilled/unskilled wage ratio will rise in both countries, offering a possible explanation for the empirical observations noted earlier in the paper. If the countries converge in relative endowments, the skilled wage and the wage ratio will rise in the skilled-labor abundant country. This may offer a partial explanation of observations regarding the USA and Europe.

## 4. Investment Liberalization and Falling Trade Costs

Consider first investment liberalization in our two-country world. By "investment" here, we mean exploiting (transferring) the services of firm-specific capital to foreign branch plants, not the transfer of primary factors of production. This analysis requires some well-specified counterfactual. What we have done is to re-compute the model suppressing or "banning" types-$m_h$ and $m_f$ multinational firms. The resulting regime looks similar to the top panel of Figure 2, except that the two shaded regions expand toward the middle and overlap considerably. We then compare the values of variables in this restricted equilibrium to the unrestricted case in Figures 1 and 2 ($\tau = 0.15$).

The effects of removing the investment barrier on the wage of skilled labor are shown in Figure 4. Liberalization always raises the wage of skilled labor in the skilled-labor abundant country and raises the skilled-labor wage in both countries over a considerable range of parameter values. The latter tends to occur when the countries are rather different in relative endowments.

Consider first the darker shaded region in Figure 4 where $v_h$ increases but $v_f$ falls. Referring back to Figure 1 and to the lower panel of Figure 2, the effect of liberalization is to allow type-$m_h$ firms to enter in equilibrium. This creates a shift from predomi-

444   *James Markusen and Anthony Venables*

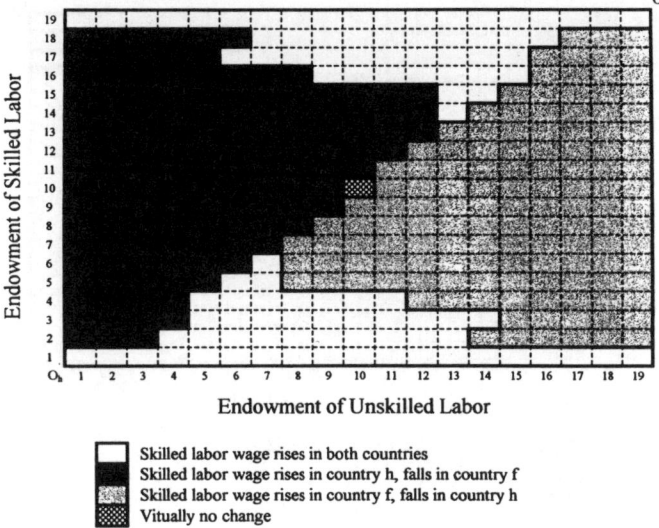

Figure legend:
- ☐ Skilled labor wage rises in both countries
- ■ Skilled labor wage rises in country h, falls in country f
- ▨ Skilled labor wage rises in country f, falls in country h
- ▒ Vitually no change

*Figure 4.  Investment Liberalization, τ = 0.15*

nantly type-$n_f$ firms but also from some type-$n_h$ firms in part of the dark-shaded region. Both shifts, but particularly the former, result in an increased demand for country $h$ skilled labor and an increase in $v_h$ in equilibrium. Country $f$, on the other hand, loses type-$n_f$ firms which are replaced by type-$m_h$ firms in equilibrium. This causes a fall in the demand for skilled labor in country $f$, as domestic firms are displaced by branch plants of country $h$ multinationals, the latter demanding significantly less country $f$ skilled labor than the displaced national firms. $v_f$ falls in equilibrium.

The explanation for the unshaded regions in Figure 4 in which the skilled-labor wage rises in both countries is a bit more subtle. Consider the upper unshaded region. When investment is banned, type-$n_h$ firms are the dominant type and in most cells the only firm type active in equilibrium. Investment liberalization leads to the entry of type-$m_h$ firms, displacing some of the type-$n_h$ firms. This increases the demand for skilled labor in country $h$ since the multinational firms are more skilled-labor intensive than national firms, even considering just their home-country demands. But the demand for skilled labor also increases in country $f$, since the branch plants of type-$m_h$ firms are drawing resources from the unskilled-labor intensive $Y$ sector, not from type-$n_f$ or $m_f$ firms.

Now consider a fall in trade costs (with multinationals initially permitted), the effects of which are shown in Figure 5. This contrasts sharply with Figure 4. In the latter, there are regions in which the real wage of skilled labor rises in both countries, while in Figure 5 there are regions in which the wage falls in both countries. In addition, the locations of the areas in which one country's wage rises and the other falls are reversed. For example, in Figure 4, $v_h$ rises and $v_f$ falls when country $h$ is skilled-labor abundant and small, while in Figure 5 the same results hold when country $h$ is large and unskilled-labor abundant.

There are three factors at work that tend to affect factor prices when trade costs fall.

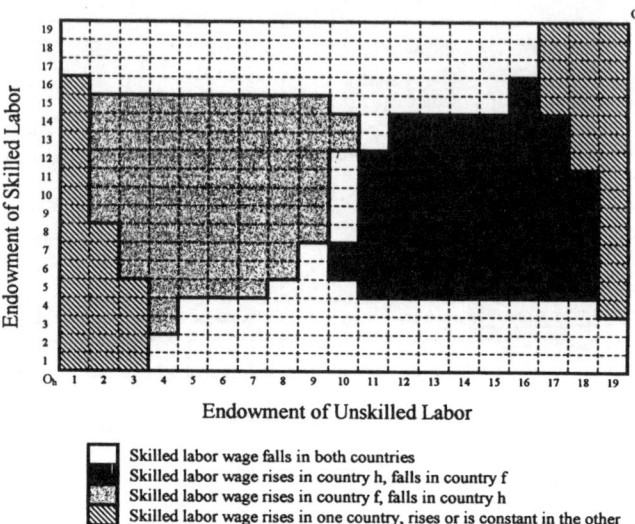

Endowment of Unskilled Labor

☐  Skilled labor wage falls in both countries
■  Skilled labor wage rises in country h, falls in country f
▒  Skilled labor wage rises in country f, falls in country h
▨  Skilled labor wage rises in one country, rises or is constant in the other

*Figure 5.  Trade Liberalization,  $\tau = 0.15$*

First, multinational firms may be displaced by less-skilled-labor intensive national firms, which may depress the skilled-labor wage in both countries, but particularly in the skilled-labor abundant country which tends to be the headquarters country for most multinational firms. The skilled-labor wage could rise in a larger, skilled-labor scarce country if its national firms displace foreign branch plants. Third, if one country basically specializes in $X$ production before and after liberalization, the real wage of skilled labor could rise in that country as trade liberalization expands its $X$ sector. But the real wage in the other country could rise as well as the price index falls. This is a possible case where the real wages of both factors rise but their ratio does not change.

These effects collectively explain the results in Figure 5. Both $v_h$ and $v_f$ fall in the unshaded regions. These are regions in which, at $\tau = 0.15$, production is dominated by type-$m_h$ firms (upper region) or type-$m_f$ firms (lower region). Trade liberalization displaces these firms with type-$n_h$ and type-$n_f$ firms respectively, causing a fall in the demand for skilled labor in both countries (essentially opposite to the effect of investment liberalization discussed above).

In the lighter-shaded region of Figure 5, type-$m_h$ firms tend to be displaced by type-$n_f$ firms, resulting in an increased demand for skilled labor in country $f$ and a fall in country $h$. The converse applies to the darker shaded region of Figure 5, in which type-$m_f$ firms tend to be displaced by type-$n_h$. The fall in trade costs creates a home-market advantage for national firms in the large, skilled-labor scarce country displacing less-skilled-labor intensive branch plants of firms headquartered in the small country.

The hatched regions of Figure 5 are areas in which the skilled-labor wage rises in both countries. Consider the left-hand hatched region. At the initial high level of trade costs, almost all production is by type-$n_f$ firms owing to a strong home-market advantage (there is a very small amount of production by type-$m_h$ firms at the uppermost of these points). Trade liberalization has little effect on the number or types of firms in country $h$ in this region, and on $X$ sector output. But it does have a price-index effect, in that trade liberalization lowers the price of $X$. The ratio of skilled to unskilled wages is essentially unaffected in country $h$, but the real wage of skilled labor rises in $h$. From country $f$'s point of view, trade liberalization expands the size of the market for $X$, its export good, and the general-equilibrium effect of expanding the $X$ sector is to increase $v_f$.

## 5. Growth in the World Economy

One reasonable hypothesis about the wage gap, particularly the observation that it has grown in developing countries as well as in advanced economies, is that some feature of growth in the world economy has caused the change. Various aspects of technical change could of course be responsible, but a goal of this paper is explicitly to suggest other possibilities, especially in light of some economists' tendency to use technical change as a sort of *deus ex machina* when some other explanation fails.

A good reference scenario to consider here is simply to allow the world economy to grow in its endowment of all factors of production. While this is surely not a very accurate characterization of world growth in recent decades, such a scenario is useful in pointing out some of the opposing forces at work.

Figure 6 plots the effects of a 100% growth in the world supply of both factors on the real wage of skilled labor in both countries. The upper panel does this for a trade cost of $\tau = 0.15$ while the bottom panel does this for a trade cost of $\tau = 0.03$. In the top panel, the *initial* regime is as given in Figure 1. In the bottom panel, the *initial* regime is composed almost solely of types-$n_h$ and $n_f$ firms, as in the top panel of Figure 2 except that the shaded areas cover the entire parameter space and intersect.

The unshaded regions of both diagrams are areas in which the skilled labor wage falls in both countries. This dominates the top panel, but is far less important in the bottom panel. The reason lies in the observation that in the top panel, multinational firms are already fairly dominant in equilibrium before growth. The effects of growth are largely that firm scale increases, which implies that the demand for skilled labor grows more slowly than the supply.[9] In the lower panel, national firms are dominant before growth. Growth results in considerable shifting from national to multinational firms, the latter being more skilled-labor intensive than national firms, and hence the demand for skilled labor grows faster than the supply, at least in the country which tends to be chosen as headquarters of the new multinational firms. Thus a firm-scale effect strongly influences the top panel while a regime-switching effect strongly influences the bottom panel. Thus the effects of growth depend closely on where we start; in particular, whether national or multinational firms are initially dominant.

A few more specific comments about Figure 6 are in order. In the top panel, the dark-shaded area in the SW corner (and up each axis) is an area where the increase in $v_h$ is due to a price index effect as discussed in the previous section (the *ratio* of the skilled to unskilled wage $v_h/w_h$ does not rise). The area in the NW corner is due to the substitution of some type-$m_h$ firms for type-$n_h$ firms, the former being more skilled-labor intensive. There is a small hatched area in the top of this panel (and a much larger one in the bottom panel) in which the skilled-labor wage increases in both countries, owing to the substitution of type-$m_h$ firms for type-$n_h$ firms, increasing the demand for skilled labor in both countries. Similarly, the hatched area at the bottom is a substitution of type-$m_f$ firms for type-$n_f$ firms.

The bottom panel results are the consequence of more regime shifting from national

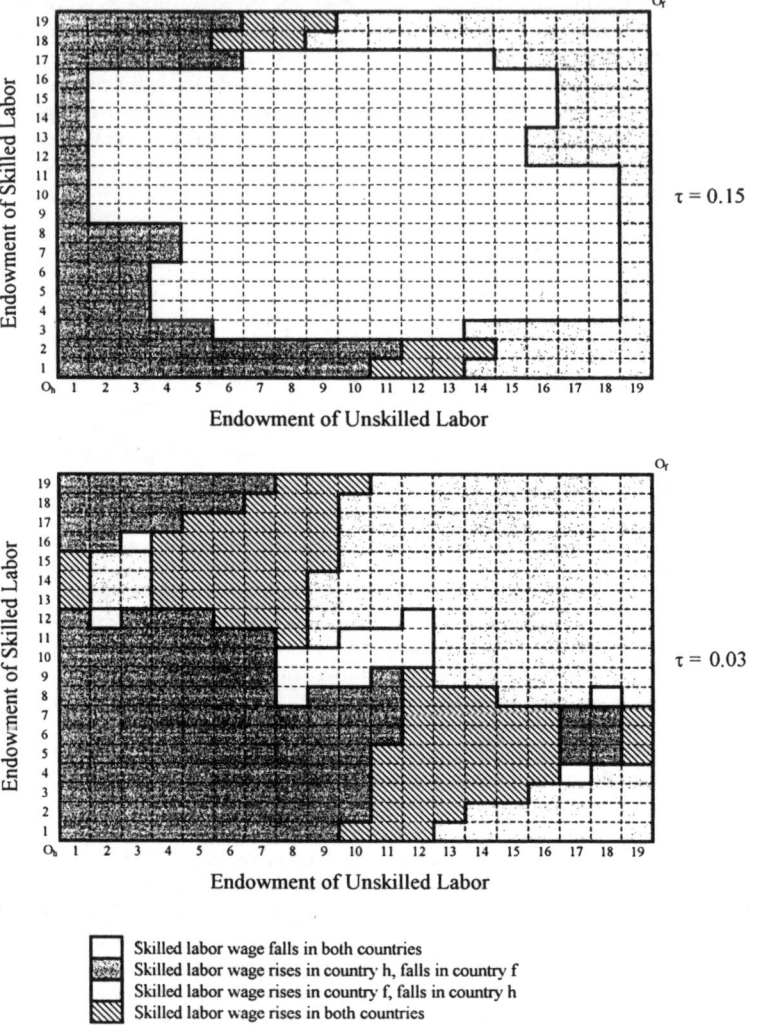

*Figure 6. Effect of 100% Growth, $\tau = 0.15$ (top), $\tau = 0.03$ (lower)*

to multinational firms as noted, but the price index effect is important in and near the SW and NE corners. The interesting result here is that the small country tends to experience a rise in the return to skilled labor regardless of whether or not it is skilled-labor abundant or scarce. Different effects dominate in different sections of the dark-shaded region in the lower panel (and correspondingly in the light-shaded region). But basically they are the same effects noted in the previous paragraph with more regime shifting in the hatched areas of the box. The small set of points in the NW area where $v_h$ falls is due to the displacement of type-$m_h$ firms by type-$n_f$ firms.

448   *James Markusen and Anthony Venables*

In summary, the effects of "neutral" growth in world factor supplies are a tension between firm-scale effects and regime-shifting effects in the model. The more dominant that national firms are initially, the more likely that growth results in increases in the return to skilled labor in at least one country. That country will generally be the smaller of the two countries. If country $h$ is small and is skilled-labor abundant, there is a substitution of type-$m_h$ firms for type-$n_h$ firms, and if it is skilled-labor scarce, there is price-index effect (fall in the price of $X$ with no change in relative factor prices). In the latter case, both factors obviously gain from growth.

## 6. Conclusions

The purpose of this paper is to adapt our earlier work to consider what role multinational firms might have in influencing factor prices, in particular the difference between skilled and unskilled wages. Multinational firms fragment production geographically, and the crucial assumptions of the paper involve how factor intensities differ among different aspects of production. Drawing on extensive empirical literature, we assume that the rankings of skilled–unskilled ratios among activities and firm types is:

[firm-level fixed costs] > [plant-level fixed costs] > [integrated $X$ production]
> [branch plant $X$ production] > [$Y$ production]

[multinational firms] > [national firms] (at common output scale).

Results in the paper depend fundamentally on these factor-intensity rankings, but extensive numbers of simulations suggest that they are not very sensitive to specific numerical values (retaining these rankings). These results are as follows.

(1) Multinational firms are more likely to arise in equilibrium when two countries are similar in both relative factor endowments and in size, and when trade costs are moderate to high.

(2) Convergence in country size and in relative endowments holding world endowments constant raises the real wage of skilled labor and the skilled–unskilled wage gap in the skilled-labor abundant country. When convergence is in country size, the skilled wage and the wage ratio can rise in both countries as more skilled-labor intensive multinational firms replace less-skilled-labor intensive national firms.

(3) Investment liberalization raises the real wage of skilled labor and the wage ratio in the skilled-labor abundant country as new multinational firms headquartered there displace its own national firms or foreign-headquartered national firms. Over a significant portion of parameter space the skilled wage rises in both countries. Assuming country $h$ is the skilled-labor abundant country, this occurs when type-$m_h$ firms displace type-$n_f$ firms, and the branch plants in country $f$ draw resources from the $Y$ sector, not from type-$n_f$ firms.[10]

(4) Falling trade costs tend to have the opposite effect in some loose sense. Trade liberalization puts downward pressure on the skilled-labor wage for two reasons. First, less-skilled-labor intensive national firms can displace more skilled-labor-intensive multinational firms; and second, a pro-competitive effect can raise firm scale, lowering skilled-labor intensity. The wage of skilled labor rises in a large, unskilled-labor abundant country as some national firms in that country displace foreign branch plants. The only case in which falling trade costs raises the skilled wage in both countries occurs when they are very different in size so that all $X$ production is by national firms in the larger country. Then liberalization expands the $X$ sector in the large country and has a

favorable effect in the small country via a fall in the price index (with no change in the wage ratio).

(5) Neutral growth in all factors in the world economy has effects that depend in large part on whether national or multinational firms are dominant initially. If national firms are dominant initially, then growth results in regime switching to multinational firms with the skilled wage rising in one or both countries. If multinational firms are already dominant initially, then growth results in pro-competitive effects leading to an increase in firm scale, so that skilled-labor demand does not grow in proportion to supply. The skilled-labor wage then falls over significant portions of parameter space.

To summarize, the results provide motivation for empirical work on the role of multinationals in the wage-gap problem. If country characteristics are converging and if indeed investment restrictions have fallen faster than trade costs (including tariffs), then multinationals may explain some part of the wage-gap phenomenon.

## References

Berman, Eli, Stephen Machin, and John Bound, "Implications of Skill Biased Technological Change: International Evidence," working paper, 1995.

Bernard, Andrew B. and J. Bradford Jensen, "Exporters, Skill Upgrading, and the Wage Gap," MIT working paper, 1995.

Brainard, S. Lael, "An Empirical Assessment of the Factor Proportions Explanation of Multinationals Sales," NBER working paper 4583, 1993a.

———, "An Empirical Assessment of the Proximity–Concentration Tradeoff between Multinational Sales and Trade," NBER working paper 4580, 1993b.

Caves, Richard E., *Multinational Enterprise and Economic Analysis*, London: Cambridge University Press, 1996 (2nd edn).

Cragg, Michael Ian and Mario Epelbaum, "The Premium for Skills in LDCs: Evidence from Mexico," working paper, 1995.

Eaton, Jonathan and Akiko Tamura, "Bilateralism and Regionalism in Japanese and US Trade and Direct Foreign Investment Patterns," *Journal of the Japanese and International Economies* 8 (1994):478–510.

Ekholm, Karolina, *Multinational Production and Trade in Technological Knowledge*, Lund Economic Studies, no. 58, 1995.

Feenstra, Robert C. and Gordon H. Hanson, "Foreign Investment, Outsourcing, and Relative Wages," working paper, 1995a.

———, "Foreign Direct Investment and Relative Wages: Evidence from Mexico's Maquiladoras," working paper, 1995b.

Freeman, Richard B., "Are Your Wages Set in Beijing?" *Journal of Economic Perspectives* 9 (1995):15–32.

Hanson, Gordon H. and Ann Harrison, "Trade, Technology, and Wage Inequality," NBER working paper 5110, 1995.

Helpman, Elhanan and Paul Krugman, *Market Structure and Foreign Trade*, Cambridge: MIT Press, 1985.

Krugman, Paul R., "Technology, Trade, and Factor Prices," NBER working paper 5355, 1995.

Krugman, Paul and Robert Lawrence, "Trade, Jobs, and Wages," NBER working paper 4478, 1993.

Lawrence, Robert and Mathew Slaughter, "International Trade and American Wages," *Brookings Papers on Economic Activity* (1993):161–226.

Leamer, Edward E., "Wage Effects of a US–Mexican Free Trade Agreement," in Peter M. Garber (ed.), *The Mexico–US Free Trade Agreement*, Cambridge: MIT Press, 1993:57–125.

450   *James Markusen and Anthony Venables*

——, "Trade, Wages, and Revolving Door Ideas," NBER working paper 4716, 1994.

——, "In Search of Stolper–Samuelson Effects on US Wages," NBER working paper 5427, 1996a.

——, "What's the Use of Factor Content Calculations?" NBER working paper 5448, 1996b.

Markusen, James R., "The Boundaries of Multinational Enterprises and the Theory of International Trade," *Journal of Economic Perspectives* 9 (1995):169–89.

Markusen, James R. and Anthony J. Venables, "Multinational Firms and the New Trade Theory," NBER working paper 5036, 1995.

——, "Multinational Production, Skilled Labor, and Real Wages," NBER working paper 5483, 1996a.

——, "The Theory of Endowment, Intra-Industry and Multinational Trade," NBER working paper 5529, 1996b.

Pissarides, Christopher A., "Trade and the Returns to Human Capital in Developing Countries," LSE working paper, 1995.

Richardson, J. David, "Income Inequality and Trade: What to Think, What to Conclude," *Journal of Economic Perspectives* 9 (1995):33–56.

Riker, David and S. Lael Brainard, "US Multinationals and Competition from Low Wage Countries," MIT working paper, 1996.

Robbins, Donald J., "Earnings Dispersions in Chile after Trade Liberalization," manuscript, 1994.

——, "Wage Dispersion and Trade in Columbia: An Analysis of Greater Bogota: 1976–1989," manuscript, 1995.

Rutherford, Thomas F., "Applied General-Equilibrium Modelling with MPS/GE as a GAMS Subsystem," working paper, 1994.

Slaughter, Matthew J., "Multinational Corporations, Outsourcing, and American Relative Wage Divergence," NBER working paper 5253, 1995.

Tan, Hong and Geeta Batra, "Technology and Industry Wage Differentials: Evidence from Three Developing Countries," World Bank working paper, 1995.

Teece, David, *The Multinational Corporation and the Resource Cost of International Technology Transfer*, Cambridge: Ballinger, 1986.

Wood, Adrian, *North–South Trade, Employment and Inequality*, Oxford: Clarendon Press, 1994.

——, "How Trade Hurt Unskilled Workers," *Journal of Economic Perspectives* 9 (1995): 57–80.

## Notes

1. The role of trade in explaining the growing gap in skilled–unskilled wages has been an important policy issue in the United States. An excellent discussion of the evidence and conceptual arguments is present in articles by Freeman, Richardson, and Wood in a recent issue of the *Journal of Economic Perspectives* (summer 1995). No role for multinationals is identified by these authors. This paper suggests that such a role should be considered, especially owing to the empirical fact that direct investment has grown much more rapidly than trade over the last two decades.

2. Extensive empirical work is reviewed in Caves (1996) and Markusen (1995). Assumptions presented below are motivated by direct observations on the characteristics of multinational firms: they tend to be R&D intensive, produce new and/or technically complex products, have large numbers of scientific, technical, and other non-production workers, and have high degrees of product differentiation. Our characterization that parent firms are more skilled-labor intensive than subsidiaries is motivated by Slaughter (1995). Other motivations are more indirect. Our model has implications (Markusen and Venables, 1995, 1996a, 1996b) that fit well with results from studies that relate bilateral investment stocks to country characteristics. These include Brainard (1993a, 1993b), Eaton and Tamura (1994), and Ekholm (1995). In particular, bilateral investment is high between countries that are similar in size and in relative endowments, and outward direct investment is strongly associated with a country's human capital endowment.

3. We decided to model trade barriers as real costs rather than tariffs in the paper for a couple of reasons. First, it may well be that real costs have fallen faster than tariffs during the last two decades. Second, we can make the incidence of trade costs on factor markets more clear (since factor intensities are explicit) than with tariffs, which have indirect effects.

4. Rising skilled–unskilled wage gaps in both north and south have been discussed, modelled, and hypotheses tested in a number of recent papers, including Feenstra and Hanson (1995a, 1995b), Hanson and Harrison (1995), Robbins (1994, 1995), Tan and Batra (1995), Pissarides (1995), Cragg and Epelbaum (1995), and Berman et al. (1995). Related questions are explored by Bernard and Jensen (1995), and Riker and Brainard (1996).

5. The technology-transfer cost ($\gamma > 0$) is motivated by empirical results, especially those of Teece (1986), that direct investments require significant further investments in skilled-labor intensive activities for multinational firms. The assumption that the branch-plant's (affiliate's) fixed costs are significantly less skilled-labor intensive than the parent's is motivated by the findings of Slaughter (1995) that the share of nonproduction workers is much higher in parents than in affiliates.

6. An exception can occur when the two countries are *very similar*. The removal of an investment barrier leads, in equilibrium, to multinational firms with significantly higher output per firm than the national firms they displace, a type of pro-competitive effect. Since final output is unskilled-labor intensive, the difference in equilibrium firm scale contributes toward making the multinational firms less skilled-labor intensive. In the simulation results we report, this firm-scale effect approximately cancels out the fixed-cost effect (making multinationals more skilled-labor intensive at common scale) so that the equilibrium skilled-labor wage and the skilled–unskilled wage gap are essentially unaffected by the removal of an investment ban when the countries are identical.

7. Changes in the real wage of skilled labor are almost always associated with the same direction of change in the skilled–unskilled wage ratio. This does not have to be the case owing to scale economies. The real wage of both skilled and unskilled labor could rise at the same time that the relative wage of skilled labor falls. But the only time something like this actually occurs in our model, is when a country is specialized in Y, so some change affects the real wage of both factors, but not their ratio. This is discussed in connection with Figures 5 and 6.

8. This is a somewhat artificial exercise, since in practice convergence generally involves lower-income countries catching up to the high-income countries, so total world absolute and relative endowments are changing. This adds complicated firm-scale effects to this model which in turn complicate the results. A discussion of overall growth in the world economy is postponed until a later section.

9. Again, there may be some discomfort in the notion that an increase in firm scale implies lower skilled-labor intensity. But while we may have a good intuitive feel for physical capital to unskilled or semi-skilled labor ratios in relation to plant scale, it is not obvious that we have good evidence about human capital intensity. Does doubling plant scale require doubling the number of scientists, engineers, and managers? We don't know. Allowing for some required increase in the demand for skilled labor as plant scale increases should shrink the unshaded regions in both panels of Figure 6.

10. There are a number of cases in which the real wage of unskilled labor rises even though its relative wage falls. This is due to the industrial organization features of the model, with endogenous markups and firm scale. Growth or liberalization has a pro-competitive effect that lowers markups and increases firm scale (lowers average cost), thereby possibly benefiting both factors.

# Name Index